Creativity Theory and Action in Education

Volume 6

CW00740790

Series Editors
Ronald A. Beghetto, Arizona State University, Tempe, AZ, USA
Bharath Sriraman, Department of Mathematical Sciences
The University of Montana, Missoula, MT, USA

Educational settings represent sites of creative possibility. They also represent the manifestation of some of the most persistent and dogmatic beliefs about teaching and learning. This series aims to push the frontiers of creativity theory, research, and practice in educational settings. Specifically, this series endeavors to provide a venue for disseminating the kinds of provocative thinking and cutting-edge research that can promote more creative approaches to teaching and learning. The focus of the series is on mainstream (rather than gifted or other specialized) educational settings. Another aspect worthy of exploration is domain specific or domain general view of creativity- one that has hitherto been the speculation of cognitive science but one that can be brought to the forefront of existing treatments of creativity. A final (and general) area of investigation is artistic, ecological, cultural and anthropological aspects of creativity that have been ignored by the community.

This Series:

- Capitalizes on the growing international interest and concern about the breakdown of creativity in everyday schools and classrooms
- Provides fresh thinking on complex issues and challenges pertaining to theory and practice aimed at promoting creativity in educational settings
- Challenges existing dogmas and overly narrow conceptions of teaching, learning, and creativity (e.g., creativity being separated from academic learning and linked to gifted education)
- Spotlights new theories, methodologies and approaches to studying and enacting creativity in a variety of domains, contexts, and levels (early childhood through higher education)

The Editors of this Series welcome proposals for edited and authored volumes that provide provocative and original explorations of creative theory, methodology and action in educational settings. This includes international and multidisciplinary perspectives on creativity across and within K-12, university, online and informal educational settings (e.g., museums, organizations, clubs, and groups). The audience for this series includes creativity and educational researchers, graduate students, practicing educators, and educational thought leaders.

Other Forthcoming volumes:

Reflections on the Future of Creativity, Technology and Education - In between the Good, the Bad, the Unimagined, and the Unintended, edited by Danah Henriksen and Punya Mishra (2022).

Proposal Review Process:

All proposals are reviewed by series and acquisition editors. There are two types of review: *expedited* and *extended*. Expedited reviews occur in cases where the series and acquisition editors have determined that a project should or should not move forward based on the fit and potential of proposal to contribute to the series. Extended reviews occur in cases where proposals take on more specialized topics and would benefit from additional input provided by experts serving on the series advisory board and, in some cases, relevant external reviewers who can make a recommendation about the potential merit of a particular project. Extended reviews may also include an exit review of the completed work by board members or external reviewers.

Ronald A. Beghetto • Garrett J. Jaeger
Editors

Uncertainty: A Catalyst for Creativity, Learning and Development

 Springer

Editors
Ronald A. Beghetto
Arizona State University
Tempe, AZ, USA

Garrett J. Jaeger
LEGO Foundation
Billund, Denmark

ISSN 2509-5781   ISSN 2509-579X   (electronic)
Creativity Theory and Action in Education
ISBN 978-3-030-98731-2   ISBN 978-3-030-98729-9   (eBook)
https://doi.org/10.1007/978-3-030-98729-9

This Springer imprint is published by the registered company Springer Nature Switzerland AG
The registered company address is: Gewerbestrasse 11, 6330 Cham, Switzerland

For my mother, Teresa, who always maintained grace, humor, and hope in the face of even the most profound of life's uncertainties.
--- Ronald A. Beghetto
For my mentor, Tommy, who taught me that uncertainty is an invitation
to make familiar worlds that once seemed foreign.
--- Garrett J. Jaeger

Book Series Foreword

The goal of the book series Creativity Theory and Action in Education is to explore new frontiers in creative theory, research, and practice in educational settings. The series therefore endeavors to provide an international forum for thinkers from various disciplinary and methodological perspectives to build on existing work in the field and offer new, alternative, and even speculative directions for creative theory, research, and practice in education.

In this way, the series is a creative experiment of sorts, one that is aimed at providing an opportunity for those engaged and interested in the broader project of understanding creativity in education to generate, develop, test out, and learn from new possibilities and multiple perspectives on all manner of creative phenomena in education. Such an experiment has potential implications for how we think about creativity in education and also for how we act on creative opportunities afforded by educational situations and settings.

Arizona State University   Ronald A. Beghetto
Tempe, AZ, USA

Acknowledgments

The authors would like thank Natalie Rieborn from Springer for support and encouragement of this project. We'd also like to thank all the members of our advisory board, colleagues at our institutions, family, and friends.

Contents

Chapter 1
Introduction

Ronald A. Beghetto and Garrett J. Jaeger

Abstract In this introductory chapter we provide an overview of the aims of this edited volume, which has the primary goal of introducing readers to perspectives and practices that focus on the role uncertainty plays in creative expression, learning, and human development. More specifically, we introduce the five organizing themes of the chapters: *understanding uncertainty; transforming uncertainty into creativity; uncertainty and creativity in science and mathematics; uncertainty in learning and development;* and *transforming education in response to uncertainty).* We also briefly introduce each chapter organized under each of these five themes.

1.1 Overview

Uncertainty is sometimes conceptualized and experienced as something that should be avoided or, at least, quickly resolved; however, it's an undeniable and indelible feature of learning and life. Rather than attempt to avoid uncertainty, the contributors of this book aim to help us better understand and more productively engage with uncertainty. Indeed, the primary goal of this book is to introduce readers to perspectives and practices that focus on the role uncertainty plays in creative expression, learning, and human development. Although, this volume has an educational focus, formal educational settings serve more as the backdrop as the ideas developed and presented in this volume offer new ways of thinking about, studying and engaging with uncertainty in and beyond educational settings.

The essays collected in this volume represent a plurality of perspectives, from scholars working in diverse contexts and fields of study. Many of the essays draw on well-established   programs   of   research,   whereas   others   are   more

R. A. Beghetto (✉)
Arizona State University, Tempe, AZ, USA
e-mail: Ronald.Beghetto@asu.edu

G. J. Jaeger
LEGO Foundation, Boston, MA, USA

© Springer Nature Switzerland AG 2022
R. A. Beghetto, G. J. Jaeger (eds.), *Uncertainty: A Catalyst for Creativity, Learning and Development*, Creativity Theory and Action in Education 6,
https://doi.org/10.1007/978-3-030-98729-9_1

speculative – offering researchers and practitioners with new possibilities and provocations for considering how uncertainty manifests, animates and can sustain creativity, learning and development.

It is worth noting that we proposed and embarked on this project prior to and during the COVID-19 global pandemic. Consequently, the ideas developed and explored in this volume were situated in a time of heighted, and at times profound, uncertainty. This volume therefore reflects somewhat of a serendipitous exploration of how people might think and act in the face of a broad range of uncertainties – from everyday uncertainties to deeply destabilizing uncertainties. We hope readers will take-up the ideas presented herein to think and act in new and different new ways when encountering, studying, and learning with uncertainty in their professional work and lives.

We also hope that the ideas presented in this volume help us consider how we might better anticipate and be more open to the possibilities that encounters with uncertainty can offer to our learning, creativity, and lives. We see this as particularly important as doing so can help us and others approach any educational experience or creative endeavor with a willingness to engage, inquire into, play with, and ultimately learn and grow from encounters with uncertainty.

Although the contributions in this volume can be read in any sequence or order, we have arranged them in what we feel is a sequence that moves readers through five overarching themes: *understanding uncertainty; transforming uncertainty into creativity; uncertainty and creativity in science and mathematics; uncertainty in learning and development;* and *transforming education in response to uncertainty.*

1.2   Understanding Uncertainty

How might we come to better understand the uncertainties we face? This question is somewhat paradoxical in that uncertainty is about not knowing. Therefore, how might we come to know more about states of not knowing? This question is addressed with the opening chapter of the volume. More specifically, **Glăveanu (Chap. 2)** opens with an exploration of the varieties of knowing experience, including: the anxiety of uncertain not knowing, the trust of certain knowing, the curiosity of uncertain knowing, and the wonder of certain not knowing. Next, **Runco (Chap. 3)**, invites us to consider how uncertainty is a part of all creative efforts and the implications for understanding how uncertainty might play a more central role in creative thinking and creativity research. In the final chapter of this first section, **Schulz and colleagues (Chap. 4),** help us better understand how "just-right" amounts of uncertainty can support young people's motivation, curiosity, enjoyment and learning. Taken together, the three chapters in this section provide a basis for broadening our conceptions of uncertainty and its role in creativity, learning, and development.

1.3 Transforming Uncertainty into Creativity

If uncertainty is necessary for creativity, then how might we better transform uncertainty into creativity? This question is taken up by the contributors in the second section of this volume. Specifically, **Hoffmann and colleagues (Chap. 5)** explore the intersection between creativity and emotional intelligence in an effort to help us consider how emotions in the face of uncertainty can be converted into creative productivity. Next, **Zielińska and Karwowski (Chap. 6)** discuss how uncertainty characterizes all creative acts and how creative self-regulation is used by people to successfully navigate and work with uncertainty as part of the creative process. **Henriksen and colleagues (Chap. 7)** then invite us to explore how mindfulness can help alleviate the fears we might have when facing uncertainties and how mindfulness can help us move toward new, creative possibilities in learning. **Gabora and Steel (Chap. 8)** conclude this section by illustrating how uncertainty can be resolved and transformed into insight through the application of an autocatalytic framework.

1.4 Uncertainty and Creativity in Science and Mathematics

Some experiences and subject areas, particularly in school settings, may seem to be more uncertain than others. In school settings, many students may, for instance, experience school-based representations of science and mathematics as somewhat fixed. However, as the contributors in this section demonstrate there is much uncertainty to be creatively engaged with in these domains. **Anderson and colleagues (Chap. 9)** open this section by proposing methods by which we can teach the scientific process that integrates uncertainty as a means for creative sense-making. Next, **Chamberlin (Chap. 10)** proposes that uncertainty should be encouraged as it contributes to creativity in learning mathematics and in solving mathematical problems more creatively. Finally, in **Chap. 11, Sriraman** describes how educators can "engineer uncertainty" in the mathematics classroom and outlines ways in which (axiomatic) rules themselves can be engineered to provoke uncertainty, ambiguity and creative learning in mathematics.

1.5 Uncertainty in Learning and Development

Childhood is often viewed as a key period of human development during which a great deal of novelty and uncertainty is experienced because we are newcomers to the human experience. There is much for us to learn with respect to uncertainty in relation to human development during these early years and throughout the lifespan. **Benton and Sobel (Chap. 12)** draw on developmental psychology research to help us understand how uncertainty provokes children's early use of causal reasoning and probabilities to predict outcomes in the world around them. **Evans and colleagues (Chap. 13)** share further insights from developmental psychology to illustrate how uncertainty, curiosity, and exploration – particularly through play -- are central to promoting preschool children's creativity. Next, **Jirout and Matthews (Chap. 14)** discuss how uncertainty animates the intellectual virtue of curiosity and the importance of engaging in educational practices that support curiosity in educational contexts. Finally, **Lebuda (Chap. 15)** presents a discussion of the importance of considering how professional artists and scientists learn to embrace the uncertainty inherent in the social validation of their work and how educators might establish more supportive learning environments that can help young people develop resilient social and personal identities.

1.6   Transforming Education in Response to Uncertainty

Encounters with uncertainty can orient us toward new possibilities and futures. Although it is true that we can and do experience uncertainties about past and present experiences, those uncertainties can still be thought of as re-orienting us toward future thoughts and actions. Educational efforts are also ultimately future oriented (e.g., preparing young people for uncertain futures). The essays in this final section offer new insights and considerations for how we can take on this future orientation through the transformation of educational efforts. **Houmann (Chap. 16)** opens this section by describing how educators can make important transformations to educational practice by using tools, such as *uncertainty field books* to help young people become more aware of the ways in which they conceptualize and work through the complexities of uncertain knowledge. **Leahy and colleagues (Chap. 17)** focus on transformations and strategies that educational leaders can draw on to better prepare educational systems for engaging with the deep uncertainties and challenges presented in the midst of *the Fourth Industrial Revolution*. In the final chapter of the volume, **Barr and colleagues (Chap. 18)** discuss the uncertainties and collective responsibilities facing higher education in the age of the Anthropocene, including the implications for transforming the broader project of education during this challenging epoch (**Chap. 18, Barr et al.**).

Taken together, we hope you find the essays in this volume provocative and inspiring in your own efforts to understand and navigate uncertainties presented in learning and everyday life. We invite you to engage with the broader themes and ideas presented herein -- particularly those ideas that disrupt your existing assumptions about the nature of uncertainty in relation to learning, creativity and development. Although you may encounter perspectives, assertions, and speculations that you disagree with in the essays collected in this volume, we hope you will approach them with what John Dewey called an *attitude of suspended conclusion*, such that you can maintain a willingness to meaningfully engage with the perspectives offered by our contributors. In this way, these essays can serve as waypoints (rather than end points) as you continue your own sensemaking-journey with uncertainty and the role it can play in learning, professional work, and life itself.

Part I
Understanding Uncertainty

Chapter 2
Not Knowing

Vlad P. Glăveanu

Abstract This chapter focuses on the role and value of not knowing for creativity, learning and development. More specifically, it proposes a typology of states that are conducive, in different ways, for creative learning, including certain knowing, uncertain not knowing, uncertain knowing, and certain not knowing. They are discussed, in turn, in relation to four associated experiences: trust, anxiety, curiosity and wonder, respectively. Towards the end, two models are proposed that specify how and when these experiences contribute to the process of creative learning. The first is focused on macro stages, the second on micro processes. While the former starts from uncertain not knowing, goes through the interplay between uncertain knowing and certain not knowing, and ends in certain knowledge, the processual model reveals the intricate relations between these experiences in each and every instance of creative learning. The developmental and educational implications of revaluing not knowing as a generate state are discussed in the end.

2.1 Introduction

This chapter focuses on the experience of not knowing as it relates to that of uncertainty and, more broadly, to human development. Most of all, it aims to develop a broader argument as to how lacking knowledge can be an important developmental resource for creativity and learning, just as important as possessing knowledge, if not more.

There are clear connections between not knowing and uncertainty, so much so that one can easily assume that being uncertain necessarily involves various forms of not knowing (e.g., about what is happening at the moment, about how things will evolve, about what the current state of affairs means for oneself and for others, and

V. P. Glăveanu (✉)
Webster University Geneva, Geneva, Switzerland

University of Bergen, Bergen, Norway
e-mail: glaveanu@webster.ch

© Springer Nature Switzerland AG 2022
R. A. Beghetto, G. J. Jaeger (eds.), *Uncertainty: A Catalyst for Creativity, Learning and Development*, Creativity Theory and Action in Education 6,
https://doi.org/10.1007/978-3-030-98729-9_2

so on). At the same time, there are experiences of not knowing that don't presuppose uncertainty, and the other way around – for instance, someone can be sure that he or she doesn't know something (Dönmez and Grote 2013) or be unsure of existing knowledge (Woozley 1952). From these examples, it would seem that not knowing is a wider category than uncertainty; and yet, we can also imagine ways of being uncertain that don't relate to knowledge, e.g., more emotional or existential ones (Gerard 1963; Van den Bos 2009).

One would be forgiven to think that both uncertainty and not knowing are either undesirable states or tolerated for as long as they are temporary in nature (for a critique, see Beghetto 2017a; Anderson Blea and Welsh 2020). This is because they could lead to anxiety and depression when sustained for a long time or to losing the desire to know or to understand, driving the person to either nihilism or skepticism. In contrast, certainty and knowing are typically considered virtues in a wide range of environments, from past and present classrooms to the workplace. In the end, why would anyone learn anything if there is no prospect of attaining certain knowledge about it? Or how can decisions be taken in contexts in which every path leads to more unknowns?

There are, of course, many voices raised against these easy assumptions, particularly coming from creativity, innovation, curiosity and wonder research. Unsurprisingly, those scholars and practitioners who focus on processes premised on not knowing or processes that require uncertainty and its management, are much less inclined to perceive either as negative. On the contrary, their accounts point to the fact that uncertainty and not knowing are key experiences that are of great values to creative people in all domains and across the life course, as well as for students and teachers alike (e.g., Duckworth 1975; Jones 2013; Beghetto 2020). They also propose a more refined way of understanding these experiences by sidestepping the polar tendencies to vilify or romanticize. In doing so, they call into question our societal (and educational) obsession with pre-planned, intentional actions and the glorification of knowledge that is certain, universal, definitive.

I will join these voices in the present chapter by adding what I hope are new arguments for why not knowing and uncertainty not only matter, but are truly instrumental for all those processes that make us human, from our capacity to wonder to the development of a sense of self. In supporting this claim, I will build on a small typology of 'states of mind' that exist at the intersection between our phenomena of interest: *certain knowledge* and the experience of trust, *uncertain not knowing* and the experience of anxiety, *uncertain knowing* and the experience of curiosity, and *certain not knowing* and the experience of wonder. These broadly connect to other typologies, such as the distinction between known knowns, unknown knowns, known unknowns, unknown unknowns (e.g., Collins and Cruickshank 2014), without any one to one mapping. I will start by reviewing, in turn, how each state relates to creativity, learning, and development. In order to recognize the inter-dependence between these phenomena, I will refer most often to 'creative learning' following Beghetto's (2016, p. 9) definition of it as "a combination of intrapsychological and interpsychological processes that result in new and personally meaningful understandings for oneself and others".

My main aim, however, is to portray the four states of mind as dynamic forms of connecting person and world that reflect their constant co-evolution. It is, in other words, the 'movement' between certain knowledge, uncertain not knowing, uncertain knowing, and certain not knowing that interests me most. Towards the end, I will propose both a phase and a process-based model of creative learning, models that are premised on the interplay between the four main experiences referred to above (trust, anxiety, curiosity, and wonder). Instead of replacing certain knowledge with uncertain forms of not knowing on the pedestal of education and human development, it is more fruitful to notice how both of these – and all the states and processes in between – contribute to living full, creative, and dignified lives. With these considerations in mind, let's begin.

2.2   Certain Knowing

There are few things as comforting as the experience of certain knowledge, a security we often seek in everyday life (Koriat 2012). Being sure that what we know is correct helps us navigate situations smoothly and make quick and informed decisions. It also boosts self-esteem and self-efficacy by potentially increasing speed and performance. Those who don't have to doubt themselves or the validity of their knowledge tend to act fast and trust that they will reach the preferred outcome. Whether or not the certainty associated with this kind of knowledge passes the test of time and practical action is another matter (Schommer 1990). In the moment of doing, there is confidence and little delay.

Most educational systems across history and across the world list the acquisition of certain knowledge as their end goal. Schooling itself is based on the implicit assumption that those who attend and are willing to learn will acquire useful information about the world, information that has been tested or verified and proven to be correct. Certainty is a key value for teachers as well, who are meant to reflect it both in what and how they teach (see Nolan and Molla 2017). In exchange, students are expected to be confident in their answers and not to question the validity of the wisdom they are imparted. Instead, the questioning is done by the teacher and most of the times it serves the purpose of steering the student away from false conclusions and towards the correct answer (Gall 1970).

This approach has certainly come under considerable criticism over time for not encouraging critical and creative thinking (see Sternberg 2012). When resting on the assumption of certain knowledge, students and teachers alike are less likely to question implicit assumptions or notice taken for granted elements in their own thinking. And yet, this doesn't mean that there is no place for this kind of knowing within a learning or creative process. Following in the footsteps of Descartes (1937/1968), we can note that at least one point of certainty is needed in order to engage in a sustained inquiry of our knowledge. Lacking the possibility of certain knowledge is disempowering and can discourage the person from thinking further.

The question is, thus, what is the true place and role of certain knowledge in education and, more broadly, in human development.

To answer this, we need to understand what the experience of this kind of knowledge feels like. One way to describe this experience is to reflect on the notion of trust. Feeling trust means placing one's confidence in a person, process or outcome and being reassured that they will act predictably or reflect reality truthfully. Importantly, trust is not an individual state of mind, but a phenomenon that is constantly framed by wider social, cultural and political factors (Markova and Gillespie 2008). It is also an essential experience for the healthy psychological development of the person (Winnicott 1971), creating the necessary conditions of safety and comfort that enable the passage from dependence to independence vis a vis caregivers. Interpersonal trust is associated with various positive outcomes for both the person who trusts and the person who is trusted (Govier 1993; Frost et al. 1978). Interestingly, these positive effects extend to how people create together (Bidault and Castello 2009; Boies et al. 2015) since self-trust appears to correlate with creative self-efficacy (Puente-Díaz 2016).

I propose here that the experience of trust is essential for creativity and learning beyond groupwork and self-efficacy. While, in creative learning, we can trust others and their inputs, trust our own evaluation criteria, trust that the materials we work with have the expected affordances, trust that risk-taking will pay off as a strategy, etc., there is a more fundamental level at which certain knowledge supports a developmental process. Since this kind of knowledge gives us the confidence to proceed, it is a key motivator for pursuing a course of action. It's not the trust that the chosen action is 'correct' that I'm referring to here, but that it will lead to interesting and potentially useful outcomes. Even in the most exploratory forms of creativity or experiential forms of learning, trust rests in the certain knowledge that new things will always emerge and that this emergence is positive and needs to be cultivated. Instead of placing certain knowledge as the end goal of education or development, we are well advised to see it as an enabler for both.

2.3 Uncertain Not Knowing

It is often in the act of letting go of certain knowledge that we discover new possibilities able to fuel creativity, learning and development. But, as always, it depends on how much uncertainty and not knowing we infuse into our thinking and action. Experiencing uncertain forms of not knowing represents, in many ways, the polar opposite of the category before. It is a state in which we don't only miss a clear understanding of things, but we are also uncertain about what exactly it is that we don't know. It is an unsettling experience that many individuals try to avoid on a daily basis. This is how, for example, the construct of 'intolerance of uncertainty' has been formulated and studied especially in its relation to worries and worrying (e.g., Ladouceur et al. 2000), in terms of its valid measurement (e.g., Carleton et al. 2007), etc. Here, I consider uncertain knowing in view of the experience of anxiety vis a vis what is not (yet) known and what remains uncertain for the individual. While anxiety has a wider scope than not knowing and uncertainty, it is one of the chief responses to both (so much so that different authors talk about uncertainty-related anxiety; see Hirsh et al. 2012).

Uncertain not knowing is not an experience that can be sustained for a long time without leaving a negative mark on the emotional and cognitive state of the person (a fact that has been documented for a long time, see Breggin 1964). Even when it does not concern issues of existential importance, this kind of uncertainty is experienced as unpleasant and defense mechanisms are employed against it (Perna 2013). One of them is ignoring things that we don't know about (and are uncertain as to what exactly we don't know about them or whether we could ever get to know more) or trivializing them. Another reaction could be to try, as much as possible, to eliminate either the uncertainty or the not knowing, even through incomplete, temporary explanations that take us closer to certainty and to knowledge. Yet another way is to contain this kind of anxiety and focus on what we do know or are certain about as a way of moving forward and continuing to act decisively.

While adaptive to different degrees, these reactions ignore the transformative potential of uncertain not knowing and its role within creativity and learning. Creative action often originates in both uncertainty and not knowing (Cremin 2006; Zelinski 1994) and it depends, to some extent, on how well the creator can withstand these states of mind and delay making quick and fast decisions. For learners, uncertain not knowing can be both a departing point and an experience that returns, again and again, whenever the learner is confronted with the new limits of his or her understanding. The anxiety that often accompanies such moments is in itself informative as it points to everything that lies beyond our understanding and view of the world. And this is precisely how uncertain not knowing becomes a key developmental resource. By focusing us on what is not within our grasp and making us unsure of what is, it directs our attention towards the great beyond vis a vis our usual thinking, action, and way of being.

It is not by coincidence that Heidegger (1927/2010) related existential anxiety with the reality of being in the world and with an existence that is open to a multitude of potentialities. Becoming aware of this openness and the many unknowns it presents us with can be destabilizing but it is a kind of instability that helps us remain open to the future (should we accept it). What we learn from uncertain not knowing is not knowledge about the world as much as knowledge about the self and its nature. The end goal of this experience is not to be replaced by certain knowledge, but to be used as a springboard for new ways of being. Anxieties due to uncertain unknowing are an ever-present companion of creative learning and they are not primarily an obstacle (as often believed), but a resource. We become more conscious of this when we don't deal only with the antinomy of certain knowing–uncertain not knowing; it is the 'mixed' states of uncertain knowing and certain not knowing that build bridges between these two poles and turn them into dynamic, recursive, integrative experiences rather than black and white states.

2.4 Uncertain Knowing

Some of the most productive experiences for creativity, learning and development combine elements of certainty and uncertainty, knowing and not knowing. For example, we can think about uncertain knowing or being certain about not knowing as generative for our thinking and being in the world. Focusing on the former, we can conclude that all our knowing is described by different degrees of associated uncertainty. We might be sure of what we know and yet still eager to double check facts or think about what remains ambiguous to us. And it is these ambiguities that make us curious about what we could or should learn next, what we might be able to create or to think differently about. Curiosity, in this context, is a natural drive towards acquiring new understandings of ourselves, other people, and the world we share (Loewenstein 1994).

And yet, for as natural as this experience is, we rarely question our knowledge on a regular basis, except when ongoing events make it unsustainable to be certain about it. This is why, for example, curiosity is born out of encountering surprising or unfamiliar stimuli in our environment (Berlyne 1954). These stimuli create tension or disequilibrium, a temporary state of not knowing that we are actively trying to replace with new knowledge. This is a key characteristic of curiosity and, more generally, the state of uncertain knowing – the fact that it prompts the person to explore things further in an effort to move from not understanding to understanding. These explorations can be imaginative (Swain 2018) and/or highly embodied, taking the form of tinkering and experimentation (Poce et al. 2019). In the end, curiosity needs to be 'satisfied' and the uncertainty 'resolved'. But, in the process, new questions emerge that led to new occasions to be curious and, as we shall see later, to wonder about things.

Curiosity is considered today a highly desirable trait and process (Lindholm 2018). It is seen as important not only for the cognitive development of the person, but also for creativity (Karwowski 2012) and even psychological health and well-being (Gallagher and Lopez 2007). The 'responsibility' to cultivate a curious approach to self and world lies, from early on, with caregivers and teachers. There is a sustained criticism, however, addressed to schools in particular for not doing more to foster students' curiosity as an essential driver of learning and creativity (Engel 2011). By not offering enough opportunities to be uncertain about their knowledge, especially when this knowledge is acquired directly from books or the teacher, we are effectively eliminating the possibility of inquiry-based learning in favor of what Paolo Freire called 'the banking metaphor of education' (Freire 1968). The interest is, here, to create 'deposits' of (certain) knowledge in the minds of students rather than allow them to think for themselves. And, more broadly, it is not only students but teachers as well who are lacking opportunities to be curious and uncertain about their knowledge, teaching practice or the curriculum that guides them. Lesson unplanning and other similar strategies made to infuse a degree of uncertainty in education (Beghetto 2017b) can go a long way in fighting the banking tendency and embracing new pedagogies of the possible (Glăveanu 2020a).

But there are also limits as to what curiosity can help us accomplish. Perhaps unfairly, philosophers like Edmund Burke (1958) and Martin Heidegger (1994) have been exceedingly critical of this experience. They noted that curiosity easily changes its topic of interest, can make us distracted and, most of all, it can be a superficial state of mind. By aiming to take us from uncertain knowing to certain knowing, it is a process that tames unfamiliarity rather than cultivate it. And, in doing this, it misses some of the deeper, more transformative qualities of other processes such as wonder. But, instead of comparing curiosity and wonder, we should try to reflect rather on the place of uncertain knowledge within the broader picture of our ongoing transactions with the world. In this regard, the uncertainty of knowledge is a step within a wider process, one that can remove uncertainty but can also maintain it. Curiosity doesn't always have to be satisfied and this is how, for example, we can find individuals who dedicate a lifetime to an overarching question (Gruber and Barrett 1974), driven by the knowledge they don't yet have.

2.5 Certain Not Knowing

From the different experiences discussed before, certain not knowing stands out as the most peculiar. While knowledge itself comes with its uncertainties, it is rare for not knowing to be 'certain' and lead to a recognition of one's limits (Martin 2004). There are many things we don't know well but few we are ready to accept not knowing anything about. It is more comforting to either ignore the latter or, prompted by curiosity, to gain some understanding of them. Accepting with conviction that you don't know and dwelling on this state seems like the practice of skeptics and nihilists. The first question everything to the point of eliminating certain knowledge, the second deny the possibility of this knowledge in the first place.

And yet, it is certain not knowing and the experience of wonder it invites that hold the key to becoming aware of and experiencing human possibility (Glăveanu 2020b). This is because, ultimately, knowledge describes the world in a specific way and often fails to keep it open to a myriad of interpretations. In the lack of knowledge there is potential to know more and, especially, to know different. For building knowledge commits us to a given reading of reality, one that makes other readings unlikely or labels them as wrong. Not knowing, on the contrary, excludes singular constructions of the world and, as such, escapes easy, dominant or hegemonic ones. In recognizing one's lack of knowledge rests the humility to learn from various perspectives and to still question each of them, in turn.

This was, essentially, the core feature of the Socratic method of inquiry (Seeskin 1987). Socrates' aim was to shake our taken-for-granted assumptions and help us look at ourselves and at reality with genuine wonderment. This is also why he famously noted that philosophy, the love of wisdom, is born in wonder (Plato 1903). Paradoxically, the discipline that studies the nature and role of knowledge itself finds its origin in not knowing and, more than this, in being certain of it ("I know that I know nothing", Socrates is supposed to have said). There is a deeper lesson here for learning and creativity researchers, many of whom consider certain knowledge as the end point for human development, even when one has to overcome uncertainty and not knowing in order to reach this state. For Socrates and Heidegger, the twentieth century philosopher who tried to recover the meaning and value of Socratic wonder (see Heidegger 1994, 2010), it was dwelling in the unknown that had the best chances of teaching us about self and world.

Wonder is, itself, contradictory in nature. It both makes us passive (wondering at) and active (wondering about), immersed (flow) and detached (reflective) about our experience (for details, see Glăveanu 2020b). Wondering can be subjectively experienced as a heightened state of openness, an exalted way of being, or as a maddening return to the same question without reaching any clearer answer. It was the latter, after all, that prompted the Athenian polis to sentence Socrates to death for corrupting the minds of youth and filling them up with paralyzing doubt instead of reassured certainty. But the doubting associated with wondering is only infuriating and paralyzing for those who wonder for the sake of reaching a final, definitive understandings of the world; the people who are certain about not knowing merely in order to know more and to know better.

The developmental value of maintaining a state of not knowing and learning from this experience rests precisely in delaying closure and avoiding pre-conceived ideas. There is consistent evidence, in the literature on creativity, that tolerating ambiguity and uncertainty (for a difference between the two, see Grenier et al. 2005) is associated with an increased likelihood of creative expression (including later on in life; see Csikszentmihalyi and Getzels 1971). But, in order to make the most of wonder, one needs to be prepared to accept not knowing not as a negative but positive state, not as a means but as a goal in itself, not as a momentary, fleeing event but the basis of a unique, fruitful approach to life. And one must also notice the complex interplay between this special way of being and the trust, anxiety and curiosity discussed before. In the end, creativity and learning require all these different manners of relating to self, world and knowledge – when, how and why they become necessary is what I focus on next.

2.6   The Creative Learning Process

As I argued above, each one of the four experiences discussed in this chapter – i.e., certain knowing, uncertain not knowing, uncertain knowing and certain not knowing – have a part to play in creativity and learning. In the following, I will refer to *creative learning* not as a new, third phenomenon, but use this term in recognition of the fact that each creative episode offers opportunities to learn and that moments of learning involve the creative appropriation of new meanings and practices (see also Beghetto 2016; Glăveanu et al. 2019). Moreover, this notion draws our attention to the intimate relation between creativity and learning, on the hand, and knowledge and uncertainty on the other. Traditionally, learning has been associated with the acquisition of knowledge while creativity, at least in its initial stages, with the experience of uncertainty. While some past research explored the connection between creativity and knowledge, its scope was mainly to consider how the latter either supports or inhibits the former (Weisberg 1999). Equally, past discussions of learning and uncertainty considered the latter as springboard, a transitional stage to be overcome by the time learning is complete (Gallagher and Reid 1981). In this chapter, I want to argue that (not) knowing and (un)certainty are part and parcel of creative learning processes and they are not merely triggers, preconditions, end points or consequences of creativity and learning.

In making this claim, I propose here two 'models' of creative learning that formulate this phenomenon in terms of the interplay between trust, anxiety, curiosity and wonder, models that recognize the significant contribution of not knowing and uncertainty to human development. The first one is structural in nature and considers the main stages of creative learning seen in a rather linear manner. The second one is dynamic and tries to unpack the relations between these different experiences within each moment and stage.

Stage models have been highly popular in both the psychology of creativity and that of learning and development. We can be reminded here, for instance, of Wallas's (1926) well-known phases of the creative process, including preparation, incubation, illumination and verification. Or the even more famous stage model of Piaget (1972), focused on the development of intelligence and moving from sensorimotor and preoperational to concrete and formal operations. Over the past decades, such linear models have been contested in both fields (see Glăveanu 2014; Robberecht 2007) and the emphasis has shifted towards constituting processes rather than distinct stages (see Lubart 2001). One of the main points of contention is the fact that real-life episodes of creative learning have a much more recursive nature than stage models tend to suggest (and it is worth remembering that, for Piaget, the qualitative jumps made between stages of development are irreversible). More and more models of creativity and learning start to recognize the unstructured and intrinsically 'messy' nature of the processes involved (see Parks 2008; Jones 2018). And yet, we should avoid throwing out the baby with the bath water in this regard. Stage models are necessary to guide our macro-view of the process and, when they make room for internal differentiations and back and forth movements, they can be very useful tools for researchers and practitioners alike (see, for example Ness's model of group creativity formalized as 'the room of opportunity' in Ness and Søreide 2014).

How does a stage model of creative learning look like from the perspective developed here? Fig. 2.1 proposes a view of this phenomenon that starts from the experience of anxiety triggered by the uncertainties of not knowing or not understanding something. It then proceeds by reflecting on existing knowledge, even if uncertain, and engaging in curious exploration. This exploration leads, often, to a clear and certain realization of what is not known and, thus, to the experience of wonder. It is the back and forth between questioning existing knowledge and wondering about the unknown that pushes creative learning forward, eventually gaining trust in what has been created or learnt and a sense of certainty vis a vis the knowledge acquired throughout the process.

Fig. 2.1 A structural
model of creative learning

Fig. 2.2 A dynamic model
of creative learning

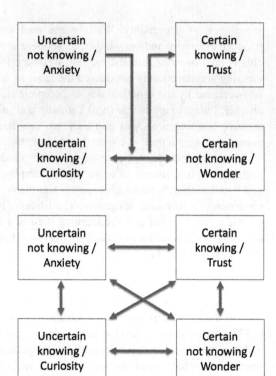

This is not to say, of course, that every single act of creative learning needs to start with a rupture in our understanding of the world and end with overcoming it and restoring a state of serenity and trust. We also learn creatively about things we are already familiar with and, at times, end the process in a state of doubt and dissatisfaction with what has been achieved. In fact, most artists would claim that they almost never reach a state of certainty in relation to their creative activity, something demonstrated by the fact that many find it difficult to say when exactly the work is finished (Landi 2014). At the same time, it is rare for any authentic forms of creative learning to not originate in a gap or problem that cannot be solved with usual, familiar means (Torrance 1988). This is, after all, how we become aware of the fact that we need to learn something new and to create things or procedures we didn't use before. The end of the process – however we define it; e.g., for the artist it might be when the work is sold or presented in an exhibition – could leave us dissatisfied but still certain about what has been produced and knowing what exactly makes us unhappy. For as long as we dwell on uncertainty and not knowing, the processes of creative learning are ongoing.

This last observation is the basis for what I call the dynamic 'model', a zooming in on the different phases of creative learning that reveals, as depicted in Fig. 2.2, the variable interrelation between trust, anxiety, curiosity and wonder. As the double arrows between the four experiences suggest, there is little regularity, at a micro level, when it comes to the movement between knowing and not knowing, certainty and uncertainty. In fact, the defining characteristics of creative learning remain its non-linearity and open-endedness (see Glăveanu and Beghetto 2020). To take some concrete examples, we can focus first on the interplay between curiosity and wonder. As argued above, these represent two different and yet inter-related moves. The first one makes the unfamiliar familiar by confronting us with uncertain knowledge that requires further exploration. The second one does the reverse, making the familiar unfamiliar or, in other words, helping us question taken-for-granted, familiar assumptions, opening us up to the certainties of not knowing. While these are two distinct experiences (see also Glăveanu 2020b), they are often intertwined in creative learning. This is because the questions raised during curious explorations of uncertain knowledge can easily lead us to deeper unknowns, including about things we considered familiar and unsurprising. Equally, wondering about the unknown can turn into the gradual construction of knowledge, including knowledge (we feel) we can trust. Certain knowledge and uncertain not knowing stand in a similar dialogical relation with each other. In the midst of the anxiety of a rupture in our experience of knowing and of certainty, we can still place our trust in specific ideas, bodies of knowledge, including in ourselves and in other people. In fact, this background experience of trust is necessary in order to confront our anxieties and learn from them (Winnicott 1971). Conversely, certain knowledge beyond any possibility of doubt or openness to not knowing is unproductive, at least from a creative learning perspective.

In the end, *creative learning itself can be defined as a fluid movement between certainty and uncertainty, knowing and not knowing that requires, at every stage, a balance between anxiety, trust, curiosity and wonder.* While, at different moments and for different people, depending on domain and personal characteristics, specific states might dominate and even overwhelm the person (think, for instance, about intense moments of wondering or all-consuming curiosity), it is important to appreciate the role and intrinsic value of each one of these states. Uncertainty and not knowing, in particular, reveal themselves as important constructs for creativity, learning and development, illuminating a wide range of possibilities and keeping us open to multiple perspectives and a future that is yet to come (Glăveanu and Beghetto 2020).

2.7   Implications

In the end, it's helpful to raise the question of why all these distinctions and models matter. Is it useful to re-describe the creative learning process in new terms, added to an already long list of concepts available in the literature, e.g., assimilation and accommodation (Piaget 1972), generation and exploration (Smith et al. 1995), blind variation and selective retention (Simonton 1998), divergent and convergent thinking (de Vries and Lubart 2019), bisociation (Koestler 1964), position exchange and perspective taking (Glăveanu 2015)? The answer is an emphatic yes, especially given the fact that these new lenses to examine creativity and learning are not meant to replace existing conceptions but to add to them a reflection on (not) knowing and (un)certainty. Why do we need this new focus? Because integrating in particular uncertainty and not knowing within our theories and models of creative thinking and human development is long overdue. Most developmental research, for instance, is built on the often-implicit assumption that we move from 'less' to 'more', from simple to complex, from not knowing to knowing (see Shaw 1996). These theories ignore the intrinsically 'messy' and open-ended nature of our being in the world (Heidegger 2010). And, in doing so, they fail to prepare us for the fast-changing, uncertain times we live in.

Placing not knowing and uncertainty – as generative states – at the heart of education is specific for the recently proposed 'pedagogies of the possible' (see Glăveanu 2020a) which are ways of designing for possibility and creative experience in the classroom (Glăveanu and Beghetto 2020). These pedagogies encourage teachers and students alike to go beyond what 'is' present, in the here and now, and explore 'what could be', 'what could have been', 'what will be' and 'what might never be', all spaces of possibility premised on the close interplay between knowing and not knowing. It is only by embracing this interplay that we can co-create knowledge and push development further.

How would a teacher, for example, prepare his or her classes when guided by the structural and dynamic frameworks proposed in this chapter? Most probably, in strikingly new ways that make room for anxiety (uncertain not knowing) and wonder (certain not knowing) in the classroom, instead of the more familiar states of curiosity (uncertain knowing) and trust (certain knowing). He or she would allow students to dwell more in the unknown and embrace its various uncertainties. More than this, the teacher him or herself would do the same, allowing the unexpected and unfamiliar to irrupt within teaching and learning and transform both (Beghetto 2017a, b). This is not, to be sure, a call for promoting disruption for the sake of disruption. As I argued before, certainty and knowledge are and remain important, formative experiences. Anxiety needs to be balanced by trust, curiosity by wonder and, ultimately, the most successful experiences of creative learning, from a developmental standpoint, need to keep these states in dialogue and tension with each other (see, for this, the dialogical writings of Bakhtin 2010). In a world obsessed with recipes for how to create or learn, this chapter and the rest of the book represent open invitations to let go of absolute certainties and enjoy not knowing. If the arguments above hold, we will get to know more and to know different because of it.

References

Anderson Blea, W., & Welsh, T. (2020). The art of not knowing: a mastering of anxiety and depression. *ReSEARCH Dialogues Conference proceedings*. Available from: https://scholar.utc.edu/research-dialogues/2020/day2_presentations/48.

Bakhtin, M. M. (2010). *The dialogic imagination: Four essays*. Austin, TX: University of Texas Press.

Beghetto, R. A. (2016). Creative learning: A fresh look. *Journal of Cognitive Education and Psychology, 15*(1), 6–23.

Beghetto, R. A. (2017a). Inviting uncertainty into the classroom. *Educational Leadership, 75*(2), 20–25.

Beghetto, R. A. (2017b). Lesson unplanning: toward transforming routine tasks into non-routine problems. *ZDM, 49*(7), 987–993.

Beghetto, R. A. (2020). Uncertainty: A gateway to the possible. In V. P. Glaveanu (ed.) *The Palgrave encyclopedia of the possible*. Palgrave: Cham.

Berlyne, D. E. (1954). A theory of human curiosity. *British Journal of Psychology, 45*(3), 180–191.

Bidault, F., & Castello, A. (2009). Trust and creativity: understanding the role of trust in creativity-oriented joint developments. *R&D Management, 39*(3), 259–270.

Boies, K., Fiset, J., & Gill, H. (2015). Communication and trust are key: Unlocking the relationship between leadership and team performance and creativity. *The Leadership Quarterly, 26*(6), 1080–1094.

Breggin, P. R. (1964). The psychophysiology of anxiety. *Journal of Nervous and Mental Disease, 139*(6), 558–568.

Burke, E. (1958). *A philosophical enquiry into the origin of our ideas of the sublime and beautiful*. London: Routledge & Kegan Paul.

Carleton, R. N., Norton, M. P. J., & Asmundson, G. J. (2007). Fearing the unknown: A short version of the Intolerance of Uncertainty Scale. *Journal of Anxiety Disorders, 21*(1), 105–117.

Collins, R. A., & Cruickshank, R. H. (2014). Known knowns, known unknowns, unknown unknowns and unknown knowns in DNA barcoding: a comment on Dowton et al. *Systematic Biology, 63*(6), 1005–1009.

Cremin, T. (2006). Creativity, uncertainty and discomfort: Teachers as writers. *Cambridge Journal of Education, 36*(3), 415–433.

Csikszentmihalyi, M., & Getzels, J. W. (1971). Discovery-oriented behavior and the originality of creative products: A study with artists. *Journal of Personality and Social Psychology, 19*(1), 47–52.

de Vries, H. B., & Lubart, T. I. (2019). Scientific creativity: divergent and convergent thinking and the impact of culture. *The Journal of Creative Behavior, 53*(2), 145–155.

Descartes, R. (1968). *Discourse on method and the meditations*. Harmondsworth: Penguin. (Original work published 1637)

Dönmez, D., & Grote, G. (2013). The practice of not knowing for sure: How agile teams manage uncertainties. In H. Baumeister & B. Weber (eds.), *Agile processes in software engineering and extreme programming* (pp. 61–75). Berlin: Springer.

Duckworth, E. (1975). The virtues of not knowing. *National Elementary Principal, 54*(4), 63–66.

Engel, S. (2011). Children's need to know: Curiosity in schools. *Harvard Educational Review, 81*(4), 625–645.

Freire, P. (1968). *Pedagogy of the oppressed*. New York, NY: Seabury.

Frost, T., Stimpson, D. V., & Maughan, M. R. (1978). Some correlates of trust. *Journal of Psychology, 99*(1), 103–108.

Gall, M. D. (1970). The use of questions in teaching. *Review of Educational Research, 40*(5), 707–721.

Gallagher, J., & Reid, K. (1981). *The learning theory of Piaget and Inhelder*. Austin, TX: PRO-ED.

Gallagher, M. W., & Lopez, S. J. (2007). Curiosity and well-being. *The Journal of Positive Psychology, 2*(4), 236–248.

Gerard, H. B. (1963). Emotional uncertainty and social comparison. *The Journal of Abnormal and Social Psychology, 66*(6), 568–573.

Glăveanu, V. P. (2014). The psychology of creativity: A critical reading. *Creativity: Theories–Research–Applications, 1*(1), 10–32.

Glăveanu, V. P. (2015). Creativity as a sociocultural act. *Journal of Creative Behavior*, *49*(3), 165–180.

Glăveanu, V. P. (2020a). *The possible: A sociocultural theory*. New York, NY: Oxford University Press.

Glăveanu, V. P. (2020b). *Wonder: The extraordinary power of an ordinary experience*. London: Bloomsbury Press.

Glăveanu, V. P., & Beghetto, R. A. (2020). Creative experience: A non-standard definition of creativity. *Creativity Research Journal*, early view.

Glăveanu, V. P., Johanne Ness, I., Wasson, B., & Lubart, T. (2019). Sociocultural perspectives on creativity, learning, and technology. In C. A. Mullen (Ed.), *Creativity under duress in education? Resistive theories, practices, and actions* (pp. 63–82). New York, NY: Springer.

Govier, T. (1993). Self-trust, autonomy, and self-esteem. *Hypatia*, *8*(1), 99–120.

Grenier, S., Barrette, A. M., & Ladouceur, R. (2005). Intolerance of uncertainty and intolerance of ambiguity: Similarities and differences. *Personality and Individual Differences*, *39*(3), 593–600.

Gruber, H. E., & Barrett, P. H. (1974). *Darwin on man: A psychological study of scientific creativity*. New York: EP Dutton.

Heidegger, M. (1994). *Basic questions of philosophy*. Translated by R Rojcewicz & A. Schuwer. Bloomington: Indiana University Press.

Heidegger, M. (2010). *Being and time* (J. Stambaugh, Trans, revised by D. J. Schmidt). Albany, NY: State University of New York Press. (Originally published in 1927)

Hirsh, J. B., Mar, R. A., & Peterson, J. B. (2012). Psychological entropy: A framework for understanding uncertainty-related anxiety. *Psychological Review*, *119*(2), 304–320.

Jones, R. (2018). Messy creativity. *Language Sciences*, *65*, 82–86.

Jones, R. (2013). On the value of not knowing: Wonder, beginning again and letting be. In E. Fisher & R. Fortnum (eds.), *On Not Knowing: How Artists Think* (pp. 6–31). London: Black Dog Publishing.

Karwowski, M. (2012). Did curiosity kill the cat? Relationship between trait curiosity, creative self-efficacy and creative personal identity. *Europe's Journal of Psychology*, *8*(4), 547–558.

Koestler, A. (1964). *The act of creation*. New York, NY: Penguin Books.

Koriat, A. (2012). The subjective confidence in one's knowledge and judgments: some metatheoretical considerations. In M. Beran, J. L. Brandl, J. Perner, & J. Proust (Eds.), *The foundations of metacognition* (pp. 213–233). Oxford: Oxford University Press.

Ladouceur, R., Gosselin, P., & Dugas, M. J. (2000). Experimental manipulation of intolerance of uncertainty: A study of a theoretical model of worry. *Behaviour Research and Therapy*, *38*(9), 933–941.

Landi, A. (2014). When Is an Artwork Finished? *ARTnews*, February, 79–83.

Lindholm, M. (2018). Promoting Curiosity? *Science & Education*, *27*(9–10), 987–1002.

Loewenstein, G. (1994). The psychology of curiosity: A review and reinterpretation. *Psychological Bulletin*, *116*(1), 75–98.

Lubart, T. I. (2001). Models of the creative process: Past, present and future. *Creativity Research Journal*, *13*(3–4), 295–308.

Markova, I., & Gillespie, A. (2008). *Trust and distrust: Sociocultural perspectives*. Charlotte, NC: Information Age Publishing.

Martin, M. G. (2004). The limits of self-awareness. *Philosophical Studies: An International Journal for Philosophy in the Analytic Tradition*, *120*(1/3), 37–89.

Ness, I. J., & Søreide, G. E. (2014). The room of opportunity: understanding phases of creative knowledge processes in innovation. *Journal of Workplace Learning*, *26*(8), 545–560

Nolan, A., & Molla, T. (2017). Teacher confidence and professional capital. *Teaching and Teacher Education*, *62*, 10–18.

Parks, A. N. (2008). Messy learning: Preservice teachers' lesson-study conversations about mathematics and students. *Teaching and Teacher Education*, *24*(5), 1200–1216.

Perna, G. (2013). Understanding anxiety disorders: the psychology and the psychopathology of defence mechanisms against threats. *Rivista di Psichiatria, 48*(1), 73–75.

Piaget, J. (1972). *The psychology of intelligence.* Totowa, NJ: Littlefield Adams.

Plato (1903). Theaetetus. In *Platonis Opera*, Edited by John Burnet. Oxford University Press. Perseus Digital Library.

Poce, A., Amenduni, F., & Medio, C. De. (2019). From tinkering to thinkering. Tinkering as critical and creative thinking enhancer. *Journal of E-Learning and Knowledge Society, 15*(2), 101–112.

Puente-Díaz, R. (2016). Creative self-efficacy: An exploration of its antecedents, consequences, and applied implications. *The Journal of Psychology, 150*(2), 175–195.

Robberecht, R. (2007). Interactive Nonlinear Learning Environments. *Electronic Journal of e-learning, 5*(1), 59–68.

Schommer, M. (1990). Effects of beliefs about the nature of knowledge on comprehension. *Journal of Educational Psychology, 82*(3), 498–504.

Seeskin, K. (1987). *Dialogue and discovery: A study in Socratic method.* New York, NY: SUNY Press.

Shaw, I. (1996). Unbroken voices: Children, young people and qualitative methods. In I. Butler & I. Shaw (eds.), *A case of neglect? Children's experiences and the sociology of childhood* (pp. 19–36). Aldershot: Avebury.

Simonton, D. K. (1998). Donald Campbell's model of the creative process: Creativity as blind variation and selective retention. *The Journal of Creative Behavior, 32*(3), 153–158.

Smith, S. M., Ward, T. B., & Finke, R. A. (eds.). (1995). *The creative cognition approach.* Cambridge, MA: MIT Press.

Sternberg, R. J. (2012). What is the purpose of schooling? In D. Ambrose & R. J. Sternberg (Eds.), *How dogmatic beliefs harm creativity and higher level thinking* (pp. 207–219). London: Routledge.

Swain, K. (2018). Wonder-full: Curiosity Cabinets and imagination in education. *The Lancet Child & Adolescent Health, 2*(12), 852–862.

Torrance, E. P. (1988). The nature of creativity as manifest in its testing. In R. J. Sternberg (ed.), *The nature of creativity: Contemporary psychological perspectives* (pp. 43–75). Cambridge, England: Cambridge University Press.

Van den Bos, K. (2009). Making sense of life: The existential self trying to deal with personal uncertainty. *Psychological Inquiry, 20*(4), 197–217.

Wallas, G. (1926). *The art of thought.* London: Jonathan Cape.

Weisburg, R. W. (1999). Creativity and knowledge: a challenge to theories. In R. J. Sternberg (Ed.), Handbook of creativity (pp. 226–259). Cambridge: Cambridge University Press.

Winnicott, D. (1971). *Playing and reality.* London: Routledge

Woozley, A. D. (1952, January). Knowing and not knowing. In *Proceedings of the Aristotelian Society* (Vol. *53*, pp. 151–172). Aristotelian Society, Wiley.

Zelinski, E. J. (1994). *The joy of not knowing it all: Profiting from creativity at work or play.* Chicago: VIP Books.

Chapter 3
Uncertainty Makes Creativity Possible

Mark A. Runco

Abstract The topic of uncertainty has not received the attention it deserves. This chapter develops the view that uncertainty is a part of all creative efforts, first by going into some detail about how creativity is defined, then turning to several kinds of research on creativity that support that view. The first section about the definition of creativity is a bit abstract but draws from respected theories of associative processes and problem solving. The next section is more concrete and practical, with material on education and testing. Next is a discussion of some lessons learned from studies of physics and creativity, as well as implications of recent studies of politics and creativity. The final section might be the simplest because it discusses Future Studies, and of course the future is an uncertain thing. The role of creative thinking for the future is explored immediately before the concluding comments.

3.1 Introduction

The topic of uncertainty has not received the attention it deserves. More attention should be devoted to it because uncertainty is inherent in all creative efforts. It is a part of the creative process, or more accurately, part of the context in which the creative process is possible. This chapter develops the view that uncertainty is a part of all creative efforts, first by going into some detail about how creativity is defined, then turning to several kinds of research on creativity that support that view. The first section about the definition of creativity is a bit abstract but draws from respected theories of associative processes and problem solving. The next section is more concrete and practical, with material on education and testing. Next is a discussion of some lessons learned from studies of physics and creativity, as well as implications of recent studies of politics and creativity. The final section might be the simplest because it discusses Future Studies, and of course the future is an

M. A. Runco (✉)
Creativity Research & Programming, Southern Oregon University, Ashland, OR, USA
e-mail: RuncoM@sou.edu

© Springer Nature Switzerland AG 2022
R. A. Beghetto, G. J. Jaeger (eds.), *Uncertainty: A Catalyst for Creativity,
Learning and Development*, Creativity Theory and Action in Education 6,
https://doi.org/10.1007/978-3-030-98729-9_3

uncertain thing. The role of creative thinking for the future is explored immediately before the concluding comments.

3.2 The Uncertainty Required for Creativity

The obvious starting point is to look more closely at why uncertainty is inherent in creative efforts. This claim follows from the *standard definition of creativity* (Runco and Jaeger 2012) which has two requirements: originality and effectiveness. The claim about uncertainty being inherent in all creative efforts is actually supported by any definition that emphasizes originality, not just the standard definition. That is because originality implies that something new is produced. Before any new idea or product is offered, there is an unknown. The unknown may involve a problem with an unknown solution or it may be a gap and effective bridges to close that gap are unknown. If an idea or product is new, which it must be to qualify as original, it has not existed previously. If it did not exist previously it is unlikely that it could be predicted. One way or another there is uncertainty.

These ideas should be put into a broader context. After all, (a) there is more to creativity than originality and (b) there are definitions of creativity which do not put as much emphasis on originality as does the standard definition. On that first point, that there is more to creativity than originality, consider wildly original ideas that are not effective. They may be crazy and worthless. All they are is original. Often they are original for a reason: they have no value (Weisberg 2015). A creative idea or product, on the other hand, must be in some way new, but it must also somehow solve a problem or fit with an existing context. This is why effectiveness is also included in the standard definition, along with originality. It also explains why various authors have suggested that *value* is a requirement for creativity.

There is latitude in how originality and effectiveness are each defined. In fact, both originality and effectiveness are umbrella terms. Originality may be novelty, but it may also be apparent in uniqueness, rarity, or unusualness. Effectiveness, on the other hand, may be defined as a solution that solves a problem in a satisfactory fashion, or it may be apparent in that the new idea or product is fitting, apt, or somehow appropriate to the situation at hand. A very detailed analysis of effectiveness was presented by Bruner (1962). He described different kinds of effectiveness, including (a) predictive effectiveness, which occurs when we look back and see the benefits of the creation, (b) formal effectiveness, which is a matter of logic and mathematics, and (c) metaphorical effectiveness, where different domains of experience that were apart are connected. As an example of the last of these Bruner described a work of art, Santa Maria Alba, with a face showing her as "virgin, strumpet, flirt, daughter, wife, and mother all at the same time." Bruner also quoted Poincare (1905) on the idea that creative thinking may effectively use combinations that "reveal to us unsuspected kingships between… facts long known but wrongly believed to be strangers to one another" (p. 5). A final form of effectiveness is aesthetic, which may fit under the label "fit" or aptness, but being in the aesthetic realm there may be a personal conception of what is felicitous.

Although the connection to uncertainty is clearest in the originality requirement of the standard definition it is also important to recognize that there are other definitions of creativity. One set of them requires *authenticity* for creativity. Authenticity makes a great deal of sense in part because it fits well with cross cultural views of creativity. Simplifying some, in the East creativity is often seen as an authentic expression of oneself. There, originality is unimportant, or at least less important than predicated by the standard definition (Kharkhurin 2014). Authenticity is also a serious consideration for a definition because it fits so well with humanistic views of creativity. Maslow (1973) and Rogers (1959), for example, felt that creativity was inextricable from *self actualization*; and self actualization requires that the individual is honest about and accepting of him- or herself. This implies a kind of authenticity. Other definitions of creativity have been presented by Acar et al. (2017), Weisberg (2015), Harrington (2018), and Corazza (2016). The point here is that the claim that uncertainty is inherent in creativity assumes a definition, and in particular a definition that emphasizes originality, but (a) there is more to creativity than just originality, and (b) there are definitions that do not put originality as a key requirement.

3.3 Uncertainty in the Creative Process

It is useful to think about creativity as a process where the individual is thinking and interacting with the environment as he or she moves through time. The individual may be thinking associatively, with ideas coming one after another (Mednick 1962; Russ and Hoffman 2020). This chain of associations may be in response to some challenge or problem, but it heads into the unknown. The individual does not know which remote associates will be found when he or she first begins to think about the problem or challenge. Another way to view the process is with the problem solving model that describes individuals exploring a *problem space*. Here uncertainty is implied by the fact that there is space. It is not like there is one possible solution or idea. In fact, often it is not even like there is one way to view the problem! I am thinking here of the role of *problem finding*, which often occurs at the beginning of the problem solving process (Reiter-Palmon et al. 1997; Runco 1994). Here too there may be various perspectives, alternatives, or associations, and hence uncertainty.

A related take on this involves the creative process as originally described by Wallas (1926). This process assumes that an idea or solution is produced (after preparation and then incubation), but then some verification (Wallas 1926) or evaluation (Runco 2003) is required. Above I described how a person may use a cognitive process but is uncertain about the outcome, but once there is an outcome, in the form of an idea or solution, there is additional uncertainty about that outcome. Is the outcome adequate, apt, and effective? These questions can only be answered after there is some evaluation. Empirical research has targeted this step of the process and examined how well people are able to evaluate ideas. Some of this research asks participants to judge the originality of the ideas they themselves have generated, and some asks for judgments about creativity or appropriateness. Sometimes the judgments are inter- rather than intrapersonal. Runco (1990), for example, had parents and teachers evaluate ideas which had been previously generated by children. The inaccuracy of judgments is somewhat surprising. For the present purposes the key findings may be those where individuals judge their own ideas for originality—and are only accurate at about 50% of the time. In other words when they have an original idea they are only aware of it about 50% of the time.

There are two implications of the research on idea evaluations. One is that a person may be trying to solve a problem in a creative way and thus put some time into ideation, perhaps producing a set of options. Given the marginal evaluative accuracy mentioned above, that person is likely to be uncertain about which ideas are the most original. This is unfortunate, at least if the standard definition applies and originality is required for creativity. The situation is even more bleak because when a person selects an idea early in the process, he or she may then follow that idea and see where it leads. But what if the first idea selected, before associations are explored, and is not a good one? You might say that this individual has chosen the wrong node in an associative network, or that the person is solving the wrong problem.

Another unfortunate situation may occur when solving problems in a group. That is because an individual may contribute by offering an idea, but there is uncertainty. This time it is uncertainty about how the group will react. The group may see the value or creativity of an idea and appreciate it, or they may not see any value in an idea. The person offering the idea will be uncertain about the interpersonal judgments of the group, especially when the idea is an original one. This can dramatically influence the effectiveness of group work. Rubenson and Runco (1995) discussed this situation and predicted that a person working alone is likely to be most original because he or she need not consider interpersonal judgments. A person working in a dyad is likely to be slightly more inhibited and is therefore likely to offer fewer wild ideas. The other person in the dyad may not see value in wild ideas, and the wild ones are the ideas that make it difficult to predict reactions. Predictions by any one individual about interpersonal judgments will be the most difficult as group size increases, and individuals are thus unlikely to be their most original in large groups. Moreover, the penalty for being highly original is the most severe when the group is large (more people may disrespect a person who gives ideas that are judged to be inappropriate). This kind of uncertainty is about group reactions. Rubenson and Runco suggested that organizations avoid relying on teamwork, including brainstorming groups, for these reasons.

3.4 Educational and Testing

There are several other important practical implications of the idea that uncertainty is inherent in creative work. One involves education. If you think about an educator supervising a classroom full of students, he or she may have a planned curriculum that very well could involve tasks presented to the students which the teacher believes will lead students to learn certain things. The teacher expects certain outcomes. The teacher may assume that the students will learn both by working through the tasks—that is, the process of working through the tasks could be beneficial to the students—but it may also be that the educator holds a constructivist view and believes that knowledge is only meaningful when students discover or create it for themselves. Piaget (1976) described this process when he wrote his wonderful monograph, *To Understand is to Invent.* The relevant thing is that the teacher may present tasks with expectations about the outcomes.

What happens if students respond to tasks presented by the teacher with an unexpected idea? Unexpected, that is, in terms of the curriculum plan. Such a thing is likely if students think creatively. They very well could offer an idea or solution that the teacher did not foresee nor expect. The uncertainty here is experienced by the teacher. He or she may be surprised by what is offered by the students, if they are creative students or if the curriculum is such that it allows students to think for themselves. This situation is not easy for teachers—yet they should appreciate it if they hope to support the creativity of their students. Teachers may minimize the possibility that students will give unexpected ideas, but of course this also means that students are not given an opportunity to be creative. If a teacher hopes to support the creativity of students, he or she should be prepared to deal with uncertainty and surprises.

There are parallel implications for testing. An educator or psychometrician may present closed-test items, such as multiple choice, which means there are very specific answers deemed correct and given high grades. Creativity is not rewarded when the test contains only closed ended (e.g., multiple choice) questions. Open ended tasks allow students to think creatively and produce original and new ideas, but there is a difficulty, namely finding an objective way to score the test. This is one area where the creativity research has recently blossomed. For years, there have been methods for scoring open ended tasks, such as divergent thinking tasks, in a reliable fashion. These methods focused on the fluency of ideas, the variety or flexibility of ideas, and the statistical in frequency of the ideas, which is taken to be indicative of originality. If one student in a group comes up with an idea that others did not think of, assuming it is an appropriate or fitting idea, it may be original and effective—and therefore creative. This method has worked quite well for many years, but lately computer scoring has evolved and been applied to open ended tasks, including essays (Runco et al. (2017b), and divergent thinking tests (Acar and Runco 2019; Beketayev and Runco 2016; Dumas and Runco 2020; Hass 2020).

Very important, the originality that an educator or psychometrician may see in students is indicative of creative *potential*. Originality is not sufficient an index of potential, just as it is not a sufficient a criterion of creativity. Potential involves motivation and attitude, as well as the cognitive capacity to produce original ideas. It is multifaceted and thus a bit of a challenge. Yet there is no more important target for education than potential. There are several reasons for this. First, it is possible for the creative potential of students to mature, and eventually to be expressed in actual creative performances and achievements. Education can go a long way to making this happen (Beghetto 2020; Runco 2017). Second, creative potential may be universal. Very likely all students have creative potential. The range of possible expressions may vary, but still, they each have the potential to be creative.

The claim that creative potential may be fulfilled and eventually allow students to perform in unambiguously creative ways led me to reject an idea that is quite common in the creativity literature. I am referring to the idea that *Big C creativity* is distinct from *Little c creativity*. Too often this idea represents a false dichotomy (Runco 2017). When it does, it implies that students, and anyone else who only express mundane or everyday forms of creativity, are unable to or unlikely to translate their potential such that they perform in a socially-recognized, high level creative manner. To my thinking it is best for educators and researchers to view creativity as a continuum, rather than any sort of dichotomous or categorical variable. It is easier to see the creative potentials of students possibly leading to unambiguous creativity (and perhaps Big C creativity) when it is treated as a continuous variable.

It is sometimes useful to look at the creativity of eminent individuals. One way of doing that uses case studies. Admittedly, there are concerns about case studies, but Gruber (1996) and others have refined the case study method such that cases can uncover things that are valuable to others. This is important because too often case studies have limited generalizability. This means that what we find with eminent cases may not help us understand other individuals. Case studies done right can be helpful. For one thing they can suggest hypotheses that can later be tested with more traditional experimental methods. I also use case studies to illustrate things about creativity which have already been supported by experimental methods.

Consider Edwin Schrödinger, a contemporary of Einstein's. The two of them used a method involving visual experiments. Einstein is famous for suggesting that we can learn about relativity by visualizing that we are riding a train or riding on a beam of light. One's perception of the world changes when in motion—especially if moving close to the speed of light. Schrödinger may be best known for his experiment where there is a cat inside a box. Physicists used "Schrödinger Cat" as a critique of the Copenhagen Interpretation of Quantum Mechanics, but for the rest of us the cat merely demonstrates the role of uncertainty in quantum physics. The uncertainty is most obvious if the cat dies. Since the cat is in a box and cannot be observed, someone outside of the box will not know precisely when the cat has died. Indeed, there is probably a point in time when the person outside of the box believes that the cat is still alive, but in fact, inside the box, unbeknownst to the human, the cat is actually dead. At that point in time there is uncertainty about the cat's status. There is a difference between what goes on in the box and what is known by those outside of the box.

Physicists discussed Schrödinger's cat at length because one implication is that there is unavoidable uncertainty, at least if you give any weight to the beliefs of an observer, and that of course is a huge part of modern physics. Things depend on what can be observed and what is observed. It may be that uncertainty is unavoidable. This conclusion, supported by Schrödinger and others, led to a creative breakthrough and a new way of thinking about physics. Simplifying a great deal, the idea is that uncertainty is inherent in the physical world and therefore science should be very wary of absolutes.

This is all quite consistent with the uncertainty surrounding our understanding of light. There is evidence that light involves quanta and behaves like particles streams, but also evidence that light behaves in a wavelight fashion. These views are not compatible with each other, and that creates a kind of uncertainty. Then there is the Heisenberg uncertainty principle, which tells us that we cannot know both the position of a particle and, at the same time, its speed. If we know its speed, the particle is moving and the location is changing and not fixed. Location is uncertain. If we know the particle's location, it must be stopped, fixed in space, and it has no speed.

Physicists learned a great deal from visual experiments and new perspectives on particles and waves. More broadly, they learned a great deal by tolerating the uncertainty. That can be seen in the breakthroughs of Schrödinger, Heisenberg, and others. As a matter of fact this is one lesson that can be learned from these particular cases—there is value in uncertainty. True, it may be that it is difficult to tolerate uncertainty. Most of the time, certainty is more tolerable. It makes our lives easier, but it may not be realistic. No wonder *tolerance of ambiguity* is one of the core characteristics of creative people (Merrotsy 2020) and research that demonstrates that creative people actually prefer uncertainty.

3.5 Uncertainty as Motive

These ideas about tolerance of uncertainty and a preference for uncertainty have been reported a number of times. Merrotsy (2020) put it this way: "In taxonomies of recurrent attitudes and traits of creative people, tolerance for ambiguity tends to be described as a tolerance of disorder and an attraction to complexity, and it is set alongside other traits such as attraction to the numinous, the mysterious, the asymmetrical, and the incongruous" (p. 645). Uncertainty is implied by several of these preferences. Along the same lines Barron (1963) suggested that creative individuals not only tolerate uncertainty and complexity; they may in fact relish it. He reached this conclusion after examining the lives of individuals who had difficult backgrounds. As they grew up some individuals learned that when a situation involves uncertainty and complexity, there is an opportunity to be creative. Quoting Barron (1963),

the creative artist and scientist appear, when one reads biographical accounts, to have experienced an unusual amount of grief and ordeal in life and to have shouldered burdens of pain
that most commonly disable the individual....the creative individual is one who has learned
to prefer irregularities and apparent disorder and to trust himself to make a new order.
(p. 157)

Barron also described how "the motive is thus generated for searching out other
situations which would seem to defy rational construction, with some degree of
confidence that after much deprivation, tension, and pain a superior form of pleasure will be attained" (p. 157). Barron's pointing to tension, irregularities, and disorder implies that his conclusions may apply to uncertainty as well. There may very
well be a benefit to looking at uncertainty the same way creative people look at
tension and disorder, as opportunities for creativity. That is consistent with Barron's
(1963) view and also follows from the situation described early in this chapter
whereby the originality that is necessary for creativity may depend on uncertainty.

One more thing about the lesson that may be learned from a difficult childhood
(i.e., complexity and uncertainty indicate opportunity). It assumes that the individual is not overwhelmed by the complexity and uncertainty. A particular disposition,
attitude, or coping mechanism may be necessary to learn from a difficult childhood.
Much the same can be said about all stressful events. Stress is not a part of our experiences. It is not imposed upon us. It is instead is the result of how we interpret
experience (Runco 2012). The situation where there is early life complexity and
some individuals are able to cope and even and relish later uncertain situations
assumes that they will interpret those situations as opportunities rather than as
stressful and something to avoid. This in turn suggests that equilibrium is not the
sole objective of creative activity. As Barron (1964) pointed out, it may be that novelty is what individuals seek, rather than homeostasis.

Corazza's (2021) ideas about "inconclusiveness" parallel Barron's (1963) view
of the value of uncertainty. Corazza pointed to famous cases where inconclusiveness seems to have played a role in the creative process. He named Steve Jobs,
Thomas Edison, Guglielmo Marconi, Jean-Baptiste Lamarck, Vincent van Gogh,
and Leonardo.

Of considerable significance in the quotation above is the recognition of the active
role played by the individual. The "searching out" Barron (1963) described is entirely
compatible with the theory that creative individuals actively pursue appropriate intellectual investments (Rubenson and Runco 1992). This in turn could be related to
descriptions of creativity as a proactive (rather than reactive), meta-cognitive, mindful
endeavor. It may also benefit from the openness provided by a liberal orientation.

3.6   Liberalism and Conservatism

There is another important disposition, in addition to the tolerance of uncertainty,
that should be explored. It involves the *liberalism-conservatism* continuum. We can
start with conservatism. That label is often used in political discussions, but it is

described here as a disposition because conservatism often shows itself outside of the political area. Conservatism is from the verb "conserve," and to conserve is to maintain and protect. What is maintained? It certainly is admirable to conserve natural resources and thus help the environment, but often conservatives look more broadly towards maintaining the status quo. This is relevant to the present discussion because a strong conservative is therefore likely to resist change in order to keep things the way they are. The connection to creativity is obvious, given that creativity leads to change and new things, such as innovations. In short, conservatism and creativity are antithetical.

There are data that support the idea that conservatives prefer the status quo and do not like change. These data show that individuals with a conservative slant display less creative behavior than those with a liberal slant. Some of the evidence focuses on correlates of creativity rather than measuring creativity per se. Jost et al. (2003), for example, conducted a meta-analysis of empirical research involving measures of conservatism. This meta-analysis indicated that conservatism was related to cognitive closure, the need for structure, a tendency to follow rules, the avoidance of uncertainty, and intolerance of ambiguity. In addition to the avoidance of the unknown, which could easily lead to missing opportunities for creativity, the tendency to follow rules is also easy to relate to creativity. That is because creative behavior frequently requires breaking or bending rules. Creative behavior is often a form of contrarianism (Runco 2011).

McCann (2011) offered even more compelling findings. He obtained data on the number of patents granted for each US State, and then compared States which voted for the conservative Presidential candidate in the 2008 election to those voting for the more liberal candidate. McCann controlled SES, degree of urbanization, and IQ and found that there were significantly fewer patents in the conservative States compared to the liberal States. Patents have been used many times as indicators of creativity (Tadik 2020). Runco et al. (2017a) extended this by examining patents granted on the County level rather than the State level. This added to the statistical power of their analyses; but the results were much the same. Fewer patents were granted in the more conservative counties.

As noted above the label conservative can be treated as a disposition and not just as a political orientation. True, some of the research above uses voting patterns, but those were used as proxies of the disposition to conservatism. Alternatively, it may be useful to think of this as an example of the "third variable" situation that is discussed in books on correlational statistical methods. In the present discussion conservatism is a causal variable and seems to lead directly to particular voting patterns. In addition, independently of voting, conservatism inhibits invention, patents, and the tendency to submit patents. Conservatism is very likely the causal variable in other situations involving politics, and situations involving creativity as well. Keep in mind that this is pertinent because conservatism is likely to lead a person towards the way things are and away from trying new things, where there is a degree of uncertainty.

3.7 Future Studies

The relationship of creativity with uncertainty is especially clear in future studies (Baumeister and Lim, 2021; Beghetto 2020; Montuori and Donnelly 2020; Leahy, Chap. 17, this volume). Montuori and Donnelly put it this way:

> Human creativity shapes the future. Creativity is how the future comes into being, and human beings are only beginning to see how they are creating the future. The creativity of the modern age led to tremendous progress in science and technology, leading to rapid social change. The very forces that led to progress are now viewed as contributing to the great problems currently facing humanity, whether environmental, economic, or social. Creativity and innovation are drivers of the economy, and there is an increasing awareness of the importance of creativity. Creativity is central to futures visioning processes and to scenario planning. But there is also debate and questioning about how creativity is being used, what kind of futures are being created, to what ends, and by whom.

The first point in that quotation, about creativity shaping the future, is probably an obvious one. Nonetheless evidence is always good, and there is plenty of it. One kind of evidence was presented by Boorstin (1992). He examined the impact of creativity on the unfolding of history. He concluded that creativity has had an enormous impact on progress in the past and there is no reason to think that it will not have the same impact on the future. In fact, if anything, we can expect creativity to have an even larger impact on the future, compared with the past, given reports that creativity has surpassed knowledge as key for innovation, progress, and the economy (Florida and Adler 2020). They main point here is that the future is uncertain and, as Montuori and Donnelly (2020) put it, is shaped by human creativity.

The last point in that quotation from Montuori and Donnelly (2020), about how creativity is being used, and by whom, is less obvious but quite intriguing. One answer to "how and by whom" points to the possibility of creativity sometimes being used to malevolent ends (Cropley et al. 2010; Runco 2019). I point this out because there is a very important implication that follows from the ideas presented in this chapter and exemplified by malevolent creativity. In fact the same idea is suggested by the research on divergent thinking (Runco 2010, in press-a, in press-b): the creativity that is possible in uncertain situations may lead to good ideas or bad. It may lead to effective ideas or ineffective ideas; it may lead to benevolence or malevolence; but if we want to support creativity, we must recognize that it is maximized in situations where there is freedom, latitude, and the opportunity to consider divergent options, some of which may not fit our own values or expectations. If we do anything that imposes our expectations or directs the creative thinking only towards our own values, we will probably stifle the creativity. This follows from the idea of *literal divergence* (Acar and Runco 2015) as well as the research showing that expectations tend to inhibit the expression of creativity (Amabile 1990).

Montuori and Donnelly (2020) went on to say something about modern society and uncertainty:

> The world is currently in a period of significant transition, an in-between state that is marked by the frequent use of the prefix "post-" to describe it, such as post-industrial and post-modern....As a result of this transition society is now in postnormal times. In postnor-

mal times, nothing seems "normal" anymore and chaos, complexity, and contradictions are its defining characteristics....Society has left one age behind but has by no means settled into a new order, if indeed there will be one. Modernity has exhausted itself, in this view. Science, technology, industry, appeared to provide solutions for the challenges of existence and were seen as sources of a bright future. They were the drivers of progress. But the seemingly limitless faith in humanity's capacity for betterment has increasingly turned to skepticism and even distrust, with an awareness that science and technology, and visions of progress cannot be insulated from human greed, errors, and illusions. *Futurists and social commentators agree that as a result of this transition, this in-between state, the future is increasingly uncertain.* Any number of terms have been used to capture the uncertainty. The Polish sociologist Zygmunt Bauman refers to current times as Liquid, fluid and ever-changing, leaving behind the Solid world of Modernity. The US Army War College uses the acronym VUCA, which stands for *Volatile, Uncertain, Complex and Ambiguous* to describe the current global situation. (p. 251, italics added)

These ideas support the suggestion above that creativity is more important today than ever before. There is more uncertainty in the future, and it is coming at us faster and faster (Gleick 2011; Wurman 1989), so we must be as adaptable as possible. Not just adaptable in the sense of responding well to changes imposed, but also adaptable in a proactive and creative fashion, where we systematically expand the range of options and look ahead before it is too late.

Before closing there is one other topic, strongly related to Future Studies, that should be mentioned. It focuses on the question, "What is Possible?" As a matter of fact my thoughts about malevolent creativity, cited above, were first explored in my own contribution to that 2020 volume. Much of that volume is relevant to Future Studies and to creativity vis-a-vis uncertainty because the answer to "what is possible" is likely to entail the future. As noted above, any consideration of the future must recognize that there is uncertainty; and as is probably obvious, my own feeling is that it would be wise to think creatively about what is possible in the future.

3.8 Conclusions

Uncertainty is a part of life. Earth and everything on it is moving through time, and the future is unknown. A person may relish the uncertainty and see it as adding richness to life. Others may be fearful of the unknown. The difference between these two options may be partly dispositional, but no doubt much is matter of choice. Creativity is involved because creative things require originality, and originality requires something new. It would be difficult to appreciate new things if there is a preference for certainty. New things would be avoided. Not surprisingly, there is research suggesting that individuals who embrace the unknown often display creative tendencies.

One suggestion from this chapter is that educators should tolerate uncertainty if they are to best support the creative potentials of their students. That is because by definition the creative potential of students is not manifest. There is an uncertain quality to it. There may be indicators of it, such as originality, a creative attitude, and intrinsic motivation, but there is no guarantee that a student who has these things will in fact eventually behave in a socially-recognized creative fashion. There is a difference between creative potential and creative performance, and there is much more uncertainty about the former because it is not expressed as the latter.

This chapter drew from creative studies, future studies, physics, economics, and politics. Each of these suggested that creativity may be necessary when dealing with uncertainty, at least if good decisions are to be made. Physicists use uncertainty because any explanation of the way things work will be incomplete without it. The brief foray into politics in this chapter looked even more directly at decision making and suggested that certain political orientations, namely those with a conservative slant, have difficulty with uncertainty and prefer that things are certain and remain unchanged. Both Ferris (2010) and Runco (in press-a, in press-b) went into much more detail about the opposite tendencies of liberalism, which embraces change and creativity and uncertainty.

I will close with an observation: This was an odd chapter to write. That is because research is cited and summarized, but most of that previous research did not point specifically to uncertainty. It pointed to patents, idea evaluation, teamwork, testing considerations, or some related topic where uncertainty was involved but not the primary concern. Much of what I did in this chapter was look back at research that assumed or briefly mentioned uncertainty, and I brought implications for creativity to the fore. Uncertainty was suggested by all of the work discussed herein but, in most of the work I cited, not considered in any depth. In a sense this chapter looked in detail about what previous research had assumed, namely that uncertainty is related in various ways creativity. We can hope that uncertainty will receive more focused attention that it has in the past. The present volume represents an excellent step in that direction.

References

Acar, S., Burnett, C., & Cabra, J. F. (2017) Ingredients of Creativity: Originality and more. *Creativity Research Journal, 29,* 133–144. https://doi.org/10.1080/10400419.2017.1302776

Acar, S., & Runco, M. A. (2015). Thinking in multiple directions: Hyperspace categories in divergent thinking. Psychology of Art, Creativity, and Aesthetics, 9, 41–53.

Acar, S., & Runco, M. A. (2019). Divergent thinking: New methods, recent research, and extended theory. Psychology of Aesthetics, Creativity, and the Arts, 13, 153–158. https://doi.org/10.1037/aca0000231

Amabile, T. M. (1990). Within you, without you: The social psychology of creativity, and beyond. In M. A. Runco & R. S. Albert (Eds.), Theories of creativity (rev. ed.). Cresskill, NJ: Hampton Press.

Barron, F. (1963). The need for order and for disorder as motives in creative activity. In C. W. Taylor & F. Barron (Ed.), *Scientific creativity: Its recognition and development* (pp. 153–160). New York: Wiley.

Baumeister R.F., Lim K. (2021) Prospection. In: Glaveanu V.P. (eds) *The Palgrave Encyclopedia of the Possible*. Palgrave Macmillan, Cham. https://doi.org/10.1007/978-3-319-98390-5_138-1

Beghetto R.A. (2020) Uncertainty. In V. Glaveanu (Ed.), *The Palgrave Encyclopedia of the Possible*. Palgrave Macmillan. https://doi.org/10.1007/978-3-319-98390-5_122-1

Beketayev, K., & Runco, M. A. (2016). Scoring divergent thinking tests with a semantics-based algorithm. Europe's Journal of Psychology, 12(2), 210–220. https://doi.org/10.5964/ejop.v12i2.1127

Boorstin, D. J. (1992). *The creators: A history of heroes of the imagination*. New York: Random House.

Bruner, J. (1962). The conditions of creativity. In H.E. Gruber, G. Terell, & M. Wertheimer (Eds.), *Contemporary approaches to creative thinking* (pp. 1–30). New York: Atherton.

Corazza, G. E. (2016) Potential Originality and Effectiveness: The Dynamic Definition of Creativity, Creativity Research Journal, 28:3, 258–267, https://doi.org/10.1080/1040041 9.2016.1195627

Corazza G.E. (2021) Creative Inconclusiveness. In: Glaveanu V.P. (eds) *The Palgrave Encyclopedia of the Possible*. Palgrave Macmillan. https://doi.org/10.1007/978-3-319-98390-5_61-1

Cropley, D. H., A. J. Cropley, J. C. Kaufman, & M. A. Runco (Eds.). (2010). *The dark side of creativity*. New York: Cambridge University Press.

Dumas, D., & Runco, M. A. (2018). Objectively scoring divergent thinking tests for originality: A re-analysis and extension. Creativity Research Journal, 30, 466–468.

Ferris, T. (2010). The science of liberty.

Florida, R., & Adler, P. (2020). Creative class and creative economy. In M. A. Runco & S. Pritzker (Eds)., *Encyclopedia of creativity*. Oxford: Elsevier.

Gleick, J. (2011). *The information*. New York: Vintage.

Gruber, H. E. (1996) The life space of a scientist: The visionary function and other aspects of Jean Piaget's thinking, *Creativity Research Journal, 9*, 251–265, https://doi.org/10.1080/1040041 9.1996.9651176

Hass, R. (2020). Computerized Creativity Testing and Scoring. In M. A. Runco & S. R. Pritzker (Eds.), Encyclopedia of creativity (3rd ed.). Oxford, UK: Elsevier.

Harrington, D. M. (2018) On the usefulness of "value" in the definition of creativity: A commentary, *Creativity Research Journal, 30*, 118–121, https://doi.org/10.1080/10400419.2018.1411432

Jost, J. T., Glaser, J., Kruglanski, A. W., & Sulloway, F. J. (2003). Political conservatism as motivated social cognition. Psychological Bulletin, 129, 339–75. https://doi.org/10.1037/0033-2909.129.3.339

Kharkhurin, A. V. (2014). Creativity.4in1: Four-Criterion Construct of Creativity. Creativity Research Journal, 26, 338–352.

Maslow, A. H. (1973). Creativity in self-actualizing people. In A. Rothenberg and C. R. Hausman (Eds.), The creative question (pp. 86–92). Durham, NC: Duke University Press

McCann, S. (2011). Conservatism, Openness, and Creativity: Patents Granted to Residents of American States. *Creativity Research Journal, 23*, 339–345.

Mednick, S. (1962). The associative basis of the creative process. *Psychological Review, 69*, 220–232.

Merrotsy, P. (2020). Tolerance for ambiguity. In M. A. Runco & S. Pritzker (Eds.), *Encyclopedia of creativity*. Oxford: Elsevier.

Montuori, A., & Donnelly, (2020). Creativity and the future. In M. A. Runco & S. Pritzker (Eds.), *Encyclopedia of creativity*. Oxford: Elsevier.

Piaget, J. (1976). To understand is to invent. New York: Penguin.

Poincare, H. (1905). Science and Hypothesis .London: Walter Scott Publishing.

Reiter-Palmon, R., Mumford, M. D., O'Connor Boes, J., & Runco, M. A. (1997). Problem construction and creativity: The role of ability, cue consistency, and active processing. *Creativity Research Journal, 10*, 9–23.

Rogers, C. R. (1959). Toward a theory of creativity. In H. H. Anderson (Ed.), *Creativity and its cultivation* (pp. 69–82). New York: Harper & Row.

Rubenson, D. L., & Runco, M. A. (1992). The psychoeconomic approach to creativity. New Ideas in Psychology, 10, 131–147.

Rubenson, D. L., & Runco, M. A. (1995). The psychoeconomic view of creative work in groups and organizations. Creativity and Innovation Management, 4, 232–241.

Runco, M. A. (1989). Parents' and teachers' ratings of the creativity of children. Journal of Social Behavior and Personality, 4, 73–83.

Runco, M. A. (1994). Conclusions concerning problem finding, problem solving, and creativity. In M. A. Runco (Ed.), *Problem finding, problem solving, and creativity* (pp. 272–290). Norwood, NJ: Ablex.

Runco, M. A. (2003). Idea evaluation, divergent thinking, and creativity. In M. A. Runco (Ed.). *Critical creative processes* (pp. 69–94). Cresskill, NJ: Hampton Press.

Runco, M. A. (2010). Creativity has no dark side. In D. H. Cropley, A. J. Cropley, J. C. Kaufman, & M. A. Runco (Eds.), *The dark side of creativity* (pp. 15–32). New York: Cambridge University Press.

Runco, M. A. (2011). Contrarianism. In M. A. Runco & S. Pritzker (Eds.), Encyclopedia of creativity (2nd ed., pp. 261-263). San Diego, CA: Elsevier.

Runco, M. A. (2012). Creativity, stress, and suicide: Interpretation as moderator. In M. A. Runco (Ed.), *Creativity research handbook* (vol. 3, pp. 163–191). Cresskill, NJ: Hampton Press.

Runco, M. A. (Ed.). (2017). Major works on creativity and education. London: Sage Publications.

Runco, M. A. (2020). Malevolent creativity. In V. Glaveanu (Eds.), The encyclopedia of the possible. New York: Palgrave. https://doi.org/10.1007/978-3-319-98390-5_80-1

Runco, M. A. (in press-a). Divergent thinking. In V. Glaveneau (Eds.), *The encyclopedia of the possible*. New York: Palgrave. https://doi.org/10.1007/978-3-319-98390-5

Runco, M. A. (in press-b). Malevolent creativity. In V. Glaveanu (Eds.), *The encyclopedia of the possible*. New York: Palgrave. https://doi.org/10.1007/978-3-319-98390-5

Runco, M. A., Acar, S., & Cayirdag, N. (2017a). Further evidence that creativity and innovation are inhibited by conservative thinking: Analyses of the 2016 Presidential election. *Creativity Research Journal, 29*, 331–336.

Runco, M. A., Turkman, B., Acar, S., & Nural, M. V. (2017b). Idea density and the creativity of written works. Journal of Genius and Eminence, 2, 26–31.

Runco, M. A., & Jaeger, G. (2012). The standard definition of creativity. *Creativity Research Journal*, 24, 92–96.

Russ, S., & Hoffman, J. (2020). Associative theory. In M. A. Runco & S. Pritzker (Eds.), *Encyclopedia of creativity*. Oxford: Elsevier.

Tadik, H. (2020). Patents. In M. A. Runco & S. R. Pritzker (Eds.), Encyclopedia of creativity (3rd ed.). Oxford, UK: Elsevier. https://doi.org/10.1016/B978-0-12-809324-5.23689-4

Wallas, G. (1926). The art of thought. New York: Harcourt Brace & World.

Weisberg, R. (2015) On the Usefulness of "Value" in the Definition of Creativity, Creativity Research Journal, 27:2, 111–124, https://doi.org/10.1080/10400419.2015.1030320

Wurman, R. (1989). *Information anxiety*. Doubleday.

Chapter 4
Play, Reflection, and the Quest for Uncertainty

Tjarde Savhannah Schulz, Marc Malmdorf Andersen, and Andreas Roepstorff

Abstract Principles of alignment, predictability and certainty have become corner-stones in modern day conceptions of high-quality education. Yet, in recent years, educational progressives who argue for the importance of uncertainty in formal learning environments are increasingly getting support from developmental psychology and cognitive neuroscience. In this chapter, we review evidence suggesting that play is characterised by agents naturally seeking or creating just-right amounts of uncertainty, which in turn has profound effects on their motivation, curiosity, enjoyment and learning. Extending on these findings, we argue for an increased focus on playful approaches in formal educational settings, placing emphasis on learners' agency and natural tendency to optimise learning strategies through the creation of manageable niches of uncertainty. We draw on examples from existing educational settings to illustrate how such approaches could be realised and identify important implications for the role of the teacher in facilitating uncertain environments and supportive reflective practices.

4.1 Introduction

Throughout the late 19th and early 20th century, a proliferation of progressive educational ideas took hold over the European and American continents. Driven by democratic ideals and informed by newly acquired accounts in developmental psychology, these philosophers and educators critiqued the contemporary, traditional education present at the time (e.g., Dewey 2011; Isaacs 2014; or Montessori as discussed in Lillard 2016). They rejected the so-called 'parrot-like' approach to teaching, or rote-learning, and instead advocated for an approach that would attend towards the whole child, i.e., a child's intellectual, physical, and emotional growth

T. S. Schulz (✉) · M. M. Andersen · A. Roepstorff
Interacting Minds Centre, Aarhus University, Aarhus, Denmark

School of Culture and Society, Aarhus University, Aarhus, Denmark
e-mail: savhannah@cas.au.dk

© Springer Nature Switzerland AG 2022
R. A. Beghetto, G. J. Jaeger (eds.), *Uncertainty: A Catalyst for Creativity, Learning and Development*, Creativity Theory and Action in Education 6,
https://doi.org/10.1007/978-3-030-98729-9_4

through experiential, child- and play-centred learning (Reese 2001; Progressive education 2021).

4.1.1 John Dewey's Ideas of Uncertainty

A central argument for adopting such an experience-based and child-centred approach was put forward by the American pragmatist John Dewey, one of the most influential progressive thinkers of his time (Cremin 1959). Inspired by new developmental accounts of learning, Dewey proposed that formal learning should focus on harnessing children's innate curiosity and agency.

> The curious mind is constantly alert and exploring, seeking material for thought, as a vigorous and healthy body is on the qui vive for nutriment. Eagerness for experience, for new and varied contacts, is found where wonder is found. Such curiosity is the only sure guarantee of the acquisition of the primary facts upon which inference must base itself (Dewey 1910, 31).

Dewey believed that a learner's agency and curiosity are what prompts learning, and that a primary elicitor of curiosity is the encountering of doubt or uncertainty. The experience of unexpected events creates a succession of thought that starts with a surprise, moves to formulating a problem and active inquiry, and ultimately leads to new experiences, or learning (e.g., Dewey 1910, 73). This process is what Dewey refers to as the 'reflective process', and indeed the ideal mode of thinking which should be trained and practiced in any formalized learning environment (Dewey 1910). By reflecting on surprising events, a learner can explicitly engage with knowledge violations, and navigate them by formulating problems and actively working towards their solution. In learning to reflect, children thus gain the ability to withhold jumping to conclusions; they practice scientific inquiry by considering alternative explanations, searching for additional information, and testing hypotheses.

Dewey argued that schools, therefore, should be environments where children can follow their innate curiosity and encounter "new (and hence uncertain or problematic") situations, (Dewey 2011, 167), all whilst being guided and supported through materials that allow them to encounter desirable unexpected experiences — or "educative experiences" in Deweyian terms (Dewey 1910; Dewey 2011). Hence, the role of the teacher should be to design learning environments that foster and scaffold the child's intrinsic drive to learning in contrast to merely supplying or 'spoon-feeding' information to children, as was the case during Dewey's own lifetime (Dewey 1910, 2011). For Dewey, this form of educational scaffolding required close attention to learners' curiosity, and with this the traits, habits and interests of the individual learner and related learning group (1910, p. 46-47). Correspondingly, Dewey held that a teacher's training should focus not only on a given school subject (such as math or history), but more fundamentally on how to create and support the conditions for surprise-induced learning to occur (Dewey 1910).

4.1.2 The Paradoxical Relationship of Uncertainty and Modern Education

A good century later, we can follow the traces in educational history to see how many of the ideas proposed in the progressive era of the early 20th century found their integration into modern schooling. For instance, in educational reforms during the 1970s and 1980s, many European and especially Scandinavian countries redesigned their primary and secondary education to be more egalitarian systems (e.g., Finland, Aho et al. 2006; Denmark, France, The Netherlands, Garrouste 2010). With the ratification of the 1990s UN *On the Rights of the Child* convention and especially its article 31 specifying a child's right to "engage in play" and "participate freely in cultural life" (UN General Assembly 1989), playful and child-centred learning have begun finding their way into early childhood education on a global scale (e.g., in the UK, Shier 2001; in China and Hong Kong, Pui-Wah et al. 2015). In addition, a few progressive forms of education like those conceived by Maria Montessori and Rudolf Steiner have found success in spreading across the globe. In May 2020, for instance, there were more than a thousand Waldorf and Rudolf Steiner schools spread across 67 countries (International Forum for Steiner/Waldorf Education 2020). Taking all of this into account, it is interesting to find that the debate about if — and, more specifically how — to integrate, *active* (Drew and Mackie 2011), *experience-based* (Morris 2020), *project-based* (Kokotsaki et al. 2016), and specifically *playful learning* (Kuschner 2012; Pyle et al. 2017) still persists. Even though many institutions and governments that shape education today have incorporated progressive ideas into their policies and state curriculums, formal learning environments continue to face a challenge:

In the effort to make schools more egalitarian and accessible to everyone, schools left little space for curiosity-informed and self-driven learning to take place. With centralised curricula and standardized testing[1], in which all students are required to engage with the same content, and need to meet specific thresholds (e.g., Year 2 national tests as part of "the national curriculum" in the United Kingdom, The national curriculum 2021), schools have increasingly become centered on creating safe and predictable environments that provide equal learning conditions to all learners. This development becomes visible in expectation for teachers to adhere and explicitly communicate clear learning objectives and assessment criteria (e.g., Reed 2012), as well as in the observation of current learning environments that are designed to be calm and well-structured spaces that limit potentials for distraction (e.g., white walls, immovable furniture and table arrangements, as well as fixed lesson plans and curricula). Subjects are hereby often taught with a single-study focus and pre-scheduled length (e.g., 2 hours math, followed by 1 hour of English), allowing learners to focus on problem spaces that can be resolved within the given

---

[1] e.g., almost all EU members follow a single structure or common core curriculum across primary and lower secondary education (European Commission/EACEA/Eurydice 2018)

timeframe. As a result, predictability and alignment have become the focus of modern education.

In fact, in aiming to improve fairness and communication towards students, many modern school environments inadvertently represent the exact antithesis to what Dewey had envisioned. Instead of being environments where children learn to navigate unexpected experiences, children are methodically protected from uncertainty. This is especially paradoxical when considering the larger educational tasks that the OECD has set out in their *The Future of Education and Skills 2030* project (Howells 2018) as a response to ever growing unprecedented challenges — social, economic and environmental — and a generally uncertain future of the globalized world. The ambition of mission 2030 is to provide children with the tools "to navigate through [...] uncertainty" and to "equip learners with agency and a sense of purpose, and the competencies they need, to shape their own lives and contribute to the lives of others" (Howells 2018, 2). Yet, by stripping uncertainty from school, children will unlikely be able to gain these skills. In this chapter, we argue that encountering and navigating uncertainty should be a key element of modern education. We do so by first pointing towards recent findings from developmental psychology and neuroscience that add a new perspective to the Deweyian argument for incorporating spaces of uncertainty and play in education. This perspective indicates the special role of play and reflection in creating a viable and effective route to harness children's intrinsic drive for learning. We then illustrate how these ideas can be realised in formal education by providing four examples from play-oriented approaches across the world (i.e., Anji Play, Opal School, Pedagogy of Play, and Scratch).

4.2   Uncertainty and Surprise in the Predictive Mind

In recent years, cognitive and computational neuroscience have increased attention to uncertainty and surprise as key concepts to understanding the intricate workings of the human brain and nervous system. These concepts have recently been formalized in a unifying neurocognitive framework for the human brain and mind, commonly referred to as *predictive processing* (PP). This framework starts from the premise that to be an organism is to survive in an uncertain and often highly volatile world. The core idea is that to do this, the agent constantly attempts to predict what will happen next in the environment (Friston 2010; Hohwy 2013; Clark 2015).

Specifically, PP depicts the human brain as an organ intricately designed to handle and minimise surprise (Hohwy 2013; Clark 2015; Wiese and Metzinger 2017; Clark 2018). It does so through a simple, yet highly efficient mechanism, commonly referred to as *prediction error minimisation*. The way this works is that the brain continuosly constructs and updates a multilayered hierarchical model of the environment, where layers predict changes on multiple temporal and spatial scales. If there are mismatches between how the brain predicts the world to be and how the world actually is, prediction error signals are generated, which the brain is then forced to deal with. It can do so in two ways: It can either act upon the world in order to change the input it is receiving, or, it can form new predictions about the world, i.e., learn about the world in order to better predict it (Feldman and Friston 2010; Friston 2010). In doing so, the agent is effectively able to detect and reduce surprise.

When the brain forms predictions, they are accompanied by dynamic estimates of confidence (also termed *precision*). In other words, the brain not only makes predictions about what ought to happen in the world, it also makes estimates about how confident it is in its own predictions (Feldman and Friston 2010; Friston 2010). The more confident an agent is in its predictions, the more surprised it will be if the prediction turns out to be wrong. In poorly lit environments, for example, precision is often estimated to be low, meaning that agents do not have confidence in the sensory input they receive, forcing agents to lean more on prior knowledge than sensory input. The idea of confidence applies to action as well, so that agents will have more or less confidence in whether sequences of action (also termed *action policies*) will bring about expected outcomes. When an agent encounters a novel object for example, action precision is often set low, meaning that the agent is not confident about what will happen when it interacts with the object. As the agent interacts with the object, precision on action policies will often increase, meaning that the agent grows more confident predicting the consequences of its actions. Over time, agents learn that certain things in the world are highly predictable, in which case predictions are often associated with estimates of high precision and it is such phenomena that are often associated with habit formation in humans.

The PP framework makes an intriguing case of how *affect* is associated with the intricate error dynamics of the predictive mind. According to the framework, the agent is predicting and tracking its own performance in surprise reduction, by predicting how effective its own strategies for minimising surprise will be over time. When the agent is doing better than estimated in predicting the world, i.e., in reducing prediction error, the agent increases its confidence in the current strategies employed. Such instances of doing better than expected is associated with reward and experientially feels really good. Conversely, when the agent is doing worse than predicted, the agent loses confidence in current strategies, which in turn is often experientially associated with frustration and negative emotions (Kiverstein et al. 2019; Hesp et al. 2021).

A crucial upshot of this idea is that agents will tend to seek situations that are associated with moderate amounts of expected surprise, because these are often the situations where agents can optimise their strategies for surprise reduction and perform better than expected (Kiverstein et al. 2019; Hesp et al. 2021; Andersen et al. 2022). This means that agents will often become curious at the prospects of encountering moderate levels of uncertainty, because such situations represent potential rewarding opportunities for improving strategies for surprise reduction (Kiverstein et al. 2019; Miller et al. 2021). In the following, we argue that this form of agency driven surprise reduction optimization is a central part of humans' natural proclivity to play and that it holds great potential for designing formal educational settings.

4.2.1 Play and Surprise in Predictive Minds

The predictive processing framework has recently been applied to play and playfulness. According to this account, play can be seen as an expression of the natural human tendency to find or create information streams with a just-right level of expected surprise (uncertainty).[2] Such efforts are due to the slope-chasing nature of humans, constantly on the lookout for reducing error faster than expected, which feels good and rewarding (Andersen et al. 2022).

From the perspective of PP, play is perhaps one of the most striking displays of how agents effectively deal with uncertainty, develop and update their prior knowledge, constantly optimise their strategies for error reduction, all while enjoying themselves over prolonged periods of time. Humans are born with the capacity and natural proclivity to play, and children can do so without adult supervision, uninterrupted for hours on end, and often in a novel and varied way each and every time.

It has been known for many years that, from infanthood, humans respond reliably and systematically to surprises, i.e., violations of their predictions. Indeed, one of the most widely used paradigms from developmental psychology applied to infants is the so-called violation of expectancy paradigm, where researchers show children certain sequences of events involving objects (e.g., a ball rolling down a slide), with predictable (e.g., the ball stops when hitting another solid object) or unpredictable (e.g., the ball rolls *through* another solid object) outcomes. In these paradigms (e.g., Baillargeon et al. 1985; Werker et al. 1997; Scherer et al. 2004), children will often exhibit increased looking time when presented with an unpredictable event compared with the predictable one. Intriguingly, if allowed to *play* with the object after having been exposed to an unpredictable event, infants will selectively explore the particular aspects of the object that caused them to be surprised. Other experiments, controlling for increased looking time, have in addition shown how breaches of expectation not only prompts selective exploration, but simply make children learn by virtue of being surprising (Schulz 2015; Stahl and Feigenson 2015).

Similarly, the idea that humans are experientially attracted to just-right doses of surprise, uncertainty, arousal or novelty, has been suggested by numerous researchers and scholars over the years (e.g., Berlyne 1970; Loewenstein 1994; Schulz 2015; Oudeyer and Smith 2016; Kiverstein et al. 2019). This has been formulated as the *Goldilocks principle*, a human preference for stimuli that are neither too simple, nor too complex relative to their current representation of the world. Such preferences have recently been documented in infants, who, when presented with the opportunity to look at pictures with different levels of complexity, prefer looking at pictures with a moderate amount of complexity (Kidd et al. 2012).

In this perspective playful exploration can be characterised as the creation — or search for — situations that hold a just-right amount of uncertainty and surprise. A PP account of play expands on this narrative by explaining *why* humans are attracted

---

[2] "Expected surprise" and "uncertainty" are treated as synonyms in this literature.

to moderate amounts of uncertainty and *why* play feels so fun (Andersen et al. 2022). Humans are attracted by moderate amounts of uncertainty because these are the situations that hold the highest likelihood of improving slopes of error reduction. When agents reduce error faster than expected, they feel good, and thus the reason why play is so fun and rewarding is because agents are doing just that (Kiverstein et al. 2019; Hesp et al. 2021). Improvements of error reduction slopes are not only seen in play, but in a plethora of rewarding states that are all characterised by human engagement, curiosity and exploration (e.g., film consumption, Miller et al. 2021).

There are several lines of evidence that support the idea that a moderate amount of uncertainty and surprise is a prime driver in children's play (Andersen et al. 2022). For instance, play is often characterised experientially by the immersive 'flow' state, something which tends to occur during tasks which are just within one's reach of ability (Csikszentmihalyi 1997; Bateson and Martin 2013). Similarly, curiosity, which is widely believed to be a main component in children's play, has been characterised as 'children's preferred level of uncertainty' (Jirout and Klahr 2012).Other examples include studies of peek-a-boo, where just-right deviations from the overall pattern of the game has similarly been found to elicit enhanced smiling and laughing in children (Parrott and Gleitman 1989). Similarly, in studies of risky play in preschool children, just-right states of heightened arousal have been suggested to be central to children maintaining their play engagement (Sandseter 2010). Such findings are echoed in a recent study on how older children and adults play with fear. Visitors to a haunted attraction were equipped with heart rate monitors and asked to report on their experience of fear and enjoyment. First, participants agreed that the experience was a form of play. Second, the study found an inverted u-shaped relationship between self-reported enjoyment and fear as well as an inverted u-shaped relationship between participant enjoyment and small-scale heart rate fluctuations. Such results support the claim that play is related to just-right amounts of uncertainty and surprise (Andersen et al. 2020).

Analysing the variety of strategies children employ to ensure that they stay within the bounds of their Goldilocks Zone is an interesting task. One strategy, it would seem, is that children are experts at making boring tasks fun by increasing their difficulty setting and cost. For example, in a series of recent experiments by Chu and Schulz (2020), four- to five-year-old children were shown to take apparently unnecessary costs and perform inefficient actions when encouraged to perform an instrumental action as a part of playing. For example, children were asked to fetch a pencil, either framed as a help to the experimenter or as part of playing a game. To get the pencil, children could approach either a small desk with a cup filled with pencils or a wall with pencils attached by Velcro at three different heights. On this wall, some pencils were easily within reach, whereas other pencils required jumping to reach. In the instrumental condition, most children made efficient actions on their first retrieval attempts, whereas most children in the play condition used inefficient actions, thus making the task harder than it needed to be.

Other strategies for staying in the Goldilocks Zone include self-handicapping, a behavior often seen in rough-n-tumble play, where stronger players inhibit themselves, thus making the play engaging and challenging for both parties (Spinka et al. 2001; Bateson and Martin 2013). Relatedly, the characteristic pattern of play where children enjoy repetitions with variations can be seen as another strategy for staying in the zone (Andersen et al. 2022). In pretend play, it has similarly been pointed out that children typically only change a few parameters of their imagined reality (Lillard 2001), keeping surprises on a just-right level.

From the perspective of the PP account of play, these strategies share that the agent seeks or creates conditions characterised by just-right levels of uncertainty in a combined effort to learn and have fun. Crucially, the reason play is fun is *because* agents improve their strategies for reducing uncertainty and error, which feels rewarding. Thus, according to this understanding of play, not only are human enjoyment and learning intimately linked, humans are also highly sensitive to uncertainty and to how well their strategies for navigating it are going.

These insights have important implications for designing educational settings. They suggest that 'having fun' is a metacognitive signal within learners when they are in the process of optimising their learning strategies. Below we detail how this is an argument for handing over agency to the learners, trusting that they themselves can sense how well their strategies for improving error reduction are working, and that they are sensitive to identifying environments with just-right levels of uncertainty. In the following, we explore these ideas and highlight prominent examples of educational practices, where we believe the facilitation of such learning behaviors are successfully facilitated.

4.3 Play and Uncertainty in Education

How might the insights just discussed be used in formal educational settings? First and foremost, in a PP account, learners are highly sensitive to the relative uncertainty within their environment.

They expect various amounts of surprise from their surrounding environment and will have their curiosity piquet at just-right amounts of expected surprise. This not only bodes carefulness in terms of ensuring that formal education will not be associated with too little ("School is boring") or too much ("School is too hard") expected surprise for learners, but might also suggest to educators that they place more trust in the sensitivity of learners and hand over more agency to them in the educational setting. Doing so affords the opportunity for the learner to seek out positively valenced situations where learning slopes and strategies for minimising error are being optimised. For educational settings then, educators may consider having an extra focus on concepts such as agency, surprise and enjoyment as indicators of importance and/or central design principles. In the following, we highlight four examples of prominent educational approaches, tasks and pedagogies that we believe are compatible with these ideas and present suggestions for how they could provide scalable pedagogical practices that use surprise as a guiding design principle.

In the Anji Play approach, first established in the public early childhood programs of Anji County, Zhejiang Province, China, kindergarteners (ages 3–6) are
constructing their own playgrounds and environments on a daily basis. Being provided with open-ended materials such as wooden blocks, ladders and planks, the
children can engage in free, self-guided play, building whatever they can envision.
Children manage their own safety while engaging in ongoing problem-solving and
the construction of new manageable goals and ideas (Fang 2018). The minimally-
structured outdoor spaces hereby present a vast variety of opportunities, integrating
the affordances of each kindergarten environment. For instance, kindergartens in
rural areas draw on the local resources by integrating farming tools and bamboo in
their set of playing materials. When water access is available, this likewise finds its
way into the playground. In these environments, children are given the agency to
organize and create playground structures and invent accompanying rules to govern
their use. For example, during our own observations during school visits in 2019, a
group of children enthusiastically built a slide and accompanying climbing frame,
using a variety of planks, ladders, and other wooden materials (see Fig. 4.1).
Experimenting with different angles, the involved children encountered a series of
surprising outcomes as they repeatedly tried to figure out how various changes in
the slope of the slide affected their sliding experience. Ensuring their own safety, the
children held the ladder when the construction got wobblier, and even placed mats
when setting the slide to steep angles. Allowing the children to engage in this kind
of free play and exploration, the role of the teacher in the didactical approach set out
by Anji Play is to be a close and attentive observer, who documents the ongoing
learning processes but does not directly intervene. In the just mentioned ladder
example, this entails to trust the young children to take risks appropriate to their
abilities and do not engage unless asked to (e.g., "Can you hold this for us?") or
absolutely needed. The teacher documents this playful learning process in the form
of images and videos, combined with drawings created by the children about their
experiences. This documentation is later used to engage the children in shared
reflections about the experience, or 'play sharing' as it is referred to by practitioners
of the Anji play approach. Here, teachers can build upon the children's observations
and their expressed surprises, or challenges they faced (e.g., trying to let a ball roll
down the slide without dropping off the side). Supported by their teachers, children
can then debate their understanding of the experience, and come up with possible
solutions to try in future play sessions (see Fig. 4.1., right). Listening to the experiences of the other children, children may sometimes experience new surprising
puzzles and conundrums to inspire ongoing play activities.

In another type of learning environment, the online coding platform Scratch
(Maloney et al. 2010), learners can build their own games, animations and stories
through the use of predefined coding blocks (see Fig. 4.2). Scratch removes entry
barriers to coding by providing basic building blocks that students can easily combine to create games, or animated videos to tell stories. In these, learners can either
use predefined structures (e.g., sounds, animations, characters, or even whole projects) and change them to their own liking, or choose to build their own from the
ground up (for instance by recording sounds from their own environment or

Fig. 4.1 Children co-constructing their own slides and climbing structure (left). Child explaining his observations during a play-sharing session (right)

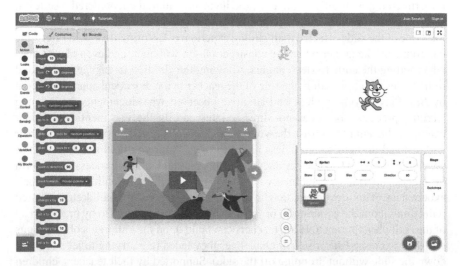

Fig. 4.2 A screenshot of the scratch user interface

drawing their own characters). Scratch thus encourages agency, experimentation and exploration, letting students explore at their own pace what happens when they introduce new blocks or change certain parameters. This regularly leads to surprising (and sometimes frustrating) moments, when a newly added feature does not behave in the way that the learner predicted — for example, an avatar might move in the opposite direction than what was intended. Working through frustrations and engaging in iterations of trial and error can lead to experiences of joy and pride when a problem is suddenly resolved or a function is better understood. Scratch additionally provides a community platform where students can share and engage with the creations of others, and support each other by sharing solutions to problems. A remix function hereby allows users to extend and amend projects shared by others, integrate elements of other projects into their own, or collaborate on larger scale projects by embedding elements from different users into a larger meta-project. In this way, students not only learn important principles of game design and animation, but also more classic curriculum oriented content including math, logic (e.g., 'if-then' statements), as well as collaboration and communication skills.

Our third example is taken from the Opal School of Portland Children's Museum (Oregon, US) in 2019 — a former[3] pre-school and K-5 public charter school that was deeply influenced by the Italian Reggio Emilia approach (e.g., Edwards 1993) and integrated a playful inquiry-focused pedagogy into their practice (About Opal School 2021; Mardell 2021). Opal emphasised normalizing uncertainty in the classroom by engaging children in conversations around 'unanswerable' questions — questions with no single or commonly accepted answer. Formalized teaching practices such as 'Doing Serendipity' were developed as a way to encourage "children to anticipate the possibility of surprise and delight in moments of uncertainty" (Inspiring Agents of Change Project 2019a). Furthermore, the didactical framework emphasised children taking ownership of their own learning with little or no adult guidance (e.g., "Snapping Ideas Together", Inspiring Agents of Change Project 2019b). For example, we observed a fourth-grade language classroom, where a teacher constructed a class around word suffixes, first introducing the general concept of word endings and then letting students practice by identifying root words from a worksheet. On this worksheet, the teacher purposefully included words that challenged the children's available knowledge, such as 'emotion'. Not knowing the root word 'emote', students were surprised, puzzled and turned to the teacher for help. Instead of supplying an answer, the teacher supported the students with guiding questions to allow them to take agency and further inquire into the problem, which they solved by consulting a dictionary. Intrigued by their finding that the word emote was categorized as a back-formation (i.e., a verb that has been created by removing supposed affixes from a noun), the learners along with their teacher decided to seek further information in the next classroom session and find other examples of back-formations.

A final example is taken from the Nova Pioneer Ormonde school in South Africa, which is one of the research sites of the Pedagogy of Play (PoP) project. Through *playful participatory research* (Baker et al. 2016) with schools in Denmark, the US, South Africa, and Columbia, the group aims to understand what playful learning looks and feels like in classrooms and schools across the world, as well as how educators can set up the conditions where playful learning thrives (Mardell et al. 2016). The school research sites are chosen based on their special emphasis and ability to support playful learning (Mardell et al. 2016; Solis et al. 2019) and follow a range of different curricula. Notably, PoP has identified that learning through play

---

[3] Severely impacted by the pandemic, Opal School, it's accompanying Centre for Learning, and Portland Children's Museum, closed permanently in June 2021.

in their South African project schools involves the "interrelated experiences of ownership, curiosity, and enjoyment" (Solis et al. 2019), as well as ubuntu.[4] At the Nova Pioneer Ormonde School, these indicators have been observed, for instance, in the use of an open-ended pre-constructed learning task. In a fifth grade classroom, students were asked as part of a larger unit (see Solis et al. 2019) to write an encyclopedic entry for an imaginary species of their choosing and categorise it according to established ethological standards. To be able to accomplish this, learners needed to extend on their already existing knowledge of biology (e.g., types of species such as mammals, insects, or amphibians), as well as gather new information in order to categorize their inventions as carnivores, herbivores or omnivores. In addition, students conjointly had to use or expand their geographical knowledge in order to envision a suitable habitat and location for their animal, whilst extending their English language skills by practicing writing formal, informational and fictional texts. In this, students were able to adapt the complexity of the task to their own ability either by staying close to a familiar animal or by venturing into uncertain territories (e.g., unknown habitats, imaginary abilities). Following their own curiosity, students could playfully navigate spaces of uncertainty by seeking out their own information, discovering different facts along the way. As one student described the experience of the unit: "It was fun that we get to do this. Well, everything is fun about it because like we get to invent something that is different. We get to create. It's just like really exciting. They [the invented creatures] are ours" (Solis et al. 2019, 32).

4.3.1   Learner Agency, the Setting of Uncertainty and the Role of the Teacher

The educational approaches above may seem relatively divergent. For example, not only do Anji Play and Pedagogy of Play represent different traditions of playful learning[5] (Mardell et al. 2016; Coffino and Bailey 2019), they also span different age groups, cultures, and, in the examples provided, diverge in terms of the targeted learning modalities. Yet, what all of these cases have in common is that they yield high amounts of agency to learners. Trusting that learners are sensitive to improvement in their learning rate, handing over agency to students in the construction of learning environments and tasks, enables learners to create scenarios that fit their own skill set and interests. In doing so, the practices become more engaging to

---

[4] A local South African term and philosophy that derives from the Zulu expression 'Umuntu ngumuntu ngabantu', which describes the community experience of *being* through others (translates approximately as: A person is a person because of people).

[5] Whilst Anji Play refers to guided play as false play and advocates for a free play or true play approach, the Pedagogy of Play research argues that play in school needs to have a clear purpose and thus incorporates both guided and free play.

learners and may more easily provide experiences of enjoyment in more or less formal settings.

What these approaches also have in common is the role they ascribe to the teacher. The role of the teacher in the presented examples has changed from a mere information-providing entity that supplies direct instruction to a facilitating guide. In Anji Play, for instance, teachers supply resources and general building tools for the environment, as well as ensure the general health and safety of the children. In addition, they document children's behaviour, facilitate shared reflection spaces, and support observed patterns of interests by supplying additional materials. Similarly, in the Scratch learning platform, the role of the teacher (or more accurately 'facilitator' in this case) is constructing and introducing the overall environment, thus setting up the conditions for agency based learning to occur. When Scratch is integrated into a formal learning context, teachers can additionally create general directions of exploration (e.g., "Create a story about the history of your country."), much like in the South African example of creating entries for imaginary creatures. Even in cases where environments and tasks are not open-ended, as seen in the Opal example, children can still be supported in their agency by helping them to seek out and resolve surprises by themselves (e.g., looking up the word *emote* in the dictionary). The teacher can assist in situations where students encounter frustration, not by giving solutions, but rather by supporting students in formalizing their ideas more concretely, directing them towards places where more information can be found, or connecting them with others for peer-sharing of knowledge and inspiration.

Educators thus may consider facilitating the construction of learning spaces with various levels of uncertainty. One concept to think about as a design element here may be the concept of 'surprise'. In many cases when we think about education, we think about it as an activity that should strive to minimise surprise in order to maximise clarity. Yet, activities designed specifically to minimize surprise often quickly induce boredom in students, a feeling which in the PP framework should be considered a metacognitive signal that the rate of error reduction is slowing down relative to what the agent was expecting. The specificity at which surprise can be used as a design element is, however, dependent on the teacher's grasp of the current level of the learners' knowledge as well as their understanding of a given problem space. If the teacher has a rich understanding of the students' knowledge, it may be possible to purposefully use surprise as a design element to target its boundaries (e.g., Opal's language class). Yet, in instances where educational settings and tasks need to be surprising to a large number of students across different skill levels and tailored to a vast variety of interests, this presents a challenge. Here, it can be helpful to allow students to design these environments themselves, or to introduce them to rich open-ended tasks (e.g., PoP example) that allow them to adapt the amount of complexity to their current needs.

One approach to facilitating open-ended tasks has perhaps been most accessible formulated by Seymour Papert, a pioneer of the constructionist movement. Papert emphasised the importance of designing tasks and learning environments that allow for easy entry points to get started with ('low floors'), but also the opportunity to

50   T. S. Schulz et al.

reach sophisticated levels of complexity ('high ceilings'). Mitch Resnick, in his *Lifelong Kindergarten* work and writings, extended this design metaphor and principle to also include 'wide walls', the opportunity to connect the floors with the ceilings in a wide range of pathways (Resnick and Robinson 2017). In other words, great learning tasks distinguish themselves by being accessible to students at all skill levels, being extendable to incorporate large amounts of complexity over time, as well as solvable in a variety of ways. Children on the Anji playground, for instance, could build a ladder and a climbing structure that was adjusted to their own height and capabilities, extend and amend this structure as their understanding of how slopes work grew over time, build the slide in a multitude of ways, and even create an entirely different construction during the next day with the same building blocks. Correspondingly, students in the classroom of Nova Pioneer Ormonde could invent following their own interests and existing knowledge, seek out unfamiliar territories in one subject area (e.g., geography) and stay closer to their comfort zone in another (e.g., biology). Similarly, in Scratch, a coding language that has been co-developed by Mitch Resnick, children can create projects with minimal prerequisite knowledge, yet with a wide variety of pathways to develop ideas which can lead to elaborate games but also small animations that explore the intricacies of the different coding blocks. Through this, learners can gain knowledge about what algorithms are, and how to use them in order to design programs that accomplish specific goals set by the learners themselves.

In summary, teachers can facilitate experience spaces that allow learners to build their own niches within learning environments by following their own curiosity and enjoyment. From the perspective of PP, learners will always be naturally inclined to seek or create situations where they optimise their strategies for reducing error (surprise) simply because such optimization feels good and rewarding to the agent. The role of the teacher thus becomes facilitating suitable frames, where the potential surprises held within the environment are deemed fruitful and suitable for the concrete school context.

Indeed, schools are not context-free environments, but are shaped by cultural norms and expectations about what children should know and learn about. Curiosity driven learning is required to abide by certain moral and cultural standards the same way as other forms of formalised learning in educational institutions. This is important to remember since the PP account in itself is a value-free framework that argues for a human drive to seek out right amounts of surprise in order to engage in optimisation of long term prediction error minimization. Thus, PP does not tell us anything about the ethical implications of a curiosity or playfully driven activity. For instance, bullying could feel joyful to the bully as they learn to predict their victims responses. This illustrates that not all enjoyable playful activities will (or should) be tolerated and teachers hold a crucial position here. The facilitation of surprising environments therefore includes the setting of norms for acceptable behavior by the teacher in consultation with the children. Similarly, the teacher needs to ensure that the surprises that children can seek out and learn from in the environment are also deemed valuable by society at large.

4.3.2   The Role of Reflection to Navigate and Share Uncertainties

While learners may be sensitive to just-right amounts of uncertainty and in constant pursuit of rewarding and optimising states to inhabit, even the most skilled learners are bound to encounter unresolvable surprises or fail to encounter surprises at all at some point. Sometimes, a slide will just not stay in place; sometimes, a series of coding blocks just won't do as you would like them to; and sometimes you just don't seem to be able to think about any creative imaginary creature other than an orange giraffe. A final point that we want to address here is how teachers can support learners in such situations by consolidating unresolvable uncertainty or help generate surprise in the first place. We argue that this can be done through — indeed may be *the* most suited place for — reflective practice.

In most formal forms of education, reflective practice refers to various forms of retrospective evaluations of learning experiences (Moon 2013). The learner is asked to assess their current understanding of a given topic or revisit curriculum content by responding to prompts provided by the teacher (e.g., "What have you learned today?"). Alternatively, teachers may also require their students to relate past learning experiences to potential futures (e.g., "How does your study group experience affect how you want to act in the future?"). However, as such, the tasks on which students are asked to reflect are often not accompanied by perplexing experiences that still require solving on the part of the student.

We argue that when reflection practices and prompts are not grounded in unresolved problems for the students, there is a danger that students may not find reflection practices intrinsically motivating. This aligns with Dewey's and current understandings of reflection, according to which reflection necessitates active involvement on the part of the learner and is elicited through an unexpected and often perplexing experience (Dewey 1910; Rogers 2001). In other words, unresolved surprise is often central for learners to meaningfully engage in intrinsically motivated forms of reflection. From the perspective of PP, social forms of reflection in educational settings could be thought of as an opportunity for agents to share their currently best performing models and strategies for resolving errors. Such sharing could allow the adoption, rejection, combination and forming of new models across agents, such that they can engage in a form of collective prediction error reduction.

In the above mentioned examples of educational practices with high-agency, enjoyment-driven forms of learning, reflection is an integrated key component in the pedagogical approaches. This allows learners to either consolidate unresolved surprise, or share uncertainties with others. Anji, for instance, facilitates daily 'play sharing' opportunities where children are asked to share their experiences and observations from their free play time with each other. In these play sharings, hearing about the different perspectives of their peers can result in the sharing of surprises that can then be discussed and resolved in the community. Correspondingly, Opal had adopted a pedagogical approach that ongoingly embedded reflection spaces into the classroom and attended closely towards learners' expressed curiosity and extended it during class. In the language class we observed, the teacher attended towards an expressed surprise (i.e., a student proclaiming loudly "emotion is broken") and recognised the opportunity to share this uncertainty, facilitate a discussion amongst the learners, and direct them to further resources. Notably, the teacher did not simply provide answers but instead highlighted the structures that allowed the children to engage in a shared reflection and collectively resolve surprise.

By attending closely to students' expression of emotions, particularly surprise and frustration, teachers can facilitate moments of internally motivated reflection and learning. Frustration serves as a helpful signal that learners are resolving surprises slower than they were expecting, possibly due to an exceeding or unresolvable amount of surprise. In classrooms, this is often expressed by students through various kinds of emotionally negative statements of frustration ("This is stupid!"), hopelessness ("I'll never make this work"), or personal insecurity ("I am just not good at math"). A continued experience of exceeding amounts of uncertainty thereby can have dire consequences for learning progression and students future expectations about themselves as learners. For these reasons, expressions of surprise and frustration are important signals for educators to be attentive to. Surprise presents a powerful entry point to potential reflection processes, whilst frustration can indicate that the students are not able to navigate uncertainty as well as they expected.

In summary, inviting uncertainty and play into the classroom can benefit from being accompanied with practices and spaces in which students can create, share, reflect and resolve uncertainty together. Over time, a habitualized practice of reflection in the classroom may make the inclination to engage in social forms of reflection more frequent as learners encounter unresolvable problems, both inside and outside the classroom.

4.4   Conclusion

It has now been more than a century since Dewey and like-minded progressisve scholars of his time set out their arguments for curiosity and uncertainty-based forms of education. Yet, educational reforms have tended to increasingly introduce elements of predictability and certainty into modern forms of education. We have argued that the sensitivity of learning agents towards manageable amounts of uncertainty and surprise bodes for reconsidering the integration of uncertainty into formal educational settings on a broader scale.

This implies an increased focus on playful and agency-based forms of learning, where learners are encouraged to create or seek their own enjoyable and surprising niches within broader learning environments. Such an approach also entails an emphasis on the educator as a facilitating guide that manages suitable and rich learning environments where potential surprises are deemed fruitful and suitable for the concrete school context, as well as an increased attention towards signs of surprise and frustration as opportunities for collective reflection.

References

About Opal School. 2021. Opal School Online. https://opalschool.org/about-opal-school/. Accessed June 29 2021.

Aho, Erkki, Kari Pitkanen, and Pasi Sahlberg. 2006. Policy Development and Reform Principles of Basic and Secondary Education in Finland Since 1968. Education Working Paper Series. Number 2. Human Development Network Education. ERIC.

Andersen, Marc Malmdorf, Julian Kiverstein, Mark Miller, and Andreas Roepstorff. 2022. Play in Predictive Minds: A Cognitive Theory of Play. *Psychological Review*.

Andersen, Marc Malmdorf, Uffe Schjoedt, Henry Price, Fernando E. Rosas, Coltan Scrivner, and Mathias Clasen. 2020. Playing with fear: a field study in recreational horror. *Psychological science* 31. SAGE Publications Sage CA: Los Angeles, CA: 1497–1510. https://doi. org/10.1177/0956797620972116

Baillargeon, Renee, Elizabeth S. Spelke, and Stanley Wasserman. 1985. Object permanence in five-month-old infants. *Cognition* 20. Elsevier: 191–208. https://doi. org/10.1016/0010-0277(85)90008-3

Baker, Megina, Mara Krechevsky, Katie Ertel, Jen Ryan, Daniel Wilson, and Ben Mardell. 2016. Playful Participatory Research: An emerging methodology for developing a pedagogy of play. http://www.pz.harvard.edu/sites/default/files/Playful%20Participatory%20Research.pdf. Accessed 25 March 2022.

Bateson, Patrick, and Paul Martin. 2013. Play, playfulness, creativity and innovation. Cambridge University Press.

Berlyne, Daniel E. 1970. Novelty, complexity, and hedonic value. *Perception & psychophysics* 8. Springer: 279–286. https://doi.org/10.3758/BF03212593.

Chu, Junyi, and Laura E. Schulz. 2020. Play, curiosity, and cognition. *Annual Review of Developmental Psychology* 2. Annual Reviews: 317–343. https://doi.org/10.1146/annurev-devpsych-070120-014806

Clark, Andy. 2015. Surfing Uncertainty: Prediction, Action, and the Embodied Mind. Oxford University Press.

Clark, Andy. 2018. A nice surprise? Predictive processing and the active pursuit of novelty. *Phenomenology and the Cognitive Sciences* 17. Springer: 521–534. https://doi.org/10.1007/s11097-017-9525-z

Coffino, Jesse Robert, and Chelsea Bailey. 2019. The Anji Play ecology of early learning. Childhood Education 95. Taylor & Francis: 3–9.

Cremin, Lawrence A. 1959. John Dewey and the Progressive-Education Movement, 1915-1952. The School Review 67. The University of Chicago Press: 160–173. https://doi.org/10.1086/442489

Csikszentmihalyi, Mihaly. 1997. Finding flow: The psychology of engagement with everyday life. Finding Flow: The Psychology of Engagement with Everyday Life. New York, NY, US: Basic Books.

Dewey, John. 1910. How We Think. D.C. HEATH & CO.

Dewey, John. 2011. Democracy and Education. reprint. Simon & Brown.

Drew, Valerie, and Lorele Mackie. 2011. Extending the constructs of active learning: implications for teachers' pedagogy and practice. *The Curriculum Journal* 22. Routledge: 451–467. https://doi.org/10.1080/09585176.2011.627204

Edwards, Carolyn, ed. 1993. The hundred languages of children: The Reggio Emilia approach to early childhood education. ERIC.

European Commission/EACEA/Eurydice. 2018. The Structure of the European Education Systems 2018/19: Schematic Diagrams. Eurydice Facts and Figures. Luxembourg: Publications Office of the European Union. https://op.europa.eu/s/vWYY. Accessed 25 March 2022.

Fang, Jun-Jun. 2018. EARLY CHILDHOOD EDUCATION IN CHINA. Handbook of International Perspectives on Early Childhood Education. Routledge: 162.

Feldman, Harriet, and Karl Friston. 2010. Attention, uncertainty, and free-energy. *Frontiers in human neuroscience* 4. Frontiers: 215. https://doi.org/10.3389/fnhum.2010.00215

Friston, Karl. 2010. The free-energy principle: a unified brain theory? Nature reviews neuroscience 11. Nature publishing group: 127–138.

Garrouste, Christelle. 2010. 100 years of educational reforms in Europe: A contextual database.

Hesp, Casper, Ryan Smith, Thomas Parr, Micah Allen, Karl J. Friston, and Maxwell J.D. Ramstead. 2021. Deeply felt affect: The emergence of valence in deep active inference. *Neural Computation* 33. MIT Press: 1–49. https://doi.org/10.1162/neco_a_01341

Hohwy, Jakob. 2013. The predictive mind. First edition. Oxford, United Kingdom ; New York, NY, United States of America: Oxford University Press.

Howells, K. 2018. The future of education and skills: education 2030: the future we want. OECD.

Inspiring Agents of Change Project. 2019a. Doing Serendipity. Project Zero Webpage. http://www.pz.harvard.edu/resources/doing-serendipity. Accessed 25 March 2022.

Inspiring Agents of Change Project. 2019b. Snapping Ideas Together. Project Zero Webpage. http://www.pz.harvard.edu/resources/snapping-ideas-together. Accessed 25 March 2022.

International Forum for Steiner/Waldorf Education, ed. 2020. Waldorf Word List. https://www.waldorf-international.org/en/waldorf-world-list/. Accessed 25 March 2022.

Isaacs, Susan. 2014. Intellectual Growth In Young Children. reprint. Routledge.

Jirout, Jamie, and David Klahr. 2012. Children's scientific curiosity: In search of an operational definition of an elusive concept. Developmental review 32. Elsevier: 125–160.

Kidd, Celeste, Steven T. Piantadosi, and Richard N. Aslin. 2012. The Goldilocks effect: Human Infants Allocate Attention to Visual Sequences That Are Neither Too Simple Nor Too Complex. *PLOS ONE* 7. Public Library of Science: e36399. https://doi.org/10.1371/journal.pone.0036399.

Kiverstein, Julian, Mark Miller, and Erik Rietveld. 2019. The feeling of grip: novelty, error dynamics, and the predictive brain. Synthese 196. Springer: 2847–2869.

Kokotsaki, Dimitra, Victoria Menzies, and Andy Wiggins. 2016. Project-based learning: A review of the literature. Improving schools 19. SAGE Publications Sage UK: London, England: 267–277.

Kuschner, David. 2012. Play is natural to childhood but school is not: The problem of integrating play into the curriculum. International Journal of Play 1. Taylor & Francis: 242–249.

Lillard, Angeline. 2001. Pretend play as twin earth: A social-cognitive analysis. Developmental Review 21. Elsevier: 495–531.

Lillard, Angeline. 2016. Montessori: The science behind the genius. Oxford University Press.

Loewenstein, George. 1994. The psychology of curiosity: A review and reinterpretation. *Psychological bulletin 116*. American Psychological Association: 75.

Maloney, John, Mitchel Resnick, Natalie Rusk, Brian Silverman, and Evelyn Eastmond. 2010. The scratch programming language and environment. ACM Transactions on Computing Education (TOCE) 10. ACM New York, NY, USA: 1–15.

Mardell, Ben. 2021. Thank you Opal School. Pedagogy of Play blog. https://www.popatplay.org/post/thank-you-opal-school. Accessed May 19 2021.

Mardell, Ben, Daniel Wilson, Jen Ryan, Katie Ertel, Mara Krechevsky, and Megina Baker. 2016. Towards a pedagogy of play. Project Zero Webpage. http://www.pz.harvard.edu/sites/default/files/Towards%20a%20Pedagogy%20of%20Play.pdf. Accessed 25 March 2022.

Miller, Mark, Marc Malmdorf Andersen, Felix Schoeller, and Julian Kiverstein. 2021. Getting a Kick Out of Film: Aesthetic Pleasure and Play in Prediction Error Minimizing Agents. forthcoming.

Moon, Jennifer Ann. 2013. *Reflection in Learning and Professional Development: Theory and Practice*. Routledge.

Morris, Thomas Howard. 2020. Experiential learning–a systematic review and revision of Kolb's model. Interactive Learning Environments 28. Taylor & Francis: 1064-1077.

Oudeyer, Pierre-Yves, and Linda B Smith. 2016. How evolution may work through curiosity-driven developmental process. Topics in Cognitive Science 8. Wiley Online Library: 492–502.

Parrott, W Gerrod, and Henry Gleitman. 1989. Infants' expectations in play: The joy of peek-a-boo. Cognition & Emotion 3. Taylor & Francis: 291–311.

Progressive education. 2021. Encyclopedia Britannica. https://www.britannica.com/topic/progressive-education. Accessed February 15 2022.

Pui-Wah, Doris Cheng, Jyrki Reunamo, Paul Cooper, Karen Liu, and Keang-ieng Peggy Vong. 2015. Children's agentive orientations in play-based and academically focused preschools in Hong Kong. Early Child Development and Care 185. Routledge: 1828–1844. https://doi.org/10.1080/03004430.2015.1028400.

Pyle, Angela, Christopher DeLuca, and Erica Danniels. 2017. A scoping review of research on play-based pedagogies in kindergarten education. Review of Education 5. Wiley Online Library: 311–351

Reed, Deborah K. 2012. Clearly communicating the learning objective matters! Clearly communicating lesson objectives supports student learning and positive behavior. *Middle School Journal* 43. Taylor & Francis: 16–24.

Reese, William J. 2001. The origins of progressive education. *History of education quarterly* 41. Wiley Online Library: 1–24.

Resnick, Mitchel, and Ken Robinson. 2017. *Lifelong kindergarten: Cultivating creativity through projects, passion, peers, and play*. MIT press.

Rogers, Russell R. 2001. Reflection in higher education: A concept analysis. *Innovative higher education* 26. Springer: 37–57.

Sandseter, Ellen Beate Hansen. 2010. Scaryfunny: A qualitative study of risky play among preschool children. NTNU.

Scherer, Klaus R, Marcel R Zentner, and Daniel Stern. 2004. Beyond surprise: the puzzle of infants' expressive reactions to expectancy violation. *Emotion* 4. American Psychological Association: 389.

Schulz, Laura. 2015. Infants explore the unexpected. *Science* 348. American Association for the Advancement of Science: 42–43.

Shier, Harry. 2001. Pathways to participation: Openings, opportunities and obligations. *Children & society* 15. Wiley Online Library: 107–117.

Solis, Lynneth, Kgopotso Khumalo, Stephanie Nowack, Elizabeth Blythe-Davidson, and Ben Mardell. 2019. Toward a South African Pedagogy of Play. http://www.pz.harvard.edu/resources/toward-a-south-african-pedagogy-of-play. Accessed 25 March 2022.

Spinka, Marek, Ruth C Newberry, and Marc Bekoff. 2001. Mammalian play: training for the unexpected. *The Quarterly review of biology* 76. University of Chicago Press: 141–168.

Stahl, Aimee E., and Lisa Feigenson. 2015. Observing the unexpected enhances infants' learning and exploration. *Science* 348: 91. https://doi.org/10.1126/science.aaa3799

The national curriculum. 2021. *GOV.UK*. https://www.gov.uk/national-curriculum. Accessed June 30 2021.

UN General Assembly. 1989. Convention on the Rights of the Child. *United Nations, Treaty Series* 1577: 1–23.

Werker, Janet F., Linda Polka, and Judith E. Pegg. 1997. The conditioned head turn procedure as a method for testing infant speech perception. *Infant and Child Development* 6. Wiley Online Library: 171–178. https://doi.org/10.1002/(SICI)1099-0917(199709/12)6:3/4<171::AID-EDP156>3.0.CO;2-H

Wiese, Wanja, and Thomas Metzinger. 2017. Vanilla PP for Philosophers: A Primer on Predictive Processing: 18. https://doi.org/10.15502/9783958573024

Part II
Transforming Uncertainty into Creativity

Chapter 5
Beyond Tolerating Ambiguity: How Emotionally Intelligent People Can Channel Uncertainty into Creativity

Jessica D. Hoffmann, Julie McGarry, and Jennifer Seibyl

Abstract In this chapter, we will focus on the intersection of creativity and emotional intelligence, and how those who are skilled in understanding and managing their emotions can convert, channel, and regulate even unpleasant, unwanted feelings - like uncertainty - to support their creative productivity. We will apply our theory to examples throughout the creative process – from problem finding to idea generation and execution – and discuss how such emotion skills can be integrated into creativity training programs to foster the next generation of creators: our secondary school students.

5.1 Introduction

> Today we must abandon competition and secure cooperation...Past thinking and methods did not prevent world wars. Future thinking must prevent wars…These and a hundred other questions concerning the desirable evolution of the world seem to be getting very little attention. (Albert Einstein 1946, p. 23)

From recent challenges surrounding COVID-19, to other global issues such as climate change, gun violence, or persistent inequities, the need for those who can produce creative solutions has never been greater. Resilience, stress tolerance, flexibility, and emotional intelligence are all listed as skills which employers are seeking. The 2020 Future of Jobs Report put out by the World Economic Forum lists the top 15 workplace skills predicted to be in high demand for 2025, with innovation, complex problem solving, and creativity all included. Yet, solving complex problems calls not only for creative thinkers on a cognitive level, but for those with the social and emotional skills to work collaboratively, persist in the face of setbacks, and perhaps most importantly, be brave enough to take creative risks in the first place (Sternberg 2000).

J. D. Hoffmann (✉) · J. McGarry · J. Seibyl
Yale Center for Emotional Intelligence, Yale University, New Haven, CT, USA
e-mail: jessica.hoffmann@yale.edu

© Springer Nature Switzerland AG 2022   59
R. A. Beghetto, G. J. Jaeger (eds.), *Uncertainty: A Catalyst for Creativity,*
Learning and Development, Creativity Theory and Action in Education 6,
https://doi.org/10.1007/978-3-030-98729-9_5

Creative problem solving, whether on a global scale or in one's own workplace, school, or home, can be fraught with uncertainty: from ambiguity in what processes might lead to solutions to the self-doubt or perceived social risk that can come from being unconventional. As written by Stoycheva (2003) describing such situations, "...we have to act with lack of clarity or lack of information, and novel or uncommon situations where our true and tried, learned ways of thinking and acting do not solve the problem" (p. 31). In this chapter, we will focus on the intersection of creativity and emotional intelligence, and how those who are skilled in understanding and managing their emotions can convert, channel, and regulate even unpleasant, unwanted feelings - like uncertainty - to support their creative productivity. We will apply our theory to examples throughout the creative process – from problem finding to idea generation and execution – and discuss how such emotion skills can be integrated into creativity training programs to foster the next generation of creators: our secondary school students.

5.2   Emotions and Creativity

Emotions are the fuel of creativity. Amazement at a beautiful sunset can inspire an iconic photograph. Feelings of betrayal may lead to hit song lyrics. But can all emotions contribute to creativity or only some of them? What about uncertainty? Can feeling unsure, confused, ambivalent, or doubtful really lead to creative outcomes just like awe, passion, or inspiration? Here, we assert that any emotion – even uncertainty – has creative value; it all depends on how the person uses it. Emotions may be fuel, but generating a creative idea and converting it into a creative product needs a skilled driver.

Historically, research on the role of emotions in creativity focused on the enhancing effect of pleasant (or positive) emotions, like happiness (e.g. Abele-Brehm 1992; Isen et al. 1985; Isen et al. 2004; Isen et al. 1987). Early mood induction studies by Isen and colleagues (Isen et al. 1985; Isen et al. 1987) found that mild states of happiness (induced through either receiving a free gift or watching a comedic film), led to broader and more flexible thinking, more remote associations, and more successful creative solutions to problems. The effects of positive affect on creative thinking were explained by theories such as the broaden-and-build model in which positive emotions expand one's thinking and subsequent actions (Fredrickson 2004). In contrast, unpleasant emotions, such as anxiety or fear, were thought to narrow one's thinking, leading to either fight or flight responses and habitual reactions rather than creative ones.

However, the benefits of pleasant emotions and the downsides of unpleasant emotions has never been considered universal; throughout the same research period, studies finding the reverse – that negative affect benefitted creativity or that positive affect was a hindrance – continued to emerge. For example, in a study asking participants to combine randomly generated letters into as many combinations as possible, Anderson et al. (1995) found that positive mood had a negative effect on performance compared to neutral mood. Kaufmann and Vosburg (2002) found that when positive, neutral, or negative mood was induced through various video clips, there was a critical interaction with time: positive mood was beneficial to early idea production but yielded the lowest number of ideas in late production, whereas both neutral and negative mood led to superior creative performance later in the task.

Alternative theoretical pathways described these perhaps counterintuitive findings. Martin et al. (1993) proposed a "mood-as-input" model in which negative affect is a cue to the creator that something is not quite right. In this model, people might continue to persist longer in the creative process when feeling unpleasant, whereas positive affect would signal to a person that their goal was achieved and they could stop (George and Zhou 2002). Schwarz's (1990) "feelings-as-information" theory posited that pleasant mood could lead to a more playful approach enhancing divergent thinking tasks, whereas unpleasant mood signals a need for increased effort and systematic thinking, supporting creative tasks in which identifying an optimal solution (i.e. insight tasks) is needed.

Other critical components in understanding the associations between creativity and emotions have also emerged, such as the impact of setting (laboratory or real-world), and time restrictions or lack-there-of attached to certain creative tasks. In a 2008 meta-analysis, Baas et al. commented on the well-documented benefits of positive affect on creative thought, but ultimately concluded that the effect is relatively small and is limited to the first few minutes of idea generation. Research outside of the laboratory shows that distress-related variables, such as job dissatisfaction, group conflicts, or budget shortages, can stimulate innovation (Anderson et al. 2004). Certain levels of dissatisfaction or frustration might inspire exploration and problem finding (Berrone et al. 2013; Runco 1994), which are crucial to the creative process (Csikszentmihalyi and Getzels 1971; Runco 1994). Russ (1993) distinguished between negative mood as a result of an external event and a negative mood that is purposeful, such as during fantasy play. When negative mood is induced, one might expect reduced motivation or productivity; but in the case of intentional accessing of primary process thinking, fantastical or imaginative thought, or regression in the service of the ego, negative affect could be harnessed for the purposes of broadening associations and idea generation, just as positive affect might. This suggests again, that the emotional skills of the creator, specifically self-awareness and emotion regulation abilities, are a critical component of whether unpleasant feelings aid creative potential or squelch it.

5.3 Using Emotions Wisely for Creativity

What if it's not the specific emotion that matters so much as the person and how they understand and manage that emotion? If this were the case, then even an emotion like uncertainty, typically expected to cause pause, doubt, or paralysis, or to increase the sense of creative risk, could be a catalyst for creativity. How artists and others might channel their emotions into creative products has many historical connections. Freud (1958/1925) wrote of the defense mechanism sublimation – the process by which socially unacceptable impulses or feelings are expressed through socially desirable behaviors (e.g. when sexual desire or aggressive thoughts are expressed through the arts). Psychoanalyst Ernst Kris (1936/1952) referred to regression in the service of the ego –intentional non-pathological regression, allowing otherwise hidden or unavailable impulses and drives to help an artist achieve inspiration. Modern laboratory studies support the idea that people can intentionally use or convert their emotions (even unwanted ones) towards a creative outcome or product (Cohen and Andrade 2004; Hoffmann and Russ 2016; Kim et al. 2013).

In this section, we explore this possibility further, beginning with a review of existing research on emotional intelligence and creativity, and then conducting an exercise in which we apply the theorized emotional intelligence and creativity connections specifically to emotions of uncertainty as a catalyst.

5.3.1 Emotional Intelligence and Creativity

Emotional intelligence is defined as the ability to perceive and express emotion, assimilate emotion in thought, understand and reason with emotion, and regulate emotion in the self and others (Mayer and Salovey 1997). Within the theory of emotional intelligence, emotions are conceptualized as information. This idea is in contrast to classical thinking which placed emotions in conflict with cognition, logic, or reason (see Lazarus 1999). Perceiving one's emotions as information is liberating, allowing one to understand and use emotions – even the unpleasant, unwanted ones – to his or her benefit, instead of feeling at the mercy of them. For example, anxiety before an exam signals that you are not prepared and may compel you to study, which will in turn reduce the intensity of the feeling. Brackett et al. (2019) describe five distinct skills that make up one's emotional intelligence, and form the acronym RULER: *recognizing* emotions in oneself and others, *understanding* the causes of emotions, *labeling* emotions with a nuanced vocabulary, *expressing* emotions in effective ways given one's context, and *regulating* emotions with helpful strategies.

Theory would suggest that people who are higher in emotional intelligence would be able to sustain their positive mood states more effectively, which would in turn benefit their idea generation, and allow them to be more capable of channeling their negative affect into solutions, which could also potentially be creative (Parke et al. 2015; Lea et al. 2018; Xu et al. 2019). When tested empirically however, the relationships between emotional intelligence and creative thought and creative production do not appear to be so clear-cut. In a recent meta-analysis, Xu et al. (2019) sought to assess the overall correlation between emotional intelligence and creativity, analyzing 96 correlations obtained from 75 studies. While a statistically significant correlation was found ($r = .032$, 95% CI, 0.26–0.38, $p < .01$), moderation analyses showed that the relationship was stronger when emotional intelligence and creativity were measured using subject self-reports (in other words, measures of trait emotional intelligence were used rather than ability tests, and measures of creative behavior or creative personality were used rather than divergent thinking, remote associations tests, or ratings of creative products). When emotional intelligence and creativity were both measured by more objective ability tests, the association between the two was significantly weaker.

While Xu et al. (2019) suggest that these weaker results with ability tests may be due to the narrowness of the tests themselves (i.e. those that only measure emotion perception of faces, or knowledge of emotion vocabulary), another possibility is there truly is not as direct a connection between emotional intelligence and creativity. Literature indicates that people tend to be poor judges of their emotional intelligence abilities (e.g. Brackett et al. 2006; Dunn et al. 2007), therefore it is possible that correlations between emotional intelligence and creativity based on self-report are inflated.

Ivcevic and Brackett (2015) provide a different view, suggesting that one facet of emotional intelligence, emotion regulation – the processes of monitoring, influencing, and changing emotions and emotional reactions in order to reach a goal (Gross 1998; Gross 2008) – is related to creativity. Studies with elementary school children have shown connections between emotion regulation and pretend play which is a precursor of later creativity (Hoffmann and Russ 2012; Russ 2014). Furthermore, Ivcevic and Brackett (2015) found that emotion regulation was associated with creativity in high school students, but only for those who were already moderately or highly prone towards creative thought in the first place, as measured by self-reported openness to experience. The relationship between openness to experience and emotion regulation was mediated by teacher reported student passion and persistence. The authors write:

> Collectively, these results provide insight into the role of emotion regulation in bridging the gap between creative disposition and behavior; the results address both when emotion regulation is predictive of creativity and describe one mechanism of this influence. Emotion regulation ability by itself does not "make" one more creative—it does not help one to connect remotely associated ideas or generate original ideas...However, emotion regulation ability appears to help individuals with high openness to transform their preference for new ideas and intellectual or artistic interests into creative behavior (Ivcevic and Brackett 2015, p. 484).

5.3.2 Applying Emotional Intelligence to Uncertainty in the Service of Creativity

What does converting uncertainty into a catalyst for creativity look like outside of the laboratory? We can begin by applying the previously described RULER skills to feelings of uncertainty. One can imagine a painter working on a mural for a public space. As the artist works, she begins to experience an unpleasant sensation, a vague uncertainty that something is wrong with the mural. *Recognizing* this new emotion, the artist pauses to examine the cause of her feeling. With a few minutes reflection, the artist is sure the looming feeling is coming from her mural and not something else (hunger, anticipation of evening plans), and begins to *understand* that she is doubtful of the color palette she has chosen. While she had put much thought into it conceptually, seeing it on the wall, in large scale, is making her question her original decision. The artist *labels* her feeling as uncertainty: uncertainty about the colors and whether they will convey the meaning she had intended to the audience. At this point, the artist faces a choice in how such uncertainty will be *expressed* and *regulated* in her behavior. She could procrastinate or become disengaged from the project, reluctant to keep going but equally reluctant to start over. She could also choose to ignore the emotion, suppress her thoughts of uncertainty, and press on, finishing the project on time and as originally proposed. She might alternatively choose to seek support from others and gain validation that she is headed in the right direction, or confirmation that she has identified a flaw and should begin again. She may also choose to engage in positive self-talk or problem solving, choosing to convince herself the feeling of uncertainty was fleeting or motivating herself to start anew. Regardless of the artist's next step, honoring her uncertainty has the potential to strengthen her decision-making and the quality of the final piece.

Another way to examine how feelings of uncertainty can be channeled into creativity is to explore the different phases or stages of the creative process and how uncertainty could arise at any of them. Theories on the stages of the creative process vary, but most agree that the process includes some aspect of problem finding (or noticing an opportunity), idea generation, idea evaluation, and execution. Ivcevic and Hoffmann (2019) outline how emotional intelligence (in particular using and regulating one's emotions wisely) can play a role at each of these stages. In their comprehensive model of emotions and creativity, Ivcevic and Hoffmann synthesize existing research on the creative personality (i.e. how traits like openness to experience are known to be associated with creative potential), and emotion states (i.e. laboratory research on associations between discrete emotions and creative thought). They then go further, to explore the role of emotion abilities, such as the capacity to process emotion-laden information. This stance towards emotion abilities and creativity "acknowledges individual agency in relation to emotions – people are able to influence the course of their emotions and mobilize them in the service of both hedonic and instrumental goals" (Ivcevic and Hoffmann 2019, p. 287).

In the next sections, we conduct an exercise examining how uncertainty might be skillfully understood, channeled, and/or regulated in the service of creativity, including the most recent research that supports this theory.

5.3.2.1   Uncertainty as a Signal of a Creative Opportunity

The first time in the creative process at which uncertainty might be useful is right at the beginning: when a person recognizes that there is an opportunity to do something in a creative way. Imagine a person struggling to see roadway signage in the dark and looking for a way to make it more visible, as was the case with Harry Heltzer. In 1937, Heltzer, an inventor, was tasked with making the center striping of

Minneapolis highways more visible at night, eventually earning him six patents for reflective highway inventions. Or consider in 2018 when Google Chrome released their password generator that automatically creates and stores passwords for each user, relieving them of the too-often-experienced forgotten password, and subsequent guesswork and frustration.

Emotional intelligence includes recognizing, understanding and managing emotions not only in oneself, but also in others (Salovey and Mayer 1990). This is particularly important when working with children, whose emotional intelligence skills are still developing, and adults modeling and co-regulating are key ways to support that growth. We have seen educators across the country devise creative ways of helping incoming students to feel more secure during the mass uncertainty created by COVID-19 in the 2020–21 school year. Edutopia, a reputable resource in the education field, published a list of flexible ideas for elementary school teachers to utilize, including a group story writing activity in which the teacher mails a journal to a different student each week for them to add to a collaborative story (Desautels 2020). Others have given their creative teaching an artistic spin, such as two high school teachers in Atlanta, Georgia who wrote and choreographed a back-to-school rap video for their students addressing virtual learning and COVID-19 safety precautions (Treisman 2020).

The examples used here demonstrate that uncertainty can trigger creativity in multiple ways. Feeling uncertain can lead one to recognize there is a better way of doing something resulting in a creative response; or knowing that a situation is high in uncertainty can lead a person to use creative strategies to regulate the emotion. Glaveanu (this volume) further unpacks how different emotions and creative behaviors can result based on the cause and type of uncertainty. For example, uncertainty and *not* knowing can lead to anxiety which focuses our attention, while uncertainty and knowing lead to curiosity and motivation for exploration. In all these cases, a key link between the feeling of uncertainty and the recognition of opportunities to behave in a new, creative way, is self-awareness, defined by "the abilities to understand one's own emotions, thoughts, and values and how they influence behavior across contexts" (CASEL 2021). In other words, to convert uncertainty into a catalyst for creativity, a person must first accurately recognize and label their feeling as uncertainty and understand its cause.

5.3.2.2 Uncertainty and Problem Construction

Once an opportunity to be creative has been identified, the step of the creative process most often overlooked begins: problem construction – the process by which individuals give structure to an ill-defined problem and thereby identify the specific goals of their subsequent problem-solving efforts (Mumford et al. 1994; Reiter-Palmon and Murugavel 2018). Problem construction is a time for asking questions; "Do we fully understand the challenge?" or "What is really being asked of us?". One might think of this as ensuring accurate diagnosis of an ailment before trying to cure it.

Research confirms that time spent on problem identification and construction lead to more creative outcomes, beginning with the frequently cited work of Getzels and Csikszentmihalyi (1975, 1976) in which art students were tasked with painting a still life and those who took more time to handle and select unique objects produced more original and aesthetically pleasing paintings. Measures of how people engage in problem identification and construction have also been linked with professional success (Csikszentmihalyi 1990; Rostan 1994; Voss et al. 1991), and the quality and originality of solutions to real-world problems of adults (Mumford et al. 1997; Reiter-Palmon et al. 1997; Reiter-Palmon et al. 1998). In children, problem finding has been found to be the best predictor of creative accomplishment beyond creative problem solving and divergent thinking (Okuda et al. 1991). Moreover, it is important to note that research has found individual differences in people's ability to construct problems beyond what could be explained by intelligence alone (e.g. Smilansky 1984).

So how might emotional intelligence, uncertainty, and the benefits of problem construction all come together? For some, problem construction may happen quickly and subconsciously, especially when a problem is perceived as not particularly novel. For example, a teacher may notice from formative assessment data that students are not displaying mastery of material, and without much consideration decide to spend another day reviewing key concepts. However, other considerations besides issues of mastery, are possible. For example, students performed below their ability out of boredom, or the assessment was a poor gauge for the content. Taking extra time to ensure that the problem has been conceptualized accurately leads to a higher quality solution in the end. Thus, a person could use their emotion regulation skills to purposefully conjure feelings of doubt or skepticism. Temporarily feeling uncertain about the parameters that have been placed on a problem takes problem construction from an automatic process to an intentional one. Indeed, a study examining how leaders might impact the creative thinking of their teams found that when the instructions are altered to encourage active processing (e.g. having participants take time to write down all the possible problems and considerations before moving on to problem solving), more creative solutions were generated (Redmond et al. 1993).

5.3.2.3   Uncertainty and Creative Idea Generation

The research on the benefits of pleasant emotions and divergent thinking might make idea generation an unlikely phase for which uncertainty could be helpful; yet, several lines of research make the case for why negative moods (which would include uncertainty) might be beneficial. The first reason is motivational: negative moods can cause people to be more critical, skeptical, and discerning (George and Zhou 2002). An individual might therefore take the creative endeavor more seriously and exert more effort (Verhaeghen et al. 2005), or understand their negative mood to be providing information (Martin 2001; Martin and Stoner 1996), such that a person uncertain of the answer to the question, "Is my idea creative enough?"

would be more likely to persist longer in the pursuit of a higher quality creative idea (Davis 2009). The serial order effect which states that ideas tend to get more original as time passes (Christensen et al. 1957), suggests that the first idea is generally not the most creative. Feeling uncertain, or at least not overly confident, and spending longer pushing oneself to think of more ideas could be beneficial.

A second connection between unpleasant emotions and idea generation exists in Davis' (2009) call for additional research that goes beyond the typical idea generation tasks to more "real world" applicable situations. For example, we can imagine how it might be easier to generate a longer and more original list of answers to questions such as "what are all the possible ways this could go wrong?" or "what are the obstacles we might face in pulling off this idea?" when one is feeling more uncertain, skeptical, or doubtful, rather than happy or confident. Schuldberg (2011) suggests exactly this: there are likely optimal matches between affective states and types of creative tasks. Insight tasks, or those in which one must pick the optimal solution, have been theorized to benefit from unpleasant emotions that enhance attention to detail and critical thinking (Russ 1993; Schwarz 1990). One can think of a medical diagnosis as a version of a Remote Associates Test: what do a set of symptoms all have in common? Such insight tasks are not helped by efficiency or overconfidence, but rather by systematic thinking that often comes with mild negative affect.

The connection between a willingness to experience uncertainty and creative achievement is most often studied as a personality trait: tolerance of ambiguity (e.g. Comadena 1984; Zenasni et al. 2008). We conceptualize the idea slightly differently, borrowing the concept of adopting an "emotions matter mindset", a key tenant of RULER, which in addition to being an acronym for the skills of emotional intelligence (described previously), is the name of a whole-school approach to social and emotional learning in which people learn that emotions influence attention, memory, learning, relationships, decision-making, physical and mental health, and creativity (Brackett et al. 2019). Therefore, it follows that even uncomfortable emotions, including uncertainty, come to hold value and are no longer threatening or to be immediately regulated away. Making space and taking time for non-judgmental attention towards our unpleasant emotions, as described here, is closely linked with the practice of mindfulness (see also Henriksen et al., this volume).

Understanding the benefits of spending time with our uncertainty is the first step towards building skills and confidence in harnessing the power of uncertainty. In a study of 99 artists (Ivcevic and Hoffmann 2016) looking at the role of emotion skills in creative processes, one artist summarized her process:

> ...when you create enough, you realize that doubt, feeling paralyzed, is a part of the process. You can remember when you felt it before, but nothing cathartic happens if you leave the work. That brings a different set of emotions centered around guilt and the feeling that the world will overwhelm you. Art, even in the feeblest sense, is a testimony to an individual trying to react and respond to the world we live in and the emotions we feel. I've done enough pieces to know that failure, feelings of uncertainty, can be overcome in ways that are not always immediately visible.

5.3.2.4 Uncertainty and Evaluating Creative Ideas

Evaluating the creative quality of an idea is perhaps the most obvious place that uncertainty would be beneficial. Generating a large number of ideas may increase the chances that some are higher quality (e.g. Osborn 1953), but it is no guarantee (MacCrimmon and Wagner 1994). The quality of idea will depend largely on the task at hand, though Dean et al. (2006) suggest that a quality idea contains three characteristics: it should be relevant, effective, and implementable. Other potential criteria for quality can also include workability (that the idea does not violate any known constraints) and thoroughness (that all the details of the idea have been worked out; MacCrimmon and Wagner 1994). Note that this definition of quality does not require that an idea be creative; thus, a high-quality *creative* idea would not only be relevant, effective, implementable, workable, and thorough, but also be novel or original.

The majority of the work on idea evaluation has been in the building of scales or rubrics to support outside raters in evaluating ideas reliably. Yet outside of laboratory studies, in many cases the idea generator is also (at least) the initial idea evaluator (e.g. a writer with a new idea for her book or a quilter designing a new pattern). As Silvia (2008) writes,

> Discernment - the ability to evaluate the creativity of one's ideas - is an important part of theories of creativity. Sociocultural theories distinguish between having an idea, which is easy, and developing an idea so that the domain's gatekeepers and audience accept it, which is hard (Sawyer 2006; Sternberg 2006).

Here, the role of uncertainty and emotional intelligence is in supporting the idea evaluation process. Healthy skepticism, or the self-regulation to pause and ask questions, should support creators in taking the time to consider whether an idea is a "good" one, or which idea is "the best". Uncertainty might appear in the form of a nagging feeling or general unease, worthy of further exploration. Alternatively, uncertainty can be generated purposefully by placing oneself in a critical or doubtful mood to question the idea's quality. Initiating a new emotion takes skill in emotion regulation, especially when trying to generate uncertainty if the creative idea is an exciting one. Emotion regulation strategies can be deployed, such as pausing or waiting a day before making a decision, or using breathing or self-talk to calm one's energy and leave space to examine the idea for any flaws.

5.3.2.5 Uncertainty and Creative Idea Execution

Noticing an opportunity to be creative, and even coming up with a creative idea, does not guarantee that the creative idea comes to fruition. Uncertainty next comes into play when a person decides whether to act on a creative idea and to share it with the world. Doing something creative is a risk. Will the idea be met with admiration or scorn? Will spending resources on a new product or process pay off in the end? As Sternberg (2000) so astutely writes: "creativity is a decision"; and in a 2003

President's Column for APA Monitor, he continues, "People are creative largely by dint of their decision to go their own way. They make decisions that others lack the will or even the courage to make…" (p. 5). Sternberg (2003) goes on to list behaviors, many of which one might tie to the emotion skills covered by the construct of emotional intelligence: self-reflection of one's ideas, persuading people to accept ideas, overcoming obstacles, tolerating ambiguity, willingness to grow, and realizing that others may have different perspectives.

Thus, emotional intelligence skills can surely play a role in ensuring that uncertainty does not paralyze the creative process through regulation strategies such as positive self-talk. Can the skills also turn uncertainty into a benefit? One way might be found in the day-to-day execution of creative projects. Again, in the Ivcevic and Hoffmann (2016) study, researchers asked artists to discuss their creative process, including their day-to-day working experiences and challenges they faced. What they found were consistent descriptions of times in which uncertainty during idea execution led artists to try new mediums, scrap drafts and start again, and to recognize when a strategy was not working and shift techniques.

A visual artist: *"The piece was originally fabricated in a matter of hours, and the remodeling of the material took about the same amount of time a few days later. I kept looking at the original piece during the days in between, trying to think of a way to salvage what I saw as a disaster. It was only when I let go of the original design concept completely that I saw the opportunity for turning the piece into something quite different."*

A jewelry maker: *"My emotions also fuel my perfectionist mentality, driving me to continue to look at my work from every relevant angle until I am fully proud of the finished product."*

A sculptor: *"I have to feel a visceral reaction to the forms I make or I reject them. This reaction cannot be described as a single emotion but instead an undifferentiated conglomerate. If I can feel that these emotions are in balance then the work feels strong, but if they are somehow out of sync then I have to go back to the drawing board"*.

A choreographer: *"I try to be very sensitive to how I feel about my work, because I want to be as happy and proud of it as I can be. Therefore, I trust my gut when I think something isn't right or have a feeling things need to be a different way."*

Even during the execution of an idea, persistence, grit in the short term, or the self-control to "power through" are not the only paths to high quality work. While further research in this area is required, Grohman et al. (2017) have begun to examine how persistence that predicts achievement in well-structured settings may be less applicable to creativity which is generally more loosely structured. They write, "At each decision point, a person is facing multiple options and often has to make decisions based on incomplete or ambiguous information…Such decision points involve weighing different options and often redefining goals and even abandoning what one has started in favor of a new approach or idea" (p. 382).

5.4   Teaching Emotional Intelligence for Creativity

One reason that emotional intelligence is such a viable target for helping to improve creative achievement is the fact that emotional intelligence can be conceptualized as a clearly defined set of skills that can be taught and improved through training and practice (Brackett et al. 2019). In their study of emotion regulation ability and creative outcomes, Ivcevic and Brackett (2015) point out that,

> One practical implication of this research is that developing emotion regulation ability could aid in channeling creative dispositions, such as high openness, into creative behavior and reduce creative underachievement. The importance of this finding is underscored by the fact that emotion regulation is typically not represented in creativity training programs (Bull et al. 1995; Scott et al. 2004)...our research shows that this ability has the potential to help one sustain passion and persistence in pursuing goals of creative work. (p. 485).

Several studies have been conducted to begin testing how emotional intelligence and creativity can be taught in concert, each enhancing the other. For example, in a series of courses, Hoffmann and colleagues successfully combined creativity and emotional intelligence skills training through the visual arts in samples of children (Hoffmann et al. 2020), adolescents (Maliakkal et al. 2016), adults (Hoffmann et al. 2018), and families (Maliakkal et al. 2017). Specific to handling feelings of uncertainty, Caratozzolo et al. (2020) describe a study in which engineering students were given creative thinking instructions meant to help them shift between different modes of thought, cope with uncertainty, and navigate interpersonal challenges. The authors call for the need to train meta-cognitive awareness and related "soft skills" to develop not only students' domain-specific thinking in their area of expertise, but domain-general thinking skills needed for interdisciplinary approaches, creative problem solving, and career success in cutting edge fields.   Emotional   intelligence skills, as they relate to supporting creative outcomes, should be, at least in part, domain general. While many creativity skills have been determined to be domain-specific, and in some cases hyper domain specific (see Baer 1998, 2010), studies have begun to uncover how emotional intelligence may support creativity across creative domains (e.g. pretend play and storytelling: Hoffmann and Russ 2012; everyday, scientific, scholarly, performance, and artistic: Tu et al. 2020). We can imagine how skills related to labeling emotions accurately learned through poetry, will continue to apply if said artist takes up screenwriting and uses their nuanced and rich emotion vocabulary in this new medium. A scientist who has employed positive self-talk when gearing up to propose a novel idea to a group of skeptics, can continue to use that positive self-talk to bolster themselves when auditioning for community theater. The fashion designer who works with women who have a range of body types and has developed a keen ability to sense how others are feeling simply through their body language, will still be able to apply that finely honed emotion perception ability while working as a volunteer in a music therapy club for teens.

5.4.1   The inspirED Process: Compassionate, Collaborative, Creative Change

Returning to the call made at the beginning of this chapter for a generation of citizens who can harness their emotion and creativity skills to solve big challenges, we conclude this chapter with a demonstration of what such training might look like, using examples from a youth empowerment program called inspirED. inspirED is a free program for middle and high school students that walks them through a four-step, A-B-C-D, process to: *assess* their school's emotional climate, *brainstorm* project ideas, commit to and *complete* a chosen project, and *debrief* their impact and personal growth. inspirED provides teams of students with training and support at each step of the process, and is grounded in both the theory of emotional intelligence and a creative problem solving framework, seeking to amplify the benefits of each set of skills through their combination (see Hoffmann et al., in press-a for a full review of the theory of change).

During the *assess* phase, inspirED teams engage in emotionally intelligent problem-finding, collecting school climate data (or review existing data), and tapping into their unpleasant emotions to identify possible areas for improvement. They might ask what makes us feel disappointed, frustrated, angry, or bored at school. Students navigate both self-awareness (recognizing and using these emotions as information) and problem-finding (identifying what to change to decrease these unpleasant emotions). In the 2019–2020 and 2020–2021 school years, students faced a new emotional experience: uncertainty around how COVID-19 might impact their school experience, relationships, families, health, and futures. As with other feeling states, inspirED students were encouraged to recognize and label their uncertainty, reflect on the cause, and consider whether it signalled an opportunity for creativity. For example, one team whose school had shifted to all-remote learning asked, "How will this impact our seniors? Will they get the graduation ceremony they've been dreaming of?" They then capitalized on their empathy for the loss experienced by the graduating senior class and endeavored to replicate the celebratory and recognition events. The inspirED team created handmade, personalized lawn signs for each senior with their name, graduation year, and any sports or extra-curriculars, and delivered the signs to each senior's home.

Uncertainty can also enter the *assess* phase through intentional emotion regulation to a place of wondering and exploring the unknown. In exploring their climate data, students are prompted to consider what they still don't know or understand about their climate data before jumping to interpretations or solutions. A tool recently designed to support students in taking that pause, and spending additional time invested in problem finding is the School Climate Walkthrough (Cipriano et al. 2019; Hoffmann 2019; Hoffmann et al., in press-b). This web-based survey allows for whole-school reporting of students' experiences of school climate and culture. It provides overall scores on relationships, safety, and school quality, and highlights places in which various demographic groups have disagreed (e.g. male students report feeling safer than female students; students of one race or ethnicity disagree about whether rules are enforced fairly or consistently in comparison to another). Through reflection, and independent review before group discussion, students ask: Do other people see the school the way I do? What don't I know yet about this data? Who's voice is missing from these data? Who else do we need in the conversation to bring clarity? Extended problem construction often prompts inspirED teams to engage in additional data collection, such as one team who built an app for tracking students emotions more continuously and consistently across time.

Next, in the *brainstorm* phase of the inspirED process, students are faced with the uncertainty of the open-ended possibilities for their project. By design, inspirED provides minimal programmatic direction for students, instead allowing them wide leeway in responding to their data as they see fit. See Beghetto (2020) for more on structured uncertainty – deliberately leaving a task open-ended, with what will be done, how it will be done, the outcomes that will result, and the criteria for success all left to-be-determined. Students are encouraged to be aware that first ideas are not always the most creative and are invited to overcome this by setting an ambitious time goal to brainstorm, perhaps 30 minutes or longer. After drafting a preliminary list of project ideas, students participate in an activity entitled "What If We?" where they deliberately iterate and build upon each other's ideas, search for ideas that could potentially be combined, and consider ways to involve more people. For example, at one school students wanted to hold an empathy conference. Such an ambitious project was met with skepticism about feasibility, and doubt around success. The school began with what they entitled "low input, high impact projects" such as decorating the front entrance with sidewalk chalk and putting sticky notes with positive messages on every locker to generate momentum. By the time they held their empathy conference, they were ready. It was such a success that the following year they hosted an even larger conference and invited teams of students and educators from surrounding schools to attend.

When it comes to the *complete* phase of a project, students are further embarking on a journey of uncertainty, experimenting with an idea that has no guarantee of effectiveness or positive reception by their peers. They must regulate this uncertainty through strategies like careful and intentional planning and emotion management strategies to initiate feelings of bravery, confidence, and determination. One school decided to tackle an ambitious project with no guaranteed outcome: petitioning school leaders to convert from a traditional, daily bell schedule to alternating-day block schedule in response to student reports of stress caused by their homework load. They convinced adults in positions of power to suspend their own uncertainty about this completely novel approach with assurances of a pre-determined method for evaluating the project's impact. The inspirED team committed to gathering evidence of the effectiveness of the change through surveying their peers, and it was agreed that the schedule change would undergo a pilot semester. In the end, students' self-reports of stress, overwhelm, and academic fatigue decreased, and the block schedule were implemented permanently. In situations such as these, inspirED teams are faced with a dilemma of proof: they can't know if it will work until they try it. inspirED was built to encourage the experiential learning of embracing the uncertainty and pushing through it to turn the uncertainty from a roadblock to a catalyst for action. Students have the opportunity to experience the learning that comes from trying something ambitious even when they are unsure and as a result, and regardless of the ultimate outcome, which translates into becoming more confident and capable over time.

The *debriefing* phase includes thinking about a project's success and impact; students must grapple with an uncertain reality about goal attainment. Perhaps they achieved their goal completely, only partially, or not at all. This reality can result in students feeling uncertain if they made a meaningful difference in their school, potentially leaving them to channel this uncertainty into motivation to gather post-test data, reflect on shortcomings, begin again, or double down and persevere. Further, given the finite nature of the high school journey, graduating students may need to confront uncertainty regarding whether the progress they've set in place will continue after they leave, accept that they will not see the fullest realization of their goals before moving on, or simply cope with not knowing the extent of the mark they made. Rather than allowing these feelings to be self-defeating and lead to considering the experience a waste, students can reappraise the uncertainty of their impact on school into reflecting on the ways they have grown personally, take the long view that their contributions are part of a greater effort to continue to move the needle of school improvement, or perceive their efforts as a beginning but not an ending. Far from being an automatic process, this type of reflection requires careful and intentional contemplation as the new skills, mindsets, and abilities may not always be obvious, especially if one is left with a sense that they did not accomplish their goal. One student, who exemplifies this well, endeavored to address racism and intolerance at her school during her time as inspirED club president. Her work did not completely eradicate systemic racism in her school and community, and uncertainty appeared in the form of thoughts such as, "What did my efforts really accomplish?" In recognition of this emotion, the student could engage in more intentional reflection, realizing that she did raise critical awareness of the harm caused by racism, create a structure for student activism by recruiting allies, speak publicly at a school board meeting, and successfully organize a protest. She leaves a legacy of perseverance, challenging the status quo, and uniting in service of a common cause; she takes with her increased skills of advocacy, leadership, assertive communication, and community organizing.

5.5   Conclusion

Uncertainty will always be a part of the human experience; when the struggles of today have faded or been resolved, new ones will arise. Employers are already asking for employees who are flexible, collaborative, and innovative; so, what is next for research on the specific training and development of the social and emotional skills in adolescents to face the today's challenges and those we cannot yet anticipate?

First and foremost, any training program must pay attention to transfer effects. Students who participate in inspirED often speak of the benefits to themselves and their peers: *"Our biggest wins were how much we were able to learn and accomplish in the time given. We believe this helped influence a change in mood in our students from tired, stressed, and bored to happy hopeful, and supported"* (Anonymous inspirED Team, personal communication, June, 2021). Yet, the question remains, do students recognize that they have built creativity skills that they can apply to navigating uncertainty in other areas of their lives, such as in relationships, employment, or hobbies? Studies in which student teams can pick their own projects, select different measures of success, and work in diverse communities is messy, but needed. We too as researchers must find our creative courage to test new programs and try new research methodologies that can answer our big questions.

Second, how can adults more explicitly model and coach students to purposefully employ their emotional intelligence through the stages of creative problem-solving? In Rumi's (1995) poem *The Guest House,* he writes, "This being human is a guest house. Every morning a new arrival. A joy, a depression, a meanness....Be grateful for whatever comes, because each has been sent as a guide from beyond." This mindset, that all emotions hold tremendous value, is a powerful stance. In this chapter we have applied this mindset specifically to how emotion skills can convert uncertainty into a catalyst for creativity, wherever it might emerge. What adult social and emotional skills must be fostered, and how can mindsets about emotions be shifted?

The eminent creators among us have captured the power of emotions in their writings, paintings, and performances for centuries; yet, just in the last several decades have we begun to understand through scientific inquiry that creativity and emotional intelligence are not simply natural talents, with haves and have-nots; they are skills which can be taught through training, improved with practice, and developed in children. Though studies to determine best practices for combining creativity training and emotional intelligence training are just beginning to emerge, there is great promise that through these efforts, future generations of students will possess the skills they need to solve big challenges and thrive in the twenty-first century and beyond.

References

Abele-Brehm, A. (1992). Positive and negative mood influences on creativity: Evidence of asymmetrical effects. *Polish Psychological Bulletin, 23,* 203-221.

Anderson, R. E., Arlett, C. & Tarrant, L. (1995). Effects of instructions and mood on creative mental synthesis. In G. Kaufman, T. Helstrup, & K. H. Teigen (Eds.), *Problem solving and cognitive processes* (pp. 183-195). Fagbokforlaget.

Anderson, N., De Dreu, C. K., & Nijstad, B. A. (2004). The routinization of innovation research: A constructively critical review of the state-of-the-science. *Journal of Organizational Behavior,* 25(2), 147-173. https://doi.org/10.1002/job.236

Baer, J. (1998). The case for domain specificity of creativity. *Creativity Research Journal, 11*(2), 173-177. https://doi.org/10.1207/s15326934crj1102_7

Baer, J. (2010). Is creativity domain specific? In J. C. Kaufman, & R. J. Sternberg (Eds.), *Cambridge handbook of creativity* (pp. 321-341). Cambridge University Press.

Baas, M., De Dreu, C. K. W. & Nijstad, B. A. (2008). A meta-analysis of 25 years of mood-creativity research: Hedonic tone, activation, or regulatory focus? *Psychological Bulletin, 134,* 779-806. https://doi.org/10.1037/a0012815

Beghetto R. A. (2020) Uncertainty. In V. Glăveanu (Ed.), *The Palgrave Encyclopedia of the Possible*. Palgrave Macmillan, Cham. https://doi.org/10.1007/978-3-319-98390-5_122-1

Berrone, P., Fosfuri, A., Gelabert, L., & Gomez-Mejia, L. R. (2013). Necessity as the mother of 'green' inventions: Institutional pressures and environmental innovations. *Strategic Management Journal, 34*(8), 891-909. https://doi.org/10.1002/smj.2041

Brackett, M. A., Bailey, C. S., Hoffmann, J. D., & Simmons, D. N. (2019). RULER: A theory-driven, systemic approach to social, emotional, and academic learning. *Educational Psychologist, 54*(3), 144-161. https://doi.org/10.1080/00461520.2019.1614447

Brackett, M. A., Rivers, S. E., Shiffman, S., Lerner, N., & Salovey, P. (2006). Relating emotional abilities to social functioning: A comparison of self-report and performance measures of emotional intelligence. *Journal of Personality and Social Psychology, 91,* 780–795. https://doi.org/10.1037/0022-3514.91.4.780

Bull, K. S., Montgomery, D., & Baloche, L. (1995). Teaching creativity at the college level: A synthesis of curricular components perceived as important by instructors. *Creativity Research Journal, 8*(1), 83-89. https://doi.org/10.1207/s15326934crj0801_7

Caratozzolo, P., Alvarez-Delgado, A., & Hosseini, S. (2020, April). Metacognitive Awareness and Creative Thinking: the capacity to cope with uncertainty in engineering. In *2020 IEEE Global Engineering Education Conference (EDUCON)* (pp. 638-643). IEEE.

Cipriano, C., Floman, J., Hoffmann, J., & Willner, C. (2019, October). *Building the assessments we need: The development of new actionable SEL data-points for teachers* [Presentation]. CASEL SEL Exchange, Chicago, IL.

CASEL, Collaborative for Academic, Social, and Emotional Learning (2021, February 2). *SEL: What are the core competence areas and where are they promoted?* CASEL. https://casel.org/sel-framework/

Christensen, P. R., Guilford, J. P., & Wilson, R. C. (1957). Relations of creative responses to working time and instructions. *Journal of Experimental Psychology, 53*(2), 82-88. https://doi.org/10.1037/h0045461

Cohen, J. B., & Andrade, E. B. (2004). Affective intuition and task-contingent affect regulation. *Journal of Consumer Research, 31*(2), 358-367. https://doi.org/10.1086/422114

Comadena, M. E. (1984). Brainstorming groups : Ambiguity tolerance, communication, apprehension, task attraction, and individual productivity. *Small Group Behavior, 15,* 251-264. https://doi.org/10.1177/104649648401500207

Csikszentmihalyi, M. (1990). The domain of creativity. In M. A. Runco & R. S. Albert (Eds.), *Sage focus editions, Vol. 115. Theories of creativity* (pp. 190–212). Sage Publications, Inc.

Csikszentmihalyi, M., & Getzels, J. W. (1971). Discovery-oriented behavior and the originality of creative products: A study with artists. *Journal of Personality and Social Psychology, 19*(1), 47. https://doi.org/10.1037/h0031106

Davis, M. A. (2009). Understanding the relationship between mood and creativity: A meta-analysis. *Organizational Behavior and Human Decision Processes, 108*(1), 25-38. https://doi.org/10.1016/j.obhdp.2008.04.001

Dean, D. L., Hender, J. M., Rodgers, T. L., and Santanen E. (2006). Identifying good ideas: Constructs and scales for idea evaluation. *Journal of Association for Information Systems, 7(10),* 646-699. https://doi.org/10.17705/1jais.00106

Desautels, L. (2020, June 24). *4 strategies to help students feel calm during distance learning*. Edutopia. https://www.edutopia.org/article/4-strategies-help-students-feel-calm-during-distance-learning

Dunn, E. W., Brackett, M. A., Ashton-James, C., Schneiderman, E., & Salovey, P. (2007). On emotionally intelligent time travel: Individual differences in affective forecasting ability. *Personality and Social Psychology Bulletin, 33*, 85–93. https://doi.org/10.1177/0146167206294201

Einstein, A. (1946). The real problem is in the hearts of men. *New York Times Magazine*, 23.

Fredrickson, B. L. (2004). The broaden–and–build theory of positive emotions. *Philosophical Transactions of the Royal Society of London. Series B: Biological Sciences, 359*(1449), 1367-1377. https://doi.org/10.1098/rstb.2004.1512

Freud, S. (1958). *On creativity and the unconscious*: *Papers on the psychology of art, literature, love, religion*. Harper. (Original work published in 1925).

George, J. M. & Zhou, J. (2002). Understanding when bad moods foster creativity and good ones don't: The role of context and clarity of feelings. *Journal of Applied Psychology, 87*, 687-697. https://doi.org/10.1037/0021-9010.87.4.687

Getzels, J. W., & Csikszentmihalyi, M. (1975). From problem solving to problem finding. In I. A. Taylor & J. W. Getzels (Eds.), *Perspectives in creativity* (pp. 90-116). Chicago, IL: Aldine.

Getzels, J. W., & Csikszentmihalyi, M. (1976). *The creative vision: A longitudinal study of problem finding in art*. Wiley.

Grohman, M. G., Ivcevic, Z., Silvia, P., Kaufman, S. B., Reiter-Palmon, R., Tinio, P., Goldstein, T. & Vartanian, O. (2017). The Role of Passion and Persistence in Creativity. *Psychology of Aesthetics, Creativity, and the Arts, 11*(4), 376–385. doi: https://doi.org/10.1037/aca0000121.

Gross, J. J. (1998). The emerging field of emotion regulation: An integrative review. *Review of General Psychology, 2*, 271–299. https://doi.org/10.1037/1089-2680.2.3.271

Gross, J. J. (2008). Emotion regulation. In M. Lewis, J. M. Haviland-Jones, & L. F. Barrett (Eds.), *Handbook of emotions* (pp. 497–512). Guilford Press.

Hoffmann, J. D. (2019, November). *The importance of a person-centered approach to measuring school climate: Raising every student's voice* [Presentation]. The International Bullying Prevention Association Conference, Chicago, IL.

Hoffmann, J. D., Ivcevic, Z., & Maliakkal, N. (2018). Creative thinking strategies for life: A course for professional adults using art. *Journal of Creative Behavior, 1*, 1-18. https://doi.org/10.1002/jocb.366

Hoffmann, J. D., Ivcevic, Z., & Maliakkal, N. (2020). Emotions, creativity, and the arts: Evaluating a course for children. *Empirical Studies of the Arts*, 1-26. https://doi.org/10.1177/0276237420907864

Hoffmann, J. D., McGarry, J. A., Baumsteiger, R., Seibyl, J., & Brackett, M. A. (in press-a). Emotional empowerment in high school life. In G. Misra & I. Misra (Eds.). *Emotions in Cultural Context*. Springer.

Hoffmann, J. D., Baumsteiger, R., Seibyl, J., Hills, E., Bradley, C., Cipriano, C., & Brackett, M. A. (in press-b). Building useful, web-based educational assessment tools for students, with students: A demonstration with the school climate walkthrough. *Assessment in Education: Principles, Policy & Practice*.

Hoffmann, J. D., & Russ, S. (2012). Pretend play, creativity, and emotion regulation in children. *Psychology of Aesthetics, Creativity, and the Arts, 6*(2), 175. https://doi.org/10.1037/a0026299

Hoffmann, J. D. & Russ, S. W. (2016, August). Adaptive regression: Emotion ability for creativity? In E. Nusbaum (Chair), *Looking back to look forward: Re-examining and re-imagining historical ideas in creativity research* [Symposium]. American Psychological Association Annual Meeting, Denver, CO.

Isen, A. M., Daubman, K. A., & Nowicki, G. P. (1987). Positive affect facilitates creative problem solving. *Journal of Personality and Social Psychology, 52*(6), 1122–1131. https://doi.org/10.1037/0022-3514.52.6.1122

Isen, A. M., Johnson, M. M., Mertz, E., & Robinson, G. F. (1985). The influence of positive affect on the unusualness of word associations. *Journal of Personality and Social Psychology, 48*(6), 1413. https://doi.org/10.1037/0022-3514.48.6.1413

Isen, A. M., Labroo, A. A., & Durlach, P. (2004). An influence of product and brand name on positive affect: Implicit and explicit measures. *Motivation and Emotion, 28*(1), 43-63. https://doi.org/10.1023/b:moem.0000027277.98917.9a

Ivcevic, Z., & Brackett, M. A. (2015). Predicting creativity: Interactive effects of openness to experience and emotion regulation ability. *Psychology of Aesthetics, Creativity, and the Arts, 9*(4), 480. https://doi.org/10.1037/a0039826

Ivcevic, Z., & Hoffmann, J. D. (2016). Emotion skills in the creative process: Artist perspectives. [Unpublished data set].

Ivcevic, Z., & Hoffmann, J. D. (2019). Emotions and creativity: From process to person and product. In J. C. Kaufman & R. S. Sternberg (Eds.), *Cambridge handbook of creativity* (pp. 273-295). Cambridge University Press.

Kaufmann, G. & Vosburg, S. K. (2002). The effects of mood on early and late idea production. *Creativity Research Journal, 14*(3-4), 317-330. https://doi.org/10.1207/s15326934crj1434_3

Kim, E., Zeppenfeld, V., & Cohen, D. (2013). Sublimation, culture, and creativity. *Journal of Personality and Social Psychology, 105*(4), 639. https://doi.org/10.1037/a0033487

Kris, E. (1952). The psychology of caricature. *Psychoanalytic explorations in art* (pp. 173–188). International Universities Press. (Original work published 1936)

Lazarus, R. S. (1999). The cognition-emotion debate: A bit of history. In T. Dalgleish & M. J. Power (Eds.), *Handbook of cognition and emotion* (pp. 3–19). John Wiley & Sons Ltd.

Lea, R. G., Qualter, P., Davis, S. K., Pérez-González, J. C., & Bangee, M. (2018). Trait emotional intelligence and attentional bias for positive emotion: An eye tracking study. *Personality and Individual Differences, 128*, 88-93. https://doi.org/10.1016/j.paid.2018.02.017

MacCrimmon, K. R. & Wagner , C. (1994). Stimulating ideas through creative software. *Management Science (40)*11, 1514-1532. https://doi.org/10.1287/mnsc.40.11.1514

Maliakkal, N., Hoffmann, J., Ivcevic, Z., & Brackett, M. (2016). Teaching emotion and creativity skills through art: A workshop for adolescents. *International Journal of Creativity and Problem Solving, 26*, 69-83.

Maliakkal, N., Hoffmann, J., Ivcevic, Z., & Brackett, M. (2017). An art-based workshop for families: learning emotion skills and choosing creativity. *International Journal of Creativity and Problem Solving, 27*, 45-60.

Martin, L. L., Ward, D. W., Achee, J. W., & Wyer, R. S. (1993). Mood as input: People have to interpret the motivational implications of their moods. *Journal of Personality and Social Psychology, 64*(3), 317. https://doi.org/10.1037/0022-3514.64.3.317

Martin, L. L., & Stoner, P. (1996). Mood as input: What we think about how we feel determines how we think. In L. L. Martin & A. Tesser (Eds.), *Striving and feeling: Interactions among goals, affect, and self-regulation* (pp. 279–301). Lawrence Erlbaum Associates, Inc.

Martin, L. L. (2001). Mood as input: A configural view of mood effects. In L. L. Martin & G. L. Clore (Eds.), *Theories of mood and cognition: A user's guidebook* (pp. 135–157). Lawrence Erlbaum Associates Publishers.

Mayer J. D., & Salovey P. (1997). What is emotional intelligence? In P. Salovey & D. Sluyter (Eds.), *Emotional development and emotional intelligence: Educational implications* (pp. 3–31). Basic Books.

Mumford, M. D., Reiter-Palmon, R., & Redmond, M. R. (1994). Problem construction and cognition: Applying problem representations in ill-defined domains. In M. A. Runco (Ed.), *Creativity research. Problem finding, problem solving, and creativity* (pp. 3–39). Ablex Publishing.

Mumford, M. D., Supinski, E. P., Baughman, W. A., Costanza, D. P., & Threlfall, K. V. (1997). Process-based measures of creative problem-solving skills: V. Overall prediction. *Creativity Research Journal, 10*(1), 73-85. https://doi.org/10.1207/s15326934crj1001_8

Okuda, S. M., Runco, M. A., & Berger, D. E. (1991). Creativity and the finding and solving of real-world problems. *Journal of Psychoeducational Assessment, 9*(1), 45-53. https://doi.org/10.1177/073428299100900104

Osborn, A. F. (1953). *Applied imagination, 1st Edition.* Scribner.

Parke, M.R., Seo, M.G., & Sherf, E.N. (2015). Regulating and facilitating: The role of emotional intelligence in maintaining and using positive affect for creativity. *Journal of Applied Psychology, 100,* 917–934. https://doi.org/10.1037/a0038452

Redmond, M. R., Mumford, M. D., & Teach, R. (1993). Putting creativity to work: Effects of leader behavior on subordinate creativity. *Organizational Behavior and Human Decision Processes, 55*(1), 120-151. https://doi.org/10.1006/obhd.1993.1027

Reiter-Palmon, R., & Murugavel, V. (2018). The effect of problem construction on team process and creativity. *Frontiers in Psychology, 9,* 2098. https://doi.org/10.3389/fpsyg.2018.02098

Reiter-Palmon, R., Mumford, M. D., O'Connor Boes, J., & Runco, M. A. (1997). Problem construction and creativity: The role of ability, cue consistency, and active processing. *Creativity Research Journal, 10*(1), 9-23. https://doi.org/10.1207/s15326934crj1001_2

Reiter-Palmon, R., Mumford, M. D., & Threlfall, K. V. (1998). Solving everyday problems creatively: The role of problem construction and personality type. *Creativity Research Journal, 11*(3), 187-197. https://doi.org/10.1207/s15326934crj1103_1

Rostan, S. M. (1994). Problem finding, problem solving, and cognitive controls: An empirical investigation of critically acclaimed productivity. *Creativity Research Journal, 7*(2), 97-110. https://doi.org/10.1080/10400419409534517

Rumi, J. (1995). The guest house. C. Barks with J. Moyne, AJ Arberry & R. Nicholson (Trans., p. 109). *The essential Rumi.* San Francisco: Harper.

Runco, M. A. (Ed.). (1994). *Problem finding, problem solving, and creativity.* Greenwood Publishing Group.

Russ, S. W. (1993). *Affect and creativity: The role of affect and play in the creative process.* Erlbaum.

Russ, S. W. (2014). *Pretend play in childhood: Foundation of adult creativity.* Washington, DC: APA Books.

Salovey, P., & Mayer, J. D. (1990). Emotional intelligence. *Imagination, Cognition and Personality, 9*(3), 185-211. https://doi.org/10.2190/dugg-p24e-52wk-6cdg

Sawyer, R. K. (2006). *Explaining creativity: The science of human innovation.* Oxford University Press.

Schuldberg, D. (2011). Chaos theory and creativity. In M. A. Runco & S. R. Pritzker (Eds.), *Encyclopedia of creativity, second edition* (pp. 183–191). Elsevier Inc.

Schwarz, N. (1990). Feelings as information: Informational and motivational functions of affective states. In E. T. Huggins & R. M. Sorrentino (Eds.), *Handbook of motivation and cognition* (Vol. 2, pp. 527-561). Guilford Press.

Scott, G., Leritz, L. E., & Mumford, M. D. (2004). The effectiveness of creativity training: A quantitative review. *Creativity Research Journal, 16,* 361–388. https://doi.org/10.1080/10400410409534549

Silvia, P. J. (2008). Discernment and creativity: How well can people identify their most creative ideas?. *Psychology of Aesthetics, Creativity, and the Arts, 2*(3), 139-146. https://doi.org/10.1037/1931-3896.2.3.139

Smilansky, J. (1984). Problem solving and the quality of invention: An empirical investigation. *Journal of Educational Psychology, 76,* 377-386.

Sternberg, R.J. (2000). Creativity is a decision. In A.L. Costa (Ed.), *Teaching for intelligence II* (pp. 85-106). Skylight Training and Publishing Inc.

Sternberg, R. J. (2003, November). President's column--Creativity is a decision. *Monitor on Psychology, 34*(10). http://www.apa.org/monitor/nov03/pc

Sternberg, R. J. (2006). The nature of creativity. *Creativity Research Journal, 18,* 87–98.

Stoycheva, K. (2003). Talent, science and education: How do we cope with uncertainty and ambiguities? In P. Csermely & L. Lederman (Eds.), *NATO science series, Volume V=38: Science education: Talent recruitment and public understanding* (pp. 31–43). IOS Press.

Treisman, R. (2020, August 19). *Georgia teachers' back-to-school rap about virtual learning goes viral.* NPR. https://www.npr.org/sections/coronavirus-live-updates/2020/08/19/903980599/georgia-high-school-teachers-back-to-school-rap-about-virtual-learning-goes-viral

Tu, C., Guo, J., Hatcher, R. C., & Kaufman, J. C. (2020). The relationship between emotional intelligence and domain-specific and domain-general creativity. *The Journal of Creative Behavior*, *54*(2), 337-349. https://doi.org/10.1002/jocb.369

Verhaeghen, P., Joorman, J., & Khan, R. (2005). Why we sing the blues: The relation between self-reflective rumination, mood, and creativity. *Emotion*, *5*(2), 226. https://doi.org/10.1037/1528-3542.5.2.226

Voss, J. F., Wolfe, C. R., Lawrence, J. A., & Engle, R. A. (1991). From representation to decision: An analysis of problem solving in international relations. In R. J. Sternberg & P. A. Frensch (Eds.), *Complex problem solving: Principles and mechanisms* (pp. 119–158). Lawrence Erlbaum Associates, Inc.

Xu, X., Liu, W., & Pang, W. (2019). Are emotionally intelligent people more creative? A meta-analysis of the emotional intelligence–creativity link. *Sustainability*, *11*(21), 6123. https://doi.org/10.3390/su11216123

Zenasni, F., Besancon, M., & Lubart, T. (2008). Creativity and tolerance of ambiguity: An empirical study. *The Journal of Creative Behavior*, *42*(1), 61-73. https://doi.org/10.1002/j.2162-6057.2008.tb01080.x

Chapter 6
Living with Uncertainty in the Creative Process: A Self-Regulatory Perspective

Aleksandra Zielińska and Maciej Karwowski

Abstract Uncertainty characterizes almost all creative acts. In this chapter, we discuss how uncertainty can be tamed and used to benefit the creative process. We analyze the agentic nature of creativity and explore how processes and strategies associated with creative self-regulation can help organize and manage creative actions. While we neither believe nor postulate that uncertainty can be eradicated from creative actions, we see creative self-regulation as one way to harness uncertainty in the creative process.

6.1 Introduction

Laypeople tend to associate creativity with spontaneous, uncontrolled behavior that results in insights or discoveries (Beghetto et al. 2013). Yet, current research challenges this bottom-up perspective and shows that creativity is mostly driven by top-down processes (Benedek and Jauk 2019). These include intelligence (Forthmann et al. 2019), working memory (Benedek et al. 2014; Lee and Therriault 2013), executive functions (Beaty et al. 2014), or metacognition (Kaufman and Beghetto 2013), but also motivational factors that result in confidence (Karwowski et al. 2020a), and applying effective strategies while creating or solving problems. Importantly, being top-down does not mean that there is no space for uncertainty in creativity. Quite the opposite, accepting uncertainty (or avoiding it) may be considered one of the strategies employed in creative processes. Naturally, uncertainty is almost always present when creativity is analyzed. Indeed, the creative process is never fully defined and specified; neither is its outcome.

The presence of uncertainty, however, should not imply that creativity is messy or chaotic. While sometimes it might seem so, the more effective creative thinkers

A. Zielińska (✉) · M. Karwowski
Institute of Psychology, University of Wrocław, Wrocław, Poland
e-mail: Aleksandra.Zielinska@uwr.edu.pl; Maciej.Karwowski@uwr.edu.pl

© Springer Nature Switzerland AG 2022
R. A. Beghetto, G. J. Jaeger (eds.), *Uncertainty: A Catalyst for Creativity, Learning and Development*, Creativity Theory and Action in Education 6,
https://doi.org/10.1007/978-3-030-98729-9_6

can manage the chaos and transform it in favor of the process. This is why we posit that creative self-regulation tames creative action's uncertainty and makes it both acceptable and manageable.

This chapter focuses on creative self-regulation as an overlooked element in current discussions about learning and creativity. While there is rich literature on cognitive mechanisms engaged in learning or problem solving (e.g., Finke et al. 1992; Mumford et al. 1994), how people plan, monitor, and assess their ideas is far less known. We see uncertainty as the engine and springboard that motivates people to search for new possibilities of thinking and to act (consider, for example, a recent Model of Actionable Uncertainty; Beghetto under review). We are also interested in what happens when a person, motivated by a state of genuine doubt, finally starts to act. What does this process look like? What does it mean to bring a creative idea to life? How do people regulate the creative process—inextricably bound up with uncertainty—as a whole? These questions address creative self-regulation.

While interest in self-regulation is not new in creativity literature (see Pesut 1990), the current theorizing is mostly inspired by two research traditions. The first is based on works devoted to creative self-beliefs (Beghetto and Karwowski 2017; Karwowski and Kaufman 2017) and—more generally—to the agentic perspective on creativity (Karwowski and Beghetto 2019). This line of work equates creative behavior with a particular decision to act (Sternberg 2002) and an effort taken by actors (individuals, groups; Glăveanu 2013) who value creativity and are confident that they can effectively solve problems. Self-regulation forms a natural next step in this agentic theorizing; a step needed to provide the answer to the question of *how* creative activity occurs. The other research line, inspired by educational psychology and works on self-regulated learning, sees creativity and learning as related processes and applies the theories developed to explain differences in the learning process to the creative process (Rubenstein et al. 2018). These two lines of thinking intersect in new works that build on both these traditions (see, e.g., Zielińska et al. 2022a).

Psychological research leads to a good understanding of how people pursue well-defined goals (e.g., Delose et al. 2015; Dohle et al. 2018; Rabinovich and Webley 2007). However, these findings' generalization to creativity is tricky precisely because of the uncertainty embedded in the creative process. A crucial element that makes creative endeavors distinct from other goal-oriented and better-structured activities is the enormous importance of problem finding (Csikszentmihalyi 1988; Csikszentmihalyi and Getzels 1971). Creativity is often associated with exploring the pool of initial concepts and ideas and then exploiting those that seem to be most promising (Finke et al. 1992). As the exploration-exploitation trade-off (Mehlhorn et al. 2015) suggests, people often choose uncertain options in the exploration phase, while the exploitation phase leads to minimizing uncertainty. Importantly, however, the transition between exploration and exploitation is neither linear nor straightforward. Exploration and exploitation dynamically intertwine and self-regulation is required to manage them.

6.2 Exploring Creative Self-Regulation

We understand creative self-regulation as a *set of processes, subprocesses, and strategies people use to make their creative process more effective*. This includes pursuing goals and planning how to obtain them, monitoring and calibrating the activity, and evaluating the effects. While not always consciously applied, creative self-regulation normally requires some sort of awareness of what is needed and what works in a problem-solving situation. That may include emotion regulation strategies, using heuristics that worked in the past, reframing goals, or self-motivation in the face of challenges.

Creative self-regulation shares some essential characteristics of dynamically theorized creative self-beliefs (Beghetto and Karwowski 2017). Indeed, how people deal with creative challenges might differ from task to task and domain to domain, similarly to their task-specific creative self-efficacy (see also Karwowski et al. 2019a). At the same time, however, there are reasons to expect that some stable positive and negative predictors of creative thinking and creative activity may similarly link with creative self-regulation. The former likely include openness to experience (e.g., Silvia et al. 2009), trait-like creative confidence, valuing creativity (Karwowski and Beghetto 2019), tolerance for ambiguity (e.g., Merrotsy 2013; Tegano 1990; Zenasni et al. 2008), or growth creative mindset (e.g., Karwowski 2014; Puente-Díaz and Cavazos-Arroyo 2017). The latter, among others, may include neuroticism (Clark and DeYoung 2014; Hirsh and Inzlicht 2008; Perkins et al. 2015), need for closure (Chirumbolo et al. 2004; Wronska et al. 2019), or fixed creative mindset (Hass et al. 2016; Karwowski et al. 2019b). Indeed, people who are more open, confident in their creative potential, and willing to engage in creative activity are very likely the same people who use more effective strategies while creating. However, what seems particularly important, is understanding the dynamic nature of creative self-regulation as embedded in creative acts. To do so, some parallels between creativity and self-regulated learning seem promising.

6.3 Creative Self-Regulation and Self-Regulated Learning

The sequential and recursive nature of the creative process is well-visible when one takes the perspective of self-regulated learning (SRL) (Rubenstein et al. 2018). Following Zimmerman's model (Zimmerman 2000), self-regulation's cyclicity is theorized as arising from three self-oriented feedback loops, wherein a person monitors behavioral, environmental, and covert (personal) adjustments. Such a view underscores the importance of metacognition (Winne 2018) and a personal agency shaped by self-beliefs and affective reactions (Zimmerman 2000).

This confluence of thoughts, beliefs, feelings, and actions forms a process that goes through three interrelated phases: forethought, performance, and self-reflection (Zimmerman 2000). They correspond to the specific—but non-linear—time points when an individual attempts to attain personally valued goals, such as learning a new skill, developing it, or only using this ability in different situations. Forethought refers to preparation, a prelude to the action itself. It involves subprocesses employed by an individual before task engagement—such as goal setting or strategic planning—as well as underlying self-beliefs (e.g., self-efficacy). The performance phase depicts multiple strategies that support learners during task performance by focalizing on proper actions and optimizing the effort while simultaneously tracking the whole activity and its affordances. Finally, when a task is completed, self-reflection on the outcome starts. These three phases follow cyclically and mutually influence each other so that forethought subprocesses equip an individual to perform a task efficiently, which consequently determines the course of the self-reflection stage, and eventually impacts preparation for the next activity (and another forethought stage).

It was recently demonstrated that specific SRL processes predict creative problem solving (Callan et al. 2019). Callan and colleagues adapted an event measurement technique, which is widely used by SRL researchers, but rarely applied in the field of creativity. They tracked the process using SRL microanalysis: a structured interview that consists of short, open-ended, task- and context-specific questions a person answers before, during, and after completing a particular task. Creative performance was measured as fluency, flexibility, originality, and usefulness of responses provided. Efficiency of idea generation (assessed as fluency and flexibility) was predicted by participants' pre-task strategies, namely strategic planning focused on solving a problem and their self-efficacy (operationalized as a perception of one's ability to generate many solutions to the problem). The differences in fluency were also explained by strategic planning that concerned anticipated ways of encountering a challenge and dealing with creative blocks. Furthermore, originality was associated with a richer repertoire of strategies planned before solving a task. The post-task process of self-evaluation was also related to generating the responses that were scored as more useful.

Identifying self-regulation mechanisms that support creative performance brings essential insights about how an individual can effectively approach creative activities of short duration. However, a real-life creative process rarely restricts itself to short-term tasks that need to be creatively solved, once and for all (Ivcevic and Nusbaum 2017). It instead extends over time, which makes this process resource-intensive and sometimes demanding sacrifices even in an interpersonal relationship sphere (Lebuda and Csikszentmihalyi 2020). Also, the results obtained by an individual are usually the subject of self-reflection that might lead to secondary outcomes (Beghetto under review) or open a new cycle of self-regulation for creativity (Zimmerman 2000). Hence, it seems mandatory for creativity researchers to investigate the underlying self-regulative strategies that a creator applies on the road from ideation to implementation (Ivcevic and Nusbaum 2017).

We believe that the most insightful creative self-regulation models capture its cyclical, recursive, and non-linear character (see Fig. 6.1). Such an approach would apply to small creative events taking place within minutes and large creative projects stretched over time, consequently making it more ecologically valid.

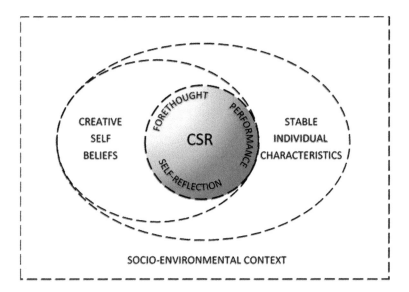

Fig. 6.1 Dynamic model of creative self-regulation (CSR) embedded in creative activity

The heart of our model reflects the non-linear and recursive character of creative self-regulation: there is no clear beginning of this process, and the phases (forethought, performance, self-reflection) melt into each other (like the color gradient). The deeper the color saturation, the more completed and perceptible the outcome of a creative activity is. Creative self-regulation is inextricably entwined with creative self-beliefs, as they mutually influence each other. These dynamic processes are—to some extent—grounded in relatively stable characteristics of a creator, such as: openness to experience, trait-like creative confidence and valuing creativity, tolerance for ambiguity, growth or fixed creative mindset, neuroticism, and need for closure, that either enhance the effectiveness of creative self-regulation, or hamper any movement. Finally, a creative act occurs within a socio-environmental context, which on the one hand enables this process and on the other, constrains it; also, this context serves as a recipient of the outcomes and reacts to them simultaneously. Note that all the boundaries are dashed as the processes included are open to many mutual exchanges.

We further conceptualize creative self-regulation (CSR) as composed of specific behaviors and strategies employed by an individual before engaging in actual activity, during the activity, and after obtaining the more or less perceptible product (Zielińska et al. 2022a). Specifically, pre-task strategies include, among others: (1) Obstacles Expectations, and (2) Uncertainty Acceptance, then during-task strategies are designated by (3) Adjusting Approach, (4) Managing and Reframing Ambiguous Goals, and (5) Emotion Regulation and Dealing with Obstacles. Finally, post-task strategies involve (6) Improving Approach, and (7) Readiness for Sharing (see also Ivcevic and Nusbaum 2017; Ivcevic et al. 2020). In what follows, we discuss in more detail these self-regulatory strategies (for an overview see Table 6.1) that might be further classified into two broad groups of processes: revising and re-strategizing, and sustaining and maintaining (Ivcevic and Nusbaum 2017).

Table 6.1 An overview of the key concepts discussed in this chapter

Construct	Description
Self-Regulation	Broad range of psychological processes through which people regulate their thoughts, emotions, and behaviors to achieve the desired goal; such self-regulatory processes include, among others, executive functioning (Miyake and Friedman 2012), effortful control (Petersen and Posner 2012), self-control (Duckworth and Gross 2014), and emotion regulation (Gross 2014).
Creative Self-Regulation (CSR)	Set of processes, subprocesses, and strategies through which people shape their thoughts, emotions, and behaviors to make their creative process more effective. CSR goes cyclically across three phases: forethought, performance, and self-reflection.
Forethought	The preparatory phase of the creative process when people—driven by motivational beliefs and attitudes—set initial goals and plan how to achieve them; essential strategies employed in this phase include Obstacles Expectations and Uncertainty Acceptance.
Obstacles Expectations	Pre-task CSR strategy that is built on the awareness of the upcoming—challenging and frustrating—yet inevitable parts of the creative process that a person will have to overcome.
Uncertainty Acceptance	Pre-task CSR strategy of anticipating uncertainties and doubts during the creative process, which bolsters people's readiness to handle any unforeseen circumstances.
Performance	The performative phase of the creative process during which people pursue the activity, regulate their effort, and monitor and adjust the course of action. Key strategies that constitute CSR in the performance phase are: Adjusting Approach, Managing and Reframing Ambiguous Goals, and Emotion Regulation and Dealing with Obstacles.
Adjusting Approach	During-task CSR strategy focused on making flexible adjustments in acting due to constraints, obstacles, or opportunities in the creative process.
Managing and Reframing Ambiguous Goals	During-task CSR strategy that refers to changing and refining set goals: transforming those initially vague into more specific ones as time goes by, pursuing new promising ideas even at the cost of progress already made, and disengaging from the unsuccessful attempts and unrealizable goals.
Emotion Regulation and Dealing with Obstacles	During-task CSR strategy focused on one's emotions, mainly using them in the creative process and adapting to difficulties encountered.
Self-Reflection	Post-task, self-reflective phase of the creative process that involves evaluating own performance, making causal attributions about the outcomes, and building an adaptive vs. defensive approach towards future creative pursuits; at this stage, an effective CSR may depend on utilizing strategies of Improving Approach and Readiness for Sharing.
Improving Approach	Post-task CSR strategy through which people consider whether any scope for improvement in the results obtained is; such reflective and evaluative processing may—in turn—encourage one to retake similar creative activity in the future.
Readiness for Sharing	Post-task CSR strategy of seeking opportunities to share the effects of own work with other people.

6.3.1 Forethought: Process Expectations

Before diving into creative activity, a person often indulges in thinking and planning processes to analyze the forthcoming action and motivate oneself to act in consonance with their own beliefs about personal capacities and situational opportunities (Usher and Schunk 2018; Zimmerman 2000). However, such creative task analysis rarely has organized goal-setting or strategic planning, like in the case of more structured and goal-oriented pursuits that still require effective self-regulation (such as losing weight, Dohle et al. 2018; or saving money, Rabinovich and Webley 2007). The creative process is instead less settled and highly unpredictable, and for this reason alone, its initial, preparatory phase largely rests on the unique strategies of *Uncertainty Acceptance* and *Obstacles Expectations*.

During the forethought stage, effective creative self-regulators are often aware that their initial ideas or products may not be the ones they end up with. Imagine a composer who comes up with a brilliant musical theme and eventually changes this construction's rhythmic aspect to make it more playable for instrumentalists. Think about a professional cook who, at the last moment decides to completely change the form of the signature dish and then plates it in a deconstructed way. While working on a creative project, it is not always possible to have a clear picture of the outcome or predict all the steps leading to a successful end. Of course, reasons for reformulating initial ideas are usually diverse, but the very anticipation of such possible alterations is what characterizes skilled self-regulators. *Uncertainty Acceptance* translates into an understanding that sometimes the best way to behave is to discard the foregoing work and explore other possibilities (Mehlhorn et al. 2015). For example, once scientists discover a new, promising perspective on an important issue, they often start to polemize against their own, earlier published theses.

Among all the uncertainties that a person forecasts even before engaging in a creative endeavor, one thing should be taken as a given: the creative process is full of difficulties, obstacles, backsets, and blocks. Many elements of creative work are not only unenjoyable but downright dull, frustrating, or painful. Professional creators working in different areas struggle with many inconveniences. Inspiration blocks are shared across various domains; deadlines, budget constraints, or a lack of adequate tools and materials are other gripes (Glăveanu et al. 2013). However, it would be naïve to think that it is easier to act creatively without any constraints or criteria. Creative products are not merely novel, but also useful, so they are original and appropriate at the same time (see, e.g., Runco and Jaeger 2012). Creativity appears within certain constraints, inside the box (Beghetto 2019a). As for the creative process, criteria are necessary, challenges, and ambiguities—inevitable. While preparing for creative performance, it is both strategic and wise to expect uncertainties and obstacles. Ironically, uncertainty itself could diminish creativity in certain circumstances: although the state of doubt serves as a catalyst for creative thought and action (Beghetto 2020, 2019a, b), it may also make people less able to recognize creativity and accurately evaluate creative ideas (Mueller et al. 2012).

6.3.2 Performance: Adjusting, Managing Goals and Emotion Regulation

Considering all the likely uncertainties and obstacles, a reasonable self-regulatory strategy is to adopt the *Adjusting Approach*. It is hard to expect continuous creative growth from a creator who persistently uses the same work methods. A painter who consistently presents all objects or landscapes from the same perspective would be eventually called predictable and their works—unattractive. Conventionality and commonplaceness preclude originality. During the creative process, many aspects of acting require adjustments and readiness to change what is already known or tried, which seems to be one of the primary sources of uncertainty (Beghetto 2020). Once creative individuals realize that the old ways of operating fail, they start looking for some new and useful solutions, or—to put it another way—they begin to think creatively. Importantly, however, people express the adjusting approach as a balance between pursuing new, tempting ideas and sticking to previous goals and commitments. Effective self-regulation during creative performance implies an ability to recognize meaningful opportunities and take advantage of them even at the expense of progress already made (Ivcevic and Nusbaum 2017).

The strategy of *Managing and Reframing Ambiguous Goals* encompasses willingness to revise and rearrange the aims of creative endeavors. At the outset of the creative process, an individual often starts with vague goals and then—as time goes by—makes them more specific and elaborate. At some point, the envisioned initial ideas might be dropped entirely and sacrificed for new and promising opportunities. Other times, a creator realizes that the possibility of attaining the preconceived goal is pretty low or even considers this outcome unfeasible. In such a case, it is not an encounter with ambiguity anymore; it is a pursuit doomed to failure. Managing such unrealizable goals effectively requires disengaging from them. The creative process is intrinsically risky, uncertain in many respects. Thus, risk-taking tendencies are often associated with creativity (Beghetto et al. 2020); however, this relationship is neither well-stated nor straightforward (Harada 2020). Furthermore, researchers seem to confound the concepts of risk and uncertainty, which are conceptually and empirically distinct (De Groot and Thurik 2018). Nevertheless, pursuing goals that are ambiguous, risky, challenging, and attuned to the high level of skills may lead to the peak-performance state of flow (Csikszentmihalyi 1996) related to both the more creative results and the intrinsic enjoyment of undertaken activity. People engage in different kinds of risky behaviors, but intellectual risk-taking is necessary for creativity (Beghetto et al. 2020). It describes adaptive behavior favorable for learning while simultaneously exposing an individual to the possibility of failure or making a wrong impression (Beghetto 2009). People who are willing to take such intellectual risks have a stronger belief in their ability to be creative (i.e., creative confidence), which translates into creative activities and achievement (Beghetto et al. 2020). Furthermore, although the role of creative confidence in actualizing creative potential is crucial (Karwowski and Beghetto 2019), the low level of intellectual risk-taking may keep a person away from transforming this confidence into creative behavior altogether (Beghetto et al. 2020).

It is also hard to imagine a creative process without having emotions involved. Certain mood states push a person to act creatively, which leads to experiencing a variety of emotions during a creative pursuit. The role of positive moods in creativity, especially those with high or medium activation levels, is well-established (Baas et al. 2008; Davis 2009). When people feel happy, excited, concentrated, interested, energetic, and enthusiastic, they are more likely to engage in a creative activity (Conner and Silvia 2015; Han et al. 2019). However, negative and active moods, such as being upset, ashamed, angry, and anxious, may also benefit creativity (To et al. 2012). Interestingly, the role of positive and negative mood might differ depending on the phase of the creative problem-solving. Positive emotions seem to increase fluency in the early idea production, while negative emotions enhance creative task performance in the later—more exploitative—phase of creative problem solving (Kaufmann and Vosburg 2002).

Artists describe their creative process as simultaneously facilitated and inhibited by their work's emotional component (Botella et al. 2013). It is not very surprising, since people are influenced by a wealth of emotions in their creative pursuits. During the creative process, artists experience various emotional states, including positive (e.g., love, happiness, joy), negative (e.g., sadness, fear), but also more complex emotions, such as nostalgia (Glăveanu et al. 2013). However, their daily work—be it the process of implementing or completing a creative idea—is mostly filled with frustration and accompanied by happiness, joy, and excitement (Glăveanu et al. 2013). In one of his last interviews, Francis Bacon—twentieth-century figurative painter—summed up this emotionally versatile nature of the creative process: "Before I start painting I have a slightly ambiguous feeling: happiness is a special excitement because unhappiness is always possible a moment later." In the face of such a multitude of floating emotions, people handle them differently and with diverse effectiveness. Thus, the creative process is demanding when it comes to emotion regulation and dealing with encountered obstacles.

Emotion regulation involves processes by which people influence their emotions when encountering them as well as how they experience and manifest these emotions (Gross 1998, 2014). An impact on one's own emotional state can be construed as a goal-directed behavior that employs particular strategies of pursuing this goal and, consequently, results in immediate and long-term outcomes. According to an instrumental approach to emotion regulation (Tamir 2005, 2009, 2011), people influence their mood to achieve any prioritized goal, not necessarily focused on attaining a positive emotional state. Instead, an adaptive regulation embodies targeting those emotions whose functions are most useful and applicable to a specific context. For example, before negotiating, people who were experimentally motivated to confront their partners—instead of collaborating with them—increased their anger assuming that it will be more useful (Tamir and Ford 2012). Importantly, instrumental emotion regulation was found to have some pragmatic implications in the field of creativity. For example, people with higher neuroticism prefer to recall worrisome events while expecting to perform a demanding creativity task (Leung et al. 2014). Furthermore, those more neurotic individuals—in whom unsettling emotions were experimentally induced—received higher peer-ratings for their creative products; they also provided more flexible and unusual uses of a common object when the additional cognitive load was introduced (Leung et al. 2014).

So, how emotion regulation might look like in the case of creative activities? Given that the creative process is inherently bonded with the state of uncertainty—which may intensify other affective reactions (Bar-Anan et al. 2009)—it seems reasonable that people need to accept any emerging yet unexpected circumstances to move on. Such cognitive change allows modifying an experienced situation's emotional charge by altering one's mindset regarding either the situation itself or one's own ability to handle its demands (Gross 2014; Peña-Sarrionandia et al. 2019). Hence—in the face of obstacles and challenges—individuals might remind themselves of their capacity to manage those difficulties effectively, which results in reappraisal of their self-efficacy. Similarly, people may influence their emotions by changing how they think about certain situations, such as by reinterpreting committed mistakes as learning opportunities. Finally, because the creative process is usually long-lasting and demanding in many other respects, it is likely that one may feel discouraged or unimaginative at some point of this journey. Finding ways to stay motivated and inspired to create stimulates people to perseveringly bring their creative ideas into fruition (Thrash et al. 2010).

6.3.3 Self-Reflection: Improving and Sharing Ideas

After performance, people engage in reflective processes to assess the obtained results and react to them. Self-evaluation of the outcomes may be conducted with different references, including mastery criteria, previous performance, social comparisons, or fulfilling a specific role while working in a team (Zimmerman 2000). Such reflective self-judgments are also related to causal attributions that people make about their performance: they view the achieved effects as resulting from either their abilities or the effort put in a particular activity. When it comes to creative self-evaluation, creative metacognition (Kaufman et al. 2016) comes to play. Generally, when self-assessing their creative ideas, people—especially those who are more creative, intelligent or open to experience—are quite accurate (Karwowski et al. 2020a; Silvia 2008). However, certain metacognitive feelings, such as ease of processing or recalling information, are linked with a person's tendency to overestimate the level of creativity of generated ideas, which—in turn—has negative consequences for the accuracy of idea selection (Puente-Díaz et al. 2021). It seems that the more objective the measures of creativity (e.g., creative problem-solving tasks, achievement-based scales) are used, the weaker their relationship with self-perceptions of creative abilities is (Reiter-Palmon et al. 2012). Nevertheless, it was demonstrated that engaging in the idea evaluation task—compared with the distraction task—improves originality of ideas during the later idea production stage (Hao et al. 2016), which reflects the cyclical nature of the creative process.

All self-assessment processes influence a person's reactions to performance efforts, which may be rife with satisfaction or dissatisfaction and other related affective states. Sometimes, a creative process brings outcomes that are not necessarily as original or effective as expected and can be rather identified as inconclusive (Corazza 2016). Even so, they still represent one's creative experience, which is often marked by the lack of exact final points or the apparent result (Glăveanu and Beghetto 2020). Artists tend to perceive their products as "never finished" and foresee potential reworkings (Glăveanu et al. 2013). Thus, during such self-reflective judgments, one may have this sense of incompleteness, which provokes thoughts of changing one's self-regulatory approach while engaging in future creative endeavors. These conclusions may be adaptive—when they redirect a person to a more efficient way of acting and thinking—or somewhat defensive: generating helplessness and inclining people to disengage from subsequent activities (Zimmerman 2000). We argue that creative self-regulation may benefit from the post-task *Improving Approach*. When applying this strategy, a person wonders whether something could be done even better and ultimately decides to try it again. It seems crucial that feeling able to improve one's potential failure in one creative task reduces the detrimental effect of self-evaluation (i.e., increased self-awareness and working under an objective standard of performance) on creativity expressed in subsequent attempts (Silvia and Phillips 2004).

Yet despite the self-oriented character of the reflection phase, it must be noted that creativity is not only an individual attribute—characterizing either those with exceptional abilities and features (He-paradigm; Glăveanu 2010) or basically every human being (I-paradigm). Many creativity scientists tend to adopt a more holistic and comprehensive approach (We-paradigm), in which creativity is interpreted as a social phenomenon (Lebuda and Glăveanu 2019). Indeed, the creative process is embedded within the social context, influenced by many environmental factors and—on its own—bringing consequences for the creator's surroundings. Thus, the creative action is directed at some environment or audience and responds to others' reactions (Glăveanu et al. 2013). Among people contributing to one's creative expression (Glăveanu and Lubart 2014) we can find the so-called familiar and immediate others (e.g., parents, siblings, friends, collaborators, competitors), who usually have a strong, intimate relationship with the creator, as well as institutional or distant others (gatekeepers, reviewers, critics, audience), or even internalized others that a person inner-dialogue with (Glăveanu 2017).

Participation and contribution of other people in one's creative work play a fourfold role: formative, regulatory, motivational, and informational (Glăveanu and Lubart 2014). Those influences are not mutually exclusive: social context may simultaneously impact a person's creative development, set necessary constraints and guidelines, foster eagerness to continue the activity, and finally bring a new angle to perceiving own work. Others' informative function suggests that sharing creative outcomes is somewhat associated with risk for one's reputation (Ivcevic and Nusbaum 2017). Of course, gaining social recognition gives pleasure to authors (Glăveanu et al. 2013); however, getting both positive and negative feedback may also benefit a person's creativity (e.g., Hoever et al. 2017; Kim and Kim 2020).

Feedback-seeking behavior—a self-regulatory tactic in which people proactively look for evaluating their performance (Ashford and Tsui 1991)—has been identified as an essential intermediary factor in attaining creative outcomes. Feedback inquiries at work partially mediate the effects of employee cognitive style and perceived organizational support for creativity on creative performance rated by the supervisor (De Stobbeleir et al. 2011). Also, proactive search for feedback is a mechanism that underlies the relationship between creative self-efficacy and creativity expressed in the work environment (Chen and Zhang 2019). Thus, we assert that *Readiness for Sharing* one's creative outcomes plays an important role during the creative process's self-reflection phase. Being proud of what was achieved in the creative endeavor and showing these results to others bravely and happily indicates successful post-task self-regulation.

6.4 Creative Self-Regulation and Creative Behavior

One natural question that comes to mind is whether using all the strategies we described above results in more creative effects. A large study on adolescents (see Zielińska et al. 2022a) provides a confirming response, albeit with some nuances. In this investigation, more than seven hundred Polish adolescents described their most creative project realized during the last year and answered a set of retrospectively framed self-regulation items that referred to this specific project. Creative self-regulation was predicted by creative self-concept, growth creative mindset, and—less systematically—by personality factors. Importantly, when self-regulation in more-versus-less creative projects was examined, it became apparent that, indeed, people who were more effective self-regulators were able to create more creative projects (see Fig. 6.2).

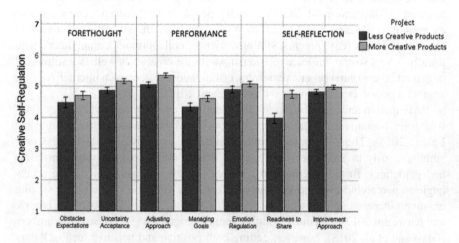

Fig. 6.2 Creative self-regulation strategies among people who developed more who developed more and less creative products. (Adapted from Zielińska et al. 2022a)

Another set of studies (Zielińska et al. under review) examined whether creative self-regulation explain differences in creative activity, achievement, and declared future engagement across domains. This was exactly the case: creative self-regulation added to our understanding of the level of activity, accomplishment, and aspirations in arts, science, and everyday creativity.

Although preliminary and correlational, these results are promising as they might open a new avenue for studying and enhancing creative activity. If helping people self-regulate makes them more effective creative thinkers, self-regulation may be considered a meaningful way to promote and support creativity. We briefly discuss such possibilities below.

6.5   How to Study and Support Creative Self-Regulation

As mentioned, creative self-regulation may be studied using retrospectively framed questionnaires (Ivcevic et al. 2020; Zielińska et al. 2022a, under review). Such measures usually either ask about a concrete activity: a process leading to a specific project (Zielińska et al. 2022a), or the most common way of working in a particular domain (Zielińska et al. under review). Data presented so far attest to a reasonable factor structure of such instruments (with strategies presented during forethought, performance, and self-reflection phases), consistent associations with creativity-relevant variables, as well as incremental validity beyond other predictors when explaining creative activity and achievement.

Not surprisingly, however, given the dynamic nature of creative self-regulation, more processual and dynamic measures might serve as an even more valid approach to study it. Previous research has shown the benefits of using on-task thinking aloud protocols (Gilhooly et al. 2007), sometimes complemented by eye-tracking (Jankowska et al. 2018). Retrospective interviews used together with recorded ways of working on tasks as a prompt were also used (Glăveanu 2015). What seems to be underused in creative self-regulation studies are such microlongitudinal designs as experience sampling measurement (Silvia et al. 2014), diary studies (Conner and Silvia 2015; Karwowski et al. 2017), and day reconstruction methods (Kahneman et al. 2004). As recently offered by Beghetto and Karwowski (2019), relying on such methodological solutions allows scholars to *unfreeze creativity* and provide an even more dynamic picture of the activity. These dynamic approaches based on experience sampling (Baumeister et al. 2019; Hofmann et al. 2012; Mrazek et al. 2018) and diaries (Schmitz and Perels 2011) were applied to study self-regulation in contexts other than creativity. In creativity literature, however, such attempts are limited and usually quite indirect, namely focusing only on certain aspects important for self-regulation (mainly affect or emotions; see for example, Benedek et al. 2017; Karwowski et al. 2020b). We see dynamic methods as well-suited to capture creative self-regulation and expect that such studies will grow in the years to come.

6.6   Toward Improving Creative Self-Regulation by Wise Interventions

Thirty years ago, Pesut (1990) posited that the effectiveness of creativity train-ing might be attributed more (or at least equally) to changes in creative self-regulation than to changes in creative abilities. This interesting and provocative thought was a little bit overlooked, given the modest number of citations of this article (113 according to Google Scholar as of March 2022). Yet, as Pesut argued, during creativity training, people develop not only their creative abili-ties or skills but also creative metacognition and the conviction that creativity is important. This idea may shed some new light on the evidence showing that creativity training is generally effective (see Ma 2006; Scott et al. 2004; Valgeirsdottir and Onarheim 2017), as the mechanisms behind the growth in creative thinking are not entirely understood. Indeed, some works that focused on developing creativity demonstrated that such training can make students' creativity beliefs less biased (Morias et al. 2015) or build their confidence in creativity and creative self-efficacy (Meinel et al. 2019; Poon et al. 2014; Vally et al. 2019).

Therefore, the open question for future studies is to what extent we are able to improve students' or employees' creativity by wise interventions (see e.g., Walton and Wilson 2018) that focus more on creative self-beliefs and self-regu-lation than on creative abilities. Is it possible to develop students' willingness to engage in creative activities by strengthening their perceived importance of cre-ativity? According to the creative behavior as agentic action model (Karwowski and Beghetto 2019), valuing creativity is a necessary factor that makes creative potential translatable into observable behavior. One recent daily diary study (Zielińska et al. 2022b) tested over 2 weeks whether days when students were prompted by simple messages and tasks about the importance of creativity, were also the days characterized by a higher level of subjectively assessed creative behavior and more intense engagement in creative activity. This was precisely the case: even brief and straightforward tasks (taking about 5–10 minutes per day) were associated with the improvement of subjectively assessed creativity and a higher level of declared everyday creative behaviors (e.g., decorating a room, cooking an original dish, preparing an original gift for someone). While this diary intervention focused more on creative self-beliefs than creative self-regulation *per se* (e.g., the tasks engaged participants' creative self-concepts and concentrated them on the value and prevalence of creativity), future works would benefit from using similar solutions to study the possibilities of improv-ing creative self-regulation as well. Creativity researchers may find inspiration in educational psychology interventions to develop self-regulated learning (see e.g., Dörrenbächer and Perels 2016; Schmitz and Perels 2011; Schmitz and Wiese 2006).

6.7 Future Directions

Potentially any situation in which people act under uncertainty abounds with creative opportunities. Having a sense of dubiety challenges one's existing knowledge or abilities and pushes one to look for a new course of action. In this way, uncertainty has the power of putting creative thinking in motion and boosting the ongoing creative process. However, being motivated to act differently than planned or learned does not guarantee that a person will persevere in the undertaken activity, nor that the attained goal will be as creative as expected. Our perspective underscores the importance of manageable and agentic aspects of the creative process that enable people to translate creative potential into behaviors and outcomes. In this chapter, we presented creative self-regulation as a means to tame uncertainty, incorporate it into the creative process, and use it as a power-up.

As was recently highlighted (Benedek and Fink 2019; Silvia 2018), creativity is built around top-down processes: executive abilities that are highly controllable. Although myths and misconceptions about the chaotic and spontaneous nature of creativity are still shared by many laypersons (Benedek et al. 2021), both professional creators and ordinary people apply different strategies to pursue their creative goals more effectively. We reviewed these processes as ranging from the initial, preparatory phase of the creative action, to the performance itself, to self-reflective behaviors after completing the activity. Importantly, there is always room for uncertainty and its potential benefits during all of these stages. Forethought is all about accepting the inevitable ambiguity: one may start at one point and end at a completely different one through continuous trials and false starts. The performance phase and—especially—adjusting approach relates to finding problems, revising, and reformulating them. Yet, it would be impossible without some uncertainty involved, as it performs an informative function telling that such new opportunities of acting are needed (Beghetto 2020). Finally, self-reflective processes carry two-fold risks and ambiguities: how the results will inspire their own future creative activities and the response of others to these outcomes.

Considering the new line of studies that associate effective self-regulation with a higher level of creative performance and achievement (Zielińska et al. 2022a, under review), we proposed that self-regulation is a fruitful way to promote and enhance creativity. Despite the preliminary and not fully conclusive (in terms of causality) nature of these studies, we believe that designing wise interventions that support creative self-beliefs and creative self-regulation may lead to actual creative engagement. Being able to regulate creative activity builds agency and capability to succeed in a creative endeavor. In turn, it makes a person more efficient in facing uncertainty as it becomes less profound and ungraspable, but more actionable and worthy of one's effort (Beghetto 2020).

As long as creative self-regulation research will consider its dynamic and non-linear character, scholars' knowledge of this complex process will systematically grow. Our theorizing, then, not only provides a useful framework for developing assessment tools of creative self-regulation, but also fits well in the recent postulate of *unfreezing creativity* (Beghetto and Karwowski 2019). This requires new methods of studying creative self-regulation and new methods to enhance it. As there are insightful inspirations in related fields, particularly in educational psychology, creativity research may benefit from exploring the possibilities offered by their fellow researchers in these domains.

To conclude, let us emphasize once again that in the modern, dynamically changing world, people encounter uncertainty on day-to-day basis. Although it may be perceived as an unpleasant state, this lack of clarity or surety holds the potential to push them to act creatively. Indeed, uncertainty and creativity are inseparable. Thanks to creative self-regulation a creative synergy of their co-existence is more likely to happen.

Acknowledgment Maciej Karwowski was supported by a grant from the National Science Centre (UMO-2016/22/E/HS6/00118). The authors report no conflict of interest.

References

Ashford, S. J., & Tsui, A. S. (1991). Self-regulation for managerial effectiveness: The role of active feedback seeking. *Academy of Management Journal, 34*, 251–280. https://doi.org/10.2307/256442

Baas, M., De Dreu, C. K. W., & Nijstad, B. A. (2008). A meta-analysis of 25 years of mood-creativity research: Hedonic tone, activation, or regulatory focus? *Psychological Bulletin, 134*, 779–806. https://doi.org/10.1037/a0012815

Bar-Anan, Y., Wilson, T. D., & Gilbert, D. T. (2009). The feeling of uncertainty intensifies affective reactions. *Emotion, 9*, 123–127. https://doi.org/10.1037/a0014607

Baumeister, R. F., Wright, B. R. E., & Carreon, D. (2019). Self-control "in the wild": Experience sampling study of trait and state self-regulation. *Self and Identity, 18*, 494–528, https://doi.org/10.1080/15298868.2018.1478324

Beaty, R. E., Silvia, P. J., Nusbaum, E. C., Jauk, E., & Benedek, M. (2014). The roles of associative and executive processes in creative cognition. *Memory & Cognition, 42*, 1186–1197.

Beghetto, R. A. (2009). Correlates of intellectual risk taking in elementary school science. *Journal of Research in Science Teaching, 46*, 210–223. https://doi.org/10.1002/tea.20270

Beghetto, R. A. (2019a). Structured uncertainty: How creativity thrives under constraints and uncertainty. In C. A. Mullen (Ed.), *Creativity under duress in education?* (Vol. 3, pp. 27–40). Springer International Publishing. https://doi.org/10.1007/978-3-319-90272-2_2

Beghetto, R. A. (2019b). Abductive reasoning and the genesis of new ideas: Charles S. Peirce. In V. P. Glăveanu (Ed.), *Creativity Reader* (pp. 157–170). Oxford University Press.

Beghetto, R. A. (2020). Uncertainty. In V. Glăveanu (Ed.) *The Palgrave Encyclopedia of the Possible*. Palgrave Macmillan. https://doi.org/10.1007/978-3-319-98390-5_122-1

Beghetto, R. A. (under review). Actionable uncertainty: An agentic perspective.

Beghetto, R. A., Barbee, B., Brooks, S., Franklin-Phipps, A., Fukuda, E., Gardner-Allers, N. L., Hood, D., Raza, N., Uusitalo, N., & White Eyes, C. (2013). Light bulbs, Bill Evans, and cat hair: Exploring representations of creativity and education in images, videos, and blogs. *Psychology of Popular Media Culture, 2*, 188–206. https://doi.org/10.1037/ppm0000003

Beghetto, R. A., & Karwowski, M. (2017). Toward untangling creative self-beliefs. In M. Karwowski and J. C. Kaufman (Eds.), *The creative self* (pp. 3-22). Academic Press.

Beghetto, R. A., & Karwowski, M. (2019). Unfreezing creativity: A dynamic micro-longitudinal approach. In R. A. Beghetto and G. Corazza (Eds.), *Dynamic perspectives on creativity* (pp. 7-25). Springer.

Beghetto, R. A., Karwowski, M., & Reiter-Palmon, R. (2020). Intellectual risk taking: A moderating link between creative confidence and creative behavior? *Psychology of Aesthetics, Creativity, and the Arts*. Advance online publication. https://doi.org/10.1037/aca0000323

Benedek, M., & Fink, A. (2019). Toward a neurocognitive framework of creative cognition: The role of memory, attention, and cognitive control. *Current Opinion in Behavioral Sciences, 27*, 116–122. https://doi.org/10.1016/j.cobeha.2018.11.002

Benedek, M., & Jauk, E. (2019). Creativity and cognitive control. In J. Kaufman & R. Sternberg (Eds.), *The Cambridge handbook of creativity* (pp. 200–223). Cambridge University Press. https://doi.org/10.1017/9781316979839.012

Benedek, M., Jauk, E., Kerschenbauer, K., Anderwald, R., & Grond, L. (2017). Creating art: An experience sampling study in the domain of moving image art. *Psychology of Aesthetics, Creativity, and the Arts, 11*, 325–334. https://doi.org/10.1037/aca0000102

Benedek, M., Jauk, E., Sommer, M., Arendasy, M., & Neubauer, A. C. (2014). Intelligence, creativity, and cognitive control: The common and differential involvement of executive functions in intelligence and creativity. *Intelligence, 46*, 73–83.

Benedek, M., Karstendiek, M., Ceh, S., Grabner, R., Krammer, G., Lebuda, I., Silvia, P., Cotter, K., Li, Y., Martskvishvili, K., & Kaufman, J. (2021). Creativity myths: Prevalence and correlates of misconceptions on creativity. *Personality and Individual Differences, 182*, Article 111068. https://doi.org/10.1016/j.paid.2021.111068

Botella, M., Glăveanu, V., Zenasni, F., Storme, M., Myszkowski, N., Wolff, M., & Lubart, T. (2013). How artists create: Creative process and multivariate factors. *Learning and Individual Differences, 26*, 161–170. https://doi.org/10.1016/j.lindif.2013.02.008

Callan, G. L., Rubenstein, L. D., Ridgley, L. M., & McCall, J. R. (2019). Measuring self-regulated learning during creative problem-solving with SRL microanalysis. *Psychology of Aesthetics, Creativity, and the Arts*. Advance online publication. https://doi.org/10.1037/aca0000238

Chen, Y., & Zhang, L. (2019). Be creative as proactive? The impact of creative self-efficacy on employee creativity: A proactive perspective. *Current Psychology, 38*, 589–598.

Chirumbolo, A., Livi, S., Mannetti, L., Pierro, A., & Kruglanski, A. W. (2004). Effects of need for closure on creativity in small group interactions. *European Journal of Personality, 18*, 265–278. https://doi.org/10.1002/per.518

Clark, R., & DeYoung, C. (2014). Creativity and the aspects of neuroticism. *Personality and Individual Differences, 60*, S54. https://doi.org/10.1016/j.paid.2013.07.224.

Conner, T. S., & Silvia, P. J. (2015). Creative days: A daily diary study of emotion, personality and everyday creativity. *Psychology of Aesthetics, Creativity, and the Arts, 9*, 463–470. https://doi.org/10.1037/aca0000022

Corazza, G. E. (2016). Potential originality and effectiveness: The dynamic definition of creativity. *Creativity Research Journal, 28*, 258–267. https://doi.org/10.1080/10400419.2016.1195627

Csikszentmihalyi, M. (1988). Motivation and creativity: toward a synthesis of structural and energistic approaches to cognition. *New Ideas in Psychology, 6*, 159–176.

Csikszentmihalyi, M. (1996). *Flow and the psychology of discovery and invention*. Harper Collins.

Csikszentmihalyi, M., & Getzels, J. W. (1971). Discovery-oriented behavior and the originality of creative products: a study with artists. *Journal of Personality and Social Psychology, 19*, 47–52.

Davis, M. A. (2009). Understanding the relationship between mood and creativity: A meta-analysis. *Organizational Behavior and Human Decision Processes, 108*, 25–38. https://doi.org/10.1016/j.obhdp.2008.04.001

De Groot, K., & Thurik, R. (2018). Disentangling risk and uncertainty: When risk-taking measures are not about risk. *Frontiers in Psychology, 9*, Article 2194. https://doi.org/10.3389/fpsyg.2018.02194

Delose, J. E., vanDellen, M. R., & Hoyle, R. H. (2015). First on the List: Effectiveness at self-regulation and prioritizing difficult exercise goal pursuit. *Self and identity, 14*, 271–289. https://doi.org/10.1080/15298868.2014.983442

De Stobbeleir, K. E. M., Ashford, S. J., & Buyens, D. (2011). Self-regulation of creativity at work: The role of feedback-seeking behavior in creative performance. *Academy of Management Journal, 54*(4), 811–831. https://doi.org/10.5465/AMJ.2011.64870144

Dohle, S., Diel, K., & Hofmann, W. (2018). Executive functions and the self-regulation of eating behavior: A review. *Appetite, 124*, 4–9. https://doi.org/10.1016/j.appet.2017.05.041

Dörrenbächer, L., & Perels, F. (2016). More is more? Evaluation of interventions to foster self-regulated learning in college. *International Journal of Educational Research, 78*, 50–65. https://doi.org/10.1016/j.ijer.2016.05.010

Duckworth, A., & Gross, J. J. (2014). Self-Control and Grit: Related but Separable Determinants of Success. *Current Directions in Psychological Science, 23*(5), 319–325. https://doi.org/10.1177/0963721414541462

Finke, R. A., Ward, T. B., & Smith, S. M. (1992). *Creative cognition: Theory, research, and applications*. The MIT Press.

Forthmann, B., Jendryczko, D., Scharfen, J., Kleinkorres, R., Benedek, M., & Holling, H. (2019). Creative ideation, broad retrieval ability, and processing speed: A confirmatory study of nested cognitive abilities. *Intelligence, 75*, 59–72.

Gilhooly, K. J., Fioratou, E., Anthony, S. H., & Wynn, V. (2007). Divergent thinking: Strategies and executive involvement in generating novel uses for familiar objects. *British Journal of Psychology, 98*, 611–625.

Glăveanu, V. P. (2010). Paradigms in the study of creativity: Introducing the perspective of cultural psychology, *New Ideas in Psychology, 28*, 79–93, https://doi.org/10.1016/j.newideapsych.2009.07.007

Glăveanu, V. P. (2013). Rewriting the Language of Creativity: The Five A's Framework. *Review of General Psychology, 17*(1), 69-81. https://doi.org/10.1037/a0029528

Glăveanu, V. P. (2015). Creativity as a sociocultural act. *The Journal of Creative Behavior, 49*(3), 165–180.

Glăveanu, V. P. (2017). The creative self in dialogue. In M. Karwowski & J. C. Kaufman (Eds.), *Explorations in creativity research. The creative self: Effect of beliefs, self-efficacy, mindset, and identity* (pp. 117–135). Academic Press. https://doi.org/10.1016/B978-0-12-809790-8.00007-8

Glăveanu, V. P., & Beghetto, R. A. (2020). Creative experience: A non-standard definition of creativity, *Creativity Research Journal*. https://doi.org/10.1080/10400419.2020.1827606

Glăveanu, V. P., & Lubart, T. (2014). Decentring the creative self. *Creativity and Innovation Management, 23*, 29–43. https://doi.org/10.1111/caim.12049

Glăveanu, V. P., Lubart, T., Bonnardel, N., Botella, M., de Biaisi, P. M., Desainte-Catherine, M., Georgsdottir, A., Guillou, K., Kurtag, G., Mouchiroud, C., Storme, M., Wojtczuk, A., & Zenasni, F. (2013). Creativity as action: findings from five creative domains. *Frontiers in Psychology, 4*(176), 1–14.

Gross, J. J. (1998). The emerging field of emotion regulation: An integrative review. *Review of General Psychology, 2*, 271–299. https://doi.org/10.1037/1089-2680.2.3.271

Gross, J. J. (2014). Emotion regulation: Conceptual and empirical foundations. In J. J. Gross (Ed.), *Handbook of emotion regulation* (3–20). The Guilford Press.

Han, W., Feng, X., Zhang, M., Peng, K., & Zhang, D. (2019). Mood states and everyday creativity: Employing an experience sampling method and a day reconstruction method. *Frontiers in Psychology, 10*, 1698. https://doi.org/10.3389/fpsyg.2019.0169

Hao, N., Ku, Y., Liu, M., Hu, Y., Bodner, M., Grabner, R., & Fink, A. (2016). Reflection enhances creativity: Beneficial effects of idea evaluation on idea generation. *Brain and cognition, 103*, 30-37. https://doi.org/10.1016/j.bandc.2016.01.005

Harada, T. (2020). The effects of risk-taking, exploitation, and exploration on creativity. *PloS one, 15*(7), e0235698. https://doi.org/10.1371/journal.pone.0235698

Hass, R. W., Katz-Buonincontro, J., & Reiter-Palmon, R. (2016). Disentangling creative mindsets from creative self-efficacy and creative identity: Do people hold fixed and growth theories of creativity? *Psychology of Aesthetics, Creativity, and the Arts, 10*(4), 436–446. https://doi.org/10.1037/aca0000081

Hirsh, J. B., & Inzlicht, M. (2008). The devil you know: Neuroticism predicts neural response to uncertainty. *Psychological Science, 19*, 962–967. https://doi.org/10.1111/j.1467-9280.2008.02183.x

Hoever, I. J., Zhou, J., & van Knippenberg, D. L. (2017). Different strokes for different teams: The contingent effects of positive and negative feedback on the creativity of informationally homogeneous and diverse teams. *Academy of Management Journal, 61*(6), 2159–2181. https://doi.org/10.5465/amj.2016.0642

Hofmann, W., Baumeister, R. F., Förster, G., & Vohs, K. D. (2012). Everyday temptations: an experience sampling study of desire, conflict, and self-control. *Journal of Personality and Social Psychology, 102*, 1318–1335.

Ivcevic, Z., & Nusbaum, E. C. (2017). From having an idea to doing something with it: Self regulation for creativity. In M. Karwowski & J. C. Kaufman (Eds.), *The creative self: Effects of beliefs, self-efficacy, mindset, and identity* (pp. 343–365). Academic Press. https://doi.org/10.1016/B978-0-12-809790-8.00020-0

Ivcevic, Z., Cotter, K. N., Nusbaum, E. C., & Silvia, P. J. (2020). Self-regulation for creativity: The how of the creative process. *Unpublished manuscript.*

Jankowska, D. M., Czerwonka, M., Lebuda, I., & Karwowski, M. (2018). Exploring the creative process: integrating psychometric and eye-tracking approaches. *Frontiers in Psychology, 9*, 1931.

Kahneman, D., Krueger, A., Schkade, D., Schwarz, N., & Stone, A. (2004). A survey method for characterizing daily life experience: The day reconstruction method. *Science, 306*, 1776–1780. https://doi.org/10.1126/science.1103572

Karwowski, M. (2014). Creative mindsets: Measurement, correlates, consequences. *Psychology of Aesthetics, Creativity, and the Arts, 8*(1), 62–70. https://doi.org/10.1037/a0034898

Karwowski, M., & Beghetto, R. A. (2019). Creative behavior as agentic action. *Psychology of Aesthetics, Creativity, and the Arts, 13*(4), 402–415. https://doi.org/10.1037/aca0000190

Karwowski, M., & Kaufman, J. C. (2017). *The creative self: Effects of beliefs, self-efficacy, mindset, and identity.* Academic Press.

Karwowski, M., Han, M. H., & Beghetto, R. A. (2019a). Toward dynamizing the measurement of creative confidence beliefs. *Psychology of Aesthetics, Creativity, and the Arts, 13*(2), 193–202. https://doi.org/10.1037/aca0000229

Karwowski, M., Royston, R. P., & Reiter-Palmon, R. (2019b). Exploring creative mindsets: Variable and person-centered approaches. *Psychology of Aesthetics, Creativity, and the Arts, 13*(1), 36–48. https://doi.org/10.1037/aca0000170

Karwowski, M., Czerwonka, M., & Kaufman, J. C. (2020a). Does intelligence strengthen creative metacognition? *Psychology of Aesthetics, Creativity, and the Arts, 14*, 353–360. https://doi.org/10.1037/aca0000208

Karwowski, M., Zielińska, A., Jankowska, D., Strutyńska, E., Omelańczuk, I., & Lebuda, I. (2020b). Creative lockdown? A daily diary study of creative activity during pandemics. *Frontiers in Psychology.*

Karwowski, M., Lebuda, I., Szumski, G., & Firkowska-Mankiewicz, A. (2017). From moment-to-moment to day-to-day: Experience sampling and diary investigations in adults' everyday creativity. *Psychology of Aesthetics, Creativity, and the Arts, 11*(3), 309–324. https://doi.org/10.1037/aca0000127

Kaufman, J. C., & Beghetto, R. A. (2013). In praise of Clark Kent: Creative metacognition and the importance of teaching kids when (not) to be creative. *Roeper Review, 35*, 155–165.

Kaufman, J. C., Beghetto, R. A., & Watson, C. (2016). Creative metacognition and self-ratings of creative performance: A 4-C perspective. *Learning and Individual Differences, 51*, 394–399. https://doi.org/10.1016/j.lindif.2015.05.004

Kaufmann, G., & Vosburg, S. K. (2002). The effects of mood on early and late idea production. *Creativity Research Journal, 14*, 317–330. https://doi.org/10.1207/S15326934CRJ1434_3

Kim, Y. J., & Kim, J. (2020). Does negative feedback benefit (or harm) recipient creativity? The role of the direction of feedback flow. *Academy of Management Journal, 63*, 584–612.

Lebuda, I., & Csikszentmihalyi, M. (2020). All you need is love: The importance of partner and family relations to highly creative individuals' well-being and success. *Journal of Creative Behavior, 54*, 100–114.

Lebuda, I., & Glăveanu, V. P. (2019) Re/searching the social in creativity, past, present and future: An introduction to the Palgrave handbook of social creativity research. In Lebuda I., Glăveanu V. (Eds.) *The Palgrave handbook of social creativity research* (pp. 1–9). Palgrave Macmillan. https://doi.org/10.1007/978-3-319-95498-1_1

Lee, C. S., & Therriault, D. J. (2013). The cognitive underpinnings of creative thought: A latent variable analysis exploring the roles of intelligence and working memory in three creative thinking processes. *Intelligence, 41*, 306–320.

Leung, A. K.-Y., Liou, S., Qiu, L., Kwan, L. Y.-Y., Chiu, C.-y., & Yong, J. C. (2014). The role of instrumental emotion regulation in the emotions–creativity link: How worries render individuals with high neuroticism more creative. *Emotion, 14*, 846–856. https://doi.org/10.1037/a0036965

Ma, H. (2006). A synthetic analysis of the effectiveness of single components and packages in creativity training programs. *Creativity Research Journal, 18*, 435–446. https://doi.org/10.1207/s15326934crj1804_3

Mehlhorn, K., Newell, B. R., Todd, P. M., Lee, M. D., Morgan, K., Braithwaite, V. A., Hausmann, D., Fiedler, K., & Gonzalez, C. (2015). Unpacking the exploration–exploitation tradeoff: A synthesis of human and animal literatures. *Decision, 2*, 191–215. https://doi.org/10.1037/dec0000033

Meinel, M., Wagner, T. F., Baccarella, C. V., & Voigt, K. I. (2019). Exploring the effects of creativity training on creative performance and creative self-efficacy: Evidence from a longitudinal study. *The Journal of Creative Behavior, 53*, 546–558. https://doi.org/10.1002/jocb.234

Merrotsy, P. (2013). Tolerance of ambiguity: A trait of the creative personality? *Creativity Research Journal, 25*, 232–237. https://doi.org/10.1080/10400419.2013.783762

Miyake, A., & Friedman, N. P. (2012). The Nature and Organization of Individual Differences in Executive Functions: Four General Conclusions. *Current Directions in Psychological Science, 21*(1), 8–14. https://doi.org/10.1177/0963721411429458

Morias, M., de Jesus, S. N., Azevedo, I., & Viseu, J. N. (2015). Intervention program on adolescent's creativity representations and academic motivation. *Paidéia, 25*, 289–297.

Mrazek, A. J., Ihm, E. D., Molden, D. C., Mrazek, M. D., Zedelius, C. M., & Schooler, J. W. (2018). Expanding minds: Growth mindsets of self-regulation and the influences on effort and perseverance. *Journal of Experimental Social Psychology, 79*, 164–180.

Mueller, J. S., Melwani, S., & Goncalo, J. A. (2012). The bias against creativity: Why people desire but reject creative ideas. *Psychological Science, 23*, 13–17. https://doi.org/10.1177/0956797611421018

Mumford, M. D., Reiter-Palmon, R., & Redmond, M. R. (1994). Problem construction and cognition: Applying problem representations in ill-defined domains. In M. A. Runco (Ed.), *Creativity research. Problem finding, problem solving, and creativity* (pp. 3–39). Ablex Publishing.

Peña-Sarrionandia, A., Mikolajczak, M., & Gross, J. J. (2019). Integrating emotion regulation and emotional intelligence traditions: A meta-analysis: Corrigendum. *Frontiers in Psychology, 10*, Article 2610. https://doi.org/10.3389/fpsyg.2019.02610

Perkins, A. M., Arnone, D., Smallwood, J., & Mobbs, D. (2015). Thinking too much: self-generated thought as the engine of neuroticism, *Trends in Cognitive Sciences, 19*, 492–498. https://doi.org/10.1016/j.tics.2015.07.003

Pesut, D. J. (1990). Creative thinking as a self-regulatory metacognitive process: A model for education, training and further research. *The Journal of Creative Behavior, 24*, 105–110. https://doi.org/10.1002/j.2162-6057.1990.tb00532.x

Petersen, S. E., & Posner, M. I. (2012). The Attention System of the Human Brain: 20 Years After. *Annual Review of Neuroscience, 35*(1), 73–89. https://doi.org/10.1146/annurev-neuro-062111-150525

Poon, J. C., Au, A. Y., Tong, T. Y., & Lau, S. (2014). The feasibility of enhancement of knowledge and self-confidence in creativity: a pilot study of a three-hour SCAMPER workshop on secondary students. *Thinking Skills and Creativity, 14*, 32–40. https://doi.org/10.1016/j.tsc.2014.06.006

Puente-Díaz, R., & Cavazos-Arroyo, J. (2017). The influence of creative mindsets on achievement goals, enjoyment, creative self-efficacy and performance among business students. *Thinking Skills and Creativity, 24*, 1–11. https://doi.org/10.1016/j.tsc.2017.02.007

Puente-Díaz, R., Cavazos-Arroyo, J., & Vargas-Barrera, F. (2021). Metacognitive feelings as a source of information in the evaluation and selection of creative ideas, *Thinking Skills and Creativity, 39*, 100767, https://doi.org/10.1016/j.tsc.2020.100767

Rabinovich, A., & Webley, P. (2007). Filling the gap between planning and doing: Psychological factors involved in the successful implementation of saving intention. *Journal of Economic Psychology, 28*, 444–461. https://doi.org/10.1016/j.joep.2006.09.002

Reiter-Palmon, R., Robinson-Morral, E. J., Kaufman, J. C., & Santo, J. B. (2012). Evaluation of self-perceptions of creativity: Is it a useful criterion? *Creativity Research Journal, 24*, 107–114. https://doi.org/10.1080/10400419.2012.676980

Rubenstein, L. D., Callan, G. L., & Ridgley, L. M. (2018). Anchoring the creative process within a self-regulated learning framework: Inspiring assessment methods and future research. *Educational Psychology Review, 30*, 921–945.

Runco, M. A., & Jaeger, G. J. (2012). The standard definition of creativity. *Creativity Research Journal, 24*, 92–96. https://doi.org/10.1080/10400419.2012.650092

Schmitz, B., & Perels, F. (2011). Self-monitoring of self-regulation during math homework behaviour using standardized diaries. *Metacognition and Learning 6*, 255–273. https://doi.org/10.1007/s11409-011-9076-6

Schmitz, B., & Wiese, B. S. (2006). New perspectives for the evaluation of training sessions in self-regulated learning: Time-series analyses of diary data. *Contemporary Educational Psychology, 31*, 64–96. https://doi.org/10.1016/j.cedpsych.2005.02.002

Scott, G., Leritz, L. E., & Mumford, M. D. (2004). The effectiveness of creativity training: A quantitative review. *Creativity Research Journal, 16*, 361–388. https://doi.org/10.1207/s15326934crj1604_1

Silvia, P. J. (2008). Discernment and creativity: How well can people identify their most creative ideas? *Psychology of Aesthetics, Creativity, and the Arts, 2*, 139–146. https://doi.org/10.1037/1931-3896.2.3.139

Silvia, P. J. (2018). Creativity is undefinable, controllable and everywhere. In R. J. Sternberg. & J. C. Kaufman (Eds.), *The nature of human creativity* (pp. 291–301). Cambridge University Press.

Silvia, P. J., Beaty, R. E., Nusbaum, E.C., Eddington, K.M., Levin-Aspenson, H., Kwapil, T.R. (2014). Everyday creativity in daily life: An experience-sampling study of "little c" creativity. *Psychology of Aesthetics, Creativity, and the Arts, 8*, 183–188. https://doi.org/10.1037/a0035722

Silvia, P. J., Nusbaum, E. C., Berg, C., Martin, C., & O'Connor, A. (2009). Openness to experience, plasticity, and creativity: Exploring lower-order, high-order, and interactive effects. *Journal of Research in Personality, 43*, 1087–1090.

Silvia, P. J., & Phillips, A. G. (2004). Self-awareness, self-evaluation, and creativity. *Personality and Social Psychology Bulletin, 30*, 1009–1017. https://doi.org/10.1177/0146167204264073

Sternberg, R. J. (2002). Creativity as a decision. *American Psychologist, 57*, 376. https://doi.org/10.1037/0003-066X.57.5.376a

Tamir, M. (2005). Don't worry, be happy? Neuroticism, trait-consistent affect regulation, and performance. *Journal of Personality and Social Psychology, 89*, 449–461. https://doi.org/10.1037/0022-3514.89.3.449

Tamir, M. (2009). What do people want to feel and why?: Pleasure and utility in emotion regulation. *Current Directions in Psychological Science, 18*, 101–105. https://doi.org/10.1111/j.1467-8721.2009.01617.x

Tamir, M. (2011). The maturing field of emotion regulation [Editorial]. *Emotion Review, 3*, 3–7. https://doi.org/10.1177/1754073910388685

Tamir, M., & Ford, B. Q. (2012). When feeling bad is expected to be good: Emotion regulation and outcome expectancies in social conflicts. *Emotion, 12*, 807–816. https://doi.org/10.1037/a0024443

Tegano, D. W. (1990). Relationship of tolerance of ambiguity and playfulness to creativity. *Psychological Reports, 66*, 1047–1056. https://doi.org/10.2466/PR0.66.3.1047-1056

Thrash, T. M., Maruskin, L. A., Cassidy, S. E., Fryer, J. W., & Ryan, R. M. (2010). Mediating between the muse and the masses: Inspiration and the actualization of creative ideas. *Journal of Personality and Social Psychology, 98*, 469–487. https://doi.org/10.1037/a0017907

To, M. L., Fisher, C. D., Ashkanasy, N. M., & Rowe, P. A. (2012). Within-person relationships between mood and creativity. *Journal of Applied Psychology, 97*, 599–612. https://doi.org/10.1037/a0026097

Usher, E. L., & Schunk, D. H. (2018). Social cognitive theoretical perspective of self-regulation. In D. H. Schunk & J. A. Greene (Eds.), *Educational psychology handbook series. Handbook of self-regulation of learning and performance* (pp. 19–35). Routledge.

Valgeirsdottir, D., & Onarheim, B. (2017). Studying creativity training programs: A methodological analysis. *Creativity and Innovation Management, 26*, 430–439. https://doi.org/10.1111/caim.12245

Vally, Z., Salloum, L., AlQedra, D., El Shazly, S., Albloshi, M., Alsheraifi, S., & Alkaabi, A. (2019). Examining the effects of creativity training on creative production, creative self-efficacy, and neuro-executive functioning. *Thinking Skills and Creativity, 31*, 70–78. https://doi.org/10.1016/j.tsc.2018.11.003

Walton, G. M., & Wilson, T. D. (2018). Wise interventions: Psychological remedies for social and personal problems. *Psychological Review, 125*, 617–655. https://doi.org/10.1037/rev0000115

Winne, P. H. (2018). Cognition and metacognition within self-regulated learning. In D. H. Schunk & J. A. Greene (Eds.), *Educational psychology handbook series. Handbook of self-regulation of learning and performance* (pp. 36–48). Routledge.

Wronska, M. K., Bujacz, A., Gocłowska, M. A., Rietzschel, E. F., & Nijstad, B. A. (2019). Person-task fit: Emotional consequences of performing divergent versus convergent thinking tasks depend on need for cognitive closure. *Personality and Individual Differences, 142*, 172–178. https://doi.org/10.1016/j.paid.2018.09.018

Zenasni, F., Besançon, M., & Lubart, T. (2008). Creativity and tolerance of ambiguity: An empirical study. *The Journal of Creative Behavior, 42*, 61–73. https://doi.org/10.1002/j.2162-6057.2008.tb01080.x

Zielińska, A., Lebuda, I., Ivcevic, Z., & Karwowski, M. (2022a). How adolescents develop and implement their ideas? On self-regulation of creative action. *Thinking Skills and Creativity, 43*, 100998. https://doi.org/10.1016/j.tsc.2022.100998

Zielińska, A., Forthmann, B., Lebuda, I., & Karwowski, M. (under review). Self-regulation for creative activity: The same or different across domains?

Zielińska, A., Lebuda, I., & Karwowski, M. (2022b). Simple, yet wise? Students' creative engagement benefits from a daily intervention. *Translational Issues in Psychological Sciences, 8*(1), 6–23. https://doi.org/10.1037/tps0000289

Zimmerman, B. J. (2000). Attaining self-regulation: a social-cognitive perspective. In M. Boekaerts, P. R. Pintrich, & M. Zeidner (Eds.), *Handbook of self-regulation* (pp. 13–39). Academic Press.

Chapter 7
The Uncertainty of Creativity: Opening Possibilities and Reducing Restrictions Through Mindfulness

Danah Henriksen, Carmen Richardson, Natalie Gruber, and Punya Mishra

Abstract This chapter explores the pivotal role that uncertainty plays in creative learning, with a focus on mindfulness as an approach to working with uncertainty and supporting creativity. Creativity is a highly sought capacity across disciplines, and creative thinking operates as a force that drives new knowledge and ideas, advancing growth and change in society. We live in an uncertain world of rapid, often accelerating, change and instability. Creativity offers us ways of thinking that prepare us to manage and address unexpected situations and consider fresh perspectives or possibilities to devise better outcomes. However, creativity can be uncomfortable for some, given the uncertainty inherent in the creative process, as well as the risk of embarrassment that comes with failure. Thus, people may hold back and hesitate to engage creatively. Such risk-aversion can be ramped up in traditional educational environments or school settings, which tend to focus on one-right-answer approaches and punitive responses to mistakes or failures. In this chapter, we explore the critical and complex relationship between creativity and uncertainty, suggesting mindfulness as a valuable approach to supporting creativity in school settings and addressing the perception of risk associated with failure. We discuss existing research around the relationship between mindfulness and creativity, and position mindfulness as a way to ameliorate fears, allow for uncertainty and open up new creative possibilities—particularly by changing one's relationship to uncertainty, becoming a better observer of the world, enabling greater openness to experience, and expanding empathy. We conclude with a call-to-action for creativity in learning settings, recognizing the need for uncertainty as part of the process, as well as the challenges that uncertainty presents to the human psyche and in school processes. We offer strategies for mindfulness in learning settings that can reduce restrictions on creativity, by supporting mindsets that are geared toward allowing and working with uncertainty.

D. Henriksen (✉) · C. Richardson · N. Gruber · P. Mishra
Mary Lou Fulton Teachers College, Arizona State University, Tempe, AZ, USA
e-mail: danah.henriksen@asu.edu

© Springer Nature Switzerland AG 2022
R. A. Beghetto, G. J. Jaeger (eds.), *Uncertainty: A Catalyst for Creativity, Learning and Development*, Creativity Theory and Action in Education 6, https://doi.org/10.1007/978-3-030-98729-9_7

"No problem can be solved from the same consciousness that created it. We must learn to see the world anew."
~ Albert Einstein

7.1 Introduction

We live in a volatile, uncertain, complicated, and ambiguous (VUCA) world. The future is inherently uncertain, heightened by unprecedented change in society, and driven by rapid technological evolution, globalization, shifting demographics, and fluctuating economies (Zhao 2012). Patterns and solutions that worked in the past are unreliable guides to uncertain futures. Complex problems require new ways of seeing the world—of identifying new patterns, and developing novel, unique and contextually grounded solutions. In addition, learners need appropriate knowledge, skills and mindsets to face these complex challenges with equanimity, see the emerging contexts through "new" eyes, and devise creative solutions to these problems (Peschl 2019). Therefore, creativity—the ability to devise novel and effective ideas and solutions (Runco and Jaeger 2012)—combined with an ability to 'see' the world, a willingness to suspend judgment and an openness for the new, is essential in addressing the uncertainty of complex global and societal challenges (e.g., climate change, wealth inequality, racial injustice, and countless others).

Although creativity is considered a desirable and coveted trait, its value becomes even more prescient to addressing complex challenges in an often-chaotic world (Glăveanu et al. 2020). Creativity is one of the most critical factors in futures-thinking, as a response to the uncertainty of the future (Heinonen and Hiltunen 2012). Yet while uncertainty can be addressed through creative thinking and solutions, the creative process itself can also fall prey to uncertainty. The inherent open-endedness of creative challenges as compared to highly structured problems, the entry into new ideas and spaces, and the need for risk-taking with the potential for failure, all may generate uncertainty and discomfort. It is no surprise, then, that individuals or institutions sometimes avoid creative choices or behaviors (as well as uncertainty and risk of failure) in favor of known solutions, preferring problems with predictable parameters to novel challenges.

In this chapter, we examine the relationship between creativity and uncertainty, wherein creativity is both a solution to dealing with the external uncertainties of our world, as well as a cause of internal uncertainty. In this, creativity and uncertainty coexist in a complex but essential tension. Uncertainty drives the need for creativity, while creativity can be the generator of uncertainty too. While uncertainty may have negative connotations, given the psychological stress that often accompanies not knowing, it may be a neutral reality, given the limited reach of control humans possess in a VUCA world. We suggest that mindfulness may be one way of addressing this tension by transforming one's outlook; providing new ways of both being in and observing the world, which allows us to contend with the ambiguity that coexists with uncertainty. This ability to embrace ambiguity offers a way of learning to navigate through uncertainty, providing the possibility for fundamentally changing our relationship to it, as neither a good nor bad condition, but a state of reality. This is critical to genuine dialogic engagement with the world, allowing us to be both an observer as well as a participant. It recognizes that we are working on understanding the world around us, even as we try to act on improving it.

Education—as a force that prepares students for the future—must have a pivotal role in supporting creativity and the ability to deal with uncertainty. We focus on mindfulness as a valuable approach or mindset toward this end. We discuss research findings around the connection between mindfulness and creativity, and position mindfulness as a way to ameliorate the fears and discomfort of uncertainty and open up creative possibilities. This can occur through reducing fear of judgment, enabling greater openness to experience, and expanding empathy. We end with a call to action for creativity in learning, focusing on the need to recognize uncertainty as an inherent part of creative processes, as well as the challenges that uncertainty presents within the human psyche and institutions of schooling. We offer strategies for mindfulness in learning settings that can reduce restrictions on creativity, by supporting practices that are geared toward allowing and working with uncertainty.

7.2   The Role of Uncertainty and Creativity in Learning

The aim of education is to prepare students for the future. In times of turbulence, where predicting the future is difficult if not impossible, the role of education must be to develop mindsets that allow students to respond to unexpected challenges with thoughtful yet flexible applications of their knowledge and skills. This is the domain of creativity—the ability to devise novel, effective and organically whole solutions to unexpected problems (Csikszentmihalyi and Wolfe 2014; Henriksen et al. 2015). Most educational systems, however, do little to address creative development, instead focusing on problems that have been important in the past (Craft 2010). It may be argued that in many cases, educational systems do the opposite of developing, expressing, and exercising creativity among learners. Rather, they repress it, by instilling a fear of risk and failure, and favoring following exact instructions over the ability to see possibilities, consider the unexpected, deal with real-world messiness, and manage multiple perspectives (or even handle conflicting information) (Henriksen et al. 2020). Educational systems are often built around an artificial separation between subjects, focusing on the development of abstract disciplinary knowledge divorced from the complexities of the real world. There may be little, if any, requirement to collaborate with others and manage the inevitable conflict of opinions or information that characterize current societal problems. Clearly, responding to uncertainty requires bringing creativity into the educational context.

Creativity and learning have often been seen as related to each other (Dewey 1934/2005). Starko (1995) suggested that learning is an inherent part of the creative process, while Guilford (1950) argued that creativity itself is an example of learning. More current conceptualizations integrate these perspectives and suggest that creativity and learning are interdependent (Beghetto 2016; Sawyer 2012). Creative learning, in our use of the term, covers a range of concepts and ideas. First, it is acceptance that academic knowledge and skills alone will not allow our society to meet the needs of a rapidly changing world. Rather, it will be the ability to both learn creatively as well as the creative application of knowledge in new (often ambiguous, uncertain) contexts (Beghetto 2020). Second, it is the rejection of the standard one-right answer approach to education which often provides a false sense of certainty. Thus, creative learning recognizes and embraces both the uncertainty inherent in the learning process and emphasizes the value of spending time in spaces that may be uncomfortable and the self-doubt that often follows. Third, and finally, creative learning focuses on the development of creative identities that are not invested in compliance and conformity, but rather those that identify and accept the messiness inherent in the process.

Creativity inevitably requires a sense of open-endedness, in allowing the risk of engaging with the new and managing undefined parameters and outcomes. Creative endeavors touch on social risk because of the potential embarrassment or discomfort in sharing ideas with others, especially if there are possible negative outcomes. With this uncertainty many people experience a sense of fear or uneasiness around creativity—fear of failure, risk, embarrassment, mistakes, or punitive outcomes—thus they may instinctively hold back and avoid creative endeavors (Erez and Nouri 2010). Yet, in an uncertain future and unstable world, holding back and sticking with known solutions or avoiding change is a recipe for trouble. Although creativity does not endorse or denote "dangerous" or haphazard risk—risk-taking (as an openness to experience and willingness to try new things) is essential to conceptualizations of creativity (Dewett 2007); and risk is unavoidable in creative learning given the potential (and inevitable) fear of failure.

Despite this, risk is often viewed negatively in educational settings. Policies tuned to standardization and metrics promote narrow norms and algorithmically driven responses. School environments, driven by policy and high-stakes assessment framings, often designate failures punitively (Luke 2011). Creativity can be uncomfortable to engage with, not only because of our human tendency to want to stay in the "comfort zone" of experience; but also, education systems may ignore creativity because of the inherent uncertainty that exists in creative spaces and action (Cremin 2006), which are difficult to standardize, measure and evaluate. Current educational systems, with their focus on the predictable and the known, have a difficult time integrating creativity, a process which looks directly into the unknown, with its focus on the new.

Creative processes inherently engage with the novel. After an act of creation, the uncertainty persists because it is "difficult to know the consequences of something truly new" (Moran 2010, p. 76). Uncertainty can linger beyond the creative act or precede it through a fear of failure. As Sternberg and Kaufman (2010) note:

> Individuals may decide against creativity, merely because it exposes them to risk that they deem unacceptable. Why risk your job when you can do it a little less creatively or perhaps a lot less so, and retain it? Why risk your grades in classrooms when, by taking fewer creative risks, you are likely to please teachers more, not less?" (p. 475).

This suggests the need for processes or constructs that support creativity toward solutions for our uncertain future, and also offer a path through the inherent uncertainty of the creative landscape. We assert that *mindfulness*, a trained practice of paying attention to the present moment with curious, non-judgmental awareness, is a critical connection point to uncertainty and creativity in education. It does this both by reducing setback factors that uncertainty may produce (e.g., reducing fear of judgment, stress, anxiety, fear of failure, and similar derailing factors), and increasing factors that can support creativity (e.g., openness to experience, empathy and perspective taking, ability to observe one's thoughts). Moreover, we suggest how mindfulness practice can support creativity by developing an ability to both participate in the world and see it, noticing and considering all possibilities and developing the creative self. Because mindfulness can help people to allow, persist and sit with whatever feelings they may experience, it may have the ability to change one's relationship to uncertainty. If we can recognize or allow the experience of uncertainty, we can also allow the open space of new possibilities that comes with uncertainty, allowing creativity to emerge (Beghetto 2020). As follows, we define mindfulness and discuss research findings on its connection to creativity, synthesizing this with the possibilities of working with uncertainty and supporting creativity in learning.

7.3 Mindfulness: Bridging Between Uncertainty and Creativity

Mindfulness is the practice of purposefully placing awareness or attention on the present moment, with open, non-judgmental awareness (Kabat-Zinn 2013). Shapiro et al. (2006) point out three axioms to this practice—intention (purposefully), attention (engaging awareness), and attitude (with openness/non-judgment). Mindfulness is not about seeking a specific outcome or experience. It is not the absence of thoughts or trying to control or push away thoughts. Mindfulness involves recognizing your experience, inside and outside of your body, in the present moment, with a particular attitude of openness, curiosity, or non-judgmental awareness (Kudesia 2019). Such an orientation may be helpful in recognizing and allowing for the uncertainty within creative experience, or in facing uncertain situations with an openness to allow for creativity.

Although the practice of mindfulness originated in Buddhist teachings approximately 2,500 years ago, it has made its way into current Western culture and highly secular settings and practices. Jon Kabat-Zinn is often credited with developing mindfulness as a secular wellness practice, through the creation of his Mindfulness Based Stress Reduction (MBSR) at the University of Massachusetts General Hospital. Research demonstrates that in developing awareness of one's own mind and body in the present, people experience less anxiety, more positive emotions and engagement, and other mental and emotional benefits (Weinstein et al. 2009). In learning settings, students can become more skilled at navigating thought processes in psychologically healthy ways (Bennett and Dorjee 2016), as mindfulness increases self-efficacy, concentration, mood, self-regulation, and engagement; and as we will discuss, creative thinking skills (Kudesia 2019).

Typically, mindfulness is learned through seated meditation. There are many structured practices available for learning mindfulness, which can be accessed through books, guided recordings on websites, retreats, classes, and apps. Different guided meditations can focus on targeted areas, such as cultivating concentration, reducing stress, self-acceptance, letting go of the past, among others. In addition to seated meditation, other formal practices can involve attending to experience in activities of daily life, such as walking meditation, eating meditation, and listening meditation. The goal of these formal meditation practices is to practice mindfulness, or moment to moment awareness with open attention, in moments of daily living. Whether engaging in ordinary, mundane life experiences, such as waiting in line at the post office, or more intense situations, such as engaging in a difficult conversation, this sense of open awareness, brought to direct experience, can be cultivated through formal practice and informally brought into daily life.

Practitioners of mindfulness consider the breath as the gateway to presence. As the breath connects with and steadies the mind, the five sensation pathways of the body connect the body and the outside world. Attuning to the breath and body allows space to notice thoughts and emotions. Engaging in this over time presents the opportunity to become more self-aware and gain awareness of repetitive thought streams, patterns of emotional responses, and ways of relating to others.

Shapiro et al. (2006) termed the phenomenon of "waking up" to one's thoughts and inner experiences and noticing that internal experience is separate from the self, as a kind of "reappraisal." This can be thought of as a positive coping mechanism and the opposite of suppression, a defense mechanism (Garland et. al. 2011). Over time, through the process of reappraisal, emotions and thoughts take on less power as the individual begins to understand that they are not their thoughts, their thoughts are separate from who they are. This is an extension of the natural developmental process of subject versus object identification (Kegan 1982). A child's first experiences others through subject identification, as not separate from the self. The child does not recognize that their mother, for example, has feelings or needs separate from their own. As the child grows older, they move through the process of recognizing the self as separate from others, with their own needs, feelings, etc. into a state of object identification. Through the process of reappraisal, an individual begins to see that they are not fused with their experiences, internal or external (Shapiro et al. 2006). This experience of reappraisal, can result in a profound shifting of outlook as the relationship with oneself and by extension, experience in the world begins to change. This changing perspective can allow practitioners to see more clearly into the true nature of phenomena as they are, including the fleeting or ephemeral nature of all things (Fisher 2021) In seeing clearly into the impermanent nature of things as they are, practitioners may begin to see that certainty itself may be an illusion to some extent, thereby changing their relationship with uncertainty.

7.3.1 Research Outcomes Related to Mindfulness and Creativity

Outcomes of mindfulness practice are related to intentions for practicing mindfulness (Shapiro et al. 2006). Relevant to the discussion of addressing uncertainty and obstacles to creativity, mindfulness practice is associated with decreased states of self-judgment, and increased feelings of empathy and compassion towards others and oneself. Mindfulness and creativity are independent constructs, but there is a theoretical basis for presuming a relationship between them. They are both areas of human psychology which connect to emotions, attention, stress, and awareness of one's own self and the surrounding world (Baas et al. 2014). Studies have shown that mindfulness improves a person's ability to concentrate (Sedlmeier et al. 2012). It also may decrease fear of judgment, and enhance open-minded thinking while reducing aversive self-conscious thinking (Brown et al. 2007). These factors relate directly to characteristics of creative thinking habits, including: relaxation or flow states (improved concentration), risk-taking (requiring a lack of fear about judgment), and curiosity or open-mindedness/openness to experience (reducing self-conscious experience) (Prabhu et al. 2008). Several aspects of trait mindfulness (or skills developed with mindfulness training) are linked with creativity. For instance, mindfulness has been associated with increased perspective-taking ability as it expands empathy and open-mindedness (Carson and Langer 2006). Moore and Malinowski (2009) found that mindfulness also increases a person's capacity to respond to situations in non-habitual ways from fresh perspectives, which is essential to creativity. Mindfulness also reduces fear of judgment, which is particularly conducive to creativity. Similarly, its ability to improve working memory is supportive of creative habits of mind (Chiesa et al. 2011). Experienced meditators have often proven to be better problem solvers and score better in verbal creativity (Greenberg et al. 2012). Jedrczak et al. (1985) found that meditation of any length has a positive effect on creativity, meaning that even short meditation breaks can effectively stimulate creative abilities.

Looking to the overall nature and direction of the mindfulness-creativity relationship, Lebuda et al. (2016) conducted a meta-analysis of quantitative research on the relationship between these constructs. Their review hypothesized a positive relationship between mindfulness and creativity, and they used statistical meta-analysis to examine 20 peer-reviewed, quantitative studies with direct measures of mindfulness and creativity—seeking to measure the relationship between the two and consider the role of moderators. The study estimated the correlation between mindfulness and creativity at $r = .22$ ($r = .18$ without correction for attenuation), and they found a significant but heterogeneous correlation. Their work suggests that creativity correlates with mindfulness significantly, with a small-to-medium effect size. Although this effect was not moderated by study design, it was stronger when creativity measurement was based on insight or problem-solving tasks and certain meditation practices (such as 'open monitoring' meditation, a practice in which the meditator aims to observe and notice all objects or experiences that emerge in consciousness, including thoughts and all five senses).

Going beyond removing hindrances to creativity, and acknowledging or accepting the role of uncertainty, there are also theoretical foundations connecting mindfulness and creativity related to observing and understanding the world. It may offer ways of noticing possibilities without being clouded by mental blinders or limiting stories. Fisher (2006) suggests that mindfulness may be most vital for young people who are most often affected by a lack of control over the uncertain world they inhabit. He notes:

> For many children childhood is not a carefree time. In a materialistic, competitive world they are subject to many of the same stresses and strains as adults. They are bombarded by an information overload of words, images and noise. They are prey to the frustration and anger of others and often experience negative emotions more deeply and intensely than adults (p. 148).

Fisher points out that such stressors are common blocks to learning and creativity, and suggests mindfulness as a beneficial psychological support for creativity. He notes that among the ancient Greeks and Romans, a quiet mind was believed to serve as an opening to the creative muse. Contemporary psychology reflects how meditation engages the mind in non-verbal ways, offering new and different ways of thinking or experiencing. Our conscious minds are caught up in language, yet the brain's linguistic structures can restrict the scope of human knowledge and action. Meditation can offer an experience of the mind that is not purely linguistic, expanding creativity by tapping into subconscious and intuitive thought. Claxton (1997) referred to this as the "under-mind" and Gladwell (2005) termed it as the "adaptive subconscious." Such intuitive experience is essential to creativity and requires a mind that is focused upon the present moment and free of distractions, fears, and immediate desires. As Justo et al. (2014) note:

> Mindfulness is a technique which allows introspective and perceptual awareness, encouraging the awareness towards our psychological processes and habits. It increases the inter-hemispheric communication, which is typical of creativity states, since the individual who meditates is able to perceive more and more subtle details of the stream of consciousness and mental processes (p. 233).

Mindfulness and creativity are not yet fully understood, neurologically or psychologically. Both are inherently complex and variable constructs, but much research investigating their relationship points in a positive and beneficial direction (Henriksen et al. 2020). Mindfulness may help to manage the uncertainty surrounding creativity, and also support creative habits of mind, which in turn are key to addressing the challenges of an uncertain world. Even beyond the existing research, there are theoretical foundations that reflect how mindfulness may develop creativity by shifting perceptions of the self.

7.3.2   Mindfulness, Creativity, and the Self: Moving into Wholeness

Human beings possess the innate capacity to engage in both mindfulness and creativity. Both require practitioners to become more open to and aware of what arises in the present moment, whether that is a prominent emotion or a spark of the imagination. The creative process and mindfulness practices have the capacity to enhance and support each other when used effectively. Ultimately, the self is at the forefront of each practice. Mindfulness and creativity can lead to the process of self-discovery, transcendence of the self through creation of something new, or they may bring aspects of the self that serve as stumbling blocks into direct awareness.

Mindfulness and creativity both have the capacity to help practitioners develop the ability to discover what is here in the present moment, within the self, and all that is occurring. Cassou and Cubley (1995, p. 109) write the following about the creative process: "you cannot know what you are going to express. What is really creative is bound to be a surprise because it is something you couldn't have thought of." Creative expression goes beyond the thinking mind and comes from the space between the thoughts or demands of the conscious mind (Cassou and Cubley 1995). This is the same state of presence mindfulness practitioners become attuned to through the practice of mindfulness. Creativity emerges from presence: "...you open yourself to the unknown experience. You connect with the background of life, and at moments your boundaries dissolve. You become one with the movement of all things" (Cassou and Cubley 1995, p. 170).

A person cannot do their best creative work if their autonomic nervous system is in 'flight or fight' mode, which the body automatically goes into under stress, real or imagined (Kabat-Zinn 2013). In this mode, the sympathetic nervous system is activated and the body is tense and constricted, blood pressure is elevated; intense emotions, like anxiety, shame and anger are likely to arise, and the individual is in a state of physical and psychological alertness, ready to respond to environmental threats (Kabat-Zinn 2013). The practice of mindfulness, especially when paired with intentional breathing, has the capacity to move a person from this "fight or flight" response to the "relaxation response" (Bensen 1993)—an alert but relaxed state mediated by the parasympathetic nervous system. As the parasympathetic nervous system is activated, feelings of safety generated from this relaxed state create space within the nervous system for new experiences and ideas (Menakem 2017). Creativity, as an expression of the new, arguably requires feelings of safety, both emotionally and physically. Conversely, creativity also has the potential to bring the person into the present moment, initiating the relaxation response generated by being in a present state, calling to mind the kind of flow states noted by Csikszentmihalyi (1997). Together, the practices of mindfulness and creativity are a potent combination for changing an individual's internal and external experiences, opening up the possibility of the creation of truly original work—allowing and managing the experience of an uncertain world.

Mindfulness, and creative expression, can facilitate the process of coming into wholeness, a state of knowing oneself fully. Carl Jung suggested the creation of spontaneous images in psychotherapy was useful in "digging up again the fantasy images of the unconscious" and breaking down of "rationalistic walls" held within the mind that cause distortions to relationships with the outer world (Abbenante 1994). From a Jungian perspective, creative expression, like mindfulness practice, has the potential to go beyond the "sheltered walls of self-protection" to reveal the authentic, inner personality (Lev-Aladgem 1998, p. 242). Going beyond the recognized aspects of the personality, these practices can reveal what Jung called the shadow, parts or aspects of the hidden self "that interfere with a more satisfying life" (Abbenante 1994). Jung stated that this process of self-realization must occur in relation to the outside world: "the self is relatedness…The self only exists in as much as you appear. Not that you are, but that you do the self. The self appears in your deeds and deeds always mean relationships" (Schmidt 2005, p. 598).

Some work suggests that engaging in creativity may offer a way to heal the relationship with the self and the outside world (Forgeard and Elstein 2014; Shah 2020). This process can become a powerful vehicle for what Jung called individuation, the result of full self-realization. When the individual has recognized the expressed and repressed aspects of the self, the individual can come into a state of wholeness, which ultimately leads to a recognition of one's purpose in life, while having access to all parts of the self, including creativity, bringing one's gifts and potential in a state of self-realization and self-actualization. When one knows themselves fully and acts from this stance, and has a deep understanding of their place in the world, the relationship to judgment and fear changes and the capacity for creativity grows. That is, if the practitioner is not identified with their thoughts or mistakes but something greater, there is increased energy, ability to connect with creativity, and less fearfulness, with more acceptance in relation to uncertainty.

7.3.3 Mindfulness, Creativity, and Uncertainty: How Mindfulness Engages Hindrances

One of the most difficult obstacles to work with in both meditation and the creative process is uncertainty. In his book on the creative process, McNiff (1998, p.1) states, "A person's license to create is irrevocable, and it opens to every corner of daily life. But it is always hard to see that doubt, fear, and indirectness are eternal aspects of the creative path."

In educational settings, creativity and uncertainty co-exist, which leads practitioners to "invariably confront the way in which people have been conditioned to expect certainties in learning situations. There is an expectation that something concrete will be delivered by the teacher to the learner" (McNiff 1998, p. 26). Challenges which arise within a mindfulness meditation practice could also be characterized in a similar way. Yet this practice provides tools for working with this emotion. When uncertainty arises, the doubt or fear associated with it can be dealt with first by identifying it and recognizing it as such. Doubt, or uncertainty about the merits of practicing mindfulness is so common that doubt is identified as one of the seven hindrances to practicing mindfulness. Doubt, along with sleepiness, restlessness, craving, aversion, boredom, and fear are other hindrances that have been recognized over the last 2,500 years, since the creation of the Buddhist practice of mindfulness (Smalley and Winston 2010).

Labeling an emotion as it arises, like uncertainty and any fear or doubt surrounding it, is a form of mindfulness. The act of labeling thoughts and/or emotions creates space between the practitioner and the mental state, as it calms the "emotional circuitry in the brain" (Smalley and Winston 2010). UCLA researcher Golnaz Taibiana explains that when mindfulness practitioners label their emotions, they are engaging in activity that activates the prefrontal cortex, which is associated with higher levels of thought and decision-making, while decreasing the activity of the amygdala, the fear response center in the brain (as cited by Ellenberg and Hanson 2020). After labeling the emotion of doubt or uncertainty, the practitioner can then remind themselves of their reasons for practicing meditation or engaging in the creative process (Smalley and Winston 2010). Generally, as practitioners of mindfulness begin to recognize that emotions and thoughts are ephemeral states and recognize and name them as they arise, these states have less power to pull the practitioner in and get lost in their undertow. As McNiff (1998) writes about the creative process, "if we are to stay with a situation, it will carry us to a new place." He further writes that, "Trusting the (creative) process is based on a belief that something valuable will emerge when we step into the unknown…The ego is willing to relinquish plans and expectations in order to receive an unanticipated result" (p. 27). The practice of engaging with a blank page or sitting on a meditation cushion may be fraught with uncertainty for the practitioner. Afterall, when we open ourselves up to experience, we do not know what will happen. Just as we do not know what will happen as we are trying to create a new business model or painting.

7.4   Mindfulness, Creativity, and Uncertainty in Education

Being mindful of the important role that uncertainty plays in creativity can provide an assurance that the time spent in spaces of uncomfortableness and self-doubt is actually time well spent in teaching and learning. Through mindfulness techniques, we can approach the creative process with a renewed sense of engagement and purpose. This is especially applicable in learning environments where there is often limited time to spend in periods of open-endedness or experimentation and where there is a push to cover content. Academic knowledge and skills alone will not allow our society to meet the needs of a rapidly changing world.

7.4.1 Allowing Uncertainty Without Judgment

An initial step to embracing creative thinking is to be mindful of the importance of uncertainty in any creative undertaking and to allow it to be present without judgment and harsh or unfair expectations. The non-judgmental quality of mindfulness allows for experiences and thoughts that might otherwise be discarded or suppressed. Through the act of being non-judgmentally aware of our own engagement in the creative process, we can recognize the need for uncertainty and make intentional decisions about how we will react to the inevitable moments of discomfort and creative risk. Practicing mindfulness in moments of uncertainty then, means being fully present in the moment, and recognizing that the uncertainty need not cause fear, alarm, or a sense of overwhelm, but rather that it is a natural part of the process (Williams and Kabat-Zinn 2011).

While it may sound simple, this practice is easier said than done. Meditation is one foundational way to practice the skill of being present in the moment, recognizing what is happening, and pausing before making decisions about how to react. Research has shown that meditation techniques that help people connect with the present moment can lead to reduced anxiety and positive emotions (Weinstein et al. 2009). Rather than avoiding the creative act because of fear of failure, or quitting partway through the process because we are not satisfied with our progress, we can use mindfulness techniques to pause, become aware of what is occurring in the moment, recognize the need for this space, and reset our thinking so that we are not overwhelmed. An increased awareness of one's own creative process, the recognition of risk-taking and uncomfortable spaces, and the non-judgmental navigation of feelings of uncertainty, is beneficial to the success of many creative professionals (Preiss and Cosmelli 2017).

7.4.2 Managing Uncertainty in Schools

There has been a call by psychologists and educational experts for years for the support of creativity in schools (Beghetto 2010; Robinson 2011). Beyond the personal judgment that prevents many people from engaging in creative acts, those who attempt to support creativity in learning environments are faced with multiple challenges driven by the uncertainty that "experimenting" with learning brings.

Glăveanu and Tanggaard (2014) describe schools as places that deny creative identities in students and teachers. However, research shows that while schools may not always support creativity, school-aged children are at an important stage in the development of their own creative self-concept. Symonds and Hargreaves (2014) explored adolescent transitions in school and found that adolescents felt that the environment of school engenders negative emotions. Few students in their study felt comfortable exploring or participating in creative endeavors in school. Adolescents are among the most susceptible to what Beghetto and Dilley (2016) termed creative mortification, in which negative feedback after a creative act can result in disengagement and loss of interest and self-efficacy in creative endeavors.

Stevenson et al. (2014) found that adolescence is a period of enhanced susceptibility for experiences that can impact creative potential, and that this stage provides a favorable time for progression into creative thinking and ideation. The challenge then, is overcoming the uncertainty that comes with engaging students in nontraditional strategies or taking social risks in sharing and expressing. Although the United States has focused heavily on test scores, still, in comparison to other countries American students are seen as performing poorly. The answer to this has been to test more frequently, which has led to a curricular narrowing as teachers spend time teaching to tests. Other countries (i.e., Australia, Canada, China, to name a few) have begun to engage policies that call for schools to support students' creative potential (Beghetto 2010). It is indeed a substantial risk for a teacher or administrator to decide to implement an unfamiliar pedagogical strategy involving risk. This fear of the unknown results in convergent teaching practices, where the teacher does most of the talking and "teaching" while students are the receivers of information (Beghetto 2010). In this type of environment students have little opportunity to share ideas, collaborate, or create.

Holistic education, on the other hand, embraces mindfulness as a core value and practice. It emphasizes the growth and development of wholeness among students and recognizes the interdependence of life through the teaching of six major areas of connectivity: subject connections (e.g., interdisciplinary lessons), earth connections (e.g., lessons on humanity and its connections to the Earth), community connections, (e.g., beginning with emphasis on positive community in the classroom, extending out to into the world, eventually students seeing themselves as global citizens), thinking connections (e.g., integration of brain hemispheres through symbolism, imagery, etc.), body mind connections (e.g., helping students develop a positive relationship with their bodies through movement practices like yoga), and soul connections (e.g., recognizing and encouraging the student's inner life, through meditation, visualization, etc.) (Miller 2010). Through this model of education, children learn with their "thinking hearts" and come to know themselves as individuals, part of a community and greater society at large, with an awareness of unity and the interconnectedness of life (Miller 2010).

For many educators, any departure from convention might be avoided as a risky endeavor. Much research has investigated pedagogical strategies that support creative thinking, including problem-based learning, place-based learning, or project-based learning. These instructional strategies may support student creativity, and also result in learning experiences where students learn content in deep and meaningful ways (Craft et al. 2014). Mindfulness allows for the mitigation of the psychological distress surrounding uncertainty, transforming one's relationship to it, through the intentional act of recognizing the importance of supporting creativity, and taking the necessary risks to make it a reality. We share some direct strategies as follows.

7.4.3 Strategies for Teaching and Learning Mindfulness

Mindfulness, or moment-to-moment awareness, can be taught and practiced by students and teachers, both as a way to mitigate uncertainty and to support teacher well-being. The normalization of risk-taking as a routine learning activity has the potential to turn an atmosphere that restricts creativity into one that nourishes creativity. An atmosphere in which students feel safe to take risks and make mistakes is essential, as students begin to see that feelings of uncertainty, and even self-doubt, are normal feelings that they can experience while still being successful (Chan and Yuen 2014).

It is important that teachers not only encourage the sharing of novel ideas, but also give students the time and space to explore and develop them, with tools, like mindfulness, to prepare the mind to deal with the process. We offer a few possible ways of incorporating mindfulness into the normal processes of schooling, that educators can teach and practice with their students.

7.4.3.1 Practicing in the Moment Awareness with Meditation Moments

Mindfulness encompasses a diverse range of practices, of which meditation is a common entry point. Basic meditation practices can be done with few moments of class time (even as little as one minute), either at the start of any class or at strategic points during a lesson or a school day (Henriksen and Shack 2020). This simply requires guiding students through a few moments of heightened awareness and attention to a specific focus (e.g., their own breathing, a phrase, a feeling, an image, etc.). There are a variety of tools available to guide such practice. In a meditation that focuses on in the moment awareness, the teacher, or a mindfulness app or tool (i.e., apps like Calm or Headspace), can guide the group through an exercise that brings awareness to the present moment by focusing on the breath, an image, or a phrase. As the mind wanders, vocal cues can help the group bring awareness back to the focus of the meditation and to the present moment. As people practice being in the moment they are able to separate themselves from thoughts of inadequacy or fear of the unknown, and are thus able to better manage times of uncertainty. The practice of meditation with a focus on increasing in the moment awareness helps learners process their realities in psychologically healthy ways (Bennett and Dorjee 2016).

For instance, Equinox Holistic Alternative School in Toronto, Canada, which follows a curriculum based on the holistic education scholarship of John P. Miller, uses mindfulness in the classroom and illustrates how mindfulness can be embedded into daily classroom activities (Miller 2016). Some teachers here use mindfulness twice a day, once at the beginning of the day and then after lunch (Miller 2016). This routine can help students orient themselves to being at school and set an intention for their school day right at the start. Practicing mindfulness after lunch can have a settling effect on students, allowing them to feel focused and ready to learn.

The type of state of relaxed alertness is reminiscent of Csikszentmihalyi's (1997) work on flow and creativity, pointing to a state of being that allows the mind and body to feel more immersed in what is happening in the moment.

Teachers can be creative with these practices and even empower students to get involved with leadership roles. In one Equinox classroom, students are often called to lead mindfulness practices with their classmates (Miller 2016). The teacher provides the guidelines and parameters with regards to time and anchor (e.g., the breath, body, sounds, etc.) and the child leads the meditation (Miller 2016). Structured mindfulness practices like these can be as brief as a minute, depending on the amount of time available and age group of the students. Another teacher routinely leads students through meditation and mindful movement outdoors (Miller 2016). After lunch, students practice "noble silence," in addition to practicing mindful listening during class time to help students hone their ability to deeply listen (Miller 2016). This kind of practice has implications for developing the kind of deep awareness and observational powers (be it through listening, seeing, touching or engaging any of the five senses), that are linked to creative perceptions of the world (Root-Bernstein and Root-Bernstein 2013). Creative people often take in more stimuli and observe more from the world around them, providing fertile grounds for imagination and inspiration (Carson et al. 2003). Certain mindfulness practices, such as open-monitoring meditation, offer direct training into the practice of noticing one's experience—not only one's own thoughts, but anything or everything that may be available to observe through the senses in the moment. Furthermore, there are a range of mindfulness practices related to meditation, that provide learners with training in observation of direct experience. For instance, mindful eating can help people, particularly young children, to hone in on what they notice and observe through sense of taste; or mindful walking may focus closely on the experience of touch, pressure, weight, the movements of the body, or anything else occurring during the act of walking. Any of these offer a kind of unique support to creative being, through learning to see the world, as well as wellness practices that allow for and manage feelings that arise around uncertainty.

Techniques like noble silence, guided mindfulness practice, and mindful movements can be used throughout the day at key transition times or even during moments when the classroom environment is unsettled. Teachers may have a bell on hand, commonly used to signal the beginning or end of a mindfulness session, to call students' attention. When the class needs a reminder to settle, the sound of the bell may be used to alert children that it is time to go into silence and stop what they are doing to follow the sound of the bell. Teachers may also choose to bring their students' awareness into their bodies throughout the day. For instance, during a time when the teacher is reading aloud to their students, they may say something like: "as I am reading this, see if you can pay attention to your breath or your seat in your chair, etc." Or, "as we are listening to this recording, see if you can place your entire attention on the words and sounds of this recording…As you are writing, notice the pencil in your hand."

Mindful stretching might be done throughout the day in moments of restlessness. Emotion labeling can be used during social emotional sharing time. The teacher may even model this by sharing their particular emotion or mood of the day (as appropriate), even noting where they feel the emotion within their body. Or as noted, mindful eating could be introduced as a fun activity with a special snack and mindful walking could be cultivated in hallways between classrooms.

7.4.3.2   Coloring Mandalas

According to Jungian theory, a mandala is a circular image that represents "wholeness and unity of the archetypal Self" (van der Vennet and Serice 2012). Jung wrote about his own experience of creating mandalas to reduce the activity of the thinking mind and cultivate a sense of inner peace (van der Vennet and Serice 2012). Jung believed all people should have the experience of coloring mandalas. Research suggests that coloring mandalas is an effective tool for reducing anxiety, which is closely related to uncertainty. Drawing original mandalas (Henderson et al. 2007; van der Vennet and Serice 2012) or coloring already existing mandalas (Curry and Kasser 2005; van der Vennet and Serice 2012) have both been empirically shown to be effective ways to decrease anxiety.

Mandala images are relatively easy for teachers to access for their students. There are mandala coloring books available in bookstores and for order online (as well as freely available for online printing on various sites, e.g., https://printmandala.com/). Teachers may also direct students to draw their own images within a circle template. Drawings may be free form or a directive might be provided, linking images to a pre-existing aspect of curriculum content. Original representations of mandalas could also be used to have children represent their experiences in a new way. Instead of writing in a journal, students could generate a book of mandalas to express their thoughts, emotions, and experiences. Mandalas could also be used for purposes of enjoyment during choice time or for their calming effect as a way to center students before taking a test or approaching a difficult task.

Learning, exploration, or relaxation derived through mandala making or coloring could be further reinforced by identification of mandala-like images found in the outside world. For example, mandalas are prolific in the natural world or part of everyday life, such as the circle students may sit in on the carpet for circle time. This focus on individual and also collectively experienced mandalas mirrors the individual working with mandalas on their own, experiencing their own wholeness and unity, while also connecting with a sense of unity in the external world.

7.4.3.3   Saying Positive Affirmations

The practice of saying positive affirmations is something that can be implemented easily as it can take as little as 30 seconds a day. Positive affirmations are phrases that an individual recites to oneself. Examples of positive affirmations that students could use include: "I am proud of my creative hard work and can overcome the challenges in front of me;" "The mistakes I made yesterday are helping me do better today;" "My creativity grows when I take risks;" and "I give myself permission to fail." By engaging in the practice of saying positive affirmations, learners are learning a new way to talk to themselves. This has the potential to decrease damaging self-talk and reduce self-conscious thinking (Brown et al. 2007). The practice has the power to change negative thinking patterns and re-wire the brain, creating space for positive thinking (Stinson and Arthur 2013).

7.4.3.4   The Voice of Judgment

Another creativity-focused mindfulness concept is the "Voice of Judgment" (or VOJ) (see Henriksen and Shack 2020 or Workmon 2018). Conceptually, it is described by psychologists as an internal monologue (more prevalent for older children, secondary students, and adults, more so than young children). This internal voice critically judges our thoughts and actions, and affects our willingness to engage creatively (Ray and Myers 1989). Human beings have thousands of thoughts every day, and while some are helpful, many are counterproductive. These are paired with our own internal-mental voice that judges and filters personal experience. Ray and Myers (1989) describe this Voice of Judgment as central to creative identity. Creative identity is a continual and developmental process in life, and reducing or quieting self-judgment increases capacity for creative engagement.

One arts-based activity which can be done in almost any curriculum where students are being asked to create (described in Henriksen and Shack 2020), allows people to identify and persevere through the VOJ. Given the abstract nature of this, it may work better with older students (though conceptually it may be adapted for younger students). In this, each student creates a visual of their own design to represent their own VOJ as a person or a physical object/idea (through sketching, drawing, or any other simple arts-based means). Workmon (2018) showed how the technique may help students to identify limiting or self-defeating narratives in their own mind. By objectifying thoughts through an external personification, learners may be more comfortable in separating and letting go of negative self-narratives or other unhelpful thoughts. When used with arts and design students, this allowed more creative thinking to emerge in their project work. Such activities may be most effective when couched in discussion with students about their self-beliefs related to creativity, or feelings about their work in school and other settings.

Another related activity which can also 'flip the script' of the VOJ, is the Voice of Persistence (VOP) (Workmon 2018). Here, students identify an internal narrative or representation that helps them persevere and keep going when they are struggling, when they are unsure, or experiencing discomfort and uncertainty. In personifying that voice in an external or visual representation (e.g., a friend or family member, a person who inspires them, or even something like a sensation of sunshine or feeling of a warm glow). Activities such as this can be helpful because in letting students discuss and represent their inner monologues, they can become more mindfully aware of them, and more able to manage them through uncertainty and toward creativity.

7.5   Getting Started: Suggestions and Implications

With any change in practice, it can be challenging to figure out how or where to begin. An important first step before implementing any of these ideas is to accept that an adjustment in practice comes with inherent risk and uncertainty, so the most essential first step is accepting and even embracing the knowledge that uncomfortable spaces are ones where positive change can emerge. In embracing creativity and uncertainty, we suggest that educators reflect on the reason for change and the goals they have for students. Then, educators can use the suggestions we have provided, or others, to identify the change in behavior, practice, or thinking that they would like to see. We suggest that educators pick one small thing to implement that will help bring about this change. For example, if an identified goal is to support high schoolers with the management of stress, a simple change might be to include a few minutes in each class period for students to self-reflect on their VOJ and to engage in some positive self-affirmations that they create or are provided by the teacher. Large scale change may be overwhelming, and many K-12 educators simply do not have the power to make huge changes to curriculum or practice. But, small changes to daily routines that are easy to implement can add up to powerful practices over time and provide important opportunities to support students.

7.6   Conclusion

We inhabit an uncertain world, in a complex society, with an unpredictable future. Learners must be prepared to act creatively through this uncertainty, to develop unique and unexpected solutions to problems we may not yet have encountered (in addition to the ones we already face). While we need learners to be creatively prepared to be novel thinkers and flexible agents in the world, uncertainty can upend creative processes and turn people away from their own creative potential. Schools rarely ameliorate this, instead exacerbating it through a focus on getting the correct answer, as opposed to pushing through the discomfort into the open-ended nature of creative challenges. The kinds of open-ended, project-based, transdisciplinary creative challenges that allow for creativity are clearly needed in educational settings, and along the way, teachers and students may be served by mindfulness practices to recognize, allow and support uncertainty. These practices may also support creative development through increased ability to observe the world, and to relate to the self in ways that allow for fresh framings and creative development, along with an evolving relationship to uncertainty itself.

Engaging in creative work involves risk and uncertainty, bringing possible fears of failure, negative self-judgment, and withdrawal or refusal to engage in creative acts. Mindfulness offers a way to mitigate these feelings by supporting one's own recognition of the value of these moments and the role that they play in the creative process. Our collective future depends on the creative potential of everyone. Educational systems must support the creative development of young people, and eschew the tendency towards compliance and conformity. By recognizing and allowing uncertainty, and providing the tools and practices of mindfulness, educators can start to create spaces where risk-taking is normalized and creativity is practiced intentionally.

References

Abbenante, J., (1994). Review [Review of the book *Photo Art Therapy: A Jungian Perspective,* 1992 by Jerry L Fryrear and Irene E. Corbit]. *American Journal of Art Therapy, 33,* 22-24.

Baas, M., Nevicka, B., & Ten Velden, F. S. (2014). Specific mindfulness skills differentially predict creative performance. *Personality and Social Psychology Bulletin, 40*(9), 1092-1106.

Beghetto, R. (2010). Creativity in the classroom. In J. C. Kaufman & R. J. Sternberg (Eds). *The Cambridge Handbook of Creativity* (pp. 447-459). Cambridge University Press.

Beghetto, R. A. (2016). Creative learning: A fresh look. *Journal of Cognitive Education and Psychology,* 15, pp. 6-23.

Beghetto, R. A., & Dilley, A. E. (2016). Creative aspirations or pipe dreams? Toward understanding creative mortification in children and adolescents: Creative aspirations or pipe dreams? *New Directions for Child and Adolescent Development, 2016* (151), 85–95.

Beghetto R.A. (2020) Uncertainty. In: Glăveanu V. (eds) The Palgrave Encyclopedia of the Possible. Palgrave Macmillan, Cham. doi:https://doi.org/10.1007/978-3-319-98390-5_122-1

Bennett, K., & Dorjee, D. (2016). The impact of a mindfulness-based stress reduction course (MBSR) on well-being and academic attainment of sixth-form students. *Mindfulness, 7*(1), 105-114.

Bensen, H., (1993). The relaxation response. In Goleman, D., & Gurin, J. (Eds.), *Mind Body Medicine How to Use Your Mind for Better Health,* pp. 125-149.

Brown, K. W., Ryan, R. M., & Creswell, J. D. (2007). Mindfulness: Theoretical foundations and evidence for its salutary effects. *Psychological Inquiry, 18*(4), 211–237.

Carson, S. H., Peterson, J. B., & Higgins, D. M. (2003). Decreased latent inhibition is associated with increased creative achievement in high-functioning individuals. *Journal of personality and social psychology, 85*(3), 499.

Carson, S. H., & Langer, E. J. (2006). Mindfulness and self-acceptance. *Journal of rational-emotive and cognitive-behavior therapy, 24*(1), 29-43.

Cassou, M., & Cubley, S., (1995). *Life, paint, and passion: Reclaiming the magic of spontaneous expression.* Tarcher Penguin.

Chan, S., & Yuen, M. (2014). Personal and environmental factors affecting teachers' creativity-fostering practices in Hong Kong. *Thinking Skills and Creativity, 12,* 69–77.

Chiesa, A., Calati, R., & Serretti, A. (2011). Does mindfulness training improve cognitive abilities? A systematic review of neuropsychological findings. *Clinical psychology review, 31*(3), 449-464.

Claxton, G. (1997). *Hare brain, tortoise mind.* Fourth Estate.

Craft, A. (2010). *Creativity and education futures: Learning in a digital age.* Trentham Books Ltd.

Craft, A., Hall, E., & Costello, R. (2014). Passion: Engine of creative teaching in an English university. *Thinking Skills and Creativity,* 13, 91–105.

Cremin, T. (2006). Creativity, uncertainty and discomfort: Teachers as writers. *Cambridge Journal of Education, 36*(3), 415-433.

Csikszentmihalyi, M. (1997). *Flow and the psychology of discovery and invention.* Harper Perennial.

Csikszentmihalyi, M., & Wolfe, R. (2014). New conceptions and research approaches to creativity: Implications of a systems perspective for creativity in education. In *The systems model of creativity* (pp. 161-184). Springer.

Curry, N. A., & Kasser, T. (2005). Can coloring mandalas reduce anxiety?. *Art Therapy*, *22*(2), 81-85.

Dewett, T. (2007). Linking intrinsic motivation, risk taking, and employee creativity in an R&D environment. *R&d Management*, *37*(3), 197–208.

Dewey, J. (1934/2005). *Art as experience*. Perigee Books.

Ellenberg, D., & Hanson, R. (2020). Friendly and fearless: Combining kindness and assertiveness in important relationships [PowerPoint slides.] Greater Good Science Center, UC Berkeley.

Erez, M., & Nouri, R. (2010). Creativity: The influence of cultural, social, and work contexts. *Management and Organization Review*, *6*(3), 351-370.

Fisher, N., (2021, June 15). What is impermanence in Buddha nature. Lion's Roar Foundation. https://www.lionsroar.com/impermanence-is-buddha-nature-embrace-changemay-2012/

Fisher, R. (2006). Still thinking: The case for meditation with children. *Thinking skills and creativity*, *1*(2), 146-151.

Forgeard, M. J., & Elstein, J. G. (2014). Advancing the clinical science of creativity. *Frontiers in psychology*, *5*, 613.

Garland, E. L., Gaylord, S.A., Fredrickson, B.L., (2011). Positive reapparaisal mediates the stress-reductive effects of mindfulness: An upward spiral process. *Mindfulness, 2*, 59-67.

Gladwell, M. (2005). *Blink: The power of thinking without thinking*. New York, NY: Little, Brown and Company.

Glăveanu, V. P., & Tanggaard, L. (2014). Creativity, identity, and representation: Towards a socio-cultural theory of creative identity. *New Ideas in Psychology*, *34*, 12–21.

Glăveanu, V. P., Hanchett Hanson, M., Baer, J., Barbot, B., Clapp, E. P., Corazza, G. E., ... & Sternberg, R. J. (2020). Advancing creativity theory and research: Asocio-cultural manifesto. *The Journal of Creative Behavior, 54*(3), 741–745.

Greenberg, J., Reiner, K., & Meiran, N. (2012). "Mind the trap": Mindfulness practice reduces cognitive rigidity. *PloS one*, *7*(5), e36206.

Guilford, J. P. (1950). Creativity. *American Psychologist*. 5. 444-454.

Heinonen, S., & Hiltunen, E. (2012). Creative foresight space and the futures window: Using visual weak signals to enhance anticipation and innovation. *Futures*, *44*(3), 248-256.

Henderson, P., Rosen, D., & Mascaro, N. (2007). Empirical study on the healing nature of mandalas. *Psychology of Aesthetics, Creativity, and the Arts*, *1*(3), 148.

Henriksen, D., Henderson, M., Creely, E., Carvalho, A. A., Cernochova, M., Dash, D., Davis, T. & Mishra, P. (2021). Creativity and risk-taking in teaching and learning settings: Insights from six international narratives. *International Journal of Educational Research Open*, 2.

Henriksen, D., Mishra, P., & Mehta, R. (2015). Novel, effective, whole: Toward a NEW framework for evaluations of creative products. *Journal of Technology and Teacher Education*, *23*(3), 455-478.

Henriksen, D., Richardson, C., & Shack, K. (2020). Mindfulness and creativity: Implications for thinking and learning. *Thinking Skills and Creativity, 37,* 1-10.

Henriksen, D., & Shack, K. (2020). Creativity-focused mindfulness for student well-being. Kappa Delta Pi Record, 56(4), 170-175.

Jedrczak, A., Beresford, M., & Clements, G. (1985). The TM-Sidhi program, pure consciousness, creativity and intelligence. *The Journal of Creative Behavior*, 19, 270-275.

Justo, C. F., Mañas, I. M., & Ayala, E. S. (2014). Improving the graphic creativity levels of Latin American high school students currently living in Spain by means of a mindfulness program. Procedia-Social and Behavioral Sciences, 132, 229-234.

Kabat-Zinn, J., (2013). *Full catastrophe living: Using the wisdom of your body and mind to face stress, pain, and illness*. Bantam Books.

Kudesia, R. S. (2019). Mindfulness as metacognitive practice. *Academy of Management Review*, *44*(2), 405-423.

Lebuda, I., Zabelina, D. L., & Karwowski, M. (2016). Mind full of ideas: A meta-analysis of the mindfulness–creativity link. *Personality and Individual Differences, 93*, 22-26.

Lev-Aladgem, S., (1998). Creating a therapeutic playful dialogue with a patient suffering from Parkinson's Disease. *The Arts in Psychotherapy, 25*(4), 237-243.

Luke, A. (2011). Generalizing across borders: Policy and the limits of educational science. *Educational researcher, 40*(8), 367-377.

Miller, J. P., (2010). Educating for wisdom. In Brantmeier, E.J., Lin, J., & Miller, J.P., (Eds.), *Spirituality, Religion, and Peace Education,* pp. 261-275. Information Age Publishing, Inc.

Miller, J.P., (2016). Equinox: portrait of a holistic school. *International Journal of Children's Spirituality.* 21(3-4), 283-301.

McNiff, S., (1998). *Trust the process: An artist's guide to letting go.* Publications.

Menakem, R., (2017). *My grandmother's hands: Racialized trauma and the pathway to mending our hearts and bodies.* Central Recovery Press.

Moore, A., & Malinowski, P. (2009). Meditation, mindfulness and cognitive flexibility. *Consciousness and cognition, 18*(1), 176-186.

Moran, S. (2010). The roles of creativity in society. In J. C. Kaufman & R. J. Sternberg (Eds). *The Cambridge Handbook of Creativity* (p. 74-90). Cambridge University Press.

Peschl, M. F. (2019). Design and innovation as co-creating and co-becoming with the future. *Design Management Journal, 14*(1), 4-14.

Prabhu, V., Sutton, C., & Sauser, W. (2008). Creativity and certain personality traits: Understanding the mediating effect of intrinsic motivation. *Creativity Research Journal, 20*(1), 53-66.

Preiss, D. D., & Cosmelli, D. (2017). Mind wandering, creative writing, and the self. In M. Karwowski & J. Kaufman (Eds.). *The Creative Self* (pp. 301-313). Academic Press.

Ray, M. L., & Myers, R. (1989). *Creativity in business.* Main Street Books.

Robinson, K. (2011). *Out of our minds.* Capstone Publishing.

Root-Bernstein, R., & Root-Bernstein, M. (2013). *Sparks of genius: The 13 thinking tools of the world's most creative people.* HMH.

Runco, M. A., & Jaeger, G. J. (2012). The standard definition of creativity. *Creativity research journal, 24*(1), 92-96.

Sawyer, R. K. (2012). *Explaining creativity: The science of human innovation (2nd ed.)* Oxford University Press.

Schmidt, M., (2005). Individuation: Finding oneself in analysis – taking risks and making sacrifices. *Journal of Analytical Psychology, 50*(5), 595-616.

Sedlmeier, P., Eberth, J., Schwarz, M., Zimmermann, D., Haarig, F., Jaeger, S., & Kunze, S. (2012). The psychological effects of meditation: a meta-analysis. *Psychological bulletin, 138*(6), 1139.

Shah, P., (2020). *What is a chakra? A primer of the chakra system.* https://chopra.com/articles/what-is-a-chakra

Shapiro, S. L., Carlson, L. E., Astin, J. A., & Freedman, B. (2006). Mechanisms of mindfulness. *Journal of clinical psychology, 62*(3), 373-386.

Smalley, S. L., & Winston, D. (2010). *Fully present: The science, art, and practice of mindfulness.* DaCapo Press.

Starko, A. J. (1995). *Creativity in the classroom: Schools of curious delight.* Longman.

Sternberg, R.J., & Kaufman, J. C.. (2010). Constraints on creativity: obvious and not so obvious. In J. C. Kaufman & R. J. Sternberg (Eds). *The Cambridge Handbook of Creativity.* 467-482. Cambridge University Press.

Stevenson, C. E., Kleibeuker, S. W., de Dreu, C. K. W., & Crone, E. A. (2014). Training creative cognition: adolescence as a flexible period for improving creativity. *Frontiers in Human Neuroscience, 8.*

Stinson, B., & Arthur, D. (2013). A novel EEG for alpha brain state training, neurobiofeedback and behavior change. *Complementary therapies in clinical practice, 19*(3), 114-118.

Symonds, J., & Hargreaves, L. (2014). Emotional and motivational engagement at school transition: A qualitative stage-environment fit study. *The Journal of Early Adolescence*, 36(1), 54-85.

van der Vennet, R., & Serice, S., (2012). Can coloring mandalas reduce anxiety? A replication study. *Art Therapy: Journal of the American Art Therapy Association, 29*(2), 87-92.

Weinstein, N., Brown, K. W., & Ryan, R. M. (2009). A multi-method examination of the effects of mindfulness on stress attribution, coping, and emotional well-being. *Journal of research in personality, 43*(3), 374-385.

Williams, J. M. G., & Kabat-Zinn, J. (2011). Mindfulness: Diverse perspectives on its meaning, origins, and multiple applications at the intersection of science and dharma. *Contemporary Buddhism, 12*(1), 1-18.

Workmon, M. (2018). The failure project: Self-efficacy, mindset, grit and navigating perceived failures in design and the arts. Arizona State University. Retrieved from ProQuest Dissertations and Theses.

Zhao, Y. (2012). *World class learners: Educating creative and entrepreneurial students.* Corwin Press.

Chapter 8
From Uncertainty to Insight: An Autocatalytic Framework

Liane Gabora and Mike Steel

Abstract We show how uncertainty and insight can be modeled using Reflexively Autocatalytic Foodset-generated (RAF) networks. RAF networks have been used to model the self-organization of adaptive networks associated with the origin and early evolution of both biological life, and the kind of cognitive structure necessary for cultural evolution. The RAF approach is applicable in these seemingly disparate cases because it provides a theoretical framework for formally describing systems composed of elements that interact to form new elements, and for studying under what conditions these (initial + new) elements collectively become integrated wholes of various types. Here, the elements are mental representations, and the whole is a conceptual network. The initial components—referred to as *foodset items*—are mental representations that are innate, or were acquired through social learning or individual learning (of *pre-existing* information). The new elements—referred to as *foodset-derived items*—are mental representations that result from creative thought (resulting in *new* information). The demarcation into foodset versus foodset-derived elements provides a natural means of (i) grounding abstract concepts in direct experiences (foodset-derived elements emerge through 'reactions' that can be traced back to foodset items), and (ii) precisely describing and tracking how new ideas emerge from earlier ones. Thus, RAFs can model how endogenous conceptual restructuring results in new conduits by which uncertainties can be resolved. A source of uncertainty is modeled as an element that resists integration into the conceptual network. This is described in terms of a *maxRAF* containing the bulk of the individual's mental representations. Uncertainty produces arousal, which catalyzes one or more interactions amongst mental representations. We illustrate the approach using the historical example of Kekulé's realization that benzene (Benzene is an organic chemical compound composed of six carbon atoms

L. Gabora (✉)
Department of Psychology, University of British Columbia Fipke Centre for Innovative Research, Kelowna, British Columbia, Canada
e-mail: liane.gabora@ubc.ca

M. Steel
University of Canterbury, Christchurch, New Zealand

© Springer Nature Switzerland AG 2022
R. A. Beghetto, G. J. Jaeger (eds.), *Uncertainty: A Catalyst for Creativity, Learning and Development*, Creativity Theory and Action in Education 6, https://doi.org/10.1007/978-3-030-98729-9_8

joined in a planar ring with one hydrogen atom attached to each.) is ring-shaped through a reverie of a snake biting its tail. We show how a single conceptual change can precipitate a cascade of reiterated cognitive 'reactions' (self-organized critical-ity) that affect the network's global structure, and discuss why this may help explain why cognitive restructuring can be therapeutic. Finally, we discuss educational implications of the RAF approach.

8.1 Introduction

Creativity flourishes in situations that involve both constraints and uncertainty (Beghetto 2019), or what has been referred to as *enabling constraints* (Kauffman 2016). Ultimately, both the constraints and the uncertainty originate in the potential-ity of *concepts:* mental constructs such as DOG or FREEDOM that enable us to interpret new situations in terms of similar previous ones. By the *potentiality* of concepts, we mean their capacity to shift in meaning in ways that are often non-trivial, or even defy classical logic, when they combine or serve as contexts for one another (Aerts et al. 2009, 2013, 2016; Hampton 1988; Osherson and Smith 1981). For example, though a seemingly defining property of the concept ISLAND is the property 'surrounded by water,' in the context 'kitchen,' as in KITCHEN ISLAND, the property 'surrounded by water' is not only unusual, but a sign of trouble!

Accordingly, our group has invested considerable effort into mathematically modeling how creativity derives from such shifts in meaning when concepts com-bine (Gabora 2017; Gabora and Carbert 2015; Gabora and Kitto 2017), and synthe-sizing these results with what happens during concept combination at the neural level (Gabora 2010, 2018; Gabora and Ranjan 2013). In such models, *constraints arise* because concepts usually appear in predictable contexts; for example, typical contexts for ISLAND are DESERT (as in DESERT ISLAND), or REMOTE (as in REMOTE ISLAND). *Potentiality arises* from the fact that concepts often appear in atypical contexts, and indeed there is no way of circumscribing the possible con-texts for any given concept. Moreover, as the KITCHEN ISLAND example shows, atypical contexts can dramatically alter the properties of a given concept, and the KITCHEN ISLAND example is far from extraordinary. For example, it would seem that all instances of ISLAND have the property 'larger than a breadbox' but TOY ISLAND does not; similarly, one might expect that all instances of the concept BUNNY possess the property 'has a heart,' but of course CHOCOLATE BUNNY does not. *Uncertainty arises* because to the extent that one cannot completely describe a situation in terms of all relevant concepts and how they mutually serve as contexts for each other (including order effects), one cannot precisely know how to act in that situation, or accurately predict what will happen.

Although in creativity research one often comes across the term 'problem domain,' concepts readily 'jump' domains; for example, BUNNY is in the ANIMAL domain, but CHOCOLATE is in the FOOD domain. This is particularly true when concepts are used creatively, as occurs in metaphor (Lakoff 1993), analogy (Gentner

Fig. 8.1 Photograph of ambiguous wood-cuttings taken from the front cover of (Hofstadter 1979). The top 'trip-let' (as the author refers to them) is not simply a rotated version of the one below it; it is a different shape. (Used with permission)

1983; Holyoak and Thagard 1996), or cross-domain transfer, in which a source from one domain (e.g., music) inspires or influences a creative work in another (e.g., painting) (Ranjan et al. 2013; Scotney et al. 2019). For example, George Mestral's invention of Velcro was inspired by analogy to burdock root seeds (Freeman and Golden 1997) which, in turn, inspired 'shoelace-less runners' (or sneakers). Ingredients for the creative process can come from just about anywhere. Therefore, understanding what happens when concepts come together in unusual ways is only part of the story of how a creator creates. Another part is: why does the creator bring certain concepts together in the first place? How is it that the creator comes to look at a problem from a particular perspective? To answer this we must know something about the overall organization of the mind.

The relationship between uncertainty and creativity, and what it means to approach it at the concept-combination level versus the global conceptual network level, can be understood metaphorically by examining the photograph in Fig. 8.1 of woodcuttings with light shining on them from three different directions, yielding three differently shaped shadows: that of a G, an E, and a B. Without going into the details of why this metaphor is particularly apt,[1] consider the situation in which you cannot see the woodcutting, and have to guess its shape by examining the two-dimensional shadows cast. Three different shadows are all projections of the same underlying object. You are in a state of uncertainty regarding its three-dimensional shape, but the two-dimensional shadows provide constraints on the space of viable answers. In the language of the above-mentioned concept combination models (which use a mathematical framework that was first used in quantum mechanics), we can refer to the state of the woodcutting when no light is shining on it as its *ground state*. We would say that the woodcutting has the potentiality to *actualize* different ways, and to actualize in one of these ways requires a *context*, in this case, light shining from a particular direction.

---

[1] This is done elsewhere (Scotney et al. 2020).

Figure 8.1 sheds light (so to speak) on many aspects of the creative process. Consider first the upper woodcutting. Your uncertainty regarding the problem solution or creative output is represented by your uncertainty as to the actual shape of the woodcutting. The process of coming to better understand it by looking at it from different perspectives is represented by the act of shining a light on it from different angles. First, this metaphor suggests a way of understanding the underlying form or conception of a creative idea that is consistent with the models of concept combination. Since the different sketches of a painting, or prototypes of an invention, take different forms when expressed in the physical world, it is tempting to assume that that they derive from different underlying conceptions in the mind. Thus, it seems self-evident that a stream of creative thought entails the generation of multiple distinct, separate ideas. However, much as the three shadows of each wood-cutting are projections of the same underlying object, there may be a single underlying as-yet-poorly articulated vision of the creative project that manifests as different sketch or prototype ideas when looked at from different perspectives.

Second, the woodcutting metaphor suggests a way of envisioning what is happening as you hone or 'reflect on' an idea. Midway through a creative process, you may have an inkling of how to proceed, but not yet know whether, or exactly how, it could work; the idea is 'half-baked.' You entertain wildly different ways of looking at it, and these different perspectives yield wildly different 'takes' on the idea, much as shining light on the woodcutting from different directions yields different shadow-letters. However, over time, your reflections on the problem converge. You start looking at it in similar ways, and the images that come to mind overlap more, and seem less like 'different ideas' and more like 'variants of one idea,' much as shining light on the upper woodcarving from the right at slightly different angles would yield similar shadows. Although some might be wobbly or distorted, they would all be G-shaped.

Third, the woodcutting metaphor provides a nice visual explanation of why we cannot understand the creative process without investigating the global structure of the creator's conceptual network. Note that the two wood-cuttings in Fig. 8.1 have different shapes, yet they yield the same three shadows. To distinguish the shape of the woodcutting above from the one below would require that light be shown on them from still more angles, casting shadows that would not look like any particular letters we know. Similarly, the more complex one's unborn creative idea, the more honing steps required to discern its underlying form.

Note also that the situation in creativity may be more complex than the woodcuttings scenario because each time you think about the creative problem from a particular angle, that thought may feed back and alter your conception of the problem. (It's as if each time you cast a shadow on a woodcarving, that slightly altered the shape of the woodcarving.) In this case, the order of the perspectives from which the problem was looked at alters the solution to the problem. The upshot is that to understand the creative process we need to understand how and why the creator looks at the problem from a particular sequence of contexts, in a particular order. In turn, to understand this, we must look beyond models of concept combination to the global structure of how a creator's concepts are woven together into a conceptual network, and how this network is restructured, fueled by the creator's needs, goals, and desires. For this, creativity research must turn to network science (Kenett 2018).

This chapter proposes a method for modelling creative insight and its origins in uncertainty using a certain kind of network, referred to as the Reflexively Autocatalytic Foodset Generated (RAF) network. The term *reflexively* is used in its mathematical sense, meaning that each part is related to the whole. The term *autocatalytic* will be defined more precisely shortly, but for now it refers to the fact that the whole can be reconstituted through interactions amongst its parts. The term *foodset* refers to the elements that are initially present, as opposed to those that are the products of interactions amongst them. In the RAF model developed here, these elements are *mental representations* (MRs)[2] composed of one or more concepts, and the network is a conceptual network: a web of shared properties, contexts, associations, and relationships of logic, causation, and so forth, that bind them together. The chapter begins with a brief introduction to the literature on analogy and cross-domain thinking. Next, we introduce RAF networks and their application to cognition, and present a RAF network model of insight through cross-domain analogical transfer. We close with some thoughts on educational applications of the model, followed by conclusions, and suggestions for future research. A glossary of terms is provided in Appendix A, and a list of acronyms is provided in Appendix B.

8.2   The Relationship Between Uncertainty and Insight

We now discuss the creative processes that will be modeled in this chapter: cross-domain transfer, analogy, and self-organized criticality.

8.2.1   Analogy and Cross-Domain Transfer

Cross-domain thinking is ubiquitous in the history of innovation (Enkel and Gassmann 2010; Feinstein 2006; Kalogerakis et al. 2010). Cross-domain thinking often takes the form of analogy, which involves reducing uncertainty by mapping correspondences between something you don't understand and something else that you do understand which shares its deep structure. Analogy is central to our human-ness (Hofstadter and Sander 2013; Holyoak and Thagard 1996). A well-known example of analogical transfer is Kekulé's discovery of the structure of benzene by visual analogy to a snake biting its tail (Findlay 1965). This example reveals an interesting aspect of the phenomenon: the information from the source domain is

---

[2] Although we use the terms 'mental representation,' we are sympathetic with the view (common amongst ecological psychologists and in the quantum cognition community) that what we call mental representations do not 'represent,' but act as contextually elicited bridges between the mind and the world.

not always retrieved from memory in the form it was originally encoded. MRs from memory may need to be modified to be useful as a source (Holyoak and Thagard 1996). (Kekulé had likely never seen a snake bite its tail (though he may have encountered the symbol of the uroboros); however, his daydreaming mind modified the concept SNAKE in a way that elicited this insight.) Alternatively, the cross-domain source material may arise by noticing something in the environment. For example, the concept of wing warping—the key insight in the invention of the air-plane—occurred to Wilbur Wright as he idly twisted an inner tube box (Heppenheimer 2003). He realized that by twisting the trailing edges of the wings in opposite direc-tions it would be possible to control the direction of the aircraft, thereby removing the remaining fundamental obstacle to human flight.

Cross-domain inspiration is also prevalent in the arts; indeed, a film score attempts to translate the emotional tone of an unfolding plot into music. A well-known example of cross-domain inspiration in music is Schubert's 'Hymn to Mary', also known as 'Ellens dritter Gesang' ('Ellen's Third Song') or (more famously) 'Ave Maria.' This song from the opera *The Lady of the Lake* was inspired by Sir Walter Scott's epic poem of the same name (Deutsch 1928). Indeed, the phenome-non of cross-domain creativity may go back much further, as the earliest stringed instrument may have been derived from the bow and arrow (Montagu 2017).

The cross-domain thought that goes into a creative work is not always evident in the work itself. The prevalence of cross-domain influences on creativity was exam-ined in two studies, one with creative experts, and the other with undergraduate stu-dents from diverse academic backgrounds (Scotney et al. 2019). Participants listed both their creative outputs, and the influences (sources of inspiration) associated with each of these outputs. In both studies, cross-domain influences on creativity were found to be widespread, and indeed more frequent than within-domain sources of inspiration. In another study in which painters were instructed to paint what a par-ticular piece of music would 'look like' if it were a painting, naïve participants were able to correctly identify at significantly above chance which piece of music inspired which painting (Ranjan et al. 2013). Although the medium of expression was may be different, something of its essence remained sufficiently intact for people to detect a resemblance between the new creative output and its inspirational source (Ganesh & Gabora, 2022). These studies show that even when the creative output lies squarely in one domain, the process giving rise to it may be rooted in another.

Analogy plays a role not only in the discovery and development of ideas, but in the pedagogical process by which they are transmitted and learned by others (Holyoak and Thagard 1996). Analogies are often used by parents and educators to explain abstract, or unfamiliar ideas, in terms of concrete or familiar ones. For example, analogy to existing methods of gene editing played a role in the discovery of CRISPR-Cas9 technology (Doudna and Charpentier 2014)[3], and its discoverers

---

[3] We note that the invention of the CRISPR–Cas9 gene-editing tool is hotly contested; although Doudna and Charpentier were awarded the Nobel prize for its discovery, Feng Zhang at the Broad Institute of MIT and Harvard, has won several key decisions by the US Patent and Trademark Office (USPTO)."

explain how it works through analogies to a weapons defence system and a Swiss army knife (Doudna and Sternberg 2017; Thagard 2019). Thus, analogies influence—sometimes misleadingly—how new concepts are understood, and developed further. Only network models can account for such lines of creative influence.

8.2.2   Self-Organized Criticality

Innovation may be indicative of a cognitive phase transition arising through self-organized criticality (SOC) (Gabora 1998, 2017; Schilling 2005; Stephen et al. 2009). SOC is a phenomenon wherein, through simple local interactions, complex systems tend to find a critical state poised at the cusp of a transition between order and chaos, from which a single small perturbation occasionally exerts a disproportionately large effect (Bak et al. 1988). In a sense, self-organized criticality in cognitive enterprises is like kicking the uncertainty down the road; answering one scientific question (or developing a piece of art or technology) leads to another, which leads to another, and so forth.

The signature of SOC is an inverse power law relationship between the magnitude of a critical event, and the frequency of critical events of that magnitude. Perhaps the best-known example of SOC is the theory of *punctuated equilibrium,* which posits that change in biological species is restricted to rare, rapid events interspersed amongst prolonged periods of stasis (Eldridge and Gould 1972). It has been suggested that insight constitutes a form of punctuated equilibrium (Gabora 2017). SOC gives rise to structure that exhibits sparse connectivity, short average path lengths, and strong local clustering. Other indications of SOC include long-range correlations in space and time, and rapid reconfiguration in response to external inputs. There is evidence of SOC in the human brain, e.g., with respect to phase synchronisation of large-scale functional networks (Kitzbichler et al. 2009). There is also evidence of SOC at the cognitive level; word association studies have shown that concepts are clustered and sparsely connected, with some having many associates and others few (Nelson et al. 1998, 2013). Thus, conceptual networks exhibit the sparse connectivity, short average path lengths, and strong local clustering characteristic of self-organized complexity, and exhibit some aspects of 'small world' structure (Bassett and Bullmore 2006; Steyvers and Tenenbaum 2005; Zurn and Bassett 2020). Like other SOC systems, a mind may function within a regime midway between order (systematic progression of thoughts), and chaos (everything reminds one of everything else). Much as most perturbations in SOC systems have little effect but the occasional perturbation has a dramatic effect, most thoughts also have little effect on one's worldview, but occasionally, one thought triggers another, which triggers another, and so forth in a chain reaction of conceptual change. This is consistent with findings that large-scale creative conceptual change often follows a series of small conceptual changes (Ward et al. 1997), and with evidence that power laws and catastrophe models are applicable to the diffusion of innovations (Jacobsen and Guastello 2011).

8.3 Reflexively Autocatalytic and Foodset Generated (RAF) Networks

We now introduce the networks that we will use to model analogical cross-domain transfer, beginning with the rationale and basic idea behind the approach, followed by the mathematical framework.

8.3.1 Rationale for the Approach

The RAF approach offers a number of benefits over other conceptual network, semantic network, and neural network models:

1. **Semantic grounding.** The distinction between foodset elements and foodset-derived elements provides a natural means of grounding abstract concepts in direct experiences; foodset-derived elements emerge through interactions (which for historical reasons are sometimes referred to as 'reactions'), that can be traced back to foodset elements.
2. **Reactivity of ideas.** The extent to which one MR modifies the meaning of another is referred to here as its *reactivity*. A given MR's reactivity varies depending on the other MRs present in working memory.[4] MRs activate, or 'react with' each other by aligning with needs (e.g., the need to resolve uncertainty or cognitive dissonance, or to solve a problem), and the emotions they elicit. Thus, whereas conventional node-and-edge network models generally require external input to continue processing, RAF networks 'catalyze' conceptual change endogenously, resulting in new conduits by which needs and goals can be met. A RAF network self-organizes through conceptual restructuring, the effects of which can percolate throughout the network, altering its global structure. By recursively inciting interactions amongst each other (which, again for historical reasons, is sometimes referred to as not inciting but *catalyzing*), MRs self-organize into new arrangements that can be formally described. Treating MRs as not merely passive participants in spreading activation, but active catalysts of conceptual change is central to our strategy for capturing the flexibility of human cognition. It enables RAFs to be used to model cognitive development during childhood of the kind of conceptual structure that actively participates in the generation of the cultural novelty (Gabora et al. 2022). MRs are not only activated by stimuli, and participate in pattern learning, but form a network that is self-organizing and entropy-reducing, and conceptual restructuring can percolate well beyond the problem domain and affect the network's global structure

---

[4] For example, the degree to which PYLON qualifies as an instance of HAT increases in the context 'worn to be funny' Veloz et al. (2011).

including one's self-concept, and thereby affect wellbeing. This is consistent with findings that immersion in a creative task can be therapeutic, and accompanied by a sense of release (Barron 1963; Forgeard 2013).

3. **Tracking innovation within and across conceptual networks.** The RAF approach tags mental representations with their source, i.e., whether they were (1) innate, or acquired through social learning or individual learning (of *pre-existing* information), or (2) the result of creative thought (resulting in *new* information). This demarcation makes it possible to trace innovations back to the individuals that generated them, and describe and track how new ideas and creative outputs emerge from previous ones.[5] Creative thought gets lumped in with individual learning, but there is an important distinction between them. In *individual learning*—obtaining pre-existing information from the environment by nonsocial means through direct perception—the information does not change form once the individual knows it. Noticing for oneself that lightning tends to be followed by thunder is an example of individual learning. In contrast, in *abstract thought*—the processing of internally sourced mental contents—the information is in flux (Barsalou 2005), and when this incremental honing process results in the generation of new and useful or pleasing ideas, behaviour, or artifacts, it is said to be *creative* (Basadur 1995; Chan and Schunn 2015a; Feinstein 2006; Gabora 2017).

   Distinguishing between individual learning and creative thought enables us to monitor at what point in a cultural lineage each new idea (or idea component) first arose, assess the relative contribution of these different sources on the emerging conceptual networks of individuals and social groups, and track cumulative change step by step.

4. **Integrative framework.** The RAF approach offers an established formal framework for integrating creativity research with the explosively growing field of network science, and embedding this synthesis in the study of self-organizing structures and their role in evolutionary processes. RAFs replicate and evolve, as demonstrated (both in theory and in simulation studies), which makes them a viable candidate for explaining how cultural information replicates and evolves (Gabora and Steel 2017, 2020a, b, 2021; Ganesh and Gabora, in press). Indeed, the fact that autocatalytic networks (such as RAFs) have proven useful for modelling the origins of both biological (Hordijk and Steel 2016; Steel et al. 2019; Vasas et al. 2012; Xavier et al. 2020), and cultural evolution (Gabora 1998, 2000; Gabora and Steel 2017, 2020a, b, 2021)[6], suggests that RAF theory may provide a broad conceptual framework that is applicable to the origins and early stages of

---

[5] We note that in the cultural evolution literature, much has been made of 'Rogers' paradox' (that social learning can invade a population without increasing its fitness). However, the apparent 'paradox' is an artifact of assumptions built into Rogers' simulation (Gabora and Tseng 2017; Kharratzadeh et al. 2017), including that it incorporates social learning and individual learning (of existing information) but not the creative generation of new information. In the real world, whether or not the environment is temporally varying, we benefit from finding creative new ways of conceptualizing and responding to this world.

[6] For related approaches, see (Andersson and Törnberg 2019; Cabell and Valsiner 2013; Muthukrishna et al. 2018).

any evolutionary process (Gabora and Steel 2021). The framework is consistent with the theory that humans possess two levels of complex, adaptive structure: an organismal level, and a psychological level, with the mind playing the role in cultural evolution that the soma plays in biological evolution (Barton 1994; Gabora 2004; Maturana and Varela 1973). The self-sustaining, self-protecting nature of a conceptual network is evident in the tendency to reduce cognitive dissonance, resolve inconsistencies, and preserve existing schemas in the face of new information. This is not merely an extension of organismal needs; indeed, these two levels of endogenous control can be at odds (e.g., a scientist immersed in solving a problem may neglect offspring or forget to eat). Although the contents of a conceptual network change over time, it maintains integrity as a relatively coherent whole. Conceptual structure replicates and evolves, in a piecemeal manner, when individuals share ideas and perspectives.

Because a RAF captures the nature of a structure *as a whole,* a cognitive RAF is, by necessity, abstract. It does not distinguish between semantic memory (memory of words, concepts, propositions, and world knowledge) and episodic memory (memory of personal experiences); indeed, we are sympathetic to the view that these are not as distinct as once thought (Kwantes 2005). For a detailed comparison between cognitive RAFs and other models used in cognitive science, we refer the reader to papers in which RAFs have been used to model the origin of cultural evolution (Gabora and Steel 2017, 2020a), and the transition to behavioural and cognitive modernity (Gabora and Steel 2020b).

8.3.2   Autocatalytic Networks

The theory of autocatalytic networks grew out of studies of the statistical properties of *random graphs* consisting of nodes randomly connected by edges (Erdös and Rényi 1960). As the ratio of edges to nodes increases, the size of the largest cluster increases, and the probability of a phase transition resulting in a single giant connected cluster also increases. The recognition that connected graphs exhibit phase transitions[7] led to their application to efforts to develop a formal model of the origin of life (OOL), i.e., how abiogenic catalytic molecules crossed the threshold to the kind of collectively self-sustaining, self-replicating, evolving structure we call 'alive' Kauffman (1986, 1993). In the application of graph theory to the OOL, nodes represent catalytic molecules, and edges represent reactions. It is exceedingly improbable that any catalytic molecule present in the primordial soup of Earth's early atmosphere catalyzed its own formation. However, reactions generate new molecules that catalyze new reactions, and as the variety of molecules increases, the variety of reactions increases faster. As the ratio of reactions to molecules increases, the probability that the system will undergo a phase transition increases. When, for

---

[7] A phase transition is a rapid transition from one state to another.

each molecule, there is a catalytic pathway to its formation, the set of molecules is said to be collectively *autocatalytic*, and the process by which this state is achieved has been referred to as *autocatalytic closure* (Kauffman 1993). Graph theory was also used to model how discrete MRs coalesce into an integrated understanding of the world capable of generating creative novelty (Gabora 1998). In this application, nodes represent, not catalytic molecules, but MRs, and the edges represent interactions amongst MRs, such as through associative learning or concept combination. The catalyst is an internal construct or external stimulus that triggers or facilitates a thought that would otherwise be very unlikely. It often takes the form of a problem, desire, or need. It may be a biological need, such as the need for food or shelter, or produced by some earlier 'reaction', as when solving one problem leads to another. Very often, a reaction that transforms one MR is catalyzed by another MR that has become aligned with the underlying need. For example, although Wilbur Wright's invention of wing warping was ultimately motivated by the need to create a flying machine, it was directly 'catalyzed' by the sight of a bending box (and most likely as well by the act of bending the box).

Autocatalytic networks have been developed mathematically in the theory of Reflexively Autocatalytic and Foodset-generated (RAF) networks (Hordijk and Steel 2016; Steel et al. 2019). The term *reflexively* is used in its mathematical sense to mean that every element is related to the whole. The term *foodset* refers to the reactants that are initially present, as opposed to those that are the products of catalyzed reactions. RAF theory has been used to model the emergence of a self-sustaining, self-replicating structure (i.e., a living protocell (Hordijk and Steel 2015)). Thus, RAFs offer a promising avenue for modelling the OOL, and thereby understanding how biological evolution began (Hordijk and Steel 2016; Steel et al. 2019; Vasas et al. 2012; Xavier et al. 2020), and (as mentioned earlier) they have also been used to model cognitive transitions underlying cultural evolution (Gabora and Steel 2017, 2020a, b). Table 8.1 summarizes how RAF theory terminology applies in biological and cultural/cognitive settings. The fact that RAFs have proven useful in both these domains suggests that RAF theory may provide a broad conceptual framework that is applicable to the origins and early stages of diverse evolutionary processes.

We now summarize the key concepts of RAF theory. A network of interrelated parts, such as a conceptual network, is referred to as a *catalytic reaction system* (CRS), and is modeled as a tuple $Q = (X, R, C, F)$ consisting of a set X of interacting elements, a set R of reactions, a catalysis set C indicating which types of elements

Table 8.1 Application of graph theoretic concepts in biology and culture, respectively

RAF theory	Biology	Culture and cognition
Node	Catalytic molecule	Mental representation (MR)
Edge	Reaction pathway	Association
Cluster	Molecules connected via reactions	MRs connected via associations
Connected graph	Autocatalytic closure (Kauffman 1986, 1993)	Conceptual closure[10] (Gabora 1998)

catalyze which reactions, and a subset F of X called the foodset. A *Reflexively Autocatalytic and F-generated* set—i.e., a RAF—is a non-empty subset $R' \subseteq R$ of reactions that satisfies the following two properties:

1. *Reflexively autocatalytic*: each reaction $r \in R'$ is catalyzed by at least one element type that is either produced by R' or is present in the foodset F ; and
2. *F-generated*: each reactant of each reaction in R' is either present in the foodset F or it can be generated from F through a series of reactions in R' itself.

A set of reactions that forms a RAF is simultaneously self-sustaining (by the F-generated condition) and (collectively) autocatalytic (by the RA condition) because each of its reactions is catalyzed by a molecule associated with the RAF. RAF theory has proven useful for identifying how phase transitions might occur, and at what parameter values. In the OOL context, a RAF emerges in systems of polymers (molecules consisting of repeated units called monomers) when the complexity of these polymers (as measured by maximum length) reaches a certain threshold (Kauffman 1993; Mossel and Steel 2005). The phase transition from no RAF to a RAF incorporating most or all of the molecules depends on (1) the probability of any one polymer catalyzing the reaction by which a given other polymer was formed, and (2) the maximum length (number of monomers) of polymers in the system. This transition has been formalized and analyzed (mathematically, and using simulations) and applied to real biochemical systems (Hordijk et al. 2010, 2011; Hordijk and Steel 2004, 2016; Mossel and Steel 2005), as well as cognitive systems (Gabora and Steel 2017, 2020a, b). Because of the deep structural or algorithmic similarity between the OOL and the OOC (as discussed above), much of this analysis can be readily imported from the former to the latter.

8.3.3 Hierarchical RAF Structure

There are three ways in which subRAFs can combine and expand (Steel et al. 2020):

1. If a CRS (such as a network of catalytic molecules or a conceptual network) contains a RAF, then the collection of all its RAFs forms a partially ordered set (i.e., a poset) under set inclusion, with a unique maximal element: the *maxRAF*. The maxRAF is the largest RAF in the network, and it includes all other RAFs. A CRS need not have a RAF, but when it does there is a unique maxRAF. The fact that the maxRAF may contain many RAFs enables RAFs to evolve, as demonstrated (both in theory and in simulation studies) through selective proliferation and drift[8] acting on possible subRAFs of the maxRAF (Hordijk and Steel 2016; Vasas et al. 2012). The remaining RAFs are called *subRAFs*. The

---

[8] Drift refers to the stabilization of certain traits due to statistical sampling error. Thus, all inhabitants of a small island may end up with the same eye color despite that there is no adaptive benefit to that eye color, due to drift.

union of any two (or more) subRAFs is a RAF (which explains why there is a unique maximal RAF). There may be a large number of irreducible RAFs, referred to as *irrRAFs*: RAFs that cannot be broken down into smaller RAFs. It is computationally straightforward to determine if a conceptual network has a one or more unique irrRAFs.

2. Some RAFs have the additional property of being *closed*, meaning that they are stable unless the reaction or foodset changes. Formally, a closed RAF is a RAF that contains every reaction in the network that has each of its reactants and at least one catalyst present either in the foodset or as a product of some reaction in the RAF. The maxRAF is always closed. A subRAF that is not closed is said to be *transient*. A transient RAF may add additional reactions until it becomes closed. The *closure* of any subRAF will contain the original subRAF, and be larger (unless the original subRAF was already closed). In Fig. 8.2, the RAF $\{r_1\}$ is not closed, but $\{r_1, r_2\}$ is (note that reaction r_3 does not become available until later, as it takes place in the mind of a different individual).

3. R' may combine with a *co-RAF*: a nonempty set of reactions that is not a RAF on its own, but that forms a RAF when combined with R'.

These are the only intrinsic processes by which RAFs can expand. Expansion can also be extrinsically driven by a change in the foodset, due to the presence of a new environmental stimulus, or through social learning processes. Extrinsic expansion can also arise due to a change in the permitted reactions, such as when participants in an experiment are instructed to 'think creatively'. Computationally, it is straightforward to determine if a RAF is the union of two smaller RAFs, and if a set of reactions is a co-RAF (Smith et al. 2014).

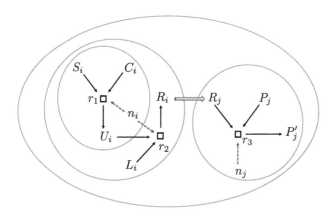

Fig. 8.2 The RAF consisting of the three reactions r_1, r_2, r_3 described by Eqs. (8.4), (8.5) and (8.6), respectively. Square boxes indicate representational redescription events (modeled as 'reactions'), and dashed blue arrows indicate the needs, desires, or contexts that elicit these events (modeled as 'catalysis events'). (For example, n_i is the desire to explain the behaviour of the benzene molecule), and n_j is the desire to understand the role of the unconscious on creativity.) This RAF contains precisely three subRAFs, namely $\{r_1\}$, and $\{r_1, r_2\}$, and $\{r_3\}$, which describe nested CCPs in the mind of Kekulé and the CCP in the mind of Jung

8.4   Application of RAF Networks to Creative Cognition

We now introduce the mathematical framework and terminology used in applications of RAF theory to creative cognition. We emphasize that this is not merely an *analogy* to the OOL scenario. The mathematical framework could have been applied to cognition before it was applied to early life; it is simply a way of formalizing the emergence of structure with the above-mentioned key properties, irrespective of the specifics with which that structure is realized.

All mental representations (MRs) in a given individual i are denoted X_i, and a particular MR $x = x_i$ in X_i is denoted by writing $x \in X_i$. The *foodset* for individual i, denoted F_i, encompasses MRs that are either innate, or that result from direct experience in the world, including natural, artificial, and social stimuli. F_i includes everything in individual i's long-term memory that did not directly result from thinking something through for oneself.

F_i also includes information obtained by i through individual learning by nonsocial means, so long as this information retains the form in which it was originally perceived, and is not redescribed or restructured through abstract thought. The crucial distinction between foodset and foodset-generated (i.e., non-foodset) items is not whether another person was involved, nor whether the MR was originally obtained through abstract thought (by *someone*), but whether the abstract thought process originated in the mind of the individual i in question. Thus, F_i has two components:

- S_i denotes the set of MRs arising through direct experience encoded in individual i's memory, including MRs obtained through social learning of an MR x_h by another individual h, denoted $S_i[x_h]$, and MRs obtained through individual learning, denoted $S_i[l]$.
- I_i denotes any *innate knowledge* with which individual i is born.

The term *foodset derived*, denoted $\neg F_i$, refers to mental contents that are *not* part of F_i (i.e. $\neg F_i$ consists of all the products $b \in B$ of all reactions $r \in R_i$). They are the result of abstract thought processes such as deduction, induction, divergent thinking, analogical thinking, and cross-domain transfer. A single instance of conceptual restructuring, or *representational redescription* (RR) in individual i is referred to as a *reaction,* and denoted $r \in R_i$. A stream of abstract thought, involving the generation of representations that go beyond what has been directly perceived, is modeled as a sequence of catalytic events. Following Gabora and Steel (2017), we refer to this as a *cognitive catalytic process* (CCP). Self-organized criticality, discussed above, describes a CCP consisting of recursive RR events, resulting in a cascade of conceptual change.

The set of reactions that can be catalyzed by a given MR x in individual i is denoted $C_i[x]$. The entire set of MRs either *undergoing* or *resulting from r* is denoted A or B, respectively, and a member of the set of MRs undergoing or resulting from reaction r is denoted $a \in A$ or $b \in B$. In particular, $\neg F_i$ includes the products of any reactions derived from F_i. Its contents come about through mental operations—RR events—on the foodset. Thus, $\neg F_i$ includes everything in memory that *was* the result of one's own CCPs. $\neg F_i$ may include a MR in which social learning played a role, so long as the most recent modification to it was a catalytic event, i.e., involved RR.[9] Note that F_i includes information obtained through social learning from *someone else* who obtained it through RR. Thus, if h invents a game and teaches it to i, this knowledge is part of F_i but it is part of $\neg F_h$.

The set of *all* possible reactions in individual i is denoted R_i. The mental contents of the mind, including all MRs and all RR events, is denoted $X_i \oplus R_i$. This includes F_i and $\neg F_i$. Recall that the set of all MRs in individual i, including both the foodset and elements derived from that foodset, is denoted X_i. R_i and C_i are not prescribed in advance; because C_i includes remindings and associations on the basis of shared properties, different CCPs can occur through interactions amongst MRs. Nevertheless, it makes perfect mathematical sense to talk about R_i and C_i as sets. Table 8.2 summarizes the terminology and correspondences between the OOL and the OOC.

Cognitive RAFs include elements of cognition that have no obvious parallel in the original application of RAFs to the OOL. We denote the subject of attention at time t as w_t^o. It may be an external stimulus, or a MR retrieved from memory. Any other contents of $X_i \oplus R_i$ that are accessible to working memory, such as close associates of w_t^o, or recently attended MRs, are denoted W_t, with W_t constituting a very small subset of $X_i \oplus R_i$.

Table 8.2 Terminology and correspondences between the application of RAFs in biology and cognition/culture

Term	Biology	Cognition/culture
X_i	all molecule types in protocell i	all mental representations (MRs) in individual i
$x \in X_i$	a molecule in X_i	a MR in X_i
F_i	foodset for protocell i	MRs that are innate or directly experienced by i
$r \in R_i$	a particular reaction in i	a particular representational redescription (RR) in i
$C_i[x]$	reactions catalyzed by x in i	RR events 'catalyzed' by x in i
$(x, r) \in C$	x catalyzes r	x 'catalyzes' redescription of r
$a \in A$	member of the set of reactants in r	member of the set of MRs undergoing r
$b \in B$	member of the set of products of r	member of the set of MRs resulting from r
$\neg F_i$	non foodset for i (i.e., all B of R_i)	MRs resulting from R_i (i.e., all B of R_i)

---

[9] This distinction between foodset MRs and foodset-derived MRs may not be so black and white, but for simplicity, we avoid that subtlety for now.

8.5   Modelling Insight

We now show how creative insight through analogical transfer can be modeled using RAF networks. The focus is not on the mechanisms underlying analogy itself; thus, the model is consistent with theories that emphasize different aspects of analogy such as structure mapping (Gentner 1983), constraint satisfaction (Holyoak and Thagard 1996), and potentiality and honing (Scotney et al. 2020). We keep the internal structure of MRs and their associative links—which can be modeled using existing methods—to a minimum, so as to lay bare the proposed approach to modeling creativity.

8.5.1   Cross-Domain Transfer in Discovery by Analogy

We explain the approach using the simple, striking, and well-known example mentioned earlier: Kekulé's realization that benzene must consist of a chain of carbon molecules that is circular in shape, inspired by a reverie in which he envisioned a snake biting its tail (Findlay 1965). This insight marked a significant departure from earlier thinking in chemistry, and was critical to founding the field of organic chemistry. We now present a RAF model of Kekulé's insight process. This innovation process is summarized in Fig. 8.3, and depicted in Fig. 8.4.

Absorbing the Relevant Background Knowledge Kekulé's insight was preceded by a lengthy period sometimes referred to in the creativity literature as *preparation*. This stage involves the acquisition of knowledge of the target domain. In the case of analogy, it would also include learning of the source domain from which the analogy will be obtained. In our example, the target domain is organic chemistry,

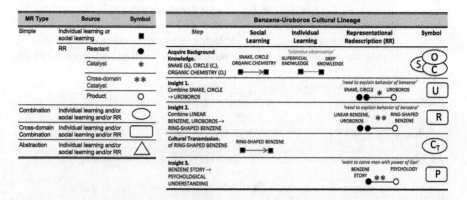

Fig. 8.3 Left: Sources of mental representations and symbols used here to depict them. Right: MRs participating in the fragment of the benzene–uroboros 'lineage' described in the text. Each instance of social learning (Column 2) has been preceded at some point in the lineage by a relevant instance of individual learning (Column 3) or representational redescription (RR) (Column 4)

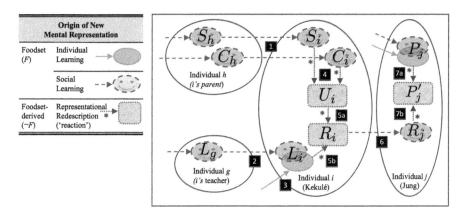

Fig. 8.4 Steps in the discovery of the ring-shaped structure of benzene. The meanings of symbols are provided in Fig. 8.3. Steps 4, 5, and 7 are representational redescription events, modeled as reactions, corresponding to Insights 1, 2, and 3 in Fig. 8.3. Note that since individual i obtained R_i through representational redescription, it is a food-set derived item in i, but that very same MR is a food-set item in j because j obtained it from i through social learning. Note also when R reaches individual j (as R_i), it participates in a reaction (step 7) that was not possible in individual i

specifically, knowledge of the structure and behaviour of carbon-based molecules. One source domain is herpetology, specifically, knowledge of the elongated shape and flexibility of snakes. Another source domain is geometry, specifically the knowledge of circular shapes. Since information from the reptile domain, specifically knowledge of the physical features of snakes featured prominently in Kekulé's insight, they are part of the cultural lineage to which he contributed.

We represent the social transmission of general knowledge of snakes and circles, denoted S and C respectively, from a parent, individual h, to young Kekulé, individual i, as follows:

$$F_i \mapsto F_i \cup \{S_i, C_i\}, \ S_i, C_i \in \mathbf{S}_i[S_h, C_h].$$

(8.1)

There is no evidence that Kekulé was exceptional with respect to his knowledge of snakes, but he was undeniably exceptional with respect to his knowledge of organic chemistry, and his drive to understand what kind of structure benzene must have to explain its anomalous behaviour. We represent the social transmission from the teacher, individual g, to Kekulé, individual i, of knowledge pertaining to organic chemistry, denoted O, as follows:

$$F_i \mapsto F_i \cup \{O_i\}, \ O_i \in \mathbf{S}_i[O_g].$$

(8.2)

Kekulé also engaged in individual learning of organic chemistry, and this is represented as follows:

$$F_i \mapsto F_i \cup \{O_i\}, \; O_i \in \mathbf{S}_i[l].$$

(8.3)

Kekulé probably also engaged in individual learning of information pertaining to snakes and circles, but to a lesser degree than individual learning of organic chemistry, so we omit that detail here.

Insight Creative honing is often (though not always) stimulated by *problem finding* (Abdulla et al. 2020), which begins with a sense of uncertainty, incompletion, inconsistency, or need, accompanied by a lingering feeling that compels the exploration and expression of ideas (Feinstein 2006). In this case, the uncertainty concerned the shape of benzene. Insight by way of analogy began with mapping correspondences between the long, skinny shape of a snake, and its potential to bite its tail and thereby form a circular shape, to the long, skinny shape of the benzene molecule, and its potential to similarly close in on itself and form a circular shape. We model this as a CCP consisting of two reactions. The first involves modification of the MR of a snake to give a snake biting its tail. The second involves redescription of the MR of benzene as a linear molecule with a chain of carbon atoms as its backbone, resulting in a circular structure for benzene. (Note: if (as suggested previously in this chapter) Kekulé was already familiar with the symbolic image of a serpent swallowing its tail, commonly referred to as the *uroboros* (or ouroboros), the uroboros MR would already be part of his foodset, and there would be no need to derive it from scratch.)

A reaction results in a new F-generated (non-foodset) item, i.e., it transforms an element of F_k into an element of $\neg F_k$. In general, for an individual k (where $k = i, j$), we write $a_k \xrightarrow{b_k} c_k$ to denote the reaction that transforms one $MR(a_k)$ to a resulting MR c_k (in $\neg F_k$) by catalyst b_k, and we let $a_k + a'_k \xrightarrow{b_k} c_k$ denote a reaction that combines and transforms two MRs $\left(a_k, a'_k\right)$ to a resulting MR c_k (in $\neg F_k$) by catalyst b_k. In our example, both catalysis events were provoked by the context: *need to explain the behaviour of the benzene molecule*, which we denote n_i. In the first reaction, r_1, the concepts SNAKE and CIRCLE denoted S_i and C_i, serve as the reactants. They undergo restructuring during a RR event resulting in a product, the MR of a snake biting its tail, i.e., a UROBOROS, denoted $U_i \in S_i(l)$. We describe this as follows:

$$S_i + C_i \xrightarrow{n_i} U_i, \; F_i \mapsto F_i \cup \{U_i\},$$

(8.4)

The second reaction involves modification of the *reactants* U_i and LINEAR–BENZENE, denoted L_i, to generate the *product*: RING-SHAPED–BENZENE, denoted $R_i \in S_i(l)$. We model this as a reaction, r_2, and describe it as follows:

$$U_i + L_i \xrightarrow{n_i} R_i, \; F_i, \mapsto F_i, \cup \{R_i\},$$

(8.5)

Since RING-SHAPED–BENZENE is associatively linked to the more abstract concept MOLECULE, this event expands the affordances of MOLECULE (i.e., it is now perceived as something that can be circular). Affordances are a kind of association and, as such, they increase the connectivity of the conceptual network.

Conceptual Network Expansion Kekulé's insight integrated other isolated fragments of conceptual structure—specifically, mental representations of seemingly inexplicable experimental results—into Kekulé maxRAF. The inertness of the benzene molecule was due to the stability afforded by its ring-shaped structure. In light of this, his experimental results with benzene now made sense. In addition, the insight bridged the domains of geometry, herpetology, and chemistry, increasing the density of connections in his conceptual network.

The insight was followed by a *honing and verification* stage: development of the idea, as well as evaluation. This involved assessing and testing the hypothesis that benzene is circular in shape. The thought processes underlying these activities brought about further expansion of the maxRAF.

Teaching and Social Learning Once Kekulé was confident in the correctness of the idea, the next stage was to share it with others. This involved teaching and social learning of the knowledge of benzene's shape with students and peers. Kekulé's insight altered the structure of their maxRAFs, as it had for Kekulé himself. Note, however, that in the RAF approach, the impact of this insight is described and depicted quite differently for Kekulé's students and peers than for Kekulé himself. For Kekulé the knowledge of benzene's ring-shaped structure was obtained through RR, modeled as a 'reaction' and therefore it expanded the set of foodset-derived MRs, $\neg F$. In contrast, for Kekulé's peers and students, this knowledge is obtained as a result of social learning, i.e., it expands the set F of foodset MRs.

Kekule's insight fueled a new lineage of cultural knowledge to which others added subsequent insights (such as quantum analyses of benzene (Jaffe and Smith 1996)). Not only did Kekulé's insight impact the field of chemistry, but it impacted thinking in psychology as well, by influencing Jung's views on the role of the unconscious in creative thought (Jung et al. 1964). Let us look briefly at this branch of the benzene–uroboros cultural lineage.

Jung had extensive training in psychology, acquired through both social learning and individual learning. We omit these here, but they could be described exactly as was done above for individual i. We denote Jung's knowledge of psychology prior to his contemplation of the benzene discovery as P_j. Jung intuited that the unconscious plays a role in creativity; his uncertainty stemmed from lack of a concrete example of the unconscious presenting its knowledge to the conscious mind. We denote his new understanding of psychology as a result of the benzene–uroboros story, as P_j'. The context that 'catalyzed' these insights was his *desire to understand the role of the unconscious on creativity*, which we denote n_j. We model this line of influence as a reaction, r_3, and describe it as follows:

$$R_j + P_j \xrightarrow{n_j} P'_j, \; F_j \mapsto F_j \cup \{P'_j\}$$

$$(8.6)$$

The set of nested subRAFs depicting Kekulé insight into benzene is illustrated in Fig. 8.2. Recall that an irrRAF is a RAF that cannot be broken down into smaller RAFs. Both $\{r_1\}$ and $\{r_3\}$ are irrRAFs. ($\{r_3\}$ is a RAF because R_j and P_j are in the foodset of Jung's maxRAF). Note that $\{r_2\}$ by itself is not a subRAF, since it requires r_1 to first generate U_i in the mind of Kekulé) in order to form. Other subsets also fail to be subRAFs (for example, $\{r_2, r_3\}$). The subRAF $\{r_1, r_2\}$ is a closed subRAF, since n_j involves a different individual (Jung) from the individual (Kekulé) associated with $\{r_1, r_2\}$. On the other hand, $\{r_1\}$ is not a closed subRAF (since n_i and the reactants of r_2 were available to Kekulé after r_1 occurred, so r_2 could proceed).

Note that although the RING-SHAPED-BENZENE MR was not a member of the foodset in Kekulé's conceptual network (because it originated in his mind), it *was* a member of the foodset in Jung's mind (since he acquired it through social learning and did not have to derive it from scratch). Note also that this is not a definitive model of how the discovery of benzene's ring structure occurred. The uroboros story may have induced SOC, such that it had a 'snowball effect' on Jung's understanding of psychology, with one insight giving rise to another. The process may also have been more bidirectional than implied here; it is possible that the image of a line bending around to form a circle was initially interpreted by Kekulé's dreaming mind as a snake, and only afterward understood to be the benzene molecule. The important point is that the concept of the uroboros played a key role in this discovery, which fundamentally revolutionized our understanding of organic chemistry, and impacted psychology, and thus constitutes a critical juncture in our collective history. More generally, analogies have played a significant role in the insights and discoveries that mark transition points in human history, and this model provides a means of formally describing them. A valuable feature of this model is that, by enabling MRs to align with needs and desires, and thereby play the role of a catalyst that prompts the occurrence of a particular thought process, each new idea (or modification of an existing idea) can be traced to its point of origin. Thus, each contribution to a particular 'lineage' of creative thought retains its connection with a particular innovator in a particular set of motivating circumstances, despite that it may change form drastically as it 'encounters' the conceptual networks of other individuals.

8.6 Collaborative Learning Environments as Higher-Level RAFs

A complementary process to that of learning *from* others, is learning *with* others (Kittur et al. 2019; Shteynberg et al. 2020; Tomasello et al. 1993), as often occurs in an educational context. Transitions in understanding often result not from the efforts of single individuals but from diads or larger groups, with or without an explicit teacher, and RAFs are well-suited to model this.

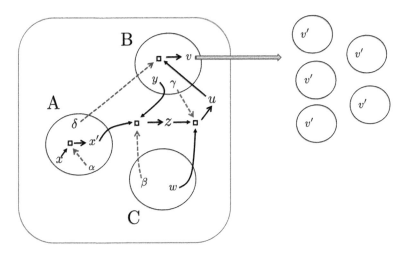

Fig. 8.5 An example of a hypothetical collaboration among three people, described by a RAF that involves four reactions. Individual A is motivated to consider a concept x from a new perspective, which results in x' (with the motivation being an internal catalyst α, such as 'curiosity'). This first reaction $\left(x \overset{\alpha}{\to} x' \right)$ in Individual A is verbally transmitted to Individuals B and C. A question raised by C catalyzes a further realisation that combining the new idea, x', with a concept from B (namely, y) yields the superior idea, (z). This second reaction $\left(x' + y \overset{\beta}{\to} z \right)$ results from the collaboration among three individuals, with C providing the catalyst, and the other two supplying the reactants. As such, we can consider the RAF that extends across the three group members. Further prompting by B (catalyst γ) allows for this idea to be developed further (with input from C via w) to produce an even better idea, u. This third reaction $\left(w + z \overset{\gamma}{\to} u \right)$ involves interaction between B and C. Input from A (catalyst δ) leads B to realize that an even better idea, v, is possible. This fourth reaction $\left(u \overset{\delta}{\to} v \right)$ takes place in the mind of B, following catalysis by A. This final 'product' is then communicated to the rest of the group (as v')

An illustrative example of creative insight in a collaborative learning context involving three individuals, A, B, and C, is illustrated in Fig. 8.5. This collaborative innovation is described by four reactions: the first occurs entirely in the mind of Individual A. The next reaction involves all three individuals. The third reaction involves B and C, and the fourth takes place in the mind of B but also involves A. The resulting group-level collaboration is described by a maxRAF consisting of several subRAFs.

8.7   Insights Arising from a Continuous Process

The RAFs examined thus far have provided a mechanism for the sudden transitions in understanding, yet the underlying model involves dynamics based on continuous-time cognitive processes. This is not so surprising in light of self-organized critical-ity (discussed earlier), and related phenomena associated with nonlinear processes.

The emergence of a new creative insight occurs when certain critical factors coinciding within an individual mind—or in the case of collaborative learning environments, a group of minds—to allow a cognitive RAF to proceed once, after which it serves as catalyst and/or reactant) in subsequent interactions (within an individual, or between individuals). For example, in Kekulé's mind, the fortuitous occurrence of the first reaction r_1 allowed the second r_2 to proceed; for the collaboration shown in Fig. 8.5, several interactions of particular MRs, in a certain order were required in the path towards the new concept v. We now describe more formally how a simple stochastic model based on RAFs predicts discontinuous bursts (or cascades).

A simple null model of continuous cognitive change over time would model the appearance of new creative outputs by a standard Poisson process at a constant rate λ. In this case, the times between events are independently exponentially distributed with an expected value of $\dfrac{1}{\lambda}$.

Modifying this null model to incorporate cognitive RAFs allows for the emergence of 'bursts' of cognitive change, i.e., self-organized criticality. To see this, first observe that the null model ignores the possibility that a new creative output from some individual in G (or collaboration within G) can rapidly become the catalyst (or a reactant) for a cognitive reaction within the mind of one (or more) other individuals in G, resulting in a new creative output that, in turn, can spark further cognitive reactions (and so on). A simple way to model this cascade effect is to assume that each new creative output has a probability q of enabling a new cognitive reaction to take place in the mind of at least one other individual in G (and the resulting creative output can then independently give rise to a further reaction in at least one other individual, again with probability q, and so on). Thus, each new creative output arising from a background Poisson process (with rate λ) gives rise to a burst of $N = 1$, 2, 3, … creative outputs (including the original item from the Poisson process). The size of these bursts (N) is variable; in fact, under this simple model N follows a geometric distribution with parameter $p = 1 - q$. It is therefore described by $P(N = k) = p^{k-1}(1 - p)$, and so N has an expected value $\mu = 1/p = 1/(1 - q)$ and a variance of $\sigma^2 = (1 - p)/p^2 = q/(1 - q)^2$ (Grimmett and Stirzaker 2020). In particular, for q close to 1, the bursts can be large, and highly variable in size.

8.8   Discussion and Conclusion

To understand how a creator dissolves uncertainty by thinking ideas through from new perspectives requires a theoretical framework that incorporates individual differences in the structuring of knowledge and experience. This chapter presents a new approach to modeling creative insight and the process by which new ideas emerge from previous ones, using RAF networks. RAFs provide a means of formalizing the notion that conceptual change is prompted by uncertainty, cognitive dissonance, questions, or gaps in understanding, which trigger the restructuring or redescription of representations, modeled as conceptual interactions, or 'reactions.'

The approach differentiates between (1) foodset MRs (knowledge that is either innate, or that results from social learning or individual learning of *existing* information), and (2) foodset-generated (i.e., non-foodset) MRs (*new* information that results from abstract thought, or interactions amongst other MRs). Treating MRs as 'reactants', 'catalysts', or 'products' enables us to model the ideation process step by step. This in turn enables us to track trajectories of conceptual change within and across individuals, and to better understand what prompts creative thought, and how ideas shape, and are shaped by, the conceptual structure that bear them. Creative thinking alters the hierarchical structure of RAFs, and provides avenues by which isolated fragments of knowledge can be assimilated into the maxRAF.

8.8.1 New Directions and Testable Predictions

We mentioned that the RAF approach has been used to model key transitions in the origins of cultural evolution (Gabora and Steel 2017, 2020a, b). In keeping with the dictum 'ontogeny recapitulates phylogeny,' the application of autocatalytic networks to the cognitive underpinnings of cultural evolution lays the groundwork for an autocatalytic framework for conceptual change (Gabora et al. 2022). In the course of development, a child must acquire a coherent, integrated, flexible conceptual network capable of adapting ideas to new situations, and combining knowledge in appropriate and meaningful ways. Thus, RAFs can be used to model transitions in cognitive development during childhood, culminating in the emergence of new participants in the creative culture-generating 'machinery.'

The RAF approach could also be used to investigate a number of other issues related to creativity, learning, and development, such as the relationship between expertise and creativity, the impact of individual differences on creativity, the relationship between creativity and the half-life of a creator's contributions, and whether conceptual network diversity among members of a social group affects the rate or quality of innovation. It could be used to model the impact of different kinds of learning experiences on conceptual network structure, and the impact of this structure on creativity. It would be interesting to study whether individual differences in reliance on foodset versus foodset-derived information sourcies (i.e., the propensity to think things through for oneself) sources may culminate in different kinds of conceptual networks and concomitant learning and/or personality trajectories.

The RAF approach also generates testable predictions. It predicts that the conceptual networks of highly innovative individuals have large maxRAFs, and a high ratio of foodset-derived to foodset MRs. It further predicts that in successful groups and organizations, such individuals are counterbalanced by individuals with a low ratio of foodset-derived to foodset MRs, so as not to compromise the capacity to preserve proven effective solutions.

The RAF framework also predicts that there may be individuals whose conceptual networks contain roughly the same *concepts* and *associations* but who nevertheless think and behave quite differently, resulting in markedly different creative outputs. A possible example would be Mozart and Salieri; while they had similar environments, experiences, and social circles, their compositions and impact were markedly different. Standard node-and-link semantic network approaches provide no obvious way of explaining this because there is no uncertainty-driven 'catalysis' of MRs. In the RAF approach, individual differences in MR reactivities and in relative reliance on foodset versus foodset-derived knowledge are expected to impact the shape of their conceptual networks, and the result in differences in the number, kind, and impact of creative outputs. We suggest that the difference between Mozart and Salieri reflects, not differences in their knowledge of music and understanding of the rules of composition, but in their proclivity to access life experiences and emotions, mull them over, and allow them to serve as reactants and catalysts in the domain of music. Differences in reactivity may help explain why intelligence is a necessary but not sufficient condition for creativity (Jauk et al. 2013).

It has been suggested that creative breakthroughs are more likely to arise from conceptually distant sources than from conceptually close ones (Gentner and Markman 1997; Holyoak and Thagard 1996; Poze 1983; Ward 1998). There is evidence that individuals from different (often adjacent) fields produce the most creative solutions (Franke et al. 2014; Jeppesen and Lakhani 2010; Wiley 1998). Some studies have also shown an advantage of conceptually distant sources over near ones with respect to novelty, quality, and flexibility of ideation (Chan et al. 2011; Chiu and Shu 2012; Dahl and Moreau 2002; Goncalves et al. 2013; Hender et al. 2002), while other studies concluded that there was no such advantage (Chan and Schunn 2015b; Dunbar 1997), or were inconclusive (Enkel and Gassmann 2010; Malaga 2000). Despite their potential benefit, distant sources may be harder to find, and require more iterative processing (Chan and Schunn 2015b). A related prediction derived from the RAF approach is that creative collaborations require not just overlapping yet different conceptual structures, but compatible levels of MR reactivity. If their joint reactivity is too low, new ideas fail to emerge, but if it is too high, they lose the thread of continuity necessary for cumulative change.

RAF networks have been used to model the origins of evolutionary processes, biological (the origin of life) as well as cultural (the origin of cumulative innovation). We think this is not coincidental; indeed, elsewhere, we showed that both the evolution of early life and cultural evolution are instantiations of a primitive form of evolution—i.e., cumulative, adaptive, open-ended change—referred to as Self-Other Reorganization (SOR) (Gabora 2019). Instead of replication using a self-assembly code, SOR entails internal self-organising and self-maintaining processes within entities, as well as interaction between entities. The argument for SOR bolsters the argument that they share a deep structure, and thus strengthens the rationale for applying RAFs in both domains. In any case, the RAF approach to creative cognition is consistent with the theory that humans possess two levels of complex, adaptive, self-organizing structure: an organismal level and a psychological level (Barton 1994; Gabora 2004; Maturana and Varela 1973). Psychological research tends to be data rich and theory poor (Fried 2020), and psychological theorizing remains fragmented (Teo 2018). Theories about creativity are disconnected from theories about the relationship between domain-specific abilities and general intelligence (e.g., (Kovacs and Conway 2016)), which are disconnected from theories about how attitudes or personality traits relate to the structuring of knowledge and experience (Dalege et al. 2018). The RAF approach offers an established mathematical framework for integrating research on creative cognition with research on semantic networks, and the kinds of structures that exhibit cumulative, adaptive, open-ended change, i.e., that evolve. Though still in its infancy, the RAF approach has the potential to provide a new way of understanding how human history unfolds, one that embeds creativity research in the formal study of self-organizing structures and their role in evolutionary processes, and that places creative cognition centre stage.

Acknowledgements We thank Marcel Montrey for comments on an early version of the manuscript.

Funding LG acknowledges funding from Grant **62R06523** from the Natural Sciences and Engineering Research Council of Canada.

Appendices

Appendix A: Glossary of Terms and Acronyms

Abstract thought: the processing of internally sourced mental contents.

Autocatalytic: the whole can be reconstituted through interactions amongst its parts.

Benzene: an organic chemical compound composed of six carbon atoms joined in a planar ring with one hydrogen atom attached to each.

Catalyst: facilitates a transition that would otherwise be highly unlikely to occur. Here, the role of catalyst is played by a problem, desire, or need, or a realization or external stimuli that trigger a thought that would be highly unlikely to occur otherwise. For example, if a stranger on the street reminds you of a deceased relative, and this triggers a memory of being with that person, the stranger (or more precisely, your mental representation of the stranger) plays the role of a catalyst.)

Catalytic reaction system: a network of interrelated parts, such as a conceptual network.

Cognitive catalytic process (CCP): a stream of abstract thought.

Closed RAF: a RAF that is stable unless the foodset changes or the reactions they take part in changes. (Formally, a closed RAF is a RAF that contains every reaction in the network that has each of its reactants and at least one catalyst present either in the foodset or as a product of some reaction in the RAF.) The maxRAF is always closed. The *closure* of any subRAF will contain the original subRAF, and be larger (unless the original subRAF was already closed).

Conceptual network: a web of shared properties, contexts, associations, and relationships of logic, causation, and so forth, that bind them together.

Co-RAF: a nonempty set of reactions that is not a RAF on its own, but that forms a RAF when combined with an existing set of reactions.

Catalytic reaction system: a network of components, such as a network of catalytic molecules, or a conceptual network.

Foodset, F : the elements that are initially present, as opposed to those that are the products of interactions amongst them.

Foodset-generated (sometimes called F-generated, or foodset-derived), $\neg F$: an element that can be generated from the foodset F through a series of reactions in R' itself. That is, an element of the network that is *not* part of the foodset. The term 'foodset-derived' is more often used in the cognitive application of RAFs.

Individual learning: obtaining pre-existing information from the environment by nonsocial means through direct perception.

IrrRAF: A RAF that is irreducible, i.e., cannot be broken down into smaller RAFs.

MaxRAF: the largest RAF in the network. It includes all other RAFs.

Mental representation (MR). Items in declarative or procedural memory composed of one or more concepts or percepts, and which came about through individual learning, social learning, or abstract thought. The set of all mental representations in individual i is denoted X_i. (As mentioned in the text, we emphasize that although we use the terms 'mental representation,' we are sympathetic with the view that what we call mental representations do not 'represent,' but act as contextually elicited bridges between the mind and the world.)

Reflexive: each part is related to the whole.

Reflexively autocatalytic: each reaction $r \in R'$ is catalyzed by at least one element type that is either produced by R' or is present in the foodset F .

Phase transition: rapid transition from one state to another.

Poisson process: a stochastic model for a series of discrete events wherein the average time between events is constant, but the precise timing of each event is random or variable.

Reactant: A mental representation that participates in a given 'reaction', i.e., an event that alters the structure of the conceptual network.

Reaction: a change of state or interaction between existing elements that results in a new element. The set of all possible reactions in individual i is denoted R_i.

Representational redescription (RR): Conceptual restructuring that causes a mental representation to change. In the RAF framework this is modeled as a reaction.

Self-organized criticality (SOC): a phenomenon wherein, through simple local interactions, complex systems tend to find a critical state poised at the cusp of a transition between order and chaos, from which a single small perturbation occasionally exerts a disproportionately large effect.

SubRAF: a RAF that is not the maxRAF. It is a component of the maxRAF.

Transient RAF: A subRAF that is not closed. A transient RAF may add additional reactions until it becomes closed.

Uroboros (or ouroboros): an ancient symbol depicting a serpent or dragon eating its own tail.

Appendix B: Acronyms

CCP: Cognitive catalytic process
CRS: Catalytic reaction system
RAF: reflexively autocatalytic foodset-generated network
MR: Mental representation
RR: Representational redescription
SOC: Self-organized criticality

References

Abdulla, A. M., Paek, S. H., Cramond, B., & Runco, M. A. (2020). Problem finding and creativity: A meta-analytic review. *Psychology of Aesthetics, Creativity, and the Arts, 14* (1), 3–14.

Aerts, D., Aerts, S., & Gabora, L. (2009). Experimental evidence for quantum structure in cognition. In: P. Bruza, W. Lawless, K. van Rijsbergen, & D. Sofge (Eds.) *Lecture Notes in Computer Science: Quantum Interaction* (pp. 59–79). Berlin: Springer.

Aerts, D., Broekaert, J., Gabora, L., & Sozzo, S. (2016). Generalizing prototype theory: A formal quantum framework. *Frontiers in Psychology (Cognition), 7,* 418. https://doi.org/10.3389/fpsyg.2016.00418

Aerts, D., Gabora, L., & Sozzo, S. (2013). Concepts and their dynamics: A quantum theoretical model. *Topics in Cognitive Science, 5,* 737–772. https://doi.org/10.1111/tops.12042

Andersson, C., & Törnberg, P. (2019). Toward a macroevolutionary theory of human evolution: The social protocell. *Biological Theory, 14,* 86–102. https://doi.org/10.1007/s13752-018-0313-y

Bak, P., Tang, C., & Weisenfeld, K. (1988). Self-organized criticality. *Physical Review A, 38,* 364.

Barron, F. (1963). *Creativity and psychological health.* New York: Van Nostrand.

Barsalou, L. W. (2005). Abstraction as dynamic interpretation in perceptual symbol systems. In L. Gershkoff-Stowe & D. Rakison (Eds.), *Building object categories in developmental time* (pp. 89–99, 389–431). Psychology Press: Earlbaum: Carnegie Symposium Series.

Barton, S. (1994). Chaos, self-organization, and psychology. *American Psychologist, 49,* 5–14.

Basadur, M. (1995). *The power of innovation: How to make innovation a way of life and put creative solutions to work.* London, U.K: Pitman Professional Publishing.

Bassett, D. S., & Bullmore, E. D. (2006). Small-world brain networks. *The neuroscientist, 12,* 512–523.

Beghetto, R. A. (2019). Structured uncertainty: How creativity thrives under constraints and uncertainty. In C. A. Mullen (Ed.), *Creativity under duress in education? resistive theories, practices, and actions* (pp. 27–40). Cham: Springer International Publishing. https://doi.org/10.1007/978-3-319-90272-2

Cabell, K. R., & Valsiner, J. (2013). *The catalyzing mind: Beyond models of causality (Annals of Theoretical Psychology, Volume 11).* Berlin: Springer. https://doi.org/10.1007/978-1-4614-8821-7

Chan, J., Fu, K., Schunn, C. D., Cagan, J., Wood, K. L., & Kotovsky, K. (2011). On the benefits and pitfalls of analogies for innovative design: Ideation performance based on analogical distance, commonness, and modality of examples. *Journal of Mechanical Design, 133,* 081004.

Chan, J., & Schunn, C. (2015a). The impact of analogies on creative concept generation: Lessons from an *in vivo* study in engineering design. *Cognitive Science, 39,* 126–155. https://doi.org/10.1111/cogs.12127

Chan, J., & Schunn, C. D. (2015b). The importance of iteration in creative conceptual combination. *Cognition, 145*, 104–115. https://doi.org/10.1016/j.cognition.2015.08.008

Chiu, I., & Shu, H. (2012). Investigating effects of oppositely related semantic stimuli on design concept creativity. *Journal of Engineering Design, 23*, 271–296. https://doi.org/10.108 0/09544828.2011.603298

Dahl, D. W., & Moreau, P. (2002). The influence and value of analogical thinking during new product ideation. *Journal of Marketing Research, 39*, 47–60.

Dalege, J., Borsboom, D., van Harreveld, F., & van der Maas, H. (2018). The attitudinal entropy (ae) framework as a general theory of individual attitudes. *Psychological Inquiry, 29* (4), 175–193. https://doi.org/10.1080/1047840X.2018.1537246

Deutsch, O. E. (1928). The Walter Scott songs. *Music & Letters, 9*, 330–335.

Doudna, J. A., & Charpentier, E. (2014). The new frontier of genome engineering with CRISPR-Cas9. *Science, 346*, 1258096.

Doudna, J. A., & Sternberg, S. H. (2017). *A crack in creation: Gene editing and the unthinkable power to control evolution*. New York: Houghton Mifflin Harcourt.

Dunbar, K. N. (1997). How scientists think: On-line creativity and conceptual change in science. In T. B. Ward, S. M. Smith, & J. Vaid (Eds.), *Creative thought: An investigation of conceptual structures and processes* (pp. 461–493). Washington, DC: American Psychological Association Press.

Eldridge, N., & Gould, S. J. (1972). Punctuated equilibria: an alternative to phyletic gradualism. In T. Schopf (Ed.), *Models in paleobiology* (pp. 82–115).

Enkel, E., & Gassmann, O. (2010). Creative imitation: Exploring the case of cross-industry innovation. *Research & Development Management, 40*, 256—270.

Erdös, P., & Rényi, A. (1960). On the evolution of random graphs. *Publication of the Mathematical Institute of the Hungarian Academy of Sciences, 5*, 17-61.

Feinstein, J. S. (2006). *The nature of creative development*. Stanford, CA: Stanford University Press.

Findlay, A. (1965). *A hundred years of chemistry (3rd ed.)*. London, UK: Duckworth.

Forgeard, M. (2013). Perceiving benefits after adversity: The relationship between self-reported post-traumatic growth and creativity. *Psychology of Aesthetics, Creativity, and the Arts, 7*, 245–264. https://doi.org/10.1037/a0031223

Franke, N., Poetz, M. K., & Schreier, M. (2014). Integrating problem solvers from analogous markets in new product ideation. *Management Science, 60*, 1063—1081.

Freeman, A., & Golden, B. (1997). *Why didn't I think of that? Bizarre origins of ingenious inventions we couldn't live without*. New York: Wiley.

Fried, E. I. (2020). Lack of theory building and testing impedes progress in the factor and network literature. *Psychological Inquiry, 31* (4), 271–288. https://doi.org/10.108 0/1047840X.2020.1853461

Gabora, L. (1998). Autocatalytic closure in a cognitive system: A tentative scenario for the origin of culture. *Psycoloquy, 9* (67), [adap-org/9901002].

Gabora, L. (2000). Conceptual closure: How memories are woven into an interconnected worldview. In G. Van de Vijver & J. Chandler (Eds.), *Closure: Emergent organizations and their dynamics* (pp. 42–53). Annals of the New York Academy of Sciences. https://doi.org/10.1111/j.1749-6632.2000.tb06264.x

Gabora, L. (2004). Ideas are not replicators but minds are. *Biology and Philosophy, 19*, 127–143.

Gabora, L. (2010). Revenge of the'neurds': Characterizing creative thought in terms of the structure and dynamics of human memory. *Creativity Research Journal, 22*, 1-13.

Gabora, L. (2017). Honing theory: A complex systems framework for creativity. *Nonlinear Dynamics, Psychology, and Life Sciences, 21*, 35–88.

Gabora, L. (2018). How insight emerges in a distributed, content-addressable memory. In O. Vartanian & J. Jung (Eds.), *The cambridge handbook of the neuroscience of creativity* (pp. 58–70). Cambridge, MA: MIT Press.

Gabora, L. (2019). From deep learning to deep reflection: Toward an appreciation of the integrated nature of cognition and a viable theoretical framework for cultural evolution. In L. Nadel &

D. D. Stein (Eds.), *Proceedings of the 2019 annual meeting of the Cognitive Science Society* (pp. 1801–1807). Austin TX: Cognitive Science Society.

Gabora, L., Beckage, N., & Steel, M. (2022). Modeling cognitive development with reflexively autocatalytic networks. *Topics in Cognitive Science, 14*(1), 163–188. https://doi.org/10.1111/tops.12583

Gabora, L., & Carbert, N. (2015). Cross-domain influences on creative innovation: Preliminary investigations. In R. Dale et al. (Eds.), *Proceedings of the 37th annual meeting of the cognitive science society* (pp. 758–763). Austin TX: Cognitive Science Society.

Gabora, L., & Kitto, K. (2017). Toward a quantum theory of humor. *Frontiers in Physics, 4*, 53. Retrieved from https://www.frontiersin.org/article/10.3389/fphy.2016.00053; https://doi.org/10.3389/fphy.2016.00053

Gabora, L., & Ranjan, A. (2013). How insight emerges in distributed, content-addressable memory. In A. Bristol, O. Vartanian, & J. Kaufman (Eds.), *The neuroscience of creativity* (pp. 19–43). Cambridge, MA: MIT Press.

Gabora, L., & Steel, M. (2017). Autocatalytic networks in cognition and the origin of culture. *Journal of Theoretical Biology, 431*, 87–95. https://doi.org/10.1016/j.jtbi.2017.07.022

Gabora, L., & Steel, M. (2020a). Modeling a cognitive transition at the origin of cultural evolution using autocatalytic networks. *Cognitive Science, 44*.

Gabora, L., & Steel, M. (2020b). A model of the transition to behavioral and cognitive modernity using reflexively autocatalytic networks. *Journal of the Royal Society Interface, 1720200545*.

Gabora, L. & Steel, M. (2021). An evolutionary process without variation and selection. *Journal of the Royal Society Interface, 18*(180). 20210334. https://doi.org/10.1098/rsif.2021.0334

Gabora, L., & Tseng, S. (2017). The social benefits of balancing creativity and imitation: Evidence from an agent-based model. *Psychology of Aesthetics, Creativity, and the Arts, 11*, 457–473.

Ganesh, K. & Gabora, L. (2022). Modeling discontinuous cultural evolution: The impact of cross-domain transfer. *Frontiers in Psychology – Theoretical and Philosophical Psychology, 13*, 786072. https://doi.org/10.3389/fpsyg.2022.786072

Ganesh, K. & Gabora, L. (in press). A dynamic autocatalytic network model of therapeutic change. Entropy. (Special issue edited by W. Tschacher & F. Orsucci on 'Complexity Science and Human Change.')

Gentner, D. (1983). Structure-mapping: A theoretical framework for analogy. *Cognitive Science, 7*, 155–170. https://doi.org/10.3389/fpsyg.2019.01426

Gentner, D., & Markman, A. B. (1997). Structure mapping in analogy and similarity. *American Psychologist, 52*, 45–56. https://doi.org/10.1037/0003-066X.52.1.45

Goncalves, M., Cardoso, C., & Badke-Schaub, P. (2013). Inspiration peak: Exploring the semantic distance between design problem and textual inspirational stimuli. *International Journal of Design Creativity and Innovation, 1*, 215–232.

Grimmett, G. R., & Stirzaker, D. R. (2020). *Probability and random processes (4th ed.)*. Oxford: Oxford University Press.

Hampton, J. A. (1988). Disjunction of natural concepts. *Memory and Cognition, 16*, 579–591. https://doi.org/10.3758/BF03197059

Hender, J. M., Dean, D. L., Rodgers, T. L., & Jay, F. F. (2002). An examination of the impact of stimuli type and GSS structure on creativity: Brainstorming versus non-brainstorming techniques in a gss environment. *Journal of Management Information Systems, 18*, 59–85.

Heppenheimer, T. A. (2003). *First flight: The Wright brothers and the invention of the airplane*. Hoboken NJA: Wiley.

Hofstadter, D. (1979). *Gödel, Escher, Bach: An eternal golden braid*. New York: Basic Books.

Hofstadter, D., & Sander, E. (2013). *Surfaces and essences: Analogy as the fuel and fire of thinking*. New York: Basic Books.

Holyoak, K. J., & Thagard, P. (1996). *Mental leaps: Analogy in creative thought*. Cambridge, MA: MIT Press.

Hordijk, W., Hein, J., & Steel, M. (2010). Autocatalytic sets and the origin of life. *Entropy, 12* (7), 1733–1742. https://doi.org/10.3390/e12071733

Hordijk, W., Kauffman, S. A., & Steel, M. (2011). Required levels of catalysis for emergence of autocatalytic sets in models of chemical reaction systems. *International Journal of Molecular Science, 12* (5), 3085–3101. https://doi.org/10.3390/ijms12053085

Hordijk, W., & Steel, M. (2004). Detecting autocatalytic, self-sustaining sets in chemical reaction systems. *Journal of Theoretical Biology, 227* (4), 451-461. https://doi.org/10.1016/j.jtbi.2003.11.020

Hordijk, W., & Steel, M. (2015). Autocatalytic sets and boundaries. *Journal of Systems Chemistry, 6* (1). https://doi.org/10.1186/s13322-014-0006-2

Hordijk, W., & Steel, M. (2016). Chasing the tail: The emergence of autocatalytic networks. *Biosystems, 152*, 1–10. https://doi.org/10.1016/j.biosystems.2016.12.002

Jacobsen, J. J., & Guastello, S. J. (2011). Diffusion models for innovation: S-curves, networks, power laws, catastrophes, and entropy. *Nonlinear Dynamics, Psychology, and Life Sciences, 15*, 307–333.

Jaffe, R. L., & Smith, G. D. (1996). A quantum chemistry study of benzene dimer. *The Journal of chemical physics, 105*(7), 2780–2788.

Jauk, E., Benedek, M., Beate Dunst, B., & Neubauer, A. C. (2013). The relationship between intelligence and creativity: New support for the threshold hypothesis by means of empirical breakpoint detection. *Intelligence, 41* (4), 212–221. https://doi.org/10.1016/j.intell.2013.03.003

Jeppesen, L. B., & Lakhani, K. R. (2010). Marginality and problem-solving effectiveness in broadcast search. *Organization Science, 21*, 1016–1033.

Jung, C. G., Von Franz, M. L., Henderson, J. L., Jaffé, A., & Jacobi, J. (1964). *Man and his symbols (Vol. 5183)*. New York: Dell.

Kalogerakis, K., Lu, C., & Herstatt, C. (2010). Developing innovations based on analogies: Experience from design and engineering consultants. *Journal of Product Innovation Management, 27*, 418–436.

Kauffman, S. A. (1986). Autocatalytic sets of proteins. *Journal of Theoretical Biology, 119*, 1–24. https://doi.org/10.3390/ijms12053085

Kauffman, S. A. (1993). *The origins of order*. Oxford University Press.

Kauffman, S. A. (2016). *Humanity in a creative universe*. Oxford, UK: Oxford University Press.

Kenett, Y. N. (2018). Investigating creativity from a semantic network perspective. In Z. Kapoula, E. Volle, J. Renoult, & M. Andreatta (Eds.), *Exploring transdisciplinarity in art and sciences* (pp. 49–75). Cham: Springer International Publishing.

Kharratzadeh, M., Montrey, M., Metz, A., & Shultz, T. R. (2017). Specialized hybrid learners resolve rogers' paradox about the adaptive value of social learning. *Journal of Theoretical Biology, 414*, 8--16. https://doi.org/10.1016/j.jtbi.2016.11.017

Kittur, A., Yu, L., Hope, T., Chan, J., Lifshitz-Assaf, H., Gilon, K., & Shahaf, D. (2019). Scaling up analogical innovation with crowds and ai. *Proceedings of the National Academy of Sciences, 116*, 1870–1877. https://doi.org/10.1073/pnas.1807185116

Kitzbichler, M. G., Smith, M. L., Christensen, S. R., & Bullmore, E. (2009). Broadband criticality of human brain network synchronization. *PLoS Computational Biology, 5*.

Kovacs, K., & Conway, A. R. A. (2016). Process overlap theory: A unified account of the general factor of intelligence. *Psychological Inquiry, 27* (3), 151–177. https://doi.org/10.108 0/1047840X.2016.1153946

Kwantes, P. J. (2005). Using context to build semantics. *Psychonomic Bulletin & Review, 12*, 703–710. https://doi.org/10.3758/BF03196761

Lakoff, G. (1993). The contemporary theory of metaphor. In A. Ortony (Ed.), *Metaphor and thought (2nd ed)* (p. 202—252). Cambridge, UK: Cambridge University Press.

Malaga, R. A. (2000). The effect of stimulus modes and associative distance in individual creativity support systems. *Decision Support Systems, 29*, 125—141. https://doi.org/10.1016/j.cognition.2015.08.008

Maturana, H., & Varela, F. (1973). Autopoiesis and cognition: The realization of the living. In R. S. Cohen & M. W. Wartofsky (Eds.), *Boston studies in the philosophy of science* (Vol. 42). Dordecht: Reidel.

Montagu, J. (2017). How music and instruments began: a brief overview of the origin and entire development of music, from its earliest stages. *Frontiers in Sociology*, 2, 8. https://doi.org/10.3389/fsoc.2017.00008

Mossel, E., & Steel, M. (2005). Random biochemical networks and the probability of self-sustaining autocatalysis. *Journal of Theoretical Biology*, *233*, 327–336. https://doi.org/10.1016/j.jtbi.2004.10.011

Muthukrishna, M., Doebeli, M., Chudek, M., & Henrich, J. (2018). The cultural brain hypothesis: How culture drives brain expansion, sociality, and life history. *PLoS Computational Biology*, *14*, e1006504. https://doi.org/10.1371/journal.pcbi.1006504

Nelson, D. L., Kitto, K., Galea, D., McEvoy, C. L., & Bruza, P. D. (2013). How activation, entanglement, and searching a semantic network contribute to event memory. *Memory & Cognition*, *41*, 797–819.

Nelson, D. L., McKinney, V. M., Gee, N. R., & Janczura, G. A. (1998). Interpreting the influence of implicitly activated memories on recall and recognition. *Psychological Review*, *105*, 299–324.

Osherson, D. N., & Smith, E. E. (1981). On the adequacy of prototype theory as a theory of concepts. *Cognition*, *9*, 35–58. https://doi.org/10.1016/0010-0277(81)90013-5

Poze, T. (1983). Analogical connections: The essence of creativity. *The Journal of Creative Behavior*, *17*, 240—258.

Ranjan, A., Gabora, L., & O'Connor, B. (2013). Evidence that cross-domain re-interpretations of creative ideas are recognizable. In *Proceedings of the Association for the Advancement of Artificial Intelligence (AAAI) Spring Symposium (Creativity and cognitive development: A perspective from artificial creativity, developmental artificial intelligence, and robotics)*. Menlo Park, USA: AAAI Press.

Schilling, M. A. (2005). A small-world network model of cognitive insight. *Creativity Research Journal*, *17*, 131–154.

Scotney, V., Schwartz, J., Carbert, N., Saab, A., & Gabora, L. (2020). The form of a 'half-baked' creative idea: Empirical explorations into the structure of ill-defined mental representations. *Acta Psychologica*, *202*, 102981. https://doi.org/10.1016/j.actpsy.2019.102981

Scotney, V., Weissmeyer, S., Carbert, N., & Gabora, L. (2019). The ubiquity of cross-domain thinking in the early phase of the creative process. *Frontiers in Psychology (Section: Cognitive Science, Topic: Creativity from Multiple Cognitive Science Perspectives)*, *10*, 1426. https://doi.org/10.3389/fpsyg.2019.01426

Shteynberg, G., Hirsh, J. B., Bentley, R. A., & Garthoff, J. (2020). Shared worlds and shared minds: A theory of collective learning and a psychology of common knowledge. *Psychological Review*, *127*, 918–931. https://doi.org/10.1037/rev0000200

Smith, J. I., Steel, M., & Hordijk, W. (2014). Autocatalytic sets in a partitioned biochemical network. *Journal of Systems Chemistry*, *5* (2), 1–18.

Steel, M., Hordijk, W., & Xavier, J. C. (2019). Autocatalytic networks in biology: Structural theory and algorithms. *Journal of the Royal Society Interface*, *16*, rsif.2018.0808. https://doi.org/10.1098/rsif.2018.0808

Steel, M., Xavier, J. C., & Huson, D. H. (2020). Autocatalytic networks in biology: Structural theory and algorithms. *Journal of the Royal Society Interface*, *17*, 20200488.

Stephen, D. G., Boncoddo, R. A., Magnuson, J. S., & Dixon, J. (2009). The dynamics of insight: Mathematical discovery as a phase transition. *Memory & Cognition*, *37*, 1132–1149.

Steyvers, M., & Tenenbaum, J. B. (2005). The large-scale structure of semantic networks: Statistical analyses and a model of semantic growth. *Cognitive Science*, *29*, 41–78.

Teo, T. (2018). *Outline of theoretical psychology: Critical investigations*. Berlin: Springer.

Thagard, P. (2019). *Brain-mind: From neurons to consciousness and creativity (Treatise on mind and society)*. New York: Oxford University Press.

Tomasello, M., Kruger, A. C., & Ratner, H. H. (1993). Cultural learning. *Behavioral and Brain Sciences*, *16*, 495—511. https://doi.org/10.1017/S0140525X0003123X

Vasas, V., Fernando, C., Santos, M., Kauffman, S., & Szathmáry, E. (2012). Evolution before genes. *Biol. Direct*, *7* (1).

Veloz, T., Gabora, L., Eyjolfson, M., & Aerts, D. (2011). Toward a formal model of the shifting relationship between concepts and contexts during associative thought. In D. Song, M. Melucci, I. Frommholz, P. Zhang, L. Wang, & S. Arafat (Eds.), *Proceedings of the Fifth International Symposium on Quantum Interaction* (pp. 25–34). Cognitive Science Society: Springer. https://doi.org/10.1007/978-3-642-24971-6_4

Ward, T., Smith, S., & Vaid, J. (1997). *Creative thought: An investigation of conceptual structures and processes*. Washington: American Psychological Association.

Ward, T. B. (1998). Analogical distance and purpose in creative thought: Mental leaps versus mental hops. In K. J. Holyoak, D. Gentner, & B. Kokinov (Eds.), *Advances in analogy research: Integration of theory and data from the cognitive, computational, and neural sciences* (pp. 221–230). Bulgaria: Sofia.

Wiley, J. (1998). Expertise as mental set: The effects of domain knowledge in creative problem solving. *Memory & Cognition, 26*, 716–730.

Xavier, J. C., Hordijk, W., Kauffman, S., Steel, M., & Martin, W. F. (2020). Autocatalytic chemical networks at the origin of metabolism. *Proceedings of the Royal Society of London. Series B: Biological Sciences, 287*, 20192377.

Zurn, P., & Bassett, D. (2020). Network architectures supporting learnability. *Philosophical Transactions of the Royal Society B, 3*, 7520190323. https://doi.org/10.1098/rstb.2019.0323

Part III
Uncertainty and Creativity in Science and Mathematics

Chapter 9
Grasping the Uncertainty of Scientific Phenomena: A Creative, Agentic, and Multimodal Model for Sensemaking

Ross C. Anderson, Shawn Irvin, Tracy Bousselot, Nate Beard, and Paul Beach

Abstract This chapter proposes a framework to guide future research and practice in the understudied area of scientific sensemaking—the liminal space of uncertainty with abstraction where meaning-making takes shape for learners. The chapter discusses the role of agency and creative metacognition in relation to scientific sensemaking and proposes a multimodal continuum, where linguistic metaphor, physical and gestural enactment, and 3D construction enhance the 2D graphic illustration of scientific models, typical in most science classrooms. Grounded with standards-based examples, this chapter illustrates how teachers can scaffold different types and intensities of uncertainty into the scientific sensemaking process to develop students' agency and metacognition, equitably, and provide access to different multimodal techniques.

R. C. Anderson (✉)
Inflexion, Eugene, OR, USA

Creative Engagement Lab, Eugene, OR, USA
e-mail: ross@creativeengagementlab.com

S. Irvin
University of Oregon, Eugene, OR, USA

T. Bousselot
Inflexion, Eugene, OR, USA

N. Beard
Creative Engagement Lab, Eugene, OR, USA

P. Beach
Bellweather, Nashville, TN, USA

© Springer Nature Switzerland AG 2022
R. A. Beghetto, G. J. Jaeger (eds.), *Uncertainty: A Catalyst for Creativity, Learning and Development*, Creativity Theory and Action in Education 6,
https://doi.org/10.1007/978-3-030-98729-9_9

9.1   Introduction

Picture a diverse Grade 9 science classroom working to grasp how the radioactive decay of unstable isotopes works as a source of heat in the Earth's mantle convection. The teacher is tackling a tricky standard and needs to be assured that students understand this process before moving on to more complexity. Students stir with uncertainty about what "unstable" refers to (*is it like when the kitchen table is wobbly on one leg?*) and what makes one "isotope" different from another. The teacher introduces the topic through a slideshow of diagrams alongside a short lecture and asks students to discuss the definitions found in the textbook for several minutes. Uncertainty about the concepts diminishes, while uncertainty about what is coming next begins to rise. The students know the teacher is going to ask them to make sense of the phenomena then incorporate these ideas into their own explanatory models using their bodies, found materials, and linguistic metaphorical representations. The impending creative challenge keeps a manageable state of uncertainty and doubt in flux, leaving room for new possibilities to arise.

When provided space to explore, students from culturally and linguistically diverse backgrounds will play with different modalities to grasp the meaning of abstractions such as an *unstable isotope* or the process of *radioactivity*. One student may spontaneously signify the idea of decay with hand/body gestures to grapple with the abstraction of *radioactivity*. Another student might grab a variety of found objects—paper clips, pencils, and pipe cleaners—and build a 3-D constructed model to illustrate how an unstable isotope decays to become another element. Another student might riff on linguistic metaphors to find meaning of this abstract concept—*an unstable isotope is having multiple careers in life or going through transformative rites of passage*. For a variety of reasons, in typical science instruction, teachers do not always prioritize or value the time students need to grapple with the uncertainty of abstraction in science (Weiss et al. 2003). Students experience limited space for sensemaking, and, therefore, may be managing a degree of uncertainty in science learning that becomes unsustainable over time.

The Next Generation Science Standards (NGSS) emphasizes three-dimensional learning and the use of phenomena to deepen understanding of science concepts. Science teachers often prompt students to simply copy or illustrate 2-D diagrams to demonstrate understanding, create scientific models, and provide accessible opportunities for assessment. Though this approach has merit, it still ignores the importance of other key sensemaking forms. Each form provides a different process for sensemaking and memory retention. The different forms discussed in this chapter are culturally and socially rooted and emphasize personal interpretation and creative expression in shaping meaning about abstraction in the world around us. These forms can be developed into polished sensemaking tools through scaffolded classroom routines. Specifically, embodied and metaphorical forms remain largely unconsidered, unexplored, and unrealized; yet, students use these forms naturally to grapple with the uncertainty of our unfathomably abstract, complex, and mysterious world.

While uncertainty serves as a catalyst for creative opportunities in learning, these multimodal forms represent the tools that students often use, intrinsically, and can develop with time to make and express new meaning in what they learn. Scientific learning is filled with actionable uncertainty, unexpected possibility, and creative potential at every turn. This chapter proposes a model—GrASSP: Growing Agency for Sensemaking of Scientific Phenomena—that functions as both (a) an instructional approach for routine scientific sensemaking and (b) a theoretical model for investigating the agentic and creative process of scientific sensemaking. The GrASSP model grew from collaboration between science educators, arts integration specialists, and creativity in education researchers in the ArtCore and makeSPACE projects. Both projects focused on developing teacher agency and skill to design, implement, and evolve high quality arts integrated experiences for students' creative engagement. The GrASSP model focuses specifically on the science classroom context.

9.2   Sources of Uncertainty in Science Learning

Uncertainty describes a state of doubt, of not knowing, where we feel a lack of control and predictability about what is to come (Beghetto 2019). Beghetto places uncertainty on a spectrum of intensity from mundane uncertainties that we experience throughout our days to profound uncertainties, which feel entirely unknowable. In between those extremes, we find actionable uncertainty—an invitation to creative action with possibility. When we place uncertainty in the context of our hypothetical Grade 9 science classroom where students actively make sense of complex science concepts together, the state of doubt experienced by students is actionable uncertainty on several levels.

As the antecedent of creative thought and action, these sources of uncertainty are akin to the social, internal, material, and societal-situational ruptures described by Beghetto (2020). At the internal level, each student holds some confusion and, potentially, frustration and anxiety, about the meaning of specific concepts they are expected to learn. At the social level, each student feels some doubt about whether others will put effort toward understanding their creative and potentially discrepant ideas and contributions. At the material level, considering students' bodies and any found objects as the learning medium, students may not know how to combine their ideas and materials into a cohesive action without some scaffolded guidance. Given that embracing uncertainty demands an "attitude of suspended conclusion," as Dewey suggests (as quoted in Beghetto 2020), this chapter proposes a multimodal modeling process with science concepts as an optimal practice to develop the uncertainty muscles in students and their teachers. The proposed framework can generalize to other abstract learning material, such as learning about political systems or systemic racism, and establish conditions for uncertainty to thrive.

9.2.1 Uncertainty As Space for Students' Funds of Knowledge

The approach outlined in this chapter assumes that learners have stores of intuition about the physical world. This intuition is informed by personal experience, cultural participation, schooling, and other knowledge-building activities (Dewey 1938; diSessa 1993; Duckworth 1996; Elby 2001; Hammer 2000, 2006). Many of these intuitions are *productive* and align with disciplinary norms (Hammer 1996; Harrer et al. 2013). If learning is a process of growth, then these early ideas mature through experience and exposure, eventually becoming coherent, more consistent, and fully scientific. Seminal theories of teaching and learning, such as constructivism, follow that logic to empower learners with tools for their own sensemaking of the world (e.g., Dewey 1938; Gupta et al. 2014; Montessori 1978; Piaget and Inhelder 1974; Vygotsky 1986).

Diverse students' *funds of knowledge* are often rooted in cultural and familial experiences and their engagement with the environment around them. These funds of knowledge may emerge from and be expressed through engagement in different modalities, such as visual, movement, or verbal, leveraged to explore, share and expand that knowledge (Moje et al. 2004). If curricular experiences are predetermined at every stage with little freedom to employ different modalities intentionally, opportunities are minimal for these funds of knowledge to be valued and applied in scientific sensemaking for students. Beghetto (2020) proposes that structured uncertainty can loosen the predetermined nature of most classroom learning in four different places: the *what*, the *how*, the *outcome,* and the *criteria*. The proposed GrASSP model focuses, primarily, on the *how* and on the *outcome*—the way that students explore and interpret new information and ideas and how they express their understanding.

Fundamentally, the how and the outcome of the learning approach are a sensemaking process. *Scientific sensemaking* represents the active effort toward meaning and coherence, assembled from bits of complex and abstract information. Sensemaking is a process of retrieval of relevant past ideas and the construction and reconstruction of explanations across multiple attempts at representation (Cannady et al. 2019). Within a classroom, sensemaking occurs individually and collectively through the accessing and sharing of different funds of knowledge (Zimmerman et al. 2010). Students draw from their past experiences with scientific phenomena and engage different modalities to work toward and express that understanding.

When grappling with uncertainty, students must consider the different kinds of modalities they can employ. Their awareness, contextual knowledge, self-evaluation, and strategies represent their *creative metacognition*. The cognitive, social, and cultural process activates key opportunities to develop and apply creative metacognition in science learning (Anderson & Haney 2021). As students develop more tools for scientific sensemaking, their awareness for flexible and novel approaches increases. Yet, to engage in scientific sensemaking and tap their funds of knowledge, to begin with, requires students to feel a sense of agency. Based on social-cognitive theory, that agency emerges from feeling capable to succeed, in control of learning, and personally valuing the process and the outcome (Bandura 1986, 2018). However, opportunities for students to develop agency to tap their funds of knowledge and creative meaning-making toward scientific sensemaking have been rare in secondary science classrooms (Manz et al. 2018; Weiss et al. 2003).

9.2.2 What Is The Nature of the Problem?

Focusing on scientific sensemaking at the secondary level is important for several reasons. The middle to high school transition can lead to a recursive decline in students' sense of agency and engagement in school (Anderson et al. 2019a; Benner and Wang 2014; Madjar and Chohat 2016), and presents a developmental period where social belonging is paramount (Dahl et al. 2018). Meaningful achievement gaps persist in middle and high school science for marginalized groups, such as Black/African American students as compared to their white peers (NAEP 2015; NCES 2012; Provasnik et al. 2012; Morgan et al. 2016). Male-female gender gaps begin as early as Grade 3 in science (e.g., Kohlhaas et al., 2010), resulting from stereotype threat and cultural messaging, not from ability (e.g., Good et al. 2007; Riegle-Crumb et al. 2012). To shift these malleable beliefs at key educational transition points, such as high school, requires active and disruptive practices in the classroom (Burger and Walk 2016). As this chapter describes, the GrASSP framework proposes that structured uncertainty and integrated creative modalities can serve as disruptive catalysts.

In many ways, the limited approach to scientific sensemaking in 2D illustration or written description represents a white-dominant approach focused on being regimented and procedural. This approach often ignores the development of students' own ideas (Windschitl and Calabrese Barton 2016). While agency and engagement decline for most students from middle school to high school (Anderson et al. 2019a, b), the sensemaking demands and complexity of scientific phenomena increases. Sensemaking is an essential component for learning and assessment in science (Duschl 2008). Unfortunately, the facilitated time for students to question, evaluate, and evolve ideas about science remains highly limited and absent from typical science instruction, according to classroom observation (Weiss et al. 2003). If teachers do not provide time and support for scientific sensemaking, then students' diverse funds of knowledge and varied culturally-informed ways of constructing, representing, and evaluating ideas likely remain delegitimized (Ladson-Billings 2003; Moje et al. 2004; Rosebery and Warren 2008).

Through Science and Engineering Practices, the NGSS in the United States focuses students attention on modeling ideas and phenomena. Access to modeling faces two barriers. First, teachers dominate the cultural and pedagogical aspects of learning, what Manz et al. (2018) called, *epistemic agency*. Structured uncertainty provides one intentional pathway to place control of certain aspects of learning and epistemology into the hands of students, but training is essential. For instance, studying autonomy support in science, Patall et al. (2019) identified that students don't always seek or need autonomy. The second barrier is that some students approach secondary science classrooms with little sense of agency to understand complex concepts successfully. For students marginalized due to race, ethnicity, culture, or language, education has often devalued and stigmatized their ways of knowing and expression. Other students may have performed poorly or experienced few opportunities for high-quality science learning, and carry low self-efficacy (Manz et al. 2018).

Teacher reflection on epistemic dominance can help identify opportunities to insert uncertainty and to see the different ways students productively struggle, leading to better formative sensemaking of scientific ideas (NRC 2012). Science instruction at the secondary level needs attention on these complementary components. The discrepancy between historically marginalized students' interest and participation in science could be a product of limited opportunities for agentic and creative sensemaking to access and build on funds of knowledge. Teachers aren't receiving training to address this need. Few graduate programs and professional development opportunities provide teachers with the tools and resources to employ effective sensemaking in science and integrate the creative learning process (Windschitl et al. 2018). The field needs a framework to conceptualize and operationalize these factors and practices in research and in the classroom.

9.3   The GrASSP Framework

The Fig. 9.1 framework illustrates the links between students' agency, their creative metacognition, and their process for sensemaking in science. To make sense of the uncertainty and abstraction of scientific concepts, students question, model, and

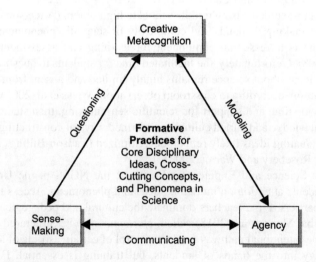

Fig. 9.1 The GrASSP framework

communicate their understanding using four different modalities that will be explored below. In the following sections, each component of the model is explained and explored in the practice of science classroom teaching.

9.3.1 Why Agency for Scientific Sensemaking?

Feeling agency to make sense of scientific ideas incorporates factors at the personal and interpersonal levels. Whereas personal agency builds from self-efficacy for future success, how in control a person feels, and how they value the task, agency at the interpersonal or proxy level, builds from vicarious experiences, modeling, and feedback (Bandura 1986, 2018). These factors shape a students' sense of agency to make meaning of complex scientific ideas and phenomena (Bandura 1986, 2018). Reeve (2013) proposed the concept of agentic engagement as the proactive process of students' shaping the learning environment to be optimally supportive of their motivation. Patall et al. (2019) found that this agentic engagement led to greater emotional, behavioral, and cognitive engagement in high school science classes in the U.S. To productively struggle after the meaning of scientific phenomena, agentic engagement emerges in a range of possible actions. Students might (a) pose clarifying questions, (b) make explanations, (c) use a non-example to solidify understanding, (d) ask for other examples from the teacher, or (e) access different modalities, such as gesture or metaphor, to explore and convey meaning to others.

Revisiting the introductory example will illustrate the role of agency in scientific sensemaking. We can assume the teacher used routine open-ended creative thinking exercises to develop students' familiarity and skill in four key modalities for sensemaking: gesture, linguistic metaphor, and 3D modeling. The routine practice with these modalities establishes conditions for students to take creative risks. The Grade 9 students work together to understand how unstable isotopes function using Helium-2 as an exemplar. The students create linguistic metaphor that represents Helium, accurately, as embodied emotions or as a character in a story. They use their own individual experiences and funds of knowledge about Helium—for example, they remember that Helium is used to inflate balloons and so must be really light in density. Through discussion, they connect those funds of knowledge to scientific characteristics. They dispel any misconceptions, attach new ideas to their own personal schema, and produce creative representations of Helium related to their own lives. To deepen their sensemaking about unstable isotopes, they explore metaphorical gestures that depict other distinct properties of Helium—colorless, odorless, tasteless, and non-toxic. By working through those initial metaphors, gestures, and details students are prepared to construct 3D representations and 2D illustrations portraying the role of unstable isotopes in the internal energy of the Earth. Looking across those steps and stages, agentic engagement manifests in how students co-create, share ideas, and expand their own scientific sensemaking tools. Proxy agency emerges in the opportunities and exposure to the different approaches taken. In this way, developing agency for scientific sensemaking becomes shared and vicarious—an important collectivist component of Bandura's (1986) conceptualization of agency.

9.4   Why Creative Learning and Metacognition?

When students in early adolescence at the cusp of high school demonstrate consistently stronger creative thinking potential for original ideas, they also demonstrate greater agentic, academic, and creative preparedness (Anderson 2019). From that perspective, to engage in creative learning in science and contribute novel and meaningful ideas in a classroom demands many of the same attitudes and self-beliefs that go into strong academic preparedness. Creative learning in science exists at the personal level of finding new possibilities in what is learned and then engaging the social and cultural setting by sharing those new possibilities with others (Anderson et al. 2019b; Beghetto 2016). A learner needs self-awareness, self-regulation, and contextual knowledge to take a risk with a new way to represent a scientific idea, even if not yet fully accurate (Anderson and Haney 2021; Karwowski and Beghetto 2018). Moreover, developing students' capacity for original thinking through practice may leverage developmental advantages for their creative learning (Anderson and Graham 2021). Creative thinking and action in science is both *meta-cognitive* and *agentic*. Accordingly, the way that students grow confidence and knowledge to use modalities, such as embodied, 3D modeling, or 2D illustration links inextricably to their creative metacognition for scientific sensemaking. In the GrASSP framework, students develop their confidence through routine and diverse applications of each modality, scaffolded carefully by the teacher. The teacher can gradually add more and more uncertainty into the process by requiring students to choose which modality they will use for a particular task. As students successfully wade into the uncertainty of modeling to make sense of abstract and complex science phenomena, their confidence can grow and lead to greater willingness to take risks and explore ways to share what they think and know.

Exploratory interactions appear to be key for more creatively supportive classrooms. When Gadja et al. (2017) observed micro-interactions in classrooms for creative behavior, more exploratory interactions between teachers and students indicated greater encouragement to work through what was being taught before moving on. The teachers demonstrated more tolerance for uncertainty by not closing down students' questions even when they appeared to be tangential from the main topic of discussion. Teachers explored seemingly unrelated and divergent ideas that students expressed about what they learned with more openness to the possible directions it could take the class. Not surprisingly, classrooms where teachers had greater flexibility in the face of uncertainty of student sensemaking also provided greater psychological safety and social-emotional support for students. In those classrooms, students were more likely to take creative risks and manage failure without being held back by the fear of not knowing the answer in front of peers

(Gadja et al. 2017). Interestingly, while active learning experiences have shown to be more effective for students (Deslauriers et al. 2019), the cognitive and emotional struggle inherent in the uncertainty that fuels creative and active learning with complex material may not feel as useful and productive to students compared to more passive learning (e.g., lecture). With this point in mind, the struggle that comes with structured uncertainty and creative use of multimodal modeling should be routinized in order for students to habituate the social, emotional, and cognitive demands.

9.4.1 Why Multimodal Modeling, Scientific Phenomena, and Metaphor?

Modeling of scientific ideas and phenomena is an integral part of scientific literacy and agency in the NGSS. Modeling fits into a continuous process of sensemaking, formative feedback, and revision within the uncertainty inherent in understanding and explaining scientific phenomena (Windschitl et al. 2018). Modeling in science typically uses 2D illustration as the primary tool for sensemaking and representation of science phenomena. That limitation results in the exclusion of the diverse culturally rooted assets and funds of knowledge students bring into their science learning through modalities such as gesture, hands-on 3D construction, linguistic metaphor, sound and rhythm, and movement, among others.

Given the lack of exploration of these modalities, the question arises as to how and why these modalities might fit into the sensemaking experience of students to shape scientific models. According to researchers, a scientific model, such as the water cycle, is "a representation that abstracts and simplifies a system by focusing on key features to explain and predict scientific phenomena" (Schwarz et al. 2009, p. 633). Complex in nature, models often include multiple relationships and interactions between parts of a scientific process. Models might also include causal mechanisms that shape a change process and rules that govern relationships within a system. Serving as anchor models, phenomena are observable events in the universe that demonstrate how models work in nature. Phenomena-based learning advocates suggest that phenomena can support students' motivation and understanding; yet phenomena remain largely underutilized in science teaching. Advocates encourage educators to use recognizable phenomena to help students figure out why or how something works or occurs as opposed to discussing a topic (Institute for Science and Math Education 2016).

Even though the NGSS emphasize scientific modeling in 2D diagrams, the standards also suggest modeling can take shape through physical replicas, mathematical representations, analogies, and computer simulations if they are used to predict or explain phenomena. Whereas 2D diagrams show explanatory models with pictures, other forms of models, such as 3D construction, physical simulation, or linguistic metaphor, explore and explain models using objects, the body, and poetic devices for illustrative purposes. Regardless of the modality employed, modeling should incorporate evidence and reasoning alongside students' interpretations of scientific phenomena and should clarify the different kinds of predictions these models make possible (Schwarz et al. 2009).

9.4.1.1 Scientific Sensemaking

Understanding the pieces that make up the scientific sensemaking process clarifies where uncertainty in the learning process—specifically the *how* and *outcome*—fit into the GrASSP framework. Cannady et al. (2019) proposed that scientific sensemaking follows a distinct process, and their research provides some support for this conceptualization. Students first ask good questions, then seek mechanistic explanations for natural and physical phenomena. Eventually, they engage in argumentation about scientific ideas, interpreting data in different forms and formats, and design investigations to elaborate and test their understanding. Of these steps, the GrASSP framework addresses *asking good questions* and *seeking mechanistic explanations* with the most attention. At the student level, these steps should include the disambiguation of related concepts through multimodal modeling—a pathway to manage uncertainty at the conceptual level. That disambiguation is critical to consider given that students show sustained difficulties differentiating related ideas and topics across science domains (McDermott and Redish 1999; Meltzer and Thornton 2012). Moreover, research supports the practice of using multiple modalities, such as explanatory embodied action (Osgood-Campbell 2018), as a process of disambiguating, or making sense of, highly related concepts (Scherr et al. 2013). As one point of evidence, Metcalfe et al. (1984) studied the effectiveness of embodied enactment of concepts related to molecular change due to heat with middle school students. They found that students using embodied, gestural enactment were able to interpret and explain the concepts at twice the rate of their peers who learned using traditional techniques.

9.4.1.2 Linguistic Metaphor

One reason that embodied enactment may be effective is through its inherent integration of a gestural form of metaphor. Metaphor generation is a powerful, cross-cultural tool of meaning-making. In fact, regularly, we may use up to four metaphors a minute without knowing. When we make and use *conceptual metaphors,* we take a *topic*, such as school, and frame the properties of that topic through a *vehicle*, or unrelated idea, which can also express values about dimensions of the topic. For instance, if a student considers school to be jail, then school contains the properties of being confined against one's will, alongside the feeling of being under the watch of authority figures and forced into subordinate thinking and behavior (Chiappe and Chiappe 2007). Often, we employ conceptual metaphor with little understanding and awareness of the power those metaphors exert on our emotions and behavior. Just consider how many words from war are included in our everyday description of arguments (e.g., an indefensible position, critique was on target, a suggestion was shot down, etc.). As Lakoff and Johnson suggest, if we described having an argument with someone using the conceptual metaphor of a *dance* between two people, we may look at conflict and disagreement differently in this culture.

The common, often unconscious everyday use of metaphor expresses cultural values and ideas and helps us make sense of and explain abstraction. The sensory-motor experiences of our bodies, such as movement and emotion, provide a primary pathway for this metaphorical generation (Lakoff and Johnson 1980). As an example, we will typically express ideas about time, such as saying we are "half-way through" the year, in a way that suggests a spatial quality to time, which provides our bodies a way to move relative to it. We use this kind of linguistic innovation to bridge—an apt metaphor, no doubt—from the everyday tangible understanding in our bodies to the abstraction and uncertainty we encounter, shaping meaning along the way.

9.4.1.3 Embodied, Gestural Modalities

The rationale to use the body to make sense of abstract concepts should be intuitive given how essential the use of gesture is to communication across cultures. For reference, try to explain something abstract and complex with your hands in your pockets. In Vanessa Van Edwards' *You are contagious* TEDx London talk, she presented research she and colleagues conducted on the use of gesture by TED speakers. They found that the most popular TED talks included, on average, 465 gestures made by the speaker to accompany their presentation of ideas and stories—twice as many as the least popular TED talks (Van Edwards 2017). When it comes to grappling with the complexities and abstraction of scientific concepts and phenomena, our bodies are likely the most underutilized and underappreciated sensemaking tools. According to ideas from embodied cognition (Amin et al. 2015), cognitive processes that occur in our minds build from knowledge structures that emerge from experiences based in our bodies—such as our emotions. These processes also recruit material, symbolic, and social structures of our bodies in relationship to our environments that actually reduce the cognitive demand on our minds.

When we make physical, embodied simulation of abstract ideas, we are essentially building empathy for non-human processes and entities, such as atoms. In that process, we visualize, we interpret, and we experience those concepts and create spatial and physical awareness—the *feeling*—of otherwise intangible, abstract ideas (Reiner and Gilbert 2000). Gesture contains a sensemaking power that remains largely understudied and misunderstood in the science of teaching and learning across content areas. One of the rare studies in this area for math instruction found that students asked to gesture during math learning, such as pointing to two sides of the equation, retained more than twice the learning of students who were told only to speak (Cook et al. 2008).

To see gestural sensemaking in action, let's reach back to our initial example around radioactivity and unstable isotopes with Helium as the star of the show. First, after practicing metaphorical gesture routines for several weeks, students might intuitively make sense of key properties of Helium with gestures that illustrate how Helium rises up using their hands, arms, and eyes. Once they have played with different embodied possibilities, groups of students might begin to build multiple scenes with their bodies aimed at telling the story of how deep in the Earth, Helium forms through radioactive decay. Students might demonstrate the release of huge quantities of Helium released by volcanic activity. These gestures are mimicking some of the non-human processes, while also tapping into some of the metaphorical possibilities that students think of to represent the properties and potential uses of Helium. For culturally diverse students, this embodied and metaphorical process may be especially powerful, given that for some, the process of imagining their bodies as part of actual science is key to exploring meaning (Rosebery and Warren 2008). For instance, properties of Helium might call forth a dance move or complicated hair style that resisted gravity. Fundamentally, the embodied element within a multimodal process may feel uncertain and vulnerable at first, but research indicates it can lead to better learning.

9.4.1.4   Three-Dimensional Construction

In a similar process to embodied enactment, building a physical model with basic materials and found objects in three dimensions is itself a physical sensemaking process. We transform those materials and common objects into a meaningful representation of an idea (Windschitl et al. 2018). Teachers and learners should focus on the modeling *process*, before, during, and after construction to identify insights and new understanding about the concepts, as well as to correct initial misconceptions. Student-generated questions, interpretations, and creative expression and extension about the phenomenon serve as the touchpoints for rigorous and useful formative feedback in the GrASSP framework. When modeling instruction integrates seamlessly into science learning, students can construct, use, compare, evaluate, and revise models in different modalities to share and enhance scientific sensemaking across a classroom of learners. When creative metacognition increases and modalities can be employed strategically, the process frees students to engage with scientific ideas using their bodies, found objects, and everyday language (see Windschitl and Calabrese Barton 2016).

9.5   Using Multimodal Sensemaking as Formative Feedback

With scaffolded supports, recent research (Anderson et al. 2021) indicates teachers can be successful with and benefit from bringing multimodal routines into their teaching, even in the distance learning format. This process can support teachers' assessment of where students get stuck and need further instruction and exploration. The process also helps to shape more adaptive beliefs and ideas about creativity for teachers and contributes to a reduction in the level of anxiety experienced when facing uncertain and open-ended experiences in teaching (Anderson et al., 2022). In the GrASSP framework and the strategies proposed, teachers develop a deeper recognition of the different ways students' express their funds of knowledge and develop a set of instructional tools that can provide different types of formative information about their students' understanding with new and complex material. Brief multimodal practices for sensemaking can provide regular practice with uncertainty in how to explore and explain scientific phenomena. These practices can be a quick and efficient way for teachers to set conditions for choice, cultivate agency, engage creative metacognition, and check for understanding. Students become agentic to recognize how and when to employ a specific modality, especially in the uncertain process of disambiguating highly related science concepts introduced in secondary school. The list below illustrates different ways to manifest the GrASSP framework, depicted in Fig. 9.1, in the routine formative feedback loops between students and teachers.

1. Teachers can incorporate live *agency checks* at regular intervals with questions such as, *show me with raised hands how **confident** you feel about your understanding from 1 to 5? Where are you stuck?*
2. Teachers can use regular creative metacognition checks with questions such as, *how many **different** ways can we explain, illustrate, or demonstrate this idea and connect it to other concepts? What **new questions** can we come up with to ask about it? How did you arrive at your understanding and what could be an **alternative** representation?*
3. Teachers can draw out students' ideas as they evolve, withholding judgment as sensemaking takes shape.
4. Teachers incorporate rapid gesture-building to represent scientific concepts, such as the periodic table of elements, with questions such as, *what is an accurate and meaningful **gesture** that can distinguish Helium from Neon and other noble gases? What about an inaccurate gesture? What is a **metaphor** for what emotions Helium might feel if it were human?*

As a formative practice, these checks for agency, creative metacognition, and multimodal sensemaking are designed to create regular opportunities for students to contribute new culturally, socially, and emotionally relevant ideas with the dual benefit of their own engagement and enhanced meaning for the whole class. With routinized practice, the uncertainty inherent in scientific understanding and multimodal sensemaking may become a catalyst for motivation and equity in scientific achievement and pursuits in high school and beyond.

9.6   The GrASSP Framework Embedded in a Science Unit

The expanded learning progression described below is grounded in three science and engineering practices from the high school NGSS key to sensemaking in science. *Asking Questions and Defining Problems* focuses on asking questions that arise from examining models or theory to clarify and/or seek additional information and relationships. *Developing and Using Models* focuses on developing, revising, and/or using evidence-based models to illustrate and/or predict relationships between systems or components. *Obtaining, Evaluating, and Communicating Information* focuses on communicating scientific and/or technical information or ideas in multiple formats and modalities, from oral presentation to graphical illustration. According to the standards, these science and engineering practices are very important. For instance, of the 67 Grade 9 NGSS performance expectations, 19 require these three practices explicitly. Of the 12 disciplinary core ideas presented for Grade 9 students, seven included these practices. And of the seven key crosscutting concepts, three incorporate these practices. Given the broad application, the development of students' agency for multimodal scientific sensemaking driven by these practices could be broadly impactful for science instruction.

The GrASSP framework can be contextualized in science curriculum through different possible learning progressions, using evidence of student learning as the lower and upper bounds of that progression . The progression described below was adapted from the Schwartz et al. (2009) approach to making scientific modeling accessible and meaningful to students. The GrASSP framework expands Schwartz and colleagues' key elements in a model-based progression by layering one possible continua of multimodal modeling, onto the two continua of the *scientific process* and *scientific purpose* shown in Fig. 9.2.

Figure 9.2 illustrates the process through which students begin to *construct* questions, models, and communication of their ideas in early iterations with the aim of *illustrating* scientific phenomena. After these early iterations, students *use* and *compare-evaluate* questions, models, and communication to *explain* scientific ideas, accurately, in exchange with one another in the classroom. After sharing and receiving feedback from peers and teachers, students *revise* questions, models, and communication with the aim of *predicting* scientific phenomena, effectively. As such, this framework interweaves the process and purpose continua with the multimodal process consisting of linguistic metaphor, embodied gestural metaphor, 3D modeling, and 2D illustration and description. For this progression to be effective, teacher and peer feedback, encouragement, suggestions, and critique should be continuous.

To fully grasp this framework in the context of a science unit and understand how students work through uncertainty in action, we can explore an illustrative example from the NGSS: PE HS-ESS2-1—*Develop a model to illustrate how Earth's internal and surface processes operate at different spatial and temporal scales to form continental and ocean-floor features*. Starting at the lower bound of the GrASSP learning progression, a teacher could ask students to *construct* a model and *illustrate* mountain-building through the subduction of internal destructive processes and volcanic growth through surficial constructive forces. Prior to illustrating the 2D model to demonstrate their understanding, students would engage with different modalities for sensemaking. The proposed progression illustrated below is one formulation of the process, but teachers and students in different contexts working with different cultural assets and science content may innovate other multimodal continua.

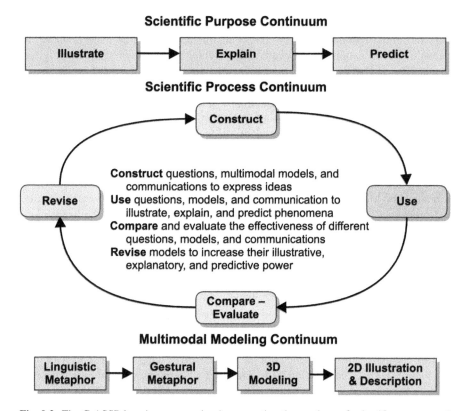

Fig. 9.2 The GrASSP learning progression incorporating the continua of scientific purpose and process adapted from Schwartz et al. (2009)

First, students would begin their sensemaking process by generating and exchanging creative linguistic metaphor around the key concepts of subduction and volcanic construction. They would use the definitions, examples, and descriptions provided by their teacher to explore different ideas from their lives and experiences, integrating their funds of knowledge. One student, hungry for lunch, might think about a giant plate of nachos and how they come to be stacked in layers and the kinds of forces at play once the plate is placed in front of a group of hungry teenagers, pulling out cheesy nacho bites carefully from the bottom of the stack. Another student might be reminded of their experience building sandcastles at the beach and watching the tide come in, slowly melting away the mounds of sand from below. With these linguistic sensemaking metaphors, students in a group can identify the aspects of a representation that are accurate and those aspects that do not match up with properties of the phenomena. In that process they gain concept attainment through examples and non-examples, develop agency, and become more comfortable with the uncertainty of this process of sensemaking of the abstract.

After developing and revising linguistic metaphor examples, students carry those ideas into gestural and embodied metaphor to represent different properties of the phenomena. For instance, one group might develop a *tableau vivants*, or series of frozen frames, with their bodies as physical simulation. The first scene describes an oceanic "plate" subducting beneath a continental plate that is comparatively less dense. The next frame illustrates the melting process that results from immense internal heat and pressure. The third frame shows bodies rising together to represent the less dense magma plume. For the final scene, students enact an embodied eruption that shows the systematic development of surficial volcanic features. In this embodied representation, one student might lay on the ground and squirm around below a blanket to show the process of subduction. Another student might splay outward to visualize melting. Several students might rise up in succession with arms opening upward and outward very slowly to portray the volcanism process of mountain-building. A third student might narrate on the side to describe these internal processes and surficial geologic features orally, providing the audience some explicit connection between the aesthetic of the dramatic enactment and the slow progression of geologic time.

Based on their creative metaphor development, another group might represent this geologic process through the emotional experience of the *five stages of grief*. They might connect the stage of denial and repression of true feelings of loss to the process of subduction. The stage of anger might be the resulting heat and energy from plate tectonic friction and surficial breaking during subduction. The stage of bargaining might reflect the process of that heat melting and building pressure for release for these students as they use the experience of the pandemic and grief from the loss of a school year with friends. The stage of depression might reflect the process of less dense magma plume rising with the continual slow release of tension and anger. As students relate their own lived experience to the process of volcanism, the final stage of acceptance and the accompanying emotional relief might feel closely connected to a volcanic eruption. Students could use facial expression and body language to represent both the stage of grief and each step in the mountain-building process. With scaffolded and routinized practice, the steps of linguistic metaphor to gesture-building for dramatic enactment can take place promptly within a class period or be inserted as short exercises across a week of class to break up a direct instruction lecture. Time constraints are important to encourage students to collaborate efficiently and develop their agency and metacognition to be creative, strategic, and confident at each stage.

After this physical enactment, teachers would direct student groups to rapidly construct these phases in sculptural 3D with found objects, making creative choices about how each material and placement align with the properties and stages of the phenomena. Though teachers could assess and assign grades using criteria for successful participation and engagement in each modality, the final step of 2D illustration and written description could provide the best opportunity for summative assessment of understanding. As this multimodal learning continuum concludes, the structured uncertainty inherent in the process has led the class of students to generate, critique, and refine an entirely new sensemaking inventory of representations of the Earth's internal and surface processes that develop continental and ocean-floor features. The performance expectation and key concepts have taken on new meaning for students through creative linguistic, embodied, and 3D multimodal extensions of the phenomena. This kind of multimodal modeling anchors understanding with enlightening social, emotional, and cultural meaning through questioning and communicating practices that prioritize the creative and interpretive aspects of scientific sensemaking .

9.7   Future Directions

GrASSP provides a framework from which multiple theoretical models can be examined. For instance, daily diary methods could document students' development of agency and creative metacognition within the multimodal sensemaking process. The diary prompts could follow a similar methodology to capture student agency and creative metacognition used by Anderson and Haney (2021). Students regular reflections could provide useful data to determine how experience in each modality contribute to students' sense of agency in their scientific sensemaking in the face of substantial uncertainty about concepts. It is possible that different arrangements of the multimodal continua could be more beneficial in different science domains, at different developmental stages, for different cultural groups, or at different stages of scientific understanding. This area of research should begin with qualitative field observations in classrooms to understand how students' agentic, creative, and metacognitive development interacts with the experience of uncertainty at the heart of the proposed GrASSP approach.

Exploring the GrASSP model with culturally diverse students can also reveal greater understanding about how different students integrate, apply, and expand the multimodal tools for sensemaking. For instance, the incorporation of the aesthetics and process of Hip Hop into the scientific sensemaking process could build naturally from the development of linguistic metaphor, enhance the participatory space for students, bring more cultural relevance, and engage different funds of knowledge than is typical in science class (Emdin 2011; Hall 2017). Similarly, the gesture building process could spin off into dance compositions to engage the aesthetics of rhythm and movement while exploring abstract scientific processes. For example, students could disambiguate *revolution* from *rotation* in astronomy through brief choreography distinguishing the two abstract ideas and exploring the nature of tides and seasons on earth.

Possibilities are limitless if we consider the numerous combinations and elaborations that build from the numerous scientific concepts and phenomena learned in high school and the multimodal tools for sensemaking. As such, uncertainty for teachers is inherent in the GrASSP model. Teachers need to develop the mindsets and skills to model and message openness and creativity in response to this uncertainty. Messaging and modeling are two of the most powerful pedagogical tools that teachers carry to develop adaptive mindsets and metacognition in students (Beach et al. 2020; Jacovidis et al. 2020). Future work can focus on how those tools can be developed and employed by teachers most effectively. Work in this area can also improve understanding about teachers' experience and comfort with uncertainty in the classroom and the kinds of professional development needed to catalyze that growth. The education field needs more models for professional development that enhance teachers' skills, knowledge, beliefs, and dispositions in order to thrive in the uncertainty that creative teaching and learning opens in the classroom. Sustained engagement of diverse learners in science learning and college and career pathways may depend on it.

Acknowledgements This research was supported by a grant from the U.S. Department of Education (U351D140063). Correspondence concerning this article should be addressed to Ross Anderson, Inflexion, 1700 Millrace, Eugene, OR 97405. E-mail: ross.anderson@inflexion.org

References

Amin, T., Jeppsson, F., & Haglund, J. (2015). Conceptual metaphor and embodied cognition in science learning: Introduction to special issue. *International Journal of Science Education, 37*(5–6), 745–758.

Anderson, R. C., & Graham, M. (2021). Creative potential in flux: The leading role of originality during early adolescent development. *Thinking Skills and Creativity, 40*, 100816. https://doi.org/10.1016/j.tsc.2021.100816

Anderson, R. C. (2019). *Becoming creative agents: Trajectories of creative development during the turbulence of early adolescence* [Dissertation]. Eugene, OR: University of Oregon.

Anderson, R. C., Bousselot, T., Katz-Buoincontro, J., & Todd, J. (2021). Generating buoyancy in a sea of uncertainty: Teachers creativity and well-being during the COVID-19 pandemic. *Frontiers in Psychology, 11*, 1–17. https://doi.org/10.3389/fpsyg.2020.614774

Anderson, R. C., Graham, M., Kennedy, P., Nelson, N., Stoolmiller, M., & Baker, S. (2019a). Student agency at the crux: Mitigating disengagement in middle and high school. *Contemporary Educational Psychology, 56*, 205–217.

Anderson, R. C., Haney, M., Pitts, C., Porter, L., & Bousselot, T. (2019b). "Mistakes can be beautiful": Creative engagement in arts integration for early adolescent learners. *Journal of Creative Behavior*. https://doi.org/10.1002/jocb.401

Anderson, R. C., & Haney, M. (2021). Reflection in the creative process of early adolescents: The mediating roles of creative metacognition, self-efficacy, and self-concept. *Psychology of the Aesthetics, Creativity, and the Arts*. https://doi.org/10.1037/aca0000324

Anderson, R.C., Katz-Buonincontro, J., Bousselot, T., Mattson, D., Beard, N., Land, J., & Livie, M. (2022). How am I a creative teacher? Beliefs, values, and affect for integrating creativity in the classroom. Teaching and Teacher Education, 110, 103583. https://doi.org/10.1016/j.tate.2021.103583

Bandura, A. (1986). *Social foundations of thought and action*. Englewood Cliffs, NJ: Prentice Hall.

Bandura, A. (2018). Toward a psychology of human agency: Pathways and reflections. *Perspectives on Psychological Science, 13*(2), 130–136. https://doi.org/10.1177/1745691617699280

Beach, P. T., Anderson, R. C., Jacovidis, J. N., & Chadwick, K. L. (2020). *Making the abstract explicit: The role of metacognition in teaching and learning*. Eugene, OR: Inflexion. Retrieved from https://ibo.org/globalassets/publications/ib-research/policy/metacognition-policy-paper.pdf

Beghetto, R. A. (2016). Creative learning: A fresh look. *Journal of Cognitive Education and Psychology, 15*(1), 6–23.

Beghetto, R. A. (2019). Structured uncertainty: How creativity thrives under constraints and uncertainty. In C. A. Mullen (Ed.), Creativity under duress in education? (pp. 27–40). Switzerland: Springer

Beghetto R.A. (2020) Uncertainty. In Glăveanu V. (ed.) The Palgrave Encyclopedia of the Possible. Palgrave Macmillan, Cham. https://doi.org/10.1007/978-3-319-98390-5_122-1

Benner, A. D., & Wang, Y. (2014). Shifting attendance trajectories from middle to high school: Influences of school transitions and changing school contexts. *Developmental Psychology*, *50*(4), 1288–1301. https://doi.org/10.1037/a0035366

Burger, K., & Walk, M. (2016). Can children break the cycle of disadvantage? Structure and agency in the transmission of education across generations. *Social Psychology of Education*, *19*(4), 695–713. https://doi.org/10.1007/s11218-016-9361-y

Cannady, M. A., Vincent-Ruz, P., Chung, J. M., & Schunn, C. D. (2019). Scientific sensemaking supports science content learning across disciplines and instructional contexts. Contemporary Educational Psychology, 59 (September), 101802. https://doi.org/10.1016/j.cedpsych.2019.

Chiappe, D. L., & Chiappe, P. (2007). The role of working memory in metaphor production and comprehension. Journal of Memory and Language, 56, 172–188. https://doi.org/10.1016/j.jml.2006.11.006

Cook, S. W., Mitchell, Z., & Goldin-Meadow, S. (2008). Gesturing makes learning last. Cognition, 106(2), 1047–1058. https://doi.org/10.1016/j.cognition.2007.04.010

Dahl, R. E., Allen, N. B., Wilbrecht, L., & Suleiman, A. B. (2018). Importance of investing in adolescence from a developmental science perspective. *Nature*, *554*(7693), 441–450. https://doi.org/10.1038/nature25770

Deslauriers, L., McCarty, L. S., Miller, K., Callaghan, K., & Kestin, G. (2019). Measuring actual learning versus feeling of learning in response to being actively engaged in the classroom. *Proceedings of the National Academy of Sciences*, *116*(39), 19251–19257. https://doi.org/10.1073/pnas.1821936116

Dewey, J. (1938). Experience and Education. *Education*, *50*(3), 96. https://doi.org/10.1017/CBO9781107415324.004

diSessa, A. A. (1993). Toward an epistemology of physics. *Cognition and Instruction*, *10*(2–3), 105–225.

Duckworth, E. (1996). *"The Having of Wonderful Ideas" and other essays on teaching and learning*. New York, NY: Teachers College Press.

Duschl, R. A. (2008). Science education in 3 part harmony: Balancing conceptual, epistemic and social learning goals. Review of Research in Education, 32, 268–291.

Elby, A. (2001). Helping physics students learn how to learn. *American Journal of Physics, Physics Education Research Supplement*, *69*(7), S54–S64.

Emdin, C. (2011). Moving beyond the boat without a paddle: Reality pedagogy, black youth, and urban science education. *Journal of Negro Education*, *80*(3), 284–295.

Gadja, A., Beghetto, R. A., & Karwowski, M. (2017). Exploring creative learning in the classroom: A multi-method approach. *Thinking Skills and Creativity*, *24*, 250–267.

Good, C., Aronson, J., & Harder, J. A. (2007). Problems in the pipeline: Stereotype threat and women's achievement in high-level math courses. Journal of Applied Developmental Psychology, 29, 17–28.

Gupta, A., Elby, A., & Conlin, L. D. (2014). How substance-based ontologies for gravity can be productive: A case study. *Physical Review - Special Topics: Physics Education Research*, *10*(010113), 1–19.

Hall, H. B. (2017). Deeper than rap: Expanding conceptions of hip-hop culture and pedagogy in the english language arts classroom. *Research in the Teaching of English*, *51*(3), 341–350.

Hammer, D. (1996). More than misconceptions: Multiple perspectives on student knowledge and reasoning, and an appropriate role for education research. *American Journal of Physics*, *64*(10), 1316–1325.

Hammer, D. (2000). Student resources for learning introductory physics. *American Journal of Physics, 68*, S52-S59.

Hammer, D. (2006). Epistemological considerations in teaching introductory physics. *Science Education, 79*(4), 393-413.

Harrer, B. W., Flood, V. J., & Wittmann, M. C. (2013). Productive resources in students' ideas about energy: An alternative analysis of Watts' original interview transcripts. *Physical Review Special Topics – Physics Education Research, 9*(2), 23101, 1–5.

Institute for Science and Math Education. (2016). Using phenomena in NGSS-designed lessons and units. Seattle, WA: STEM Learning Tools, University of Washington Institute for Science and Math Education. http://stemteachingtools.org/assets/landscapes/STT42_Using_Phenomena_in_NGSS.pdf

Jacovidis, J. N., Anderson, R. C., Beach, P. T., & Chadwick, K. L. (2020). *Growth mindset thinking and beliefs in teaching and learning.* Eugene, OR: Inflexion.

Karwowski, M., & Beghetto, R. A. (2018). Creative behavior as agentic action. *Psychology of Aesthetics, Creativity, and the Arts, 13*(4), 402–415. https://doi.org/10.1037/aca0000190

Ladson-Billings, G. (2003). *Critical race theory perspectives on the social studies: The profession, policies, and curriculum.* Greenwich, CT: Information Age Publishing.

Lakoff, G. & Johnson, M. (1980). The metaphors we live by. Chicago, IL: The University of Chicago Press.

Madjar, N., & Chohat, R. (2016). Will I succeed in middle school? A longitudinal analysis of self-efficacy in school transitions in relation to goal structures and engagement. *Educational Psychology, 3410*, 1-15. https://doi.org/10.1080/01443410.2016.1179265

Manz, E., Stroupe, D., & Berland, L. (2018). Addressing the epistemic elephant in the room: Epistemic agency and the next generation science standards. *Journal of Research in Science Teaching, 55*(7), 1053–1075. https://doi.org/10.1002/tea.21459

McDermott, L. C., & Redish, E. F. (1999). Resource letter PER-1: Physics education research. American Journal of Physics, 67(9), 755–767.

Meltzer, D. E., & Thornton, R. K. (2012). Resource letter ALIP-1: Active-learning instruction in physics. American Journal of Physics, 80(3).

Metcalfe, R. J. A., Abbott, S., Bray, P., Exley, J., & Wisnia, D. (1984). Teaching science through drama: An empirical investigation. Research in Science and Technological Education, 2(1), 77–81

Moje, E., Ciechanowski, K., Kramer, K., Ellis, L., Carrilo, R., & Collazo, T. (2004). Working toward third space in content area literacy: An examination of everyday funds of knowledge and discourse. *Reading Research Quarterly, 39*(1), 38–70.

Montessori, M. M. (1978). *The discovery of the child.* New York, NY: Ballantine Books.

Morgan, P. L., Farkas, G., Hillemeier, M. M., & Maczuga, S. (2016). Science achievement gaps begin very early, persist, and are largely explained by modifiable factors. Educational Researcher, 45(1), 18–35.

National Assessment of Educational Progress. (2015). 2015 science grades 4, 8, and 12 assessment report cards: Summary data tables for national and state average scores and achievement level results. Washington, DC: U.S. Department of Education, Institute of Education Sciences, National Center for Education Statistics.

National Center for Education Statistics. (2012). The Nation's Report Card: Science 2011 (NCES 2012–465). Washington, DC: Institute of Education Sciences, U.S. Department of Education. Institute of Education Sciences, U.S. Department of Education.

National Research Council. (2012). A framework for K-12 science education: Practices, cross-cutting concepts, and core ideas.

Osgood-Campbell, E. (2018). Investigating the educational implications of embodied cognition: A model interdisciplinary inquiry and education curricula. Mind, Brain, and Education, 9(1), 2–9.

Patall, E. A., Pituch, K. A., Steingut, R. R., Vasquez, A. C., Yates, N., & Kennedy, A. A. U. (2019). Agency and high school science students' motivation, engagement, and classroom support experiences. *Journal of Applied Developmental Psychology, 62*, 77–92. https://doi.org/10.1016/j.appdev.2019.01.004

Piaget, J., & Inhelder, B. (1974). *The child's construction of quantities: Conservation and atomism.* Routledge.

Provasnik, S., Kastberg, D., Ferraro, D., Lemanski, N., Roey, S., & Jenkins, F. (2012). Highlights from TIMSS 2011: Mathematics and science achievement of U.S. fourth- and eighth-grade students in an international context (NCES 2013-009 Revised). Washington, DC: National Center for Education Statistics, Institute of Education Sciences, U.S. Department of Education.

Reeve, J. (2013). How students create motivationally supportive learning environments for themselves: The concept of agentic engagement. *Journal of Educational Psychology, 105*(3), 579–595. https://doi.org/10.1037/a0032690

Reiner, M., & Gilbert, J. (2000). Epistemological resources for thought experimentation in science learning. International Journal of Science Education, 22(5), 489–50.

Riegle-Crumb, C., King, B., Grodsky, E., & Muller, C. (2012). The more things change, the more they stay the same? Prior achievement fails to explain gender inequality in entry into STEM college majors over time. American Educational Research Journal, 49, 1048–73.

Rosebery, A., & Warren, B. (2008). *Teaching science to English language learners.* Arlington, VA: National Science Teachers Association Press.

Scherr, R. E., Close, H. G., Close, E. W., Flood, V. J., McKagan, S. B., Robertson, A. D., . . . & Vokos, S. (2013). Negotiating energy dynamics through embodied action in a materially structured environment. Physical Review Special Topics – Physics Education Research, 9(2), 020105, 1–18.

Schwarz, C., Reiser, B., Davis, E., Kenyon, L., Acher, A., Fortus, D., Shwartz, Y., Hug, B., & Krajcik, J. (2009). Developing a learning progression for scientific modeling: Making scientific modeling accessible and meaningful for learners. Journal of Research in Science Teaching, 46(6), 632–654.

Van Edwards, V. (2017, June). You are contagious [Video]. TED Conferences. https://www.youtube.com/watch?v=cef35Fk7YD8

Vygotsky, L. S. (1986). The development of scientific concepts in childhood: The design of a working hypothesis. In A. Kozulin (Ed.), *Thought and language* (pp. 146–209). Cambridge, MA: MIT Press.

Weiss, I. R., Pasley, J. D., Smith, P. S., Banilower, E. R., & Heck, D. J. (2003). *Looking inside the classroom: A study of K-12 mathematics and science education in the United States.* Chapel Hill, NC.

Windschitl, M., & Calabrese Barton, A. (2016). Rigor and equity by design: Seeking a core of practices for the science education community. In *AERA Handbook of Research on Teaching, 5th Edition* (pp. 1099-1158).

Windschitl, M., Thompson, J., & Braaten, M. (2018). *Ambitious science teaching.* Cambridge, MA: Harvard University Press.

Zimmerman, H. T., Reeve, S., & Bell, P. (2010). Family sensemaking practices in science center conversations. Science Education, 94(3), 478–505. https://doi.org/10.1002/sce.20374

Chapter 10
The Relationship of the Five Legs of Creativity Theory and Uncertainty in the Generation of Mathematical Creativity

Scott A. Chamberlin

Abstract The Five Legs of Creativity Theory is one in which affective states are said to influence the prospect for the emergence of creative mathematical process and product (Chamberlin SA, Mann EL (2021) The relationship of affect and creativity in mathematical giftedness: how the five legs of creativity influence math talent. Prufrock Academic Press). In the Five Legs Theory, affective states called Iconoclasm, Impartiality, Investment, Intuition, and Inquisitiveness are mental states that may greatly influence the extent to which creative process is rewarded and valued in the classroom. When the aforementioned states are said to be high or positive, it is likely the case that creative thinking in mathematics may be engendered, thus enhancing the likelihood of creative products. The converse is also true. When such affective states are said to be low or predominantly negative, the likelihood for creative process and subsequently product in mathematics may be greatly compromised. The focus of this chapter pertains to the relationship of the Five Legs of Creativity Theory in relation to uncertainty in mathematical learning episodes, with a special focus on mathematical problem solving situations.

10.1 Introduction

The Five Legs of Creativity Theory is one that originated after a several year exploration and discussion of literature in mathematical creativity and affect (Chamberlin and Mann 2021). Not surprisingly, Drs. Chamberlin and Mann had completed a dissertation on affect in mathematics and creativity in mathematics respectively, and had subsequently acquired an interest in their peer's field. Thus, the theory originated from three sources. First, the theory was predicated on empirical data and

S. A. Chamberlin (✉)
University of Wyoming, Laramie, WY, USA
e-mail: scott@uwyo.edu

second, the theory originated from extensive reviews of the literature in which the relationship between the two constructs had not yet been considered with any degree of comprehensiveness. Third, discussions between Drs. Chamberlin and Mann were instrumental in conceptualizing the theory. With the exception of several chapters in edited books (e.g., Chamberlin and Mann 2014; Cropley 2017; Goldin 2009; Mann et al. 2017; Movshovitz-Hadar and Kleiner 2009) and scant empirical articles, the constructs of mathematical creativity and affect have rarely been considered as a relationship (Imai 2000; Kozlowski et al. 2019; Leu and Chiu 2015; Tuli 1980).

In this chapter, the Five Legs Theory is explicated so that readers can consider it in relation to needs in mathematics education. Second, the relationship of the Five Legs to uncertainty is discussed, with a particular emphasis on uncertainty in problem solving episodes. To conclude the chapter, three focus questions are considered. For an extended discussion of the Five Legs of Creativity Theory, please access *The Relationship of Affect and Creativity in Mathematical Giftedness: How the Five Legs of Creativity Influence Math Talent* (Chamberlin and Mann 2021). In this book, the authors provide extensive discussion of the theory and situate it in the context of classroom expectations, types of problems that should be utilized and classroom instruction, as well as applications to gifted and general population students.

10.2 The Five Legs of Creativity Theory

Prior to the discussion on the theory, several caveats are issued. First, the Five Legs Theory of Creativity was generated on empirical data, in addition to theoretical discussions about mathematical creativity (domain-specific perspective) and general creativity (a domain neutral perspective). Second, the Five Legs Theory of creativity is considered applicable to mathematics and mathematical problem solving episodes in specific, and not other domains such as literacy, science, humanities. The extent to which it is applicable to other domains is contingent upon multiple factors and should be made by scholars in non-mathematical domains. In this section, each of the Five Legs is discussed so that readers can make sense of the theory and apply it as necessary. Third, sections should be carefully read because in some situations, terminology has been adopted that may be used in a somewhat altered context and use of the terminology should be dictated by its use in mathematical contexts. Fourth, all discussions of the Five Legs are somewhat abridged versions of the more lengthy discussion, presented in *The relationship of affect and creativity in mathematics in mathematical giftedness: How the five legs of creativity influence math talent* (Chamberlin and Mann 2021).

10.2.1   *Iconoclasm*

Iconoclasm is the first subcomponent of the theory, conceptualized seven years ago (Chamberlin and Mann 2014). Initially revealed at the International Group of Mathematical Creativity and Giftedness (2014), the construct of Iconoclasm was well received by peers. In short, Iconoclasm pertains to a mathematicians' penchant to challenge commonly accepted or conventional mathematical ideas, and not to accept the standard procedure or algorithm (Chamberlin and Mann 2021). In so doing, mathematicians are not satisfied with solutions that are congruent with or patterned after those that are presented in textbooks or by instructors. If, for instance, the most commonly accepted method to divide fractions is to (1) invert the second fraction and (2) multiply it by the first fraction, a problem solver that is high in Iconoclasm might wonder why a prospective solution could not be to (1) make like denominators, and (2) divide the numerators, which of course works. This solution, however, is not the one that many instructors present because it has often not been investigated by them. Upon first sight of such a solution, open-minded instructors may look at the solution with confusion and consider its merit. A close-minded instructor, by the way, might be inclined to simply tell the problem solver that this is not a viable solution, when indeed it is. The second, less well-prepared instructor, may be negatively influencing the prospect for creative emergence among a capable young mathematician.

Instructor responses are shared because they are instrumental in understanding the affective state known as Iconoclasm. This is because Iconoclasm is based on a problem solver's interaction with an instructor and the climate produced in which to do mathematics. In this sense, there is a socio-cognitive (Bandura 1988, 1989) aspect to Iconoclasm because the individual mathematician that is making sense of mathematics and better still, prospectively engaging in creative thought, relies on a mediation process with a mentor or instructor, as well as peers in some cases. Iconoclasm is utilized when a mathematician has the courage to challenge accepted ideas, not necessarily as wrong, but as not the most efficient or most aesthetically pleasing, elegant, and/or sophisticated. In the division of fractions example, inverting the second fraction and multiplying the two values is not an incorrect approach to dividing fractions. It may be the desire then of the problem solver to try a novel approach, such as making like denominators and dividing the numerators, to see if it works. Though this may not be creative per se in the context of mathematics as a discipline, and hence not Pro C, Big C, or even Little C creativity (Kaufman and Beghetto 2009), it may well qualify as a Mini C contribution because the student, and perhaps even the teacher, were not familiar with the approach prior to it being investigated, in situ.

10.2.2   Impartiality

Somewhat closely tied to Iconoclasm is the affective state known as Impartiality. Impartiality is conceptually defined as, "an openness to appreciate and see multiple perspectives and to consider utilizing unconventional ones" (Chamberlin and Mann 2021, p. 43). In this respect, the mental state known as Impartiality may help a mathematical problem solver avoid adopting conventional ideas. Moreover, it possesses a similarity with Iconoclasm in the respect that unconventional or mathematical procedures not typically accepted or promoted in textbooks, online, or in professional development sessions are considered ideal for the emergence of creativity. With Iconoclasm, one is in a mental state of having substantial courage to share ideas and with Impartiality one is open to various ideas and not always the one creating them. It is, however, the openness to accept new ideas that may help facilitate creative thinking among problem solvers.

In addition to not being limited to one solution, the best problem solvers are not limited by one rigid style of thinking, which is another facet of impartiality. As Hersh and John-Steiner (2011) suggest, "Thus, mathematicians are not limited to a single mode of thought. They rely on intuition, logic, visual and verbal processes, inferences, and guesses (p. 56)." When problem solvers are limited by the pursuit of a single solution or a single mode of thought, they are said to have constraints imposed upon them (Öllinger et al. 2017) and may have compromised flexibility (Krutetskii 1976). Flexibility in thinking is a component discussed by Krutetskii and it is considered essential to the development of mathematically creative thoughts. Hence, this notion of an open-minded or unbiased state of mind, so-called Impartiality in this theory, is essential to enable problem solvers to have free reign of thoughts, without being impeded by externally imposed ideas or artificially imposed constraints. An analogy regarding the generation of ideas in solving mathematical problems may be providing the problem solver with the opportunity to select from endless ideas, as would be done with an essay examination, as opposed to selecting from a menu of mathematical solutions, as might be done on a selected response assessment. With the completely open-ended approach to assessment, the propensity for highly creative ideas is expanded beyond the menu approach to solving problems.

10.2.3   Investment

An affective construct that is ostensibly not related to thought process in the respect of generating ideas is the third component of the Five Legs of Creativity Theory, which is referred to as Investment. Investment in this sense is used in much the same manner as it is in the economic or business world, not as Sternberg (2006) discussed. When one makes a financial investment, be it in a business, stock or mutual fund, or in any financial endeavor, a form of commitment is made. If one opts to pursue an advanced degree, a time and financial commitment is involved. Likewise, when mathematical problem solvers commit to solving a problem, an emotional investment is made. More specifically, Chamberlin and Mann (p. 50, Chamberlin and Mann 2021) suggest that Investment in the domain of mathematical creativity pertains to, "an emotional contribution to finding a solution to a task for one or more reasons." When an emotional investment is made to virtually any endeavor, the prospects for success are enhanced. Renzulli (1978) generalized the necessity of commitment a step further in stating that it was essential as one of the three rings of giftedness.

Nearly all authors in the McLeod and Adams (1989) book on affect and mathematical problem solving refer to persistence as a requisite characteristic in success. The relationship between investment and commitment to persistence has been made (Tinto 1975) and is instrumental in facilitating creativity in problem solving episodes.

10.2.4   Intuition

The affective component known as Intuition plays a critical role in development of mathematical creativity. It was, after all, Wilder (p. 43, 1984) that stated, "Without intuition, there is no creativity in mathematics." Wilder was not using the construct intuition in precisely the same manner as it is utilized in this chapter and in the Five Legs Theory, but it was discussed in a very similar manner. In fact, Wilder referred to intuition as requisite to mathematical creativity emerging. In the Five Legs of Creativity Theory, Intuition is thought of as similarly as critical to creative process and product emerging. However, in this theory, Intuition takes on a slightly altered conception than it does in other discussions in educational and mathematical psychology. In this theory, Intuition is not considered an overt cognitive state, inasmuch as it is an affective state. Specifically, Intuition is, "An inescapable drive to be pulled to a response or solution" (p. 22, Chamberlin and Mann 2021). An analogy has been made to one driving an automobile without a map, yet relying on past experience to find a location. Unbeknownst to the driver, intuition may play a significant role in identifying previously seen landmarks and other landmarks that perhaps were not noticed on the earlier visit. In this respect, Intuition, in the Five Legs Theory, is a motive to follow a 'hunch, cognizance, or motive' in pursuing a correct solution to a perplexing mathematical problem.

Ideally, Intuition may lead to increased persistence, thus enhancing the likelihood of success in solving a problem. However, Intuition and its many positive by-products may not be limited to success in finding successful solutions, but it is theorized that it has applications to identifying particularly creative mathematical solutions. Persistence, it might be postulated, has ramifications for enhancing the likelihood of creativity, since most creative output is not a result of a small investment of time in anything that is cognitively engaging. As Wallas (1926) suggested, the necessity of persistence may be instrumental in the incubation stage. Intuition also may have applications to working in novel situations, much like a surgeon that can apply previously learned concepts from earlier work to a new situation. Mathematicians may find situations in which they have been successful solving problems in a domain and when prompted for a solution in a new domain or another area of the initial domain, insufficient knowledge exists to solve the problem. However, highly creative individuals may be in a situation to rely on Intuition to identify a successful process and product to a novel problem, based on Intuition. Finally, a high degree of Intuition may serve an advanced problem solver well in the respect that (s)he may realize that a successful solution is imminent, given their understanding of the domain, even though the problem solver may not be able to explain why a solution is forthcoming. There are instances in which a problem solver simply *knows* that (s)he is close to solving a problem.

10.2.5   Inquisitiveness

The fifth leg of the theory is referred to as Inquisitiveness. Inquisitiveness shares some characteristics with interest. When one thinks of an inquisitive mind, one may think of the inquiry process, which is jumpstarted with affective states such as wonderment, curiosity, and a desire to find answers to questions. Dyasi (1999) suggests that children are naturally curious and that curiosity is a fundamental human trait. Interest, therefore, is at the heart of reported high levels of curiosity and an inquisitive mental state (Kashdan and Silvia 2009) and there is an established relationship between interest and engagement (Flowerday and Shell 2015; Renninger and Bachrach 2015). In short, the psychological construct of Inquisitiveness encompasses several positive attributes that enhance the likelihood of mathematically creative processes and products emerging.

A component of the construct Inquisitiveness that facilitates mathematical creativity is its close relationship to Intuition, based on persistence. As suggested, creative output is not a facile or quick process per se (Penaloza and Calvillo 2012) and persistence, coupled with periodic breaks in work, is likely to provide a greater likelihood of success than working continuously. This may be a result of a reduced likelihood of fixation on behalf of the problem solver. Moreover, an individual in a highly inquisitive mental state may generate questions at a much greater rate than peers with reported low levels of interest. Such questions may serve as the drive to seek highly creative solutions in mathematical problem solving episodes.

10.3   The Relationship of the Five Legs Theory of Creativity to Uncertainty

The construct of uncertainty in creativity is an intriguing, yet a frequently dismissed one. It is, however, not to be overlooked in the generation of creative output or process in mathematical episodes. Prior to engaging in a discussion of the relationship between uncertainty and the Five Legs of Creativity Theory, it is necessary to conceptualize the construct known as uncertainty. A characteristic of many psychological constructs is that they are deemed fuzzy, or not well defined. Closely related to uncertainty is the psychological construct of doubt (Beghetto 2020). In fact, uncertainty may be considered an antecedent to doubt in mathematical problem solving episodes. Hence, learning about features associated with them can provide some understanding. In Tracey and Hutchinson's (2018) work, they suggest that uncertainty is a mental state that most individuals involved in the creative process would like to avoid altogether or resolve (Adair and Xiong 2018; Bar-Anan et al. 2009), while other researchers such as Lane and Maxfied (2005) find it highly worthwhile, or as they deemed it potent, for innovation. Menger et al. (2014), refer to uncertainty as a prerequisite mental state for creativity to emerge. In other words, the precise mental state that many experience in creativity and hope to avoid is the very same mental state that likely facilitates highly creative output. In part, the successful outcomes that may come as a consequence of uncertainty are likely a result of an intensification of emotions among problem solvers. A secondary by-product of uncertainty is likely the notion that uncertainty may precipitate additional learning in a domain to mitigate the effect of uncertainty.

Uncertainty in problem solving episodes may be marked by a lack of confidence in the outcome of the situation. It may be postulated that the construct on which uncertainty has the greatest effect is self-efficacy (Bandura 1977), because self-efficacy is conceptualized to be one's belief that an outcome can be positively influenced. When dealing with uncertainty, therefore, one must contemplate how one can deal with situations that contain unknowns, and overcome them to instill confidence to successfully obtain a positive outcome. To compound the issue, the construct of creative self-efficacy exists, which is, "an individual's beliefs that they have the ability to produce something creative" (Liu et al. 2017), and it is a prerequisite trait for creative production to occur according to Hallack et al. (2018) and Tierney and Farmer (2002). Hence, uncertainty, perhaps in the form of ill-structured problems (Sales and Wakker 2009; Stepien et al. 1993), can present a challenge with respect to uncertainty for problem solvers. It may be postulated, however, that once problem solvers can creatively solve a sufficiently challenging ill-structured problem, their creative self-efficacy, as well as their general self-efficacy, may be greatly enhanced relative to its previous state. This positive change in dealing with ill-structured problems may result in increased confidence and self-beliefs (Miller et al. 2021; Pitsia et al. 2017) in one's ability to successfully navigate and solve a mathematical problem in a creative manner. In turn, such classroom experiences may enhance problem solvers' abilities to engage in creative process and the emergence of products in mathematical learning episodes.

Moreover, one consideration that is central to the relationship of uncertainty in mathematical creativity and affect in mathematics is that each pertain to students' feelings, emotions, and dispositions. As has been suggested in the discussion of the Five Legs Theory, the more certain and confident that a problem solver is about personal affect, the greater the propensity of the problem solver to realize success in mathematics. Conversely, uncertainty naturally suggests that a mathematical problem solver is not sure about something. This something may be the environment in which the problem is solved (e.g., a classroom), the learning facilitator, the constraints of the problem, emotions, the expectations of the problem regarding assessment, or any number of remaining components. Most instrumental though may be uncertainty in identifying a solution. Any such uncertainty can have negative ramifications on problem solver self-efficacy, which could have deleterious effects on one's ability to successfully engage in cognition. Hence, the relationship of uncertainty to the Five Legs Theory of creativity in mathematics must resemble a balancing act, insofar as a problem solver must be able to maintain a delicate balance between dealing with uncertainty in identifying a creative mathematical solution and seeking positive affect. When the relationship of uncertainty and affect are said to be imbalanced, as shown below, the likelihood of positive outcomes in creativity may be reduced.

Illustration   secured   from: https://lessonpix.com/drawings/4959/100x100/seesaw.png

Without perseverance while engaging in high level mathematics, the prospect for success in solving problems, creatively or not, is likely in jeopardy. Perhaps most significant to success in finding creative solutions to mathematical problems is openness. Openness has already been established as a prerequisite characteristic to creative output and perseverance plays a considerable role in realizing full benefits of openness (Kutlu et al. 2017). Interestingly, motivation may play a role as well as an intervening variable in the equation of openness and perseverance and one outcome in which it may influence mathematical creativity pertains to the type of tasks that problem solvers attempt to solve (Nicholls 1983). This is likely because problem solvers with a high degree of motivation and intent to reach mastery goals may select more challenging mathematical problems than their peers with presumably lower, performance or achievement goals (Poortvliet 2016). Selecting in depth problems that may require greater cognitive effort than problems in which low cognitive and emotional investment are required may result in problem solvers working on problems that are rich. As a consequence, such problems may pose greater risk for failure than less engaging problems, but the result when success is achieved may be a highly insightful process and product. In turn, highly creative solutions to the problems may be the result. Hence, despite what may appear to be a tenuous relationship between affective constructs such as openness, perseverance, motivation, goals, and creative output, it is apparent that emotions play a critical role in outcomes. Still, uncertainty in solving problems would appear to be almost endemic.

This is to suggest, however, that uncertainty is inherently negative. The ability to cope with uncertainty has been known to derail problem solvers' success in finding solutions. A certain element of it though may be instrumental in ultimate goal achievement, as overcoming obstacles in identifying solutions may lead to increased confidence and advanced levels of self-efficacy in solving problems. All of this may be a result of successfully managing anxiety (Pajares 1996).

10.4 Costs and Benefits Associated with Uncertainty in Educational Settings

With virtually all efforts in improving education, costs can be a concern. In most cases, budget expenditures are not the primary concern, inasmuch as costs to related efforts are a concern. However, in overlaying the Five Legs Theory to engender creative process and product in learning episodes, the principal cost is familiarizing teachers with the approach and fundamental principles of the theory so that they can utilize adjustments in teaching philosophies and classroom atmosphere, learning theories, curricular manipulations such as types of tasks adopted, and assessment feedback. In short, costs will be minimal to have teachers invest attention to student affect and the prospective return on investment could be substantial. That is to say, the degree of creative output in mathematics classrooms could be considerable in relation to the amount of effort invested. Moreover, investing efforts in making educational changes may ideally create lasting effects in a cultural shift because problem solving will become the bedrock of mathematics instruction, as it should be (Hiebert et al. 2000).

A secondary, and rather unintended cost to mathematics efforts, may be that efforts to meet state or national mathematics standards in an attempt to perform well on standardized assessments, may be compromised. This is because creative efforts are rarely, if ever, engaged, utilized, addressed, or assessed in (inter)national assessments. Moreover, they are rarely even suggested in standards documents for several reasons. Perhaps the first reason that they are rarely mentioned in standards documents may pertain to the difficulty in assessing them. A second reason may be that minus experts in academia, quantifying the value of mathematical creativity, and for that matter creativity in general, is similarly difficult to ascertain. A third reason may be educators' lack of familiarity with mathematical creativity and when teachers are not prepared to pay attention to creativity and intentionally try to facilitate it, they may be in a challenging position to precipitate it among learners (Grégiore 2016). It is likely a safe assumption that few teachers have had (any) undergraduate coursework relevant to mathematical creativity. Until recently, it could be argued that mathematical creativity was merely a construct that academics discussed at conferences and in books. The practicality of creating scenarios that might enhance the likelihood of mathematical creativity emerging was considered not a valuable investment of time or money, when standardized assessments loomed. Simply stated, facilitating creativity in mathematics has never been an endeavor that was designed to support standardized assessment performance. Instead, aiding problem solvers in learning how to deal with uncertainty has enhanced implications for advanced mathematical understanding and solutions.

10.5 Practical Implications of Uncertainty Plays in Creativity and Learning

The practical implications for understanding the role that uncertainty plays in creativity, learning, and development are various. Regarding creativity, the better a problem solver deals with uncertainty, the greater the likelihood that the problem solver realizes success in attaining a successful and sophisticated solution. Such outcomes have a relationship to students making sense of mathematics (Hiebert et al. 2000), which speaks of true mathematical learning. Development is intricately intertwined with learning, because without conceptual understanding, often promoted through enabling students to deal with uncomfortableness and messiness, mathematical learners may not advance in development of mathematical concepts. Dealing with uncertainty successfully in mathematics is not something that may happen serendipitously. According to Grégiore (2016), uncertainty is inherent in the problem solving process among professional mathematicians and may be among younger mathematicians. The question remains, "So, what can teachers practically do in the classroom to encourage problem solvers to cope with and ideally overcome uncertainty?" The logical answer to this question is to prepare problem solvers for the rigors and expectation of uncertainty, so that they are prepared to deal with it. When uncertainty presents itself in any sort of situation and problem solvers are not expecting it, prospective outcomes could pose problems that are insurmountable to success. Helping students to overcome uncertainty by promoting, "…development of intrinsic motivation, associating positive emotions with uncertainty and exploration" (Grégiore, p. 32) can prove valuable in stimulating the development of creative cognitive thinking approaches.

10.6 Needed Directions for Future Work in Uncertainty and Creativity

The needs for research regarding uncertainty in mathematical creativity are extensive. This is because the chasm between that which is known about uncertainty and that which is known about certainty in solving problems is vast. In particular, researchers must start with developing a system for quantifying uncertainty in the context of mathematical creativity. Additional needed directions are a concrete understanding of how dealing with uncertainty positively, and perhaps negatively, influences learning and creativity in mathematics. The construct of uncertainty contains many characteristics about it that are unknown, or at best unclear in the world of mathematics learning and creativity. This position may serve to fascinate researchers and scholars in the world of mathematics education and mathematical psychology because clarifying unknown components of a psychological construct, in this case uncertainty, is the reward that experts realize for many years of efforts. From a practicality perspective, educators in the classroom may not have much tolerance for uncertainty because with it comes unknown outcomes and doubt. Practitioners may enjoy relating an input with an output, in anticipation of control of learning scenarios. However, as has been seen for over a century, dating to at least Poincaré's (1913) day, much still needs to be learned about creativity from a theoretician's perspective and how it can be engendered in classrooms from a practitioner's perspective.

10.7   Applications to Educators

Mathematics educators with an interest in investigating the Five Legs of Creativity Theory are strongly encouraged to access the complete book (Chamberlin and Mann 2021), mentioned in the introduction. As a snapshot of what should be done in the classroom, a primary focus in relation to this work, and in particular creativity and uncertainty, hastens the question, "What, precisely, is an apropos amount of uncertainty in the mathematics classroom, to engender creative process and product?" As discussed in the previous sections, uncertainty is something that is inherent in mathematical problem solving. In fact, without a modicum of uncertainty, no novelty (Chamberlin 2008) exists. Without novelty, problem solving is said to be absent (Chamberlin 2008). Hence, for creativity to emerge in mathematics and mathematical problem solving episodes, uncertainty must exist. The question remains, what constitutes a suitable amount of uncertainty and how is it managed by problem solvers. The essence of the first component pertains to mathematics problems that are developmentally appropriate (Baroody et al. 2003). Mathematically appropriate tasks are essential to foster mathematically appropriate teaching (Clements et al. 2017). Nevertheless, problem solvers must be conditioned to deal with uncertainty so that it is not a surprise to them. This struggle is likely necessary for productive thinking to transpire. If not pushed to solve a challenging problem, solvers may not engage in substantially high(er) level thinking and thus be in a position to identify and originate creative responses.

The second question pertains to how uncertainty is managed by problem solvers. Problem solvers should not merely be encouraged to cope or deal with uncertainty. Instead, they should be encouraged to embrace it because without uncertainty, the opportunity for true challenge may be compromised (Chamberlin 2002). Imperative to this process is the concept of identifying mathematical problem solving tasks that are accessible to students and solvable.

10.8   Conclusion

The lingering question after all of this discussion is, "How can creativity be facilitated in the classroom, especially in mathematics that may be fraught with uncertainty?" Twenty five years ago, Westby and Dawson (1995) provided some insight
on teachers' perception of creative individuals in stating, "One of the most consistent findings in educational studies of creativity has been that teachers dislike personality traits associated with creativity. Research has indicated that teachers prefer
traits that seem to run counter to creativity, such as conformity and unquestioning
acceptance of authority." In other words, teachers prefer working with students that
play the school game well, but highly creative individuals do not always want to
play the school game, and thus may not be accepted openly by teachers. It would
appear as though one of the ways to encourage teachers to become more amenable
to mathematical creativity is to enact a culture change, whereby it is valued. To
accomplish this, unfortunately, a much larger, seismic shift must ensue, in that
administrators will need to identify a means to maintain some element of assessment accountability in mathematics, while overlaying mathematical creativity in the
entire milieu of assessment.

Perhaps, the more salient and pragmatic question with respect to uncertainty and
mathematical creativity, or simply creativity in general, pertains to how teachers
help their students deal with uncertainty. It is important to issue the caveat that
uncertainty and anxiety, each share at least two similarities as psychological constructs. First, they are likely inherent in solving mathematical problems. Second,
they are typically a positive attribute of solving problems (Lane and Maxfied 2005),
insofar as a modicum of uncertainty and anxiety (incidentally, anxiety may well be
increased as a correlate of uncertainty), may encourage problem solvers to commit
themselves to persist in successfully finding creative solutions to mathematical
problems. Learning facilitators, generally teachers, of mathematical problem solving tasks can implement one simple approach in an attempt to aid students in dealing with uncertainty. They should psychologically prepare problem solvers for
uncertainty, and accordingly increased anxiety that may accompany uncertainty or
doubt as Beghetto (2020) calls it, by suggesting prior to problems that problems
solvers should be expected to incur a degree of uncertainty and thus anxiety, as a
result of doubt. When problem solvers realize that uncertainty is an expected by-
product of seeking creative solutions, it may serve to assuage their nervousness.

References

Adair, W. L., & Xiong, T. X. (2018). How Chinese and Caucasian Canadians conceptualize cre-
    ativity: The mediating role of uncertainty avoidance. *Journal of Cross-Cultural Psychology, 49,*
    223-238. doi:https://doi.org/10.1177/0022022117713153
Bandura, A. (1989). *Human Agency in Social Cognitive Theory. American Psychologist, 44,*
    1175–1184. doi:https://doi.org/10.1037/0003-066X.44.9.1175.

Bandura, A. *(1988)*. Organizational Application of Social Cognitive Theory. *Australian Journal of Management, 13, 275–302.*

Bandura, A. (1977). Self-efficacy: Toward a unifying theory of behavioral change. *Psychological Review, 84,* 191-215.

Bar-Anan, Y., Wilson, T. D., & Gilbert, D. T. (2009). The feeling of uncertainty intensifies affective reactions. *Emotions, 9,* 123-127.

Baroody, A. J., & Dowker, A. (Eds.). (2003). The development of arithmetic concepts and skills: Recent research and theory. Lawrence Erlbaum Associates.

Beghetto, R. (2020). *Uncertainty.* In V. Glăveanu (ed.) *The Palgrave Encyclopedia of the Possible.* Palgrave Macmillan. doi:https://doi.org/10.1007/978-3-319-98390-5_122-1

Chamberlin, S. A. (2008). What is problem solving in the mathematics classroom? *Philosophy of Mathematics Education, 23,* 1-25.

Chamberlin, S. A. (2002). Analysis of interest during and after model-eliciting activities: A comparison of gifted and general population students (Doctoral dissertation, Purdue University, 2002). *Dissertation Abstracts International, 64,* 2379. Available at: http://docs.lib.purdue.edu/dissertations/AAI3099758/

Chamberlin, S. A., & Mann, E. L. (2021). *The Relationship of Affect and Creativity in Mathematical Giftedness: How the Five Legs of Creativity Influence Math Talent.* Prufrock Academic Press.

Chamberlin, S. A., & Mann, E. L. (2014, July 27–30). *A new model of creativity in mathematical problem solving.* In Proceedings of the International Group for Mathematical Creativity and Giftedness (pp. 35–40). Denver, CO, University of Denver, CO. Available online at: http://www.igmcg.org/images/proceedings/MCG-8-proceedings.pdf

Clements, D. H., Fuson, K. C., & Sarama, J. (2017). What Is Developmentally Appropriate Teaching? *Teaching Children Mathematics, 24,* 178–188.

Cropley, D. (2017). *Psychological and Neuroscientific Perspectives on Mathematical Creativity and Giftedness.* In R. Leikin & B. Srirman (Eds.), *Creativity and Giftedness* (p. 183-199). Springer International Publishing.

Dyasi, H. (1999). *What children gain by learning through inquiry.* In National Science Foundation, *Inquiry: Thoughts, views, and strategies for the K-5 classroom* (p. 9-14). National Science Foundation.

Flowerday, T., & Shell, D. F. (2015). Disentangling the effects of interest, and choice on learning, engagement, and attitude. *Learning and Individual Differences, 40,* 134–140. doi:https://doi.org/10.1016/j.lindif.2015.05.003

Goldin, G. A. (2009). *The affective domain and students' mathematical inventiveness.* In R. Leikin, A. Berman, & B. Koichu (Eds.), *Creativity in Mathematics and the Education of Gifted Students,* (p. 149–163). Sense Publishers.

Grégoire, J. (2016). Understanding creativity in mathematics for improving mathematical education. *Journal of Cognitive Education and Psychology, 15,* 24-36. doi:https://doi.org/10.1891/1945-8959.15.1.24

Hallack, R., Assaker, G., O'Connor, P., & Lee, C. (2018). Firm performance in the upscale restaurant sector: The effects of resilience, creative self-efficacy, innovation and industry experience. *Journal of Retailing and Consumer Services, 40,* 229-240. doi:https://doi.org/10.1016/j.jretconser.2017.10.014

Hersh, R., & John-Steiner, V. (2011). *Loving and hating mathematics.* Princeton University Press.

Hiebert, J, Carpenter, T. C., Fennema, E., Fuson, K. C., Wearne, D., Murray, H., Olivier, A., & Human, P. (2000). *Making sense: Teaching and learning mathematics with understanding.* Heinemann

Imai, T. (2000). The influence of overcoming fixation in mathematics towards divergent thinking in open-ended mathematics problems on Japanese junior high school students. *International Journal of Mathematical Education in Science and Technology, 31,* 187–193. doi:https://doi.org/10.1080/002073900287246

Kashdan, T., & Silvia, P. (2009). *Curiosity and Interest: The Benefits of Thriving on Novelty and Challenge*. In, S. J. Lopez & C. R. Snyder (Eds.), *Oxford handbook of positive psychology* (p. 367-375). doi:https://doi.org/10.1093/oxfordhb/9780195187243.013.0034

Kaufman, J. C., & Beghetto, R. A. (2009). Beyond big and little: The four C model of creativity. *Review of General Psychology, 13,* 1-12. doi:https://doi.org/10.1037/a0013688

Kozlowski, J., Chamberlin, S. A., & Mann, E. L. (2019). Factors that influence mathematical creativity. *The Mathematics Enthusiast, 16,* article 26. Available at: https://scholarworks.umt.edu/tme/vol16/iss1/26/

Krutetskii, V. A. (1976). *The Psychology of Mathematical Abilities in School Children* (translated by J. Teller). University of Chicago Press.

Kutlu, O., Kula-Kartal, S., & Şimşek, N. T. (2017). Identifying the Relationships Between Perseverance, Openness to Problem Solving, and Academic Success in PISA 2012 Turkey. *Journal of Educational Sciences Research, 7,* 263-274. https://doi.org/10.22521/jesr.2017.71.9

Lane, D. A., & Maxfied, R. R. (2005). Ontological uncertainty and innovation. *Journal of Evolutionary Economics, 15,* 3-50.

Leu, Y., & Chiu, M. (2015). Creative behaviours in mathematics: Relationships with abilities, demographics, affects and gifted behaviours. *Thinking Skills and Creativity, 16,* 40–50. doi:https://doi.org/10.1016/j.tsc.2015.01.001.

Liu, W., Pan, Y., Luo, X., Wang, L., Pang, W. (2017). Active procrastination and creative ideation: The mediating role of creative self-efficacy. *Personality and Individual Differences, 119,* 227-229, doi:https://doi.org/10.1016/j.paid.2017.07.033

Mann, E. L., Chamberlin, S. A., & Graefe, A. (2017) *The Prominence of Affect in Creativity: Expanding the Conception of Creativity in Mathematical Problem Solving*. In R. Leikin & B. Srirman (Eds.), *Creativity and Giftedness* (p. 57-73). Springer International Publishing.

McLeod, D. B., & Adams, V. M. (1989). Affect and mathematical problem solving. Springer-Verlag.

Menger, P.-M., Rendall, S., Jacobs, A., Dorval, A., Eskinazi, L., Saada, E., & Karaganis, J. (2014). *The economics of creativity: Art and achievement under uncertainty*. Harvard University Press. doi:https://doi.org/10.4159/harvard.9780674726451

Miller, C. J., Perera, H. N., & Maghsoudlou, A. (2021). Students' multidimensional profiles of math engagement: Predictors and outcomes from a self-system motivational perspective. *British Journal of Educational Psychology, 91,* 261–285. doi:https://doi.org/10.1111/bjep.12358

Movshovitz-Hadar, N., & Kleiner, I. (2009). *Intellectual courage and mathematical creativity*. In R. Leikin, A. Berman, & B. Koichu (Eds.), *Creativity in Mathematics and the Education of Gifted Students,* (p. 31-50). Sense Publishers.

Nicholls, J. (1983). *Conception of ability and achievement motivation: A theory and its implications for education*. In S. Paris, G. Olson, & H. Steveson (Eds.), *Learning and motivation in the classroom* (pp. 211-237). Erlbaum Associates.

Öllinger, M., Fedor, A., Brodt, S., & Szathmáry, E. (2017). Insight into the ten-penny problem: Guiding search by constraints and maximization. *Psychological Research, 81,* 925–938. https://doi.org/10.1007/s00426-016-0800-3

Pajares, F. (1996). Self-efficacy beliefs and mathematical problem solving of gifted students. *Contemporary Educational Psychology, 21,* 325-344. doi:https://doi.org/10.1006/ceps.1996.0025

Penaloza, A. A., & Calvillo, D. P. (2012). Incubation provides relief from artificial fixation in problem solving. *Creativity Research Journal, 24,* 338-344. doi:https://doi.org/10.1080/10400419.2012.730329

Pitsia, V., Biggart, A., & Karakolidis, A. (2017). The role of students' self-beliefs, motivation and attitudes in predicting mathematics achievement: A multilevel analysis of the Programme for International Student Assessment data. *Learning and Individual Differences, 55,* 163–173. doi:https://doi.org/10.1016/j.lindif.2017.03.014

Poincaré, H. (1913). *The foundations of science*. The Science Press.

Poortvliet P.M. (2016) Mastery Goals. In: Zeigler-Hill V., Shackelford T. (eds) Encyclopedia of Personality and Individual Differences. Springer. https://doi.org/10.1007/978-3-319-28099-8_533-1

Renninger, K. A., & Bachrach, J. E. (2015). Studying triggers for interest and engagement using observational methods. *Educational Psychologist, 50,* 58–69. doi:https://doi.org/10.1080/00461520.2014.999920

Renzulli, J. S. (n.d.). Retrieved from: https://gifted.uconn.edu/schoolwide-enrichment-model/identifygt/

Renzulli, J.S. What makes giftedness? Reexamining a definition. Phi Delta Kappan 1978, 60, 180–184.

Sales, C. M. D., & Wakker, P. P. (2009). The metric-frequency measure of similarity for ill-structured data sets, with an application to family therapy. *British Journal of Mathematical and Statistical Psychology*, *62*, 663–682. doi:https://doi.org/10.1348/000711008X376070

Stepien, W. J., Gallagher, S. A., & Workman, D. (1993). Problem-based learning for traditional and interdisciplinary classrooms. *Journal for the Education of the Gifted, 16*(4), 338–357. doi:https://doi.org/10.1177/016235329301600402

Sternberg, R. J. (2006). The nature of creativity. *Creativity Research Journal, 18,* 87-98. https://doi.org/10.1207/s15326934crj1801_10

Tierney, P., & Farmer, S. M. (2002). Creative self-efficacy: Its potential antecedents and relationship to creative performance. *The Academy of Management Journal, 45,* 1137-1148

Tinto, V. (1975) Dropout from higher education: A theoretical synthesis of recent research. *Review of Educational Research 45,* 89–125. doi:https://doi.org/10.2307/1170024.

Tracey, M. W., & Hutchinson, A. (2018). Uncertainty, agency and motivation in graduate design students. *Thinking Skills and Creativity, 29,* 196-202. doi:https://doi.org/10.1016/j.tsc.2018.07.004

Tuli, M. R. (1980). Mathematical creativity as related to aptitude for achievement in and attitude towards mathematics. (Doctoral dissertation, Panjab University, 1980). *Dissertation Abstracts International,* 42(01), 122.

Wallas, G. (1926). *The art of thought.* Cape.

Westby, E., & Dawson, V. L. (1995). Creativity: Asset or burden in the classroom. *Creativity Research Journal, 8,* 1-10. https://doi.org/10.1207/s15326934crj0801_1

Wilder, R. L. (1984). The role of intuition. In D. M. Campbell & J. C. Higgins (eds.), *Mathematics: People, problems, results, vol II* (p. 37–45). Wadsworth International.

Chapter 11
Engineering Uncertainty in the Mathematics Classroom: Implications for Classroom Tasks and Learning

Bharath Sriraman

Abstract Mathematics is a creative expression. The results of mathematics, namely its theorems have not only stood the test of time but also adapted to paradigm shifts that resulted in different systems of axioms. Axiomatic shifts result in the development of new areas of mathematics (e.g., Non-Euclidean geometries; Non-standard Analysis etc.). However, axioms are also a system of rules that can be "playfully changed" to force creative expression. The chapter addresses whether uncertainty and creative expression go hand-in-hand in mathematics and whether creativity can be fostered by engineering uncertainty. Uncertainty also exists in numerous real-life situations where a mathematical model is required to understand a problem situation. This chapter addresses promising approaches in the learning of mathematics that involves both abstract and real-life situations in the classroom that result in ambiguity and uncertainty. Implications of the creativity that results from such an approach is discussed.

> *The uncertainty where to look for the next opening of discovery brings the pain of conflict and the debility of indecision."* Alexander Bain (1818–1903)

11.1 Introduction

Uncertainty is a buzzword in the present day exacerbated by global events like Covid19, mixed and often contrarian messages from media, and the advent of oxymoronic phrases like "alternative facts." In mathematics oxymoronic phrases such as the one stated earlier do not exist. Mathematical facts are also called theorems-namely statements that have been proven using deductive logic. This certainty in

B. Sriraman (✉)
Department of Mathematical Sciences, University of Montana-Missoula, Missoula, MT, USA
e-mail: sriramanb@mso.umt.edu

© Springer Nature Switzerland AG 2022
R. A. Beghetto, G. J. Jaeger (eds.), *Uncertainty: A Catalyst for Creativity, Learning and Development*, Creativity Theory and Action in Education 6,
https://doi.org/10.1007/978-3-030-98729-9_11

mathematics is one face of the coin, which hides "uncertainty", namely the process or means via which one arrives at the discovery of a theorem that becomes mathematical fact once the burden of proof has been met (Sriraman 2021). The dynamic between certainty of a proved theorem and the uncertainty which led to its discovery, is well known among practitioners of mathematics, however textbooks and teaching methods more often than not obscure this. This is even true in advanced mathematics where proof obscures uncertainty as opposed to shedding light on how it was overcome? Davis and Hersh (1981) describe this as follows when an "ideal mathematician" is asked to describe what a proof is.

> Well, this whole thing was cleared up by the logician Tarski, I guess, and some others, maybe Russell or Peano. Anyhow, what you do is, you write down the axioms of your theory in a formal language with a given list of symbols or alphabet. Then you write down the hypothesis of your theorem in the same symbolism. Then you show that you can transform the hypothesis step by step, using the rules of logic, till you get the conclusion. That's a proof.

This quote reveals the nature of mathematics presented or learned in its traditional form, which Reuben Hersh (1927–2020) an eminent philosopher of mathematics described as the front side of mathematics; the front side is compared to the orderly nature of entering and ordering a meal at a restaurant. This hides the bustle and frenzied activity in the kitchen, namely its backside, which more often than not is chaotic. Similar views are echoed by many researchers in the domain of creativity. Beghetto and Corazza (2019) suggest inconclusiveness and uncertainty are important ingredients in any dynamic conceptualization of creativity. They criticize traditional views "tend to privilege static creative achievement and fixed creative traits, rather than focus on the more dynamic, developing, and variable nature of creative thought and action" (p.2).

In this chapter, the meaning of uncertainty in mathematics is unpacked with the aim of both understanding it and engineering it in the classroom to foster creativity. First, we need to define what we mean by mathematical creativity. Sriraman (2019) posits that mathematical creativity is catalyzed by five factors:

1. Knowledge of what is already known (labelled Prolonged Preparation)
2. Questions encountered at the boundaries of what is known that are unanswerable due to domain limitations with existing tools/techniques (labelled Constraints)
3. Uncertainty in what is possible with the questions that spur the development of something new, or what is not possible that imposes constraints on the development of something new (labelled Uncertainty).
4. The creation or new tools/techniques that are hitherto unknown to the field or the adaptation of what is known, and their confrontation with the gatekeepers of the field (labelled Risk taking).
5. The convergence or divergence of the new theorem/technique/result with other results in that particular area of research or inquiry (that lend Coherence) and can lead to other areas of research.

These five factors are captured in terms of a cyclical process that catalyzes mathematical creativity (in Fig. 11.1) under the designated labels.

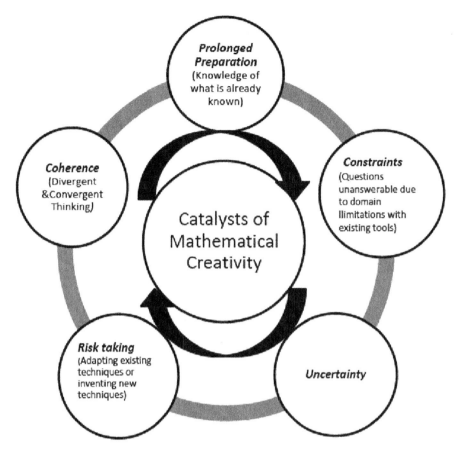

Fig. 11.1 The catalysts of mathematical creativity. (Sriraman 2019)

Beghetto (2007) viewed classroom creativity as a dynamic between task constraints (or restrictions) and original expression. This dynamic is present in this model of the catalysts of mathematical creativity. It also contains elements of Glaveanu's (2016) nuanced view of creativity as "both a troublesome noun" suggesting "an object it designates in the world" (p.205) as well as "a quality of human action- to create means to act in a flexible, novel and meaningful way in a given context … a useful verb." (p.210). The model also incorporates Corazza's (2016) view of creativity as characterized by *change*. In mathematics, this is particularly true when a new question requires one to adapt previously available tools or in some cases create new tools to solve a problem. Corazza (2016) also adds that "potentially creative outcomes" change and are influenced by socio-cultural and historical conditions. For instance, problems from physics that required Isaac Newton to create the mathematics of Calculus as a viable tool, is now the purview of university freshmen. What was once new is no longer new and completely devoid of the context in which the language of Calculus is situated. Problem situations in mathematics can range from the mundane – applying a known technique to the exciting – where everything is unknown. Andrew Wiles, who solved the long standing Fermat's Last Theorem remarked:

> Perhaps I could best describe my experience of doing mathematics in terms of entering a dark mansion. You go into the first room and it's dark, completely dark. You stumble around, bumping into the furniture. Gradually, you learn where each piece of furniture is. And finally, after six months or so, you find the light switch and turn it on. Suddenly, it's all illuminated and you can see exactly where you were. Then you enter the next dark room…

Although Wiles was describing his 7-year journey into solving one of the outstanding problems of mathematics, the quote can resonate with learners of mathematics. For many students confronting a problem is like entering a dark mansion and making sense of it and attempting the problem results in stumbles that often results is many giving up. The quote is metaphorical – one can interpret furniture as things that one is familiar with (a mathematical knowledge base and toolkit). The "light switch" can mean several things, it can mean "illumination" in the Gestalt sense or it could be the invention of a new tool necessary for solving the problem.

11.2 Engineering Uncertainty in Mathematics: A Study of Contrasts

One can trace the origins of uncertainty in mathematics by examining the 13 books of Euclid's Elements, which begin with 23 definitions, 5 common notions and 5 axioms and proceed to prove an "orderly" chain of 465 propositions. The Elements epitomizes ancient Greek mathematics at its best, in that it is not only an astonishing feat of axiomatic-deductive mathematics with an emphasis on proof, but also an elevation of mathematics into an abstract plane of thought. In contrast to Euclid's Elements, stands the ancient Chinese classic The Nine Chapters on the Mathematical Art. Like Euclid's Elements which is a compendium that incorporated work done prior to Euclid's time period, the Nine Chapters is also a compendium of Chinese mathematics from 10 BCE- 2 CE with one major commentary in 3 CE by Liu Hui. The contrast lies in the fact that the Nine chapters is written in the style of problem, followed by solution and an explanation of the solution. A modern reader of this book is often astonished at the similarity in the structure of the book to the mathematics learned today in the elementary and high school curriculum. The emphasis is on practical problems that involve measurement, storage of grains and rice, proportional distributions, fair levies, and engineering (construction). The 246 problems of the Nine Chapters represent an apotheosis of Chinese mathematics that suggests mathematics not as an abstract discipline based on axiomatic-deductive thought but mathematics as a way of making sense of the world around us- practically oriented and sophisticated in the types of algorithms and formulas that needed to be developed to solve real world problems.

Zeilberger (2017) looks back at Greek mathematics with the satirical statement "Beware of Greeks bearing mathematical gifts" (p.140). He goes on to admonish Greek mathematics and its pernicious influence on the history of mathematics "as a sequence of (unsuccessfully!) trying to answer stupid questions." (p.140). An explanation is warranted for the uninitiated reader to understand Zeilberger's admonishment. The questions in question here deal with being hemmed in by an axiomatic system. For instance proving the parallel postulate (the fifth axiom in Euclid's Elements) was an impossibility, and the assumption that it could be false (1800 years later) led to the development of non-Euclidean geometries. Similarly the so-called Delian problems that ask whether (1) is it possible to square a circle; (2) is it possible to trisect any angle; and (3) is it possible to double a cube (i.e., construct a new cube with double the given volume) are also impossible when one is "bound by the Euclidean party line" (Zeilberger, p.140). In Euclidean geometry, the axioms bind one to use a straightedge (with no marks, unlike a ruler) and a compass for all constructions. Staying within the axiomatic system made it impossible to solve the aforementioned problems, but led to some very interesting mathematics. In fact, the entire edifice of classical abstract algebra can be viewed as being built on these three problems. On the other hand tweaking the axioms to allow what it not permissible by the Euclidean axioms leads one to interesting mathematics as well. For instance, it led to the development of the geometry of mathematical curves, as well as Origami mathematics (that has Paper folding axioms) which makes the Delian problems solvable. The only additional axioms in this case are folding axioms, which allow 3-dimensional moves in a 2- dimensional surface – which are not permissible in Euclidean geometry. It is clear that uncertainty in the validity of the solution to these problems depends on the choice of axioms. This is true of research mathematics.

The larger question in mathematics is:

1. Are we discovering/inventing something new by tweaking axioms?
2. What can be considered new in mathematics? And who decides something is new?

These questions are beyond the scope of this chapter and are dealt with elsewhere (e.g., Sriraman (2021). However the creativity of mathematicians comes into focus in their ability to either work within an axiomatic system by inventing new tools to tackle an existing problem, or go beyond the domain limitations by tweaking the axioms. Uncertainty spurs this creativity. In the next section, we attempt to engineer uncertainty in a classroom setting and analyze the creativity that manifests.

11.3 Engineering Uncertainty in a Mathematics Classroom

Unlike the traditional geometry curricula that is still anchored in Euclid's Elements, most modern geometry curricula in K-12 includes transformational geometry, analytical geometry as well as measurement. Measurement has more emphasis in the K-8 curricula. In one of the courses taught by the author that is required for prospective elementary school teachers, the topic of measurement figures prominently in the syllabus. After students learn the differences between the U.S customary units (the English system of measurement) and metric units, the focus shifts to real world situations where measurement topics are present and relevant. Over the course of the last decade, one of the investigations in this course focused on environmental issues- particularly the rate at which "trash" was produced and disposed in landfills across the U.S. Measurement units and mathematical modeling were emphasized in this investigation. The problem was presented in a form that created uncertainty and the need to create a mathematical model to resolve the uncertainty. The underlying hope is that students will also be creative in the ways in which they resolve the problem, mathematical or otherwise. While students are encouraged to work in groups in the classroom, the final write up is done individually by students.

11.3.1 The Measurement Problem

The "measurement" problem has been presented in different formats. One format is as follows:

> Consider the following graphical representation of trash from the Environmental Protection Agency (Fig. 11.2). Does the number 14.3 tons per person seem reasonable for the State of Montana?

Another format for the problem is:

> The local newspaper reports that Montanans throw away 7.26 pounds of trash per person per day, but the rest of the country only throws away an average of 4.38 pounds. Is this believable? Create a mathematical model that can help us make sense of the situation.

A third format for the same problem is:

> Republic Services, our local waste management company, says it has purchased 100 years of airspace for its landfill. Our goal is to determine what this means, and if this "amount of space" is adequate for Missoula's needs?

In all three formats, the problem has sufficient uncertainty (or even incredulity) that students are motivated to dig in (no pun intended). Classroom discussion of the task before group work was veered towards what is known versus what is unknown in this particular problem. The following checklist was triggered by the problem:

(a) What does "air space" mean in the landfill vocabulary?
(b) What type of a unit is it? [length, area, volume, weight]? Explain
(c) Find other examples of Landfills that have acquired airspace. Be specific about their location and how much airspace has been purchased?
(d) Is your standard trashcan and other trash containers around campus examples of airspace? Which unit of measurement would you use to describe these objects

Fig. 11.2 Retrieved from https://www.saveonenergy.com/land-of-waste/ (Original source https://www3.epa.gov/lmop/projects-candidates/)

Response 1:

a) air space = the projected cubic yards filled by waste

b) unit = volume, cubic yards

c) 1. Las Vegas - 2,200 acres - Apex Regional 300 t/n

   2. PA, Green Tree landfill - 3,000 c/d = 12⁹ t/n

d) yes it is, cubic yards (but only the big dumpsters)

These questions were typically followed with groups of students "finding the answers (sample response of which is found above) or in other cases students wanting to simply solve the problem by scaling up the numbers for 100 years. One sample response follows:

Response 2:

Obversely, there were students who questioned the validity of the numbers found in different sources. "Does 14.3 tons per person mean the total trash over a lifetime, a year?" This was based on the observation that 7.26 lbs per person per day only scaled up to around 2650 lbs per year which was slightly more than 1 ton. Several students called the company that managed the landfill to find out that 14.3 tons meant the waste per capita in a state based on all the solid waste that was present in all the landfills. Several students remarked, "The EPA sources have numbers that are inflated compared to what the landfill company has." This led to an important discussion on what was defined as "waste", and what facts were accumulated by different sources before publishing their numbers.

11.3.2   Sources of Uncertainty and Determining Certainty

Different sources found gave different rates at which landfills were filled up. There was also uncertainty in what was determined as "waste or trash" and how much volume a ton of trash would fill up since this depended on the density of the disposed waste. Eventually the definition of "municipal solid waste (MSW)" from the EPA was used as the guideline, as well as the average density given by the EPA for MSW as approximately 318 kg/m³. Another parameter of uncertainty was the shape of the landfill and its dimensions. Research on different landfills in different parts of the country led to a determination of a landfill having roughly the shape of a half cylinder (see Fig. 11.3). In this modeling of the volume of a landfill, dimensions of 2000 feet × 800 feet × 1000 feet was assumed which were then converted to yards. These starting assumptions were later adjusted when students found that the largest landfill in the U.S, namely Puente Hills had a height (depth) of 500 feet.

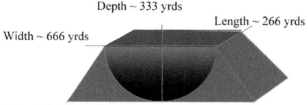

This looks like half a cylinder. If we find the volume for the whole cylinder and divide that in half we can get an estimate for the landfill. The solution for the volume of a cylinder is

$$V = \pi r^2 h$$

$$\pi \cdot 333^2 \cdot 266 = 92{,}665{,}827.8 \text{ cubic yards}$$
$$92{,}665{,}827.8 \ / \ 2 = 46{,}332{,}913.9 \text{ cubic yards}$$

Fig. 11.3 Determining the shape of a landfill

11.3.3   What About Creativity?

As stated earlier, there are nuances in the way mathematics is viewed depending on the cultural context. The Nine Chapters on the Mathematical Art contains problems, which are contextual and oriented towards a "measurement" approach to mathematics. However there are cases in "which an original problem or a class of problems...[s]olved presents opportunities for axiomatization and a mathematical theory can develop out of it." (Lindström and Sriraman 2021). In this case, the classroom example of "the measurement problem" involving the landfill led to a variety of approaches and called into questions what definitions and "measures" could be used to systematize a solution. Once this was accomplished abstraction occurred in ways the volume of the landfill could be visualized through ideal geometric objects such as a prism (where the volume is simply the product of length, width and height) or a half-cylinder. For instance, as in the geometry of Euclid "the abstraction level is high enough to allow an analysis of the problems outside their original context (Lindström and Sriraman 2021). However, creativity manifested in the questions that could be posed and mathematically answered. One of the questions posed was "Can we calculate the area of the landfill?" which was followed up with the suggestion that "we can check if we are correct using Google Earth." To complete such a calculation, the following assumptions were made:

1. The rate of solid waste production from the local newspaper sources was deemed accurate and scaled up for 100 years. This amounted to approximately 2.7×10^{10} lbs, which converted to approximately 1.22×10^{10} kg.
2. The density of municipal solid waste from the EPA was used, namely 318 kg/m^3 Since, density = mass/volume, this meant the total volume of the solid waste for Missoula for 100 years was mass/density; namely 1.22×10^{10} kg divided by its density 318 kg/m^3 which resulted in approximately 3.8×10^7 m^3 of space occupied.

3. Since Volume = Surface area x depth, if the depth of the landfill were known, then the surface area could be calculated. By calling the landfill company, the depth was determined to be roughly 300 feet, which converted to roughly 100 meters.
   Therefore the surface area of the landfill was equal to $3.8 \times 10^7/100$ which was approximately equal to 3.8×10^5 square meters or 380,000 square meters.
4. Now the accuracy of this calculation was checked on Google Earth, by using the polygon measurement feature to determine the surface area (see Fig. 11.4).

It turned out that the answer found on Google Earth for the surface area was much lower than the expected value from the calculation. This discrepancy between the calculated value and the actual value led to considerable cognitive dissonance and brought uncertainty back into the foreground of this problem. As Beghetto (2020) stated "Given that uncertainty is associated with lack of clarity, control and determinateness, it tends to be viewed as an unpleasant state that should be quickly resolved." Two ways were proposed to resolve the uncertainty:

(a) Revisit the assumptions made in the measures used in the calculation
(b) Call the landfill to determine if the area chosen was correct or incorrect.

The assumptions were deemed to be correct, which meant that the polygon used to determine the landfill area must have been incorrect. Another phone call to the landfill manager led to the realization that the "future" airspace of the landfill was yet to be excavated. This led to constructing another polygon on Google Earth that marked the boundaries of the land acquired for the future airspace (see Fig. 11.5), which led to compatibility of the two answers, the theoretical value being 380,000 square

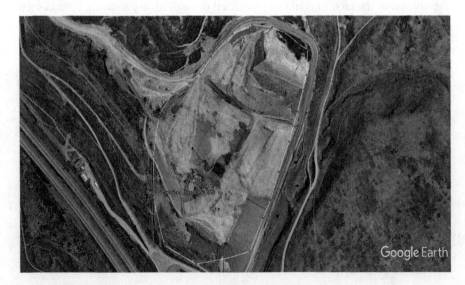

Fig. 11.4 Polygon showing the present area of the local Landfill

Fig. 11.5 Polygon showing the area of the "future Landfill"

meters, and the value on Google Earth being 385,000 square meters. The margin of error was under 2%.

Once this was accomplished "the method" devised to solve the local landfill problem could be applied to other landfills around the country to determine if "the method" generalized to other similar measurement situations involving landfill.

11.4 The Catalysts of Creativity

The measurement problem used to engineer creativity presents uncertainty in the definitions needed and the accuracy of the sources for measuring the different quantities. The ensuing mathematical model created to determine the volume in a landfill is dependent on the "airspace" that is available for the waste material. In terms of the model proposed by Sriraman (2019) on the catalysts of mathematical creativity, these classroom episodes can also be analyzed through that theoretical lens. The question of what "airspace" in a landfill meant was at the boundary of what the elementary education students had encountered. In other words, this particular question was at the periphery of what was known or answerable to them based on their background in measurement units (Prolonged Preparation). The uncertainty of answering the question led them into the development of a mathematical model based on what their knowledge base, but pushed them beyond it in determining densities of objects that are never encountered in textbooks. The resources they encountered in their quest to find different measurement quantities relevant for the problem also included an element of risk – what should one believe? The internet is rife with misinformation especially with respect to numerical data, as the last 5 years have revealed, since anyone is able to "post" legitimate looking information without any evidence or fact to back it up. Thus, students were confronted with information that was hitherto unknown to them and had to take a calculated risk (pun intended) on what information and numerical values were credible and relevant for the problem. Finally, the aspect of coherence was achieved when the discrepancy between the theoretical value and the actual value was resolved, and the realization that the type of modeling that was accomplished was generalizable to other "airspace" problems involving solid waste in landfills. We conclude this section with several quotes from students on this investigation as well as some observations from the author to support this approach to engineering uncertainty.

- "This activity allows students to explore future problems that humans face. It raises ideas of sustainability that are connected to a student's community."
- "It was surprising how much trash is created in Missoula, MT. Even when comparing the amount of trash Missoula to larger cities like Chicago, Los Angeles, and Vegas it is staggering. This investigation was an eye opener about the importance of being proactive in the recycling and buying items that are reusable instead of disposable."
- "Units like airspace and solid waste density were new for me. These are not found in any books! Also having conflicting numbers from different agencies was aggravating for me. The most surprising aspect for me was to actually call up different landfills around the country for information and realizing that they were not willing to readily part with information that the public has a right to know."
- "I wish I had learned about this in elementary school. As a future teacher, I am going to bring relevant topics in measurement and combine this with field trips to the recycling centers or even the landfill."
- "Comparing our consumption to other countries shows the disparity that exists in the world. Isn't it true that the cheap goods we consume are produced elsewhere and often shipped halfway around the world! The local movements here are more relevant than I thought."

11.5   Coda

The landfill problem was used over the period 2010–2020 with 12 different groups of pre-service elementary teachers (roughly 250 students). The exit surveys completed by students after engaging in this activity suggested a naiveté with what constituted "data" in the real world and a lack of awareness on credible sources of data for such a problem. However, as the existential threat of climate change became more prevalent over the course of the last decade especially in student awareness of this threat, the landfill problem was one that students engaged in with interest and resulted in strong affective reactions. There was an element of surprise at how much waste was actually produced by a small community in a rural State in comparison to larger urban areas in other States. Hans Rosling's visual statistics available at gapminder.org was another source introduced by the author to the students to find reliable data related to consumption lifestyles in different countries. Comparing U.S data to developing countries produced a profound awareness in the disparities in lifestyles in different parts of the world and sometimes resulted in a contentious discussion on whether or not the lifestyle of one country came at the expense of poverty and industrial pollution in other countries that were part of the supply chain.

Earlier in the chapter, a comparison was made between two ancient and iconic mathematical texts, namely Euclid's Elements and the Chinese Nine Chapters on the Mathematical Art. The former is iconic for its axiomatic and deductive presentation of mathematics, whereas the latter is more representative about mathematics as it is encountered in the real world with an emphasis on calculation and modeling. The mathematics encountered by elementary education majors contains both these aspects of mathematics since it includes curricula that emphasizes measurement topics besides the classical topics from Euclid. However, measurement as encountered in the curricula does not offer any contemporary challenges with problems that are actually encountered in the real world. Instead, many measurement problems are still mired in the comparison of American customary units with the Metric system. Uncertainty is difficult to engineer with problems that do not include an element of surprise. The example presented in this chapter is one instance where the element of surprise is created, and where both Euclid's Elements and the Nine Chapters on the Mathematical Art are relevant.

As the world is confronted with problems due to Climate Change, the mathematics curricula for elementary students needs to adapt and include problems that are relevant for the world they will inherit. To wit, uncertainty is increasingly present in the world and requires human ingenuity to adapt to the planetary changes. Clearly, our creativity comes to the forefront when we encounter problems that threaten our existence. The example presented in this chapter offers a glimpse into engineering uncertainty and fostering creativity in the context of elementary classroom mathematics. It also provides opportunities for interdisciplinary explorations involving environmental issues within a community that could include field trips to the locations for students.

References

Beghetto, R. A. (2007). Ideational code-switching: Walking the talk about supporting student creativity in the classroom. *Roeper Review, 29*, 265–270.

Beghetto, R. A & Corazza, G. E. (2019). *Dynamic perspective on creativity*. Springer Switzerland.

Beghetto R. A. (2020) Uncertainty. In: Glăveanu V. (Ed) *The Palgrave Encyclopedia of the Possible*. Palgrave Macmillan, Cham.

Corazza, G. E. (2016). Potential originality and effectiveness: The dynamic definition of creativity. *Creativity Research Journal, 28*, 258–267.

Davis, P. J., & Hersh, R. (1981). *The Mathematical Experience*. Birkhäuser.

Glaveanu, V. P. (2016). The psychology of creating: A cultural developmental approach to key dichotomies within creativity studies. In V.P. Glaveanu (Ed). *The Palgrave Handbook of Creativity and Culture Research* (pp. 205–223). Palgrave Macmillian.

Lindström T., Sriraman B. (2021) Mathematics, Science, and Dynamical Systems: An Introduction. In: Sriraman B. (eds) *Handbook of the Mathematics of the Arts and Sciences*. Springer, Cham. https://doi.org/10.1007/978-3-319-70658-0_143-1

Shen, K., Crossley, J., & Lun, A. (1999). The Nine Chapters on the Mathematical Art. Oxford University Press.

Sriraman, B. (2019). Uncertainty as a catalyst for mathematical creativity. In M. Nolte (Ed), *Including the Highly Gifted and Creative Students-Current Ideas and Future Directions. Proceedings of the 11th International Conference on Mathematical Creativity and Giftedness* (MCG 11), pp. 32–51. Universitaet Hamburg, Germany. WTM Verlag Muenster.

Sriraman, B. (2021). Uncertainty as a catalyst and condition for creativity: the case of mathematics. *ZDM Mathematics Education*. https://doi.org/10.1007/s11858-021-01287-6

Zeilberger, D. (2017). What is mathematics and what should it be? In B. Sriraman (Ed). *Humanizing Mathematics and its Philosophy* (pp. 139–150). Birkhäuser.

Part IV
Uncertainty in Learning and Development

Chapter 12
Do Children Think *Alea Iacta Est?*: Developing Concepts of Uncertainty in Causal Reasoning

Deon T. Benton and David M. Sobel

Abstract A fundamental question in cognitive development is when young children are capable of incorporating probabilities into their inferences about everyday behaviors and how they represent knowledge of probability. In this chapter, we will focus on how children understand probability in an explicit manner – examples in which children must incorporate probabilistic data into their inferences.

12.1 Introduction

To make predictions, explain actions, and reason about alternate possibilities, we need to reason about probabilities – the likelihood that particular events will occur or have occurred. To act adaptively, we must also be able to construct actions that maximize the likelihood of desirable outcomes. This again requires probabilistic reasoning about the relation between our choices and their consequences. A fundamental question in cognitive development is when young children are capable of incorporating probabilities into their inferences about everyday behaviors and how they represent knowledge of probability. In this chapter, we will focus on how children understand probability in an explicit manner – examples in which children must incorporate probabilistic data into their inferences (see Bryant and Nunes (2012) for a description of other problems that rely on probabilistic reasoning).

Investigations into this aspect of young children's probabilistic reasoning have been divided into two categories. Dating back to Piaget (1930) and Piaget and Inhelder (1975), the ability to recognize and reason across probabilities can be

D. T. Benton (✉)
Department of Psychology, Swarthmore College, Swarthmore, PA, USA
e-mail: dbenton2@swarthmore.edu

D. M. Sobel
Brown University, Providence, RI, USA

© Springer Nature Switzerland AG 2022
R. A. Beghetto, G. J. Jaeger (eds.), *Uncertainty: A Catalyst for Creativity, Learning and Development*, Creativity Theory and Action in Education 6,
https://doi.org/10.1007/978-3-030-98729-9_12

thought of as an explicit, slow-developing capacity, emerging relatively late in development. More recently, however, there is evidence that young infants are sensitive to probabilities (e.g., Denison and Xu 2010; Téglás et al. 2007; Xu and Garcia 2008). Below, we briefly summarize these two literatures and then present our goal to integrate them through the subsequent discussion.

12.2   Early Emerging Statistical Learning Capacities

Some of the earliest theories of causal inference begin with associative learning. The crux of this perspective is that infants possess an early-emerging capacity to detect cooccurrence relations between and among features, objects, and entities and use those relations to make inferences about causality based on statistical regularity information. This ability to register cooccurrences not only enables children to make causal inferences based on statistical and correlational information, but is an ability that is thought to be evolutionarily ancient and is and shared with lower animals (see e.g., Cramer et al. 2002; Dickinson 2001; Dickinson and Shanks 1995; Wagner and Rescorla 1972).

There is substantial evidence that shows that children possess sophisticated capacities for picking out statistical regularities in the environment early in infancy (e.g., Fiser and Aslin 2003; Goldstein et al. 2009; Haith et al. 1993; Kirkham et al. 2002; Saffran et al. 1996). For example, Saffran et al. (1996; see also Aslin et al. 1998) showed that infants recognize the transitional probabilities among sounds that make up words. That is, regular exposure to a language indicates that certain syllables occur after others within a word, while other syllable transitions can only occur between words. Thus, on this view, infants can learn to detect where words end and begin by attending to dips in the transitional probabilities between sounds, syllables, and words. Eight-month-old infants showed heightened attention when presented with part-words that violated the transitional probability between sounds than words that adhered to the transitional probability structure. This aspect of language learning not only helps infants learn where word boundaries exist but to detect word boundaries over entire speech streams. Subsequent research by Kirkham et al. (2002) showed that this capacity to register transitional probabilities is not specific to the domain of language learning, but also generalizes to visual stimuli.

Detecting and learning statistical regularities provide a powerful mechanism for interpreting the world, but it is limited. The well-known "Poverty of the Stimulus" argument (part of Chomsky's (1980) review of Skinner's (1957) *Verbal Behavior*) is an extreme example. A less extreme, though similar argument, is that provided by Keil (1989), which he called *Original Sim*. On this account, statistical and associative learning mechanisms are deemed to be insufficient processes because they do not provide a way to determine which (of potentially many) real-world correlations are relevant for category learning. Language learning and category formation are different from causal inference, and our goal is not to try to rebut the Poverty of the Stimulus or Original Sim arguments (in fact, we do not want to); rather, we want to suggest that domain-general statistical learning mechanisms are not the baby to be thrown out with the proverbial bathwater.

For associative learning to be a good representation of causal structure, you need to go beyond detecting, encoding, and registering the associative link between features that are shown together through spatiotemporal contiguity: you need to be able to make inferences about features that are only indirectly related. For example, infants can register correlations among spatiotemporally contiguous static object features by 10 months of age (Younger and Cohen 1983) and among dynamic features by 18 months of age (e.g., Rakison and Poulin-Dubois 2002). Previous research has also established that young infants can encode the relation between biologically-plausible stimuli. For example, infants between 3½ and 6 months of age can register that hands (but not other objects, like occupational therapy claws) produce goal-directed actions (e.g., Leslie 1982; Sommerville et al. 2005; Woodward 1998). In addition, research with 9½-month-old infants (e.g., Saxe et al. 2005, 2007) has shown that they understand that things with eyes, but not inanimate objects that lack these features such as toy trucks or blocks, can cause "ballistic" motion (Saxe et al. 2005, p. 156 – for example, a beanbag being thrown over a wall). Crucially, in each of these studies, infants are shown features that occur together. An open question is whether infants can infer the relation between two features that rarely, if ever, occur together. For example, can infer that objects with heads, eyes, or hands will engage in goal-directed actions, even if these features are not observed together? This capacity to infer the relation between two features that are only indirectly related is called *second-order correlation* learning. Note that this relates to our notion of associations being stacked, one on another. This is learning mechanism is important because infants cannot possibly encode all of the correlations and associations to which they are exposed in the real world. Powerful inferential processes such as second-order correlation learning can enable young learners to overcome this difficulty.

Several studies have demonstrated that infants and toddlers can detect second-order correlations among static features of objects (Cuevas et al. 2006; Yermolayeva and Rakison 2016) as well as dynamic features (Rakison and Benton 2019). Benton et al. (2021) extended this research to show that 2- and 3-year-olds can use second-order correlations to make causal inferences about the relation between and among arbitrary features. They introduced children to two objects that differed in shape, color, and size (objects A and B). Object A had a unique feature (C), whereas object B had a different unique feature (D). The two objects were situated next to each other on a stage and remained motionless for approximately 10 seconds.

Children were then shown two new objects—which did not possess the aforementioned unique features—and then were introduced to a novel machine. Object A and B were put on the machine one at a time. One of them made the machine activate (it lit up and played music when the object came in contact with it) and the other did not (the machine just stayed inert).

Children then observed two new identical objects. These objects differed in shape and color from the previous ones but were identical in shape and color to each other. Critically, one of these new objects had unique feature C, whereas the other had unique feature D from the first two object pairs. Children were asked to make the machine go. Benton et al. (2021) reasoned that children should place the novel object that possessed the feature that was indirectly associated with the machine's activation on the machine. For example, if children learned that object A possessed feature C during the first phase of the experiment and then that object A—without feature C—made the machine activate during the second phase of the experiment, then they should use the novel object with feature C to make the machine go but not the novel object with feature D. Children's responses indicated that they detected the second-order correlation that embodied the indirect relation between one of the features and the machine's activation. In the case that Object A—without feature C—made the machine activate, they chose the novel object with feature C to make the machine go.

These data suggest that relatively young children can use second-order correlation learning to detect the relation between stimuli that are indirectly related, but they also point to a problem with positing that causal reasoning is produced only through simple, first-order associative learning mechanisms (mechanisms in which features are paired with one another only through observed spatiotemporal contingency). This is not to say that higher-order correlational learning cannot produce rational behaviors. For instance, children could simply put both objects on the machine. If they do not know which one makes it go, or if they even have the slightest uncertainty, putting both objects on the machine is a reasonable thing to do, simply because children have never seen an instance of the machine activating with nothing on it. But critically, they never do this. Detecting, encoding, and recognizing second-order correlations in the environment allows children to understand that features and relations can be linked even if they do not directly observe those relations together. What second-order correlation learning does not do, however, is allow children to represent multiple possibilities (i.e., that a feature could be a cause or could not be a cause). Inferring that two indirectly related features go together through a second-order correlation is not the same thing as knowing whether a given feature causes or produces an outcome (e.g., machine activation). Children might be reasoning about the statistical relations among events, but not the uncertainty of any particular feature's causal status.

12.3   The Slow Emergence of Explicit Probabilistic Reasoning

What understanding second-order correlation does suggest is that children need not see features paired together to infer a relation between them. However, we also know that children can engage in probabilistic reasoning. Understanding probability involves understanding the nature of the relation between two events. My understanding of how likely I can draw a black ball from an urn involves calculating the proportion of black balls in the urn to balls of other colors. There is now a great deal of work suggesting that infants and very young children have an implicit understanding of such probabilistic inferences (e.g., Téglás et al. 2007; Xu and Denison 2009; Xu and Garcia 2008) and can even use statistical learning to make inferences about others (Denison and Xu 2010; Kushnir et al. 2010; Sobel and Kirkham 2012).

These data all suggest that children might have implicit learning capacities, but there is a difference between registering implicit relations among events and explicitly reasoning about probability in terms of numerical quantities. Historically, this has led several researchers to posit that children have difficulty reasoning about probability. For example, Hoemann and Ross (1971) presented 4- through 10-year-old children with spinners, divided into different areas of black and white. They asked children questions about magnitude of the colors on the spinners or questions that involved a probability judgment. In the magnitude condition, they showed children two spinners (with the pointers removed) and asked children which spinner had more of a target color (e.g. black). Children of all ages correctly answered these questions. In the probability condition, they showed children one spinner and asked them to predict the color where the pointer would land. Children under age 6 chose colors randomly; older children demonstrated an emerging understanding of probability. These results confirmed Piaget and Inhelder's (1975) proposal that preoperational children only processed surface associations and led Hoemann and Ross (1982) to suggest that 3–5-year-olds do not have even "a glimmer of probability understanding" (p. 116).

Similar studies have also suggested that preschoolers have difficulty reasoning about probability. Perner (1979) presented 4–5-year-olds with two spinners that varied the frequency of two colors and told them that they would win a prize if they spun a particular color; the children chose which spinner they wanted to use. Children chose correctly only when contrasting a spinner that represented the target color at a 7–1 proportion with one that did so at a 1–7 proportion. Further, Perner (1979) demonstrated that 4–5-year-olds responded at chance on a similar measure using 'deceptive spinners,' in which the color of lower probability had greater area (by increasing its width). In a follow-up experiment using non-deceptive spinners, 4- and 5-year-olds did show a learning effect: correct performance on probability judgments was more likely at the end of the experimental session after children saw the results of the same spinner used 24 times. However, this learning effect was modest – when the spinners varied in probability, performance did not improve over the session.

The fact that preschoolers could learn about the outcome of a single spinner over an experimental session suggests that young children might have *some* access to probabilistic knowledge. For example, Fischbein (1975) demonstrated that with training, 6-year-olds could integrate frequency information into their probability judgments. 'Training' in this context took the form of explicit instruction, reinforcement via reward, or simply allowing children to see the outcomes of their choices. These demonstrations suggest that children's judgments about probability might improve if the questions are presented using an accessible and engaging method.

In line with this hypothesis, Kuzmak and Gelman (1986) presented 3-, 4-, and 5-year-olds with two machines. One randomly spit out marbles of different colors; the other did so in a predictable sequence. Children were shown the mechanisms underlying each machine and were asked whether they could predict the color of the next marble. Three-year-olds showed an emerging understanding of the difference between the two mechanisms; 4-year-olds correctly answered that they could predict the outcome of the deterministic device but not of the random one; and 5-year-olds were able both to distinguish between the two types of mechanisms and to justify their answers appropriately. This suggests that providing children with a context for understanding probabilistic information might aid their ability to make probabilistic judgments.

12.4   The Importance of Mechanism

The Kuzmak and Gelman (1986) study suggests that children's probabilistic reasoning might be aided by causal contexts. Why might this be the case? One possible reason is that children come to appreciate the nature of causal mechanisms, which in turn helps them reason about probabilities. In causal reasoning, there are numerous examples of children discounting potential causes based on observing conditional probability information (e.g., Gopnik et al. 2001; Schulz and Gopnik 2004; Sobel and Kirkham 2006). For example, Gopnik et al. (2001) showed 2- to 4-year-olds a novel machine called a "blicket detector," which is a box that lights up and plays music when objects (controlled by the experimenter) are placed on it (in some of the initial studies, the objects that activated the machine were given the label "blicket", and thus the moniker "blicket detector" stuck). Children saw two objects (A and B). Object A activated the machine by itself; object B did not, and then both were placed on the machine together twice, which activated both times. Children easily recognized that object A had the efficacy to make the machine go, while object B did not, and were not simply making judgments about causal efficacy based on the statistical relation between the objects and the machine's activation. If this were the case, and children recognized that object A activated the machine just one more time than object B, then they should consider both objects to be causally efficacious. Indeed, in a control condition that involved removing the conditional independence information between objects B and the machine's activation (e.g., by placing both objects on the machine with the same pattern of efficacy), children judged both objects to be efficacious. Thus, when children observe that object B only activates the machine in the presence, but not the absence of object A, they recognize that A is the actual cause, and B is just "along for the ride."

Sobel et al. (2004) took this paradigm one step further. They introduced children to the machine in the same manner but asked them to make retrospective inferences, which involved some uncertainty. Initially, they showed 3- and 4-year-olds two objects (A and B) activate the machine together, and then placed object A on the machine alone, which either did or did not activate it. When object A does not activate the machine by itself, children should make a similar inference as in the above situation. A was 'along for the ride' and B was efficacious; this was exactly the inference that children made.   The more interesting case is when A activates the machine by itself. Now, what is the efficacy of object B? If you are reading closely, the answer should be, "I have no idea." This is because object B's causal efficacious is not unambiguously known. This is how children responded, although there were some age-related changes in their responses. Three-year-olds guessed: they said object B was a blicket 50% of the time. Four-year-olds made a subsequent inference: object B was judged to be efficacious only 13% of the time. Basically, they responded with a version of the gambler's fallacy—you have shown me that only half of these objects make the machine go, so if there are two objects and one of them definitely makes the machine, the other probably does not.

Sobel et al. (2004) ran a second experiment with 4-year-olds that replicated the first experiment with an added twist. Prior to the critical test trial, they showed children two more objects that activated the machine – so now, beforehand, *more* than half of the objects that children saw made the machine go (and it also was not the case that whenever children saw two objects in a pair, exactly one made the machine go and the other did not, which might have led to making an inference based solely on a higher-order correlation). Again, they showed children the novel objects A and B together activate the machine, and then A activate it by itself. Children now said that B was efficacious 34% of the time. It is still less than half, but it is definitely more than the 13% in the previous experiment.

This led them to ask a critical question—can children reason about base rates? Traditionally, adults often failed to use base rates in their decision-making (e.g., Kahneman and Tversky 1973). When adults are shown the base rates directly, however, their base rate neglect is reduced (e.g., Betsch et al. 1998; Christensen-Szalanski and Bushyhead 1981). So, it might be the case that even young children were registering the likelihood with which objects activated the machine from their direct observations. In their third experiment, they introduced children to a box containing a large set of identical objects. They pulled 12 of those objects out of the box, one at a time, and showed the children that either 2 or 10 of those 12 objects individually made the machine activate. They then repeated their procedure with the 13th and 14th objects (A and B), which together made the machine go. Object A was then shown alone to be causally efficacious. Interestingly, when causal efficacy was rare, 4-year-olds judged object B to be causally efficacious approximately 16% of the time. When efficacy was common, 4-year-olds judged object B to be causally efficacious approximately 83% of the time. This is almost identical to the base rates. But here's where the real development happened—3-year-olds did not make this inference; they just said B was efficacious in both conditions.

What these data suggest is that 4-year-olds are paying attention to the base rate with which objects have causal efficacy— they are tracking explicit probabilities in the world and using those data to make inferences. Are 3-year-olds not doing this? Maybe. But another possibility is that 3-year-olds can track base rates but cannot apply that knowledge to make the causal inference because they do not understand the relation between the probabilistic information and the mechanism with which an object activates the machine.

Sobel et al. (2004) referred to this as the "activation law" (following Tenenbaum and Griffiths 2001) – the idea is that in order for children to reason probabilistically, they had to recognize that there was something to reason about – they had to be able to posit that there was *something* that connected the machine's activation to the object. That 'something' was a kind of non-obvious property that the object possessed. A candidate placeholder was the internal properties of the object. Sobel et al. (2007) tested this by presenting 4-year-olds with two objects. One made the same "blicket machine" activate, and the other did not. The one that made the machine go had an internal property (a weighted top, similar to what the main character in *Inception* uses to keep his grip on reality); the one that did not activate the machine was empty. When the top was transferred from one object to the other, the majority of children thought the causal efficacy of the object would transfer as well.

The more critical experiment involved showing 3- and 4-year-olds three objects. Two were identical; one was unique. One of the two identical objects and the unique object activated the machine. The other object did not. Children were then shown that the member of the identical pair that activated the machine had an internal property. They were asked which other object had the same internal part. Four-year-olds responded based on the causal efficacy and chose the perceptually unique object; 3-year-olds, in contrast, responded based on perceptual similarity. These data suggest that between the ages of 3–4, children are developing the understanding that there is something about the objects that makes the machine go.

Sobel and Munro (2009) connected these two experiments. They replicated the Sobel et al. (2004) "rare" procedure and the Sobel et al. (2007) "insides" procedure and found strong correlations, controlling for age. It did not matter if children were 3 or 4; what mattered was their understanding of the relation between causes and insides. If children registered that an object's causal efficacy related to their internal properties, then they were likely to recognize the base rate information, and say that object B in the "rare" procedure was not efficacious. Critically, Sobel and Munro (2009) also manipulated the cover story behind the machine's activation (sometime it was a machine; other times it was an agent – "Mr. Blicket" – who indicated what he "liked", a mental state easily accessible to 3-year-olds). This latter manipulation boosted 3-year-olds' performance dramatically, but still preserved the correlation. As a control, when Mr. Blicket's activation referred to mental states that were difficult for 3-year-olds to understand (like his beliefs, see Wellman et al. 2001), 3-year-olds' performance was similar to the blicket machine condition, but again the correlation was preserved. The general idea was that if children understood that there might be a reason why objects have their causal properties, which is stable and intrinsic to the object, they might have the ability to reason about an activation law.

These data all suggest that children might be more sensitive to probabilistic information in the environment than previously thought. This work has also been used to describe Bayesian Inference as a mechanism for causal learning and reasoning (e.g., Griffiths et al. 2011), but that is beyond the scope of this chapter. Instead, we'd like to turn to different, but related set of data – one that suggest children's understanding of explicit probability and uncertainty in causal reasoning is not as robust, as well as why this might be the case.

12.5   Probability vs. Uncertainty

So far, we have discussed causal reasoning tasks in which there might be probabilities to think about, although there is not a great deal of uncertainty. Children usually see what happens when individual objects are placed on the machine, and the assumption behind the activation law is that children believe the machine's effects are deterministic. Indeed, when the machine's effects are not deterministic – when the same object sometimes makes the machine go and sometimes does not, children struggle with making appropriate probabilistic inferences until they are about 5 (e.g., Kushnir and Gopnik 2005; Sobel et al. 2009; Walker et al. 2017).

It is important to distinguish between probabilistic reasoning and reasoning about uncertainty. The distinction we want to draw is between estimating the probability of a causal relation that one already knows about, and the ability to hold multiple possibilities in mind about a situation. The latter might be more difficult than the former. Beck et al. (2006, Experiment 2) asked 4- and 6-year-olds to make counterfactual inferences that were based on actual events. They showed children a ball that was placed down an upside-down Y tube, so it could come out in one of two locations. Children observed the ball fall and land in one of the two possible locations. They were then asked standard counterfactual questions – if the ball had gone down the other chute, where would it have landed. Children at all ages were really good at answering this question. They also asked children two other kinds of questions. The first were more open-ended counterfactual questions – whether a different outcome was possible. Only the older children were good at answering this question. Similarly, they asked children another kind of *underdetermined* question. On these trials, children had to prepare for all the possible outcomes when the ball went into the Y tube (namely, they had to recognize that it could emerge from either of the bottom parts). Four-year-olds struggled with answering this question correctly, whereas 6-year-olds were much better at doing so.

The rare condition with the blicket detector that we described in the previous section (Sobel et al. 2004) focuses on reasoning about probabilities—how likely is an object to have efficacy—given that I've observed ambiguous evidence. But that is not the same as asking children to hold multiple potential causes in place at the same time when that efficacy is unknown. In other words, we have shown that the presence of potential causes whose efficacy is unknown can seriously compromise children's abilities to reason about a causal system (e.g., Fernbach et al. 2012; Erb and Sobel 2014; Sobel et al. 2017).

As an example, Sobel et al. (2017) showed 3- to 7-year-olds a blicket detector and a set of four objects (A, B, C, and D). In one trial, children saw each object go on the machine by itself. Object A activated the machine, making it light up and play music. Object B did not. Objects C and D also activated the machine. The experimenter then brought out a piece of cardboard, and occluded the machine and the objects from the child's view. He said to the children that he was putting one of the objects on the machine, and the machine activated, which children could confirm because they heard the music. In reality, the experimenter did not actually move any of the objects, and just activated the machine remotely, so that the children would not have any cues as to which object had been moved, to make a guess later on.

The experimenter then removed the occluder and asked children which object he had used to activate the machine. Whichever object they chose, the experimenter corrected them by saying, "That's a good guess, but it's not right." He removed the object children chose from the table and asked them to guess again. This was repeated, and children were "wrong" again, regardless of what they chose. Finally, they made a third "guess" with only two objects left on the table.

The authors were interested in whether children picked the object that they saw fail to activate the machine (B). Three- and 4-year-olds picked this object about half the time at some point in their guessing (including often on the first trial), and overall responded no different from chance levels. Five-, 6- and 7-year-olds, however, tended to avoid choosing this object. Critically, the chance-level performance by the 3- and 4-year-olds did not result from their inability to remember which objects were causally efficacious and which objects were not. In a separate trial, they could make predictions about what would happen if each object (with the same efficacy) was placed on the machine. This showed they remembered what each object did when it was placed on the machine.

What is interesting is comparing performance on this trial with two other trials. In another trial in this same experiment, children saw four new objects (E, F, G, H). Object E made the machine activate (same as A), F did not (same as B), G made it activate (same as C), but H was never put on the machine. So, children had no idea what it did. The third trial involved a similar pattern (one made it go, one did not, but now the other two were never placed on the machine so their efficacy was uncertain). We used the same 'three guesses' set of test questions to assess whether children could handle this uncertainty.

The main finding was that children's age was correlated with the amount of uncertainty they could handle. Three- and 4-year-olds performed poorly on all of these trials. As mentioned, 5-year-olds were fine at avoiding the object that did not make the machine go when there was no uncertainty, but once uncertainty was introduced, they looked just like the 3–4-year-olds. But what was really interesting is that as children got older, specifically between the ages of 5 and 7, they were able to handle more and more uncertainty in their inferences, becoming less and less likely to choose the inefficacious object. Indeed, after children's seventh birthday, their performance on this task was well above chance.

We think that this ability to understand uncertainty is one of a set of cognitive capacities that allows children to make certain kinds of more complex causal inferences. This ability to reason about uncertainty and entertain multiple possibilities may also underlie creativity. As an example, consider that following demonstration: Four objects (A, B, C and D) activate the machine one color (Green). Three of those objects (A, B, and D) activates the machine a different way (Red), as does another set of three objects (A, C, and D). Object A does not make the machine go at all by itself. Then, suppose we ask which pair of objects would make the machine go green: A and D, A and C, or B and C?

Informally, we did this with a group of adults. Most adults pick B and C, but have a hard time justifying it, but if they can, it's because they must recognize that B and C have to combine in some way to make the Green activation. It's the only combination that could, because the other combinations revealed different patterns of activation. But more importantly, it's an example of discrete additive causality; B and C each individually make the machine go red, but together they have an additive effect (We also did this formally with an adult sample and got the same results, Weisberg and Sobel 2022).

When we presented this problem to 5- to 8-year-olds, 5- and 6-year-olds responded to this test question at chance levels, but 7- and 8-year-olds were above chance – they could choose the BC pair as the one that made the machine go green (Sobel et al. 2017). In a larger-scale replication of this study, we observed the same developmental difference and even showed that some 7- and 8-year-olds could justify why they chose B and C in terms of language that looked like they understood the causal structure (e.g., "because gray and orange <the colors of B and C> were in this when it made green", see Weisberg et al. 2020). These data suggest that around age 7 children use their appreciation of uncertainty to understand additive causality. Such a finding is consistent with some other investigations; using a different paradigm (one about merit-based reward), Koskuba et al. (2018) also showed that only starting around age 7 did children appreciate additive causal structure (particularly in the rules of a game that children had to learn). It should also be noted before closing that this ability to reason about uncertainty may also underlie creativity more broadly, but this is beyond the scope of this chapter so we will not discuss this issue further (for work on this topic, see Stricker and Sobel 2020).

12.6   Do Children Think the Die Is Cast?

Alea iacta est (roughly translated to "the die is cast") is the popularized version of what Caesar allegedly said before he crossed the Rubicon and brought his army into Rome. It refers to the idea that one has come to a point of no return. The die will land a certain way because it is determined to do so. The general argument of this chapter is that children use sophisticated statistical learning mechanisms, which may provide the origin for their representations of causal knowledge (see Sobel and Kirkham 2012; Sobel and Legare 2014, for more details about this argument). These statistical learning capacities, however, seem to be independent from children's explicit understanding of probability. Statistical learning is an implicit learning system available to infants and it might be a foundational cognitive capacity for children's causal learning and inference. Asking children to reason about explicit probabilistic contrasts, however, might involve separate cognitive mechanisms, which have a much slower developmental trajectory.

Consider how children learn from other sources of information. There is a large literature that suggests children track the reliability of others as sources of knowledge, and use others' epistemic competence to determine whether they will adopt new knowledge those informants generated (e.g., Koenig and Harris 2005). For instance, if you introduce children to two informants, one who always labels familiar objects correctly and the other who labels familiar objects incorrectly, children as young as 18 months will rely on the accurate speaker's novel label for novel objects (Brooker and Poulin-Dubois 2013; Koenig and Woodward 2010; Luchkina et al. 2018).

But how rare is it to interact with an individual who is always inaccurate (and even a stopped clock is accurate twice a day). Moreover, ask any parent of preschool-aged children, stressed and harried through their existence, and you will find that they occasionally err in their labeling of even the most familiar of objects. Pasquini et al. (2007) presented 3- and 4-year-olds with two informants who varied in their level of accuracy when establishing their reliability. Four-year-olds would rely on the probability with which informants generated information – so if one informant was accurate 75% of the time and the other was accurate 25% of the time, children at this age used the information generated by the informant with the higher likelihood. Three-year-olds, in contrast, could not reason about these probabilities. Instead, they reasoned that once an informant was inaccurate, they were an unreliable source. The 3-year-olds in that study only trusted the information generated by informants who were 100% accurate. They trusted the information generated by the 75% and 25% informants equally, but preferred a 100% accurate informant to a 25% accurate one.

There's a broader idea here, which is that children are *causal determinists* – they believe that stochastic events indicate deterministic or hidden mechanisms. Instead of simply positing a probabilistic causal structure, children might posit the existence of hidden inhibitors, which exist as part of the causal mechanism. Such an idea is inherent in work by Schulz and Sommerville (2006). They showed 4- and 5-year-olds a machine that activates via a switch. The machine also had a ring on top of it. Children saw that the machine would activate if the switch was flipped (three times). Then, they saw three trials in which the ring on top was removed, and the machine would not activate when the switch was flipped.

In the final phase of the demonstration, the ring was placed back on the machine, and the switch was then flipped a number of times. Sometimes the machine activated and sometimes it did not. The experimenter then revealed that she had a flashlight in her hands the whole time. She placed the flashlight next to the machine and announced that she would flip the switch. Children were asked to make sure the machine would not turn on. Most of the children chose to activate the flashlight, even though they had never seen its efficacy, and removing the ring had been established as an inhibitor.

Buchanan and Sobel (2014) also suggested that when young children observe stochastic data, they represent such data as indicating the presence of hidden inhibitors. In the Schulz and Sommerville (2006) case, children do not have difficulty recognizing the flashlight is an inhibitor because the stochastic data primed the presence of one (their control condition involved the machine always activating when the switch was flipped, instead of it activating sporadically, and in this case, children went to remove the ring and ignore the flashlight). Buchanan and Sobel (2014) demonstrated that one can incorporate these assumptions of determinism into representations of causal structure, which enables children to reason about probabilities as well as uncertainty. They presented a broad computational framework for modeling causal determinism, as well as a set of effects that emerge from this framework (see e.g., Erb et al. 2013).

To conclude, we have suggested that children possess sophisticated statistical learning capacities, which motivate much of their initial interaction with the world. There is a great deal of statistical regularity in the world, and early development is motivated by acquiring an understanding of that regularity. Attentional and memory processes play a large role in the acquisition of such knowledge (e.g., Richardson and Kirkham 2004; Slone and Johnson 2015; Smith and Yu 2013; Vlach and Johnson 2013). Statistical learning processes potentially form the basis of how children represent causal knowledge (Sobel and Kirkham 2012; Sobel and Legare 2014), and are part of the acquisition of new pieces of causal knowledge. Explicit understanding of probability and the capacity to reason about uncertainty in causal structure, has a more prolonged developmental trajectory. The difficulty young children might have with reasoning about uncertainty might make them believe in a form of determinism – that events can only unfold the way they have unfolded – but this is speculative and requires further investigation. Although a great deal is now known about infants' and children's statistical learning capacities, as we have demonstrated in this chapter, there remains several open questions. One such question concerns what the precise mechanisms and processes are that underpin children's reasoning about hidden mechanisms, uncertainty, and probability. We have shown that children do possess the capacity to reason about these features, and that it undergoes significant development during early childhood, but it is not yet known *how* children reason about these features of causality. This may be an open issue for which the die is not yet cast.

Acknowledgements The authors were supported by NSF (1661068, 1917639 and 2033368 to DMS) during the writing of this chapter. We thank Emily Blumenthal, David Buchanan, and David Rakison who provided helpful discussion during the development of some of the research described in this chapter.

Appendix: Summary of the Key Learning Mechanisms Discussed in This Chapter

Learning mechanisms	Definitions of learning abilities	Key studies	Age of acquisition
Associative & Statistical learning	**Associative learning:** The process in which learners link two (or more) spatiotemporally contiguous, cooccurring features. **Statistical learning:** The process in which learners detect transitional probabilities between visual or auditory elements.	Kirkham et al. (2002); Rakison and Poulin-Dubois (2002), Saffran et al. (1996), Younger and Cohen (1983)	Statistical learning for auditory and visual sequences between 2–8 months of age. Associative learning for static stimuli between 4–10 months of age. Associative learning for dynamic stimuli between 10–18 months of age.
Second-order correlation (SOC) learning	The process in which learners detect and link two features that are neither spatially nor temporally contiguous.	Benton et al. (2021); Rakison and Benton (2019); Yermolayeva and Rakison (2016)	SOC learning of static stimuli between 7 and 11 months of age and between 20 and 26 months of age for dynamic stimuli. SOC learning for dynamic stimuli: 20–26 months of age
Probabilistic reasoning	The process in which learners determine the likelihood of an event taking place or occurring.	Denison and Xu (2010), Kushnir et al. (2010), Sobel and Kirkham (2012), Xu and Denison (2009), Xu and Garcia (2008)	8–12 months of age.
Uncertainty	The process in which learners must determine which of a number of possible outcomes is the correct one.	Beck et al. (2006), Sobel et al. (2017)	3–7 years of age.

References

Aslin, R. N., Saffran, J. R., & Newport, E. L. (1998). Computation of conditional probability statistics by 8-month-old infants. Psychological Science, 9(4), 321–324. https://doi.org/10.1111/1467-9280.00063

Beck, S. R., Robinson, E. J., Carroll, D. J., & Apperly, I. A. (2006). Children's thinking about counterfactuals and future hypotheticals as possibilities. *Child Development, 77*(2), 413–426. https://doi.org/10.1111/j.1467-8624.2006.00879.x

Benton, D.T., Rakison, D.H., & Sobel, D.M. (2021). When Correlation Equals Causation: Using Behavioral Experiments and Computational Modeling to Examine Children's Causal Inferences from Second-Order Correlations. https://doi.org/10.1016/j.jecp.2020.105008

Betsch, T., Biel, G. M., Eddelbüttel, C., & Mock, A. (1998). Natural sampling and base-rate neglect. European Journal of Social Psychology, 28(2), 269–273. https://doi.org/10.1002/(SICI)1099-0992(199803/04)28:2%3C269::AID-EJSP872%3E3.0.CO;2-U

Brooker, I., & Poulin-Dubois, D. (2013). Is a bird an apple? The effect of speaker labeling accuracy on infants' word learning, imitation, and helping behaviors. *Infancy, 18*, E46–E68. https://doi.org/10.1111/infa.12027

Bryant, P., & Nunes, T. (2012). *Children's understanding of probability: A literature review (full report).* London: Nuffield Foundation.

Buchanan, D. W., & Sobel, D. M. (2014). Edge Replacement and Minimality as Models of Causal Inference in Children. In Advances in child development and behavior (Vol. 46, pp. 183–213). JAI. https://doi.org/10.1016/B978-0-12-800285-8.00007-8

Chomsky, N. (1980). A review of BF Skinner's Verbal Behavior. Readings in Philosophy of Psychology, 1, 48–63. https://doi.org/10.4159/harvard.9780674594623

Christensen-Szalanski, J. J., & Bushyhead, J. B. (1981). Physicians' use of probabilistic information in a real clinical setting. Journal of Experimental Psychology: Human Perception and Performance, 7(4), 928. https://psycnet.apa.org/doi/10.1037/0096-1523.7.4.928

Cramer, R. E., Weiss, R. F., William, R., Reid, S., Nieri, L., & Manning-Ryan, B. (2002). Human agency and associative learning: Pavlovian principles govern social process in causal relationship detection. The Quarterly Journal of Experimental Psychology: Section B, 55(3), 241–266. https://doi.org/10.1080/02724990143000289

Cuevas, K., Rovee-Collier, C., & Learmonth, A. E. (2006). Infants form associations between memory representations of stimuli that are absent. Psychological Science, 17(6), 543–549. https://doi.org/10.1111/j.1467-9280.2006.01741.x

Denison, S., & Xu, F. (2010). Twelve-to 14-month-old infants can predict single-event probability with large set sizes. Developmental Science, 13(5), 798–803. https://doi.org/10.1111/j.1467-7687.2009.00943.x

Dickinson, A. (2001). The 28th Bartlett memorial lecture causal learning: An associative analysis. The Quarterly Journal of Experimental Psychology Section B, 54(1b), 3–25. https://doi.org/10.1080/713932741

Dickinson, A., & Shanks, D. (1995). Instrumental action and causal representation. In D. Sperber, D. Premack, & A. J. Premack (Eds.), Symposia of the Fyssen Foundation. Causal cognition: A multidisciplinary debate (p. 5–25). Clarendon Press/Oxford University Press.

Erb, C. D., Buchanan, D. W., & Sobel, D. M. (2013). Children's developing understanding of the relation between variable causal efficacy and mechanistic complexity. *Cognition, 129*(3), 494–500. https://doi.org/10.1016/j.cognition.2013.08.002

Erb, C. D., & Sobel, D. M. (2014). The development of diagnostic reasoning about uncertain events between ages 4–7. PloS One, 9(3), e92285. https://doi.org/10.1371/journal.pone.0092285

Fernbach, P. M., Macris, D. M., & Sobel, D. M. (2012). Which one made it go? The emergence of diagnostic reasoning in preschoolers. Cognitive Development, 27(1), 39–53. https://doi.org/10.1016/j.cogdev.2011.10.002

Fischbein, H. (1975). The intuitive sources of probabilistic thinking in children (Vol. 85). Springer Science & Business Media.

Fiser, J., & Aslin, R. N. (2003). Element predictability not high occurrence frequency determines feature learning from multi-element scenes. Journal of Vision, 3(9), 163–163. https://doi.org/10.1167/3.9.163

Goldstein, M. H., Schwade, J. A., & Bornstein, M. H. (2009). The value of vocalizing: Five-month-old infants associate their own noncry vocalizations with responses from caregivers. Child development, 80(3), 636–644. https://doi.org/10.1111/j.1467-8624.2009.01287.x

Gopnik, A., Sobel, D. M., Schulz, L. E., & Glymour, C. (2001). Causal learning mechanisms in very young children: Two-, three-, and four-year-olds infer causal relations from patterns of variation and covariation. Developmental Psychology, 37(5), 620. https://psycnet.apa.org/doi/10.1037/0012-1649.37.5.620

Griffiths, T. L., Sobel, D. M., Tenenbaum, J. B., & Gopnik, A. (2011). Bayes and blickets: Effects of knowledge on causal induction in children and adults. Cognitive Science, 35(8), 1407–1455. https://doi.org/10.1111/j.1551-6709.2011.01203.x

Haith, M. M., Wentworth, N., & Canfield, R. L. (1993). The formation of expectations in early infancy. Advances in infancy research.

Hoemann, H. W., & Ross, B. M. (1971). Children's understanding of probability concepts. Child Development, 221–236. https://doi.org/10.2307/1127077

Hoemann, H. W., & Ross, B. M. (1982). Children's Concepts of Chance and Probability. In: Brainerd, C.J. (eds) Children's Logical and Mathematical Cognition. Springer Series in Cognitive Development. Springer, New York, NY. https://doi.org/10.1007/978-1-4613-9466-2_3

Kahneman, D., & Tversky, A. (1973). On the psychology of prediction. Psychological Review, 80(4), 237. https://psycnet.apa.org/doi/10.1037/h0034747

Keil, F. C. (1989), Concepts, Kinds and Cognitive Development. Cambridge, MA: Bradford/ MIT Press.

Kushnir, T., & Gopnik, A. (2005). Young children infer causal strength from probabilities and interventions. Psychological Science, 16(9), 678–683. https://doi.org/10.1111/j.1467-9280.2005.01595.x

Kirkham, N. Z., Slemmer, J. A., & Johnson, S. P. (2002). Visual statistical learning in infancy: Evidence for a domain general learning mechanism. Cognition, 83(2), B35–B42.

Koenig, M. A., & Harris, P. L. (2005). Preschoolers mistrust ignorant and inaccurate speakers. Child Development, 76(6), 1261–1277. https://doi.org/10.1016/S0010-0277(02)00004-5

Koenig, M. A., & Woodward, A. L. (2010). Sensitivity of 24-month-olds to the prior inaccuracy of the source: possible mechanisms. Developmental Psychology, 46(4), 815. https://psycnet.apa.org/doi/10.1037/a0019664

Koskuba, K., Gerstenberg, T., Gordon, H., Lagnado, D., & Schlottmann, A. (2018). What's fair? How children assign reward to members of teams with differing causal structures. Cognition, 177, 234–248. https://doi.org/10.1016/j.cognition.2018.03.016

Kushnir, T., Xu, F., & Wellman, H. M. (2010). Young children use statistical sampling to infer the preferences of other people. Psychological Science, 21(8), 1134–1140. https://doi.org/10.1177/0956797610376652

Kuzmak, S. D., & Gelman, R. (1986). Young children's understanding of random phenomena. Child Development, 559–566. https://doi.org/10.2307/1130336

Leslie, A. M. (1982). The perception of causality in infants. Perception, 11(2), 173–186. https://doi.org/10.1068/p110173

Luchkina, E., Sobel, D. M., & Morgan, J. L. (2018). Eighteen-month-olds selectively generalize words from accurate speakers to novel contexts. Developmental Science, 21(6), e12663. https://doi.org/10.1111/desc.12663

Pasquini, E. S., Corriveau, K. H., Koenig, M., & Harris, P. L. (2007). Preschoolers monitor the relative accuracy of informants. Developmental Psychology, 43(5), 1216. https://psycnet.apa.org/doi/10.1037/0012-1649.43.5.1216

Piaget, J. (1930). The child's conception of physical causality (M. Gabain, Trans.). London: Lund Humphries.

Piaget, J., & Inhelder, B. (1975). The origins of the idea of chance in children (L. Leake, Jr., P. Burrell, & H. Fischbein, Trans.). New York: Norton. (Original work published in 1951).

Perner, J. (1979). Discrepant results in experimental studies of young children's understanding of probability. Child Development, 1121–1127. https://doi.org/10.2307/1129339

Rakison, D. H., & Benton, D. T. (2019). Second-order correlation learning of dynamic stimuli: Evidence from infants and computational modeling. Infancy, 24(1), 57–78. https://doi.org/10.1111/infa.12274

Rakison, D. H., & Poulin-Dubois, D. (2002). You go this way and I'll go that way: Developmental changes in infants' detection of correlations among static and dynamic features in motion events. Child Development, 73(3), 682–699. https://doi.org/10.1111/1467-8624.00432

Richardson, D. C., & Kirkham, N. Z. (2004). Multimodal events and moving locations: Eye movements of adults and 6-month-olds reveal dynamic spatial indexing. Journal of Experimental Psychology: General, 133(1), 46. https://psycnet.apa.org/doi/10.1037/0096-3445.133.1.46

Saffran, J. R., Newport, E. L., & Aslin, R. N. (1996). Word segmentation: The role of distributional cues. Journal of Memory and Language, 35(4), 606–621. https://doi.org/10.1006/jmla.1996.0032

Saxe, R., Tenenbaum, J. B., & Carey, S. (2005). Secret agents: Inferences about hidden causes by 10-and 12-month-old infants. Psychological Science, 16(12), 995–1001. https://doi.org/10.1111/j.1467-9280.2005.01649.x

Saxe, R., Tzelnic, T., & Carey, S. (2007). Knowing who dunnit: Infants identify the causal agent in an unseen causal interaction. Developmental Psychology, 43(1), 149. https://psycnet.apa.org/doi/10.1037/0012-1649.43.1.149

Schulz, L. E., & Gopnik, A. (2004). Causal learning across domains. Developmental Psychology, 40(2), 162. https://psycnet.apa.org/doi/10.1037/0012-1649.40.2.162

Schulz, L. E., & Sommerville, J. (2006). God does not play dice: Causal determinism and preschoolers' causal inferences. Child Development, 77(2), 427–442. https://doi.org/10.1111/j.1467-8624.2006.00880.x

Skinner, B. F. (1957). Verbal behavior. New York: Appleton- Century-Crofts.

Slone, L. K., & Johnson, S. P. (2015). Infants' statistical learning: 2-and 5-month-olds' segmentation of continuous visual sequences. Journal of Experimental Child Psychology, 133, 47–56. https://doi.org/10.1016/j.jecp.2015.01.007

Smith, L. B., & Yu, C. (2013). Visual attention is not enough: Individual differences in statistical word-referent learning in infants. Language Learning and Development, 9(1), 25–49. https://doi.org/10.1080/15475441.2012.707104

Sobel, D. M., Erb, C. D., Tassin, T., & Weisberg, D. S. (2017). The development of diagnostic inference about uncertain causes. Journal of Cognition and Development, 18(5), 556–576. https://doi.org/10.1080/15248372.2017.1387117

Sobel, D. M., & Kirkham, N. Z. (2006). Blickets and babies: the development of causal reasoning in toddlers and infants. Developmental Psychology, 42(6), 1103. https://psycnet.apa.org/doi/10.1037/0012-1649.42.6.1103

Sobel, D. M., & Kirkham, N. Z. (2012). The influence of social information on children's statistical and causal inferences. In Advances in child development and behavior (Vol. 43, pp. 321–350). JAI. https://doi.org/10.1016/B978-0-12-397919-3.00012-5

Sobel, D. M., & Legare, C. H. (2014). Causal learning in children. Wiley Interdisciplinary Reviews: Cognitive Science, 5(4), 413–427. https://doi.org/10.1002/wcs.1291

Sobel, D. M., & Munro, S. E. (2009). Domain generality and specificity in children's causal inference about ambiguous data. Developmental Psychology, 45(2), 511. https://psycnet.apa.org/doi/10.1037/a0014944

Sobel, D. M., Sommerville, J. A., Travers, L. V., Blumenthal, E. J., & Stoddard, E. (2009). The role of probability and intentionality in preschoolers' causal generalizations. Journal of Cognition and Development, 10(4), 262–284. https://doi.org/10.1080/15248370903389416

Sobel, D. M., Tenenbaum, J. B., & Gopnik, A. (2004). Children's causal inferences from indirect evidence: Backwards blocking and Bayesian reasoning in preschoolers. Cognitive Science, 28(3), 303–333.

Sobel, D. M., Yoachim, C. M., Gopnik, A., Meltzoff, A. N., & Blumenthal, E. J. (2007). The blicket within: Preschoolers' inferences about insides and causes. Journal of Cognition and Development, 8(2), 159–182. https://doi.org/10.1080/15248370701202356

Sommerville, J. A., Woodward, A. L., & Needham, A. (2005). Action experience alters 3-month-old infants' perception of others' actions. Cognition, 96(1), B1–B11. https://doi.org/10.1016/j.cognition.2004.07.004

Stricker, L. W., & Sobel, D. M. (2020). Children's developing reflections on and understanding of creativity. *Cognitive Development*, *55*(3), 100916. https://doi.org/10.1016/j.cogdev.2020.100916

Téglás, E., Girotto, V., Gonzalez, M., & Bonatti, L. L. (2007). Intuitions of probabilities shape expectations about the future at 12 months and beyond. Proceedings of the National Academy of Sciences, 104(48), 19156–19159. https://doi.org/10.1073/pnas.0700271104

Tenenbaum, J. B., & Griffiths, T. L. (2001). Generalization, similarity, and Bayesian inference. Behavioral and Brain Sciences, 24(4), 629. https://doi.org/10.1017/S0140525X01000061

Vlach, H. A., & Johnson, S. P. (2013). Memory constraints on infants' cross-situational statistical learning. Cognition, 127(3), 375–382. https://doi.org/10.1016/j.cognition.2013.02.015

Wagner, A. R., & Rescorla, R. A. (1972). Inhibition in Pavlovian conditioning: Application of a theory. Inhibition and Learning, 301–336.

Walker, C. M., Lombrozo, T., Williams, J. J., Rafferty, A. N., & Gopnik, A. (2017). Explaining constrains causal learning in childhood. Child Development, 88(1), 229–246. https://doi.org/10.1111/cdev.12590

Weisberg, D. S., Choi, E., & Sobel, D. M. (2020). Of Blickets, Butterflies, and Baby Dinosaurs: Children's Diagnostic Reasoning Across Domains. Frontiers in Psychology, 11, 2210. https://doi.org/10.3389/fpsyg.2020.02210

Weisberg, D. S., & Sobel, D. M. (2022). Constructing science: Connecting causal reasoning to scientific thinking in young children. MIT Press.

Wellman, H. M., Cross, D., & Watson, J. (2001). Meta-analysis of theory-of-mind development: The truth about false belief. Child development, 72(3), 655–684. https://doi.org/10.1111/1467-8624.00304

Woodward, A. L. (1998). Infants selectively encode the goal object of an actor's reach. Cognition, 69(1), 1–34. https://doi.org/10.1016/S0010-0277(98)00058-4

Xu, F., & Denison, S. (2009). Statistical inference and sensitivity to sampling in 11-month-old infants. Cognition, 112(1), 97–104. https://doi.org/10.1016/j.cognition.2009.04.006

Xu, F., & Garcia, V. (2008). Intuitive statistics by 8-month-old infants. Proceedings of the National Academy of Sciences, 105(13), 5012–5015. https://doi.org/10.1073/pnas.0704450105

Yermolayeva, Y., & Rakison, D. H. (2016). Seeing the unseen: Second-order correlation learning in 7-to 11-month-olds. Cognition, 152, 87–100. https://doi.org/10.1016/j.cognition.2016.03.012

Younger, B. A., & Cohen, L. B. (1983). Infant perception of correlations among attributes. Child Development, 858–867. https://doi.org/10.2307/1129890

Chapter 13
Getting Comfortable with Uncertainty: The Road to Creativity in Preschool Children

Natalie S. Evans, Rachael D. Todaro, Roberta Michnick Golinkoff, and Kathy Hirsh-Pasek

Abstract There is a great interest in studying creativity in children. Yet, the current literature on preschool creativity is sparse. Extending on work in the innovation literature, we propose that uncertainty, curiosity, and exploration are vital components of a larger model of creativity. In the current chapter, we examine this new model of creativity and its implications for preschool children. Specifically, we propose that play is an ideal context for supporting the components of the creativity model. We investigate challenges in implementing the model in educational settings and explore outstanding questions in the field of preschool creativity.

13.1 Introduction

Creativity is one of the most essential twenty-first century skills related to professional success (Craft et al., 2012; Golinkoff and Hirsh-Pasek 2016; IBM 2010). This attention on creativity research in the field of psychology has the potential to benefit intellectual, educational, and professional development (Plucker et al. 2004). Generating new, original ideas is key to economic (Davies et al. 2002), educational (Craft 2005), and technological competitiveness, which ignites public and corporate interest and investment. It is also integral in solving ambiguous problems with uncertain solutions that emerge in a fast-changing world (Shaheen 2010). Moving creativity from the fringes to a core aspect of early education shapes one's "human

Authors Natalie S. Evans, Rachael D. Todaro have equally contributed to this chapter.

N. S. Evans (✉) · R. D. Todaro · K. Hirsh-Pasek
Temple University, Philadelphia, PA, USA
e-mail: natalie.evans@temple.edu

R. M. Golinkoff
University of Delaware, Newark, DE, USA

© Springer Nature Switzerland AG 2022
R. A. Beghetto, G. J. Jaeger (eds.), *Uncertainty: A Catalyst for Creativity,
Learning and Development*, Creativity Theory and Action in Education 6,
https://doi.org/10.1007/978-3-030-98729-9_13

capital" and quality of life (Tan et al. 2019). Promoting creativity during the preschool years has the potential to build the foundation for well-being, coping strategies, socio-emotional growth, and improved inter- and intrapersonal relationships later in life (Plucker et al. 2004).

Although creativity is considered valuable, there is a paucity of research investigating creativity and the ways to support it in preschool children (Evans et al. 2021a). This divide between the interest in creativity across many fields and disciplines and the lack of research to support it is aptly dubbed "the creativity gap" (Makel 2009). This gap reflects a paradox in understanding creativity as the term used in public discourse oversimplifies the complexity that has been revealed in scientific studies (Plucker et al. 2004). The lack of a uniform definition for the field of creativity is compounded by the broad spectrum of measures used within and across different disciplines, which do not always index the complex and evolving components of creativity. The multidimensional nature of creativity requires that we move beyond the traditional field and look to other areas of research for insight. Research done in the areas of uncertainty, curiosity, exploration, and innovation will advance the study of creativity and ultimately help researchers and educators gain new perspectives on how to cultivate the components that comprise and impact preschool children's creativity. Leveraging uncertainty is central to supporting creativity in children and adults.

13.1.1 Chapter Aims

Carr et al. (2016) suggest that curiosity and exploration allow people to engage in creativity. In Carr's model, *curiosity,* or the desire to close a gap of information or uncertainty (Jirout and Klahr 2012; Loewenstein 1994), sparks *exploration*, the process in which children investigate their immediate environment (Gopnik and Wellman 2012). As children explore to address their curiosity, they engage in *divergent thinking* and are able to generate multiple ideas through investigation. Whereas divergent thinking is an essential aspect of creativity, most definitions suggest that creativity also requires honing in on one idea or solution, known as *convergent thinking* (Guilford 1950). Creativity is not a static, unidimensional construct, but is rather reliant on several dynamic processes and factors.

While curiosity and exploration may lead to creativity, *uncertainty* forms the foundation of this model. Uncertainty can be defined as the awareness of a lack of knowledge, information, or understanding (Anderson et al. 2019). It represents a key component that drives curiosity and exploration (Jirout and Klahr 2012). While uncertainty is an uncomfortable state of disequilibrium for children and adults, environments that include optimal levels of uncertainty support children's curiosity and exploration, which in turn cultivates creativity. After a brief survey of traditional creativity research in preschool children, we discuss the implications of a creativity model borne from uncertainty (pictured in Fig. 13.1). Creativity is often studied in play paradigms (Russ and Wallace 2013) suggesting that play is an ideal context for

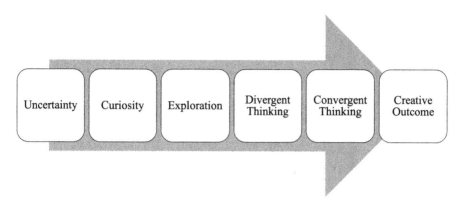

Fig. 13.1 Uncertainty-based creativity model

supporting the proposed model. We discuss existing challenges to integrating this model into current educational settings.

13.2 Defining and Measuring Creativity

Creativity was first defined by Guilford as a combination of divergent and convergent thinking (1950). *Divergent thinking* refers to the ability to generate multiple original ideas or solutions to a prompt or problem, whereas *convergent thinking* is the ability to hone in on one idea or solution. More recent definitions build on Guilford's foundation and recognize that creativity represents a balance between processes, such as divergent thinking, and outcomes, that are the result of convergent thinking (Barbot et al. 2016; Lubart et al. 2013). To be considered creative, outcomes must be both novel and useful (Runco and Jaeger 2012). Creativity outcomes are also influenced by personal factors, such as temperament (Diener et al. 2016), and environmental factors such as societal expectations (Glăveanu 2018). These components were first suggested by Rhodes in 1961, and are summarized in Plucker et al.' (2004) definition, "Creativity is the interaction among aptitude, process, and environment by which an individual or group produces a perceptible product that is both novel and successful as defined within a social context" (p. 90). These definitions highlight the complex and multidimensional nature of creativity but are limited by measurement tools that narrowly assess, and thereby define, creativity as divergent thinking (Baer 2011).

Divergent thinking assessments are the most common form of creativity measurement for both adults (Said-Metwaly et al. 2017) and children (Evans et al. 2021a). These tests tap the ability to generate multiple original ideas and are most commonly conducted in verbal, figural, and motor modalities. Verbal tests, such as the Alternative Uses and Instances tasks (Wallach and Kogan 1965), ask participants to generate solutions to a verbal prompt such as, "Name all the things you can think of that roll on wheels". Figural tests such as the Torrance Test of Creative Thinking (TTCT; Torrance 1972), present participants with abstract shapes or lines and ask them to complete a drawing. Finally, in tests in the motor modality such as the Thinking Creatively in Action and Movement test (TCAM; Torrance 1981), participants are asked to act out scenarios with their bodies, such as moving across a room in as many different ways as possible. Recently, a new divergent thinking test was designed for children as young as 2-years-old. In the Unusual Box task (Bijvoet-van den Berg and Hoicka 2014), children are presented with a multifunctional box and novel objects, and generate as many actions as possible. One of the major advantages of using the Unusual Box task or the TCAM to assess young children's creativity is that they do not rely on verbal ability, which may be limited in the preschool years (Bijvoet-van den Berg and Hoicka 2014). Divergent thinking tasks are typically scored on *fluency*, the total number of ideas or actions generated, and *originality*, the number of unique ideas or actions as compared to the full sample. Some studies also score participants' responses for the number of distinct categories they generate (*flexibility*); for example, using a cup to carry rocks or to carry sand belong to the same category, but using a cup to carry rocks or wearing it as a hat would count as two categories.

Importantly, divergent thinking and creativity are not synonymous (Baer 2011; Plucker et al. 2004). Guilford's (1950) research reminds us that the definition of creativity introduces both divergent *and* convergent thinking. Many traditional measures do not capture convergent thinking, but recent measures are designed to capture both components. The Evaluation of Potential Creativity (EPoC; Barbot et al. 2016), for instance, is designed for children and adolescents, and assesses both divergent and convergent thinking in verbal and figural modalities. In a verbal divergent thinking task, children are asked to write many possible endings to a story, whereas in a verbal convergent thinking task they are asked to write a single story based on a given title.

Designed for younger children, the Ball and Jar Task relies on non-verbal responses and assesses both divergent and convergent thinking (Evans et al. 2021b). Children are tasked with removing a ball from a jar using a selection of everyday objects such as a pipe cleaner, spoon, or sticky clay. Researchers measure how children explore and manipulate objects to generate solutions for retrieving the ball (divergent thinking), and how they select solutions that are ultimately used in attempts to retrieve the ball (convergent thinking). The Ball and Jar Task is among the first measures to consider and assess the breadth of creativity in young children.

The Consensual Assessment Technique (CAT; Amabile and Gitomer 1984; Hennessey and Amabile 1988), also assesses creative outcomes that are both divergent and convergent. Participants produce a tangible creative product such as collage or a story, and a set of judges then assesses the outcome based on a predetermined rubric. As part of a study conducted by Fehr and Russ (2016), children were asked to tell a story, and this story was assessed for creativity on a 5-point scale by a set of judges in accordance with procedures designed by Hennessey and Amabile (1988).

13.3   Creativity in Preschool Children

Extant creativity research examines interventions meant to foster creativity in preschool children. Interventions relying on drawing lead to increases in figural divergent thinking (Dziedziewicz et al. 2013; Garaigordobil and Berrueco 2011; Khatena 1971), motor interventions increase motor divergent thinking (Zachopoulou et al. 2006), and verbal interventions increase verbal divergent thinking (Garaigordobil and Berrueco 2011). Thus, these interventions often "teach to the test," (Simons et al. 2016) in that the tasks meant to evaluate the intervention are in the same domain as the intervention itself. Occasionally, even when training and testing modalities are matched there is no increase in divergent thinking. Children in a storytelling intervention group did not perform better than the control group on a subsequent storytelling task or verbal divergent thinking task (Fehr and Russ 2016). When the training modality (e.g., verbal) does not match the testing modality (e.g., figural), there is little transfer to divergent thinking (Christie 1983; Cliatt et al. 1980). Further, it is difficult to generalize the effects of interventions on creativity, as there is no uniformity in the overall number, distribution, or length of interventions.

Research on creativity in preschool children is most commonly studied in the context of play. Vygotsky (1967) was one of the first to suggest a link between play and creativity, describing both as interrelated processes that naturally occur during childhood. Recent work suggests that play and creativity share similar underlying cognitive processes, such as divergent thinking, perspective taking, and cognitive flexibility (Russ and Wallace 2013). Despite the seemingly obvious connections between play and creativity, research findings are mixed. Many studies have specifically examined the connection between play and divergent thinking (Dansky and Silverman 1973, 1975; Dansky 1980; Fehr and Russ 2016).

The relation between play and divergent thinking in preschoolers is tenuous. Experiments have found that engaging in play supports preschoolers' divergent thinking, as assessed by the Alternative Uses Task (Dansky and Silverman 1973, 1975; Dansky 1980). However, an extensive review by Lillard et al. (2013) notes that these studies contain methodological flaws, namely potentially biased experimenters, that make the findings difficult to interpret and extend. A study that addressed these flaws, by including an experimenter unaware of condition, did not find a relation between play and divergent thinking (Smith and Whitney 1987). Recent correlational work also failed to note a relation between play and divergent thinking. Bijvoet-van den Berg and Hoicka (2019) examined children's object substitution, a common event in pretend play where children use an object for a use other than its intended function, such as using a banana as a phone (Tomasello et al. 1999). Children's object substitution did not correlate with divergent thinking.

In contrast, correlational work indicates that pretend play is linked to creativity in preschoolers when assessed through the Consensual Assessment Technique (CAT; Amabile and Gitomer 1984; Hennessey and Amabile 1988) on storytelling and drawing tasks. Fehr and Russ (2016) found that young children's pretend play scores modestly correlated with storytelling task scores and with originality scores, but not fluency scores, on a verbal divergent thinking task (Multidimensional Stimulus Fluency Measure). Mottweiler and Taylor (2014) also noted that children's elaborated role play (i.e., pretend play that involves acting out imaginary personas, playing with an imaginary friend, or pretending to adopt the properties of an object) was correlated with both storytelling and drawing creativity as assessed through the CAT. Based on these findings, there is evidence that play may relate to creativity when assessed through artistic products, such as storytelling or drawing, measured with the CAT. There is inconsistent evidence that play is related to preschooler's divergent thinking performance.

Children are naturally drawn to play. Despite mixed findings regarding effective play interventions on preschool children's creativity, we argue that play can serve as a context for promoting curiosity and exploration, especially when children experience uncertainty.

13.4   Building the Base of the Creativity Model: Linking Uncertainty with Curiosity and Exploration

Uncertainty, curiosity, and exploration form the foundation of our new creativity model. A brief overview of extant research on uncertainty, curiosity, and exploration and how their relation to one another demonstrates progress through this model.

13.4.1   Uncertainty

Uncertainty refers to the awareness of a lack of knowledge, information, or understanding regarding how the future may unfold, what the present means, or how to interpret past events (Jordan and McDaniel 2014). Uncertainty is distinct from ignorance, which is when one is *unaware* of lacking knowledge, information, or understanding (Anderson et al. 2019). Uncertainty is a *cognitive feeling* (Jordan and McDaniel 2014) deeply rooted in philosophy and widely studied in the context of evolutionary psychology (Gigerenzer and Hoffrage 1995), organizational psychology, cognitive psychology (Anderson 1998; Tversky and Kahneman 1974), metacognition (Dunlosky and Nelson 1997; Nelson and Narens 1990; Smith et al. 2003), language translation research (Angelone 2010), medical decision making (Hall 2002; Karni 2009), mental health and well-being (Satici et al. 2020), and much more. Interdisciplinary work demonstrates that various fields pose different questions about how humans (and primates) deal with uncertainty, implement different methods of measuring uncertainty, and assess behaviors which follow their recognition of uncertainty.

Feelings of uncertainty about our knowledge and understanding inform judgement and decision making (Afifi and Afifi 2009; Ghetti et al. 2013; Koriat and Goldsmith 1996; Nelson and Narens 1990). Individuals first introspect on the current state of their cognitive operations, using the output of this monitoring to regulate these operations. Uncertain situations can prompt individuals to introspect on aspects of their cognition and regulate functioning as a result (Ghetti et al. 2013).

Responses to uncertainty differ depending on the degree. The U-Shaped curve theory of uncertainty (Loewenstein 1994) posits that varying levels of uncertainty may elicit different responses. If a situation is only slightly uncertain, then it may not be salient enough to promote curiosity. On the other hand, if a situation is incredibly uncertain, individuals may conclude that no amount of curiosity or exploration will be sufficient to resolve the uncertainty. Situations in which there is a moderate amount of uncertainty, enough to spark exploration but not enough to be overwhelmed, represent *actionable* uncertainty (Beghetto 2020).

13.4.2   Curiosity

Curiosity is notoriously difficult to define (Kidd and Hayden 2015). One element consistently found amongst the various definitions is uncertainty (Berlyne 1962). Loewenstein's information gap theory (1994) states that curiosity arises when an individual realizes their own uncertainty and is motivated to resolve this gap in knowledge, information, or understanding. The motivation to close this information gap distinguishes curiosity from uncertainty, the latter referring to the awareness of the gap's existence.

Curiosity can be understood as both a trait or a state. Trait curiosity refers to a personality characteristic that motivates an individual to pursue knowledge and information (Jirout and Klahr 2012; Shah et al. 2018). State curiosity is more consistent with Loewenstein's information gap theory (1994), and describes a drive to reduce uncertainty. State curiosity may be easier to measure than trait curiosity, as most state measures rely on behavioral outcomes, whereas trait measures rely on self-report questionnaires (Hassinger-Das and Hirsh-Pasek 2018). Evidence suggests that trait and state curiosity are related to one another (Grossnickle 2016; Reio and Callahan 2004), although more work is needed to understand this relation (Hassinger-Das and Hirsh-Pasek 2018). The role of child interest and its relation to curiosity is also highly debated (Grossnickle 2016; Hidi and Renninger 2019, 2020; Schmidt and Rotgans 2020; Shin et al. 2019). Schmidt and Rotgans (2020) argue that the same psychological mechanism underlies both constructs: an information gap that needs to be resolved.

13.4.3   Exploration

Exploration is the behavioral indicator of state curiosity, or an individual's desire to seek information and reduce uncertainty (Jirout and Klahr 2012). If curiosity is an itch, then exploration is the scratch that seeks to remedy it. In one of the few studies that examine curiosity and exploration distinctly, children's curiosity scores were positively linked to their exploration behaviors, which resulted in increased knowledge acquisition in a scientific causal learning context (van Schijndel et al. 2018).

The study of exploration examines how individuals actively engage with and manipulate their surroundings to better understand them (Gopnik and Wellman 2012). Exploration is described as both specific and diverse. Specific exploration refers to actions that seek to solve a particular problem or answer a particular question, with diversive exploration referring to exploration for exploration's sake (Berlyne 1960). Exploration is commonly studied in the field of causal learning, which examines how children learn about cause and effect relationships (see for review Gopnik and Wellman 2012; Gopnik et al. 2017). Exploration is also studied in the context of decision making, particularly in the explore-exploit paradigm (Hills et al. 2015; Mehlhorn et al. 2015). In this paradigm, an individual either prioritizes gaining rewards over seeking new information (exploit) or chooses to sacrifice rewards in favor of gaining new information (explore).

Uncertainty and curiosity spark exploration that encourages divergent thinking as children practice generating multiple explanations and solutions to events and problems they encounter. A creative outcome occurs when children unite divergent thinking with convergent thinking and hone in on an answer or solution (Guilford 1950). This desire to find an answer or solution was first ignited by a sense of uncertainty. Uncertainty, curiosity, and exploration taken together overlap with the broader concept of "wonder". Wonder refers to, "a particular type of experience whereby the person becomes … aware of an expanded field of possibility for thought and/or action and engages (more or less actively) in exploring this field" (Glăveanu 2017, p.172). Whereas uncertainty represents an awareness of a lack of knowledge, wonder is driven by an awareness of multiple possibilities and perspectives. Both can spur excitement, curiosity, and exploration behaviors that lead to creative outcomes.

13.5   Uncertainty as a Foundation of Curiosity, Exploration, and Creativity with Preschool Children

Even with foundational components defined, questions remain as to how we can put our model to the test with preschool children. Are young children even aware of their uncertainty? Do they address uncertainty through curiosity and exploration? These questions lie at the heart of our creativity model.

13.5.1 Are Young Children Aware of Their Own Uncertainty?

Children at 2.5-years-old know what they do not know, as evidenced in queries about word meaning (Marazita and Merriman 2004). Preschoolers also recognize degrees of uncertainty, as indicated by their confidence about what they know (Lyons and Ghetti 2011). When children withhold answers, take longer to respond, waver between response options, spend more time making eye contact with experimenters (Patterson et al. 1980), ask questions (Chouinard 2007), request clarification, or ask to hear or see content again, they are demonstrating their knowledge of uncertainty (Patterson et al. 1980; Pratt and Bates 1982).

Uncertainty in the form of novelty or surprise is also attractive to infants and children. Children are more likely to engage with objects when they experience a phenomenon that violates their current knowledge or beliefs and offer special opportunities for learning (Stahl and Feigenson 2015, 2017, 2019). For example, 3- to 6-year-old children were more likely to learn a novel verb after experiencing an unexpected event, such as seeing a toy appear in an impossible location (Stahl and Feigenson 2017).

13.5.2 Responding to Uncertainty

What do children do when they encounter uncertainty that sparks their curiosity? Research indicates that children seek answers by searching for information through explanations and exploration (Busch et al. 2018; Liquin and Lombrozo 2020; Sobel and Letourneau 2018).

13.5.2.1 Explanation

Children often turn to adults for assistance and explanation when they encounter uncertainty that they cannot resolve through their own interventions. In one study, children ages 3- to 5-years were presented with degraded images and asked to rate their confidence in identifying the pictures. Children were given the option of help from an adult when trying to identify the images. Children were more likely to ask for help on items that they previously rated as low confidence. This finding indicates that children's recognition of their own uncertainty prompted requests for help (Coughlin et al. 2015). These bids for explanation also often take the form of question-asking (Liquin and Lombrozo 2020; for review see Ronfard et al. 2018). Children ask questions in direct response to their level of uncertainty (Chouinard 2007; Ghetti et al. 2013; Patterson et al. 1980) but take adult knowledge into account when asking questions. When adults display uncertainty, children are less likely to perceive them as trustworthy (Jaswal and Malone 2007). Furthermore, children are more likely to seek information from a source they perceive as knowledgeable and reliable (Koenig and Harris 2005; Pasquini et al. 2007).

13.5.2.2 Exploration

Like "little scientists" children engage in exploration behaviors to investigate and understand their environment (Gopnik and Wellman 2012). Through their own exploratory play, children discern simple causal structures. In a causal learning task, 3-year-olds learned the rules of a novel machine through self-directed exploration just as well as being directly trained on the rules of the task by adults (Sim and Xu 2017). Children in both conditions were equally able to generalize their causal learning to a novel machine. Therefore, when faced with uncertainty young children independently engage in exploration behaviors that drive their own learning.

Preschool children display the ability to recognize uncertainty and use exploration as a strategy to disambiguate information. In one study, 2- to 6-year-olds were presented with interlocking beads that could make a machine play music (Cook et al. 2011). In the *certain* condition, children were aware that all four beads could activate the machine. In the *uncertain* condition, children knew that only two of the four beads could activate the machine. To ascertain which beads made the machine work, children needed to separate the beads and test them one at a time instead of in pairs. The children in the uncertain condition were more likely to test the beads one at a time when compared to children in the certain condition. Schulz and Bonawitz (2007) also found evidence that children adjust their exploration behavior when confronted with ambiguous information. In their study, 3- and 4-year-olds were shown a jack-in-the-box toy with two puppets and two levers. In the *unconfounded* condition, children were shown that each of the levers made one of the puppets appear. In the *confounded* condition, the experimenter pressed both levers at the same time revealing both of the puppets. After the demonstration, all children were given the option of playing with a new toy or continuing to explore the previous toy. Children in the confounded condition were more likely to return to the previous toy, presumably so that they could examine its causal mechanism. Finally, Lapidow et al. (2020) presented children ages 3- to 4-years with shapes behind clear, partially obscured, and full obscured windows. When given the opportunity to explore the windows and reveal the shapes, children were more likely to choose the fully obscured windows -- the windows with the maximum amount of uncertainty.

Children are more likely to engage in exploration behaviors than adults (Gopnik et al. 2017; Gopnik 2020), even when exploration comes at the cost of rewards (Blanco and Sloutsky 2020; Liquin and Gopnik 2022; Schulz et al. 2019; Sumner et al. 2019). Most studies utilize a variation of the multiarmed bandit task in which participants are given a set number of options to choose from that provide consistent rewards. Adults engaged in the minimal exploration necessary to discover the choices that yielded the most rewards and then exploited these options for the remainder of the task while children from 4- to 12-years of age explored more than adults (Blanco and Sloutsky 2019; Schulz et al. 2019; Sumner et al. 2019). Further analyses revealed that children did not randomly select options but instead chose those that represented greater uncertainty (Blanko and Sloutsky 2019; Schulz et al. 2019). Children found more value in exploring and reducing uncertainty in their environment than exploiting rewards. These findings align with a classic theory of perceptual development posed by Gibson (1969) who argued that children explore their environment to reduce their uncertainty.

Children explore more than adults because they experience more uncertainty and require more exploration to gather appropriate knowledge (Liquin and Gopnik 2022). In one study, adult participants were presented with a machine and told that some blocks would make the machine light up and others would not. Participants were given four stars, which would later be exchanged for money, and were told that selecting a block that made the machine work would earn them one more star, whereas choosing an incorrect block would cost two stars. Children ages 4- to 7-years participated in a similar task and received stickers instead of stars and money. Critically, embedded in this task was a "learning trap". Two rules could make the machine work instead of one, which could only be discovered through further exploration. Specifically, the blocks could be sorted by color *or* pattern. Similar to the findings of the multiarmed bandit studies, adults explored fewer blocks than children in favor of selecting blocks they knew to work. Consequently, children were more likely than adults to learn that the blocks could be sorted based on two rules (Liquin and Gopnik 2022).

13.5.2.3 From Exploration to Creativity

Exploration serves as a bridge between uncertainty and creativity in young children. Uncertainty sparks curiosity that can lead to exploration, which in turn is beneficial to creativity as it supports the discovery of new information and drives the generation of new ideas (Carr et al. 2016; Sutton-Smith 1997). Exploration with the direct intent to reduce uncertainty emerges during preschool (Sobel and Letourneau 2018). As exploration behaviors develop, children not only explore to reduce uncertainty, but use the information gained during exploration to inform future actions. This behavior fully develops in later adolescence (Somerville et al. 2017).

Increased exploration behaviors predict children's success on a creative problem-solving task (Evans et al. 2021b). In the Ball and Jar Task, children ages 4- to 6-years were asked to remove a ball from a tall jar using a variety of everyday objects. Children's actions were labeled as exploration behaviors if they investigated an object's properties or combined objects together. The number of exploration behaviors positively predicted success at retrieving the ball from the jar. We also examined the number of attempts at retrieving the ball each child made. Attempts may be understood as *exploitation* behaviors, as children were utilizing an object or set of objects to achieve an end – retrieving the ball. There were no differences in the number of attempts made between children who successfully retrieved the ball and those who did not. Yet, we found that children who retrieved the ball spent significantly less time on attempts than those who failed to retrieve the ball.

Children who were successful spent less time engaging in exploitation behaviors and more time exploring. Put differently, understanding the properties of the objects gave children an edge over those who simply attempted to solve the problem. These studies provide evidence that leveraging children's eagerness to explore uncertain objects and situations is a promising way to encourage young children's creativity.

Measures like the Ball and Jar Task not only assess creative outcomes, but also capture children's creative processes. While the task directly measures creative outcomes, such as whether the child retrieves the ball from the jar, an equally important purpose of the task is that it evaluates *how* children try to retrieve the ball through exploring and generating new ideas. The Ball and Jar Task aligns with newer non-standard definitions of creativity that suggest it is time to move away from measures that only examine creative outcomes in favor of measures that capture creative processes and experiences (Glăveanu and Beghetto 2020). By shifting the primary focus away from outcomes, it is possible to examine and value creativity as a non-linear process. While our proposed model portrays a step-by-step progression where each step builds upon the previous, children need not progress linearly from a place of uncertainty to a creative outcome. For instance, while seeking the solution to the Ball and Jar Task, children encountered novel items during their exploration, such as a wooden spool, placing them back into a state of uncertainty that sparked curiosity and drove further exploration. Moreover, all children failed to retrieve the ball on their first attempt, which required them to continue exploring and generating new ideas about the objects (Evans et al. 2021b). Our creativity model embraces children's iterative behaviors and emphasizes that curiosity and exploration behaviors are just as essential as divergent thinking and creative outcomes.

13.6   Connecting the Dots: Uncertainty during Play Cultivates Creativity

Decades of research demonstrate that play is related to creative thinking. Play gives children access to freely explore and tinker with their environment. Uncertainty during play prompts children to explore, provides a safe space to fail where there is no right answer, and allows them to openly wonder "what if?" (Sutton-Smith 1997).

The definition of play is inextricably woven to the definition of creativity. Zosh et al. (2018) suggests that play lies on a spectrum that ranges from free play to direct instruction. Free play is characterized by the child setting up and engaging in their own play. During direct instruction, the adult initiates and directs the activity. Between free play and direct instruction lies guided play, a child-directed activity that is initiated and further supported by an adult.

Free play allows children to act on their own environment and explore for the sake of exploring, which demonstrates positive effects on divergent thinking (Howard-Jones et al. 2002). Sutton-Smith (1967) showed that children were more likely to imagine multiple purposes for objects after playing with them. In free play children are unbounded. They encounter uncertainty, indulge their curiosity, and engage in exploration. Yet, free play by itself does not always lead to a *novel* and *useful* outcome (Runco and Jaeger 2012) because no clear goal has been articulated. Free play contains so much uncertainty that children struggle to reach creative solutions to problems without adult support (Beck et al. 2011; Cutting et al. 2011, 2014; Nielsen et al. 2014). Children ages 3- to 11-years were asked to remove a small bucket from a tall tube using a pipe cleaner. To succeed, children needed to devise a hook from the pipe cleaner. Most 3- to 5-year-old children found this task impossible whereas children ages 8 and older performed as well as adults. Once 3- to 5-year-old children were shown how to fashion the pipe cleaner into a hook by an adult, most successfully solved the task. Tasks with a high degree of uncertainty may foster preschool children's exploration, but adult support is crucial for achieving a goal (Beck et al. 2011).

Direct instruction from adults eliminates uncertainty, and too much adult guidance can hinder creativity. With less agency, children are less likely to engage in exploration behaviors. When adults remove agency, they reduce children's motivation to explore. Bonawitz et al. (2011) presented children with a novel toy that included several hidden features, such as a squeaker or a button that could turn on a light. In the direct instruction condition, an adult taught children how to activate the squeaker. In the other conditions, children saw the adult activate the squeaker by accident, or received no information about the toy. Afterward, all children were given the opportunity to play with the toy. Children in the direct instruction condition played with the toy for less time and discovered fewer hidden features than children in other conditions. In a museum study, parent-child interaction and exploration behaviors were coded in a gear machine exhibit. Children engaged in less exploration when the interaction was driven by the parent in contrast to child-led and jointly engaged interactions (Callanan et al. 2020). Children are highly attuned to information provided to them by adults, and too much reduction of uncertainty may stifle exploration.

In guided play, adults can support children's curiosity and exploration by modifying the level of uncertainty in the environment. Yu et al. (2018) conducted a follow-up study using the novel toy paradigm (Bonawitz et al. 2011) to examine the impact of guided play on preschool children's exploration. In the guided play condition, adults showed children a button that could activate the toy, and posed a pedagogical question to the child, "I am asking you, what does this button do?". Children in the direct instruction condition were told exactly how to activate one of the features of the toy, "Press this button". Children in the guided play condition explored the toy for longer and discovered more features than the children in the direct instruction condition. Both conditions directed children towards a button. The guided play demonstration, however, left room for uncertainty thereby prompting curiosity and exploration. Evans et al. (2021b) found that children's exploration behaviors were also positively associated with fluency scores on the Alternative Uses Task. Furthermore, Evans et al. (in preparation) found that children who built a structure in a guided play condition demonstrated higher divergent thinking scores than children who built structures in direct instruction and free play conditions.

Envisioning play on a spectrum also allows us to imagine uncertainty on a spectrum. The parallel here suggests that different types of play vary in their ability to jump start curiosity, exploration, and creativity.

13.7 Existing Challenges to the Creativity Model: How Some Education Systems Dampen Uncertainty and Play

"For some reason, we have deemed creative development and performance extremely important in the professional world of adults, but appear to minimize it in children" (Makel 2009, p. 38).

To the extent that uncertainty breeds curiosity and exploration, it offers a potential first step towards creative outcomes. Oddly, education systems around the world tend to downplay both the roles of uncertainty and curiosity. Many schools "teach to the test" or "drill, kill and bubble fill" (Goyle 2012) and actively deter children from finding different pathways to an answer or from treating failure as a step towards ultimate creative success (Mueller and Dweck 1998). This presents us with an ultimate paradox. On the one hand, teachers report that creativity is an important skill to nurture, and businesses list creativity as an important twenty-first century skill (Golinkoff and Hirsh-Pasek 2016; IBM 2010). At the same time, educators are restricted by policies that endorse knowing the right answer, leaving little room for uncertainty. Indeed, with playtime cut for test preparation (Jacobson 2008; Miller and Almon 2009) – even for 5-year-olds – kindergarten has become "the new First Grade" (Bassok et al. 2016). Under these circumstances, direct instruction, rather than guided play, becomes the norm.

Around the world societies are rethinking the reliance on standardized testing and elevating their focus on playful learning and children's creativity. Reducing our reliance on standardized testing and increasing play within education has powerful implications for young children's creativity. Countries such as Finland, Sweden, Singapore, Chile, and India are dropping standardized testing and focusing on play, creativity, and child education (Hirsh-Pasek et al. 2020). For example, India's Ministry of Human Resource Development includes in their National Education Policy (2020), "… certain subjects and skills should be learned by all students to become good, successful, innovative, adaptable, and productive human beings in today's rapidly-changing world. In addition to proficiency in languages, these skills include … creativity and innovativeness". Science shows us that traditional academic subjects can be learned in tandem with creativity. Indeed, creativity builds upon having a sufficient knowledge base on which to innovate. Around the world, people are understanding that children can learn traditional academic subjects *and* become creative thinkers and innovators.

13.8   Conclusion

The literature is ripe with discussions about creativity. Young children are curious, they want to explore, and they are capable of generating new ideas and finding solutions to the problems they encounter. We suggest that creative outcomes are just one part of an iterative, non-linear model that is borne from uncertainty. Our uncertainty-based model unites theories of uncertainty, curiosity, and exploration with traditional definitions of creativity that include divergent and convergent thinking. The model also offers a new frontier for rethinking measurements of creativity and the contexts that enable children to develop it. To promote creativity at home and in classrooms, caregivers and educators can cultivate playful environments embedded with elements of uncertainty that drive children to act on their own curiosity. Adults can further support children by modeling comfort with uncertainty, and demonstrating productive responses such as exploration or question-asking. Environments that combine optimal levels of uncertainty with adult support provide children the freedom to progress through each stage of the model and arrive at a creative outcome. Finally, we invite researchers to investigate this model and the relations between each of the components to better understand the development of creativity in preschool children.

References

Afifi, W. A., & Afifi, T. D. (2009). Avoidance among adolescents in conversations about their parents' relationship: Applying the theory of motivated information management. *Journal of Social and Personal Relationships*, 26(4), 488–511. https://doi-org.libproxy.temple.edu/10.1177/0265407509350869

Amabile, T. M., & Gitomer, J. (1984). Children's artistic creativity effects of choice in task materials. *Personality and Social Psychology Bulletin, 10*(2), 209–215. https://doi.org/10.1177/0146167284102006

Anderson, E. W. (1998). Customer Satisfaction and Word of Mouth. *Journal of Service Research, 1*(1), 5–17. https://doi-org.libproxy.temple.edu/10.1177/109467059800100102

Anderson, E. C., Carleton, R. N., Diefenbach, M., & Han, P. K. J. (2019). The relationship between uncertainty and affect. *Frontiers in Psychology*, 10. https://doi-org.libproxy.temple.edu/10.3389/fpsyg.2019.02504

Angelone, Erik. (2010). Uncertainty management and metacognitive problem solving. In G. Shreve & E. Anderson (Eds.), *Translation and Cognition* (pp. 17–40). Amsterdam: John Benjamins.

Baer, J. (2011). How divergent thinking tests mislead us: Are the Torrance Tests still relevant in the 21st century? The Division 10 debate. *Psychology of Aesthetics, Creativity, and the Arts, 5*(4), 309–313. doi:https://doi.org/10.1037/a0025210

Barbot, B., Besançon, M., & Lubart, T. (2016). The generality-specificity of creativity: Exploring the structure of creative potential with EPoC. *Learning and Individual Differences, 52*, 178–187. https://doi.org/10.1016/j.lindif.2016.06.005

Bassok, D., Latham, S., & Rorem, A. (2016). Is kindergarten the new first grade? *AERA Open, 1*(4), 1–31. https://doi.org/10.1177/2332858415616358

Beck, S. R., Apperly, I. A., Chappell, J., Guthrie, C., & Cutting, N. (2011). Making tools isn't child's play. *Cognition, 119*(2), 301–306. https://doi.org.libproxy.temple.edu/10.1016/j.cognition.2011.01.003

Beghetto R.A. (2020) Uncertainty. In Glăveanu V. (eds) *The Palgrave Encyclopedia of the Possible*. Palgrave Macmillan. https://doi.org/10.1007/978-3-319-98390-5_122-1

Berlyne, D. E. (1960). *Conflict, arousal, and curiosity*. New York, NY: McGraw-Hill.

Berlyne, D. E. (1962). Uncertainty and epistemic curiosity. British Journal of Psychology, 53(1), 27–34.

Bijvoet-van den Berg, S., & Hoicka, E. (2014). Individual differences and age-related changes in divergent thinking in toddlers and preschoolers. *Developmental Psychology, 50*(6),1629–1639. doi:https://doi.org/10.1037/a0036131

Bijvoet-van den Berg, S., & Hoicka, E. (2019). Preschoolers understand and generate pretend actions using object substitution. *Journal of Experimental Child Psychology, 177*, 313–334. https://doi-org.libproxy.temple.edu/10.1016/j.jecp.2018.08.008

Blanco, N. J., & Sloutsky, V. M. (2019). Adaptive flexibility in category learning? Young children exhibit smaller costs of selective attention than adults. Developmental psychology, 55(10), 2060.

Blanco, N. J., & Sloutsky, V. M. (2020). Systematic exploration and uncertainty dominate young children's choices. *Developmental Science*. https://doi-org.libproxy.temple.edu/10.1111/desc.13026

Bonawitz, E., Shafto, P., Gweon, H., Goodman, N. D., Spelke, E., & Schulz, L. (2011). The double-edged sword of pedagogy: Instruction limits spontaneous exploration and discovery. *Cognition, 120*(3), 322–330. https://doi-org.libproxy.temple.edu/10.1016/j.cognition.2010.10.001

Busch, J. T., Willard, A. K., & Legare, C. H. (2018). Explanation scaffolds causal learning and problem solving in childhood. In M. M. Saylor & P. A. Ganea (Eds.), *Active learning from infancy to childhood* (pp. 113–127). Champaign, IL: Springer. https://doi.org/10.1007/978-3-319-77182-3_7

Callanan, M. A., Legare, C. H., Sobel, D. M., Jaeger, G. J., Letourneau, S., McHugh, S. R., Willard, A., Brinkman, A., Finiasz, Z., Rubio, E., Barnett, A., Gose, R., Martin, J. L., Meisner, R., & Watson, J. (2020). Exploration, explanation, and parent–child interaction in museums. Monographs of the Society for Research in Child Development, 85(1), 7–137. https://doi-org.libproxy.temple.edu/10.1111/mono.12412

Carr, K., Kendal, R. L., & Flynn, E. G. (2016). Eureka!: What is innovation, how does it develop, and who does it? *Child Development, 87*(5), 1505–1519. https://doi-org.libproxy.temple.edu/10.1111/cdev.12549

Chouinard, M. M. (2007). Children's questions: A mechanism for cognitive development. *Monographs of the Society for Research in Child Development, 72*(1), 1–13. https://doi-org.libproxy.temple.edu/10.1111/j.1540-5834.2007.00413.x

Christie, J. F. (1983). The effects of play tutoring on young children's cognitive performance. *The Journal of Educational Research, 76*(6), 326–330. https://doi.org/10.1080/00220671.1983.10885477

Cliatt, M. J., Shaw, J. M., & Sherwood, J. M. (1980). Effects of training on the divergent-thinking abilities of kindergarten children. *Child Development, 51*(4), 1061–1064.doi:https://doi.org/10.2307/1129544

Cook, C., Goodman, N. D., & Schulz, L. E. (2011). Where science starts: Spontaneous experiments in preschoolers' exploratory play. *Cognition, 120*(3), 341–349. https://doi-org.libproxy.temple.edu/10.1016/j.cognition.2011.03.003

Coughlin, C., Hembacher, E., Lyons, K. E., & Ghetti, S. (2015). Introspection on uncertainty and judicious help-seeking during the preschool years. *Developmental Science, 18*(6), 957–971. https://doi-org.libproxy.temple.edu/10.1111/desc.12271

Craft, A. (2005). *Creativity in schools: Tensions and dilemmas*. Psychology Press.

Craft, A., McConnon, L., & Matthews, A. (2012). Child-initiated play and professional creativity: Enabling four-year-olds' possibility thinking. *Thinking Skills and Creativity, 7*(1), 48–61.

Cutting, N., Apperly, I. A., Chappell, J., & Beck, S. R. (2014). The puzzling difficulty of tool innovation: Why can't children piece their knowledge together? *Journal of Experimental Child Psychology, 125*, 110–117. https://doi-org.libproxy.temple.edu/10.1016/j.jecp.2013.11.010

Cutting, N., Apperly, I. A., & Beck, S. R. (2011). Why do children lack the flexibility to innovate tools? *Journal of Experimental Child Psychology, 109*(4), 497–511. https://doi-org.libproxy.temple.edu/10.1016/j.jecp.2011.02.012

Dansky, J. L. (1980). Make-believe: A mediator of the relationship between play and associative fluency. *Child Development, 51*(2), 576–579. doi:https://doi.org/10.2307/1129296

Dansky, J. L., & Silverman, I. W. (1973). Effects of play on associative fluency in preschool-aged children. *Developmental Psychology, 9*(1), 38–43. https://doi.org/10.1037/h0035076

Dansky, J. L., & Silverman, I. W. (1975). Play: A general facilitator of associative fluency. *Developmental Psychology, 11*(1), 104. doi:https://doi.org/10.1037/h0076108

Davies, P. T., Harold, G. T., Goeke-Morey, M. C., Cummings, E. M., Shelton, K., Rasi, J. A., & Jenkins, J. M. (2002). Child emotional security and interparental conflict. *Monographs of the society for research in child development*, i-127.

Diener, M. L., Wright, C., Brehl, B., & Black, T. (2016). Socioemotional correlates of creative potential in preschool age children: Thinking beyond student academic assessments. *Creativity Research Journal, 28*(4), 450–457. https://doi-org.libproxy.temple.edu/10.1080/10400419.2016.1229975

Dunlosky, J., & Nelson, T. O. (1997). Similarity between the cue for judgments of learning (JOL) and the cue for test is not the primary determinant of JOL accuracy. *Journal of Memory and Language, 36*(1), 34–49. https://doi-org.libproxy.temple.edu/10.1006/jmla.1996.2476

Dziedziewicz, D., Oledzka, D., & Karwowski, M. (2013). Developing 4- to 6-year-old children's figural creativity using a doodle-book program. *Thinking Skills and Creativity, 9*, 85–95. https://doi.org/10.1016/j.tsc.2012.09.004

Evans, N., Schlesinger, M.A., Hopkins, E.J., Jaeger, G. J., Golinkoff, R.M., Hirsh-Pasek, K. (2021a) Are preschoolers creative? A review of the literature. In J. Hoffmann, J. Kaufman, & S. Russ. *Handbook of lifespan development of creativity*. Cambridge University Press.

Evans, N., Todaro, R., Schlesinger, M. A., Golinkoff, R. M., & Hirsh-Pasek, K. (2021b). Examining the impact of children's exploration behaviors on creativity. *Journal of Experimental Child Psychology*.

Evans, N., Todaro, R., Schlesinger, M. A., Golinkoff, R. M., & Hirsh-Pasek, K. (in preparation). Building blocks of problem-solving: How guided play enhances divergent thinking

Fehr, K. K., & Russ, S. W. (2016). Pretend play and creativity in preschool-age children: Associations and brief intervention. *Psychology of Aesthetics, Creativity, and the Arts, 10*(3), 296–308. https://doi.org/10.1037/aca0000054

Garaigordobil, M., & Berrueco, L. (2011). Effects of a play program on creative thinking of pre-school children. *The Spanish Journal of Psychology, 14*(2), 608–618. https://doi.org/10.5209/rev_SJOP.2011.v14.n2.9

Ghetti, S., Hembacher, E., & Coughlin, C. A. (2013). Feeling uncertain and acting on it during the preschool years: A metacognitive approach. *Child Development Perspectives, 7*(3), 160–165. https://doi-org.libproxy.temple.edu/10.1111/cdep.12035

Gibson, E. J. (1969). Principles of perceptual learning and development.

Gigerenzer, G., & Hoffrage, U. (1995). How to improve Bayesian reasoning without instruction: Frequency formats. *Psychological Review, 102*(4), 684–704. https://doi-org.libproxy.temple.edu/10.1037/0033-295X.102.4.684

Glăveanu, V. P. (2017). Creativity and wonder. *Journal of Creative Behavior*. https://doi.org/10.1002/jocb.225

Glăveanu, V. P. (2018). Educating which creativity? *Thinking Skills and Creativity, 27*, 25–32. https://doi-org.libproxy.temple.edu/10.1016/j.tsc.2017.11.006

Glăveanu, V. P., & Beghetto, R. A. (2020). Creative experience: A non-standard definition of creativity. *Creativity Research Journal*. https://doi-org.libproxy.temple.edu/10.1080/10400419.2020.1827606

Golinkoff, R. M., & Hirsh-Pasek, K. (2016). *Becoming brilliant: What science tells us about raising successful children*. Washington, DC: American Psychological Association.

Gopnik, A. (2020). Childhood as a solution to explore–exploit tensions. *Philosophical Transactions of the Royal Society B: Biological Sciences*, 375 (1803), 20190502. https://doi.org/10.1098/rstb.2019.0502

Gopnik, A., O'Grady, S., Lucas, C. G., Griffiths, T. L., Wente, A., Bridgers, S., Aboody, R., Fung, H., & Dahl, R. E. (2017). Changes in cognitive flexibility and hypothesis search across human life history from childhood to adolescence to adulthood. *PNAS Proceedings of the National Academy of Sciences of the United States of America*, *114*(30), 7892–7899. https://doi-org.libproxy.temple.edu/10.1073/pnas.1700811114

Gopnik, A., & Wellman, H. M. (2012). Reconstructing constructivism: Causal models, Bayesian learning mechanisms, and the theory theory. *Psychological Bulletin, 138*(6), 1085–1108. https://doi-org.libproxy.temple.edu/10.1037/a0028044

Goyle, N. (2012). *One size does not fit all: A student's assessment of school*. Alternative Education Resource Organization.

Grossnickle, E. M. (2016). Disentangling curiosity: Dimensionality, definitions, and distinctions from interest in educational contexts. *Educational Psychology Review*, *28*(1), 23–60. https://doi-org.libproxy.temple.edu/10.1007/s10648-014-9294-y

Guilford, J. P. (1950). Creativity. *American Psychologist, 5*(9), 444–454. doi:https://doi.org/10.1037/h0063487

Hall, K. H. (2002). Reviewing intuitive decision-making and uncertainty: The implications for medical education. *Medical Education*, *36*(3), 216–224. https://doi-org.libproxy.temple.edu/10.1046/j.1365-2923.2002.01140.x

Hassinger-Das, B., & Hirsh-Pasek, K. (2018). Appetite for knowledge: curiosity and children's academic achievement. *Pediatric Research, 84*(3), 323–324. https://doi-org.libproxy.temple.edu/10.1038/s41390-018-0099-4

Hennessey, B. A., & Amabile, T. M. (1988). The conditions of creativity. In R. J. Sternberg (Ed.), *The nature of creativity: Contemporary psychology perspectives* (pp. 11–38). New York: Cambridge University Press.

Hidi, S. E., & Renninger, K. A. (2019). Interest development and its relation to curiosity: Needed neuroscientific research. *Educational Psychology Review*. https://doi-org.libproxy.temple.edu/10.1007/s10648-019-09491-3

Hidi, S. E., & Renninger, K. A. (2020). On educating, curiosity, and interest development. *Current Opinion in Behavioral Sciences*. https://doi.org/10.1016/j.cobeha.2020.08.002

Hills, T. T., Todd, P. M., Lazer, D., Redish, A. D., & Couzin, I. D. (2015). Exploration versus exploitation in space, mind, and society. *Trends in Cognitive Sciences*, *19*(1), 46–54. https://doi.org/10.1016/j.tics.2014.10.004

Hirsh-Pasek, K., Hadani, H., Blinkoff, E., & Golinkoff, R. M. (2020). *A new path to education reform: Playful learning promotes 21st-century skills in schools and beyond*. [Policy Brief]. Brookings. https://www.brookings.edu/policy2020/bigideas/a-new-path-to-education-reform-playful-learning-promotes-21st-century-skills-in-schools-and-beyond/

Howard-Jones, P. A., Taylor, J. R., & Sutton, L. (2002). The effect of play on the creativity of young children during subsequent activity. *Early Child Development and Care, 172*(4), 323–328. https://doi.org/10.1080/03004430212722

IBM (2010, May 18). IBM 2010 Global CEO study: Creativity selected as most crucial factor for future success. [Press release]. Retrieved from http://www-03.ibm.com/press/us/en/pressrelease/31670.wss#release.

Lillard, A. S., Lerner, M. D., Hopkins, E. J., Dore, R. A., Smith, E. D., & Palmquist, C. M. (2013). The impact of pretend play on children's development: A review of the evidence. *Psychological Bulletin, 139*(1), 1–34. doi:https://doi.org/10.1037/a0029321

Liquin, E. G. & Gopnik, A. (2022). Children are more exploratory and learn more than adults in an approach-avoid task. Cognition, 218, p.104940. Vancouver.

Liquin, E. G., & Lombrozo, T. (2020). A functional approach to explanation-seeking curiosity. *Cognitive Psychology*, *119*. https://doi-org.libproxy.temple.edu/10.1016/j.cogpsych.2020.101276

Loewenstein, G. (1994). The psychology of curiosity: A review and reinterpretation. *Psychological Bulletin*, 116(1), 75–98. https://doi.org/10.1037/0033-2909.116.1.75

Lubart, T. I., F. Zenasni, and B. Barbot. 2013. Creative potential and its measurement. *International Journal of Talent Development and Creativity* 1 (2): 41–51.

Jacobson, L. (2008). Children's lack of playtime seen as troubling health, school issue. *Education Week, 28*(14), 1, 14, 15.

Jaswal, V. K., & Malone, L. S. (2007). Turning believers into skeptics: 3-year-olds' sensitivity to cues to speaker credibility. *Journal of Cognition and Development*, 8(3), 263–283. https://doi-org.libproxy.temple.edu/10.1080/15248370701446392

Jirout, J., & Klahr, D. (2012). Children's scientific curiosity: In search of an operational definition of an elusive concept. *Developmental Review, 32*(2), 125–160. https://doi-org.libproxy.temple.edu/10.1016/j.dr.2012.04.002

Jordan, M. E., & McDaniel, R. R., Jr. (2014). Managing uncertainty during collaborative problem solving in elementary school teams: The role of peer influence in robotics engineering activity. *Journal of the Learning Sciences, 23*(4), 490–536. https://doi-org.libproxy.temple.edu/10.1080/10508406.2014.896254

Karni, E. (2009). A theory of medical decision making under uncertainty. *Journal of Risk and Uncertainty, 39*(1), 1–16. https://doi.org.libproxy.temple.edu/10.1007/s11166-009-9071-3

Khatena, J. (1971). Teaching disadvantaged preschool children to think creatively with pictures. *Journal of Educational Psychology, 62*(5), 384–386. https://doi.org.libproxy.temple.edu/10.1037/h0031634

Kidd, C. & Hayden, B. Y. (2015). The psychology and neuroscience of curiosity. *Neuron, 88*, 449–460. https://doi.org/10.1016/j.neuron.2015.09.010

Koenig, M. A., & Harris, P. L. (2005). Preschoolers mistrust ignorant and inaccurate speakers. *Child Development, 76*(6), 1261–1277. https://doi-org.libproxy.temple.edu/10.1111/j.1467-8624.2005.00849.x

Koriat, A., & Goldsmith, M. (1996). Monitoring and control processes in the strategic regulation of memory accuracy. *Psychological Review, 103*(3), 490–517. https://doi-org.libproxy.temple.edu/10.1037/0033-295X.103.3.490

Lapidow, E., Killeen, I., & Walker, C. M. (2020). Exploration Decisions Precede and Improve Explicit Uncertainty Judgments in Preschoolers. *Proceedings of the 42nd Annual Conference of the Cognitive Science Society*. Virtual Meeting: Cognitive Science Society.

Lyons, K. E., & Ghetti, S. (2011). The development of uncertainty monitoring in early childhood. *Child Development, 82*(6), 1778–1787. https://doi-org.libproxy.temple.edu/10.1111/j.1467-8624.2011.01649.x

Makel, M. C. (2009). Help us creativity researchers, you're our only hope. *Psychology of Aesthetics, Creativity, and the Arts, 3*(1), 38–42. https://doi-org.libproxy.temple.edu/10.1037/a0014919

Marazita, J. M., & Merriman, W. E. (2004). Young children's judgment of whether they know names for objects: The metalinguistic ability it reflects and the processes it involves. *Journal of Memory and Language, 51*(3), 458–472. https://doi-org.libproxy.temple.edu/10.1016/j.jml.2004.06.008

Mehlhorn, K., Newell, B. R., Todd, P. M., Lee, M. D., Morgan, K., Braithwaite, V. A., Hausmann, D., Fiedler, K., & Gonzalez, C. (2015). Unpacking the exploration–exploitation tradeoff: A synthesis of human and animal literatures. *Decision*, 2(3), 191–215. https://doi.org/10.1037/dec0000033

Miller, E., & Almon, J. (2009). *Crisis in the kindergarten: Why children need to play in school*. Alliance for Childhood (NJ3a).

Ministry of Human Resources (2020). *National Education Policy.*

Mottweiler, C. M., & Taylor, M. (2014). Elaborated role play and creativity in preschool age children. *Psychology of Aesthetics, Creativity, and the Arts, 8*(3), 277–286. https://doi.org/10.1037/a0036083

Mueller, C. M., & Dweck, C. S. (1998). Praise for intelligence can undermine children's motivation and performance. *Journal of Personality and Social Psychology, 75*(1), 33–52. https://doi-org.libproxy.temple.edu/10.1037/0022-3514.75.1.33

Nelson, T. O., & Narens, L. (1990). Metamemory: A theoretical framework and new findings. *The Psychology of Learning and Motivation, 26*, 125–173.

Nielsen, M., Tomaselli, K., Mushin, I., & Whiten, A. (2014). Exploring tool innovation: A comparison of Western and Bushman children. *Journal of Experimental Child Psychology, 126*, 384–394. https://doi-org.libproxy.temple.edu/10.1016/j.jecp.2014.05.008

Pasquini, E. S., Corriveau, K. H., Koenig, M., & Harris, P. L. (2007). Preschoolers monitor the relative accuracy of informants. *Developmental Psychology, 43*(5), 1216–1226. https://doi-org.libproxy.temple.edu/10.1037/0012-1649.43.5.1216

Patterson, C. J., Cosgrove, J. M., & O'Brien, R. G. (1980). Nonverbal indicants of comprehension and noncomprehension in children. *Developmental Psychology, 16*(1), 38–48. https://doi-org.libproxy.temple.edu/10.1037/0012-1649.16.1.38

Plucker, J. A., Beghetto, R. A., & Dow, G. T. (2004). Why isn't creativity more important to educational psychologists? Potentials, pitfalls, and future directions in creativity research. *Educational Psychologist, 39*(2), 83–96. https://doi-org.libproxy.temple.edu/10.1207/s15326985ep3902_1

Pratt, M. W., & Bates, K. R. (1982). Young editors: Preschoolers' evaluation and production of ambiguous messages. *Developmental Psychology, 18*(1), 30–42. https://doi-org.libproxy.temple.edu/10.1037/0012-1649.18.1.30

Reio, T. G., Jr., & Callahan, J. L. (2004). Affect, curiosity, and socialization-related learning: A path analysis of antecedents to job performance. *Journal of Business and Psychology, 19*(1), 3–22. https://doi-org.libproxy.temple.edu/10.1023/B:JOBU.0000040269.72795.ce

Rhodes, M. (1961). An analysis of creativity. *The Phi Delta Kappan, 42*(7), 305–310. Retrieved from http://www.jstor.org/stable/20342603

Ronfard, S., Zambrana, I. M., Hermansen, T. K., & Kelemen, D. (2018). Question-asking in childhood: A review of the literature and a framework for understanding its development. *Developmental Review, 49*, 101–120. https://doi-org.libproxy.temple.edu/10.1016/j.dr.2018.05.002

Runco, M. A., & Jaeger, G. J. (2012). The standard definition of creativity. *Creativity Research Journal, 24*(1), 92–96. https://doi.org/10.1080/10400419.2012.650092

Russ, S. W., & Wallace, C. E. (2013). Pretend play and creative processes. *American Journal of Play, 6*(1), 136–148.

Said-Metwaly, S., Van den Noortgate, W., Kyndt, E. (2017). Approaches to measuring creativity: A systematic literature review. *Creativity. Theories – Research – Applications, 4*(2), 238–275. https://doi.org/10.1515/ctra-2017-0013

Satici, B., Saricali, M., Satici, S. A., & Griffiths, M. D. (2020). Intolerance of uncertainty and mental wellbeing: Serial mediation by rumination and fear of covid-19. *International Journal of Mental Health and Addiction.* https://doi-org.libproxy.temple.edu/10.1007/s11469-020-00305-0

Schmidt, H., & Rotgans, J. (2020). Epistemic curiosity and situational interest: Distant cousins or identical twins? *Educational Psychology Review.* https://doi.org/10.1007/s10648-020-09539-9

Schulz, L. E., & Bonawitz, E. B. (2007). Serious fun: Preschoolers engage in more exploratory play when evidence is confounded. *Developmental Psychology, 43*(4), 1045–1050. https://doi-org.libproxy.temple.edu/10.1037/0012-1649.43.4.1045

Schulz, E., Wu, C. M., Ruggeri, A., & Meder, B. (2019). Searching for rewards like a child means less generalization and more directed exploration. *Psychological Science, 30*(11), 1561–1572. https://doi-org.libproxy.temple.edu/10.1177/0956797619863663

Shah, P. E., Weeks, H. M., Richards, B., & Kaciroti, N. (2018). Early childhood curiosity and kindergarten reading and math academic achievement. *Pediatric Research, 84*(3), 380–386. https://doi-org.libproxy.temple.edu/10.1038/s41390-018-0039-3

Shaheen, R. (2010). Creativity and education. *Creative Education, 1*, 166–169. https://doi.org/10.4236/ce.2010.13026

Shin, D. J. D., Lee, H. J., Lee, G., & Kim, S. (2019). The role of curiosity and interest in learning and motivation. In K. A. Renninger & S. E. Hidi (Eds.), *The Cambridge handbook of motivation and learning* (pp. 443–464). Cambridge: Cambridge University Press.

Sim, Z. L., & Xu, F. (2017). Learning higher-order generalizations through free play: Evidence from 2- and 3-year-old children. *Developmental Psychology, 53*(4), 642–651. https://doi-org.libproxy.temple.edu/10.1037/dev0000278

Simons, D. J., Boot, W. R., Charness, N., Gathercole, S. E., Chabris, C. F., Hambrick, D. Z., & Stine-Morrow, E. A. L. (2016). Do "brain-training" programs work? *Psychological Science in the Public Interest, 17*(3), 103–186. https://doi-org.libproxy.temple.edu/10.1177/1529100616661983

Smith, J. D., Shields, W. E., & Washburn, D. A. (2003). The comparative psychology of uncertainty monitoring and metacognition. *Behavioral and Brain Sciences, 26*(3), 317–373. https://doi-org.libproxy.temple.edu/10.1017/S0140525X03000086

Smith, P. K., & Whitney, S. (1987). Play and associative fluency: Experimenter effects may be responsible for previous positive findings. *Developmental Psychology, 23,* 49–53. doi:https://doi.org/10.1037/0012-1649.23.1.49

Sobel, D. M., & Letourneau, S. M. (2018). Curiosity, exploration, and children's understanding of learning. In M. Saylor & P. Ganea (Eds.), *Active learning from infancy to childhood* (pp. 57–74). Cham: Springer.

Somerville, L. H., Sasse, S. F., Garrad, M. C., Drysdale, A. T., Abi Akar, N., Insel, C., & Wilson, R. C. (2017). Charting the expansion of strategic exploratory behavior during adolescence. *Journal of Experimental Psychology: General, 146*(2), 155–164. https://doi-org.libproxy.temple.edu/10.1037/xge0000250.

Stahl, A. E., & Feigenson, L. (2015). Observing the unexpected enhances infants' learning and exploration. *Science, 348*(6230), 91–94. https://doi.org/10.1126/science.aaa3799

Stahl, A. E., & Feigenson, L. (2017). Expectancy violations promote learning in young children. *Cognition, 163,* 1–14. https://doi-org.libproxy.temple.edu/10.1016/j.cognition.2017.02.008

Stahl, A. E., & Feigenson, L. (2019). Violations of core knowledge shape early learning. *Topics in Cognitive Science, 11*(1), 136–153. https://doi-org.libproxy.temple.edu/10.1111/tops.12389

Sumner, E., Li, A. X., Perfors, A., Hayes, B., Navarro, D., & Sarnecka, B. W. (2019). *The Exploration Advantage: Children's instinct to explore allows them to find information that adults miss.* [Preprint]. PsyArXiv preprint 10.31234/osf.io/h437v. 10.31234/osf.io/h437v

Sutton-Smith, B. (1967). The role of play in cognitive development. *Young Children, 22,* 361–370.

Sutton-Smith, B. (1997). *The ambiguity of play.* Harvard University Press.

Tan, C.-S., Tan, S.-A., Mohd Hashim, I. H., Lee, M.-N., Ong, A. W.-H., & Yaacob, S. nor B. (2019). Problem-solving ability and stress mediate the relationship between creativity and happiness. *Creativity Research Journal, 31*(1), 15–25. https://doi.org.libproxy.temple.edu/10.1080/10400419.2019.1568155

Tomasello, M., Striano, T., & Rochat, P. (1999). Do young children use objects as symbols? *British Journal of Developmental Psychology, 17*(4), 563–584. https://doi.org.libproxy.temple.edu/10.1348/026151099165483

Torrance, E. P. (1972). Predictive validity of the Torrance Tests of Creative Thinking. *Journal of Creative Behavior, 6,* 236–252.

Torrance, E.P. (1981). *Thinking creatively in action and movement.* Bensenville, IL: Scholastic Testing Service.

Tversky, A., & Kahneman, D. (1974). Judgment under uncertainty: Heuristics and biases. *Science, 185*(4157), 1124–1131. https://doi-org.libproxy.temple.edu/10.1126/science.185.4157.1124

van Schijndel, T. J. P., Jansen, B. R. J., & Raijmakers, M. E. J. (2018). Do individual differences in children's curiosity relate to their inquiry-based learning? *International Journal of Science Education, 40*(9), 996–1015. https://doi-org.libproxy.temple.edu/10.1080/09500693.2018.1460772

Vygotsky, L. S. (1967). Play and its role in the mental development of the child. *Soviet Psychology, 5*(3), 6–18.

Wallach, M., & Kogan, N. (1965). *Modes of thinking in young children.* New York: Holt, Rinehart and Winston.

Yu, Y., Shafto, P., Bonawitz, E., Yang, S. C.-H., Golinkoff, R. M., Corriveau, K. H., Hirsh-Pasek, K., & Xu, F. (2018). The theoretical and methodological opportunities afforded by guided play with young children. *Frontiers in Psychology, 9.* https://doi.org.libproxy.temple.edu/10.3389/fpsyg.2018.01152

Zachopoulou, E., Trevlas, E., & Konstadinidou, E. (2006). The design and implementation of a physical education program to promote children's creativity in the early years. *International Journal of Early Years Education, 14*(3), 279–294. https://doi.org/10.1080/09669760600880043

Zosh, J. M., Hirsh-Pasek, K., Hopkins, E. J., Jensen, H., Liu, C., Neale, D., Solis, S.L., Whitebread, D. (2018). Accessing the inaccessible: Redefining play as a spectrum. *Frontiers in Psychology 9*:1124. https://doi.org/10.3389/fpsyg.2018.01124

Chapter 14
Developing Intellectual Character: An Educational Perspective on How Uncertainty-Driven Curiosity Can Support Learning

Jamie J. Jirout and Shoronda E. Matthews

> *"I think that when we know that we actually do live in uncertainty, then we ought to admit it; it is of great value to realize that we do not know the answers to different questions. This attitude of mind – this attitude of uncertainty – is vital to the scientist, and it is this attitude of mind which the student must first acquire." – Richard Feynman (Feynman, 1956)*

Abstract Uncertainty can play an important role in learning in educational settings. The realization that one does not know something can be perceived as an opportunity for learning, and the desire to seek this information is related to an important intellectual virtue: curiosity. Specifically, curiosity can be defined as desiring and persisting in information seeking and exploration, especially in response to uncertainty or information gaps. Despite the role curiosity plays in learning, uncertainty is often viewed negatively by students in educational contexts, where performance is valued and leads to performance-oriented goals, rather than mastery-oriented goals. In this chapter, we review how uncertainty-driven curiosity can support learning and develop effective learners. We include a discussion of how curiosity can also support the development of more general intellectual character through its relation to creativity, open-minded thinking, and intellectual courage. Finally, we describe how uncertainty in education can be perceived in maladaptive ways that might suppress curiosity, and give specific strategies related to approaches to uncertainty that can be applied to educational contexts to support curiosity.

J. J. Jirout (✉) · S. E. Matthews
School of Education and Human Development, University of Virginia,
Charlottesville, VA, USA
e-mail: jirout@virginia.edu

© Springer Nature Switzerland AG 2022

253

R. A. Beghetto, G. J. Jaeger (eds.), *Uncertainty: A Catalyst for Creativity, Learning and Development*, Creativity Theory and Action in Education 6,
https://doi.org/10.1007/978-3-030-98729-9_14

14.1   Introduction

In the above quote, Feynman describes an important aspect of learning: one's attitude toward uncertainty. In this chapter, we describe how a specific attitude toward
uncertainty exemplifies curiosity as we define it, in which uncertainty motivates
information seeking and, specifically, exploring in response to uncertainty. As
Feyman suggests, this attitude of mind is an important foundation for students to
support their learning. We also believe that curiosity is foundational to the development of students' intellectual character more broadly through the embracing of
uncertainty as opportunity to learn. In this chapter, we discuss the role curiosity
plays in becoming an effective learner and how curiosity can promote broader intellectual character with a focus on creativity, open-minded thinking, and intellectual
courage. We include a discussion of how approaches to uncertainty in educational
contexts can support or suppress curiosity, and what this means for educational
practice.

14.2   Curiosity as Intellectual Character

Curiosity is often conceptualized as an intellectual virtue, a kind of love of knowledge (Baehr 2013), and is one of several intellectual virtues that make up what can
be referred to as intellectual character, along with creativity and open-minded thinking, among others. Despite curiosity seeming to be a ubiquitous part of education
and learning, it is challenging to define, as it is a multidimensional and somewhat
complex construct that likely manifests in varying ways across people and contexts.
For the purpose of this chapter, we conceptualize curiosity as desiring and persevering in information seeking and exploration, especially in response to uncertainty or
information gaps, recognizing that broader definitions exist (Jirout and Klahr 2012;
Loewenstein 1994; Kidd and Hayden 2015). This definition stems from research
showing that uncertainty leads to greater levels of information seeking, with less
exploration when there is too little or too much uncertainty (Loewenstein 1994;
Litman et al. 2005; Jirout and Klahr 2012), similar to Beghetto's (2020) conceptualizing uncertainty as a present state of not knowing, with "actionable uncertainty"
leading to information seeking to resolve that uncertainty.

Prior research shows that higher curiosity (i.e., higher probability of exploration
with increasing levels of uncertainty) relates to academic persistence, question-
asking, and critical thinking (Jirout and Klahr 2012, 2020) and greater learning
under similar conditions (van Schijndel et al. 2018). Curiosity is intrinsically motivating because exploring new information and experiences, seeking out challenging
opportunities, and willingness to incur risks by approaching uncertainty is driven by
an individual's desire to fill a gap in their knowledge, rather than to achieve some

performance standard or receive something in exchange (Baehr 2013; Engel 2011; Hulme et al. 2013). This motivation to seek out what one does not know, resulting from uncertainty, can lead to a sense of fulfillment or satisfaction from closing gaps in knowledge. Importantly, curiosity in this sense involves an openness to uncertainty rather than avoiding it, focusing on the positive affective influence of uncertainty rather than the negative affect other theories have included in definitions of curiosity (Litman 2008; Litman and Spielberger 2003; Lowenstien 1994). Specifically, some theories have suggested that curiosity, or at least a type of curiosity, leads to exploration because of unpleasant feelings of not knowing, or uncertainty-induced anxiety, and behavior to resolve those unpleasant feelings (e.g., curiosity as feelings of deprivation, Litman 2008; Litman and Spielberger 2003; Bar-Anan et al. 2009; Hirsh et al. 2012). On the other hand, uncertainty can lead to quite positive feelings (Kurtz et al. 2007; Wilson et al. 2005), and when scientists are considered to be curious often this curiosity leads to further and increasingly complex curiosities (Livio 2017). If curiosity was driven by reducing anxiety or resolving the feeling of deprivation, it would be negatively reinforced by the realization that, when we feel we have learned something, we often follow up that discovery with further curiosity (Wade and Kidd 2019). At the neural level, curiosity for information leads to similar positive activation as anticipation of reward and positive engagement, while perceptual information, such as wanting to know what a blurry picture is, leads to less pleasant engagement (Livio 2017). In education, it is curiosity for information and understanding that is of interest for meaningful learning, thus curiosity can be considered a positive motivator for learning. Consistent with this, when uncertainty was used to promote curiosity, greater learning and transfer was observed, and positive affect – *not* negative affect – predicted learning (Lamnina and Chase 2019).

In addition to curiosity's direct role in supporting learning, it can also promote related intellectual virtues. Intellectual character is distinct from civic or moral virtues in its focus on dispositions and strengths related to learning, including behavior that contributes to more complete knowledge and understanding (Baehr 2017). Curiosity likely relates to, and potentially supports other aspects of intellectual character through the commonality of including attitudes of uncertainty. Specifically, creativity, open-minded thinking, and intellectual courage all involve a positive approach to uncertainty. Creativity relies on the belief that there are different, novel ways of thinking and doing that one is not necessarily aware of – that one is uncertain of. Open-minded thinking similarly relies on the active seeking of ideas and perspectives that are unknown and challenging one's own knowledge and ideas. As social beings that are motivated by the desire to feel competent and "fit in" (Ryan and Deci 2000), uncertainty can feel threatening, and one must have courage to face uncertainty for intellectual development. Developing curiosity can support these other intellectual virtues, developing the "attitude of mind" Feynman suggests learners ideally will acquire, while also supporting academic learning, and we discuss them later in this chapter within the context of this approach.

14.3   Why Curiosity Matters

From infancy, uncertainty drives the curiosity essential for learning how to learn, how the world works, and how to interact with others and the environment (Berlyne 1960; Piaget 1952). Piaget's concept of disequilibrium involves children recognizing some uncertainty in their world- something that doesn't fit within their existing knowledge and understanding, and through which they change their understanding and/or perception of the world to account for the uncertainty (Piaget 1950). Curiosity, in this way, can be observed in children's active role in seeking to understand their world as naturally curious information seekers (Engel 2011; Piaget 1952). Piaget and others consider this curiosity to be how children learn about all aspects of how their world works, from the basic awareness of surroundings in order to survive, to how to effectively interact with others around them, to becoming efficient learners of information to advance their thinking, making curiosity essential for children's basic cognitive development and learning through actively seeking out and engaging with uncertainty.

As children enter formal schooling, curiosity continues to be an important mechanism of learning. While there is little research on the development of curiosity or on curiosity in school settings, it is widely believed that learning and innovative thinking are driven by curiosity (Kashdan et al. 2013; Livio 2017). More broadly, curiosity promotes a range of positive outcomes from exploration and persistence in information seeking to academic performance and longer-term well-being (Kashdan and Silvia 2009; Kashdan and Steger 2007; von Stumm et al. 2011). For example, although a meta-analysis found that intelligence was the strongest predictor of academic performance, curiosity predicted performance beyond intelligence, even when controlling for students' effort and ability (von Stumm et al. 2011). Similarly, curiosity related to kindergarten children's academic performance even after controlling for effortful control, and the association was strongest for low-income children (Shah et al. 2018). In addition to children's curiosity, the educational context is also important to consider, as negative perceptions of school can lead to lower academic performance for higher curious students (Kashdan and Yuen 2007). Importantly, it is very likely that the educational context can influence children's curiosity more directly and their learning indirectly, though research is needed to test this empirically (Jirout et al. 2018). For example, a study of parental promotion of curiosity suggests that early promotion can have lasting impacts, with positive effects of promotion at age 8 observed in both motivation and achievement through high school (Gottfried et al. 2016).

There are several ways through which curiosity can support learning, such as motivating and directing information seeking and facilitating encoding of information at a deeper level (Jirout 2020). Curiosity can also help to develop sustained interests, and, in turn, promote self-regulation, information seeking, and motivation for learning (Hidi and Renninger 2006; Renninger 2000). Curiosity relates to engagement and persistence even when facing obstacles and setting goals (Kashdan and Steger 2007). Importantly, curiosity can be sparked at a momentary level during activities, but – as discussed above – it can also be developed as an approach to uncertainty, and this approach can likely be maintained and developed to lead to more stable curiosity. Despite the positive findings linking curiosity to general well-being, learning, and learning behaviors, and the belief that children are naturally curious (Dewey 1910; Piaget 1952), some evidence suggests that curiosity dissipates over time (Engelhard and Monsaas 1988), perhaps due to formal schooling (Engel 2015; Jirout et al. 2018), as we discuss later in this chapter. This is unfortunate, as there is reasoning to believe that in addition to promoting learning, curiosity can support other dimensions of intellectual character development as well.

14.4 Uncertainty-Driven Curiosity and Other Intellectual Character Virtues

Intellectual virtues involve a love of or desire for knowledge, truth, and/or understanding, including curiosity as well as creativity, open-mindedness, intellectual courage, and critical thinking or reasoning (Baehr 2013). While conceptually distinct from one another, these virtues all share the common characteristic of having a motivational basis to them, and this motivation relates specifically to engaging in activities that are useful in achieving an epistemic aim (Baehr 2013). For example, Watson (2018) defined a virtuously curious person as being "characteristically motivated to acquire worthwhile epistemic goods that he or she believes they lack" (Watson 2018, p. 296). Like curiosity, each of these intellectual virtues are either stimulated by or provide methods of addressing contexts involving uncertainty, suggesting an interrelatedness among them. For this reason, they may mutually influence one another. For example, curiosity and creativity together can prepare a person to be open-minded to alternative ideas, with being open-minded leading to information seeking (Haran et al. 2013). Like curiosity, intellectual courage and critical thinking involve persistence in seeking an understanding of the unknown and a willingness to question and critically analyze the information being learned (Byrnes and Dunbar 2014; Movshovitz-Hadar and Kleiner 2009).We discuss the relations between curiosity and other intellectual virtues in light of our specific definition of curiosity as desiring and persevering in information seeking and exploration, especially in response to uncertainty or information gaps.

Creativity Creativity, the act of thinking and doing things in new or different ways (Peterson and Seligman 2004), can include recognition of problems or gaps in information (Torrance 1977). Peterson and Seligman (2004) state that there are two essential components to creativity. The first is the production of original ideas or behaviors that are either novel, surprising, and/or unusual, and the second component is that the ideas and behaviors must be adaptive. Peterson and Seligman (2004) emphasize the originality of the ideas or behaviors having a positive contribution to the life of the creator or the lives of others, while Torrance emphasizes the courage to approach the unknown by ideas considered to be divergent (Torrance 1977). The motivation to approach the unknown in order to create something novel aligns with curiosity, and with scientific thinking more generally, with creativity described as "the process of sensing problems or gaps in information, forming ideas or hypotheses, testing and modifying these hypotheses, and communicating the results" (p. 7, Torrance 1977). Yet, creativity also involves novelty in thinking and doing, which can cause fear of judgement or failure to create an educational risk of creativity (Henriksen et al. this volume), similar to the risk of being curious in academic contexts discussed below. On the other hand, this creative risk could become a catalyst for creativity (Hoffman et al. this volume).

While curiosity involves desiring to explore uncertainty and seeking out information, Henrisksen and colleagues (this volume) discuss creativity and uncertainty as existing in an essential, complex tension, where the need for creativity comes from uncertainty, but with further uncertainty arising from the creative process. Torrance suggested that creativity is about the process of making sense of information and communicating it. The initial acquisition of information driven by curiosity is likely an important precursor or necessary aspect of being creative, so supporting curiosity would likely also support creativity (Starko 2013). Children's creative thinking, on the other hand, may support curiosity. Children have less experience through which to focus their attention and "exploit" their knowledge to perform specific tasks, but this lack of experience and focus can provide the benefit of supporting more creative or "out-of-the-box" thinking during information seeking, sometimes resulting in higher performance than adults (Gopnik 2016).

14.4.1 Open-Minded Thinking and Intellectual Courage

The motivation to identify gaps in one's thinking as part of becoming curious likely also relates to open-minded thinking, the inherent acceptance of and openness to alternatives to one's own thinking (Stanovich and West 1997). Asking questions generated out of their own curiosity can support students' thinking in new ways and developing new interests (Hidi and Renninger 2006). Theories of open-mindedness address the social aspect of being open to ideas outside of one's own thoughts and the importance of considering others' views, especially when they differ from one's own (Riggs 2010). Being open-minded means that one is open to any counterevidence or doubts of current beliefs (Adler 2004), and prior research shows that open-minded thinking, like curiosity, leads to information seeking (Haran et al. 2013). Yet, related risks and fears – such as the fear of being wrong or appearing ignorant by asking a question, or of doing something the 'wrong' way if that means it may be marked as incorrect on a test – are important aspects of intellectual courage. Thus, being curious may also relate to intellectual courage, defined as action and persistence toward gaining knowledge, understanding, or new ideas or perspectives when faced with risk (e.g., embarrassment or fear related to failure or ignorance; Movshovitz-Hadar and Kleiner 2009). When children avoid failure, they are more likely to disengage and have lower enjoyment of school than those who show courage (Martin 2011).

14.4.2 Critical Thinking

Finally, curiosity relies on critical thinking by critically analyzing information and prior knowledge to identify gaps or uncertainty. Critical thinking is a broad term encompassing a range of processes and skills, and, like curiosity, is almost universally included as an important "21st Century Skill". In general, critical thinking is defined as thinking that is effortful and involves the use and evaluation of information to understand or change one's thinking about a problem or topic (Miele and Wigfield 2014). Similar to open-minded thinking and intellectual courage, critical thinking involves challenging, or at least questioning, the accuracy of claims rather than passively accepting them (Byrnes and Dunbar 2014), and so similarly is likely to show some relation to curiosity. This relation is likely bidirectional, with curiosity leading to more experience practicing critical thinking by evaluating the relevance of information in addressing information gaps, and higher critical thinking ability leading to more curiosity-driven information seeking to solve problems (Şeker and Kömür 2008).

14.5 The Development of Curiosity and Potential Challenges to Curiosity-Driven Learning

Success in education is often measured by how much a student knows or has learned. In contrast, there is increasing value of and emphasis on "21st Century Skills" and character development (Duckworth and Yeager 2015; Kidd and Hayden 2015; NAP 2015; Pelligrino and Hilton 2012), suggesting that the goals of educational institutions are evolving to focus on producing "learners" rather than "learned individuals". In other words, there is increasing emphasis on students learning *how to learn*, rather than learning specific content. This emphasis on developing learners rather than focusing on acquiring specific content is consistent with developing curiosity in educational contexts and aligns well with the approach to uncertainty that young children often bring to school initially. Young children are naturally curious about the unknown and can be seen as information seekers (Engel 2011). As with adults (Loewenstein et al. 2001), when children become aware of a gap in their knowledge or are not certain about something, they seek out the information they need to fill in the gaps of their knowledge (Engel 2011). It is likely, though, that experience in educational contexts influences students' curiosity.

In educational settings, curiosity can be influenced through different teaching methods, modeling, or observational learning. For example, observations of how their teachers approach seeking answers to their own questions can shape children's approach toward uncertainty. Using different teaching methods and modeling, teachers can scaffold and encourage children to use uncertainty as a way to motivate themselves to explore without being afraid of taking risks (Engel 2011; McTighe and Lyman 1988). Curiosity can also be supported when children are given the opportunity to think and ask questions in class (Hidi and Renninger 2006), allowing them to explore and manipulate information they are learning in a way that lets them figure out what they don't know and make connections between things (Ronfard et al. 2018). In our past work, we developed a theoretical framework for how teachers can support students' comfort with uncertainty and approach to exploring uncertainty (Jirout et al. 2018). Specifically, to promote comfort with uncertainty, teachers can provide opportunities for children to acknowledge and recognize uncertainty in what they are doing and learning (see Table 14.1). In addition, educational experience can be designed to promote curiosity by using "structured uncertainty" (Beghetto 2020), where scaffolding and support is built in for students to practice thinking in new or different ways about a problem.

Children need opportunities to become curious and practice being curious, and this happens through support from teachers in becoming more comfortable with uncertainty. If students are expected to listen and learn information without pauses to actually think about it, they won't have the time needed for reflecting beyond what it is they heard to consider what it is they don't know but could be curious about, what Glăveanu and colleagues (this volume) refer to as "uncertain knowing". Further, supporting a mindful approach to thinking about uncertainty can help to open children's thinking and reduce the focus on worrying about judgement (Henriksen et al. this volume). If teachers do pause to ask a question but call on the first student who raises their hand, other students may not have enough time to be motivated to think of their own ideas or questions. On the other hand, if teachers give time after asking for questions or ideas, before students hear others' responses, they have more opportunity for their own thinking. Further, teachers can allow as many students as time permits to share ideas, questions, strategies, and answers to

Table 14.1 Categories and instructional practices to promote student curiosity

Supporting children's comfort with and awareness of curiosity
Provide opportunities to become curious by considering what they don't know and want to know
Scaffold metacognition: recognition of what a child knows and does not know
Prompt question asking explicitly or include activities designed to support questioning
Ask for more than one idea or answer to questions to show different ways of thinking
Model what curiosity looks like and one's own comfort with uncertainty
Supporting children's exploration of things they are curious about
Provide opportunities for children to explore and "figure out" in a way that connects to their curiosity
Scaffold information seeking and exploration to support children's comfort with uncertainty
Positively reinforce curious behavior and questions

Jirout et al. (2018, 2022)

demonstrate that there's rarely a single "right" way to think about or do something, and if a student does say something inaccurate the teacher can be supportive and respond in a way that makes it ok to be wrong, and to see mistakes as opportunities for learning.

Teachers can also use prompting as a way to guide students toward thinking about what they are curious to know. For example, a common phrase of teachers is the simple, "are there any questions?" – however this phrase asks for *existing* questions students may have, and often leads to no responses or procedural or clarification questions, rather than curiosity-driven questions. Alternatively, teachers could ask "what questions do you have?" and give time for students to consider this, with the simple rephrasing suggesting that students can think of questions to ask. This prompting and, importantly, time dedicated to allowing students to consider what they are curious about, can show children that questions and curiosity are valued in that classroom. Importantly, supporting curiosity won't have a lasting influence on children's attitudes of uncertainty unless it is a regular, expected pattern of behavior and expectations. This can create a classroom climate that is conducive to curiosity by de-emphasizing performance and refocusing children on the learning itself, making students comfortable with asking questions rather than being self-conscious about showing peers they don't know something (Martin 2011).

"...Even very young children are most likely making inferences about what adults care about based on multiple observations of the adults' actual behavior in context" (pg. 38, Katz 1998). Classroom climate is impacted by students' observations of what teachers care about, which can be portrayed both indirectly and directly such as through instructional language (Jirout et al. 2018). This type of climate can support focusing academic goals onto learning and mastery, and away from performance and competition. One way this can be done is through instructional language, such as the way a teacher introduces an activity to direct children's attention to the process of learning rather than the product of an exercise (e.g., focus on reflection and process and collaborative learning: "see if you can figure out how this question is different from the last one and how to solve it, and how many different ideas you all come up with" instead of focus on the solution, performance, and competition: "now we will do a different kind of problem- let's see who can get the right answer to this question"). This type of class-level refocusing can lead to less fear of failure and positive impacts on learning (Martin and Marsh 2003). More generally, de-emphasizing the goal of finding the "right" answers can help to shift students' goals away from certainty and open up their thinking to exploring uncertainty. Along with promoting curiosity, this practice of more open-ended learning focus is more relevant to the type of creative thinking needed to find solutions to real-world problems (Henriksen et al. this volume).

Teachers can also set up learning experiences in ways that facilitate exploration, such as offering choices about materials to use and asking students to figure something out, providing guidance and hints when needed, as opposed to following a given series of steps or procedures. Often, when focusing on skills and ways of thinking rather than specific content, it becomes possible to align learning experiences with what students are curious about, making the learning more meaningful.

This is the foundation for educational approaches such as Reggio Emelia, where project-based learning builds on observations of children's curiosities (Edwards et al. 1998) and Montessori approaches of allowing children autonomy in their learning and careful design of learning experiences to promote learning and curiosity (Lillard 2016). Many teachers in traditional public schools also use activities to engage students in becoming curious or to use their curiosity to promote learning, for example using a common activity known as "KWL". In KWL activities, students are instructed to quietly reflect on what they know, what they want to find out, and what they learned or still need to learn, and then discuss responses as a class. Although this was designed as a strategy for reading comprehension (Ogle 1986), it is used more generally by many teachers as a way of supporting children's metacognition and evaluation of what they do and do not know, with a prompt (what do you want to know?) that could lead to considering what they are curious about. Similar teaching methods that encourage collaboration and modeling approaches to uncertainty by both peers and teachers can similarly be used to promote curiosity in the classroom (Ciardiello 1998; McTighe and Lyman 1988). For example, in the think-pair-share teaching method, children are given time to think and come up with their own ideas before sharing those with peers (McTighe and Lyman 1988). By discussing their different ideas with one another, children make connections between what they know or don't know and are exposed to different ways of thinking, which can help to highlight gaps in their knowledge and new approaches to information seeking.

While many teachers are quite successful in supporting curiosity in their students, there are also ways that the opposite can be true, where specific language and instructional methods have the potential to suppress curiosity. This could be through behavior such as belittling students for not knowing something or asking questions, but in our own research we have found this to be quite rare (Jirout and Vitiello 2018). At a broader level, it is possible that institutional barriers exist for teachers to support curiosity, which could, over time, lead to decreases in curiosity – at least in students' curiosity in educational contexts (Post and Walma van der Molen 2018; Jirout et al. 2018). Consistent with this, research suggests curiosity is observed at quite low levels in classroom contexts (Engel 2011). The observed lack of curiosity is likely at least partially related to school and classroom rules, reward systems, perceptions, social norms, and pedagogy that is inconsistent with promoting curiosity and being curious (Post and Walma van der Molen 2018; Ronfard et al. 2018; Van Der Meij 1994). Specifically, a focus on attaining certainty – learning predetermined information corresponding to standards and assessed using standardized tests – directly conflicts with developing a positive approach to uncertainty. For example, in a context in which performance is constantly rewarded and social comparisons are emphasized, children may feel that being curious about something will be disapproved of by the people around them (Engel 2011; Post and Walma van der Molen 2018). When students are evaluated based on their performance, being curious becomes at odds with positive academic evaluation (Jirout et al. 2018).

When grades and standardized test scores are prioritized over academic exploration, curious behavior will be discouraged in favor of giving the 'right' answer

(Hulme et al. 2013; Martin 2011; Martin and Marsh 2003). In contrast to this type of performance-oriented learning, mastery orientations focus more on understanding and the learning process, rather than learning outcomes (Ames 1992), and research on student motivation has found evidence of performance focus leading to lower curiosity in college students (Hulme et al. 2013). In our own recent research, we observed a positive association between teachers' use of mastery-oriented language and their curiosity-promoting instructional practices in preschool math and science lessons, and in fifth grade lessons lower curiosity-promotion was associated with students' perceptions of higher emphasis being placed on standardized testing (Jirout and Vitiello 2018).

We are not suggesting that it is detrimental to assess students' learning and progress in school or schools' ability to be effective, but rather that the current system is driven by a very limited set of performance outcomes that are inconsistent with teaching for curiosity and the more meaningful, deep learning that could result. It is unclear whether promoting curiosity early-on would support students' performance on these outcomes, but we do believe that teachers could still focus on the material assessed on these tests using methods that more effectively spark curiosity in students. Further, students who have higher curiosity would likely still perform highly in the long term by being more intrinsically motivated -- but including outcomes related to curiosity and other character virtues on assessments could promote greater focus on these in classroom instruction, as could de-emphasizing performance-based educational goals. If meaningful learning and innovation require students to seek out the unknown and to find new, different, and better ways of understanding and doing things (Duschl and Osborne 2002; Beghetto 2020), we must prioritize promoting students' curiosity in educational contexts alongside traditional performance outcomes.

14.6 What Comes Next for Education Practice and Research?

The goals of this chapter were to argue for the importance of promoting a positive approach to uncertainty, which we describe as an important aspect of curiosity, in educational contexts. By supporting children's awareness of and comfort with uncertainty, they can become more curious learners in school settings, which can be intrinsically motivating, direct information seeking and attention, and facilitate encoding of information at a deeper level (Jirout 2020). These benefits of curiosity can promote more meaningful learning and develop longer-term interests. However, as we discussed, current educational systems that prioritize accountability measures, such as state standardized assessments, emphasize a performance-focused educational structure that creates a curiosity risk where grades and standardized test scores are prioritized over academic exploration (Engel 2011; Jirout et al. 2018). In such environments, curious behavior is discouraged in favor of giving the 'right'

answer (Hulme et al. 2013; Martin 2011; Martin and Marsh 2003). This performance emphasis likely impacts curiosity in important ways, with this curiosity risk
in which curiosity-motivated information seeking and exploration, and related support for students being curious, could come at the cost of striving for certainty --
memorizing and practicing the knowledge and skills needed to succeed on those
standardized tests. How, then, could teachers support a more positive approach to
uncertainty? Neil deGrasse Tyson gives this suggestion: "I would undervalue grades
based on knowing things and find ways to reward curiosity. In the end, it's the
people who are curious who change the world." (Tyson 2011).

How, then, are schools to contribute to developing the curious people who can
change the world? Despite the systematic challenge of educational institutions,
many teachers do promote students' curiosity and build on curiosity to make learning experiences engaging and effective. For example, teachers can give students
opportunities to notice and wonder rather than being told to simply solve given
problems or answer questions. They can model being curious and support collaborative learning where peers are encouraged to share their ideas and perspectives
and focus on the "figuring out" of learning. Continuously engaging in instructional
methods to support curiosity can create a classroom climate that encourages positive approaches to uncertainty and optimal learning orientations where failure is
seen as opportunities to learn and all students believe they can be successful learners.

That said, the broader educational system has an obvious impact on the learning
climate and the expectations placed on teachers and students. If teachers are held
accountable for students doing well on standardized tests, and if standardized tests
are used as gatekeepers for educational opportunities and focus on assessing discrete, concrete knowledge (i.e., assessing what students have learned, rather than
their ability to learn), then curiosity and associated virtues would become risks to
academic success for both teachers and students, as defined by this system.
Alternatively, some systems of assessment focus on measuring students' proficien-
cies as learners, such as the International Baccalaureate organization's "Learner
Profile", including attributes of learners as being inquirers, open-minded, and reflective among several additional attributes (International Baccalaureate Organization
2018). With the formal inclusion of this learner profile across the IB program, systems are developed for prioritizing, promoting, and assessing these attributes
explicitly.

Similarly, other educational programs are based on philosophies that guide
instructional methods to be supportive of curiosity, creativity, open-mindedness,
and critical thinking. For example, Reggio Emilia, Waldorf, and Montessori methods are all learner-focused where students have more active roles in leading their
learning experiences, with the teachers' role as supporting children's learning rather
than to teach them predetermined content (Aljabreen 2020), similar to other self-
directed methods like experiential learning (Jiusto and DiBiasio 2006). These different methods all align with some of the practices described in this chapter for
promoting curiosity. Future research can further assess the efficacy of using these
methods to promote curiosity, such as the role of support for autonomy in learning
and making connections and meaning of what is being learned. Importantly, research

should also explore what might be learned from these other education examples for supporting development of comfort with uncertainty, looking across levels of educational systems. Classroom culture is influenced by many factors outside of the classroom itself, and schools will be most successful in promoting curiosity and associated intellectual virtues if this is prioritized and supported by the alignment across educational systems in valuing this educational goal.

Acknowledgements This publication was made possible through the support of grants from the John Templeton Foundation and the Jacobs Foundation and by the Institute of Education Sciences, U.S. Department of Education, through Grant #R305B140026 to the Rectors and Visitors of the University of Virginia. The opinions expressed in this publication are those of the authors and do not necessarily reflect the views of the funding agencies.

References

Adler, J. (2004). Reconciling Open-Mindedness and Belief. *School Field, 2*(2), 127–142. https://doi.org/10.1177/1477878504043440

Aljabreen, H. (2020). Montessori, Waldorf, and Reggio Emilia: A Comparative Analysis of Alternative Models of Early Childhood Education. *International Journal of Early Childhood*, 1–17.

Ames, C. (1992). Classrooms: Goals, structures, and student motivation. *Journal of Educational Psychology, 84*(3), 261–271

Baehr, J. (2013). Educating for Intellectual Virtues: From Theory to Practice. *Journal of Philosophy of Education, 47*(2), 248–262. https://doi.org/10.1111/1467-9752.12023

Baehr, J. (2017). The Varieties of Character and Some Implications for Character Education. *Journal of Youth and Adolescence, 46*(6), 1153–1161. https://doi.org/10.1007/s10964-017-0654-z

Bar-Anan, Y., Wilson, T. D., & Gilbert, D. T. (2009). The feeling of uncertainty intensifies affective reactions. Emotion, 9(1), 123–127. https://doi.org/10.1037/a0014607.

Beghetto R.A. (2020) Uncertainty. In: Glăveanu V. (Eds) *The Palgrave Encyclopedia of the Possible*. Palgrave Macmillan, Cham. https://doi.org/10.1007/978-3-319-98390-5_122-1

Berlyne, D. E. (1960). *Conflict, arousal, and curiosity* (pp. xii, 350). McGraw-Hill Book Company. https://doi.org/10.1037/11164-000

Byrnes, J. P., & Dunbar, K. N. (2014). The nature and development of critical-analytic thinking. *Educational Psychology Review, 26*(4), 477–493.

Ciardiello, A. V. (1998). Did You Ask a Good Question Today? Alternative Cognitive and Metacognitive Strategies. *Journal of Adolescent & Adult Literacy, 42*(3), 210–219.

Dewey, J. (1910). *How we think* (pp. vi, 228). D C Heath. https://doi.org/10.1037/10903-000

Duckworth, A. L., & Yeager, D. S. (2015). Measurement Matters: Assessing Personal Qualities Other Than Cognitive Ability for Educational Purposes. *Educational Researcher (Washington, D.C.: 1972), 44*(4), 237–251. https://doi.org/10.3102/0013189X15584327

Duschl, R. A., & Osborne, J. (2002). Supporting and Promoting Argumentation Discourse in Science Education. *Studies in Science Education, 38*(1), 39–72. https://doi.org/10.1080/03057260208560187

Edwards, C. P., Giandini, L. & Forman, G. E. (1998). *The hundred languages of children: The Reggio Emilia approach--advanced reflections*. Greenwood Publishing Group.

Engel, S. (2011). Children's Need to Know: Curiosity in Schools. *Harvard Educational Review, 81*(4), 625–645. https://doi.org/10.17763/haer.81.4.h054131316473115

Engel, S. (2015). *The hungry mind: The origins of curiosity in childhood*. Harvard University Press.

Engelhard Jr, G., & Monsaas, J. A. (1988). Grade level, gender, and school-related curiosity in urban elementary schools. *The Journal of Educational Research, 82*(1), 22–26.

Feynman, R. P. (1956). The relation of science and religion. *Engineering and Science, 19*(9), 20–23.

Glăveanu, V. P. (this volume). Not Knowing. In Beghetto, R. A. & Jaeger, J. G. (Eds.) *Uncertainty: A catalyst for creativity, learning and development.* Springer International Publisher.

Gopnik, A. (2016). *The gardener and the carpenter: What the new science of child development tells us about the relationship between parents and children.* Macmillan.

Gottfried, A. E., Preston, K. S. J., Gottfried, A. W., Oliver, P. H., Delany, D. E., & Ibrahim, S. M. (2016). Pathways from parental stimulation of children's curiosity to high school science course accomplishments and science career interest and skill. *International Journal of Science Education, 38*(12), 1972–1995. https://doi.org/10.1080/09500693.2016.1220690

Haran, U., Ritov, I., & Mellers, B. A. (2013). The role of actively open-minded thinking in information acquisition, accuracy, and calibration. *Judgment and Decision Making, 8*(3), 14.

Henriksen, D., Richardson, C., Gruber, N., & Mishra, P. (this volume). The Uncertainty of Creativity: Opening Possibilities and Reducing Restrictions through Mindfulness. In Beghetto, R. A. & Jaeger, J. G. (Eds.) *Uncertainty: A catalyst for creativity, learning and development.* Springer International Publisher.

Hidi, S., & Renninger, K. A. (2006). The Four-Phase Model of Interest Development. *Educational Psychologist, 41*(2), 111–127. https://doi.org/10.1207/s15326985ep4102_4

Hirsh, J. B., Mar, R. A., & Peterson, J. B. (2012). Psychological entropy: A framework for understanding uncertainty-related anxiety. Psychological Review, 119(2), 304–320.

Hoffman, J. D., McGarry, J., & Seibyl, J. (this volume). Beyond tolerating ambiguity: How emotionally intelligent people can channel uncertainty into creativity. In Beghetto, R. A. & Jaeger, J. G. (Eds.) *Uncertainty: A catalyst for creativity, learning and development.* Springer International Publisher.

Hulme, E., Green, D. T., & Ladd, K. S. (2013). Fostering Student Engagement by Cultivating Curiosity: Fostering Student Engagement by Cultivating Curiosity. *New Directions for Student Services, 2013*(143), 53–64. https://doi.org/10.1002/ss.20060

International Baccalaureate Organization (2018). Assessment principles and practices—Quality assessments in a digital age. International Baccalaureate. https://www.ibo.org/contentassets/1c df850e366447e99b5a862aab622883/assessment-principles-and-practices-2018-en.pdf

Jirout, J., & Klahr, D. (2012). Children's scientific curiosity: In search of an operational definition of an elusive concept. Developmental review, 32(2), 125–160.

Jirout, J. & Vitiello, V. (October, 2018). *Curiosity in the classroom: promoting curiosity through classroom instruction that supports positive responses to uncertainty.* Poster presented at the SRCD Special Topics Meeting, Philadelphia, PA.

Jirout, J. J., Vitiello, V. E., & Zumbrunn, S. K. (2018). Curiosity in schools. In *The new science of curiosity* (pp. 243–265). Nova Science Publishers.

Jirout, J., & Klahr, D. (2020). Questions – And Some Answers – About Young Children's Questions. *Journal of Cognition and Development, 21*(5), 729–753. https://doi.org/10.108 0/15248372.2020.1832492

Jirout, J. J. (2020). Supporting Early Scientific Thinking Through Curiosity. *Frontiers in Psychology, 11.* https://doi.org/10.3389/fpsyg.2020.01717

Jirout, J. J., Zumbrunn, S., Evans, N., & Vitiello, V. (2022). Development and testing of the Curiosity in Classrooms Framework coding protocol. *Frontiers in Psychology.*

Jiusto, S., & DiBiasio, D. (2006). Experiential Learning Environments: Do They Prepare Our Students to be Self-Directed, Life-Long Learners? *Journal of Engineering Education, 95*(3), 195–204.

Kashdan, Todd B., Sherman, R. A., Yarbro, J., & Funder, D. C. (2013). How are Curious People Viewed and How Do they Behave in Social Situations? From the Perspectives of Self, Friends, Parents, and Unacquainted Observers. *Journal of Personality, 81*(2), 142–154. https://doi. org/10.1111/j.1467-6494.2012.00796.x

Kashdan, Todd B., & Silvia, P. J. (2009). Curiosity and Interest: The Benefits of Thriving on Novelty and Challenge. In S. J. Lopez & C. R. Snyder (Eds.), *The Oxford Handbook of*

Positive Psychology (pp. 366–374). Oxford University Press. https://doi.org/10.1093/oxfor dhb/9780195187243.013.0034

Kashdan, Todd B., & Steger, M. F. (2007). Curiosity and pathways to well-being and meaning in life: Traits, states, and everyday behaviors. *Motivation and Emotion, 31*(3), 159–173. https://doi.org/10.1007/s11031-007-9068-7

Kashdan, Todd Barrett, & Yuen, M. (2007). Whether highly curious students thrive academically depends on perceptions about the school learning environment: A study of Hong Kong adolescents. *Motivation and Emotion, 31*(4), 260–270. https://doi.org/10.1007/s11031-007-9074-9

Katz, L. G. (1998). What can we learn from Reggio Emilia. In Edwards, C. P., Giandini, L. & Forman, G. E. (Eds.). *The hundred languages of children: The Reggio Emilia approach--advanced reflections*. Greenwood Publishing Group. 27–45.

Kidd, C., & Hayden, B. Y. (2015). The Psychology and Neuroscience of Curiosity. *Neuron, 88*(3), 449–460. https://doi.org/10.1016/j.neuron.2015.09.010

Kurtz, J. L., Wilson, T. D., & Gilbert, D. T. (2007). Quantity versus uncertainty: When winning one prize is better than winning two. *Journal of Experimental Social Psychology, 43*(6), 979–985. https://doi.org/10.1016/j.jesp.2006.10.020

Lamnina, M., & Chase, C. C. (2019). Developing a thirst for knowledge: How uncertainty in the classroom influences curiosity, affect, learning, and transfer. *Contemporary Educational Psychology, 59*, 101785.

Lillard, A. S. (2016). *Montessori: The Science Behind the Genius*. Oxford University Press.

Litman, J. A. (2008). Interest and deprivation factors of epistemic curiosity. Personality and individual differences, 44(7), 1585–1595.

Litman, J. A., & Spielberger, C. D. (2003). Measuring epistemic curiosity and its divertive and specific components. Journal of Personality Assessment, 80, 75–86.

Litman, J. A., Collins, R. P., & Spielberger, C. D. (2005). The nature and measurement of sensory curiosity. *Personality and Individual Differences, 39*(6), 1123–1133.

Livio, M. (2017). *Why?* New York, NY: Simon & Schuster.

Loewenstein, G. (1994). The psychology of curiosity: A review and reinterpretation. *Psychological Bulletin, 116*(1), 75.

Loewenstein, G. F., Weber, E. U., Hsee, C. K., & Welch, N. (2001). Risk as feelings. *Psychological Bulletin, 127*(2), 267–286. https://doi.org/10.1037//0033-2909.127.2.267

Martin, A. (2011). Courage in the Classroom: Exploring a New Framework Predicting Academic Performance and Engagement. *School Psychology Quarterly, 26*, 145–160. https://doi.org/10.1037/a0023020

Martin, A. J., & Marsh, H. W. (2003). Fear of Failure: Friend or Foe? *Australian Psychologist, 38*(1), 31–38. https://doi.org/10.1080/00050060310001706997

McTighe, J., & Lyman, F. T. (1988). Cueing thinking in the classroom: The promise of theory-embedded tools. *Educational Leadership, 45*(7), 18–24.

Miele, D. B., & Wigfield, A. (2014). Quantitative and Qualitative Relations Between Motivation and Critical-Analytic Thinking. *Educational Psychology Review, 26*(4), 519–541. https://doi.org/10.1007/s10648-014-9282-2

Movshovitz-Hadar, N., & Kleiner, I. (2009). Intellectual courage and mathematical creativity. *Creativity in Mathematics and Education of Gifted Students*, 31–50.

National Academies Press. (2015). *Assessing 21st Century Skills*. Washington, DC: The National Academies Press.

Ogle, D. M. (1986). K-W-L: A Teaching Model That Develops Active Reading of Expository Text. *The Reading Teacher, 39*(6), 564–570.

Pelligrino, J., & Hilton, M. (2012). Education for life and work: Developing transferable knowledge and skills in the 21st century. Washington, D.C.: National Academies Press.

Peterson, C., & Seligman, M. E. P. (2004). *Character strengths and virtues: A handbook and classification*. American Psychological Association; Oxford University Press.

Piaget, J. (1952). The Origins of Intelligence in Children. New York: International University Press. (Original work published 1936.)

Piaget, J. (1950). The psychology of intelligence (M. Piercy & D. E. Berlyne, Trans.). London: Routledge.

Post, T., & Walma van der Molen, J. H. (2018). Do children express curiosity at school? Exploring children's experiences of curiosity inside and outside the school context. *Learning, Culture and Social Interaction, 18*, 60–71. https://doi.org/10.1016/j.lcsi.2018.03.005

Renninger, K. A. (2000). Individual interest and its implications for understanding intrinsic motivation. In *Intrinsic and extrinsic motivation* (pp. 373–404). Academic Press.

Riggs, W. (2010). Open-Mindedness. *Metaphilosophy, 41*(1/2), 172–188.

Ronfard, S., Zambrana, I. M., Hermansen, T. K., & Kelemen, D. (2018). Question-asking in childhood: A review of the literature and a framework for understanding its development. *Developmental Review, 49*, 101–120. https://doi.org/10.1016/j.dr.2018.05.002

Ryan, R. M., & Deci, E. L. (2000). Self-Determination Theory and the Facilitation of Intrinsic Motivation, Social Development, and Well-Being. *American Psychologist, 11*.

Şeker, H., & Kömür, S. (2008). The relationship between critical thinking skills and in-class questioning behaviours of English language teaching students. *European Journal of Teacher Education, 31*(4), 389–402. https://doi.org/10.1080/02619760802420784

Shah, P. E., Weeks, H. M., Richards, B., & Kaciroti, N. (2018). Early childhood curiosity and kindergarten reading and math academic achievement. *Pediatric Research, 84*(3), 380–386. https://doi.org/10.1038/s41390-018-0039-3

Stanovich, K. E., & West, R. F. (1997). Reasoning independently of prior belief and individual differences in actively open-minded thinking. *Journal of Educational Psychology, 89*(2), 342–357. https://doi.org/10.1037/0022-0663.89.2.342

Starko, A. (2013). Creativity on the brink. Educational Leadership, 70(5), 54–56.

Torrance, E. P. (1977). *Creativity in the classroom*. National Education Association.

Tyson, N. D. [neiltyson] (2011, December 17). [I am Neil deGrasse Tyson -- AMA]. Retrieved from https://www.reddit.com/r/IAmA/comments/mateq/i_am_neil_degrasse_tyson_ama

Van Der Meij, H. (1994). Student questioning: A componential analysis. Learning and Individual Differences, 6(2), 137–161. doi:https://doi.org/10.1016/1041-6080(94)90007-8

van Schijndel, T. J. P., Jansen, B. R. J., & Raijmakers, M. E. J. (2018). Do individual differences in children's curiosity relate to their inquiry-based learning? *International Journal of Science Education, 40*(9), 996–1015. https://doi.org/10.1080/09500693.2018.1460772

von Stumm, S., Hell, B., & Chamorro-Premuzic, T. (2011). The Hungry Mind: Intellectual Curiosity Is the Third Pillar of Academic Performance. *Perspectives on Psychological Science, 6*(6), 574–588. https://doi.org/10.1177/1745691611421204

Wade, S., & Kidd, C. (2019). The role of prior knowledge and curiosity in learning. *Psychonomic Bulletin & Review, 26*(4), 1377–1387. https://doi.org/10.3758/s13423-019-01598-6

Watson, L. (2018). Educating for Curiosity. In Inan, I., Watson, L., Whitcomb, D., & Yigit, S. (Eds.) *The Moral Psychology of Curiosity*. Rowman & Littlefield.

Wilson, T. D., Centerbar, D. B., Kermer, D. A., & Gilbert, D. T. (2005). The Pleasures of Uncertainty: Prolonging Positive Moods in Ways People Do Not Anticipate. *Journal of Personality and Social Psychology, 88*(1), 5–21. https://doi.org/10.1037/0022-3514.88.1.5

Chapter 15
(Un)Certain Relation Between Social Validation and Creators' Self-Concept

Izabela Lebuda

Abstract Who would feel confident being constantly evaluated? How do artists or scientists embrace the uncertainty linked to their work's social validation? In the first part of the chapter, I present meanders related to the inevitable evaluation process of professional and eminent creators. Then, I propose a theoretical model of how creators tame the uncertainty of being under radars and dealing with doubts about the results of favorable or negative evaluations of the field. The presented hypothetical mechanism combines contextual factors with individual differences to indicate the crucial role of creative self-concept, mainly social and personal identity, in creativity's social certification incessant cycle. In summary, educational and research considerations related to the proposed model are outlined.

15.1 Introduction

The link between professional creativity and uncertainty has its own chapter in the history of psychology. In 2002, Daniel Kahneman, as the first psychologist, was awarded the Nobel Prize, bestowed "for having integrated insights from psychological research into economic science, especially concerning human judgment and decision-making under uncertainty" (The Royal Swedish Academy of Sciences 2002). Kahneman's work, conducted together with Amos Tversky, described how human judgment departs from basic principles of probability. Scientists hadn't planned to conquer a new field, and as Kahneman declared, the paper in *Econometica*, which was their entry into behavioral economics, was "completely accident" (Staff 2002).

Professional creative success at the highest level, like winning a Nobel Prize, seem hard, even impossible, to be planned or predicted. As such, it could be seen as

Author's NoteIzabela Lebuda, Institute of Psychology, University of Wrocław, Dawida 1, St., 50-527 Wrocław, Poland. E-mail: izalebuda@gmail.com

I. Lebuda (✉)
University of Wrocław, Wrocław, Poland

University of Graz, Graz, Austria

© Springer Nature Switzerland AG 2022
R. A. Beghetto, G. J. Jaeger (eds.), *Uncertainty: A Catalyst for Creativity, Learning and Development*, Creativity Theory and Action in Education 6,
https://doi.org/10.1007/978-3-030-98729-9_15

a work of chance or accident (see Simonton 2011). Although uncertainty is a constant element across all creativity levels (Kaufman and Beghetto 2009), through the entire creative process, from a domain and problem choice to a presentation of product (see Carabine 2013; Zielińska and Karwowski, in this volume), in this chapter I will focus only on uncertainty as it is associated with the social validation of professional creators' works and how it links to their self-concept. In the beginning, I will present the character of creators' social certification with a focus on elements that could increase a sense of the process's unpredictability. In the next part, combining socio-cognitive and individual differences perspectives, I will present the theoretical mechanism of dealing with the uncertainty of evaluation and its results by professional and eminent authors. Last but not least, I will indicate directions for future research necessary to verify the proposed hypothetical model and potential educational implications linked to described mechanism.

15.2   Necessity of Social Validation in Professional and Eminent Creativity

Creative activities are social acts (Lebuda and Glăveanu 2019) and as such they need an audience (Glăveanu 2013). Undertaking everyday creativity, we usually have luxuries to decide whether we want to share the results of our efforts with others or not. In the case of professional creators, constant "creativity in a drawer" can lead to serious consequences, including necessity to change professions. Therefore, social verification of creative achievements is an indispensable element of their work (see Ginsburgh and Weyers 2014). In a professional creative process, it is not coming up with an idea, or even its implementation, which is in fact the last stage, but exactly the presentation of it to others when social verification indeed takes place (e.g., Botella et al. 2013; Mace and Ward 2002).

Outside recipients of professional creative works are not only the people interested in some domain of art or science, but also representatives of a field, called gatekeepers, often professionally involved in evaluating the performances of others: critics, reviewers, publishers, editors, grant and prize donors, etc. Their role is to judge and select the creative products worth to be shared with others or to become part of a domain, give a chance to pass the test of time, and stay there for the next generation to shape future creators (Csikszentmihalyi 1996). Field goal is at least threefold: inspiring and motivating creators, taking care of the development on quality of represented domain, and supporting lay recipients in their evaluation of creative artefacts. Therefore, they play a crucial role in creators' careers, but also a sociocultural function for the entire society (see Csikszentmihalyi 1996; Lebuda and Csikszentmihalyi 2019; Ma and Uzzi 2018).

As opposed to everyday creativity, in the case of which assessment is mainly in form of a direct message, in professional creativity the field expresses its opinion mainly indirectly – by means of reviews, prizes, or setting product prices. Many of these social recognition signs, like winning a prestigious prize, are perceived as forms of the highest achievement in a domain (Carson et al. 2005; Simonton 2020). In addition to psychological consequences, some of which will be discussed later in this chapter, social validation also has a pragmatic aspect. Public acclamation and acknowledgment builds reputation, confers credibility on the creator and his/her work, promotes careers, helps to get the funds, and provides financial benefits.

The way the field acts could stimulate but also hinder creativity. Most studies about the relation between external validation and creativity are devoted to motivational aspects of mini- and little-c creativity and focus on how outside judgments and prizes could influence intrinsic motivation (e.g., Amabile et al. 1986, 1990; Eisenberger and Aselage 2009; Eisenberger and Selbst 1994). A conclusion that is essential for the discussion in this chapter, and that emerges from this research, is that social validation provides relevant information to guide goal-directed behavior (for summary see Byron and Khazanchi 2012). Social validation of professional creativity reflects a social consensus about norms, criteria, and values shared in the domain, so it may serve as a reference point for creators to orient toward or deviate from (see Haslam et al. 2013).

15.3 Uncertainty in Creativity Social Validation

On the one hand, social evaluation of creative artefacts is an important message for recipients. It may reduce audience's uncertainty regarding the value of works and inform creators about the domain-applicable expectations and rules. On the other hand, many social assessment aspects could evoke and arouse uncertainty for both the assessed and the evaluators. This issue varies across disciplines. The more difficult it is to objectively operationalize creative success in a domain, the more weighty the social certification and recognition of the field are (see Fraiberger et al. 2018). This is connected with the domain-specific hierarchy of creativity domains (see Simonton 2009a). In more structured disciplines, for example more in science than in art, there is a stronger consensus between judges about what a significant contribution to a domain is (Simonton 2020). Prizes and appreciation in more structured domains are less dependent on the social context. For example, scientific Nobel Prize is less influenced by political concerns than the one in literature and peace (Simonton 2020). Moreover, formal education is necessary to fulfil the role in highly structured domains. It is impossible to be an architect without a diploma, whereas it is an acceptable scenario for a painter or sculptor, and in the case of a poet or writer, it is the only possible way. Formal education provides professional status certification for creators and almost inalienable right to be part of a professional guild (see Frith 2001; Toynbee 2000). The less structured the domain, the more possible the evaluation of creative products may raise authors' doubts about the quality of works as their qualification. For example, while looking for scientific disciplines it was found that in social science, researchers more likely than in physical science consult the results of their work with colleagues before submitting it to a journal (Suls and Fletcher 1983). Therefore, in less formal, less structured areas of creativity, social validation is linked to higher uncertainty levels.

It could be supposed that also the uncertainty about the artefacts' value among the audience is specific to the domain. However, it is not conditioned by the structuring of the creative area but more by the works' abstraction and necessity of recipients' preparation. It seems that preselection made by experts is crucial for a wider unprofessional audience in domains where understanding of works requires more specialized knowledge, like in modern art or quantum physics. Indeed, in examples of highbrow art, like opera (Simonton 1998) or modern visual art (Pénet and Lee 2014), audiences rely on professional judgments and there is consensus between expert and nonexpert creativity verdicts. The situation is not so exact in the domains where artefacts could have everyday use. Where art is also entertainment, assessment of experts and laypeople are consistent, and specialists' judgment does not adequately reflect appreciation of the general public. For example, literary prizes are not a good predictor of a book's popularity (Form 2017) or in the movie business, critics' assessments are not always in harmony with viewers' judgments (Simonton 2009b). In the case of scientific theories that are not very abstract and at the same time have or can have a direct impact on the quality of life, more likely in psychology or educational studies than in theoretical physics or chemistry, a tendency to ignore the opinions of specialists is also noticed. People tend to oversimplify information and shape opinions inconsistent with empirical evidence, based on anecdotal examples or media coverage (e.g., Baas et al. 2015; Benedek et al. 2021). It seems natural that creators have doubts about who the creative work should be addressed to, or whether it is possible to communicate in a way that will secure recognition among specialists and appreciation of lay audience. These discrepancies are sources of negative emotions among creators and raise the question about validity of field assessment (Lebuda and Pieczyńska 2018).

Considering consistency of social evaluation, it is worth to also look at consensus between professionals. Although it is easy to imagine fierce disputes, it has been shown that experts in the field, just like in research and in real-life contests, mostly agree regarding the value of the product, and the contribution of the creation to the domain (e.g., in poetry Kaufman et al. 2008; in film Simonton 2004; in opera Simonton 1998). Even though field assessments are consistent, it doesn't mean they aren't prone to various kinds of distortion due to contextual factors. It is a classic idea that creative products don't have absolute value and are dependent on context (Stein 1953).

Let us return for a moment to Kahneman and Tversky's discoveries, mentioned in the introduction, and describe tendencies in decision making. The authors presented that often, especially in uncertain situations, the decision-making and evaluation processes are based on heuristics and as such they are susceptible to some errors (Kahneman et al. 1982). The echo of this theory could be found in the attributional approach to creativity (Kasof 1995). It pointed out that characteristics attributed to a product are often a result of biases, for example, reflecting authors' distinctive characteristics. The case of an eighteenth century painting titled "The Man with the Golden Helmet" could serve as a good illustration here. The piece was attributed to Rembrandt, but when evidence emerged in the 1980s that it was another author, it lost much economic and attributed artistic values, even though nothing about the artwork itself has changed (Bonus and Ronte 1997). Less anecdotal evidence also points out that the author's perception does significantly shape assessment of an artefact. When the author's information is limited, as in many artistic and scientific contests, even a fraction of details like gender or name plays a vital role in the assessment. It was shown that where women sign scientific work, it is scored lower than when males and anonymous individuals signed the same fragment of a paper. And a piece of theory gains higher appreciation when it is attributed to a male with a common name. A unique name induces more positive notes in artistic domains like music and poetry (Lebuda and Karwowski 2013). Trends in assessments may also result from other contextual variables over which the authors very often have no influence. For example, the final ranking in musical contests has been shown to depend on the order of appearance (Ginsburgh and Van Ours 2003).

The importance of numerous variables for social evaluation, which are not directly related to the quality of the work, may significantly increase the sense of unpredictability of the results of the evaluation and, in extreme cases, subordinate its fairness. In order to appreciate more deserving artifacts, even though the creative product has no absolute value, attempts are made to establish some form of an arbitrary professional assessment rule (see Bourdieu 1983). However, in most cases, that very arbitrary professional assessment rule refers not to the value of the work itself or the creator's output, but to formal characteristics, such as the time of the creation of the work. Although the rule's legitimacy raises doubts, its consequences may be significant for creators' careers. Limitation of shared Nobel Prize recipients to three individuals is one of those explicit criteria that raises the greatest degree of doubt. Restriction of individuals who could be awarded may unfairly locate the credit for work, especially in scientific domains, raise doubts about personalizing discoveries that result from team efforts and lead to a reduction of collaboration, and strengthen rivalry (Casadevall and Fang 2013). Controversies around excluding some individuals from the Nobel Prize have been courted since the prize's inception. One of those was caused when Kitasato Shibasaburo's contributions to research into antibodies as antioxidants was not acknowledged. These controversies are ongoing. For instance, many individuals working on innate immunity were omitted when the Committee was considering the 2011 Nobel Prize (Casadevall and Fang 2013). An additional rule is that Nobel Prizes are given only to living creators (Simonton 2020); this was the reason why Tversky, who died in 1996, did not receive the Nobel Prize along with Kahneman. In the case of the Nobel Prize, other explicit criteria derived from Alfred Nobel's will were the one-year window between the discovery and prize. The rule was quickly changed (see Fortunato et al. 2014) even though it meant that Dmitri Mendeleev, one of the most eminent chemists in history, who formulated the periodic table of elements, could not receive the Prize. When the Nobel Prize was established the invention was "too old" and when "the preceding year" rule was changed it was too late for the scientist, who was already deceased.

The arbitrary nature of the criteria and changes in compliance may be a source of uncertainty for authors. It also doesn't help that in most social verification cases, little is known about the criteria for the quality of the work itself. It is often challenging to indicate criteria that would allow, without a shadow of a doubt, to distinguish famous works or achievements from the ones with a timeless, most significant impact on the given domain. It was pointed out that only history and the passage of time can verify the value of recognized creative artefacts (Kaufman and Beghetto 2009). Certainly, lasting fame and creative immortality help to distinguish eminent creative products from ephemera and could be a good selection criterion during scientific research. But this kind of "deferred success" (Moulin 1987) could be a source of uncertainty for contemporary creators – especially the beginning ones, who have to gradually accumulate their recognition into the field. An illustration of the ambiguous nature of excellence criteria could be found in the rationale for the Nobel Prize. As Alfred Nobel put in his will, these are "prizes to those, who (...) conferred the greatest benefit to humankind" (Nobel 1895/2021). This part of the decision, engraved on the Nobel medal, seems broad and presents many possibilities of interpretation. It can be assumed that this statement's enigmatic nature is one of the reasons for numerous controversies and discussions about the legitimacy of awarding or omitting creators from the Nobel Prize (see Casadevall and Fang 2013; Feldman 2000; Luttenberger 1996). Dependence of judgment on perspectives is well illustrated by the example of 1994 the Nobel Peace Prize for Yasser Arafat, who, considered by some as a freedom fighter and creator of peace in the Middle East, was seen by others as a terrorist (Philipps 2011). There is also another, vigorously discussed example of the 2016 Literature Nobel Prize going to musician and songwriter Bob Dylan – meritorious for some while a mistake for others (North 2016; O'Hagan 2016).

The lack of clear standards is one of the primary sources of uncertainty (Aspers 2018). The problem of imprecise criteria may arouse discomfort not only among creators but it may also cause increases in inaccuracy of identifying creative products (see Rietzschel et al. 2010). However, because creative works are characterized by novelty and originality, and the higher level of creativity the more surprising the works is expected to be (see Simonton 2012), it is difficult to predict and thus set unambiguous criteria of excellence. Moreover, creative products' novelty could induce tension in evaluators and let them resist revolutionary works. It was shown as not so unusual that decision-makers reject creative ideas or products even if they endorse creativity as essential (Staw 1995). The more novel and unusual the idea, the greater the chance that it would raise uncertainty about practical, useful aspects of the given work (see Rietzschel et al. 2010) and doubts concerning its value and occurrence of potential errors (Simonton 1984). That's why too original ideas can be misunderstood, objectionable, and underestimated. For illustration, we can examine the scientific peer-review process. Reviews work well for the vast majority of publications; the ones that are highest-rated before publication are most cited later. However, most groundbreaking, most cited works in the field, were desk rejected from leading journals in the domains (Siler et al. 2015). As was presented, uncertainty hinders the ability to recognize creativity (Mueller et al. 2012). The innovative character, significantly different from what was known so far, raises doubts and uncertainty about quality and therefore led to rejection during preliminary assessment. Potential experts' mistake has obvious ramifications for the creators but it can also cost a lot for evaluators who rest on their reputation as specialists in the field (see Gallotti and De Domenico 2019).

Fear of an unknown, too unusual work may be related to one more tendency in the social validation of creativity. As is known from *mere exposure effect*, people usually prefer what they know (Zajonc 2001). A creative idea can't be a copy of a previously known one; however, the potential difference of a new product may be of varying degrees. The tendency to choose more familiar products also translates into favoritism of creators who are similar to judges and share some characteristics with them (see Haslam et al. 2013). We can find the illustration of this bias both in art and in science. The Oscars prize awarded by the U.S.-based Academy of Motion Picture Arts and Science most often goes to U.S. actors and actresses than British ones. The opposite happens in the case of the BATA prize awarded by the British Academy of Film and Television Arts (Steffens et al. 2013 from Haslam et al. 2013). The national homophily, as much as political and gender one, was also presented in the scientific Nobel Prize nominations and prizes (Gallotti and De Domenico 2019).

Homophily in judgments, alongside field members' consensus in an assessment, are some of the possible explanations of the "Matthew effect" – the tendency to prize, and give credit for work, to the most famous, already appreciated ones (Merton 1968). First described in science, the effect was also corroborated in art (e.g., popular music – Chung and Cox 1994; the film industry – Collins and Hand 2006; Simonton 2004). The tendency that *success breeds success* could be illustrated by studies showing that researchers who won funding for research before tend to get funded more easily during subsequent years (Bol et al. 2018); papers of authors with high reputation gain more citations in the citation life cycle faster (Petersen et al. 2014); and the established authors' papers were less often rejected then when submitted as anonymous (Peters and Ceci 1982). Moreover, even though the number of scientific awards is continuously increasing, a smaller number of scholars, who are more closely related through genealogical and co-authorship networks, are being awarded (Ma and Uzzi 2018). Additionally, the more prestigious the award, the smaller the number of recipients: for example, till today, the Nobel Prize in Physics was awarded to 216 scientists, including only 4 women. Even a smaller group was awarded the Nobel Prize in Literature – 117 authors (of whom only 16 are women). Therefore, it seems evident that many highly creative people, with a significant impact for their domains, will never receive this or maybe any award (see Simonton 2020). We can argue that the most eminent ones will do, but because we cannot cut clear criteria and compare achievements one to one, it is hard to decide whether the winner is always the best of the nominee pool. What is known is that the history of the Nobel Prize has known cases when people with many nominations, repeated year after year, did not always win against individuals with fewer nominations. For example, Ramón Menéndez Pidal was nominated more than any other physicist (in whose cases the data on nominations was disclosed), but never won.

The problem with a small group of highly socially appreciated creators goes beyond academic debate and has real impact on creators' lives. The most eminent, appreciated creators get the most access to the broadest support system (see Magee and Galinsky 2008). Reinforced self-assurance of most prized creators could motivate them to pick up riskier and demanding problems, to increase the chances of the next breakthrough of the work (see Duguid and Goncalo 2015; Merton 1968) and in this way, the rewards may continuously recreate the same, established order (see Bourdieu 1983). As a result, it could be difficult for new people to emerge, and those who have achieved a certain status must face social expectations related to their position (Karakowsky et al. 2020; Magee and Galinsky 2008).

The argument in favor of the thesis that the system of social validation, especially in the form of awards, is intended to reflect the existing order is the tendency to empower creators who socialize well to the domain (see Csikszentmihalyi 1996; Lebuda and Csikszentmihalyi 2019); those who not only know the domain's rules but also tend to look for the values shared and promoted by the field or maybe by wider society (see Haslam et al. 2013). Before we move on to the data, we can refer to one more anecdotal example from the Nobel Prize's history. When in 1911 Maria Skłodowska-Curie was awarded her second Nobel Prize (the one in chemistry for her work with radium and polonium), turbulence in her private life became public. Publication of her love correspondence with Paul Langevin, who was married, raised a social scandal. Svante Arrhenius, a Nobel Committee member, wrote to her to skip the ceremony in Stockholm. Curie answered:

> You suggest to me… that the Academy of Stockholm, if it had been forewarned, would probably have decided not to give me the Prize, unless I could publicly explain the attacks of which I have been the object …. I must therefore act according to my convictions…. The action that you advise me would appear a grave error on my part. In fact, the Prize has been awarded for the discovery of radium and polonium. I believe there is no connection between my scientific work and the facts of private life…. I cannot accept the idea in principle that the appreciation of the value of scientific work should be influenced by libel and slander concerning private life. I am convinced that this opinion is shared by many people (Dry and Seifert 2003, p. 91–92).

Even though high independence from rules could be necessary to defy the crowd (Sternberg and Lubart 1996) and, as presented above, could help defend a work against social criticism (see Hunter and Cushenbery 2015), it could be harmful in the professional social validation process. This reflected in the recommendation to always "be nice to Swedish scientists" as one of the rules to win the Nobel Prize, which are formulated by the 1993 Nobel Prize Winner in Physiology and Medicine, Richard J. Roberts (2015). Looking for more empirical evidence, it was presented that in the case of Nobel Prize laureates, agreeableness has a positive effect on professional recognition (Lebuda and Karwowski 2021). The preferences of *safe choices* is also present in the case of the Nobel Prize in literature – even more dominant authors who were nominated for awards at a lower age had to wait for the prize longer (Lebuda and Karwowski 2016; see also Karwowski and Lebuda 2014). This above research could reflect the tendency to ignore more rebellious creators and award the more conciliatory ones. But because high professional notes of artwork were predicted by lower agreeableness of artists who were anonymous to the evaluators (Benedek et al. 2017), it is also possible that their work is more aligned with domain status quo (see Ko and Kim 2008; LePine and Van Dyne 2001) and as such their products as less revolutionary don't raise so many doubts and uncertainty, and balance well between originality and safety. The process of social evaluation of creative works may reduce uncertainty of inexperienced audiences. However, it may also potentially provide many doubts and fears to members of the field and ultimately to creators. Above, I have indicated the doubts, tendencies, and potential problems that accompany the inevitable social evaluation of professional creative works. In the next part of this chapter, I will describe a hypothetical mechanism: effects that uncertainty related to social evaluation (and its results) may have on a creator's self-concept and, consequently, on undertaking more or less risky creative challenges.

15.4 Uncertainty of Social Validation and Creators' Self-Concept

The social validation process of professional creativity could be a challenging experience, but it is also worth to notice the role that its results play for creators' careers and self-evaluation. The history of success is important for formulating creative self-beliefs (Bandura 1986; Wigfield and Eccles 2000) and it could shape the efficacy that one could handle creative challenges and that creativity is an integral part of the self (see Karwowski et al. 2019). The development of a professional's creative self is a social co-construction process (Glăveanu and Tanggaard 2014; Lebuda and Csikszentmihalyi 2017; Taylor and Littleton 2012). Messages sent by social validation in the form of appreciation or criticism and rejection, could confirm, strengthen, or shake the creator's self-concept (see promoted, denied, and problematic creative identity in Glăveanu and Tanggaard 2014). Uncertainty of professional creativity's social certification is related to the meanders of the process but also to the final result of the evaluation. In simplified terms, it can be assumed that in effect of the social creativity assessment, creators may receive one of two possible types of feedback: acceptance and accolade or lack of approval and, in extreme cases, rejection of work. Social validation, in forms of such tokens of respect as appreciation, attention, or prizes, are not motives to create, but help confirm and establish professional identity especially for young creators (Jutti and Littleton 2012; Lebuda and Csikszentmihalyi 2017). In the beginning of a creator's career, being noticed by the field serves as a crystallizing experience (Walters and Gardner 1986) and strengthens the sense of being a representative of the chosen domain (see Szen-Ziamiańska et al. 2017).

In the case of an established creator, appreciation secures them in their position in the domain. It could boost their self-efficacy (e.g., Tierney and Farmer 2002) and as a result, it can motivate them to more creative performance (e.g., Choi 2004;

Tierney and Farmer 2011), encourage picking up high-risk challenges, and lead to groundbreaking innovations (see Duguid and Goncalo 2015). Moreover, according to what was mentioned above ("Matthew effect"), it could favor them in the future and shield them from criticism (see Duguid and Goncalo 2015). However, the situation of privilege and appreciation can paradoxically raise concerns and anxiety (see Karakowsky et al. 2020). Although it has been shown that a high position helps to cope with stress and increase efficiency in tasks, it is only valid when the position held is certain and stable. In a situation of a potential threat to status, the experience of stress increases significantly and performance advantage disappears (Knight and Mehta 2017). Similarly, people with a higher position are more likely to demonstrate their superior competences, but only when they are sure that their position is not at risk (Jury et al. 2019). What's more, individuals who hold higher positions in their domains are significantly less productive upon losing it, in comparison not only with those who kept their status, but also those who held lower position and also lost them (Marr and Thau 2014). As the acclaimed art critic and writer Robert Hughes (2012) stated: "The greater the artist, the greater the doubt. Perfect confidence is granted to the less talented as a consolation prize."

Being prized, holding a high position in the domain, or being part of a prestigious group, is likely incorporated into self-concept (Marr and Thau 2014; Tajfel and Turner 1986). Being perceived as a successful, eminent, or popular creator is becoming a more central, important part of oneself. When the central part of self-concept is challenged or contradicted, people experience self-threat, and the higher their position, the higher the level of anxiety of losing this position (Baumeister et al. 1996). While research has confirmed a tendency to empower previously appreciated people, ongoing verification, in some areas even an annual cycle of environmental re-assessments (such as the Nobel Prize or Films Awards, see Simonton 2020), coupled with many, not always consistent assessment sources (see above, the assessment of competent judges and the assessment of lay audiences), along with the continually emerging new representatives, may raise concerns about a creator's position and reputation in a domain (Jury et al. 2019). When the creator's self-concept is not stable, it is likely that in a self-threatened condition, such as facing social validation in a competitive area, creators will engage in self-protection and self-enhancement action (see Alicke and Sedikides 2009; Sedikides 2012).

There are two theoretically legitimate self-protection mechanisms that are possible when a successful creator is unsure of a position and focuses on upholding their own reputation. In the case of both mechanisms, I will focus especially on how they influence originality of a creator's works in the future and hence on the development of the entire domain. The first possible mechanism is based on the assumption that the creator who wants to avoid critical evaluations will to a small extent deviate from previously valued ideas. Doing so can ensure a stable position, while producing works that meet expectations, are not radically new, will not cause uncertainty in evaluators (see the mechanism described above), and will more likely gain professional applause. Focusing on external validation, especially when the domain position is perceived to be in jeopardy, can discourage one from choosing risky projects and reduce more innovative, radical forms of creativity (Gilson and Madjar

2011; Maner et al. 2007, 2007). Indeed, it was presented that successful creators are more likely to invent new ideas, but these ideas to not diverge far from the creators' previous works and are more incremental in nature (Audia and Goncalo 2007).

The second potential mechanism describing how successful creators could embrace uncertainty and potential self-threat triggered by social validation and its results does not rule out and is not necessarily different from the first one described above. However, it could add some additional explanation of the incremental nature of professional successful creators (see Audia and Goncalo 2007). This assumption is based on knowledge that in the case of potential rejection, humans strengthen their sense of social belonging (Knowles and Gardner 2008; Swann Jr. et al. 2004). In situations when an essential part of self-concept (such as being an appreciated creator) is threatened, it could result in identity uncertainty (Hogg 2007). In light of uncertainty-identity theory, to deal with challenging experiences people strengthen their belonging in the groups that provide a clear and distinctive identity, mainly to such high-entitativity groups as artistic or scientific movements (Hogg 2000, 2007). This was observed in reports of creators who experience uncertainties of political regimes; during oppression time, they not only look strongly to referential groups of people who react to the political situation in similar ways, but also separate and distance themselves strictly from other domain representatives (Lebuda 2016). But when creators' social identity is salient, they create conforming more to group norms (see Haslam et al. 2013), so it is harder to come up with revolutionary, tradition-breaking ideas. When social identity is more central, the creative acts are more aligned with group norms and values as such are also more favorably perceived and rated by other group members (see Adarves-Yorno et al. 2006, 2007).

The above discussion was about a situation when established or successful creators (also rising stars) feel self-threatened by potential criticism in social validation. The question is how the self-concept knowledge is relevant to the situation when negative information about artefacts is really delivered. Objection or rejection of a creator's work decreases the feeling of belonging (see Gerber and Wheeler 2009). One could anticipate that a more salient personal identity contributes to more revolutionary creativity that is less fitted to group expectancies (see Haslam et al. 2013). It was shown that when people hold an independent self-concept, they are more creative after social rejection than after inclusion. Negative social judgment boosts a salient feeling of being different from others and as a result it increases creativity (Kim et al. 2013). Retaining their own uniqueness and the so-called differentiation mindset will help creators be more independent from domain and field rules, increasing the chance for more revolutionary inventions. Moreover, it could shed some light on the role creative self-concept plays in the context of failure and rejection of professional creators (see Cox 1926; Freeman 1993). In the case of creative potential the creative self-concept is the agentic element, it helps translate the possible into real-life action – undertaking creative activities and, consequently achieving successes (Dollinger et al. 2005; Helson 1967; Helson and Pals 2000; Karwowski et al. 2019; Karwowski and Beghetto 2019). Hence, it can be assumed that professional creativity and strong personal creative identity prevents creative mortification – loss of willingness to pursue creative aspiration following a negative performance outcome (Beghetto 2014). A summary of the proposed mechanism of dealing with the uncertainty of social evaluation is presented in Fig. 15.1 below.

The presented model needs empirical verification. Notwithstanding, it could serve as further support for the hypothesis that embracing uncertainty associated with professional social validation of creativity could be supported by strong and stable self-concept of the creator (see Karakowsky et al. 2020; Swann Jr. et al. 2003). Along with the development of creators' competences, personal identity and understanding of uncertainty as a permanent element of creative work are strengthened (Carabine 2013; Tracey and Hutchinson 2016). What is more, it was corroborated many times that a stronger creative self-concept is distinguishable for eminent creators compared to their less successful professional peers (e.g., Albert and Runco 1986; Barron 1983; Barron and Harrington 1981; Cox 1926; Dowd and Pinheiro 2013; Kozbelt 2007; Lebuda and Csikszentmihalyi 2020; Ochse 1990; Taylor and Barron 1963; Zuckerman 2005). What's even more important, they are independent in their professional roles and so they are likely less focused on social rules and expectations (e.g., MacKinnon 1978, 1983; also see Dudek and Hall 1991).

Response to the uncertainty of being under constant evaluation as well as response to its results are also associated not only with objective challenges but also with tendencies to perceive the context in a specific way. That's why creators' individual differences also play a significant role in reacting to the uncertainty of social validation. Whether a creator who has a long history of success will perceive their position as stable or not is due not only to the circumstances in which they find themselves, but also to a tendency to experience anxiety and a sense of threat (see Elliot and Thrash 2002). It was presented, in line with theoretical perspectives on psychological entropy, that three Big Five personality traits are almost constantly connected to response to uncertainty: openness for experience, extraversion, and neuroticism (DeYoung 2013; Hirsh et al. 2012). Openness and extraversion are

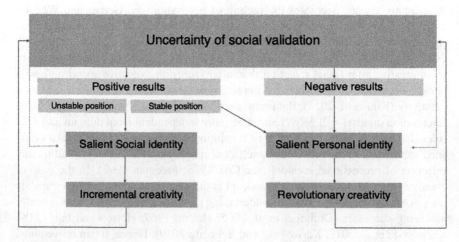

Fig. 15.1 A theoretical model of a link between social validation uncertainty, creators' self-concept and creativity

linked positively to the motivation to explore the unknown, to the need for complexity and novelty, and low level of discomfort in an ambiguous situation, when neuroticism is grounded in aversive response to uncertainty (DeYoung 2013; DeYoung 2013; Hirsh et al. 2012; Lauriola et al. 2016). Looking at personality aspects, it was found that tolerance of uncertainty is strongly related to the intellectual curiosity (more so than to aesthetic appreciation) facet of openness to experience and the assertiveness (rather than energy or sociability) facet of extraversion (Jach and Smillie 2019).

More open and extraverted people would do better at embracing the uncertainty of being under the radar, expectation of assessment results and a potentially unstable position when the more neurotic ones will look for some form of self-protection. It could be hypothesized that the self-affirmation mechanism is similar to the one described above. It is proposed that personality shapes the context's perception and social validation process, and influences self-concept (see Asendorpf and van Aken 2003). Based on meta-analytical studies, openness to experience and extraversion were the stronger of all personality traits that were positively related to creative self-beliefs when neuroticism was weaker and negatively linked to them (Karwowski and Lebuda 2016, 2017; see also Lebuda et al. 2021). What is more, neuroticism is related to a stronger reaction to any social-threat (Denissen and Penke 2008) and the feeling of being threatened or anxious typically turns to social inclusion, affiliation, strengthening of the sense of belonging (e.g., Baumeister and Leary 1995; Maner et al. 2007), and in consequence to probably making social identity more salient (see Hogg 2007). In turn, this may lead to more socially expected ideas (see Haslam et al. 2013). To sum up, it is likely that openness to experience and extraversion, with a positive reaction to uncertainty, will trigger salient personal identity and effect in more revolutionary creativity while higher neuroticism will strengthen social identity and result in more incremental creativity. If we agree that the most renowned authors have created most groundbreaking, revolutionary works, results of research on eminent creators' personalities partially confirm the above-described mechanism. Openness to experience is consistently indicated as a predictor of creative achievements across domains (Batey and Furnham 2006; Kaufman et al. 2016; Lebuda et al. 2019; Lebuda and Karwowski 2021; Silvia et al. 2009). The most eminent scientists rate significantly higher in openness than the less successful ones (Feist 1998; Feist and Gorman 1998), and are more often cited, even though they do not publish more works (Grosul and Feist 2014). But when extraversion is a consistent predictor of achievement in arts (Kaufman et al. 2016), it tends to link negatively to creativity in science (Batey and Furnham 2006). A reverse tendency is noted in the case of neuroticism, which is indicated as more conducive to artistic achievements, but harmful to scientific ones (Batey and Furnham 2006; Feist 1998), yet appreciated scientists are higher on emotional sensitivity and reactivity compared to the less successful ones (Cox 1926; Feist 1998; Grosul and Feist 2014). These personality domain-specific characteristics could be linked to the difference in the uncertainty of social validation described earlier in this chapter. However, like most of the above-described ones, this assumption requires empirical verification.

15.5 Summary

The experience of creativity's social validation is beautifully described by Rudyard Kipling (Nobel Prize in Literature, 1907) in the poem, titled Conundrum of the Workshops (1920) (http://www.kiplingsociety.co.uk/poems_conundrum.htm). The Devil as "first, most dread review", or critic, responds to human creative artefacts with the statement that "it's pretty, but is it art?" This kind of confusion hurls the author to anguish. Doubts about a work's quality and a possibility to come up with appreciated ideas could be dreadful. They could be perceived as a threat to domain position, everyday well-being, and the self-concept of being a professional creator. In the chapter, I propose a hypothetical mechanism on how the situation of being judged and dealing with validation results could make salient social or individual identity and cause more incremental or revolutionary creativity. I am far from demonizing uncertainty. In light of the presented model, uncertainty does have a motivational value and certain conditions would increase chances for breakthrough inventions. For example, for some more curious and assertive individuals, unclear and ambiguous situations and challenges could be even tempting and rewarding (see Jach and Smillie 2019). What is more, the appropriate level of uncertainty seems necessary for experiencing flow (Csikszentmihalyi 1996), which "(...) makes us feel edgy and alive, and delivers us a sense of satisfaction and mastery when we resolve such uncertainties" (Hogg 2007, p.73).

The model presented in the chapter is theoretical and as such it may arouse a feeling of uncertainty in the reader. I hope that, like most uncertainty-based challenges, it has a motivational potential and can inspire research in the proposed subject. At least some of the submitted claims require empirical verification. One of them is the domain differences in experiencing uncertainty as linked to the social validation process. An interesting question is how democratization of creativity's social validation, by spreading voting and opinionating in traditional and social media and some professional portals (such as ResearchGate for scientists or Behance for artists), could increase or decrease uncertainty of professional creative work assessment. The next one is how different assessment results (appreciation or rejection) are associated with social and personal identity of creators and whether it bears further influence on the quality of their ideas.

Education (along with professional creativity) is one more context when assessment is present almost all the time. Similarly to creators, students often perceive their work's judgments as arbitrary or even irrelevant (Struyven et al. 2005). Therefore, it seems that the proposed mechanism could also be applied in mini- and little-c creativity in school context. The way that students perceive validation determines how they approach their assignments (Struyven et al. 2005). In the case of creativity, even expectation of assessment could be significant for performance (Baer 1997) and teachers' feedback on creativity is essential for students' self-concept (Beghetto 2006). Moreover, it was presented that the role of creativity assessment depends on the condition of judgment and personality predispositions (Zhou and Oldham 2001). Therefore, it seems justifiable, considering stimulating the creative development of students by taking inspiration from the proposed model, to simultaneously take into account students' individual differences, the socio-cognitive aspects (such as beliefs about their own abilities), their image of themselves, but also the more social factors, such as a place they occupy in the social network (see Karwowski 2015; McKay et al. 2017). Furthermore, it is worth to look how peers and teachers perceive each student and whether this position allows them to take up risky creative challenges or, on the contrary, encourages them to repeat the awarded pattern. A more profound understanding of how feedback impacts pupils' creative self-concept and performance could be meaningful for creativity education. Finally, we need to connect individual and situational variables that help deal with uncertainty in creativity challenges, not to reduce it, but to tame and learn how to use it to fuel our own work (see Carabine 2013). This skill seems crucial because in the current world, nobody can feel entirely certain, only less uncertain (Pollock 2003).

Acknowledgments The project leading to this chapter has received funding from the European Union's Horizon 2020 research and innovation programme under the Marie Sklodowska-Curie grant agreement No 896518.

References

Adarves-Yorno, I., Postmes, T., & Haslam, S. A. (2006). Social identity and the recognition of creativity in groups. *British Journal of Social Psychology, 45,* 479-497. https://doi.org/10.134 8/014466605X50184

Adarves-Yorno, I., Postmes, T., & Haslam, S. A. (2007). Creative innovation or crazy irrelevance? The contribution of group norms and social identity to creative behavior. *Journal of Experimental Social Psychology, 43,* 410-416. https://doi.org/10.1016/j.jesp.2006.02.013

Amabile, T. M., Goldfarb, P., & Brackfield, S. C. (1990). Social influences on creativity: Evaluation, coaction, and surveillance. *Creativity Research Journal, 3,* 6–21. doi:https://doi.org/10.1080/10400419009534330

Amabile, T. M., Hennessey, B. A., & Grossman, B. S. (1986). Social influences on creativity: The effects of contracted-for reward. *Journal of Personality and Social Psychology, 50,* 14–23. doi:https://doi.org/10.1037/0022-3514.50.1.14

Albert, R. S., & Runco, M. A. (1986). The achievement of eminence: A model based on a longitudinal study of exceptionally gifted boys and their families. In R. J. Sternberg, & J. E Davidson (Eds.), *Conceptions of giftedness* (pp. 332–357). Cambridge University Press.

Alicke, M. D., & Sedikides, C. (2009). Self-enhancement and self-protection: What they are and what they do. *European Review of Social Psychology, 20,* 1-48. https://doi.org/10.1080/10463280802613866

Asendorpf, J. B., & van Aken, M. A. G. (2003). Personality-relationship transaction in adolescence: Core versus surface personality characteris- tics. *Journal of Personality, 71,* 629–666. https://doi.org/10.1111/1467-6494.7104005

Aspers, P. (2018). Forms of uncertainty reduction: Decision, valuation, and contest. *Theory and Society, 47,* 133–149. https://doi.org/10.1007/s11186-018-9311-0

Audia, P. G., & Goncalo, J.A. (2007). Past success and creativity over time: A study of inventors in the hard disk drive industry. *Management Science, 53,* 1–15. https://doi.org/10.1287/mnsc.1060.0593

Baas, M., Koch, S., Nijstad, B. A., & De Dreu, C. K. W. (2015). Conceiving creativity: The nature and consequences of laypeople's beliefs About the realization of creativity. *Psychology of Aesthetics, Creativity, and the Arts, 9*, 340-354.https://doi.org/10.1037/a0039420

Baer, J. (1997). Gender Differences in the Effects of Anticipated Evaluation on Creativity. *Creativity Research Journal, 10*, 25–31. https://doi.org/10.1207/s15326934crj1001_3

Bandura, A. (1986). *Social foundations of thought and action: A social cognitive theory.* Prentice-Hall.

Barron, F. (1983). Creative writers. In R. S. Albert (ed.), *Genius and eminence: The social psychology of creativity and exceptional achievement* (pp. 302–310). Pergamon Press.

Barron, F., & Harrington, D. M. (1981). Creativity, intelligence and personality. *Annual Review of Psychology, 32*, 439–476. https://doi.org/10.1146/annurev.ps.32.020181.002255

Batey, M., & Furnham, A. (2006). Creativity, Intelligence, and Personality: A Critical Review of the Scattered Literature. *Genetic, Social, and General Psychology Monographs, 132*, 355–429. https://doi.org/10.3200/MONO.132.4.355-430

Baumeister, R. F., & Leary, M. R. (1995). The need to belong: Desire for interpersonal attachments as a fundamental human motivation. *Psychological Bulletin, 111*, 497–529. doi:https://doi.org/10.1037/0033-2909.117.3.497.

Baumeister, R. F., Smart, L., & Boden, J. M. (1996). Relation of threatened egotism to violence and aggression: The dark side of high self-esteem. *Psychological Review, 103*, 5–33. https://doi.org/10.1037/0033-295X.103.1.5

Beghetto, R.A. (2006). Creative self-efficacy: correlates in middle and secondary students. *Creativity Research Journal, 18*, 447–457.

Beghetto, R. A. (2014). Creative mortification: An initial exploration. *Psychology of Aesthetics, Creativity, and the Arts, 8*, 266–276. https://doi.org/10.1037/a0036618

Benedek, M., Jauk, E., Kerschenbauer, K., Anderwald, R., & Grond, L. (2017). Creating art: An experience sampling study in the domain of moving image art. *Psychology of Aesthetics, Creativity, and the Arts, 11*, 325–334. https://doi.org/10.1037/aca0000102

Benedek, M., Karstendiek, M., Ceh, S. M., Grabner, R. H., Krammer, G., Lebuda, I., Silvia, P. J., Cotter, K. N., Li, Y., Hu, W., Martskvishvili, K., & Kaufman, J. C. (2021). Creativity myths: Prevalence and correlates of misconceptions on creativity. *Personality and Individual Differences, 182,* 111068. https://doi.org/10.1016/j.paid.2021.111068

Bol, T., de Vaan, M., van de Rijt, A. (2018). The Matthew Effect in Science Funding. *Proceedings of the National Academy of Sciences, 115*, 4887–4890. doi:https://doi.org/10.1073/pnas.1719557115.

Bonus, H., & Ronte, D. (1997)., Credibility and economic value in the visual arts. *Journal of Cultural Economics, 21*, 103. doi:https://doi.org/10.1023/A:1007338319088

Botella, M., Glaveanu, V., Zenasni, F., Storme, M., Myszkowski, N., Wolff, M., & Lubart, T. I. (2013). Creative artistic activity: Factors and stages based on interviews. *Learning and Individual Differences, 26*, 161–170. https://doi.org/10.1016/j.lindif.2013.02.008

Bourdieu, P. (1983). The field of cultural production, or the economic world reversed. *Poetics, 12*, 311–356. https://doi.org/10.1016/0304-422X(83)90012-8

Byron, K., & Khazanchi, S. (2012). Rewards and creative performance: A meta-analytic test of theoretically derived hypotheses. *Psychological Bulletin, 138*, 809–830. https://doi.org/10.1037/a0027652

Carabine, J. (2013). Creativity, Art and Learning: A Psycho-Social Exploration of Uncertainty. *International Journal of Art & Design Education, 32*(1), 33–43. https://doi.org/10.1111/j.1476-8070.2013.01745.x

Carson, S. H., Peterson, J. B., & Higgins, D. M. (2005). Reliability, Validity, and Factor Structure of the Creative Achievement Questionnaire. *Creativity Research Journal, 17*(1), 37–50. https://doi.org/10.1207/s15326934crj1701_4

Casadevall, A., & Fang, F. C. (2013). Is the Nobel Prize good for science? *FASEB Journal, 27*, 4682–4690. https://doi.org/10.1096/fj.13-238758

Choi, J.N. (2004). Individual and contextual predictors of creative performance: The mediating role of psychological processes. *Creativity Research Journal, 16*, 187–199. ttps://doi.org/1 0.1080/10400419.2004.9651452

Chung, K. H., & Cox, R. A. K. (1994). A stochastic model of super- stardom: An application of the Yule distribution. Review of Eco- nomics and Statistics, 76, 771–775.

Collins, A., & Hand, C. (2006). Vote Clustering in Tournaments: What Can Oscar Tell Us? *Creativity Research Journal, 18*, 427–434. https://doi.org/10.1207/s15326934crj1804_2

Cox, C. (1926). *The early mental traits of three hundred geniuses*. Stanford University Press.

Csikszentmihalyi, M. (1996). *Creativity. Flow and the psychology of discovery and invention*. Harper Collins.

Denissen, J. J. A., & Penke, L. (2008). Neuroticism predicts reactions to cues of social inclusion. *European Journal of Personality, 22*, 497–517. https://doi.org/10.1002/per.682

DeYoung, C. G. (2013). The neuromodulator of exploration: A unifying theory of the role of dopamine in personality. *Frontiers in Human Neuroscience, 7*, 762. https:// doi.org/10.3389/ fnhum.2013.00762.

Dollinger, S. J., Dollinger, S. M. C., & Centeno, L. (2005). Identity and creativity. *Identity: An International Journal of Theory and Research, 5*, 315–339. https://doi.org/10.1207/ s1532706xid0504_2

Dowd, T. J., & Pinheiro, D. L. (2013). The ties among the notes: the social capital of jazz musi- cians in three metro areas. *Work and Occupations, 40*, 431–464. https://doi. org/10.1177/0730888413504099

Dudek, S. Z., & Hall, W. B. (1991). Personality consistency: eminent architects 25 years later. *Creativity Research Journal, 4*, 213–231. https://doi.org/10.1080/10400419109534395

Duguid, M. M., & Goncalo, J. A. (2015). Squeezed in the middle: The middle status trade cre- ativity for focus. *Journal of Personality and Social Psychology, 109*, 589–603. https://doi. org/10.1037/a0039569

Dry, S., & Seifert, S. (2003). *Curie: Life and Times*. Haus Publishing Limited.

Eisenberger, R., & Aselage, J. (2009). Incremental effects of reward on experienced performance pressure: Positive outcomes for intrinsic interest and creativity. *Journal of Organizational Behavior, 30*, 95–117. doi:https://doi.org/10.1002/job.543

Eisenberger, R., & Selbst, M. (1994). Does reward increase or decrease creativ- ity? *Journal of Personality and Social Psychology, 66*, 1116– 1127. doi:https://doi. org/10.1037/0022-3514.66.6.1116

Elliot, A., & Thrash, T. (2002). Approach-avoidance motivation in personality: Approach and avoidance temperaments and goals. *Journal of Personality and Social Psychology, 82*, 804–818. doi: https://doi.org/10.1037//0022-3514.82.5.804

Feist, G. J. (1998). A Meta-Analysis of Personality in Scientific and Artistic Creativity. *Personality and Social Psychology Review, 2*(4), 290–309. https://doi.org/10.1207/s15327957pspr0204_5

Feist, G. J., & Gorman, M. E. (1998). The psychology of science: Review and integration of a nascent discipline. *Review of General Psychology, 2*, 3–47. https://doi.org/10.1037/1089-2680.2.1.3

Feldman, B. (2000). *The Nobel Prize: A History of Genius, Controversy, and Prestige*. Arcade.

Form, S. (2017). Measuring the Aesthetic Success of Books: Can User-driven Databases Fill the Gap? *Creativity. Theories – Research - Applications, 4*(2), 322–332. https://doi.org/10.1515/ ctra-2017-0016

Fraiberger, S. P., Sinatra, R., Resch, M., Riedl, C., & Barabási, A.-L. (2018). Quantifying reputa- tion and success in art. *Science, 362*(6416), 825–829. https://doi.org/10.1126/science.aau7224

Freeman, M. (1993). *Finding file muse: A socio-psychological inquiry into the conditions of artis- tic creativity*. Cambridge University Press.

Frith, S. (2001). The popular music industry. In S. Frith, W. Straw, & J. Street (eds.), *The Cambridge companion to pop and rock* (pp. 26–52). Cambridge University Press.

Fortunato, S. et al. (2014). Growing time lag threatens Nobels. *Nature, 508*, 186–186. doi: https:// doi.org/10.1038/508186a

Gallotti, R., & De Domenico, M. (2019). Effects of homophily and academic reputation in the nomination and selection of Nobel laureates. *Scientific Reports, 9*, 17304. https://doi.org/10.1038/s41598-019-53657-6

Gerber, J., & Wheeler, L. (2009). On being rejected: A meta-analysis of experimental research on rejection. *Perspectives on Psychological Science, 4*, 468–488. doi:https://doi.org/10.1111/j.1745-6924.2009.01158

Gilson, L. L., & Madjar, N. (2011). Radical and incremental creativity: Antecedents and processes. *Psychology of Aesthetics, Creativity, and the Arts, 5*, 21–28. https://doi.org/10.1037/a0017863

Ginsburgh, V., & Van Ours, J. (2003). Expert opinion and compensation: Evidence from a Musical Competition. *American Economic Review, 93*, 289-296. doi: https://doi.org/10.1257/000282803321455296

Ginsburgh, V., & Weyers, S. (2014). Evaluating excellence in the arts. In D. K. Simonton (Ed.), *The Wiley handbook of genius* (p. 511–532). Wiley Blackwell.

Glăveanu, V. P. (2013). Rewriting the language of creativity: The five A's framework. *Review of General Psychology, 17*, 69-81. doi:https://doi.org/10.1037/a0029528

Glăveanu, V. P., & Tanggaard, L. (2014). Creativity, identity, and representation: towards a sociocultural theory of creative identity. *New Ideas in Psychology, 34*, 12–21. doi: https://doi.org/10.1016/j.newideapsych.2014.02.002

Grosul, M., & Feist, G. J. (2014). The creative person in science. *Psychology of Aesthetics, Creativity, and the Arts, 8*, 30–43. https://doi.org/10.1037/a0034828

Hirsh, J. B., Mar, R. A., & Peterson, J. B. (2012). Psychological entropy: A framework for understanding uncertainty-related anxiety. *Psychological Review, 119,* 304. https://doi.org/10.1037/a0026767.

Haslam, S. A., Adarves-Yorno, I., Postmes, T., & Jans, L. (2013). The collective origins of valued originality: A social identity approach to creativity. *Personality and Social Psychology Review, 17*, 384-401. https://doi.org/10.1177/1088868313498001

Helson, R. (1967). Personality characteristics and developmental history of creative college women. *Genetic Psychology Monographs, 76*, 205–256.

Helson, R., & Pals, J. L. (2000). Creative potential, creative achievement, and personal growth. *Journal of Personality, 68*, 1–27. https://doi.org/10.1111/1467-6494.00089

Hogg, M. A. (2007). Uncertainty–Identity Theory. In *Advances in Experimental Social Psychology* (Vol. 39, pp. 69–126). Elsevier. https://doi.org/10.1016/S0065-2601(06)39002-8

Hogg, M. A. (2000). Subjective Uncertainty Reduction through Self-categorization: A Motivational Theory of Social Identity Processes. *European Review of Social Psychology, 11*, 223-255. doi: https://doi.org/10.1080/14792772043000040

Hughes, R. (2012). *Robert Hughes quotes: 20 of the best. https://www.theguardian.com/books/2012/aug/07/robert-hughes-quotes-best*

Hunter, S. T., & Cushenbery, L. (2015). Is Being a Jerk Necessary for Originality? Examining the Role of Disagreeableness in the Sharing and Utilization of Original Ideas. *Journal of Business and Psychology, 30*, 621–639. https://doi.org/10.1007/s10869-014-9386-1

Jach, H., K., & Smillie, L. D. (2019). To fear or fly to the unknown: Tolerance for ambiguity and Big Five personality traits. *Journal of Research in Personality, 79*, 67-78. https://doi.org/10.1016/j.jrp.2019.02.003

Jury, M., Quiamzade, A., Darnon, C., & Mugny, G. (2019). Higher and lower status individuals' performance goals: The role of hierarchy stability. *Motivation Science, 5,* 52–65. https://doi.org/10.1037/mot0000105

Jutti, S., & Littleton, K. (2012). Tracing the transition from study to a contemporary creative working life: The trajectories of professional musicians. *Vocations and Learning, 5*, 5–21. https://doi.org/10.1007/s12186-011-9062-9

Kahneman, D., Slovic, P., & Tversky, A. (1982). J*udgment Under Uncertainty: Heuristics and Biases.* Cambridge University Press.

Karakowsky, L., Kotlyar, I., & Good, J. (2020). Identifying the Double-Edged Sword of Stardom: High-Status and Creativity in the Context of Status Instability. *The Journal of Creative Behavior*, jocb.486. https://doi.org/10.1002/jocb.486

Karwowski, M. (2015). Peer Effect on Students' Creative Self-Concept. *The Journal of Creative Behavior, 49*, 211–225. https://doi.org/10.1002/jocb.102

Karwowski, M., & Beghetto, R. A. (2019). Creative behavior as agentic action. *Psychology of Aesthetics, Creativity, and the Arts, 13*, 402–415. https://doi.org/10.1037/aca0000190

Karwowski, M., & Lebuda, I. (2017). Creative Self-Concept: A Surface Characteristics of Creative Personality. In: G. J. Feist, R. Reiter-Palmon, & J. C. Kaufman (Eds.) *Cambridge Handbook of Creativity and Personality Research* (pp. 84-101). Cambridge University Press.

Karwowski, M., & Lebuda, I. (2016). The Big Five, the Huge Two, and Creative Self-Beliefs: A Meta-Analysis. *Psychology of Aesthetics, Creativity, and the Arts, 2*, 214-232, https://doi.org/10.1037/aca0000035

Karwowski, M., & Lebuda, I. (2014). Digit ratio predicts eminence of Polish actors. *Personality and Individual Differences, 64*, 30-34. https://doi.org/10.1016/j.paid.2014.02.014

Karwowski, M., Lebuda, I., & Beghetto, R. (2019). Creative Self-Beliefs. In J. Kaufman & R. Sternberg (Eds.), *The Cambridge Handbook of Creativity* (pp. 396-418). Cambridge: Cambridge University Press.

Kasof, J. (1995). Explaining creativity: The attributional perspective. *Creativity Research Journal, 8*, 311–366. https://doi.org/10.1207/s15326934crj0804_1

Kaufman, J. C., Baer, J., Cole, J. C., & Sexton, J. D. (2008). A comparison of expert and nonexpert raters using the Consensual Assessment Technique. *Creativity Research Journal, 20*, 171-178. https://doi.org/10.1080/10400410802059929

Kaufman, S. B., Quilty, L. C., Grazioplene, R. G., Hirsh, J. B., Gray, J. R., Peterson, J. B., & DeYoung, C. G. (2016). Openness to Experience and Intellect Differentially Predict Creative Achievement in the Arts and Sciences: Openness, Intellect, and Creativity. *Journal of Personality, 84*, 248–258. https://doi.org/10.1111/jopy.12156

Kaufman, J. C., & Beghetto, R. A. (2009). Beyond big and little: The four C model of creativity. *Review of General Psychology, 13*, 1-12. https://doi.org/10.1037/a0013688

Kim, S. H., Vincent, L. C., & Goncalo, J. A. (2013). Outside advantage: Can social rejection fuel creative thought? *Journal of Experimental Psychology: General, 142*, 605–611. https://doi.org/10.1037/a0029728

Knight, E. L., & Mehta, P.H. (2017). Hierarchy stability moderates the effect of status on stress and performance in humans. *Proceedings of the National Academy of Sciences, 114*, 78–83. https://doi.org/10.1073/pnas.1609811114

Knowles, M. L., & Gardner, W. L. (2008). Benefits of membership: The activation and amplification of group identities in response to social rejection. *Personality and Social Psychology Bulletin, 34*, 1200–1213. https://doi.org/10.1177/0146167208320062

Ko, Y., & Kim, J. (2008). Scientific Geniuses' Psychopathology as a Moderator in the Relation Between Creative Contribution Types and Eminence. *Creativity Research Journal, 20*, 251–261. https://doi.org/10.1080/10400410802278677

Kozbelt, A. (2007). A quantitative analysis of Beethoven as self-critic: implications for psychological theories of musical creativity. *Psychology of Music, 35*, 147–172. doi: https://doi.org/10.1177/0305735607068892

Lauriola, M., Foschi, R., Mosca, O., & Weller, J. (2016). Attitude toward ambiguity: Empirically robust factors in self-report personality scales. *Assessment, 23*, 353–373. https://doi.org/10.1177/1073191115577188.

Lebuda, I. (2016). Political pathologies and big-C creativity – Eminent polish cre- ators' experience of restrictions under the communist regime. In V. P. Glăveanu (Ed.), *The Palgrave Handbook of Creativity and Culture Research* (pp. 329–354). Palgrave Macmillan.

Lebuda, I., & Csikszentmihalyi, M. (2020). All You Need Is Love: The Importance of Partner and Family Relations to Eminent Creators' Well-Being and Success. *The Journal of Creative Behavior, 54*, 100-114. doi:https://doi.org/10.1002/jocb.348

Lebuda, I., & Csikszentmihalyi, M. (2019). Why Researches of Professional and Eminent Creators' Self Beliefs Need Social Context In: Lebuda, I. & Glăveanu, V. P. (Eds.), *The Palgrave Handbook of Social Creativity Research* (pp.585-593). Palgrave Macmillan.

Lebuda, I., & Csikszentmihalyi, M. (2017). Me, myself, I, and creativity: Self- concepts of eminent creators. In M. Karwowski & J. C. Kaufman (Eds.), *The creative self: Effects of self-efficacy, mindset and identity* (pp. 138–146). Academic.

Lebuda, I., & Glăveanu, V. P. (2019). Re/searching the Social in Creativity, Past, Present and Future: An Introduction to the Palgrave Handbook of Social Creativity Research. In: Lebuda, I. & Glăveanu, V. P. (Eds.), The Palgrave Handbook of Social Creativity Research (pp. 1-10). Palgrave Macmillan.

Lebuda, I., & Karwowski, M. (2016). Written on the Writer's Face: Facial Width-to-Height Ratio among Nominees and Laureates of the Nobel Prize in Literature. *Creativity Research Journal, 28*(2), 207–211. https://doi.org/10.1080/10400419.2016.1162572

Lebuda, I., & Karwowski, M. (2013). Tell me your name and I'll tell you how creative your work is: Author's name and gender as factors influencing assessment of product originality in four different domains. *Creativity Research Journal, 25*, 137-142. https://doi.org/10.1080/1040041 9.2013.752297

Lebuda, I., & Karwowski, M. (2021). The Personality of Nobel Prize Laureates: Differences Across Domains and the Relationship to Public Recognition. *Psychology of Aesthetics, Creativity, and the Arts.* https://doi.org/10.1037/aca0000412

Lebuda, I., Karwowski, M., Galang, A. J. R., Szumski, G., & Firkowska A. (2019). Personality predictors of creative achievement and lawbreaking behavior. *Current Psychology.* doi: https://doi.org/10.1007/s12144-019-00306-w

Lebuda, I., & Pieczyńska, M. (2018). *Emotions in a creative process based on interviews with well-known polis directors.* Presentation on Creativity Week in Webster Center for Creativity and Innovation.

Lebuda, I., Zielińska, A., Karwowski M. (2021). On Surface and Core Predictors of Real-Life Creativity. *Thinking Skills and Creativity, 42*. https://doi.org/10.1016/j.tsc.2021.100973

LePine, J. A., & Van Dyne, L. (2001). Voice and cooperative behavior as contrasting forms of contextual performance: Evidence of differential relationships with Big Five personality characteristics and cognitive ability. *Journal of Applied Psychology, 86*, 326–336. https://doi.org/10.1037/0021-9010.86.2.326

Luttenberger, F. (1996). Excellence and chance: The Nobel Prize case of E. von Behring and E. Roux. *History and Philosophy of the Life Sciences, 18*, 225–238.

Ma, Y., & Uzzi, B. (2018) Scientific prize network predicts who pushes the boundaries of science. *Proceedings of the National Academy of Sciences, 115*, 12608–12615, https://doi.org/10.1073/pnas.1800485115

Mace, M. A., & Ward, T. (2002). Modeling the creative process: A grounded theory analysis of creativity in the domain of art making. *Creativity Research Journal, 14*, 179–192. doi: https://doi.org/10.1207/S15326934CRJ1402_5

MacKinnon, D. W. (1978). *In search of human effectiveness.* Creative education Foundation.

MacKinnon, D. W. (1983). Creative architects. In R. S. Albert (Ed.), *Genius and eminence: The social psychology of creativity and exceptional achievement* (pp. 291–301). Pergamon Press.

Magee, J. C., & Galinsky, A. D. (2008). Social hierarchy: The self-reinforcing nature of power and status. *The Academy of Management Annals, 2*, 351–398. https://doi.org/10.1080/19416520802211628

Maner, J. K., DeWall, C. N., Baumeister, R. F., & Schaller, M. (2007). Does social exclusion motivate interpersonal reconnection? Resolving the "porcupine problem". *Journal of Personality and Social Psychology, 92*, 42–55. doi: https://doi.org/10.1037/0022-3514.92.1.42

Maner, J. K., Gailliot, M. T., Butz, D. A., & Peruche, B. M. (2007). Power, risk, and the status quo does power promote riskier or more conservative decision-making? *Personality and Social Psychology Bulletin, 33*, 451–462. doi:https://doi.org/10.1177/0146167206297405

Marr, J. C., & Thau, S. (2014). Falling from great (and not-so-great) heights: How initial status position influences performance after status loss. *Academy of Management Journal, 57*, 223–248. https://doi.org/10.5465/amj.2011.0909

McKay, A. S., Grygiel, P., & Karwowski, M. (2017). Connected to create: A social network analysis of friendship ties and creativity. *Psychology of Aesthetics, Creativity, and the Arts, 11*, 284–294. https://doi.org/10.1037/aca0000117

Merton, R. K. (1968). The Matthew Effect in Science. *Science, 159*, 56–63. doi:https://doi.org/10.1126/science.159.3810.56

Moulin, R. (1987). *The French Art Market: A Sociological View*. Rutgers University Press.

Mueller, J. S., Melwani, S., & Goncalo, J. A. (2012). The bias against creativity: Why people desire but reject creative ideas. *Psychological Science, 23*, 13–17. https://doi.org/10.1177/0956797611421018

Nobel, A. (1895/2021). *Full text of Alfred Nobel's will*. https://www.nobelprize.org/alfred-nobel/full-text-of-alfred-nobels-will-2/

North, A. (2016) *Why Bob Dylan Shouldn't Have Gotten a Nobel*. http://www.nytimes.com/2016/10/13/opinion/why-bob-dylan-shouldnt-have-gotten-a-nobel.html?_r=0.

Ochse, R. (1990). *Before the gates of excellence: The determinants of creative genius*. Cambridge University Press.

O'Hagan, S (2016) *Fascinating, infuriating, enduring: Bob Dylan deserves his Nobel prize*. https://www.theguardian.com/music/2016/oct/15/bob-dylan-deserves-nobel-laureate-literature-singular-talent.

Pénet, P., & Lee, K. (2014). Prize & price: The Turner Prize as a valuation device in the contemporary art market. *Poetics, 43*, 149–171. https://doi.org/10.1016/j.poetic.2014.01.003

Peters, D., & Ceci, S. J. (1982). A naturalistic study of the peer review process in psychology: The fate of published articles, resubmitted. *Behavioral and Brain Sciences, 5*, 4–17.

Petersen, A. M., et al. (2014). Reputation and impact in academic careers. *Proceedings of the National Academy of Sciences, 111*, 15316–15321. https://doi.org/10.1073/pnas.1323111111.

Philipps, J. (2011). Top 10 Nobel Prize Controversies. TIME Magazine. Retrieved 20.12.2020, http://content.time.com/time/specials/packages/article/0,28804,2096389_2096388_2096378,00.html

Pollock, H. N. (2003). *Uncertain science ... uncertain world*. Cambridge University Press.

Rietzschel, E., Nijstad, B., & Stroebe, W. (2010). The selection of creative ideas after individual idea generation: Choosing between creativity and impact. *British Journal of Psychology, 101*, 47–68. doi: https://doi.org/10.1348/000712609X414204

Roberts, R. J. (2015). Ten Simple Rules to Win a Nobel Prize. *PLoS Comput Biol, 11*. e1004084. doi:https://doi.org/10.1371/journal.pcbi.1004084

Sedikides, C. 2012. Self-protection. In M. R. Leary & J. P. Tangney (Eds.), *Handbook of self and identity* (2nd ed.pp. 327–353). Guilford.

Siler, K., Lee, K., & Bero, L. (2015). Measuring the effectiveness of scientific gatekeeping. *Proceedings of the National Academy of Sciences, 112*, 360– 365. https://doi.org/10.1073/pnas.1418218112

Silvia, P. J., Nusbaum, E. C., Berg, C., Martin, C., & O'Connor, A. (2009). Openness to experience, plasticity, and creativity: Exploring lower-order, high-order, and interactive effects. *Journal of Research in Personality, 43*(6), 1087–1090.

Simonton, D. K. (2020). Awards. In M. A. Runco & S. Pritzker (Eds.), *Encyclopedia of creativity* (3rd ed., pp. 111-117). Elsevier.

Simonton, D. K. (2012). Taking the U.S. Patent Office criteria seriously: A quantitative three-criterion creativity definition and its implications. *Creativity Research Journal, 24*, 97–106. https://doi.org/10.1080/10400419.2012.676974

Simonton, D. K. (2011). Creativity and Discovery as Blind Variation: Campbell's (1960) BVSR Model after the Half-Century Mark. *Review of General Psychology, 15*, 158–174. https://doi.org/10.1037/a0022912

Simonton, D. K. (2009a). Varieties of (Scientific) Creativity: A Hierarchical Model of Domain-Specific Disposition, Development, and Achievement. *Perspectives on Psychological Science*, *4*(5), 441–452. https://doi.org/10.1111/j.1745-6924.2009.01152.x

Simonton, D. K. (2009b). Cinematic success, aesthetics, and economics: An exploratory recursive model. *Psychology of Aesthetics, Creativity, and the Arts*, *3*(3), 128–138. https://doi.org/10.1037/a0014521

Simonton, D. K. (2004). Film awards as indicators of cinematic creativity and achievement: A quantitative comparison of the Oscars and six alternatives. *Creativity Research Journal, 16*, 163–172. https://doi.org/10.1207/s15326934crj1602&3_2

Simonton, D. K. (1998). Fickle fashion versus immortal fame: Transhistorical assessments of creative products in the opera house. *Journal of Personality and Social Psychology, 75*, 198–210. https://doi.org/10.1037/0022-3514.75.1.198

Simonton, D. K. (1984). *Genius, creativity, and leadership: Histriometric inquiries.* Harvard University Press.

Staff, D. (2002). Psychologist wins Nobel Prize. https://www.apa.org/monitor/dec02/nobel.html

Struyven, K., Dochy, F., & Janssens, S. (2005). Students' perceptions about evaluation and assessment in higher education: A review. *Assessment & Evaluation in Higher Education, 30*, 325–341. https://doi.org/10.1080/02602930500099102

Suls, J., & Fletcher, B. (1983). Social comparison in the social and physical sciences: An archival study. *Journal of Personality and Social Psychology, 44*, 575–580. https://doi.org/10.1037/0022-3514.44.3.575

Staw, B. M. (1995). Why no one really wants creativity. In C. M. Ford & D. A. Gioia (Eds.), *Creative action in organizations: Ivory tower visions and real world voices* (pp. 161–166). Sage.

Stein, M. I. (1953). Creativity and culture. *Journal of Psychology, 36*, 311–322. https://doi.org/10.1080/00223980.1953.9712897

Sternberg, R. J., & Lubart, T. (1996). *Defying the crowd.* Free Press.

Swann, W. B., Jr., Polzer, J. T., Seyle, C., & Ko, S. (2004). Finding value in diversity: Verification of personal and social self-views in diverse groups. *Academy of Management Review, 29*, 9–27. https://doi.org/10.5465/amr.2004.11851702

Swann, W. B., Jr., Rentfrow, P. J., & Guinn, J. S. (2003). Self-verification: The search for coherence. In M. R. Leary & J. P. Tangney (Eds.), *Handbook of self and identity* (pp. 367–383). Guilford.

Szen-Ziamiańska, J., Lebuda, I., & Karwowski, M. (2017). Mix and Match: Opportunities, Conditions, and Limitations of Cross-Domain Creativity. in: J. C. Kaufman, J. Baer, & V. P. Glăveanu (Eds.), *Cambridge handbook of creativity across different domains* (p. 18-40). Cambridge University Press.

Tajfel, H., & Turner, J. (1986). The social identity theory of intergroup behavior. In S. Worchel & W. Austin (Eds.), *Psychology of intergroup relations* (pp. 7–24). Nelson-Hall.

Taylor, C. W., & Barron, F. (1963). *Scientific creativity.* John Wiley & Sons, Inc.

Taylor, S., & Littleton, K. (2012). *Contemporary identities of creativity and creative work.* Ashgate Publishing Ltd.

The Royal Swedish Academy of Sciences (2002). *Press release.* https://www.nobelprize.org/prizes/economic-sciences/2002/press-release/

Tierney, P., & Farmer, S. M. (2011). Creative self-efficacy development and creative performance over time. *Journal of Applied Psychology, 96*, 277–293. https://doi.org/10.1037/a0020952

Tierney, P., & Farmer, S. M. (2002). Creative self-efficacy: its potential antecedents and relationship to creative performance. *Academy of Management Journal, 45*, 1137–1148.

Toynbee, J. (2000). Making popular music: Musicians, creativity and institutions. Arnold.

Tracey, M. W., & Hutchinson, A. (2016). Uncertainty, reflection, and designer identity development. *Design Studies, 42*, 86-109. https://doi.org/10.2307/3069429

Walters, J., & Gardner, H. (1986). The crystallizing experience: Discovering an intellectual gift. In R. J. Sternberg, & J. E. Davidson (Eds.), *Conceptions of giftedness* (pp. 306–331). Cambridge University Press.

Wigfield, A., & Eccles, J. S. (2000). Expectancy–value theory of achievement motivation. *Contemporary Educational Psychology, 25*, 68–81. https://doi.org/10.1006/ceps.1999.1015

Zajonc, R. B. (2001). Mere exposure: A gateway to the subliminal. *Current Directions in Psychological Science, 10*, 224–228. https://doi.org/10.1111/1467-8721.00154

Zhou, J., & Oldham, G. R. (2001). Enhancing Creative Performance: Effects of Expected Developmental Assessment Strategies and Creative Personality. *The Journal of Creative Behavior, 35*, 151–167. https://doi.org/10.1002/j.2162-6057.2001.tb01044.x

Zielińska, & Karwowski (in this volume). Living with Uncertainty in the Creative Process: A Self-Regulatory Perspective.

Zuckerman, E. W. (2005). Typecasting and generalism in firm and market: genre-based career concentration in the feature film industry, 1933–1995. *Research in the Sociology of Organizations, 23*, 171–214. https://doi.org/10.1016/S0733-558X(05)23005-7

Chapter 16
Exploring Uncertainty by Groaning in the Groan Zone: A Pattern for Emergent Conversation and Learning

Anna Houmann

Abstract This chapter will describe how educators can use uncertainty field books to explore students' experiences as they navigate in complex and uncertain knowledge and information spaces, to engage others, and to start, grow and sustain movements for change using the groaning in the groan zone. In describing the field book, method and practice, but foremost students' narratives, the chapter sets it up as one example among many of how uncertainty and possibility might be conceptualized and put into practice for change-making. In doing so I situate the field book as an interdisciplinary approach that encompasses and blends perspectives and ways of knowing largely from ethnography and design.

16.1 Introduction

One of my favorite hobbies is putting jigsaw puzzles together. I find great pleasure in trying different strategies to systematically or randomly assembling the pieces. One of my favorite puzzle experiences ended up in a reflection on uncertainties connected to puzzles, play and games in education. In a continuous search of new jigsaw puzzles I stumbled across the "Gold Box 'VICTORY' Jig Saw Puzzle" that had no guide picture nor illustration, but a label stating why. "To do so would destroy much of its absorbing interest. The greatest pleasure is derived from not knowing beforehand the subject which the Puzzle will make and then see the picture gradually form as the pieces are assembled". This wooden puzzle "with about 500 pieces" had no edge pieces, as you would traditionally see in a puzzle, all crooked and shapeless, as you would not traditionally see in a puzzle, no visual features, in wishy washy colors. I found it intriguing but quite overwhelming. Did I need that guiding picture?

A. Houmann (✉)
Lund University, Lund, Sweden
e-mail: anna.houmann@mhm.lu.se

© Springer Nature Switzerland AG 2022
R. A. Beghetto, G. J. Jaeger (eds.), *Uncertainty: A Catalyst for Creativity, Learning and Development*, Creativity Theory and Action in Education 6,
https://doi.org/10.1007/978-3-030-98729-9_16

This could, metaphorically speaking, be transferred to the uncertainty anyone faces entering into a situation in education, or elsewhere, where you are trying to make your way from point A to B. How much guidance do you need? Why? How do you tackle the uncertainty of not having a chart of the deep waters ahead? Do you start with edge pieces creating a framework or do you build your perception and knowledge from bottom up, from top to bottom or from the center outwards, or do just randomly put them in as you pick them up? Why? Do you need a framework? Are you sure it is towards B you are heading? How much uncertainty can you handle? Are you willing to explore it? How do you perceive uncertainty? Why? Then imagine you have all these quandaries, and then some, in and as a group. Regardless, welcome to the *groan zone*.

In knowledge work we need to manage for creativity – in effect, we don't want predictability as much as breakthrough ideas, which are inherently unpredictable. In any creative endeavor, the goal is not to incrementally improve on the past but to generate something new. This is where it becomes necessary to imagine a world; a future world that is different from our own (Greene 1995). Yet 200 years of industrial habits are embedded in our workplaces, our schools and our systems of government. How, or rather, can we change education where 'goals gone wild' (Ordóñez et al. 2009) stressing to reach point B in an effective and productive way? What if we threw everyone in the 'groan zone' (Kaner et al. 2007) and explored the uncertainty? Or perhaps, threw some gravel into the system to make us stop and groan for a while. As researchers and change-makers, we help people become aware of hidden dimensions, surface questions buried in deeply held assumptions, provide alternative perspectives and we ask what could be done differently. In such moments we grapple with uncertainty constantly, whether it is our lack of understanding the extent of complex issues or our partners in the project who are often unsure about what they are doing or how to do things in new ways. Acknowledging that uncertainty, paradoxically, plays a disruptive and generative role in our work, as we draw upon an accumulation of our experiences and thinking, and pursue how uncertainty can be embraced by turning it into focused enquiry and exploration.

Through this work I began to ask, what if we take uncertainty and put it at the core of our investigatory and change-making practice? This chapter does just that. This chapter explores uncertainty through the practice of using different models and methods focusing the groan zone. It examines how re-figuring the meaning and potential of uncertainty might enable theoretical advances and new forms of practice and understanding. Uncertainty, I argue, brings with it possibilities. It does not close down what might happen yet into predictive untruths, but rather opens up pathways of what might be next and enables us to creatively and imaginatively inhabit such worlds with possibilities. However, this chapter is not a naïve invitation to better world-making. Solnit (2016) argues that hope is not blind optimism, hence we need to have our eyes and our senses fully open "in the spaciousness of uncertainty" (p. xii) because hope calls for action. I propose that this action is a methodology that enables us to consider futures ad change-making as part of processual worlds of uncertainty and possibility. Change-making is thus seen as a form of intervention in a process that involves the opening up of many possibilities. In doing so a theoretical and methodological framework is created for the engagement of uncertainty through students' emergent conversations and learning as described in uncertainty field books.

This chapter will describe how one can use uncertainty field books to explore students' experiences as they navigate in complex and uncertain knowledge and information spaces, to engage others, and to start, grow and sustain movements for change using the groaning in the groan zone. In describing the field book, method and practice, but foremost students' narratives, the chapter sets it up as one example among many of how uncertainty and possibility might be conceptualized and put into practice for change-making. In doing so I situate the field book as an interdisciplinary approach that encompasses and blends perspectives and ways of knowing largely from ethnography and design.

16.2 Introducing the Groan Zone

Guilford (1950) distinguished two ways of thinking, divergent and convergent thinking leading to *the creative diamond model*. This model shows that as many ideas as possible must be created during the divergent phase, while later it must be narrowed down during the convergent phase. In short, divergent thinking is a thought process used to create different ideas, trying to explore as many solutions as possible, it's about expansion. On the other hand, convergent thinking is the extreme opposite of the divergent one. It is the thought process behind the ability to make choices, knowing how to select the solution that better fits the problem and problem owner (Simon 1956). This model highlights the fact that a complete creative problem-solving process requires not only the convergent thinking but also the divergent thinking in a continuing alternation.

Based on Guilford (1950) model, Tassoul and Buijs (2007) introduced an in-between step in the middle of the diamond. While Guilfords model only had divergence and convergence steps, the extended model includes a clustering part. Moreover, the model highlights the importance of having the clustering part separated from the divergence and convergence phases. Heine and Smit (2018) call this phase "reverging" and add that "clustering" is actually a technique to be used during this phase. In revergent thinking, ideas generated during divergence must be revisited and rearranged in order to "build a shared understanding about the content" (Heine and Smit 2018, p. 3). They believe that as it is the transition step between the divergent and convergent thinking, a change in participants' mood must be addressed. In order to perform the reverging phase, there are three golden rules that must be respected all the time to assist participants:

- Active participation: every facilitation session' participant must be part of the revering process.
- Responsive listening: during the reverging phase it is important to let participants listen to each other, instead of trying to reply.

- Move circular: the reverging phase in not linear, and it does not matter where to start but just to start doing the activity.

In the reverging phase, time is dedicated to let ideas grow on participants. Ideas which are poorly formulated, or seem strange at first, get more time to be considered by the entire group.

Kaner et al. (2007) also describes the importance of having a different step between the two others and introduces this step in the model *The Diamond of Participatory Decision-Making*. For Kaner this stage is more of a painful struggle process, hence called the "groan zone". A period of confusion and frustration is a natural part of group process and specifically decision-making. Once a group crosses the line from airing familiar opinions to exploring perspectives, group members have to struggle in order to integrate new and different ways of thinking with their own. Struggling to understand a wide range of foreign or opposing ideas is not a pleasant experience. Group members can be repetitious, intensive, defensive, short-tempered – and more. Sometimes the mere act of acknowledge the existence of the groan zone can be a significant step for a group to take (Kaner et al. 2014).

Within the concept of *game storming* the in-between-step is called the *challenge space* (Gray et al. 2010). After the opening and divergent act, with the purpose to opening people's minds, opening possibilities you need to do some exploration and experimentation. It is where the rubber hits the road, where you look for patterns and analogies, try to see old things in new ways, sift and sort through ideas, build and test things, and so on. The keyword for the challenge space is "emergent", hence also called the *emergent phase* (Gray et al. 2010): you want to create conditions that will allow unexpected, surprising, and delightful things to emerge. Within the community of *Art of hosting and harvesting* (2021) the emergent phase is found between chaos and order:

> Throughout the universe order exists within disorder and disorder within order. We have always thought that disorder was the absence of true state of order. But is chaos and irregularity, or is order just a brief moment seized from disorder? Linear thinking demands that we see things as separate states: One needs to be normal, the other exceptional. Yet there is a way to see this ballet of chaos and order, of change and stability, as two complementary aspects in the process of growth neither of which is primary. (Wheatley 2006, p. 23)

In entering into an inquiry or multi stakeholder conversation we operate within these three different phases. Emergence is high-order complexity arising out of chaos, in which novel, coherent structures coalesce through interactions among the diverse entities of a system. Emergence occurs when theses interactions disrupt, causing the system to differentiate and ultimately coalesce into something novel. If we are looking for innovative, new solutions we will find them in a place between chaos and order – containing and combining elements of both – called *the chaordic path* (Hock 1999).When people experience discomfort in the midst of a group decision-making process, they often take it as evidence that their group is dysfunctional. As their impatience increases, so does their disillusion and uncertainty with the process. Many projects are abandoned prematurely for exactly this reason. In such cases, it's not that the goals were ill conceived; it's that the groan zone was perceived as an insurmountable impediment rather than as a normal part of the process. The groan zone is a direct, inevitable consequence of the diversity that exists in any group. Kaner et al. (2014) further states that the act of working through these misunderstandings and uncertainties is part of what must be done to lay the foundation for sustainable agreements. Without shared understanding, meaningful collaboration is impossible. Groups that can tolerate the uncertainties of the groan zone are far more likely to discover common ground. Brown (2015) states that when we have no relevant experience or expertise, the vulnerability, uncertainty and fear of these firsts can be overwhelming. Yet, showing up and pushing ourselves past the awkward, learner stage is how we get braver. Exploring the reverging phase, challenge space, the emergent phase, the groan zone, is taking a risk opening up for vulnerability.

Understanding group dynamics is an indispensable core competency for anyone, whether teacher, facilitator, leader, or group member, who wants to help their group tap the enormous potential of participatory decision-making. Hence, to lead groups or organizations on the chaordic path we need *chaordic confidence* (Hock 2000), to have the courage to stay in the dance of order and chaos long enough to support a generative emergence, to rest in the uncertainty of not knowing before we reach new clarity, to resist the temptation to rush for certainty or grab for control.

16.2.1 Facilitating the Groan Zone

Facilitators, teachers and students use Kaner et al. (2007, 2014) model in many ways: as a diagnostic tool, a road map, or a teaching tool to provide their groups with shared language and shared point of reference (Houmann 2017). Fundamentally, though, it was created to validate and legitimize the hidden aspects of everyday life in groups. Kaner et al. (2007) see group facilitation as a whole constellation of ingredients:

> a deep belief in the wisdom and creativity of people; a search for synergy and overlapping goals; the ability to listen openly and actively; a working knowledge of group dynamics; a deep belief in the inherent power of groups and teams; a respect for individuals and their points of view; patience and a high tolerance for ambiguity to let a decision evolve and gel; strong interpersonal and collaborative problem-solving skills; an understanding of thinking process; and a flexible versus a lock step approach to resolving issues and making decisions. (p. xi)

In this sense, teachers and students could work as facilitators where they honor, enhance, and focus the wisdom and knowledge that lay dormant in most groups. Developing and articulating tools to further democratic action is essential to enable students from all walks of life to work together in more constructive and productive ways. However, a shift from conventional values to participatory values is not a simple matter of saying, 'let's become a thinking team'. It requires a change of mindset – a committed effort from a group to swim against the tide of prevailing values and assumptions (Kaner et al. 2007). A skilled teacher, or facilitator, helps a group outgrow their old familiar patterns. Specifically, the teacher encourages full participation, promotes mutual understanding, fosters inclusive solutions and cultivates shared responsibility. This builds on a faith that the wisdom to solve the problems at hand will emerge from the group, as long as people don't give up trying. It is an attitude that relates to questions linked to certainty and knowing that are highly significant, particularly to relationships between teachers and students where there exists a power differential (Shor and Freire 1987). Brown (2016) believes that we need to re-conceptualize universities and colleges as learning partnerships. "We have to all be learners, we have to all be teachers. We have to all be knowers and we have to all be open-minded inquirers" (p. 6).Once a group has expressed several diverging points of view, the members face quandary. They have entered the groan zone. They often don't understand each other's perspectives very well, yet they may not be able to resolve the issue at hand until they do understand each other. Even in groups whose members get along reasonably well, the groan zone is agonizing. People have to wrestle with foreign concepts and unfamiliar biases. They have to try to understand other people's reasoning – even when that reasoning leads to a conclusion they don't agree with. The facilitator's main objective in the groan zone is to help the group develop a shared framework of understanding. This is anything but easy. The greater the divergence of opinions in the room, the greater is the chance for confusion and misinterpretation. The facilitator should concentrate on promoting mutual understanding. This takes a lot of careful, responsive listening; at times, the facilitator may be the only person in the room who is listening at all (Kaner et al. 2014).

Whether the facilitator is helping one person stand up to pressure from others, or helping two people clear up a misunderstanding between them, or helping a whole group focus on the same thing at the same time, the overall goal remains constant: support the group to keep working (Kaner et al. 2007). A k a don't let the group give in to the temptation to make a pseudo-decision. Instead, the facilitator should help them keep struggling to integrate each other's points of view. Brown (2018) calls this "rumbling" in terms of having real conversations, even if it is tough.

Many facilitators, especially beginners, think their task is to prevent people from experiencing the pain and the frustration individuals and groups face in the groan zone. This would be a mistake. The only way to insulate a group from the groan zone is to block them from doing the hard work necessary to build a shared framework of understanding (Kaner et al. 2007). Moving through the groan zone there is certainly a lot of darkness in learning, a kind of trying to feel your way through. Facilitators have the ability to reframe the conversation into; "Look, this is a powerful experience precisely because it's so uncomfortable, and if you are really going to engage and put yourself out there, you are going to fail". Failure and feeling uncomfortable is not learning gone bad, it is not the opposite of learning. Discomfort, uncertainty and failure are part of the learning process in the groan zone.

> The quest for certainty is a quest for a peace which is assured, an object which is unqualified by risk and the shadow of fear which action casts. For it is not uncertainty *per se* which men dislike, but the fact that uncertainty involves us in perils of evils. Uncertainty that

affected only the detail of consequences to be experienced provided they had a warrant of being enjoyable would have no sting. It would bring the zest of adventure and the spice of variety. (Dewey 1984/2004, p. 7)

The process of learning, of moving beyond, calls for an inherent focus for the learner: "ordering the materials of his own life-world when dislocations occur, what was once familiar abruptly appears strange" (Greene 1997, p. 142). The contemporary person deals continuously with the transience of her life-world, of the manner in which she relates to people, ideas, art, and values. Greene's postmodern observations acknowledge that a human being may feel strange, disengaged, frustrated, and/or helpless in the face of ever-changing realities; and that a willingness to acknowledge the strangeness, the uncertainty, is part of learning. Facilitating the groan zone, in this sense, means to master the art of not disturbing the process in the groan zone or disturbing processes that are skipping or leaving the groan zone too soon.Honoring the groan zone, a new type of leadership is being called for in corporations, businesses, non-profit organizations, associations, schools, universities, communities and families (Petrie 2014; Lundquist et al. 2013). The participatory leadership. This kind of leader need to skillfully call important conversations and connect different perspectives to address complex challenges and to grow into our creative possibilities. As a leader you should be able to create opportunities where the essential knowledge present in even a large group or organization can be shared. This style of leadership generates fresh thinking and creates shared commitment to solving critical challenges in sustainable, inclusive ways. To be successful in an ever-shifting world the European Commission (through for example the VOICE project, Mazzonetto and Marino 2014), WHO (2016) and others, state that participatory leadership is shown when diverse groups are empowered and enabled to contribute freely in an inclusive, collaborative, open minded, adaptive, persuasive and receptive way. According to Hock (2000) chaordic leadership requires a much different consciousness about the leader/follower dichotomy. It comes down to both individual and collective sense of where and how people choose to be led.

> True leaders are those who epitomize the general sense of the community – who symbolize, legitimize and strengthen behavior in accordance with the sense of the community – who enable its shared purpose, values and beliefs to emerge and be transmitted. A true leader's behavior is induced by the behavior of every individual choosing where to be led. (Hock 2000, p. 21)

In this sense both chaordic leadership and participatory leadership is methods, techniques, tips, tricks, tools to evolve, to lead, to create synergy, to share experience, to lead a team, to create a transversal network, to manage a project, change processes and strategic visions. It takes time and effort to build a shared framework of understanding, and groups need different types of support at different points in the process. Facilitators who understand this will need to vary their technique to match the group's current dynamics (Kaner et al. 2014). However, there is not much literature nor research regarding the groan zone, leading also to a gap of knowledge on techniques to be used during this stage. The following sections aims to narrow that gap.

16.3   Inside the Groan Zone – Uncertainty Field Books

Akama (2015) describes how designing collaboratively with people (co-design) is to immerse in emergence and chance while attuning into "slippery, un-namable tones and expressions that can only be sensed through our feelings and bodily encounters in relation to other people, materials, and entities" (p. 262) so that we embrace that we are creating, transforming and becoming together among this heterogeneity. In co-design, we re-situate ourselves in interrelatedness hence the two letters of "co" in co-design signals "an openness to embrace the influence, interventions, disruptions, tensions and uncertainties brought to bear by other things and people. It requires the designer to step into the 'in-between' space that is dynamic, emergent and relational" (Akama and Prendeville 2013, p. 32). To capture such in-betweens both analog and digital brief-but-vivid narratives were used in this project. In spring 2020, 55 students captured their individual experiences of the groan zone in their respective *Uncertainty field book* (UFB) during a project conducted in groups of four to five students. A blended practice combining handwritten and video logs were used by the students at any given point during the five-week project.

In the project the students entered a space that was set to investigate and map the process in the three phases; divergent, emergent and convergent. During the project students used different games, models and methods to explore, examine and experiment, taking the role of the other (Mead 1934) with uncertainty as a focal point. The purpose of the project was to examine what it takes to consciously design and facilitate creative processes that deepens students' dialogue and leadership skills focusing the emergent phase, the groan zone. In this sense they were exploring the participatory and chaordic leadership, as earlier described.

Teachers in the project introduced the elements of design, mental frameworks to understand how to work with emergence and complexity, and techniques to support and disrupt the students processes. By designing games, during the project, the students then orchestrated the activities within their respective group to achieve the right harmony between creativity, reflection, thinking, disturbance, uncertainty, energy and decision making. Divergent, emergent and convergent were the core principles that helped them to orchestrate the flow and get the best possible outcome from the creative processes during the project.

The UFB's reveal that the three phases are perceived as different way of thinking and working that is complimentary and different. Some of the students used a metaphor and likened them to the phases of breathing: breathing in (lungs expanding/diverging), holding (emerging), breathing out (lungs contracting/converging). "The 'breath' of divergence and convergence is at the heart of our process design. Every process goes through several such breathing cycles so you would not have one divergent phase leading to one emergent and so forth. You would have as many as needed and group members would also be breathing different processes and phases simultaneously" (UFB, 2020:14).

The students describe the divergent phase, also named as pre-ject, as a "goal-seeking" phase where a clear and shared purpose gives the collective direction. A shared perception was that if you close the divergent phase to soon, the level of newness or innovation will be less. Ideally a group would stay in inquiry in the divergent phase until a new shared and agreed goal emerges and is seen collectively. It is non-linear and needs "chaos time" in the groan zone. It is process-oriented and needs prolonged decision time. Students described that hosting this phase well includes focusing the process, allow sufficient time, knowing that the next phases can go rapidly when this first phase is allowed to run to term. On the other hand, the convergent phase is goal-oriented and focused, linear, structured and usually subject to time constraints. It is focused on getting results and may require quick decisions. The students mention that this phase entails evaluating alternative, summarizing key points, sorting ideas into categories and arriving at general conclusions.

16.3.1 Entering the Groan Zone

After a period of divergent thinking, most of the groups enter the groan zone, but not all. Some groups were neither diverging nor converging, but instead doing both at the same time. Many UFBs describe that the members for example finish a brain-storming process and then, in theory, the group's next task seems simple: just sift through all the ideas and discuss a few more in depth. But in practice that task is perceived as grueling. Everyone has their own unique frame of reference, and com-munication can easily break down. Moreover, when people misunderstand one another, their behavior often becomes more confused, more impatient, more self-centered – more unpleasant all around. This phase of work is truly difficult to toler-ate. It is a normal, natural period – but it's still a struggle, according to the students. The effort to understand one another's perspectives and build a shared framework of understanding – this struggle in the service of integration – is defining the work of the groan zone. In an effort to avoid discomfort, end discussion, or just get to the end now, groups are often tempted to circumnavigate the groan zone by picking an idea, or a solution prematurely and develop it into "the answer".

> Some things happen when we don't embrace the uncertainty of the groan zone. We miss out on the truly important things. By prematurely closing a conversation, the essence or pattern of it often comes back. We think we made a decision, but the decision is questioned, and we end up in a new round of conversation about things we thought were settled, growing frus-tration and dissatisfaction later on. Staying with the discomfort just a bit longer might emerge a different idea or opportunity or a new understanding of where we are at. What if we became curious about where we are instead of wanting to shut it down? What might then emerge? What if we ask the question, 'what else is going on here?' What is underneath the conversation, the unrest, the uncertainties? (UFB 2020:24)

However, some students also describe this as the phase "where the magic happens". "It may require us to stretch our own understanding to hold and include other point of views. This uncomfortable stretch may feel messy, but it is also the phase where new ideas and perspectives emerges." (UFB 2020:5). Navigating the groan zone is an art of discernment in many ways and also a skill students develop, according to the UFBs. Even though it is hard or near impossible to explain succinctly where they are in their process – unsettled, a bit disconnected as a group, unclear about what all was bubbling. The next day things flow together, the group becomes more cohesive and new possibilities emerge. "I have a new story to share about the groan zone and the importance of staying in it in our process not prematurely attempting to assess the success of failure of a conversation, a training or a process. We don't just need to stay tuned to the groan zone, we need to be alert for convergence and good timing of it." (UFB 2020:27). To have the "magic happen" most groups had to navigate the groan zone with attunement, patience and awareness and whether they do it well or not, the learning is rich. Working through the groan zone it is clear that students articulate the initial state as a leap of faith. They fear that their "seeds" to new ideas will be misunderstood, dismissed or discouraged by others and thereby not revisited. Since engaging emergence involves the unknown, it is risky. "We would like to be more certain before we present an idea. Furthermore, our first impulse is to try to fit it into our existing frame of reference to make sure it fits with some previously set agenda and we miss out on getting new perspectives" (UFB 2020: 41). Facilitating these engagements or conversations was perceived more like stewarding or "hosting", allowing the solutions to emerge from the wisdom in this phase. In this process the students describe that they have used models and methods presented by teachers in the project such as the Cynefin Framework (Snowden 1999), Participatory Decision-Making (Kaner et al. 2007, 2014), Chaordic Stepping Stones (Hock 1999), Game Storming (Gray et al. 2010) and Art of Hosting and Harvesting (www.artofhosting.org). The Art of Hosting brings together a range of group process techniques: Peer Circle Process (Baldwin and Linnea 2010; Baldwin 1998), Open Space Technology (Owen 1997), World Café (Brown and Isaacs 2005), Appreciative Inquiry (Cooperrider and Srivastva 1987), and others, like Storytellling, Proaction Café, and Harvesting developed within the community of practitioners. Importantly, the techniques and practical frameworks are not owned by an institution or copyrighted. Rather, they come from an international community of practitioners committed to sharing them. Many groups have used these models and methods in combination and/or complimentary or as a point of departure to create their own, depending on respective process. Interestingly the students used them to facilitate in terms of smoothing the ride but also to disturb and disrupt the process thoroughly exploring the groan zone.

Half the battle seemed to be just recognizing that the group had entered the groan zone. Just naming the transition from divergence to convergence as a distinct, valuable, and normal phase helped to reassure many groups. One of the groups used masking tape to visualize Kaner et al. (2007) diamond shaped model on the floor which made it possible for the group to move around in the model physically. By asking "where are you in this process now?" they could individually take place in the phase they believed the group to be in and explore each experience more closely.

> Using the model more physically was a creative breakthrough for us. It gave us dialogue, collective insight rather than debate. We could define terms, unpack assumptions, explain thinking to bridge diverse disciplinary perspectives. Just by interacting this way we felt more comfortable wading into the groan zone's uncertainty and trust the process – and each

other – to carry us through to the other side. It also made it clear that some of us had already passed the groan zone, standing on the other side, impatiently waiting for the rest of us standing in the middle ready to explore. (UFB 2020:15)

Recognizing that they had a difficult problem on their hands, this group did not try to solve the problem in a meeting or two, rather they created a structure that allowed them to keep working for as long as it took to solve the problem, embracing and embodying the uncertainty of the groan zone. They saw that all members would have to agree on the final decision hence allowed them to survive the rocky start. They had to struggle to understand one another's perspectives, built a shared framework of understanding which allowed them to create a solution that incorporated everyone's point of view.

16.3.2 Creating a Container of Trust

Effective learning depends on solid foundations and strong relationships of trust and support between educator and learner and between learners (Vella 2002). When we enter an inquiry where we do not have ready or easy answers and we cannot see the obvious solution – we also enter "chaos" together. Entering the groan zone and maneuvering in the groan zone requires some thorough steps. Students describe in their UFB's that they have put much time into creating conditions that help contain or maneuver the chaos. They refer to this process as creating a "container of trust". In principle they create a container by agreeing on how they want to work together, defining some agreements or principles of co-operation during the emergence of uncertainty. These principles guide the process and serve as a touchstone to remind them of how they have agreed to act and decide together around their purpose. When the students enter an inquiry, they don't have ready or easy answers – they enter "chaos" together. In walking the chaordic path, creating a container of trust seemed to help to contain or maneuver in that chaos.

> Taking the time to create the container first seemed as a fantastic waste of time. However, entering the groan zone, it was extremely valuable to have these ground rules for communicating and behaving. It made it so much easier to be vulnerable and take risks using the chaordic path. And if needed we could always point out when people weren't following the rules. We had them posted in plain sight, so no drama, just a nod in the right direction and everyone got the message. (UFB 2020:22)

Many groups visualized their list of ground rules after a session of container building. Posted in the room they held their meeting in, groups continuously checked if anyone had something to add or adjust. Specifically, if something sensitive emerged in the group creating uncertainty (e.g. someone leaving, big changes or a group setback) groups revisited the container of trust list.

> Trust is conquered again and again by doing it. As facilitator I need to create circumstances through trust and a direction in which everyone should be able to live up to their full potential. As if I were a juggler the important thing would not be to catch but to throw in a good way so that someone actually can catch. And when the time comes, I need to let go. Trust

others and not let the instinct control what 'I know to be true today'. Trust the uncertainty of what might be and become. I discovered that my trust is a possibility maker! And still I find it so hard to let go of that control. Having trust is something that must be conquered again and again and again. (UFB 2020:11)

In the groan zone creating and maintaining shared context and strengthening relationships are the two main activities described in the UFB's. Advancing mutual understanding are described as acquiring shared experiences and language by surfacing background information and making efforts to put oneself in the other person's shoes. Great lengths went to enable people to think from each other's point of views. Hence the importance of getting to know each other by activities that support strengthening relationships within the group. A check-in is one of the most used in creating a container of trust described in the UFB's to help group members strengthen their relationships. Recognizing that they will devote most of their discussion-time to work-related issues, the check-in provided members with a gentle format for getting to know one another in greater depth as multi-dimensional human beings. A regular check-in was perceived as a solid investment in the long-term development of mutual trust.According to the UFBs the groan zone is the phase when the trust levels are low and the tension and uncertainty levels are high. Even though there was no shortage on activities to use during periods of uncertainty and misunderstanding it might not be so easy for student facilitators to obtain the group's agreement to do such activities.

I did not expect people to feel so challenged by my suggestions to do some activities to revisit and rebuilt the container of trust by sharing context or strengthening relationship. Someone even felt that the activity was a personal response to something they said or did. I think a least 40% of my activity suggestions were rejected. It was really hard to honor objections and ask the group for suggestions. In the groan zone ideas are frequently misunderstood – of course – mine will be too. What the group need is someone who trusts the process and the group members capability. Most of all the need my support and understanding. (UFB 2020:32)

In developing a container of trust the focus is on understanding perspectives. UFB's describe that the simplest way to help group members gain a deeper understanding is to encourage them to ask questions of curiosity. It could be as simple as saying: "Tell me more..". The task was to combine this with seeking out opportunities to strengthen relationships in order to counterbalance the struggles that might make the groan zone so painful and clear the uncertainty cobwebs. Broadening the context of working relationships allowed group members to see one another as real people, by creating interpersonal encounters. Relationship building strengthened the foundation of mutual understanding by clarifying boundaries, questions of reliability, accountability and integrity extending the most generous interpretation to the intentions, words, and actions of others. In creating a container of trust emergent conversations walked students from a place of curiosity, learning, and ultimately trust-building. As the group moved through the different phases the students circle back to these conversations as an intention setter and a behavioral cue or reminder to handle or rest within uncertainty.

16.3.3 Questions of Curiosity in the Groan Zone

Perhaps nothing seemed more important to exploration and discovery in the groan zone, according to the UFBs, than the art of asking questions in combination with curiosity. Covey (2020) defines his fifth habit as "seek first to understand, then to be understood" (p. 237) as a strategy to get engaged, to understand what and why. Because you so often listen autobiographically, you tend to respond by judging and then either agree or disagree, ask question from your own frame of reference, give counsel, advice, and solutions to problem and analyze other's motives and behaviors based on your own experience. Overcoming this takes a lot of self-awareness and a lot of intentionality. Students recognized that they had a tendency to understand people through their own egocentric lens and that they spend more time to fit their perspective into their own than assuming that they're seeing the world differently and try to understand it the way they themselves do.

> For me, and I believe also for the group, it was life changing magic when we started to really listen to each other's ideas and suggestions by asking questions and then...shut up! Getting behind the scene, by letting a person paint the whole picture without me filling in the blanks. To stay in that persons' narrative – moving around in that story. Still don't understand? Ask a better question. Questions. That's was truly the best learning experience ever and helped us get the most out of the groan zone. (UFB 2020:35)

Students used questions as fire-starters: "they ignited passions and energy" (UFB 2020:3), "created heat" (UFB 2020:16) and "they illuminated things that were previously obscure" (UFB 2020:39). A question is one half of a question, where the other half is usually unknown (Gray et al. 2010). If the answer is known, the equation is fulfilled, and we can draw a straight line from A to B. This would be the process answer, where we describe the path from A to B as series of steps. For the most part students described such experiences from previous schooling; the hunt for known answers or following a path of breadcrumbs were the process was smooth as "pre-chewed baby food, no chunky bits, no surprises" (UFB 2020:6). The uncertainty was imbedded in the questions of how to live up to the prescribed matrix. However, when the path from A to B is unclear, we have a different kind of challenge, and we need to face the fact that we don't know the answer. The answer in fact may be not only unknown but also unknowable. This requires a quite different mindset where the students' influenced their own learning which increased their responsibility of the same. In that sense, crossing the groan zone was perceived as a journey into the unknown, like "crossing a desert" or "sailing into unchartered waters". When you begin, it's impossible to know how near or far the answer – if there is one – may be. You are wading in uncertainty.

> It is just a matter of position, or an attitude of extreme curiosity. I would rather spend my education in the driving seat than the back seat. I don't mind asking where we are going and why or getting of track or loosing my way. But at least I have a chance to slow down when we get to a tight curve, put the pedal to the metal when needed, or just enjoy the scenery. I would be responsible for throwing the map out of the window and asking questions to my fellow travel companions or hitch hikers along the way. Teachers' enjoy the ride! The same could be said about our group. No backseat drivers, all asking questions about what roads to take and the untaken. (UFB 2020:37)

Students acknowledged curiosity as the feeling of deprivation experienced when they identified and focused on a gap in their knowledge. Hence curiosity can be uncomfortable because it requires uncertainty and vulnerability (Brown 2015). In the context of solving problems in the project, failure to be curios resulted in poor solutions, according to the students. In a sense curiosity, in the groan zone, meant focusing on the nature of the problem before even considering a solution. Curiosity was about listening and asking the right questions. Students used different sets of questions in the respective phases divergent (opening questions) – convergent (closing questions) and in the emergent phase, in the groan zone (navigating, examining, experimental questions).Opening questions were used to generate ideas and options, to provoke thought and reveal possibilities. Students describe good openings questions as opening doors to new ways of looking at a challenge: "you should just jump-start your brain! A really good opening question is a call to adventure!" (UFB 2020:43). To that end some of the students' body- and brainstormed questions about the emergent phase instead of ideas, withholding criticism and welcoming unusual or controversial ideas to work on later. Closing questions served the opposite function focusing on convergence and selection, moving towards commitment, decision, and action. If opening questions concerned opportunities, closing was about selecting which opportunities you wanted to pursue.

Navigating questions were used in helping groups underway by summarizing key points and confirmation or understanding of group alignment. When groups experienced frustration and drained on energy these questions were also used as a check-in entering the groan zone or in the groan zone: "Are we on track? Are you getting where you need to go? Are you feeling connected to the project? Is this a useful discussion to help us get where we want to?" (UFB 2020:28). Students also highlighted the risk of raising too many navigating questions as it might make people nervous if you expressed to much doubt. Often navigating questions were combined with other methods such as chaordic steppingstones which included attention to needs, purposes, principles, invitation, limiting beliefs, and implementation support.

However, sometimes, the students acknowledged that they hesitated to ask questions about each other's perspectives or the process because questions at certain times could be perceived as criticism. Another reason for not using questions was that it might create a deviation from the current track of the process or eats up precious meeting time. But the alternative – trying to proceed in the absence of understanding – ended up consuming much more time, according to the UFB's. As a fundamental key to asking questions from a perspective of curiosity was the level of participation and involvement of group members. Extensive discussions required sustained concentration and effort hence high levels of involvement pushed a group into the groan zone. Convergence and alignment together with discussions and questions about ownership and commitment required members to become able to think from each other's point of views, tolerate the tension that arose during misunderstandings with the added requirement to persevere until shared understanding and a solution that gained endorsement from all group members.

16.4 Omitting Verbal Feedback and Creating a No-Free Zone

In the stumbling moments just entering the groan zone, there were several moments described in the UFBs when the tedious and stiff conversations in the group led to people censoring themselves rather than risked being embarrassed by criticism. In acknowledging ideas there was a clear tendency to slipping into "supervisory, evaluative comments" despite their best intentions to avoid them. Hence collaborative activities tended to disintegrate. Students shared in the UFBs that they expected "first the good news, then the bad" because their past schooling and training experiences and described previous situations where they often pressured the teachers to go beyond technical feedback and give them "the real scoop", "the real story". Teachers who could not deliver "the truth" were considered weak, incompetent and left these students insecure and uncertain of their process and performance. On the other hand, you would have students describing quite the opposite feeling regarding this, tired of this "inconsiderate, fixed mindset" feedback culture just honoring the teachers' capacity to find faults. Rendering a student afraid of making mistakes.

Stone and Heen (2015) argue that we swim in an ocean of feedback; assignments, papers, tests, try outs, auditions, SAT scores, admission letters, swiping, work assessments, performance reviews, double blind peer review, just to mention a few. Analyzing the UFBs, written during the first steps into the groan zone, the conversations perceived as most difficult in the groan zone was feedback. Despite or due to previous experience, role models, training techniques, methods and models, the students describe how tough it was to give honest feedback, even when they knew it was sorely needed. Issues that went unaddressed for a while and finally were, rarely went well, leaving a group member upset and defensive, and ended up less motivated. "Given how hard it is to muster the courage and energy to give feedback in the first place, and the dispiriting results – well, who needs it?" (UFB 2020:21). However, students also described that getting feedback was not easier. The feedback was perceived as either unfair, off base, based on a misunderstanding, poorly timed and delivered or all too true. Another perspective was that giving feedback, following suggested models and checklists, resulted in a static almost robotic approach to the generated ideas. Some students reflected on why feedback makes such a conundrum:

> I thought long and hard about our initial conversations and how we responded to each others ideas, in a sense giving feedback on a multilayer level. The thing is when given response, the person receiving it isn't any good at receiving it, and when receiving it the person giving it isn't any good at giving it. It is not only what we say and how we say it. It resonates (or not) with our whole bodies and we send a clear, and yet uncertain, message just by raising an eyebrow. So, I ended up with this: who and what is the problem, is also the answer. I am. I need to become a more skillful learner. (UFB 2020:4)

Mastering the skills required to drive our own learning in the groan zone included recognizing and managing our resistance, engage in feedback conversations with confidence and curiosity, and even when the feedback seemed wrong, to find insight that might help us grow. But, according to the students UFB's, it is also about standing up for who we are, how we see the world, and ask for what we need. It's about how to learn from feedback in any shape or form. As the above quote describe it's well and good to hope for that perfect feedback, but don't put off learning until it arrives. In addition, according to the UFB's feedback sits at the intersection of two needs – our drive to learn and our longing for acceptance. To be accepted, appreciated, respected, to be seen fully, to be given the opportunity to live up to our full potential. Stone and Heen (2015) states that we can manage this tension by reducing the anxiety in the face of feedback and to learn in spite of the fear. It's about managing emotional triggers in order to take in what the other person is telling you, and being open to seeing yourself in new ways, especially in the groan zone.

> There is surely a cost of premature feedback formulated as criticism. I think we truly believe that we have been helpful in pointing out 'a flaw'. But the timing of a critical evaluation could make the difference between the life and death of an emergent idea. Rough ideas need to be clarified, researched and explored before we even start to think about 'loading our guns'. We saw a shift from people being discouraged, stopped trying, unwilling to share rough-draft thinking, practicing self-censorship to genuine curiosity about peoples thinking and ideas and by that accessing the creative thinking of the group members. (UFB 2020:11)

As a result, some of the students in this project found it necessary and important to explore omitting verbal feedback as a component in all or some of the different phases. The primary activity of the groups was planning and developing a project in pursuit of shared goals. Especially when learning strategies designed for higher-order outcomes, students needed to think through their overarching goals, as well as the specific objectives leading to them. Collaborative planning was essential if students were to divide the labor within the project. To the extent that feedback was evaluative or was perceived as evaluative, it was not meeting the projects original intention. Remarkably, omitting feedback in the process did not, according to the UFB's, depress student growth, rather greatly simplified the organization in the groups. In retrospect, it is not difficult to understand this finding. Learning to provide technical feedback requires extensive training and time and was unnecessary after groups mastered new behaviors and attitudes moving through the groan zone. The collaboration among the students of this project also exemplified the positive nature of feedback exchanged between students in response to ideas explored in groan zone. For some students, parts of the groan zone were perceived as a "no-free zone" in which all feedback should be stated positively, and all suggestions explicitly affirmed. For others, it was important to pass through this "no-free" zone into a level of comfort in which more candor about the viability of a particular suggestion was possible. In any case students seemed consistently opposed to unwarranted negativity and endorsed a positive, supportive approach to giving feedback. Though students couldn't be expected to agree on every proposed idea, giving each other's ideas a chance and sharing feedback in a way that affirmed one's group was an important part of building an environment that was comfortable enough to support creative activity. Some groups used a technique they named "15 minutes of fame" suggesting you should like everything about an idea for 15 minutes by using strategies such as "yes, and…" or "yes, what if…" before you started examining and exploring it. However, this technique did not imply agreement; it implied tolerance, making room for other people to express their ideas whilst the rest suspend their judgment. The attitude of suspended judgment is one of the most important thinking skills facilitators can teach their groups (Kaner et al. 2007). It encourages people to use their creative imagination in a process where the group set clear ground rules and a time limit. Opportunities to experience this was provided through formats such as "the trigger method" (VanGundy 1998), "brainwriting" (Geschka et al. 1976) and "turn and learn" (Brown 2018). By exercising suspended judgement and by modeling it whenever possible, a respectful, supportive facilitator created a relaxed, open atmosphere that gave fellow students permission to speak freely in the groan zone.

> I found it extremely helpful to use suspended judgment as an attitude and a catch phrase both as group member and as a facilitator and host in the groan zone. Never mind the method or approach of listing or emerging ideas using suspended judgment as a ground role in effect meant no defending, explaining, discussing or apologizing. Although there are clear differences in the specific games and procedures associated with each approach, suspending judgment remained the enduring grounding principle. Combining this with "turn and learn" where we shared input simultaneously helped us to overcome any halo effects in regard to who posted what idea. It really gave everyone a voice and a possibility to understand each other's perspectives. (UFB 2020:36)

Sustainable agreements required well-thought-out ideas that incorporated everyone's needs and goals. The struggle of the groan zone was at the heart of a sustainable agreement.

16.5 Propositions and Practical Applications – Promoting Discomfort, Disruption and Interruption

In a chapter about uncertainty there can be no final word. However, as this chapter hopefully has shown, uncertainty is an inevitable element of our lives and worlds. It can bring forms of discomfort but it can also inspire and invite us to move on beyond what we thought we knew to open up to new possibilities. Given the inevitability of uncertainty, I propose that it is absolutely necessary for us who work within education to be able to embrace it, whenever possible, with ways of moving forward and to build the capacity to depart from stagnant and normative practices that only perpetuate the status quo. Not all situations of uncertainty can happily be embraced by the development of strategies and methods outlined in this chapter. Rather I am suggesting that if we are always prepared for teaching and educating in forms of uncertainty that have the potential for becoming extreme enough to disrupt our existing assumptions this will enable us to fully participate in supporting students to become change-makers of their own futures.

Discomfort, disruptions and interruptions towards uncertainty, as shown, offer new ways to initiate and catalyze generative processes in groups, collectives, organizations, research projects and interdisciplinary investigations. I propose to nurture a culture of practitioners, equipped with an approach and orientation towards uncertainty stepping into unknown futures together, and to invite teachers, students and researchers to participate in its making. My workshop-based and field book explorations of uncertainty are propositions for its role in research and creative teaching practice. I suggest a posture or orientation towards uncertainty that treats it as generative and dynamic. Yet for uncertainty to play a generative role in education we need to also enable consensus around its form, use and appropriateness. In this chapter it has been demonstrated through the group's collective exploration, production, decision-making, sharing of individual stories, bouncing ideas, workshops co-constructed with student facilitators who actively shaped its content, structure and possible outcomes, through which various participants cross-pollinated ideas and imagination together. That is, uncertainty was productive when it was engaged (with) collectively and consensually. When planning and developing research and intervention that uses forms of uncertainty in this way, theses social, sharing and collective dimensions are significant to keep in mind.

This chapter has articulated the ways in which uncertainty is treated and the capacity it has to disrupt, invite surrender and move beyond, which is always contingent on specific circumstances and on the improvisatory opportunities that develop in relation to these. This also means errors, misinterpretations and serendipity are willingly incorporated as a central ingredient. In this sense I do not propose a template for other researchers or practitioners to copy or follow, but rather a set of principles and examples that are intended to inspire and aid in the shaping of the use of uncertainty. This means that the principle of improvisation is at the core, not only of what we expect participants might do during workshops and in field books, but also central to the work of researchers, teachers and any creative professional who whish to use an uncertainty field book. As such, the interdisciplinary applications of this chapter are manifold; engaging with uncertainty in a field book or workshop format is an approach that can be applied to explore any number of practical or scholarly questions, in particular those explicitly concerned with possibility, change, collectively and richer, more expansive ways to think about the future education. The principle of engaging (with) and harnessing uncertainty can play a key role in our learning about possible futures and change-making scenarios.

Another central theme of this chapter is emergence. This theme also reflects on what is produced by projects, and in this sense I propose thinking not of 'outputs', but of how such work can continue its presence in a dynamic and ongoing way to open to further interpretation, meaning and practice over time. At the core of this blended practice, which tended to follow the processes and to be imbued with their effects and affects, was the concept of the trace. This means that when we think of workshops as having impacts or outputs, these might not necessarily emerge in conventional or predictable forms, and might take time to gestate or become apparent. Instead it is relevant to consider how the traces of each event or activity might best be documented and then shared, and how different media, narratives and stories might become interwoven with each other. Moreover, it is significant to consider how to engage others in these stories, so that they join us in making traces through them, and continue to engage uncertainty to make change in education. The uncertainty field books contain multiple media that trace different elements of the project, including a series of performances that students produced based on their experiences and collective work at the end of our encounter.

Brown (2015) encourages educators to normalize the discomfort of learning and reframe failure as learning. Inspired by Brown I start all my courses and facilitations of workshops at the university by stating: "If you are comfortable, I'm not doing my job, because learning is not comfortable". It's a change, it's pushing against old ideas, it's challenging, it's claiming the space of uncertainty as the main learning event. In many ways, re-conceptualizing universities and colleges does, indeed, mean breaking with old quantitative models; however, countering this break is an anxiety that is driving people into what Dewey (1929/1960) called the "quest for certainty". Staying with the trouble, leaning into uncertainty by staying curious and generous when sticking with the messy middle of the groan zone has the potential to revolutionize and transform the culture of any working group.

As if the groan zone itself was not enough as an embodied disrupted practice some groups in this study experimented and explored uncertainty by introducing activities such as inviting group members to swap their smartphones. Swapping smart phones aimed to disrupt the members relationship with their familiar, reliable and somewhat innocuous technology by turning it into a tool to explore what is revealed about ourselves and each other. It also gave the opportunity to reflect on the role that smartphones play in the mediation and curation of lived experiences connected to uncertainty in the groan zone. It is interesting to note how the students, according to their UFB, developed a range of different strategies through which to cope with the activity while working with uncertainties of the groan zone. In this case group members negotiated different boundaries (go and no go zones) and improvised creatively.

As explained at the beginning of the chapter the aim has been to describe, through the uncertainty field books how uncertainty might be engaged in the groan zone, intervened to generate new forms of possibility. The examples discussed in this chapter were not always successful or manifest in the same way for all students. However, students' resistance, discomfort and disengagement were nevertheless valuable in learning about both uncertainty and its disruptive effects and affects. Uncertainty field books serve well for enabling people to reflect and improvise beyond what they already do and think they know. Yet it could be emphasized that every case of implementation is contingent upon many forces and factors that require mindful and reflexive approach. In pursuing a methodology that puts uncertainty at its center, we need to engage with the possibility of criticism and to take this as a basis for learning about what might be generated by uncertainty and about the questions' we seek to address through the process of making uncertain. Thus the impact and ultimate value of disruption in the groan zone came at different times for different people, but was ultimately generative of new ways of thinking about uncertainty and change-making.

Greene (n.d.) makes an outstanding remark, which very much highlights the central of the learning processes involved in the groan zone. "Even now it strikes me as one of those interruptions of the ordinary than can (if people are lucky and smart enough) lead to all kinds of revisions and renewals, unless too many folks are invest-ing everything in keeping things the same" (pp. 3–4). What if the struggle for mean-ing must be – always! – an interruption of the ordinary? What if the ordinary itself is always in need of occasional interruptions? What if meaning is the moment of interruption? Wouldn't that be enough to claim back meaning for everyone? Wouldn't that interruption be a way of releasing meaning?

In my view, education today must confront such tensions, as it must take into account the contradictions of this moment in history. In some way we are bound to find a mode of teaching that equips the young to deal with often unrecognized ide-ologies, provides some sense of agency, some consciousness of beginnings rather than closures. At once, we need to enhance our capacity to make sense of our own experiences, to enable those we teach to pursue meanings as they shape their own life stories, as they are aroused somehow to look through new eyes upon the world around, to listen for new frequencies, to heed shapes and nuances scarcely noticed before.

Dewey (1929/1960) spoke long ago about facts being dead and repellent things until imagination opened the way to intellectual possibilities; and indeed, imagina-tion has been called a passion for possibility. It signifies a summoning up of hereto-fore unsuspected alternatives, of road not taken, to unwritten letters to the world. Uncertainty signifies a new kind of authenticity, perhaps the return of a lost sponta-neity – an ability to retrieve meanings funded over time. Merlau-Ponty (1962) p. xxii) wrote that "we are condemned to meaning" and I think of students confronting endless ambiguities and negations, and seeking some way of translating this into a search for and, perhaps a recapturing a meanings. It may be an almost inevitable response to the crowding of contradictions, to what appears to be unanswerable. Engaged in this search, many of us turn to the several arts, not because Goya or Virginia Woolf or Toni Morrison or Mozart or Richter holds solutions the sciences and the social sciences do not, but an encounter with an art form demands a particu-lar kind of interchange or transaction between a live human consciousness and a painting, say, or a novel, or a sonata that becomes a work of art or may be realized as art depending on the reader's or perceiver's willingness and readiness to grasp what is being offered. A transformation of a sort – a changed perspective, a new mode of understanding the groaning in the groan zone.

Jigsaw puzzles have been around for nearly 250 years. An English cartographer named John Spilsbury created the very first jigsaw puzzle in 1767, when he chopped up a wooden map and challenged people to reassemble it. He named his creation a "dissected map" and it quickly became a popular tool for teaching geography. We often have a general sense of what is going on, what should be happening, by look-ing at the picture on the box – we just don't know the details. In an important way, we work backwards from solutions. Logically, we are supposed to work forward from premises, not backwards from solutions. But in real life, as in the embodied metaphor of the jigsaw puzzle, we often do not proceed logically. While as empha-sized, this chapter does not give templates, it does however present a mode of con-sidering and working with uncertainty. In this chapter uncertainty becomes a part of a comfortable environment, where students might flourish, rather than seeking to mitigate risk. They expose themselves to uncertainty rather than avoid it. It offers an instance of how individuals, as part of a shared environment, might experience uncertainty as part of a situation in which they also experience the possibility of personal gain and learning. While it is no doubt a facet of contemporary societal configurations, and a feature of global inequalities, uncertainty might also be considered to be a site for intervention, an element of process of emergence and as such an essential part of change-making processes, rather than something that change needs to be made to mitigate against. "To do so would destroy much of its absorbing interest. The greatest pleasure is derived from not knowing beforehand the subject which the Puzzle will make and then see the picture gradually form as the pieces are assembled". VICTORY.

References

Akama Y (2015) Being Awake to Ma: Designing in Between-ness as a Way of Becoming With. Co-Design: International Journal of CoCreation in Design and the Arts, 11 (3–4): 262–274.

Akama Y, Prendeville A (2013) Embodying, Enacting and Entangling Design: A Phenomenological View to Co-designing Services. *Swedish Design Research Journal, (1)*: 29-40.

Art of hosting and harvesting conversations that matter. http://www.artofhosting.org. Accessed 25 July 2021.

Baldwin C, Linnea A (2010) The Circle Way: A Leader in Every Chair. Berrett-Koehler Publishers, San Francisco.

Baldwin C (1998) Calling the Circle: The First and Future Culture. Bantam, New York.

Brown B (2015) Daring Greatly. How the courage to be vulnerable transforms the way we live, love, parent, and lead. Penguin Life, London.

Brown B (2016) Brené Brown Encourages Educators to Normalize the Discomfort of Learning and Reframe Failure as Learning. Wiley Online Library (wileyonlinelibrary.com). American College Personnel Association and Wiley Periodicals, Inc. https://doi.org/10.1002/abc.21224

Brown B (2018) Dare to Lead. Random House, New York.

Brown J, Isaacs D (2005) The World Café: Shaping Our Futures through Conversations that Matter. Berrett-Koehler, San Francisco.

Cooperrider DL, Srivastva S (1987) Appreciative Inquiry in Organizational Life, In: Pasmore W, Woodman R (eds) Research in Organization Change and Development, 1. JAI, Greenwich CT, pp. 129–170.

Covey S (2020) The 7 habits of highly effective people. Simon & Schuster Ltd, London.

Dewey J (1929/1960) The quest for Certainty: A Study of the Relation of Knowledge and Action. Capricorn Publisher, New York.

Dewey J (1984/2004) Escape from Peril. In: Boydston A (ed) John Dewey. The later works, 1925–1953. Southern Illinois University Press, Carbondale.

Geschka H, Schaude GR, Schlicksupp H (1976) Modern Techniques for Solving Problems. International Studies of Management & Organization, Volume 6 (4): pp. 45–63.

Gray D, Brown S, Macanufo, J (2010) Gamestorming. A Playbook for innovators, rulebreakers, and changemakers. O'Reilly, Sebastopol CA.

Greene M (n.d.) "Between Past and Future: The Becoming of Teachers College." Convocation address to Teachers College Columbia University. Typewritten MS. Teachers College Library Archive. Electronic access, https://pk.tc.columbia.edu/item/Between-Past-And-Future:-The-Becoming-Of-Teachers-College-A-Convocation-Address-(draft)-451?fileId=480. Accessed 25 July 2021.

Greene M (1995) Releasing the imagination. Essays on Education, the Arts, and Social Change. Jossey-Bass, San Francisco.

Greene M (1997) Curriculum and consciousness. In: Flinders DJ, Thornton SJ (eds) The curriculum studies reader. Routledge, New York, pp. 137-149.

Guilford J P (1950) Creativity. American Psychologist, 5(9): 444-454.

Heine K, Smit L (2018) The Creative Diamond revisited: Reverging, an essential transition step between Diverging and Converging. In Societal impact of knowledge and design: Proceedings of the 13th international conference of the international forum and knowledge asset dynamics 2018. IFKAD, pp. 1228–1244.

Hock D (1999) Birth of the Chaordic Age. Berrett-Koehler Publishers, San Francisco.

Hock D (2000) The Art of Chaordic Leadership. Leader to Leader. Peter F. Drucker Foundation for Nonprofit management. Jossey-Bass Publishers, San Francisco, 15, pp. 20-26.

Houmann A (2017) Do you Expect the Unexpected? Teaching for Creativity using Pedagogical Creative Improvisation. In: Girdzijauskiene R, Stakelum M (eds) Creativity and Innovation. European Perspectives on music education. European Association for Music in Schools. Helbling, Innsbruck.

Kaner S, Lind L, Fisk S (2007) Facilitator's guide to participatory decision-making (2nd edition). Wiley, San Francisco.

Kaner S, Lind L, Fisk S (2014) Facilitator's guide to participatory decision-making (3rd edition). Wiley, San Francisco.

Lundquist L, Sandfort J, Lopez C, Odor MS, Engelmann S, Bacig KZ (2013) Cultivating Change in the Academy: Practicing the Art of Hosting Conversations that Matter within the University of Minnesota. An Open Source eBook. Available from: https://conservancy.umn.edu/bitstream/handle/11299/155523/CCAoH_UMN_eBook.pdf?sequence=3&isAllowed=y. Accessed 25 July 2021.

Mazzonetto M, Marino L (eds) (2014) Voices for responsible research and innovation: Engaging citizens to shape EU research policy on urban waste. Belgium: Ecsite – the European network of science centres and museums. Available from: https://www.ecsite.eu/sites/default/files/voices_for_responsible_research_and_innovation_engaging_citizens_to_shape_eu_research_policy_on_urban_waste.pdf. Accessed 25 July 2021.

Mead GH (1934) Mind, self and society. University of Chicago Press, London.

Merlau-Ponty M (1962) Phenomenology of perception. Routledge, New York.

Ordóñez LD, Schwitzer ME, Galinsky AD, Bazerman MH (January 2009). Goals Gone Wild: The Systematic Side Effects of Over-Prescribing Goal Setting. (HBS Working paper Number: 09-083). Published by Harvard Business School. Available from: https://www.hbs.edu/faculty/Publication%20Files/09-083.pdf. Accessed 25 July 2021.

Owen H (1997) Open Space Technology: A User's Guide. Berrett-Koehler, San Francisco.

Petrie N (2014) Future Trends in Leadership Development. Center for Creative Leadership. Available from: https://leanconstruction.org/media/learning_laboratory/Leadership/Future_Trends_in_Leadership_Development.pdf. Accessed 25 July 2021.

Shor I, Freire P (1987) A pedagogy for liberation: Dialogues on transforming education. Bergin & Garvey, South Hadley MA.

Simon HA (1956) Rational choice and the structure of the environment. Psychological Review, 63(2):129–138.

Snowden D (1999) Liberating Knowledge. Liberating Knowledge. CBI Business Guide. Caspian Publishing, London.

Solnit R (2016) Hope in the Dark: Untold Histories, Wild Possibilities. Cannongate Books, Edinburgh.

Stone D, Heen S (2015) Thanks for the feedback. The Science and art of receiving feedback well. Penguin Books, New York.

Tassoul M, Buijs J (2007) Clustering: An Essential Step from Diverging to Converging. Creativity and Innovation Management, 16:16–26.

VanGundy AB (1998) Techniques of Structured Problem Solving. JohnWiley and Sons, New York.

Vella J (2002) Learning to listen, learning to teach. Jossey-Bass, San Francisco.
Wheatley M (2006) Leadership and the new science. Discovering order in a chaotic world. Berret-Koehler Publishers, San Francisco.
World Health Organization (2016) Open mindsets: Participatory leadership for health. https://apps.who.int/iris/bitstream/handle/10665/251458/9789241511360-eng.pdf;jsessionid=0C9728D2D2413E1DEF6BCCA0B31DB868?sequence=1. Accessed 25 July 2021.

Chapter 17
Creatively Confronting the Adjacent Possible: Educational Leadership and the Fourth Industrial Revolution

Sean M. Leahy, Benjamin Scragg, and Punya Mishra

Abstract In this chapter we explore the unknown possibilities that lie in the shadows of disruptions and innovations known as the adjacent possible. We frame the challenges educational leaders face when trying to prepare for an increasingly volatile, uncertain, complex, and ambiguous world that is propelled into the Fourth Industrial Revolution imbued with rapidly changing and unevenly distributed technological proliferation. Throughout our chapter, we offer strategic mindsets in design and futures thinking to combat the growing challenges of preparing educational systems that are rife with existing deep and complexly interwoven wicked problems for uncertainty. We propose that looking to the past, we can discover insights into meta-patterns and the ways we failed to predict the futures that emerged from previous discoveries and innovations. Using this frame, we discuss the potential of combining the interconnected mindsets of futures thinking and design, not to predict the future, but to prepare our educational systems for the uncertainty of the future.

> There has never been a time of greater promise, or greater peril – Professor Klaus Schwab (Hutt 2016).

17.1 Introduction

Human beings have a super-power, and that is the ability to make deliberative, long-term decisions. We plan, we strategize, we learn, we create models and stories, all with the goal of understanding the world around us, not just at this moment, but also into the future. But just as Superman has Kryptonite, our super power, our ability to prognosticate has its limitations as well. There are many reasons for this; some have to do with limitations in our cognitive capabilities, some with the kinds of networks and organizations we work within, and some have to do with the complex nature of

S. M. Leahy (✉) · B. Scragg · P. Mishra
Arizona State University, Tempe, AZ, USA
e-mail: sean.m.leahy@asu.edu

© Springer Nature Switzerland AG 2022
R. A. Beghetto, G. J. Jaeger (eds.), *Uncertainty: A Catalyst for Creativity, Learning and Development*, Creativity Theory and Action in Education 6,
https://doi.org/10.1007/978-3-030-98729-9_17

the world itself. What's more, some of these limitations appear as functions or out-comes of the very decisions we make and models we create. These limitations con-strain not just us as individuals, they constrain us collectively as well, as we seek to reorient and redesign organizations and systems to address future challenges. Taking our current educational systems as a case in point, we find ourselves challenged to reimagine and redesign these complex socio-technological infrastructures that *we* have created, to address the challenges of the future. This failure is of particular significance because the main purpose of education (and the key reason why we have educational systems) is to develop the next generation of citizens and leaders, individuals and groups who will live in, and will have to contend with, this emerg-ing future.

The philosopher George Santayana (1910) famously stated, "Those who cannot remember the past are condemned to repeat it." (p. 284). In other words, the "best" way to prepare for the future is to study the past and through that, identify patterns and trends, and then extrapolate them into the future. There is of course a fundamen-tal assumption here—that the patterns of the past will faithfully extend into the future. As we will argue, this assumption, if ever true, is not necessarily applicable in the tumultuous times in which we live. Further, we will argue that questioning this assumption is particularly important for educational leaders, given the future-facing nature of their work. The second decade of the twenty-first century continues to affirm that we are living through an incredibly rapid and volatile time of change, even beyond the global disruption of 2019's severe acute respiratory syndrome coronavirus 2 (SARS-CoV-2) and ongoing COVID-19 pandemic, which has laid bare the insufficiencies of our political, economic, and cultural institutions. While we paradoxically accept change as a constant of human existence, the pace and scale of the changes we face are wholly unique throughout human history in regard to our present moment. To give our present challenges an order of magnitude, schol-ars have described them as "planet-sized" (Gidley 2016) and even "intergalactic" (Heller 2018).

Our current collective context has been described as being volatile, uncertain, complex, and ambiguous, popularly acronymized as VUCA (Cousins 2018; Shields 2018). The VUCA frame is used extensively to study leadership and organizational dynamics and strategy across numerous sectors and facets of life (Cousins 2018; Shields 2018). We might think of VUCA as a context or state of affairs, but it also relates closely to a class of problems in the social sciences that have been identified as *wicked problems* (Rittel and Webber 1973). Such problems are characterized by incomplete or even contradictory knowledge, the wide range of people and opinions involved, and the inter-relatedness of these problems with other problems. Wicked problems are also characterized by their indeterminacy, meaning they also can appear without limit or clear forms of closure (Buchanan 1992). Addressing such problems (in fact it has been argued that wicked problems cannot be solved per se but just can be resolved temporarily) do not yield to approaches that attempt to apply existing solutions (Buchanan 1992; Zafeirakopoulos and van der Bijl-Brouwer 2018). It requires us to go beyond moving through a deductive or even an inductive form of analytical, stepwise processes that may have worked for other existing problems. Working to ameliorate such problems may require reframing them or refreshing our views on them (Fisher 2016; Pacanowsky 1995). In fact, articulating the solution is sometimes the only way to define a wicked problem. Examples of wicked problems confronting us today include financial crises, healthcare, income disparity, poverty, sustainability, and education. Recently, Levin et al. (2012) have identified global climate change as a kind of super wicked problem, where "traditional analytical techniques are ill equipped to identify solutions, even when it is well recognized that actions must take place soon to avoid catastrophic future impacts" (p. 123).

One of the key challenges in contending with wicked problems in this VUCA world we live in is uncertainty. Uncertainty, when defined as a "present state of not knowing, a future oriented inability to confidently predict what will happen in the future and a potential lack of clarity of how to make sense of past events" (Beghetto 2020, p. 1) illustrates the common understanding that feeling uncertain, or facing uncertainty is an unpleasant experience in which we as humans try to resolve or mitigate quickly to return to a more desirable state. Therefore, it is not surprising that understanding how to look for, embrace, and potentially leverage uncertainty is not a mindset or skill that comes naturally to most people. Learning to prepare for uncertainty brings with it an inherent assertation, often incorrect, that leaders or organizations know how to recognize uncertainty and where it comes from. Organizations, are often by their very nature, conservative and somewhat resistant to change. While uncertainty may be uncomfortable at the personal, organizational, or systems level, it can be a powerful catalyst for positive change. Beghetto (2020) suggests that by intentionally designing uncertainty into experiences, we can see uncertainty as a gateway to new possibilities and if we are able to suspend our inclination to quickly resolve or rescind the experience, it can become an opportunity to explore new ways of thinking and action. Later in this chapter we discuss *Futures Thinking* as a design strategy for educational leaders to intentionally engage with uncertainty through developing mindsets that seek out and discover emerging trends of disruption (including megatrends) that are taking place around the globe. Often when dealing with uncertainty, we only look to our own context: the industry we are in, the economic and psychological incentives within our spaces and so on. What is needed is the ability to intentionally cast a wide survey of new and emerging trends, thus providing us opportunities to make connections, and to imagine, and through that, explore and prepare ourselves for possible futures. It challenges us to think about how disruptions in one sector, industry, or geographic region, will impact our organization, our educational systems, our own lives. Embracing this mindset allows us to engage our imagination in thinking of ways to mitigate or leverage new opportunities in the future.

An important factor to understanding our own limitations in accurately predicting and thus preparing for our possible futures, is that we are emotional beings, and as such we ascribe affective states to our thinking. it's hard for us to think about our past (or future), without the corresponding emotional state that memory revives (or one in which we aspire to reach). This is a form of implicit bias, in which a person overestimates the intensity and duration of an affect based on their predictions of their emotional responses to a future event. This bias when employed to predict a person's future state is known as affective forecasting. Wilson and Gilbert (2003) discuss the role of impact bias in affective forecasting in which people overestimate the emotional impact of future events (positively or negatively). We are all susceptible to impact biases when it comes to imagining the future, especially our own future. Even now, as we turn our attention to the massive disruption brought on by the COVID-19 global pandemic, as we try and imagine our "new normal" in a post-pandemic world we cannot escape the emotional states we've experienced as a result in the shift in our behavior to adapt to the new routines required by the global response to the pandemic. Hammond (2020) provides an example of this bias at work in our everyday lives by proposing that we consider the future of our first train ride (or flight) or even first day back in the office after the COVID-19 pandemic is over, it is likely that we will use our most recent history to predict how we will feel about that moment. It is this impact bias that is subtly pushing our predictive thoughts to the forefront using our most recent (and potentially most heightened emotional experience) as the predictor of how we will feel although we may have taken hundreds of train rides before, or worked in the office for years, it is the most recent experience that drives our ability to predict the future. In the domain of education, this emotional response is often connected to a sense of familiarity with existing educational structures and experiences. "I went through the existing educational system and I turned out ok" is a sentiment often heard when people seek to bring transformative changes to education. This is an emotional response, connected to a sense of the familiar and distrust of change.

While we as humans may be bad at predicting our own futures, and our collective lives full of wicked problems stemming from an accelerating volatile, uncertain, complex, and ambiguous world–all hope is not lost. There is great value in our experiences with uncertainty. For it is uncertainty that becomes the shadows of the disruptions and innovations that propel our societies forward. And it is within these shadows, where the adjacent futures lie, a product of the unintended or unforeseen possibilities made possible with the arrival of a seemingly unconnected advancement or occurrence in our world. Learning to understand the multitude of explored and yet-to-be imagined ways these events will shape our futures, we can open our minds to the creative and imaginative process of exploring not just what may be–but what could be. While it might seem counterintuitive at first to discuss the benefits of uncertainty, throughout this chapter we explore the potential and the exciting possibilities that can immerge from the relationship between uncertainty and creativity. By viewing this relationship through a lens of the possible as a form of inquiry (Glaveanu 2018), the conditions combining our cognitive processes on determining the differences between the possible and the actual, and the sociocultural position of the possible (that exist outside of the individual) present an opportunity to leverage multiple perspectives that allow for (or even create) a space for novelty, creativity, and action. When thinking of "the possible" we often think forward in time (relating to the "possible future") but this is only just one instantiation of "the possible", that may coexist cognitively alongside possible worlds, pasts, and even possible selves. For us to leverage the creativity that is born of the possible, we must explore the multitude of perspectives that are at play within any system. Glaveanu (2018) argues that to experience the possible (in all its forms) "one needs to become aware of the differences in perspective and of the fact that we all live, as human beings, in a per-spectival world" (p. 527). It is from these lessons, that we can learn to stretch our understanding of "what might be" as we consider the rapidly approaching epoch of technological innovations on the horizon within the Fourth Industrial Revolution, and how educational leaders can prepare for the uncertainty this era will bring. This requires leveraging an imaginative design process and futures thinking mindset. Finally, it is important that as we turn our attention towards preparing for the future, we look to our past to learn how groundbreaking innovations paved the way for other advancements and innovations that we never could have imaged possible.

17.2 Looking Back, to Look Forward (Through a Lens Darkly)

There are two ways of looking back at the past, to understand and prepare for the future. The first, as we have written above, is to identify patterns and trends in the past and present and to simplistically extrapolate them into the future. This may work in certain stable contexts but is less reliable as a strategy in the VUCA contexts we live in today. The other approach, more diffident in its projections, but maybe more appropriate given the inherent uncertainty in VUCA contexts is to identify *meta-patterns*, and ways in which we would have failed to predict the futures that emerged. This is, what we call, an acceptance and exploration of the adjacent pos-sible. There is humility in this approach, suggesting that it is more important to accept uncertainty and to be prepared for its disruptive nature. As Robert Burns wrote, "The best-laid schemes of mice and men, go oft awry" (Burns et al. 1991, p. 228) and recognizing that, and building off from it may be the way to go.

As a global society, we have undergone three industrial revolutions that have led the collective human race through the transition of handmade goods to manufactur-ing, steam power to electricity, microprocessors to cloud computing, brought to fruition the globalization of people and ideas, and ushered the human race into the information age. Each industrial era brought with it new innovations which led to shifts in the economic capability, society, and the movement of people and ideas. Grasping the extent and scope of these changes is challenging, particularly as we look to what has been described as the approaching Fourth Industrial Revolution (4IR). In this context it may be useful, as an intellectual exercise, to step back and look at the impact of *one* technology and how it has played out across time. It will demonstrate, that even in this narrower, truncated context, just how difficult it is to predict the kinds of impact a new technology, as it plays out over time, can and will have on our lives. As computer scientist Roy Amara said, (in a quote often mis-attributed to range of other people, including, but not limited to, Peter Drucker and Bill Gates), "we overestimate the impact of technology in the short-term and underestimate the effect in the long run" (Ratcliffe 2016). In other words, the effects of particular technologies on cognition, knowledge, and society at large often are subtle and complexly woven (Salomon 1979). Cause-effect relationships are difficult to tease out. Moreover, these effects often are not immediately appreciated, but rather, show their influence on far longer time scales— decades or maybe even centuries.

For instance, consider the invention of the printing press—arguably one of the most significant technological advances of human cultural evolution. It allowed for mass literacy, and in some ways, it can be argued that, our educational system is built around the "book." The "book" and the ability it provided to inscribe and share ideas in a concrete form is what led to the renaissance, the reformation, the scientific revolution. By democratizing access to information and knowledge, the book, challenged authority, and popularized ideas such as "all men [sic] are created equal,' or "man [sic] is born free, but he is everywhere in chains" leading to transformative social change, the impact of which we feel even today.

But the impact of print technologies is more complex and greater reaching than even that—in ways big and small. One of the unintended consequences of the invention of printing was that many people realized they had poor eyesight. That had not previously been an issue because masses of people had not needed to peer at small print on a page by candlelight. Within decades after the invention of the printing press, lens makers were making spectacles and it became a booming business across Europe. A side effect of this growth of interest in glass and its refractory properties led innovators to play and experiment with them and discover new and alternative uses for lenses. And it was that undirected play, with pieces of polished glass, that led to the invention of the microscope and the telescope. With those new innovations, suddenly the infinities of the very small and the very large became revealed to us and transformed how we looked at the world and our place in it.

Furthermore, scholars of technology have argued that the influence of media can manifest itself in even more subtle ways. For instance, it has been argued that the impact of media can be best understood in the manner in which different media *prefigure* processes and structures (cognitive and social) in different ways. And it this *prefiguration* that led to the dramatic changes in all aspects of social, cultural, political and social life in Europe and, in ever expanding circles, across the world (Bolter 1990; Eisenstein 1980; McLuhan 1962, 1964; Ong 1982; Provenzo 1986). This argument is based on the idea that, as Mishra et al. (1996) write:

> Most of the significant effects of the invention and spread of print can be traced to certain specific properties of print media: In particular, print created objects that were *mobile, immutable, presentable, and readable;* and these properties led to fundamental changes in human cognition (Latour, 1990). These properties ensure (or seemed to ensure) that discussions could be carried beyond the conversational arena, that ideas could be transported without change in their essential nature, and that they could be universally and consistently understood (at least by those who knew the conventions) in a way that more mutable, "unreliable" oral re-tellings could not. The crucial argument here is that initially it was the medium, this new fixed object, that was immutable. Then the idea of immutability passed on from the medium to the message, with attendant implications of accuracy, fixedness, and truthfulness. (p. 289).

A few of the consequences of this transference of properties from the medium to the message were that it solidified the notion of ownership of ideas and the convention that arguments could be settled by invoking the appropriate text, that ideas could be "owned" and more. This is of course in sharp contrast to an oral culture, where meanings were deeply connected to speech, with no external arbitrator or authority. This idea, that the impact of a new technology or medium goes beyond the content being distributed is best captured by McLuhan's pithy quote: "the medium is the message." According to McLuhan (1964) "the 'message' of any medium or technology is the change of scale or pace or pattern that it introduces into human affairs" (p. 1). For any technology, the potential "message" it brings may have enormous impact on human affairs, even if the original intended content of that medium may only have a limited, or narrow scope of impact. McLuhan illustrates this potential (in an intentionally exaggerated claim) that when considering the power of the "message" that is brought with the advent of electric light, he argues that brain surgery and night baseball are both examples of the "content" of that electric light, and without the advent of the electric light, neither example would be possible (McLuhan 1964, p. 2). It is this deeper exploration of the power of an innovation or disruption that brings with it the inherent uncertainty of what else may be possible. What future possibility lies in the shadows of a new invention waiting to be discovered, what adjacent future is hiding in plain sight?

The advent of the Internet, and most importantly of social media, is another example of this phenomenon. In many ways social media is more akin to an oral culture than one solely based on print. We can see the relative unraveling of the ways of thinking and being that were based on a print culture as we move into a social media dominated world. We are confronting the consequences of this shift in technology at that very moment across the world. The key question of course, is what impact this will have on us in the long run, and what we can predict about the uncertainty it will bring? If anything, the complex history of print and the inherent uncertainty of its evolution and impact nudges us towards humility. This uncertainty, of course, does not mean that we don't prepare for the future, rather that we ought to do it without arrogance and by eschewing simplistic, cause-effect relationships.

This extended digression of the impact of information technologies– not just on society but on the very way we think and act in the world is what we call the *adjacent possible*. Author Steven Johnson (2014) borrowed the idea of the adjacent possible from theoretical biologist Stuart Kaufmann, and gave the construct that we build on in this chapter. Johnson (2010) writes:

> The adjacent possible is a kind of shadow future, hovering on the edges of the present state of things, a map of all the ways in which the present can reinvent itself... What the adjacent possible tells us is that at any moment the world is capable of extraordinary change, but only certain changes can happen. (p. 31).

An interesting difference to note about adjacent possibilities compared to longer more future-oriented possibilities, is that while a future oriented possibility may require a very specific occurrence of many interconnected stepwise possibilities to transpire, adjacent possibilities are the literal "ready-at-hand" possibilities for any current state. Björneborn (2020) defines adjacent possibles as "actual" possibilities that "constitute what actually is possible for a specific entity with specific capabilities in a specific setting at a specific time" (p. 11).

In summary, it is clear that with any new technology, innovation, or disruption, there lies an uncertainty within its shadows that can hold potential benefits, or even harms to human society. Uncertainty is all around us, and is ever present as we peer to the horizon. It is with this knowledge that we turn to thinking about the future, and how to handle the uncertainty it brings. *We think not in terms of predicting the future, but in preparing for it.* In short, we argue that predicting the future is a business best left to charlatans, for the rest of us, we shall work towards preparing for uncertainty. And, that requires a combination of strategy *and* creativity, particularly as we explore the implications of the next epoch of transformative advancements that are coming into reality at this very moment: what has been hailed as the Fourth Industrial Revolution.

17.3 Coming Soon, to a World Near You: The Fourth Industrial Revolution

As a global society, we now find ourselves on the precipice of the Fourth Industrial Revolution (4IR), which the World Economic Forum defines as "a range of new technologies that are fusing the physical, digital and biological worlds, impacting all disciplines, economies and industries, and even challenging ideas about what it means to be human" (Schwab n.d.).

To gain some perspective on these claims about the potential impact of the 4IR, it may help to revisit some of the effects (some of which are just beginning to be felt) of the Third Industrial Revolution. This industrial revolution which is sometimes referred to as the "digital" revolution was the era of the twentieth century that brought innovations such as the microprocessor, digital communications, and perhaps most prolific (from a global scale) the Internet. Looking at these innovations, each one of us can trace some element of our modern conveniences and our workflows to the digital transformations made possible by this Third Industrial Revolution. When we start to look more specifically at the system of education, we can draw even more lines of connection between digital innovations and the educational environments and opportunities afforded by those inventions, online learning for example. A now seemingly robust (if not a commodity) learning modality amongst higher education institutions. Access to higher education is another major effect of the collective advancements made in the Third Industrial Revolution. According to Penprase (2018) the population that had access to higher education in the United States rose from a mere 4% in 1900 to almost 70% a century later in 2000. Penprase also argues that through these advancements in digital technologies higher education institutions have been able to reach a more diverse student population that improve the traditional learning experiences through online learning, videoconferencing, and leveraging the traditional experience by offering hybrid learning environments. These impacts can be seen around the world currently, in the global response to the COVID-19 pandemic. With universities and K-12 school systems moving to fully online, hybrid, or some other combination of in-person and remote learning has enabled the educational process to continue across regions (national or local) where traditional in-person learning experiences are not safe.

As we turn our attention back to the 4IR, we can start to imagine how this new epoch of innovations and disruptions might change the way we think about education and learning. Thinking into the futures about the potential use of mature technologies that are only in their nascent stages of development today such as artificial intelligence (AI), extended reality (XR), nanotechnologies, and smart materials (to name just a few), it can be easy to get excited about the transformational possibilities. In a short essay that reimagines the futures of lifelong learning through an augmented human-cybernetic experience the reader is prompted to visualize the adjacent future of these emerging technologies that allow for a completely redefined learning environment, one that is reminiscent of a distributed-computing model, where the learning no longer takes place in the center (traditional educational model) but at the learner themselves (or the "edge") made possible by truly intelligent individualized tutoring systems (Leahy n.d.). This imagined future recounts the possibilities afforded to the learner when all spaces (physical) and technologies are aligned to provide the user with the preferred just-in-time learning and experiences, that the individual needs to progress in their personally defined learning goals. However fun and exciting this imagined future can be, we would be remiss if we did not take a moment to secure our feet to a healthy foundation of skepticism. This is not the first time in our history that we have been promised an era of transformational technological innovations that will reshape our educational institutions. In fact, we can point to nearly a century of lofty claims and predictions about the revolutionary changes a new technological innovation would have on education, only to experience weak or ineffectual realizations of the overhyped promise, yet the 4IR claims to be different. Previous examination of emerging technologies shaping the beginning of the 4IR has proposed a futures studies methodology to critically examine and challenge the assumptions of technologically proposed futures and suggests that new emergent pedagogical approaches may be more influential in informing the futures of education than technological advances alone (Leahy et al. 2019).

17.3.1 Three Pressing Challenges

The 4IR brings many lofty claims about the potential for advancement and innovation of converged digital, biological, and virtual systems on the collective human experience. Yet even at present time we cannot ignore that in parts around the world the advantages and impacts of the previous three industrial revolutions have not yet been fully realized. If we consider the futures of the 4IR, and the rapid innovation of technological advancements we must also consider our ability to adequately adapt our societies and institutions at a macro-level, as well our own norms and behaviors at a micro-level, to handle the powerful new technologies that may be just around the corner, or lurking in the shadows of the adjacent possible of tomorrow. It could be argued today, that as a society, we have not yet been able to control the power of social media or the new found power of big data and predictive analytics we've only just begun to explore in the information age. So how then can we be prepared for the next wave of disruptions that are said to outpace any previous innovations in human history? If we look to the futures of the 4IR, we must consider the challenges it represents alongside the potential for untold advancements in the human condition. In their book, Schwab and Davis (2018) propose three pressing global challenges that we must rise to meet to create a more inclusive and equitable future which we will discuss in turn, along with their implications for our educational systems: fair distribution, externalities of risk, and human-centric approach. Taking each in turn:

Fair distribution: Historically, the benefits of all three previous industrial revolutions, have not been equally and fairly distributed. In fact, it is clear that they still are not equally distributed even today. As inequities rise around the globe, the wealthiest portions of the population continue to reap the economic benefits of new innovations and advancements in access, wealth, and healthcare. This challenge, when viewed through the educational system, is all the more pressing. The educational system is no stranger to inequities of access, in fact this is still a major issue across the U.S. (and the world) at all levels. This of course raises the question of how we can prepare for the uncertainties that will arise with the onslaught of faster technological innovations, disruptions, and convergences? Schwab and Davis (2018) point out that this issue of fair distribution is far more than a moral or ethical challenge, but one that may have far reaching consequences. They write that, "the failure of many democratic systems to address disparities in wealth or opportunity stemming from their prevailing ecological models has led to entrenched social and economic imbalances that are both divisive and destabilizing" (p. 52). These ideas lead us to also consider the adjacent futures, such as what will happen to the world economic labor force when these promised advances in technology replace the human workforce. What happens to a society where the labor force is reduced or replaced by automation or AI? What does the educational system look like if there are fewer economic opportunities to prepare for? It is in this context that ideas such as Universal Basic Income (UBI) have been raised though it has mixed support. Proponents argue it that UBI will stabilize and ensure a healthy citizenry to the critics who argue it proves a disincentive to work (Parolin and Siöland 2019). All of these have significant educational implications.

Externalities of risk: Schwab and Davis (2018) argue that in the past not enough effort was devoted to protect "vulnerable populations, the natural environment and future generations from suffering as a result of unintended consequences, costs of change, second-order impacts or deliberate misuse of new capabilities" (p. 13). Looking at this challenge from the lens of educational systems, we can begin to start asking questions that can help us, not to predict what the future will hold, but help us build resiliency and adaptability into our systems to handle uncertainty. To combat this second challenge, this would be an appropriate space for educational institutions to engage in futures thinking and strategic foresight. Looking to the emergent megatrends and preparing strategic plans to mitigate possible, or plausible unintended consequences, and try to find opportunities within the uncertainty.

Human-centric approach: Due to the increasingly technological advancements and the convergence of industries and big data notions such as privacy and agency may become threatened or coerced at a level we have only begun to imagine. Schwab and Davis (2018) warn of the potential threats if we do not ensure a human-centered approach to new technology; "They can assess and make decisions based on data that no human can process, and in ways no human understands" (p. 14). This challenge calls for renewed efforts of educational leaders to engage in humanistic approaches to systems change.

17.4   Imagining Educational Leadership for a VUCA World

We have so far offered a range of ideas accounting for our current situation/context, as well as the impact that global trends, particularly technological trends, have made or are poised to make for our systems of education. We have also charted the inefficacy of rationalist, top-down planning that comes from most dominant educational leadership paradigms. As we begin to weave the narrative for how we move from challenge to solution, we can see the picture emerge with an emphasis on the adjacent possible and the important role of imagination.

What the foregoing suggests is our VUCA world, imbued as it is with its wicked problems, and emergent 4IR transformations presents tremendous challenges for educational leaders. While most education in the United States and even across the globe tends to be operated and managed at a local level, many of the existing problems and challenges are universal: the effects and complications that poverty has on students, systemic goals and bureaucratic mandates emphasizing increasing performance (and delivered with increasing punitive outcomes in the name of accountability) on standardized tests, and the ravages of inequality perpetuated by cultural and, particularly in the United States, racial discrimination. These challenges may be considered wicked in their own right, and have been nagging and pervasive sources of complication in education for decades. However, the rapid technological transformation and global interconnectedness of the 4IR brings yet another host of challenges, many of which are not predictable, and whose impact we cannot yet begin to perceive.

Thus, given the shifting demands on schools, from accountability and testing reforms to the increased demands for social services that schools must provide, leaders have plenty of wicked problems to contend with. Moreover, these problems do not exist in isolation from one another, they are deeply and complexly interwoven. It is also clear that this form of systems thinking, or learning (at a meta-level) from the past and understanding underlying transformational trends is not something that has entered the educational vernacular. It is at some level a failure of the imagination—something bureaucracies are not particularly situated to do well. In fact, this failure of the imagination was pointed to by the 9/11 Commission report as being part of the failure to prevent the attacks on the World Trade Center. The report offers that "imagination is not a gift usually associated with bureaucracies" (National Commission on Terrorist Attacks upon the United States 2004, p. 344), but that imagination as a tool for leadership must be developed and engaged routinely, perhaps even as a function of a bureaucracy. Organizational theorist Karl Weick (2005) explored this concept further, going so far as to suggest that solutions to such failures of imagination might require replacing traditional emphases on deductive reasoning with abductive reasoning, and focusing organizational design activities on sensemaking rather than only decision making. In one subsequent military analysis, Hoover (2013) even made a connection to this lack of imagination as consequence of the failures of the American educational system itself, noting that, "the dearth of imaginative thinking which is a consequence of the educational system is increasingly critical in the current world economic environment where tried and true solutions are falling short" (p. 62).

It is clear, however, that leading our complex education systems toward a place of efficacy and sustainability through the Fourth Industrial Revolution and other changes will not happen as a matter of linear sequencing or planning where all of the requirements and outcomes of change initiatives can be easily predicted and executed. Furthermore, these issues are complicated by the fact that many education systems are still enduring and mitigating the uneven instantiations of the prior industrial revolutions let alone prepared for the fourth. Perhaps articulated another way, leading change in our complex educational systems will require navigating intensely sticky and historically-laden systems that are already and always ongoing, in a VUCA world.

While the turbulence of this VUCA world and its associated wicked problems create difficulties for solving problems in traditional ways, it is not wholly without promise for educational leadership. Times of crisis transition have created opportunities to reimagine possibilities and to explore ways to solve those problems that have not yet been solved (Cook 2019; Fullan 2007; Heifetz 1994). In educational leadership, several existing theories have offered pathways to lead through the kind of uncertainties we face now and will likely face in the future. For instance, Fullan (2007) provides a framework for leading in a culture of change, in which he emphasizes leading people to ameliorate challenges that have not yet been solved. This has close connections to the work of Heifetz's (1994), Heifetz et al. 2009) work on adaptive leadership theory, which suggests that leading through the adaptive changes of a VUCA world requires new knowledge and modes of operation, including the paradigms and perspectives leaders themselves bring to the challenge (Heifetz and Linsky 2002).

In some sense then, given the difficulty of both untangling the complexities of a given problem and the contingent nature of the solutions that arise, educational leaders are beginning to look beyond traditional leadership models and strategic planning methods to address these kinds of challenges. Indeed, we might see this VUCA context as more than an occasion to castigate the inefficacies of our current leadership practices in education, but as an opportunity to use the adjacent possible as a way to explore what could be. And while our educational systems are currently mired in complexity and carry a legacy of stickiness and resistance to change it is worth recognizing that our educational systems have themselves been *designed*. As Richter and Allert (2017) wrote:

> Education and educational systems are artificial phenomena in the sense that they emanate from human intervention and effort. Irrespective of whether we look at policies, curricula, instructional measures, tools, networks, or environments, educational processes are essentially shaped by man-made inventions and artifacts. As a consequence educational processes are not uniform and lasting but contingent on the socio-material, and historical conditions in which they take place. (p. 1).

And it is recognizing the artificial and designed nature of all education that can be a starting point for redesigning the futures of education, grounded a clear-eyed acceptance of ambiguity, a knowledge of history and of current technological and global trends combined with a sense of humility. Thus, the task is to take designing as a point of departure, thereby allowing educational leaders to the imaginative and creative work of the adjacent possible, and to embrace the interconnectedness of uncertainty and creativity.

17.5   One Possible Solution: Futures Thinking

To help accomplish this, we can turn to some of the tools used in futures thinking and strategic foresight as frameworks for preparing for the future. Futures thinking is generally described as an intentional practice of thinking about the future in a structured way, guided by a range of methodologies and frameworks designed to guide the process (Prosser and Basra 2019). In addition, futures thinking can be described as a mindset or philosophy focused on the act of evaluating emerging global trends and informing strategic plans to handle future uncertainty. It is important to note that futures thinking is *not* about trying to predict the future, but rather prepare a system or organization for uncertainty.

Futures thinking embraces the emergence of new disruptions (natural or human-created) and recognizes, what the Copenhagen Institute for Futures Studies (CIFS) describes as megatrends. Megatrends, in this context, are major global areas of development that have a lifespan of 10–15 years, in which there may not be any expectation of linear development within the trend category. CIFS has identified and published a list of 14 megatrends namely: technological development, knowledge society, acceleration and complexity, polarization, individualization, immaterialism, network society, demographic development, economic growth, globalization, sustainability, focus on health, commercialization, and democratization (Copenhagen Institute for Futures Studies 2020). It is clearly untenable, given the length of this list, to become an expert or perhaps even well-versed in all of these topics. However, as we engage in thinking about our own futures, this list provides us with a "first stop" of the types of disruptions that might be happening around the world, allowing us to ask critical questions as we think about our own preparedness for uncertainty. Thus, recognizing these megatrends as sources of uncertainty, means that we can start to ask probing questions about these disruptions use these questions as a way of interrogating our preparedness to deal with this uncertainty. This allows us also to look reflexively on our own organizations or professional contexts to gauge our collective readiness to handle the uncertainties that will come. For example, considering one of the megatrends, that of acceleration and complexity, leads to a range of questions of relevance to education. For instance, one may ask how shortened business lifespans and the increasing convergence of industries impact education? Or, alternatively we may seek to ask how the presence of algorithmic bias in artificial intelligence and facial recognition systems may further exacerbate pre-existing social, racial, and economic inequities. Again, the idea is not to pretend to predict the future, but to recognize emerging global trends and strategically prepare our organizations for potential disruptions, as well as possibly identify new opportunities.

17.5.1   Futures Thinking in Practice

To illustrate the potential benefits of the practical implementation of futures thinking and strategic foresight tools, we will explore a hypothetical example of how this can be applied in the context of educational leadership. For our hypothetical case, let's consider a leadership team from a K12 school district that consists of the superintendent, school board members, executive cabinet (or council), and a selected team of invited principals and staff from the district. This team, for the sake of this example, is working to create a three-to-five-year strategic plan to support equitable student achievement for all students across their district in the wake of the COVID-19 disruption of 2020–2021. This hypothetical team, like so many real educational leadership teams may be full of members that are familiar with organizational development and leadership approaches to various forms of strategic planning that include strategic thinking and management (Fullan 2007; Heckelman 2017; Kaplan and Norton 2001; Meehan and Jonker 2017). However, in this hypothesized case, the team wants to expand their thinking beyond the immediate, by intentionally working through possible futures in a structured method to better design an agile and adaptable district system. Enter futures thinking and strategic foresight. This hypothetical case also serves to illustrate the additive nature of futures thinking, and the role of strategic foresight tools by the adoption of the intentionality in which leadership teams can incorporate these tools and frameworks into their existing organizational planning methodologies. It does not require leadership teams to abandon their existing structures and processes, but rather provides a structure to explore their planning in ways that prepare for the uncertainty of the future.

While there is no prescriptive toolset or strict methodology that a team such as our hypnotical K12 leadership team *must* follow in order to successfully engage in futures thinking, there are lots of freely available foresight tools that can provide the structure for teams to engage with the discussions and often difficult conversations that arise when challenging a set of ideas and strategic plans against the unknown. In this example, we will operate under the assumption that one (or more) of our team members have taken the lead to incorporate a foresight tool in their strategic planning meetings. As they begin thinking about the future, and possible disruptions that might emerge as stated in the aforementioned megatrends of innovation, the planning team examines the emerging trends identified as having the potential to impact or disrupt the education sector, and the possible disruptions that may impact their local economy as well, knowing these disruptions could have direct impact on their district communities. It is at this point in their planning that a foresight tool can provide a central focal point for discussion and deeper examination of their strategic plans, mapped against the list of possible disruptions. One of the challenges when engaging in strategic foresight is to visualize or otherwise map out the often hard to conceptualize "possible" disruptions.

To facilitate this next phase of their strategic planning, the member (or members) of the team that are leading the foresight work could introduce a tool generically referred to as a "cone of time" that is meant to provide leaders a way to think about time in multiple, simultaneous timelines. The Future Today Institute (n.d.) provides one such tool as one of eleven open source (licensed under Creative Commons) foresight tools that are freely available to use and build upon. The "cone of time" version from the Future Today Institute (FTI) known as a "strategic time horizon" is represented as a horizontal cone, with the closed end of the cone on the left-hand side, representing the most near-term timeframe (tactical) of one-to-two years. As the cone widens towards the righthand, it is further broken into subsequent time-frames of three-to-five years (strategy), five-to-ten (vision), and 10+ years (systems-level). As the cone widens with more distant timeframes, it represents the increased uncertainty facing the organization. For example, the uncertainty for the tactical timeframe of one-to-two years is typically less than the uncertainty at the systems-level timeframe of more than ten years. One of the key elements of this tool is to help leaders think about the spectrum of time in relation to the possible disruptions they have identified and how their organization can respond to those uncertainties.

Returning to our hypothetical team, after discussing the identified trends and mapping them according to their sense of relevance and urgency for the district, the team then employs the "cone of time" to explore the future time horizon as a *cone* of expanding uncertainties, rather than a singular, linear *path*. As the leaders discuss emerging trends, they spend time mapping several of the most prominent trends at various points in the space of the time cone and discussing the implications for the district and surrounding community should these trends come to fruition. As they plan, they begin to center in on the emergence of artificial intelligence and learning analytics, and discuss how they should best consider the proliferation of learning analytics with their equity aspirations. They ask: as more and more of our teaching and learning platforms become imbued with predictive analytics, how will we ensure that our technology partners and vendors are similarly committed to issues of equity and inclusion as we are? As a result, the planning team makes a recommendation to refresh their vendor management strategy to annually revisit their contracts and policies to ensure alignment with their vision.

To conclude this hypothetical situation, our imagined leadership team was able to successfully define a strategic plan to address their goal of increasing equity in the district by surfacing relevant disruptions and working through the potential impact of the disruption on their plans. A key takeaway, with this illustration, is again, the emphasis that this and other foresight tools are not intended to try and predict the future, but to provide an intentionality to address future uncertainty. Using a futures thinking mindset and strategic foresight tools provide leadership teams with the ability to plot known and hypothetical disruptions and discuss how possible eventualities of uncertainty can provide risk, opportunity, or growth to their organization and system.

17.6 Summary

Through this chapter, we have worked to demonstrate that while human beings contend with volatility, uncertainty, complexity, and ambiguity – as well as rapidly changing and unevenly distributed technological proliferation – we have creative and imaginative capabilities that enable us to pursue ambitious and necessary work. In the domain of education, leaders face a host of VUCA contingencies, including the challenge to innovate and redesign intractable, historically-laden systems. While the tools and methods of futures studies do not guarantee sweeping reforms and redesigns, we do believe they offer promise for supporting new ways of thinking and leading that meet the needs of the adaptive challenges education leaders face.

Embracing the adjacent possible through a combination of design and futures thinking is how we, as humans, can try to mitigate the effects of our own Kryptonite, by addressing head-on the limitations of our own ability to prognosticate. While learning futures methodologies and those of design may not inherently appear to be synergistic, we would argue that both of these approaches to preparing organizations and systems for uncertainty are interdependent. Each approach has its own set of internal mechanisms, methodologies, and skillsets, yet they share a mutual approach to uncertainty. Futures thinking and design both demonstrate a clear-eyed acceptance of uncertainty. It is the uncertainty, and the adjacent possibilities that lie within the shadows of uncertainty, that both approaches draw their optimistic mindset. This similarity is what prepares us to be resilient in the face of uncertainty, to embrace it, and design and build systems to intentionally withstand the only constant we can predict, change.

These tools, when coupled with the imaginative and creative mindsets of the adjacent possible, create necessary but likely insufficient capabilities for educational leaders who stand poised to become much more than bureaucrats, middle managers, or stewards of the status quo. Just as Santayana's adage offers a prophetic warning about the past, we hope that leaders may come to utilize the mindsets and methods of the adjacent possible in designing successful narratives of the future.

References

Beghetto, R. A. (2020). Uncertainty, In V. P. Glaveanu (Ed.), *The Palgrave encyclopedia of the possible* (pp. 1-7). Springer. https://doi.org/10.1007/978-3-319-98390-5_122-1

Björneborn, L. (2020). Adjacent possible, In V. P Glaveanu (Ed.), *The Palgrave encyclopedia of the possible* (pp. 1-12). Springer. https://doi.org/10.1007/978-3-319-98390-5_100-1

Bolter, J. D. (1990). *Writing space: The computer in the history of literacy*. Hillsdale, NJ: Erlbaum.

Buchanan, R. (1992). Wicked problems in design thinking. *Design Issues, 8*(2), 5–21.

Burns, R., Hughes, B., & Torres Ribelles, F. J. (1991). Poems. *Alicante Journal of English Studies, 4*, 228–233.

Cook, J.W. (2019). Learning at the edge of history. In J.W. Cook (Ed.), *Sustainability, human well-being, and the future of education*, pp. 1–28. Palgrave Macmillan.

Copenhagen Institute for Futures Studies. (2020). Beyond the COVID-19: How the pandemic will shape our future. https://scenario.wpengine.com/wp-content/uploads/2020/06/Quarantine-Kit.pdf

Cousins, B. (2018). Design thinking: Organizational learning in VUCA environments. *Academy of Strategic Management Journal, 17*(2), 1–18.

Eisenstein, E.L. (1980). The printing press as an agent of change: Communications and cultural transformations in early-modern Europe. Cambridge: Cambridge University Press.

Fisher, T. (2016). *Designing our way to a better world*. University of Minnesota Press.

Fullan, M. (2007). *Leading in a culture of change*. John Wiley & Sons.

Future Today Institute. (n.d.). *How to think about time*. https://futuretodayinstitute.com/strategic-time-horizons/

Gidley, J. (2016). *Postformal education: A philosophy for complex futures*. Switzerland: Springer.

Glaveanu, V. P. (2018). The possible as a field of inquiry. *Europe's Journal of Psychology, 14*(3), 519–530. https://doi.org/10.5964/ejop.v14i3.1725

Hammond, C. (2020, August 26). When you imagine how you'll feel at a future date, you're unaware of subtle but powerful biases that frame the way you think. BBC Future. https://www.bbc.com/future/article/20200825-why-predicting-our-future-feelings-is-so-difficult

Heckelman, W. (2017). Five critical principles to guide organizational change. *OD Practitioner, 49*(4), 13–21.

Heifetz, R. A. (1994). *Leadership without easy answers*. Harvard University Press.

Heifetz, R. A., Grashow, A., & Linsky, M. (2009). *The practice of adaptive leadership: Tools and tactics for changing your organization and the world*. Harvard Business Press.

Heifetz, R. A., & Linsky, M. (2002). A survival guide for leaders. *Harvard business review, 80*(6), 65-74.

Heller, C. (2018). *The intergalactic design guide: Harnessing the creative potential of social design*. Washington, D.C.: Island Press.

Hoover, D. L. (2013). A failure of imagination in the US intelligence community. *American Intelligence Journal, 31*(1), 59–71.

Hutt, R. (2016, January 23). 9 quotes that sum up the Fourth Industrial Revolution. World Economic Forum. https://www.weforum.org/agenda/2016/01/9-quotes-that-sum-up-the-fourth-industrial-revolution/

Johnson, S. (2010). *Where good ideas come from: The natural history of innovation*. London: Allen Lane.

Johnson, S. (2014). *How we got to now: Six innovations that made the modern world*. New York: Riverhead books.

Kaplan, R. S., & Norton, D. (2001). *The strategy-focused organization: How balanced scorecard companies thrive in the new business environment*. Harvard Business School Press.

Latour, B. (1990). Drawing things together. In Lynch, M., & Woolgar, S. (Eds.), Representation in Scientific Practice. (1st MIT Press ed., pp.19–68). MIT Press: Cambridge MA.

Leahy, S. (n.d.). Design our life-long-learning places for an augmented you. The Guide Project: How to Design the Future. https://howtodesignthefuture.asu.edu/design-your-life-long-learning-places-augmented-you

Leahy, S. M., Holland, C., & Ward, F. (2019). The digital frontier: Envisioning future technologies impact on the classroom. *Futures*, 113, 1–10. https://doi.org/10.1016/j.futures.2019.04.009

Levin, K., Cashore, B., Bernstein, S., & Auld, G. (2012). Overcoming the tragedy of super wicked problems: constraining our future selves to ameliorate global climate change. *Policy sciences*, 45(2), 123–152.

McLuhan, M. (1962). The Gutenberg galaxy: The making of typographic man. Toronto: University of Toronto Press.

McLuhan, M. (1964). Understanding media: The extensions of man. MIT Press.

Meehan, W. F., & Jonker, K. S. (2017). *Engine of impact: essentials of strategic leadership in the nonprofit sector*. Stanford University Press.

Mishra, P., Spiro, R. J. & Feltovich, P. (1996) Technology, representation & cognition. In von Oostendorp, H. (Ed.) Cognitive aspects of electronic text processing. (pp. 287–306). Norwood, NJ: Ablex Publishing Corporation.

National Commission on Terrorist Attacks upon the United States. (2004). *The 9/11 Commission report: final report of the National Commission on Terrorist Attacks upon the United States*. [Web.] Retrieved from the Library of Congress, https://lccn.loc.gov/2004356401.

Ong, W. (1982). Orality and literacy: The technologizing of the word. London: Methuen.

Pacanowsky, M. (1995). Team tools for wicked problems. *Organizational dynamics*, 23(3), 36–51.

Parolin, Z., & Siöland, L. (2019). Support for a universal basic income: A demand–capacity paradox? *Journal of European Social Policy*, 30(1), 5–19. https://doi.org/10.1177/0958928719886525

Penprase, B. E. (2018). The Fourth Industrial Revolution and higher education. In N. Gleason (Ed.), Higher Education in the era of the Fourth Industrial Revolution (1st ed., pp. 207–229). Springer Singapore. https://doi.org/10.1007/978-981-13-0194-0

Prosser, Z., & Basra, S. (2019, January 29). Futures thinking: A mind-set, not a method. Medium. https://medium.com/touchpoint/futures-thinking-a-mind-set-not-a-method-64c9b5f9da37

Provenzo, E. F. (1986), Beyond the Gutenberg galaxy: Microcomputers and the emergence of post-typographic culture. New York: Teachers College Press.

Ratcliffe, S. (Ed.). 2016. *Oxford essential quotations* (4th ed.). Oxford University Press.

Richter, C., & Allert, H. (2017). Design as critical engagement in and for education. *EDeR. Educational Design Research,* 1(1).

Rittel, H. W., & Webber, M. M. (1973). Dilemmas in a general theory of planning. *Policy sciences*, 4(2), 155–169.

Salomon, G. (1979). Interaction of media, cognition and learning. San Francisco: Jossey-Bass.

Santayana, G. (1910). *Reason in common sense*. United Kingdom: Constable.

Schwab, K. (n.d.) The Fourth Industrial Revolution. World Economic Forum. https://www.weforum.org/about/the-fourth-industrial-revolution-by-klaus-schwab/

Schwab, K., & Davis, N. (2018). Shaping the future of the Fourth Industrial Revolution. Currency; Penguin Random House.

Shields, C. M. (2018). *Transformative leadership in education: Equitable and socially just change in an uncertain and complex world* (3rd ed.). Routledge.

Weick, K. E. (2005). Organizing and failures of imagination. *International public management journal*, 8(3), 425–438.

Wilson, T. D., & Gilbert, D. T. (2003). Affective forecasting. *Advances in Experimental Social Psychology,* 35, 345–411.

Zafeirakopoulos, M. & van der Bijl-Brouwer, M. (2018). Exploring the transdisciplinary learning experiences of innovation professionals. *Technology Innovation Management Review*, 8(8), 50–59.

Chapter 18
Learning in An Uncertain World: Transforming Higher Education for the Anthropocene

Nathaniel Barr, Kylie Hartley, Joel A. Lopata, Brandon McFarlane, and Michael J. Mcnamara

Abstract As the Fourth Industrial Revolution rapidly changes how people live, work, and connect, and as the realities of the Anthropocene and a planet irrevocably marked by human activity come to impact all aspects of existence on Earth, our species faces great uncertainty. Social, economic, and environmental challenges, primarily of our own doing, pose grave risks with no certainties as to their resolution. In a world awash with rapid transformation, higher education has not kept pace with emergent needs. In order that higher education may help us survive, it must undergo evolution and transformation to suit the uncertainty of the Anthropocene. This chapter offers several preliminary recommendations for this endeavour. The higher education of tomorrow should be more flexible, creative, focused on critical skills, leverage constructivist pedagogical tactics, and be supported by earlier education that can help prepare students for a transformed higher education and the challenges of this epoch.

18.1 Learning in an Uncertain World

The human capacity for complex cognition, reason, metacognition, and creative ideation has led to the genesis of innovations that have transformed the way our species experiences and navigates life on Earth. Art, science, medicine, engineering, and the host of other products of the human mind, have been pivotal to our success. One of the most formidable innovations in the story of our species is the transition from informal transmission of knowledge to the development of formalized education, with higher education in particular representing the pinnacle of knowledge and

N. Barr (✉) · K. Hartley · J. A. Lopata · B. McFarlane · M. J. Mcnamara
School of Humanities and Creativity, Sheridan College, Oakville, ON, Canada
e-mail: nathaniel.barr@sheridancollege.ca

© Springer Nature Switzerland AG 2022
R. A. Beghetto, G. J. Jaeger (eds.), *Uncertainty: A Catalyst for Creativity, Learning and Development*, Creativity Theory and Action in Education 6, https://doi.org/10.1007/978-3-030-98729-9_18

skill dissemination for the purposes of propelling our collective well-being and advancement.

Throughout human history, few had the opportunity to engage in formal education. As industrialization took root and the proliferation of widespread public education became common around the world, higher education was only accessible to elites, as the structure of society was still largely dependent on manual rather than intellectual contributions from citizenry. As time progressed and the economy shifted toward a knowledge-based economy, post-war government interventions made post-secondary education broadly accessible, and global enrolment continues to skyrocket—a recent report projects an increase in global post-secondary enrollments from 214 million in 2015 to a staggering 594 million in 2040 (Calderon 2018). Higher education must maintain the status of a catalyst for the advancement of humanity.

This chapter considers the question of how higher education should be reimagined in light of this uncertainty and how to transform it for this epoch. First, the socio-economic and environmental disruption underway that are causing unprecedented uncertainty and risk on the global scale are described. The skills and knowledge required in such an uncertain era, strategies for embedding these perspectives within curriculum and in the classroom, and building accessible pathways for creative higher education in earlier education are then suggested.

18.2 Uncertainty in the Anthropocene

Over the span of the Earth's history, many species have existed, with varying degrees and duration of success. On one extreme, some have gone extinct. Others have endured but no longer enjoy widespread success. Biogeographic relict species are descendants of populations that once enjoyed much wider distribution and larger numbers, but are now constrained to a much smaller geographic region, often due to an inability to adapt to significant environmental changes (Habel et al. 2010). Contrastingly, the human species experienced massive population growth and came to inhabit vast swaths of the planet, leaving an indelible imprint along the way.

Humanity's growth is a relatively recent and incredibly rapid development. The world population went from four million in 10,000 BCE to nearly 8 billion today. This growth was far from linear. Indeed, the growth rate of the human population was only 0.04% from 10,000 BCE until around 1700, with massive growth following soon after. In the early 1800s, Earth saw a population of one billion humans for the first time, the two billion mark was reached in 1928, three billion in 1960, four billion in 1975, five billion in 1987, six billion in 1999, and crossed the mark of seven billion in 2011. Though precise projections vary, barring any catastrophic disruptions, there will be eight billion humans on Earth in but a few years. What this growth means for our species is uncertain.

It is certain that population growth, coupled with the outputs associated with our innovative capacity, have had a significant impact on Earth systems. Though the seeds of human innovative capacity took root in the Upper Paleolithic (Leakey 1984), geologists have identified 'The Great Acceleration', which began in 1950, as a turning point (Steffen et al. 2015). The effect of our growth and activity has been so great that this epoch has been dubbed the Anthropocene, a time in which the foremost defining feature of the planet is human impact (Steffen et al. 2011; Barr and Pennycook 2018). Our role as a dominating force in shaping the planet is observable in many ways, including our changing climate. An illustrative and symbolic example comes from recent analyses which show that anthropogenic mass (i.e., the total mass of material output of human activity) has surpassed the total living biomass on Earth, with an average human responsible for the production of an anthropogenic mass equal to or more than the weight of their own body each week (Elhacham et al. 2020).

Coincident is our march forth into yet another industrial revolution (IR). The First IR brought manufacturing innovation and the steam engine in the late 1700s, the Second brought electricity in the late 1800s, the Third in the late 1960s was based on information technology, and humanity now sits on the precipice of the Fourth IR, defined by artificial intelligence (AI) and a variety of biotechnological advances. Klaus Schwab, Founder and Executive Chairman of the World Economic Forum, has argued that the Fourth IR "will fundamentally alter the way we live, work, and relate to one another" (Schwab 2016). Intertwined with increasing digitization is increased disruption to our informational ecosystem, leaving citizens uncertain about what is true and false (see Lazer et al. 2018).

Biologists have observed that changes to the environment can relegate once prosperous species into the status of the relict, and there is no guarantee that humans retain our dominion over the whole of the planet, nor that humans will persist to exist at all. Nick Bostrom (2013) cites expert estimates as typically falling somewhere between 10 and 20% for total existential risk in the next century and contends that the biggest risks stem from our own innovative advances. This position echoes that of George Miller, who in his 1969 APA address, argued that the "most urgent problems of our world today are the problems we have made for ourselves … They are human problems whose solutions will require us to change our behavior and our social institutions" (p. 1063). The COVID-19 global pandemic has served as a stark reminder that our species is susceptible to risk and our prosperity is not guaranteed. The problems humans have created are diverse, dire, and will require an educated populace to address them.

Sir Ken Robinson's call to action makes clear the urgency that we face: "we are living in times of revolution… if we are to survive and flourish we have to think differently about our own abilities and make the best use of them" (2011, p. 5). Consideration of this observation brings us back to the question posed at the outset of this chapter as to how higher education can transform to suit these uncertain conditions that surround us. The precise answer is, of course, uncertain. Evidence and arguments from the social and psychological sciences, educational research, dispatches from industry leaders, and scholarship from the humanities are suggestive of the most imperative skills and knowledge to impart to students, the best curricular models and classroom activities to cultivate them, and the pathways from

K-12 education that are most likely to help our collective odds of success as a species.

18.3 Building Higher Education for the Uncertainty of the Anthropocene

The curriculum and skills-training of today must be oriented to the uncertainty that defines tomorrow. But what should we be teaching today's undergraduates to help them flourish in 2025? And what types of curriculum and skills-training programs should we be preparing now in order to support the incoming classes of 2030, or even 2035? These questions become particularly problematic with the realization that we have very little idea of what the world will look in 2025, let alone 2035. Yuval Noah Harari summarizes these prognosticating challenges when he suggests that, when it comes to the not so distant future:

> [w]e don't know what people will do for a living, we don't know how armies or bureaucracies will function, and we don't know what gender relations will be like. Some people will probably live much longer than today, and the human body itself might undergo an unprecedented revolution thanks to bioengineering and direct brain-computer interfaces. Much of what kids learn today will likely be irrelevant by 2050 (Harari 2018).

Under such conditions, what should post-secondary educators be preparing to teach our students to help them navigate this future?

Transforming higher education to this reality will require recognition that the *'pace of technological development'* under the 4IR will have a profound impact on the future of work and the skills needed by industry. Unlike any other industrial revolution before it, the 4IR is characterized by exponential rather than linear technological evolution (Schwab 2016, p. 8). Rapid proto-typing, 3-D printing, ever-evolving customization capabilities, nanotechnology and exponential growth in the development and application of new materials, as well the continued integration of technologies across physical, digital, and biological domains mean that product-life cycles will continue to shrink at unprecedented rates and technology-specific skill-sets run a greater risk of becoming obsolete before they can be adequately mastered (Schwab 2016; Thomas and Brown 2011). This quickening pace of technological disruption threatens to "swiftly outdate the shelf life of people's skillsets and the relevance of what they thought they knew about the path to social mobility and rewarding employment" (*World Economic Forum* 2018, p. 3).

Individual workers will need access to flexible skills-upgrading programs that can be continuously modified and adapted to support individuals throughout their new life-long learning and up-grading journeys. Such dynamism will demand creativity in construction of curricular offerings that go beyond traditional four-year degrees. It is already projected 50% of all employees will need reskilling by 2025 (World Economic Forum 2020); this figure is projected to increase as the labour force becomes increasingly augmented with and by new technologies to enhance productivity and worker performance (Barr and Peters 2018). In terms of technological augmentation, the World Economic Forum estimates that another 97 million new roles may emerge that are more adapted to the integration of labour between humans, machines, and algorithms (World Economic Forum 2020, pg. 5). We must prepare ourselves and our institutions to accommodate the new reality of life-long learning and continuous skills-upgrading that is demanded by the 4IR. Rather than view transformation of higher education as a metamorphosis into a new form, it is imperative to embrace an attitude of continual evolution and responsiveness. If higher education is unable to predict and prepare for the nature of the future of work in a dynamic way, the effects will be detrimental across all sectors.

Hastened by the COVID-19 pandemic, the shift toward online higher education evidences the need for dynamic evolution. Data indicates a four-fold increase in the numbers of individuals seeking opportunities for learning online, a five-fold increase in employer provision of online learning opportunities to their workers, and a nine-fold increase for learners accessing online learning through government programs (World Economic Forum 2020). Not only will curriculum need transformation to fit online environments, our curriculum and programmatic decisions will need to accommodate the '*growing harmonization and integration of technology across all disciplines and domains of work*' (Schwab 2016). Consider that by 2025, the time spent on current tasks at work by humans and machines will be equal (World Economic Forum 2020). The COVID-19 global pandemic has only hastened these projected shifts in the division of labour between humans and machines; creating a 'double disruption' that is forecasted to lead to the technological displacement of 85 million jobs within the next five years (World Economic Forum 2020).

From both a performance and neoliberal cost-savings perspective, it is apparent that the pace of this shift will not diminish. Even in realms that appear as uniquely human, technology is outperforming us—for instance, in judicial decision-making, impersonal, machine-based learning programs are now showing themselves to be far more accurate and effective in their bail-hearing decision than their human counter-parts; namely, judges (Klienberg et al. 2018). This trend is global. In the authors' country, Canada, 10.6% of workers are deemed to be at a high-risk for automation-related job displacement, while another 29.1% are at a moderate risk (Frenette and Frank 2020). While office support occupations (35.7%) and specialized service occupations (20%) are at the highest risk, even the once 'recession-proof' occupations like administration and financial supervisor occupations (11.3%) and technical occupations in health (8.2%) are not immune to displacement. Harari's prediction of a possible future where artificial-intelligence enabled technologies have replaced most forms of human labour and decision-making (Harari 2015) appears less like a dystopian hypothetical and more like the logical end to a process that is already underway (see West/Brookings Institute, 2015).

How should educators design curriculum that enables students to effectively cope with such possible trajectories? What human-performed tasks and functions will be needed and sought-after in this future? To what extent will humans offload thinking to devices and systems (e.g., Barr et al. 2015)? Where, as individuals, will we find our 'competitive advantage' in the new world of work? And how will society cope with the massive numbers of displaced workers?

While consideration of the human costs is critical, it is also paramount that any curriculum and programmatic decisions in the twenty-first century should consider, if not squarely address, the need for responses and innovations that can counter-act the biosphere destruction that characterizes life in the Anthropocene. Much has been written on the subject of education philosophy and pedagogy in the era of the Anthropocene (for example, see: Stratford 2019), but few authors better articulate the challenges confronting us than the philospher Peter Sloterdijk. In his two essays, the "Anthropocene" and "From the Domestication of Man to the Civilizing of Culture", Sloterdijk posits the urgent need for a radical politico-economic change, or what he calls "the domestication of the wild animal culture" (Sloterdijk 2018). Here, the task that education must urgently undertake is that of civilizing civilizations themselves, of inspiring imposing universal solidarity and cooperation among all humanity in response to the existential crisis confronting us. For the post-secondary sector, this means investing in programs and redesigning learning experiences such that they both emphasize the skillsets required by such an ambitious, global undertaking while simultaneously mobilizing all of our disciplines in the collective pursuit of sustainability-promoting innovation. Crises can serve as a catalyst toward creativity and innovation—higher education must bring leadership to the ongoing societal and global crises underway if it hopes to both participate in response and prepare students to contribute (see Beghetto 2020) while also mitigating the risk that post-secondary education become complicit with the systems that perpetuate disastrous change (Hollenberg 2017).

18.4   Skills and Knowledge for the Uncertainty of the Anthropocene

Given the direction that higher education is going—toward flexible, digital, and adaptive learning programming—active learning and self-management are a critical skills cluster. Due to the pace of disruption in the 4IR, simply having a technical skillset in a single domain is not sufficient to remain competitive or employable over the long-haul. Rather, individuals will need to engage in a continuous process of building and reshaping understanding as a natural consequence of their experience and interactions with the world (Grabinger and Dunlap 1995). Active learning—learning through one's active engagement with the information and experiencing they encounter—was recently identified as the second most important skillset; while other self-management skills such as resilience, stress tolerance, and flexibility were ninth on the World Economic Forum's list of the most important, employability skills for 2025 (World Economic Forum 2020). The unprecedented amount of learning online, now and into the future, will place unique demands on students in this area (see Glăveanu et al. 2020 for a conversation on creative learning in digital and virtual environments). In this era of uncertainty, being able to adapt well, cope with adversity, bounce back quickly, and proactively seek out and pursue new opportunities will be central to one's ability to successfully navigate an uncertain future.

Creativity and creative thinking skills will also be a valuable and increasingly valued asset. Creativity, our cognitive capacity for divergent thinking (Guilford 1950), associational thinking (Mednick 1962; Barr et al. 2014), ideational flexibility (Smith and Carlsson 1987), or, quite simply our capacity to generate ideas or products that are both novel and useful (e.g., Barron 1955; Runco and Jaeger 2012) is continually recognized as one of the most important employability skills in this new century (World Economic Forum 2020, 2018). In the era of rapid technological disruption and integration, creativity skills are vital to our ability to navigate ambiguity, solve complex problems, and as a fundamental precursor to the innovations of tomorrow.

In his landmark 1950 APA address, JP Guilford foresaw that as artificial intelligence comes to realize its potential, eventually about "the only economic value of brains left would be in the creative thinking of which they are capable" (p. 448). New technology will continue to create unforeseen problems that require novel thinking and critical solutions if they are to be adequately addressed. Workers across all segments of society require the capacity to respond creatively to the uncertain challenges that will arise regularly in such a dynamic working environment. Educational approaches that are primarily oriented to deriving known solutions to known challenges will be wholly inadequate in a reality defined by uncertainty. Success in navigating the Anthropocence will depend on imaginative, creative thinkers working across a wide array of disciplines, who are adaptable in the face of ambiguity, and have deep domain-specific expertise.

'*Innovation skills*' will also be of paramount significance in this new century. While creative thinkers can inspire new possibilities, ideas, and solutions, they will be insufficiently equipped to affect change absent the skills needed to effectively bring their ideas and solutions into the world (Levitt 2002). Translating concepts into tractable solutions and knowing how to design, construct, and rally support for ideas will be central to one's capacity to affect change. For these reasons, The World Economic Forum (World Economic Forum 2020) ranks 'analytical thinking and innovation' as the most important skillset for today's world of work.

Innovations skills, though varied, are typically those abilities associated with *implementation* of newly generated ideas and possibilities. In *The Innovator's DNA* (2009), Dyer, Jefferey, and Christiansen, characterize 'innovation skills' as a cluster of cognitive and behavioural abilities ranging from associating (the drawing connections between questions, problems, or ideas from unrelated fields), questioning (posing queries that challenge common wisdom), observing (scrutinizing the behavior of customers, suppliers, and competitors to identify new ways of doing things), experimenting (constructing interactive experiences and provoking unorthodox responses to see what insights emerge) and networking (meeting people with different ideas and perspectives who can help bring the idea to life). An important aspect of promoting such innovation skills will be guidance on orienting these capacities toward the challenges of the Anthropocene rather than perpetuate or exacerbate them.

Training in behavioral science can facilitate the cultivation of diverse skills and has been identified as a framework for innovation via iterative experimentation (see Peters 2020). Behavioral approaches infuse innovations, new solutions, and social interventions with insights from the psychological and behavioral sciences that can drive human behavioural responses in desired directions and are amenable to empirical testing (Thaler and Sunstein 2008; Ariely 2008). Learning about the science of psychology and behavior can help ensure that solutions are based in how people think and act, increasing their utility, and training in scientific methods enables testing solutions prior to scaling.

18.5   Uncertainty and Pedagogy

Now that the uncertainty in the current era, the sorts of curricular programming needed, and that certain skills are particularly important for higher education to emphasize have been communicated, this chapter turns to the question of what to do in the classroom. How can pedagogy be leveraged in the pursuit of attaining these aspirations? For an uncertain world, educational experiences that capitalize on uncertainty are needed. Evidence shows that creativity can thrive under uncertainty and it should be invited into the classroom (see Beghetto 2017, 2019). To understand how this can be accomplished, it is important to understand different pedagogical approaches and their relation to uncertainty.

Pedagogical certainty can be conceptualized as the likelihood that learners will acquire *correct* conceptual and procedural knowledge via pedagogical activities (e.g., lessons and exercises). Under a strict direct transmission paradigm, lessons are highly structured and teacher-centered (Ku et al. 2014). Known to be highly efficient, direct transmission methods result in high *certainty* that learners will arrive at correct conclusions and attain accepted conceptual knowledge on curricular topics. Conversely, with constructivist methods, lessons are loosely structured and learner-centered such that conceptual material, procedural sequences, and instructional feedback are all guided and directed by students (Hoover 1996; Mvududu and Thiel-Burgess 2012). Known for benefiting student interest and motivation, constructivist methods are, however, accompanied by increased *uncertainty* that learners will arrive at correct conclusions and ultimately may not attain the intended conceptual and procedural knowledge set out in curricula (Kirschner et al. 2006). Of course, real-world lessons are rarely strict on one approach or the other, and it is generally accepted that even under constructivist paradigms some degree of structure and guidance is preferred over completely unguided discovery learning (Hmelo-Silver et al. 2007).

Discovery Learning was the first, and perhaps remains the quintessential, constructivist method for actively acquiring complex conceptual knowledge (Bruner 1961; Piaget and Inhelder 2008). This method is founded on the principle that learning occurs through inductive reasoning applied towards resources in the learning environment (Holland et al. 1986). As an approach, it is operationalized in three pedagogical methods: (1) *Concept Attainment*, wherein conceptual understandings and definitions are built through the active analysis and evaluation of examples and instances, (2) *Scientific Inquiry*, wherein causal phenomenological knowledge is constructed through hypothesis testing and experimentation, and (3) *Design-based Learning*, wherein conceptual and procedural knowledge are applied towards the creation of products (Joyce & Weil, 2008; Neber 2012). Of these, the two discovery methods most applicable to creativity studies are Concept Attainment and Design-based Learning, whereas Scientific Inquiry is more applicable to STEM subjects.

When designing constructivist learning experiences, such as those utilizing the Concept Attainment and Design-based Learning methods, teachers make decisions impacting lesson *structure*—i.e., the degree of guidance—and *centre*—i.e., the degree of student- or teacher-centeredness. They make these decisions towards three lesson resources: (1) the *conceptual materials* students will negotiate, (2) the *procedural sequences* they will follow, and (3) the *instructional feedback* they will receive. Most critically, when designing lessons, teachers decide who creates the material to be worked with (i.e., the content), who outlines the actions to be taken (i.e., the procedures), and from where the confirmatory response (i.e., the feedback) derives. These decisions impact the inherent *uncertainty* in a lesson, and by intentionally considering the alternatives available to them, educators can introduce varying degrees of uncertainty to their lessons.

Educators have substantial latitude over and potential for the deliberate and artful application of uncertainty when designing learning experiences—e.g., lessons, activities. They can control this latitude through the manipulation of two pedagogical variables related to the generation of lessons resources—*resource source* and *resourcing style*. The first variable, *resource source*, speaks to who generates the materials and procedures students will work with. The second variable, *resourcing style,* speaks to how the lesson resources are generated—in an emergent or planned manner.

Teachers often make resource decisions without sufficient consideration of who generates the resources. When operating under a teacher-centered approach, they themselves supply the conceptual materials for students to work with, whereas when operating under a student-centered approach, they engage students in generating the content. While underappreciated, this decision has substantial impact on the *uncertainty* elicited in lessons.

If a teacher chooses a student-centered approach—wherein the students generate an activity's content—they introduce uncertainty. On this approach, teachers decide whether their students generate this content deliberately (e.g., via preparation and research), or emergently (e.g., via ideation); this decision is related to *resourcing style*—how lesson resources are generated. Emergent options elicit greater uncertainty than preplanned options regardless of whether delivered via a teacher- or student-centered approach, and student-centered, emergent choices lead to the *highest* uncertainty. Through their choice of lesson resource options, educators can introduce low, moderate, or high degrees of uncertainty. These choices and their impacts apply to all aspects of a lesson including those related to conceptual materials, activity procedures, and instructional feedback.

For example, when designing an activity, teachers make choices regarding cognitive and physical procedures—the sequences of mental and physical actions students take to acquire knowledge. Under a direct transmission approach, teachers outline and provide procedures for their students to follow, thereby guiding them through learning experiences with relatively high certainty that they will carry out effective and efficient actions. In such cases, the resource source is the teacher, the resourcing style is deliberate, and the resulting uncertainty is low; however, teachers may alternatively choose to provide their students the freedom to design the procedures themselves, and they can choose whether their students predetermine these procedural sequences in advance or discover it emergently.

Providing students with the freedom to decide their own learning procedures in an emergent way introduces high uncertainty to the learning climate. This is because the potential and risk of following a flawed procedural sequence may lead to the discovery of incorrect conceptual knowledge and the routinization of flawed procedural knowledge (Kirschner et al. 2006), whereas just providing freedom to generate the content may only run the risk of constructing incorrect conceptual knowledge but still correct procedural knowledge. Procedural uncertainty provides more freedom but is accompanied by increased pedagogical risk.

Operationally, when teachers generate both the conceptual material and the activity procedure, uncertainty remains low. Conversely, when students generate the conceptual material in a deliberate and preplanned way uncertainty is moderate, when they generate it emergently uncertainty is high, and when they generate both conceptual materials and activity procedures emergently, uncertainty is at its peak. In this way, by varying the resource source—teachers or students—and resourcing style—planned or emergent—teachers can modulate the uncertainty in a learning experience.

Regarding instructional feedback strategies, the same resource-related options apply. Teachers can provide feedback themselves or can shift control towards their students by using more student-centered feedback strategies such as self- and peer-assessment. Additionally, teachers can design lessons such that the environment provides feedback. In environmental feedback, student actions stimulate environmental responses that inform their understandings—e.g., baking soda reacting with vinegar provides information learners incorporate into their existing mental schema on chemical reactions. Once again, teacher-centered strategies elicit low uncertainty, whereas student-centered and environmental feedback strategies introduce greater uncertainty as the possibility of consolidating incorrect knowledge and pedagogical risk grows.

By focusing on student-centered experiences, we put students in the position to ask 'Why?' and explore rather than "reproduce knowledge" (Beghetto and Plucker 2006). By providing students with authentic experiences, we can nurture engaged learning in meaningful contexts, creative thinking and problem solving skills—e.g. divergent and convergent thinking, lateral thinking, problem and solution finding—and creative traits—e.g. open-mindedness, curiosity, tolerance for ambiguity. For example, asking students to use divergent thinking to consider, 'What are the greatest challenges facing your generation?' can be a way to facilitate engagement with uncertainty and think creatively. Perhaps this question is embedded in project or problem-based instruction or maybe it is an opportunity for the instructor to develop a curricular unit focusing on student interests. Maybe this also includes giving students time to use other resources (e.g. Legos, craft supplies), technology, and/or space (e.g. time in nature, time in other buildings) to explore their and others' ideas and perspectives.

Despite the known benefits of student-centered approaches and introducing uncertainty into the classroom, instructors in higher education have not widely adopted these approaches (Grunspan et al. 2018). Grunspan et al. conceive of the required pedagogical change as a process of cultural evolution, requiring cultural transmission and selection over time, before widespread changes can occur. They characterize this change as slow and multi-generational but offer suggestions for how to accelerate this process by intervening in key points to influence population-level change. Alternative educational paradigms that value "interconnection, flexibility, diverse epistemologies, creativity, playfulness, unknowability, and sociocultural pluralism" (Jung et al. 2014 p. 6) must find stronger footing within higher education sooner rather than later.

18.6 Evolving Beyond Industrialism Through the Creative Humanities

Sir Ken Robinson has convincingly argued that much of modern educational practice emerged as a product and emulation of the industrial revolution (see Robinson 2011). As we enter yet another industrial revolution, and creativity is rightfully recognized as an imperative for the work of the future, we must exercise caution that we do not repeat this error of attuning our transformation of the educational system in the Anthropocene entirely toward industrial aims, for "this assembly-line educational system can numb the human mind into devaluing the different ways of knowing, learning, and living" (Jung et al. 2014, p. 5). In the pursuit to construct educational approaches that foster more holistic, human creativity, the humanities hold special promise and should feature prominently in efforts to adapt higher education for an uncertain world.

The special nature of humanities creativity regards the ability to critically and creatively engage with the ambiguous past and future, particularly through the rigorous interpretation of creative works and culture. Contemporary humanities scholarship is informed by the assumption that creative works are inherently ambiguous and that the creator's intention is unknowable and/or arbitrary as audiences play an essential role in producing meaning. These assumptions were popularized via Roland Barthes's 1967 essay *The Death of the Author*, which challenged the historical notion that a literary text had a 'true' intended meaning and it was the role of the scholar to discover that meaning—a humanist was metaphorically comparable to an archeologist or a botanist who identified and described what already existed (Leddy 2009). More recent theories understand readers are co-creators who draw upon their knowledge base, personal experience, and socio-cultural context to produce novel interpretations which, in turn, socially produce meaning as members of the field or broader public accept and reject interpretations. This ability, what Hollenberg (2017) labelled critical creativity, can be broadly applied to creatively explore the ambiguous with the aim of heightening genuine novelty and mitigating disastrous change; and within the context of neoliberal higher education, instructors have a responsibility to foster critical creativity to take issue with the neoliberalization of creativity and, more broadly, society.

Humanities scholarship has taken issue with the creative turn in advanced capitalist societies by teaching students to critically evaluate the interrelationship between creativity and the systems in which creativity is conceptualized, practiced, and assessed. Anne Harris coined the term "creative turn" to describe the neoliberalization of creativity during the two decades bracketing the new millennium. Neoliberalism describes the expansion of the logic of free markets and the unfettered pursuit of individual profit to all aspects of life with little to no concern for the social good. Historically, conceptualizations of creativity emerged from the arts and crafts, in which creativity advanced social justice and the social good. For artists and creators alike, creativity was intrinsically valuable because it provided personally transformative experiences through critical engagement with artistic novelty; creativity was extrinsically valuable because works of art had the potential to challenge and expand consciousness—often with the aim of advancing progressive social, cultural, and political causes—and improved quality of life by building community and spreading joy. That all changed with the emergence of the creative economy in which influential thinkers such as Clayton Christensen, Richard Florida, and Daniel Pink theorized creativity from a neoliberal worldview, little-c and pro-c creativity were valued because they were prerequisites for commercial innovation which would drive economic growth in the twenty-first century. As neoliberalism becomes increasingly hegemonic, creativity is correspondingly being conceptualized via and reduced to its economic value. To responsibly engage with the uncertain present and future, creatives require new knowledge—how creativity is socially constructed—and new skills—how to identify, critique, and mitigate the negative second-order consequences of irresponsible innovation.

Critical creativity should be an essential competency (Hollenberg 2017). Critical creativity has two important connotations. The first regards how interpretation is a creative act and responsible interpretation necessitates critical engagement with social, historical, and political context. Consider a highly ambiguous work of art such as Marcel Duchamp's *Fountain* (1917), a mass-produced urinal that the artist flipped upside down, signed with the name "R. Mutt," and installed in the Society of Independent Artists exhibit. The work's meaning originates from the context in which it was produced, displayed, and interpreted—the world of avant-garde art—and, for contemporary students, their art history class or some similar forum in which the work is studied and interpreted. Ambiguous works, like *Fountain*, foreground the role the audience plays in creating a work through interpretation but the same principles extend to the interpretation of all creativity.

The second connotation regards the relationship between the creator and systems, to create novel works an artist must critically engage with domain-specific knowledge and the environments in which the work will be interpreted. When creators fail to apply critical creativity, they not only produce 'bad' or redundant art but also risk causing harm—such as a white comedian putting on makeup to appear black in skit (Clifton 2020). Indeed, critical creativity extends to all creative practice, see for example Dove's 2017 campaign which featured brown and black women who appeared to be transformed into Caucasians after using the product. While perhaps unintentional, the campaign evidenced an irresponsible ignorance of the racist history of skin care products and perpetuated racist tropes that continue to problematically inform caste systems in Indian and other cultures. The campaign was intended to be visually and socially novel—a celebration of diversity and social justice—but in practice it advanced what Arthur Cropley and other scholars labelled the 'dark side of creativity' (Cropley and Cropley 2010) because the marketing team failed to consider social context when speculating upon how the campaign may be interpreted. As Hollenberg concludes, there is a pertinent need to "challenge the easily digestible definitions of creativity as the production of valuable novelty" that emerged from JP Guilford's scholarship and continues to be uncritically perpetuated by creativity scholars who blinker the socio-cultural context in which a creative product is made, disseminated, interpreted, and evaluated.

While emerging from the humanities, critical creativity is an essential transdisciplinary competency. Charise (2020) examined the integration of narrativity training into healthcare curriculum to take issue with "preparedness" as a twenty-first century competency. Narrativity is an area of literary theory that examines how stories are told and interpreted; teaching medical practitioners how to tell and interpret stories has enhanced their ability to prepare for disaster by better diagnosing and, correspondingly, treating ailments—in other words, it helps practitioners manage and overcome ambiguity. What concerns Charise and Krecsy is how preparedness is increasingly being theorized and practiced as a form of creativity: "Creativity is valuable, it seems, because it allows us not only *to prepare* (a very different outcome than the making, imitation, or invention that have constituted creativity's conceptual history over the centuries) but also *to respond* to a climate of urgent and perpetual crisis." At issue is not that preparedness is bad, per se, but rather how it discourages a holistic approach to healthcare and innovation. What healthcare and, more broadly, career-orientated discourse "all too frequently foreclose are accounts of the present conditions that give rise to instability in the first place, taking the present not as a site or reform or development, but as a site of 'preparedness' to come." Consider, for example, the COVID-19 crisis. Healthcare professionals interpret stories to diagnose an infection and perform contact tracing. However, focusing exclusively on preparedness distracts from the systemic problems that have enabled COVID-19 to thrive and kill thousands in Canada: the privatization of long-term care homes, defunding of public health care, and other structural race- and class-based inequities that have resulted in a disproportionate volume of outbreaks in marginalized communities.

Others have demonstrated how the discourse of neoliberal post-secondary education similarly grooms graduates for exploitation by emphasizing 'preparation' for the gig economy rather than questioning and reforming structural inequalities. Scholars have demonstrated how neoliberalism has instrumentalized creativity studies scholarship on the creative press to reconstitute creative labour as fun that need not be compensated (Szeman 2010) and idealize "models of good work as a flexible and self-sufficient enterprise averse to social responsibility, human interdependence, and collective politics" (Brouillette 2014, p. 56). Educators should certainly prepare students for crisis and the new forms of exploitation that await them in industry—we all want doctors to be prepared for a crisis and our students to enjoy rewarding careers—but they also have a responsibility to foster genuine creativity that adopts a holistic perspective to identify and transcend systemic challenges. But, how can educators do that?

There are two emerging responses. The first advocates adopting a meta-approach that explicitly flags how the educator, course, and/or discipline conceptualizes creativity with the aim of providing students with the foundation necessary for critical evaluation and self-reflection (Hollenberg 2017; Charise 2020; Tracy 2020). Educational resources on creativity studies all too often totalize creativity via positivist epistemology while problematically delegitimizing perspectives grounded in constructivist epistemology or those originating from the arts, crafts, and humanities; similarly, resources uphold a neoliberal worldview by uncritically perpetuating popular myths about the creative economy and tropes of preparedness. Irrespective of one's political orientation or ideology, educators have a responsibility to model critical creativity and provide students with the intellectual foundation to apply critical creativity so that they can form their own conclusions and opinions. The second champions mini-c creativity as a counterpoint to creativity studies and neoliberal higher education. This perspective has been most forcefully advocated by David Gauntlett, who rejects naïve conceptualizations that reduce creativity to divergent thinking and contemporary postsecondary institutions that reduce creativity to its economic value (Gauntlett and Culpepper 2020). For Gauntlett, creativity is valuable because it facilitates community building, self-actualization, and happiness (Gauntlett 2020, 2018), and he envisions postsecondary education as a platform to facilitate and champion everyday creativity.

For higher education to meet the simultaneous demand for industry-relevant skills oriented toward the future of work and suited to the 4IR yet still cultivate critical creativity, it will be imperative that educators model paradoxical leadership (see Zhang et al. 2015), a "both-and" orientation to programming and pedagogy that incorporates diverse transdisciplinary approaches which both accurately reflect the demands of the world as it is and push students to critically and creatively imagine what it might be.

18.7   Equipping Young Learners for Transformed Higher Education

If we are to be successful at preparing students for the uncertainty in the world in higher education, it will be important to start earlier, with our youngest learners, in both formal and informal learning environments. Of the required skills discussed above, creativity seems particularly amenable for adoption in earlier curriculum and classrooms. While there are likely many nuanced ways to nurture creativity among primary and secondary students, the focus should be on integrating student-centered experiences where educators teach creatively for creativity. This holistic instruction should focus on both domain-general and domain specific creative understanding and skill building. While creativity researchers may still debate on this issue (see Baer 1998, 2011; Plucker 1998), the reality is if we can integrate creative thinking into a curriculum that values creative students and is facilitated by creative instructors, then there is time and space for both of these approaches.

In terms of skill and strategy use, equipping incoming students for creativity training in higher education should include explicit instruction of a variety of creative thinking and problem-solving skills, strategies, styles, and models. Teachers can help students develop flexible problem-solving skills and strategies (Treffinger et al. 2008). They can also teach and model different creative styles while exposing students to a variety of creative thinking and problem solving models. Running parallel to what is known about creative ideation, the more flexible students can be in using creative styles, the more likely they will be able to find and use a style, strategy, or model that is appropriate for a specific situation (Hartley and Plucker 2012). With enough practice and use, it would be appropriate to expect students arriving in higher education proficient with a variety of creative thinking and problem-solving skills, strategies, styles, and models. Educators should also be focusing on helping students better understand their creative self-beliefs, which include creative self-efficacy, creative self-concept, and creative-metacognition (Beghetto and Karwowski 2017). Through creative metacognition, students can also better understand when not to be creative (Kaufman and Beghetto 2013), an essential component to creativity education.

A critical step that should be taken early in education is the task of defining creativity (Plucker et al. 2004; Runco and Jaeger 2012) and exploring creativity as art, invention, and craft (Glăveanu 2018). Doing so can help prepare students for future capacity building on this critical skill. Equipping young learners with a framework of creative understanding emphasizing the importance of different levels of creativity—e.g. Four-C model of creativity—and types of creators—e.g. Adaptor-Innovator spectrum—will allow them nuanced understanding amenable to enhancement as they mature as learners.

Authentic student-centered experiences reflecting these typical creative prototypes stand as a useful approach. For example, while learning about the Second Industrial Revolution, students could explore creativity as art by creating art that replicates Impressionism and Post-Impressionism, two genres present during this time period. Students could build early electrical prototypes as practice in creativity as invention and learn how to knit in effort to better understand a common creative craft people engaged in during this era. This example provides an authentic environment in which to nurture creativity, creative thinking, and analysis of creativity. Students could be invited to discuss inter-connected themes and topics including the different types of creativity and their values in addition to how one might go about assessing the different products, people, processes, and culture of that time (Glăveanu 2018). Advanced learning would be greatly enhanced if students arrived to advanced training already comfortable and able to articulate which creativity is being talked about when something is labelled as creative and how it might be assessed within a specific context. This type of education may also help young people judge their own creativity in a variety of domains, which may (Kaufman et al. 2016) or may not (Kaufman et al. 2010) be a strength of theirs.

Finally, students should be exposed to the creative values of other societies and cultures to help them form an understanding and appreciation of the differences and similarities among people around the world. These learning environments should emphasize the importance of respecting culture and community while also encouraging cooperative and collaborative work, skills that are essential for local and global citizenship. It is possible that the primary and secondary creativity model recently published by Runco and Beghetto (2019) is an appropriate framework that can be a foundation in which to explore the interaction of the individual and culture.

None of these suggestions will be possible without supportive and knowledgeable others, whether they be teachers, counselors, and/or guardians. Recent research from around the world investigating pre-service teachers' and teachers' perspectives of creativity and/or creative students is nuanced, ranging from rather bleak (Gralewski 2019; Kettler et al. 2018) to more hopeful (Cropley et al. 2019; Jónsdóttir 2017; Karwowski et al. 2020; Patston et al. 2018; Rubenstein et al. 2018). Teachers' understandings, perceptions, and behaviors are probably like most things, improving in some ways and needing improvement in others (see Mullet, Willerson, N. Lamb, & Kettler, 2016 for a review of literature on teachers' perceptions from 1999–2015).

In order to facilitate nurturing creativity in the classroom, it needs to start in teacher education and continue through teacher professional development (Bolden et al. 2010; Park et al. 2006; Selkrig and Keamy 2017). In order to make space for nurturing creativity in our everyday lives, we all need to model living creatively and embodying the skills, traits, and behaviors of creative people.

18.8 Transforming Higher Education as Existential Imperative

This chapter began by characterizing higher education as representing the pinnacle of our ability to share knowledge and teach skills for the purposes of propelling our collective well-being and advancement. This has been true throughout the history of higher education but for our species to effectively navigate the uncertainty humans collectively face, transformation must ensue. Not only is this transformation about rising to meet the organizational and economic challenges of the Fourth IR, it is about navigating the existential threats of the Anthropocene, and promoting critical creativity.

Setting aside species-level concerns, it is also important to recognize the existential threat facing institutions of higher education themselves in this uncertain climate. The same technological trends transforming industry at large are impacting the marketplace of learning as well. In a remote learning environment devoid of the social and community benefits that come from campus life, many are rightly questioning the price tags for traditional post-secondary institutions relative to alternative offerings; indeed, too often arts and humanities programs are deemed useless and targeted for shuttering despite the central role they play in fostering socially-engaged critical and creative thinkers. Though estimates forecast the continued massification of higher education (Calderon 2018), there is uncertainty as to the impact that the COVID-19 pandemic and the host of other challenges outlined here may have on the continued success of traditional higher education institutions. If such institutions are to survive, they must be adapted for the Anthropocene and attuned to the uncertainty that pervades this epoch.

While uncertainty reigns, there are certain next steps that seem beneficial. Acknowledgment and understanding of the global socio-economic trends discussed here, and the rapidity with which they are evolving, mark an essential first step. Deeper conversations and collaboration with leaders outside of higher education in the private, public, and non-profit sectors will be imperative for apprehending and forecasting shifting needs. While shifts in conceptions around skills, knowledge, and pedagogical techniques have been cast as an evolutionary process, time is not on our side—the transformation of higher education must track the pace of technological and societal change. Urgency in re-imagining the essence of higher education is necessary. Educators must be afforded the opportunity, flexibility, and time necessary to implement the requisite changes to what and how we teach from administrators. The same creativity, innovation, adaptability identified as essential for students is also required for stakeholders across the higher education landscape.

In addition to the implications for education, this need for transformation suggests critical directions for research. The scientific method was a central part of our species' ascent into the Anthropocene and the arrival of the 4IR and should in turn be used to develop and test new approaches. Insights from the psychological and behavioral sciences about the human mind and behavior should inform new strategies, offerings, and pedagogical approaches aimed at attaining the novel knowledge and skill requirements of this era and be tested empirically for efficacy. Humanities scholars and qualitative researchers must delve into the social and societal anteced-ents and consequences of transformation, to help map connections and more deeply understand the implications of widespread change and uncertainty in the context of higher education.

This task will be challenging, but stands as imperative—in the words of Sir Ken Robinson: "Transforming education is not easy, but the price of failure is more than we can afford, while the benefits of success are more than we can imagine" (2011, p. 283). If universities and colleges seek to avoid becoming a relic, and if our spe-cies seeks to maintain our widespread success and continue our ascent, transforma-tion must be significant and change must be swift.

References

Ariely, D. (2008). *Predictably irrational*. New York: HarperCollins.

Baer, J. (1998). The case for domain specificity of creativity. *Creativity Research Journal, 11*(2), 173–177.

Baer, J. (2011). Why teachers should assume creativity is very domain specific. *The International Journal of Creativity and Problem Solving, 21*(2), 57–61.

Barr, N & Pennycook, G. (2018). Why reason matters: Connecting research on human reason to the challenges of the Anthropocene.. In G. Pennycook (Eds.), *The New Reflectionism in Cognitive Psychology: Why Reason Matters (2018)*. Current Issues in Thinking and Reasoning Series: Routledge.

Barr, N., Pennycook, G., Stolz, J. A., & Fugelsang, J. A. (2014). Reasoned connections: A dual-process perspective on creative thought. *Thinking & Reasoning, 21*, 61–75.

Barr, N., Pennycook, G., Stolz, J. A., & Fugelsang, J. A. (2015). The brain in your pocket: Evidence that Smartphones are used to supplant thinking. *Computers in Human Behavior, 48*, 473-480.

Barr, N., & Peters, K. (2018, January 8). Resistance is Futile: Embracing the Era of the Augmented Worker. Retrieved from Behavioural Scientist: https://behavioralscientist.org/resistance-futile-embracing-era-augmented-worker/

Barron, F. (1955). The disposition toward originality. The Journal of Abnormal and Social Psychology, 51, 478-485.

Beghetto, R. A. (2017). Inviting uncertainty into the classroom. *Educational Leadership, 75*(2), 20-25.

Beghetto, R. A. (2019). Structured uncertainty: How creativity thrives under constraints and uncer-tainty. In *Creativity Under Duress in Education?* (pp. 27-40). Springer, Cham.

Beghetto, R. (2020). How times of crisis serve as a catalyst for creative action: An agentic perspec-tive. *Frontiers in Psychology, 11*, 3735.

Beghetto, R.A., & Karwowski, M. (2017). Toward Untangling Creative Self-Beliefs. In *The Creative Self: Effect of Beliefs, Self-Efficacy, Mindset, and Identity*.

Beghetto, R.A., & Plucker, J. A. (2006). The relationship among schooling, learning, and creativ-ity. In *Creativity and reason in cognitive development* (Vol. 1, pp. 316–332).

Bolden, D. S., Harries, T. V., & Newton, D. P. (2010). Pre-service primary teachers' conceptions of creativity in mathematics. *Educational Studies in Mathematics, 73*(2), 143–157.

Bostrom, N. (2013). Existential risk prevention as global priority. *Global Policy, 4*(1), 15-31.

Brouillette, S. (2014). *Literature and the Creative Economy*. Redwood: Stanford UP.

Bruner, J. S. (1961). The act of discovery. *Harvard educational review*.

Calderon, A. (2018). Massification of higher education revisited. *Melbourne: RMIT University*.

Charise, A. & Krecsy,S. (2020). The Manual of Disaster: Creativity, Preparedness, and Writing the Emergency Room. *University of Toronto Quarterly* (online ahead of print). First published online 8 July 2020. (https://source.sheridancollege.ca/fhass_creative_humanites/4/).

Clifton, G. (2020). "Critical-Creative Literary and Creative Writing Pedagogy." *University of Toronto Quarterly* (online ahead of print). First published online 6 July 2020. (https://source.sheridancollege.ca/fhass_creative_humanities/3/).

Cropley, D. H., Cropley, A. J., Kaufman, J. C., & Runco, M. A. (Eds.). (2010). *The dark side of creativity*. Cambridge University Press.

Cropley, D. H., Patston, T., Marrone, R. L., & Kaufman, J. C. (2019). Essential, unexceptional and universal: Teacher implicit beliefs of creativity. *Thinking Skills and Creativity, 34*.

Dyer, J. H., Gregersen, H. B., & Christensen, C. M. (2009, December). The Innovator's DNA. Harvard Business Review, 87(12).

Elhacham, E., Ben-Uri, L., Grozovski, J., Bar-On, Y. M., & Milo, R. (2020). Global human-made mass exceeds all living biomass. *Nature*, 1-3.

Frenette, M., & Frank, K. (2020). *Automation and Job Transformation in Canada: Who's at Risk?* Statistics Canada, Ministry of Industry. Ottawa: Her Majesty the Queen in Right of Canada.

Gauntlett, D. (2018) *Making is Connecting*. 2nd ed. Cambridge: Polity.

Gauntlett, D. & Culpepper, M.K. (2020). All Parts of the Same Thing: Dispatches from the Creativity Everything Lab. Forthcoming from the *University of Toronto* (online ahead of print). First published 8 July 2020. (https://source.sheridancollege.ca/fhass_creative_humanities/2/).

Glăveanu, V. P. (2018). Educating which creativity? *Thinking Skills and Creativity, 27*(October 2017), 25–32.

Glăveanu, V. P., Beghetto, R. A., Benvenuti, M., Bourgeois-Bougrine, S., Chaudet, C., Chirico, A., ... & Trgalová, J. (2020). Creative Learning in Digital and Virtual Environments During COVID-19 and Beyond. *Creative Learning in Digital and Virtual Environments: Opportunities and Challenges of Technology-Enabled Learning and Creativity, 162*.

Grabinger, R. S., & Dunlap, J. C. (1995). Rich environments for active learning: a definition. *Research in Learning Technology, 3(2)*, 5-34.

Gralewski, J. (2019). Teachers' beliefs about creative students' characteristics: A qualitative study. *Thinking Skills and Creativity, 31*, 1–12. https://doi.org/10.1016/j.tsc.2018.11.008

Grunspan, D. Z., Kline, M. A., & Brownell, S. E. (2018). The lecture machine: A cultural evolutionary model of pedagogy in higher education. *CBE—Life Sciences Education, 17*(3), es6.

Guilford, J. (1950). Creativity. *American Psychologist, 5(9)*, 444-454

Habel, J. C., Assmann, T., Schmitt, T., & Avise, J. C. (2010). Relict species: from past to future. In *Relict species* (pp. 1-5). Springer, Berlin, Heidelberg.

Harari, Y. N. (2015). *Homo Deus: A Brief History of Tomorrow*. Toronto: Signal.

Harari, Y. N. (2018, August 12). Yuval Noah Harari on what the year 2050 has in store for humankind. *Wired Magazine*. Retrieved from: https://www.wired.co.uk/article/yuval-noah-harari-extract-21-lessons-for-the-21st-century

Hartley, K. A., & Plucker, J. A. (2012). Creativity and Intellectual Styles. In L. F. Zhang, R. J. Sternberg, & S. Rayner (Eds.), *Handbook of Intellectual Styles: Preferences in Cognition, Learning, and Thinking* (pp. 193–208). New York: Springer Publishing Company.

Hmelo-Silver, C. E., Duncan, R. G., & Chinn, C. A. (2007). Scaffolding and achievement in problem-based and inquiry learning: a response to Kirschner, Sweller, and. *Educational psychologist, 42(2)*, 99-107.

Holland, J. H., Holyoak, K. J., Nisbett, R. E., & Thagard, P. (1986). *Induction: Processes of Inference, Learning, and Discovery*. Cambridge: MIT Press.

Hollenberg, A. (2017). Challenging Creativity: A Critical Pedagogy of Narrative Interpretation. *English Studies in Canada, 43.1*, 45-66.

Hoover, W. A. (1996). The practice implications of constructivism. *SEDL Letter, 9(3)*, 1-2.

Jónsdóttir, S. R. (2017). Narratives of creativity: How eight teachers on four school levels integrate creativity into teaching and learning. *Thinking Skills and Creativity, 24*.

Jung, Y., Eudy, V., Wilson, G., & Jaeger, G. (2014). Four Alternative Theoretical Lenses to Change the Educational Paradigm: Systems Thinking, Informal Learning, Play Theories, and Culturally Responsive Education. *Curriculum and Pedagogy*.

Karwowski, M., Gralewski, J., Patston, T., Cropley, D. H., & Kaufman, J. C. (2020). The creative student in the eyes of a teacher: A cross-cultural study. *Thinking Skills and Creativity, 35*.

Kaufman, J. C., & Beghetto, R. A. (2013). In Praise of Clark Kent: Creative Metacognition and the Importance of Teaching Kids When (Not) to Be Creative. *Roeper Review, 35*(3), 155–165. https://doi.org/10.1080/02783193.2013.799413

Kaufman, J. C., Beghetto, R. A., & Watson, C. (2016). Creative metacognition and self-ratings of creative performance: A 4-C perspective. *Learning and Individual Differences, 51*.

Kaufman, J., Evans, M., & Baer, J. (2010). The American idol effect: Are students good judges of their creativity across domains? *Empirical Studies of the Arts, 28*(1), 3–17.

Kettler, T., Lamb, K. N., Willerson, A., & Mullet, D. R. (2018). Teachers' Perceptions of Creativity in the Classroom. *Creativity Research Journal, 30*(2).

Kirschner, P. A., Sweller, J., & Clark, R. E. (2006). Why minimal guidance during instruction does not work: An analysis of the failure of constructivist, discovery, problem-based, experiential, and inquiry-based teaching. *Educational psychologist, 41*(2), 75-86.

Ku, K. Y., Ho, I. T., Hau, K. T., & Lai, E. C. (2014). Integrating direct and inquiry-based instruction in the teaching of critical thinking: an intervention study. *Instructional Science, 42*(2), 251-269.

Klienberg, J., Lakkaraju, H., Leskovec, J., & Mullainathan, S. (2018, February). Human Decisions and Machine Predictions. *The Quarterly Journal of Economics, 133*(1), 237-293.

Lazer, D. M., Baum, M. A., Benkler, Y., Berinsky, A. J., Greenhill, K. M., Menczer, F., ... & Zittrain, J. L. (2018). The science of fake news. *Science, 359*(6380), 1094-1096.

Leakey, R. (1984). *The origins of humankind*. New York: Science Masters Basic Books.

Leddy, T. (2009). Creative Interpretation of Literary Texts. In *The Idea of Creativity*. Eds. M. Krausz, D. Dutton, & K. Bardsley. Leiden, Brill.

Levitt, T. (2002, August). Creativity is Not Enough. *Best of HBR: Harvard Business Review*, pp. 137-145.

Mednick, S. (1962). The associative basis for the creative process. *Psychological Review*, 69(3), 220-232.

Miller, G. A. (1969). Psychology as a means of promoting human welfare. *American Psychologist, 24*(12), 1063.

Mullet, D. R., Willerson, A., N. Lamb, K., & Kettler, T. (2016). Examining teacher perceptions of creativity: A systematic review of the literature. *Thinking Skills and Creativity, 21*.

Mvududu, N., & Thiel-Burgess, J. (2012). Constructivism in practice: The case for English language learners. *International Journal of Education, 4*(3), 108.

Neber, H. (2012). *Discovery learning. Encyclopedia of the Sciences of Learning*; Seel, N., Ed.; Springer: Berlin, Germany, 1009-1012.

Park, S., Lee, S. Y., Oliver, J. S., & Cramond, B. (2006). Changes in Korean science teachers' perceptions of creativity and science teaching after participating in an overseas professional development program. *Journal of Science Teacher Education, 17*(1), 37–64.

Patston, T. J., Cropley, D. H., Marrone, R. L., & Kaufman, J. C. (2018). Teacher implicit beliefs of creativity: Is there an arts bias? *Teaching and Teacher Education, 75*.

Peters, K. (2020). Behavioural Science: The Answer to Innovation? *Rotman Magazine*.

Piaget, J., & Inhelder, B. (2008). *The psychology of the child*. Basic books.

Plucker, J. A. (1998). Beware of simple conclusions: The case for content generality of creativity. *Creativity Research Journal*, Vol. 11, pp. 179–182.

Plucker, J. A., Beghetto, R. A., & Dow, G. T. (2004). Why isn't creativity more important to educational psychologists? Potentials, pitfalls, and future directions in creativity research. *Educational Psychologist, 39*(2), 83–96.

Robinson, K. (2011). Out of our minds: Learning to be creative. Capstone Publishing Ltd.

Rubenstein, L. D. V., Ridgley, L. M., Callan, G. L., Karami, S., & Ehlinger, J. (2018). How teachers perceive factors that influence creativity development: Applying a Social Cognitive Theory perspective. *Teaching and Teacher Education, 70*. https://doi.org/10.1016/j.tate.2017.11.012

Runco, M. A., & Beghetto, R. A. (2019). Primary and secondary creativity. *Current Opinion in Behavioral Sciences, 27*, 7–10. https://doi.org/10.1016/j.cobeha.2018.08.011

Runco, M. A., & Jaeger, G. J. (2012). The Standard Definition of Creativity. *Creativity Research Journal, 24*(1), 92–96.

Schwab, K. (2016). The Fourth Industrial Revolution: what it means, how to respond. *WEF*. Retrieved from: https://www.weforum.org/agenda/2016/01/the-fourth-industrial-revolution-what-it-means-and-how-to-respond/

Selkrig, M., & Keamy, R. (2017). Creative pedagogy: a case for teachers' creative learning being at the centre. *Teaching Education, 28*(3), 317–332.

Sloterdijk, P. (2018). *What Happened in the Twentieth Century?: Towards a Critique of Extreme Reason*. New Jersey: John Wiley & Sons.

Smith, G., & Carlsson, I. (1987). A new creativity test. Journal of Creative Behaviour, 21(1), 7-14.

Stratford, R. (2019). Educational philosophy, ecology and the Anthropocene. *Educational Philosophy and Theory, 51(2)*, 149-152.

Steffen, W., Broadgate, W., Deutsch, L., Gaffney, O., & Ludwig, C. (2015). The trajectory of the Anthropocene: the great acceleration. *The Anthropocene Review, 2*(1), 81-98.

Steffen, W., Grinevald, J., Crutzen, P., & McNeill, J. (2011). The Anthropocene: conceptual and historical perspectives. *Philosophical Transactions of the Royal Society of London A: Mathematical, Physical and Engineering Sciences, 369*(1938), 842-867.

Szeman, I. (2010) "Neoliberals Dressed in Black; or, the Traffic in Creativity." *English Studies in Canada, 36.1*, 15-36.

Thaler, R., & Sunstein, C. R. (2008). *Nudge: Improving decisions about health, wealth, and happiness*. New Haven, CT: Yale University Press.

Thomas, D., & Brown, J. S. (2011). *A New Culture of Learning: Cultivating the Imagination of a World of Constant Change*. Kentucky: CreateSpace Independent Publishing Platform.

Tracy, D. (2020) Tailor Made, Skylarking, and Making in the Humanities. *University of Toronto Quarterly* (online ahead of print). First published online 6 July 2020. (https://source.sheridancollege.ca/fhass_creative_ humanities/1/).

Treffinger, D. J., Selby, E. C., & Isaksen, S. G. (2008). Understanding individual problem-solving style: A key to learning and applying creative problem solving. *Learning and Individual Differences, 18*, 390–401.

World Economic Forum. (2018). *Towards a Reskilling Revolution: A Future of Jobs for All. Geneva*.

World Economic Forum. (2020). *The Future of Jobs Report*. Geneva: WEF

Zhang, Y., Waldman, D. A., Han, Y. L., & Li, X. B. (2015). Paradoxical leader behaviors in people management: Antecedents and consequences. *Academy of Management Journal, 58*(2), 538-566.

Printed by Books on Demand, Germany